Abnormal Psychology

Abnorma

Psych

Morton G. Harmatz

The University of Massachusetts at Amherst

ology

Prentice-Hall, Inc., Englewood Cliffs, New Jersey

This book is dedicated to my parents, Harry and Louise Harmatz, my wife, Marilynne, and my son, Mark.

Library of Congress Cataloging in Publication Data

Harmatz, Morton G.
  Abnormal psychology.

  Bibliography.
  Includes indexes.
  1. Psychology, Pathological.   I. Title.
RC454.H355   616.8'9   77-15947
ISBN 0-13-000885-0

Printed in the United States of America

10 9 8 7 6 5 4 3 2 1

PRENTICE-HALL INTERNATIONAL, INC., *London*
PRENTICE-HALL OF AUSTRALIA PTY. LIMITED, *Sydney*
PRENTICE-HALL OF CANADA, LTD., *Toronto*
PRENTICE-HALL OF INDIA PRIVATE LIMITED, *New Delhi*
PRENTICE-HALL OF JAPAN, INC., *Tokyo*
PRENTICE-HALL OF SOUTHEAST ASIA PTE. LTD., *Singapore*
WHITEHALL BOOKS LIMITED, *Wellington, New Zealand*

Acknowledgments for quoted material in the text
appear in the Bibliography.

Photo credits: cover, Luis Villota (foreground)/Bill
Longcore (background); Part I Opener, p. 1, Part II
Opener, p. 115, Part IV Opener, p. 473, and openers for
Chapters 1–5, 6 and 7, 19 and 20 by Luis Villota; Part III
Opener, p. 167, and openers for Chapters 8–18 by Michal
Heron.

Overview

Contents

2   The designation and classification of abnormal behavior   23

3   Psychodynamic and behavioral views of abnormal behavior   40

4 Causal, contributing, and maintaining factors of abnormal behavior 72

5 Clinical and research methods of inquiry about abnormal behavior 92

PART TWO
Psychotherapeutic Intervention 115

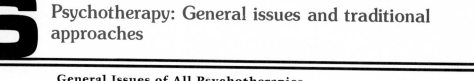

Psychotherapy: General issues and traditional approaches 116

Psychotherapy: Contemporary approaches to behavior change 140

PART THREE
Types of Abnormal Behavior

8 The neuroses

9 Psychophysiologic disorders

Schizophrenia: Background, classification, and description   230

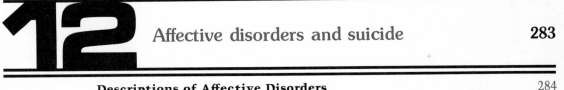

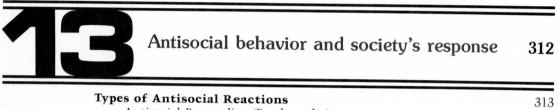

13   Antisocial behavior and society's response   312

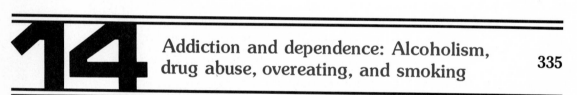

14   Addiction and dependence: Alcoholism, drug abuse, overeating, and smoking   335

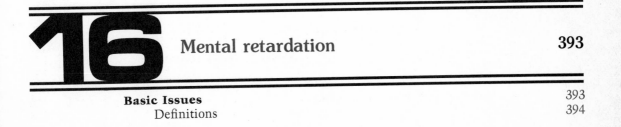

Organic brain syndrome and aging 414

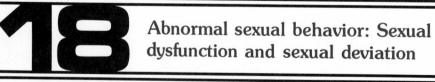

Abnormal sexual behavior: Sexual dysfunction and sexual deviation 437

PART FOUR
A Field in Transition: Emerging Approaches and Future Directions   473

19   Emerging issues in conceptualizing abnormal behavior   474

Emerging approaches to the treatment and prevention of abnormal behavior

497

Preface

Abnormal Psychology is designed as a text for the general introductory course in abnormal psychology. The book covers a broad range of topics and viewpoints. It is comprehensive rather than selective, providing the student with a firm grounding in the general subject matter while permitting the instructor the freedom to emphasize the material he or she feels is of special importance or interest.

A major goal of this textbook is to convey a sense of the excitement and dynamism of the field of abnormal psychology, which is experiencing a phase of enormous growth and change. It is truly a period of important paradigm clashes, and it would be inappropriate to present it as a fixed, descriptive science in which everything fits neatly into place.

Certain features of the book are designed to get the student involved in the excitement of discovery. These include: an emphasis on the field as an area of active inquiry both in clinical practice and in research; a complete presentation of the most important theoretical models; and an emphasis on topics that reflect contemporary interests. Each of these is discussed briefly below.

Emphasis on Inquiry About Abnormal Behavior

The emphasis on inquiry attempts to provide the student with an understanding of how workers in the field formulate and answer questions about abnormal behavior. Inquiry is stressed as the basis of both clinical and research work. The diagnostician, the researcher, and the psychotherapist are described in their roles as participants in the pursuit of knowledge. These approaches to inquiry are presented both in a chapter on clinical and research methods of inquiry (Chapter 5) and throughout the text by the use of research and case studies.

The Approach to Theoretical Models

The field of abnormal psychology is in transition. The more traditional models based on psychodynamic conceptions of man are in conflict with emerging models that stress behavioral and social psychological variables. The text attempts a clear and detailed presentation of these models.

Emphasis on Contemporary Topics

Greater than usual attention is given to some areas because they reflect the current fields of interest in abnormal psychology. Issues of sexual inadequacy (impotence and frigidity), for example, are of greater interest today than are the classical sexual deviations (fetishism and voyeurism). Therefore, I give greater weight to those issues.

Psychotherapy is one area covered in far greater depth than in most other abnormal psychology textbooks currently available. This emphasis reflects the increasing research interest in therapy during the last few years. It also reflects students' curiosity about this exciting human interaction. Finally, when conceptualized as behavior change, therapy provides an excellent way of understanding the variables that control disordered behavior. Since it is viewed as a method of inquiry, the material on psychotherapy is placed early in the book so that the variety of approaches can be referred to in later chapters. However, Part II, Psychotherapeutic Intervention, is designed to be self-contained so that it could be assigned at the end of the course if the instructor prefers.

Other topics given greater emphasis are biofeedback, community mental health, and the psychological problems associated with aging. As you read the text, still other areas of unusual emphasis will become clear to you. It is important to note that, while the text emphasizes certain areas, none of the traditional categories generally covered in an introductory abnormal psychology course are omitted.

Organization of the Text

After several years of preparing and presenting my own abnormal psychology lectures for students of extremely varied backgrounds I have come to recognize many of the problems associated with teaching this course. This textbook has grown out of this practical knowledge. It is aimed at the general upper-division college student, of any major, who is interested in abnormal psychology. I assume little technical background and present enough basic material early in the text so that research studies can be presented and discussed without difficulty. I also include a substantial amount of case material.

The text is organized into four major parts. Part I, The Foundations of Abnormal Psychology, provides the background and introduction to the field. It starts with the nature and scope of abnormal psychology, presents the difficulties of definition and the issues surrounding assessment and diagnosis, and provides a contemporary view of the labeling process. The historical perspective is aimed at showing the evolution of current views of abnormality and current treatment approaches. Contemporary models are then presented and discussed as logical extensions of this history. The current models are compared and contrasted and evaluated as to their relative importance. Chapter 4 in Part I discusses the wide variety of causal factors that are supported by contemporary research. Included is a discussion of those factors that contribute to the genesis of psychological problems or that help to maintain problem behavior. Part I ends with the chapter on clinical and research methods of inquiry described above.

Part II is devoted to psychotherapy. The chapters in this section provide a general orientation to psychotherapy, provide detailed presentation and analyses of the traditional approaches to therapy, and then review the variety of current approaches. The concept of psychotherapy is broadened beyond individual psychotherapy to all levels of therapeutic intervention, including environmental manipulations. Throughout the section there is an emphasis on how an understanding of behavior change and maintenance can increase our knowledge of abnormal psychology.

Part III discusses the various types of abnormality usually considered problems in our society. The American Psychiatric Association's *Diagnostic and Statistical Manual* (DSM-II) is used as a guide to the disorders, although earlier in the text this listing is criticized and its limitations in a contemporary approach are noted.

Part IV covers the emerging approaches to the description, conceptualization, and treatment of abnormal behavior. Particular emphasis is given to the social context of behavior. Also covered are adult life stages and crises, ecological problems, and a variety of emerging treatment models. Community mental health and community psychology are highlighted both as conceptual systems and models of intervention. Prevention through social action provides the closing topic of the textbook.

Other features of the text include a general glossary providing clear and precise definitions of terms and concepts, both a name and subject index, chapter summaries that help the student review each chapter, notations of supplementary readings for students who would like to pursue a topic in greater depth, and boxed inserts that help to illustrate points from the text by providing interesting examples or recapitulations of what has been discussed there. A complete Instructor's Manual also accompanies the text.

Acknowledgments

A large introductory textbook such as this is very much the reflection of many people. While I alone am responsible for the content, I have benefited from the energies and skills of many others.

Alice Greenwald, the editor, was an incredible source of knowledge, help, and support. Ann Greif and Brian Stagner, who served as reseachers, went far beyond the call of duty and devoted their lives and energies to the book. Because they did this along with the normally excessive demands of being graduate students, it was not only laudable, it was heroic. The final product was very much shaped by the suggestions, criticisms, and inspiration of these three people. They also supplied encouragement and enthusiasm along with their hard work, and made a difficult task far more pleasant.

Prentice-Hall provided important assistance in numerous ways. Help was provided by specialists in market analysis, production, design, editing, reviewing, writing, photo research, and copyediting. In particular I want to thank Neale Sweet, Patricia Ann Wubbe, Ruth Kugelman, Florence Silverman, and Helena Frost for their professional guidance and expertise. Toni Goldfarb, Martin Haydon, Robert Lamm, James McDonald, and Lynn Schulz each helped with the writing of various parts of the manuscript. The readability of the text was greatly enhanced by their contributions. I also want to thank Sally Ives, who did much of the typing.

The book also benefited from the helpful comments of those who reviewed it: Leonard B. Olinger, Michael D. Spiegler, William C. Crain, Daniel F. Penrod, John F. Kihlstrom, Bernard S. Gorman, Rudy V. Nydegger, Alan G. Glaros, and Perry London.

M. G. H.

Abnormal Psychology

Foundations of
Abnormal Psychology

PART ONE

Introduction to the study of abnormal behavior

Popular Views and Beliefs

As you begin the study of abnormal psychology, it is important to realize that you already have numerous ideas, attitudes, and value judgments about the subject. You are not so "naive" a student as you might be in another field of study, say, geology or physics. This will have both advantages and disadvantages when you are learning about abnormal psychology as a formal field of study. The advantage is that this knowledge indicates your already-developed interest in the subject matter—a curiosity about it and motivation to learn more. But popularly held views such as those you now hold are not only often erroneous, they may also be highly destructive when they affect the way you behave toward people with psychological problems. Much of the knowledge we bring with us is based on myths, misconceptions, and half-truths. To complicate the problem further, many of these views are formed in our earliest years and become so deeply embedded in our attitudes that by the time we reach adulthood they become unquestioned "gut-level" responses. For example, how many of the opinions in Box 1-1 do you share? Can you sense any "emotional" agreement even though you may reject the notions on an intellectual level?

Several investigators have studied the way the general public views abnormality and abnormal behavior. Nunnally (1961) surveyed 250 people in the Chicago area on their attitudes toward those showing abnormal behavior. Except for the geographical limitation, this group approximated the national population in terms of age, education, income, and other characteristics. The people surveyed were asked to judge the adjectives that best applied to a number of concepts related to mental health. The results indicated that public attitudes are generally negative toward people with psychological problems. The prevailing view among those asked was that people with psychological problems are tense, unpredictable, dirty, worthless, dangerous, and insecure. Abnormality was viewed with fear, distrust, and dislike. The more educated respondents held somewhat less extreme, but still very negative, views of abnormal behavior.

The results of many studies such as the one just mentioned indicate people with abnormal behavior continue to be targets of public disgust and rejection. Sadly enough, most of the mental patients themselves are as negative in their attitudes toward abnormal behavior as the general public. They are no better informed and show no greater tolerance for abnormality. These people often feel shame and guilt because of their problems. Indeed, the inmates of a psychiatric hospital "seldom share the rights, liberties, and satisfactions that civilians enjoy,

Box 1-1 Some Commonly Held Misconceptions

Abnormal Behavior is Always—

bizarre, irrational, strange, and violent.

clearly different from normal behavior.

inherited and will be passed on to offspring.

something to be ashamed of.

untreatable, or at least not totally curable.

a sign of a defect in a person's character.

found among artists, writers, and other creative types.

related to retardation.

a symptom of something being wrong in the brain.

People Who Exhibit Abnormal Behavior—

are capable of anything.

will have to be hospitalized.

usually commit suicide.

always hurt their family or friends without warning.

are basically helpless and need to be taken care of.

must be treated with extreme care so they are not made worse.

usually revert to abnormal behavior even after a period of normality.

could be normal if they would just use a little will power.

and on their return home they often find that being an ex-mental patient is more of a liability than being an ex-criminal in the pursuit of housing, jobs, and friends" (Rabkin, 1972, pp. 157–158).

Some rather surprising research evidence indicates that college students, when forced to choose, would rather be an ex-convict than an ex-mental hospital patient (Lamy, 1966). Ex-mental patients were viewed as permanently susceptible to breakdown under stress, and as less reliable for jobs involving responsibility.

Certainly, the public holds a more enlightened view of abnormal behavior today than it did 15 or 20 years ago. Yet research continues to show that a significant proportion of the population is still misinformed or uninformed, and that they are still frightened and repelled by their stereotyped picture of a "mental patient." Since the 1950s, there has been little evidence that people's attitudes have changed at all as far as how to cope with their own emotional difficulties. The dominant theme is self-sufficiency— the admission of one's need for professional help is perceived as a "weakness." Part of the public's reluctance to seek such help may stem from ignorance and confusion over the roles of the various mental health professionals.

The fact that a person has sought help for an emotional problem is often more of a cause for his or her rejection by society than is the problem itself. Public views condemn people who "cannot handle their own problems," rather than praise the individual who seeks assistance to maintain a favorable personal adjustment. Research attempting to illustrate this point was conducted by Phillips (1963) in interviews with 300 New England residents. In each interview, descriptions were read of various states of mental health, ranging from schizophrenia to "normality." The source of help being used was also described, ranging from no help to hospitalization. The degree of social acceptance or rejection was measured by questions such as: Would you rent to this person? work with this person? like to have this person for your neighbor? as a member of your club?

The major finding of this study was that people are increasingly rejected as they go up the hierarchy from seeking no help, to seeing a clergyman, a physician, a psychiatrist, or being hospitalized in a mental institution. The rejection is extreme and disproportionate for the last two sources of help. "Even when the normal person is described as seeing a psychiatrist, he is rejected more than a simple schizophrenic who seeks no help" (Phillips, 1963, p. 969). Thus we see that in our society, not only is a stigma attached to psychological problems, but an additional penalty is paid for seeking help for them.

A prime example of these attitudes was provided by the "Eagleton affair" of the 1972 presidential election. During the campaign, it was disclosed that Thomas F. Eagleton, the Democratic vice-presidential nominee, had been hospitalized three times between 1960 and 1966 for "nervous exhaustion and fatigue." On two occasions, he had undergone psychiatric treatment, including electroshock therapy, for "depression." His running mate, presidential candidate George McGovern, had not been aware of Eagleton's previous difficulties, but asserted that he would have chosen him even if he had known. During the week following the disclosure of Eagleton's treatment, many of Eagleton's colleagues attested to the candidate's present good state of mental health. Public discussion of the situation was intense, with much news media coverage on "nervous breakdowns," "electric shock," and "depression." Pressures mounted to replace Eagleton on the ticket, and even high Democratic sources made it plain that Eagleton's voluntary withdrawal would be appreciated. One week after his psychiatric history was made public, Thomas Eagleton, ex-mental patient, was also an ex-candidate for the vice-presidency.

Abnormal Behavior: Problems for Contemporary Society

Negative and rejecting views toward abnormal behavior are prevalent within our society and, to varying degrees, within each individual. To the extent that our views are distorted, we will react inappropriately in our dealings with abnormality. This is not a condition we should simply accept. Abnormal psychology, the field of study concerned with abnormal behavior, should be of more than just academic interest to you. As you are about to see, the problems of abnormal behavior touch us at every level of our existence. Whether we are responding as educated members of society to large issues or as individuals to the events in our own lives, our ability to respond knowledgeably to these issues becomes critical. More than in most other areas of study, it is true that what we don't know in the area of abnormal psychology *will* hurt us.

Scope of the Problem

What is the extent of the problems created by abnormal behavior? Can there be an estimate of the number of people involved? Is abnormal behavior on the increase within our society? These questions are difficult, if not impossible, to answer. First, there is the problem of choosing a method for counting people designated as abnormal. Two commonly used estimates are the prevalence and incidence rates in a given population.

A measure of *prevalence* counts all people who are under treatment at a specific point in time. As early as 1850, the U.S. Census provided data on the prevalence of abnormal behavior. Including both those hospitalized and those who were being treated on an "outpatient" basis, there were 15,610 patients. Considering the size of the total population at that time, this translates to a prevalence rate of 67.3 per 100,000 population. Data compiled in 1950, based only on patients in state mental hospitals, recorded a total of 574,881, or a prevalence rate of 391.4 per 100,000. This estimate does not include patients treated in private institutions, or as outpatients by psychiatrists or psychologists.

Over this time period, there has been a definite increase in mental health facilities, which may account for some of the apparent rise in the prevalence of abnormal behavior.

New hospitals have been built, and improved standards for treatment have been introduced. Thus we cannot definitely conclude from the increasing numbers of resident patients that there has been an increase in the frequency of abnormal behavior itself.

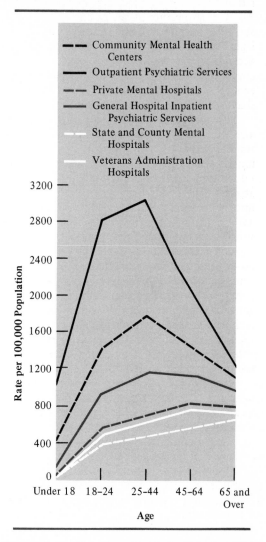

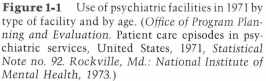

Figure 1-1 Use of psychiatric facilities in 1971 by type of facility and by age. (*Office of Program Planning and Evaluation.* Patient care episodes in psychiatric services, United States, 1971, *Statistical Note no. 92. Rockville, Md.: National Institute of Mental Health, 1973.*)

An alternative counting method considers only the number of *new* admissions to mental hospitals during a specified period of time or, as they are called, "first admissions." This is referred to as the *incidence* rate. Such data were first reported for the United States in 1922. In that year, the incidence rate was 68.2 per 100,000 population. By 1950, this figure had risen to 100.6, or an increase in incidence of 48 percent. Although the incidence rate is also affected by the growth of hospital facilities, many experts believe that the rate indeed reflects an increase in the frequency of abnormal behavior in the population (Malzberg, 1959).

The magnitude of the problem may be more obvious from some recent prevalence data collected by the National Institute of Mental Health. In 1971, the count of hospitalized mental patients plus those being treated as outpatients totaled 4,038,143. According to some estimates, 50 percent of the nation's hospital beds are taken up by those labeled as abnormal in psychological functioning!

None of these figures includes the unknown number of people with abnormal behavior who are receiving no help at all. An often-cited estimate is that 25 percent of our population is in need of help in the area of psychological functioning. This assessment is supported by the findings of an eight-year study covering 1,660 adult residents of midtown Manhattan (Srole et al., 1962). Teams of psychiatrists and sociologists carried out extensive interviews with the participants, evaluating all aspects of their mental health. The overall results indicated that only 18.5 percent of those interviewed could be classified as "well." Mild symptoms of abnormal functioning were recorded in 36.3 percent, and symptoms classified as "moderate" were observed in 21.8 percent. Regarding more serious disturbances, symptom formation was "marked" in 13.2 percent, "severe" in 7.5 percent, and "incapacitating" in 2.7 percent. These last three categories were combined under the title of "impairment" and come close to the 25 percent mark (Srole et al., 1962).

Through such research programs, we can get an estimate of the broad scope of the mental health problem. Although the 25 percent figure is quite high—and Srole et al. have been criticized for overstating the case—many people in the field believe that the problem may be even greater. Estimates have been offered that at some point during their lives, 10 percent of the population will have an incapacitating psychologic disorder, and that a total of 40 percent will have some type of psychological problem.

The Social Problem

What economic burdens are placed on society by abnormal behavior? Perhaps the largest material cost is the loss of productivity that results from the inability of individuals experiencing such problems to work, or their employment in less productive jobs than they would hold otherwise. The reduction in marketable income due to psychological problems was estimated to be in excess of $14 billion in 1966. In addition, the reduction in homemaking services was valued at $970 million, and other unpaid work at $240 million (Conley, Conwell, and Arrill, 1967).

The same sources estimated that in 1966 almost $4 billion was spent on the treatment and prevention of abnormal behavior. Other costs more difficult to quantify are the increases in undesirable and illegal behavior due to behavioral disturbances. Unfortunate consequences of such behavior often include divorce, accidents, promiscuity, alcoholism, and drug addiction. Illegal activities stemming from psychological problems are extremely costly to society, and may include assaults, thefts, and homicides.

The bulk of the cost of abnormal behavior is borne by the general population through taxation. Not only is there a loss of tax revenue from those with psychological problems, but also these individuals must be provided with financial support through social security, V.A. benefits, welfare, or charity. Furthermore, the majority of treatment facilities are sponsored by federal and state governments.

It is almost certainly an underestimate, so we may safely say that the total costs of abnormal behavior to society exceed $20 billion annually (Conley et al., 1967). This economic burden, although weighty, would be justified if the benefits to society exceeded the costs. With abnormal behavior, however, this does not seem to be the case at the present time. Our current allocation of funds may be another example of being "penny-wise but pound-foolish." Present programs provide for the incapacitated and the seriously disturbed, but place less emphasis on preventive programs, rehabilitation, and education of the general public. One factor in the high cost of psychological problems may be society's neglect of individuals who could be treated and returned to the economic system as productive participants. Reentry into society is made extremely difficult as a result of the loss of legal rights, lowered self-esteem, and the social stigmatization suffered by the former mental patient.

The Human Problem

While the number of persons affected with psychological problems and the costs to society are impressive, these are merely cold and impersonal figures. They cannot convey the anguish of the personal experience of psychological problems. It is only at the individual level that the full weight of the problem can be appreciated. One sufferer has recorded his experience as follows:

Neurasthenia, hypochondria, melancholia—hideous names for hideous things—it was these, or one of these. The symptoms, a persistent sleeplessness, a perpetual dejection, amounting at times to an intolerable mental anguish; the mind perfectly unclouded and absolutely hopeless. I tried rest cures, medicines, treatment of all kinds, waters, hypnotism. There was a month of travel, during which the lights of life seemed to be going out one by one. I . . . toiled faithfully to see beautiful things, till the whole became unutterably hideous to me, and I sickened for home. . . .

. . . the old horror rushed back into the mind, the dread of I knew not what, the anguish of life thus strangely interrupted, perhaps never to be resumed. . . . I was condemned to suffer a pain of which each minute seemed an eternity, in which

dread, disgust, repugnance, and dreariness seemed all entwined in one sickening draught. (Benson, 1912, pp. 1–6)

Would we not be justified in seeking to advance our psychological knowledge if only one person could be relieved from such pain and unhappiness? The fact that millions suffer as much or worse makes the study of abnormal behavior an absolute necessity.

Personal Reactions

We are all fascinated by the drama of other people's lives, but the experiences of those with psychological problems seem to have a special intrigue. Why are we drawn to know more about abnormality? What can we, as individuals, gain from the study of the case histories, research, and theoretical explanations that are part of the subject of abnormal psychology?

The study of any academic subject should have personal value to the student beyond the general acquisition of knowledge. The study of psychology directly extends one's knowledge about oneself. The study of *abnormal* psychology, especially as you begin to realize how "normal" abnormal behavior often is, can have profound personal significance for you. From such knowledge, we may gain a new perspective on our own and others' everyday problems. It can create the framework in which to examine our psychological functioning and to make judgments about it. This demystification of confusing, and often worrisome, aspects of our own functioning is an important goal of this textbook.

Closely linked to these benefits are the *risks* involved in the study of abnormality. You have probably heard of the "medical student syndrome." Students of medicine frequently diagnose in themselves many of the physical disorders they are studying. If you examine your own psychological status too intently in light of the material we will be discussing, you may find various pathological qualities you have in common with cases under discussion. The line between what is "normal" and what is "abnormal" is very thin indeed. Simply being aware of the tendency in you to think you have the problems you read about, and reminding yourself that it is common to think this way, will probably be sufficient reassurance of your adjustment.

Involvement in the Issues

Aside from these possible personal gains, what are the long-term advantages to the study of abnormal behavior? Students who enroll in such courses are often heading for professional careers in areas related to abnormal psychology—social work, medicine, nursing, psychology, education, etc. Knowledge of abnormal behavior is essential for professional involvement in these fields. It will prove to be equally beneficial to students entering one of the "person-related" fields such as personnel, sales, or marketing. Being a scholar of human behavior is an asset in any vocation. The practical value of this knowledge can be observed in such widely varied careers as law, acting, teaching, and politics.

A second advantage provided by your acquaintance with this field is of a more personal nature. The statistics already given on the scope of abnormal behavior suggest that even if you do not now have such problems yourself, sometime during your life you or someone close to you probably will. How will you react to help the situation? Will you be able to judge whether you or a spouse, parent, child, or friend needs outside help? If so, will you know what kind, and how to find it? A thorough involvement in the issues of mental health will have personal value for you, and, in turn, will make you a more valuable member of society.

Another warning is necessary here about becoming too involved in the problems of others. How much should you intervene in the psychological problems of those around you? With your newly acquired knowledge of abnormal psychology, you may be tempted to offer your services to others. Don't put up your "Doctor Is In" shingle just yet. Knowledge about abnormal psychology will expand your view of yourself and others, and you should feel more secure than you were before about

becoming involved in the behavior of others. But learning about abnormal psychology should also be a humbling experience as you begin to learn about the complexities of a field attempting to understand people at one of the most difficult moments of their existence—when they are experiencing psychological problems. Again, a thin line divides an appropriate from an inappropriate response on your part. This book is concerned with helping you make the best decisions possible in those circumstances.

To begin your involvement with the field, some rapid traveling through history is needed to illustrate how we have arrived at our contemporary views of "abnormality." The history is at times tragic, at times humorous, but it is a continually fascinating story.

Historical Perspective

Our concepts of abnormality have evolved with the changing values and ideas of the culture. The view of abnormal behavior taken by any particular society at a given time in its history is rooted in that society's way of explaining the world. Explanations have ranged from the supernatural to the scientific, depending on the prevailing attitudes of the civilization. The designated "experts" in matters of abnormal behavior have represented the dominant institutions of the times. Religious, medical, philosophical, legal, political, and scientific institutions at one time or another have taken the lead in defining abnormality for society.

In beginning the journey through history, be careful not to rely on your current perspectives on mental illness as the only "correct" point of view. Perhaps our attitudes are appropriate for our society at this point in time, but they must not be used as a yardstick for measuring the past or, for that matter, the future. The standards of normality and abnormality that will prevail in years to come are as unforeseeable as the future itself. Yet learning how we got where we are now may help us decide where we are going. If an ignorance of history does doom one to relive it, then we had better learn that history well. For as you will see, with

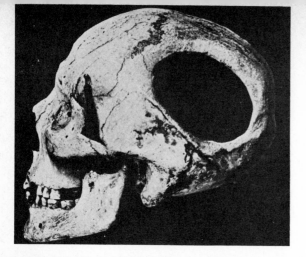

The ancient art of trephining involved boring a hole in the skull to let out the evil spirits. (*The Bettmann Archive, Inc.*)

the exception of one or two bright spots, it is not a history we would want to relive.

Primitive Supernaturalism

We study preliterate humans primarily through the artifacts they have left and by comparison with currently accessible primitive societies, such as the aborigines. Apparently, Stone Age men and women lived in a very terrifying world, full of real and imagined threats. Knowing little of reality, and only slightly more about themselves, they populated their world with imaginary creatures modeled on themselves—spirits, gods, demons, ancestors, etc. Some of these were perceived as benevolent, parallel to the good impulses in people. Others were felt to be dangerous and evil, like the darker side of our nature. This system of belief, known as *animism*, reflects a world that is "alive" with supernatural spirits, who are responsible for the ills and evils that befall men and women (Zilboorg and Henry, 1941).

We doubt that Stone Age societies made any distinction between physical disorders and mental disturbances. In both cases, primitive people knew only their emotional responses of pain and fear. Since the illnesses were attributed to supernatural causes, only magical-religious cures were thought to be effective. Demonology, which appeared in the Middle Ages,

has its roots in these early practices involving exorcism or the expulsion of evil spirits.

Although primitive "treatments" took many forms, their success depended on the patient's image of the healer as the possessor of special knowledge and skills, either as a result of training, or by divine authority. The primitive healer, or "shaman," had the full confidence of his patients because they shared the same animistic views of the world and causality. Even today, this remains an important factor in psychotherapy: the effectiveness of treatment depends, at least in part, on the degree to which therapist and patient share the same perspective of the universe. In primitive cultures, however, this requirement was more easily met than it is in today's pluralistic and complex society (Frank, 1961).

The methods employed by the primitive shaman varied enormously, from pure deception to rather advanced techniques. On the one hand, the shaman might spit out a few feathers covered with blood, representing the foreign body that had made the patient ill, but that had been magically extracted from his body (Frank, 1961). On the more sophisticated side, we note the ancient art of trepanning (or trephining)—removal of a circular section of bone from the skull—as practiced by primitive South American societies.

We know of this technique from the numerous skulls that have been found with circular holes carefully bored into them. Subsequent bone growth in these skulls demonstrates that the patients often lived on for some time after the operation, presumably in a "cured" state. Scholars have assumed that these operations were performed in the hopes of "letting out the evil spirits" from the afflicted person. Strangely enough, modern surgeons perform similar operations to relieve intercranial pressure. Yet what will future historians assume about *our* motivations? And can we really be sure of the motives of the ancient shamans?

The Golden Age: Greece and Rome

Historical evidence has it that animistic views prevailed until the time of Hippocrates, the fourth century B.C. Early Greek civilization revered Aesculapius, the god of medicine. In his temples, high priests would carry out medical treatments in impressive religious ceremonies. Oracles were a leading source of medical advice, and causation was uniformly attributed to acts of the gods. Some diseases were considered to be "divine," particularly epilepsy, and the victims were revered and granted priesthood status.

Naturalism

Hippocrates is considered to have been the first physician, and as such, he is called the father of medicine. Written records attest to his skill in clinical observation and diagnosis, as well as to his theoretical speculations. Almost single-handedly, he fought the ignorance and superstition that surrounded medicine in his day. In his book *Sacred Disease*, the then popular name for epilepsy, Hippocrates denies that it is divine, stating that it "has a natural cause from which it originates like other affections. . . . If you cut open the head, you will find the brain humid, full of sweat and smelling badly. And in this way, you may see that it is not a god which injures the body, but disease" (cited in Zilboorg and Henry, 1941, pp. 43–44).

Hippocrates' writings reflect the naturalistic view that events in the body are responsible for behavioral problems. His classic theory that imbalances of body substances or "humors" (blood, phlegm, black bile, yellow bile) are the basis of personality and abnormal behavior was inaccurate, but it at least represents a search for natural disease processes. Hippocrates also offered a very rational classification of psychologic disorders (e.g., mania, melancholia, paranoia, hysteria), which is still with us in modern psychology, although the definitions have been altered.

Early Organic Viewpoint

As illustrated by his attitude toward epilepsy, Hippocrates looked within the body for causes of all disorder, physical and psychologic. He emphasized the brain as the central organ of reason, sensation, and motor activities. His or-

ganic viewpoint and empirical approach were later shared by Aristotle, although Aristotle ascribed a more central role to the heart than to the brain.

After Hippocrates, nothing of import was contributed to the study of psychologic disorders until the middle of the first century B.C. in Rome. The Roman physician Asclepiades was a keen observer of psychological detail, and was the first to distinguish between *acute* (abrupt onset and short-term) and *chronic* (of longer duration) disease processes. He objected to popular use of the term "insanity," and preferred to define abnormal behavior as an emotional disturbance. In this, as well as other respects. Asclepiades was far ahead of his time. In methods of treatment, he showed much concern for the physical comfort of his patients, and tried to soothe them with baths, massage, music therapy, special diet, quiet, and rest. He disapproved of the old treatments of bloodletting and purging, and also strenuously objected to the confinement of the mentally ill in dark cells and dungeons.

Unfortunately, this period of Roman humanism was brief. Celsus, a physician writing during the reign of Tiberius (A.D. 14–37), suggests more unpleasant treatments for the mental patient:

> When he has said or done anything wrong, he must be chastised by hunger, chains and fetters. He must be made to attend and to learn something that he may remember, for thus it will happen that by degrees he will be led to consider what he is doing. It is also beneficial, in this malady, to make use of sudden fright, for a change may be effected by withdrawing the mind from that state in which it has been. (*De re medica*, III, 18, cited in Zilboorg and Henry, 1941, p. 70)

Celsus is inclined to see psychological disturbances as flaws in intelligence or understanding, which may be corrected by physical coercion or shock. Such views are not the error of Celsus or the ancients alone. The techniques of physical restraint, fright, and intimidation have recurred in various forms throughout the centuries. The fear and ignorance underlying such views represent a danger from which we are not totally free today.

Another Roman physician worthy of note is Aretaeus of Cappodocia, who practiced medicine in the first century A.D. He was the first to describe the stages of manic-depressive psychosis, and, in contrast to Celsus, Aretaeus stressed the importance of emotional factors in abnormal behavior. Unfortunately, Aretaeus is best remembered historically for his classically inaccurate description of the wanderings of the uterus, which he felt to be the cause of hysteria[1] in women:

> In the middle of the flanks of women lies the womb, a female viscus, closely resembling an animal, for it is moved of itself, hither and thither in the flanks, also upward in a direct line . . . and also obliquely to the right or the left . . . and it is also subject to prolapsus downward, and, in a word, is altogether erratic. It delights in fragrant smells and advances toward them; and, on the whole, the womb is like an animal within an animal. (cited in Stone, 1937, pp. 133–134)

Despite this obvious error in reasoning, Aretaeus made many accurate observations about abnormal behavior, and established a system of classification based on what the final outcome of the behavior would be, or the *prognosis* of the disease. At the end of the nineteenth century, the same basis for classification would be used in the Kraepelinian system, which will be discussed later in this chapter. Again foreshadowing the future, Aretaeus departed from previously held views that each disease has its own location in the body and affects only that site. Although the disease might stem from the abdomen, Aretaeus reasoned, the brain might become secondarily affected. This perspective was later to be shared by Galen (A.D. 130–200), who asserted that "a great many parts of a person may be affected by *consensus* . . . even though these parts are not

[1]Physical symptoms without organic explanation. Hysteria will be discussed in depth in Chapter 8.

the direct bearers of the malady" (cited in Zilboorg and Henry, 1941, p. 73).

A student of anatomy, Galen elaborated the theory that symptoms do not always indicate the organ affected, and that in abnormal behavior the brain is either directly involved or affected by "consensus" from another disturbance. Galen's work summarized the medical efforts of the Greco-Roman period, a span of seven centuries from the time of Hippocrates. Although the invasion of Rome by the barbarians did not take place until the fifth century A.D., the Dark Ages in medical history are said to have begun with the death of Galen in A.D. 200.

The Middle Ages: The Return of Supernaturalism

The fall of the Roman Empire occasioned a giant step backward for medical knowledge, and particularly for the understanding of abnormal behavior. The physician had to depend on texts translated from Greek to Arabic, then to Latin. No questioning of religious, scientific, or political authority was permissible. Thus the scholar who doubted the validity of some of the ancient medical texts was told that it was his own ignorance that prevented him from seeing the truth. Generally, it was considered wiser to accept the statements of the ancients than to propose new theories.

Demonology and Possession

Virtually the only medical practitioners of the Middle Ages were monks. The monasteries served as places of refuge for the sick and places of confinement for the insane. Medical authority, particularly over psychologic disorders, was recaptured by the religious system, and controlled by it for nearly 12 centuries. In this context, abnormal behavior was explained by a collection of ideas about demonic possession and superstition, mingled with the "humors" of Hippocrates, and early Christian theology.

In the early Middle Ages, rather mild cures were prescribed for psychological aberrations.

Sprinkling with (or immersion in) holy water, visits to shrines, and contact with relics were employed to save the afflicted. Mixed with prayers, however, we find other remedies as well: the use of herbs, applications of excrement, religious tokens, and the eating of wolf's flesh, which was highly recommended as a cure for hallucinations (Stone, 1937). It appeared that superstitious fears would soon outdistance the Christian quality of mercy.

The Church faced the dilemma of determining whether the person who behaved abnormally was a saint or a disciple of the devil. Many of the "possessions" had features of religious ecstasy, mystical raptures, revelations, and prophecies. Like the primitive shamans and the Greek epileptics, those who were "possessed" were revered at first. By the seventh century, however, even these cases were considered to be the work of the devil, and from then on abnormal behavior was equated with sin.

During this period, it is likely that the incidence of disturbed behavior was increasing, but the psychological and medical aspects of the problem were ignored by those in power— the theologians. People with psychological problems were treated as heretics (traitors to the Church) and punished severely until they "confessed" to heresy. The use of inhumane treatment was justified on the grounds that it would make the person's body an unpleasant habitat for the demons, and they would be forced to flee. To maim, torture, and, if these remedies failed, to burn the "patient" would actually be doing him a service by freeing his soul from the devil.

Mass Hysterias

Given the climate of poverty, ignorance, and authoritarian rule of the Church, the scene was set for tragedy. Europe began to be ravaged by epidemics of both physical and mental diseases. In thirteenth-century Italy, a phenomenon known as *tarantism* occurred. In large numbers, afflicted persons were compelled to dance and dance without stopping. Spreading throughout Europe, this disorder became known as *St. Vitus dance*, and could be cured only by pilgrimages to certain shrines.

Self-torturing sects known as *Flagellants* also made their appearance in the thirteenth century. Roaming the countryside in groups, the delirious Flagellants inflicted gruesome punishments on themselves to atone for their sins. Such large-scale masochism and suicidal behaviors are puzzling psychosocial phenomena to us today, but they terrorized the populace of the time and challenged the authority and control of the Church.

Providing material for our late-night horror movies, epidemics of *lycanthropy* (in which people imagine themselves to be werewolves) became frequent throughout Europe. In areas where there were no wolves, the insane variously believed themselves to be transformed into dogs, foxes, or crows. In one case recorded in 1541, "the lycanthrope told his captors in confidence that he was really a wolf but that his skin was smooth on the surface because all the hairs were inside. His extremities were amputated in order to convince him of his fallacies and mistaken notions, following which he died, unconvinced" (Stone, 1937, p. 139).

Epidemics of *cloister hysteria* began in 1609 when an Ursuline nun at Aix confessed that she was possessed by a number of demons, and that her priest had control over them. The hysteria spread rapidly among the nuns, resulting in the decision by higher Church authorities to torture the priest until he "confessed," and then to burn him at the stake. The burning of priests and many other innocent victims did nothing to slow the swelling tide of abnormal behavior.

Witchcraft

In 1484, the Pope had given permission to two "inquisitors" to organize witchcraft trials under the authority of the Church. These men, Johann Sprenger and Henry Kraemer, were Dominican monks. Together they compiled a volume entitled *Malleus Maleficarum*, or the *Evildoer's Hammer*, which for years was used as a guide and record book in witchcraft trials.

The Flagellants of the thirteenth century inflicted punishment on themselves to atone for their sins. (*Culver Pictures, Inc.*)

It provides detailed evidence of the illness of both the victims and the inquisitors. Most of the accused were women, and most were judged to be guilty. Although not all of the victims had severe psychological problems, those who did were primary targets. Thousands were burned as witches or sorcerers; in some villages, every old woman was burned. The last "witch" was executed in England in 1722, closing a chapter on 300 years of persecution.

Emerging Humanism of the Renaissance

The sixteenth century saw slowly changing attitudes toward abnormal behavior, and a lessened tendency to persecute those displaying it. Criticisms, at first veiled and later more open, were aimed at the inquisitors and their methods. Rabelais (1490–1553), a physician and monk, turned to writing satirical and ribald tales of "monkish deviltries." Couched in bawdy humor, his writings mocked the pursuers of witches and conveyed his disdain for their goals and methods. It is likely that only his careful wit and popularity saved him from being burned as a heretic.

Johann Weyer was more direct in his criticism of religious persecution. Writing in the 1560s, he systematically refuted all the superstitions surrounding witchcraft. Weyer considered the historical question of witches from Biblical references and Greek mythology, but focused on analyzing the phenomena noted in the *Malleus*. He presented the conclusion that the "witches" were simply people with psychological problems and the monks who tormented and tortured them were the ones deserving the punishment.

Weyer's overall contributions can be summarized as follows. He was the first physician to show a clinical and descriptive interest in abnormal behavior. His efforts began a trend that resulted in the formation of psychiatry as a medical specialty. Moreover, more than any other individual, he encouraged the separation of medical psychology from theology. Until this separation was complete, scientific inquiry could not proceed into areas previously held to be matters of unquestioning faith. Finally, he evaluated and accepted people as they actually were, rather than as they should be. Leaving the perfection of the soul to the Church, he dealt with the individual as a fallible creature. "Love man," he challenged, "kill errors, go into combat for truth without cruelty" (cited in Zilboorg and Henry, 1941, p. 229). Weyer richly deserves to be remembered as the first psychiatrist of the Renaissance.

Gradually, those experiencing psychological problems came to be hidden away and confined in special locations, rather than overtly tortured. Actual custodial practices were very different from the liberal theorizing expressed by Weyer. At least in the beginning, treatment in the asylums was only slightly more humane than the Inquisitors had been. A medical practitioner of the early sixteenth century recommended for "every man the whiche is madde or lunatycke . . . to be kepte in safeguarde in some close house or chamber where there is lyttle light; and that he have a keeper the whiche the madde man do feare" (Stone, 1937, p. 136). The Bethlehem Hospital in England first shows records of insane persons in 1403, when six "lunaticks" were confined there, kept in locks and chains. Iron manacles and stocks were also part of the hospital inventory, and remained in use until the early nineteenth century. The hospital name was later corrupted to "Bedlam," explaining the origins of the present meaning of the word. Many of its harmless patients were "discharged" to wander begging through the land, and were known as "tom-o-Bedlams."

The Seventeenth and Eighteenth Centuries

The next 200 years showed a gradual increase in tolerance and understanding, as the awareness of the Renaissance reached the general population. New ideas in science were espoused, frequently in opposition to the religious doctrines of the time. The study of abnormal psychology advanced to the point of recording case histories and attempting to find patterns of abnormal behavior. A main concern was with classifying and subclassifying various types of "mental disorders." In terms of treatment, however, no advances were made, other than falling back on the early Greek remedies of purgings and bloodletting.

The disturbed behavior of King George III in the late 1700s awakened public interest in insanity and provided new directions for the treatment of the disturbed. In England, a Quaker custodial facility known as the York Retreat was established on the principle that treatment should rely upon moral persuasion and kindness rather than coercion. The person most frequently credited with liberating those

The Bethlehem Hospital, commonly known as Bedlam, was one of the first, and worst, asylums for the insane. The chaos that was characteristic of Bedlam is graphically depicted in this eighteenth-century etching by Hogarth. (*National Library of Medicine.*)

displaying abnormal behavior from their chains was Philippe Pinel in France. His humanitarian reforms were widely imitated throughout Europe. The practices in American institutions of this period were generally less abusive, though physical restraint was commonly employed. The earliest facility was the Pennsylvania Hospital, which began taking patients in its Insane Department in 1752, and the mental hospital in Williamsburg, which opened in 1773 exclusively for the mentally ill.

One institutional approach that found its major expression in America and had a very successful, but short-lived, existence was *moral treatment* (Bockoven, 1963). It was an approach based on the work of Pinel and the English Quaker tradition of the York Retreat. It was not a religious approach, but one built on the moral doctrine of the time—hard work, good food, healthy atmosphere, good frame of mind, and firm conviction that the problems would be resolved. Data from the Worcester Retreat in Massachusetts showed success rates enviable even by today's standards. The expanding acceptance of an *organic* explanation,

however, eventually brought an end to the use of this approach.

The Nineteenth Century

By 1850, there were over a dozen state mental hospitals, and awareness of the problem was growing. Dorothea Dix was effective in leading the American public to a concern for improved standards of care and treatment in mental institutions. The hospital supervisors banded together in an organization that was later to become the American Psychiatric Association. In 1884, this group began publishing *The American Journal of the Insane* to stimulate discussion of all aspects of abnormal behavior.

The Scientific Approach

A period of rapid growth ensued in the scientific study of abnormal behavior. European research had identified the brain as the locus of mental functioning. Careful investiga-

Philippe Pinel, shown here at a hospital in France, was one of the first to attempt humanitarian reform in mental hospitals and to liberate the inmates from their chains. (*National Library of Medicine.*)

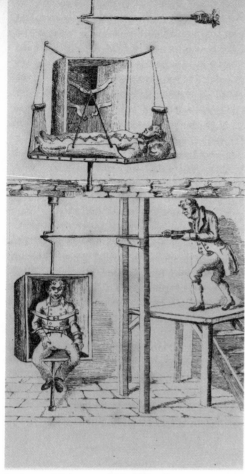

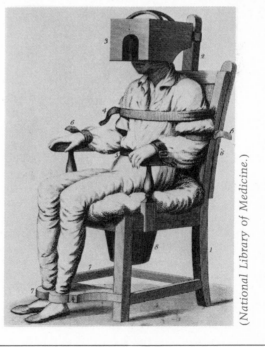

Although there was significant improvement in the standards of care and treatment in some nineteenth-century mental institutions, other hospitals relied on cruel punishments and restraining devices.

tions in anatomy and physiology had shown that specific areas of the brain are related to different physical functions. For example, stimulating a certain point in the brain with electric current consistently causes movements in a particular part of the body. Considerable effort went into the mapping of internal areas of the brain according to the functions they control.

The history of science must record its mistakes as well as its triumphs. In what now seems a parody of physiological advances, the nineteenth century witnessed the development of the pseudoscience of *phrenology*. Its advocates claimed to have mapped the external skull in correspondence to mental abilities. Bumps and prominences in certain areas were used to assess the character and personality of the individual being examined.

In addition to searching for internal and external localization of function, the nineteenth-century scientists were busy devising elaborate systems for the classification of abnormal behavior. Stimulated by the work of Linnaeus in biology, many classificatory schemes were offered. The most influential system was proposed in the 1880s by Emil Kraepelin, a German psychiatrist. The Kraepelinian system is based on observation of the symptoms and the course of the mental illness. Certain patterns of symptoms, or *syndromes*, were noted to lead to predictable outcomes. Compiling masses of observational data, Kraepelin divided abnormal behavior into two broad categories: (1) *dementia praecox* (now known as schizophrenia) and (2) *manic-depressive psychoses*. Each division had many subclassifications based on symptoms and prognosis. Kraepelin felt that patients could recover from the manic-depressive psychoses, but believed that the condition of dementia praecox would progressively deteriorate to a totally demented state that was generally incurable. The existence of Kraepelin's labels brought order out of chaos in the psychiatric field, but at the same time may have inhibited further creative thinking about abnormal behavior. For many years, psychiatric observations were molded to fit these already-established categories.

The Organic Model

Kraepelin's fatalistic view of a large segment of psychologic disorders discouraged the use of therapeutic measures to treat them. He believed the illnesses included under the general heading of *dementia praecox* reflected basic constitutional weaknesses, possibly of a metabolic nature. The faults were biological and probably incurable. His attitudes illustrate the prevailing view in German medical circles of the time, which might be briefly paraphrased as "no twisted thought without a twisted molecule."

This organic model was supported even more fanatically by Wilhelm Griesinger, another nineteenth-century German psychiatrist. According to Griesinger, *all* psychologic disorders were diseases of the brain. Rather than classifying diseases by their symptoms, Griesinger encouraged psychiatrists to look within the body for medical relationships and causes. Painstaking autopsies of mental patients were conducted in search of physiologic origins. In most cases, the quest resulted in some finding of abnormality to which the insanity was attributed. When no anatomical flaws could be found, the physician's skill was questioned rather than the organic theory. This attitude was the same as that of the Middle Ages!

In some cases, however, these scientists were on the right track. We now know that some physical diseases produce mental changes, and occasionally psychological abnormalities are the primary symptoms of these physical diseases. The organic model was supported by the exciting nineteenth-century discovery that *general paresis*, a syndrome involving mental deterioration and paralysis, was due to lesions in the brain caused by syphilis. This finding provided the first direct link between a psychologic disorder and a physical event. Many more examples were to follow, and the biophysical view of abnormality was to remain an important avenue of approach in medical science.

The organic model is also the *symptom* model, that is, the symptom is a clinical sign of some underlying disease process. For example, coughing is the sign or symptom of some more basic problem in the respiratory system; it is not the disease per se. In this view, the madness is not the disorder, it is a sign of some destructive brain process such as the work of the syphilitic germ. Thus, according to the organic model, the manifest behavior is of less importance than the underlying pathology.

The Medical Illness Model

When psychiatry, under Freud and others, was forced away from the organic view, it rejected the organic model but retained the *medical* or *illness* model upon which it was based. That is, while there may not be actual physical changes in the brain, there are underlying psychological events that are responsible for the behavioral effects of symptoms. For Freud, the abnormal behaviors were merely the outward symptoms of the deeper, underlying processes of *intrapsychic conflicts.* To treat only the symptoms would be useless, since the underlying pathological processes would still be present. More important, it would be dangerous to treat only the symptoms, since the symptoms are seen as the response the patient makes to the disturbance—an attempt to maintain balance in the system, much as a fever or inflammation is a bodily response to infection. Treating only the symptoms would result in an outcropping of new symptoms, or possible disintegration of the total personality structure. We will discuss this in greater detail in Chapter 3. For now, it is important to note that the medical or illness model became the dominant view of abnormal behavior, and has retained that position to the present time.

Abnormal Psychology as a Field of Study

The preceding historical overview has been intended to show the search people have made for ways of conceptualizing and responding to psychological problems. At a more basic level, it is the story of the individual's attempt to find order in his universe. Abnormal behavior, a disturbing and often terrifying event, has been a constant challenge to our explanatory powers. It has been perceived in many ways, depending on society's total world view at the time. The intensity of our response to "disordered" behavior, even in the twentieth century, is more easily understood when such behavior is viewed as thwarting our need to live in a rational world—a world where we can predict and control behavior, our neighbor's as well as our own.

The Scientific Method

Contemporary abnormal psychology has continued the quest to increase our understanding of abnormal behavior. From the nineteenth century, we have inherited the intellectual system of science as our method of attacking the problem. Science emerged as the dominant view because it proved to be fruitful. It advanced our knowledge and allowed a greater degree of control over previously inexplicable events.

We choose science because it has paid off. But once we choose to view issues of abnormal behavior from the scientific point of view, certain restrictions are placed on how we proceed. Observation and description are the first stages in a scientific endeavor. One of the basic rules of science is that events should be explainable in naturalistic terms, rather than in the supernatural terms we have seen throughout the ages. Descriptions and observations must also be subject to agreement of more than one observer. The same event can be perceived differently by different individuals, but science will only allow data that are held in common, that is, data that are *consensually verifiable.*

Basic to the scientific method is the goal of generating testable hypotheses. The hallmark of a good theory is that it offers plausible explanations, in this instance about abnormal behavior, that can be subjected to empirical tests of its validity. Science does not advance when all parties adhere to one theory, or when the prevailing theory is so constructed that it is impossible to disprove it. The organic model developed in Germany might be taken as an example of a theory that could not be disproved. In cases where no organic causes of abnormal behavior could be found, the proponents of the theory could always argue that their techniques were not yet sufficiently advanced to discover the "twisted molecules" at fault. Science advances when *alternative* explanations are proposed for the same phenomenon. The active controversy stimulates theoreticians and researchers on all sides of a question to muster evidence to support their particular view. These explanatory systems are variously referred to as "models," "perspectives," or "viewpoints" (Price, 1972). Much of the work of science stems from attempts to either support or refute such theoretical constructions. It is out of the "fight" of opposing theoretical views that useful approaches survive, while inappropriate ones disappear. Kuhn (1962) referred to this as a "paradigm clash."

Viewpoints, Models, and Perspectives

One of the terms most frequently used in describing ways of thinking about abnormal behavior is the word "model." The basic quality of a "model" is that it provides a means of comparison to something more familiar. For example, in using illness as a model for abnormal behavior, we are attempting to understand events that are puzzling to us by assuming that they are similar to things we find easier to comprehend, that is, physical sickness (Price, 1972).

Models help us to choose the events we consider relevant while discarding those that have no importance for the theory. Within the illness model, we will distinguish between events that are considered to be symptoms from other aspects of abnormal behavior that are observed, but have no bearing on the model itself, such as the reaction of the general public to a mentally ill patient.

A major problem with the use of models is that we often forget that they are only representations of the thing we are studying, and

that as such, they will always be incomplete and imperfect. To continue with our example, we should always be careful to say that abnormal behavior is *like* an illness, or that it may be viewed *as if* it were an illness. It is overstating the model to declare that abnormal behavior *is* an illness, just as you would not try to fly in a model airplane. In the chapters that follow, it will be important to remember that the viewpoints are not *the* reality itself, but are *representations* of that reality. They are ways of organizing the world into testable questions for the purposes of advancing our knowledge.

In dealing with the ways in which scientists have described abnormal behavior, it is more useful to speak of the various approaches as different "perspectives" or "viewpoints," rather than use the more global "model." These terms emphasize the fact that our constructions are not "finished" products. They also emphasize that different investigators can quite literally *see* the same problem in totally different ways (Price, 1972). The investigators have paid attention to those parts of the situation that have importance for them. In short, their viewpoint is consistent with the way they perceive and organize their universe. Communication among those holding various perspectives is often strained because each is concerned with different issues. Similarly, it becomes difficult to test each view to determine which is the "correct" one when each investigator is looking at different data.

Two Dominant Views of Abnormal Behavior

At present, we find several viewpoints being expressed about abnormal behavior, with two views sharing center stage: the behavioral and the psychodynamic points of view. These views differ in a number of central concepts—and these differences provide the intellectual opposition of ideas that is likely to lead to significant advancement in our knowledge about abnormal behavior. Both approaches will be described in detail in Chapter 3, but it will be useful for us to briefly summarize each view and their important differences at this point.

The Psychodynamic Viewpoint

The contributions of Sigmund Freud had great impact in the developing field of abnormal psychology. At the end of the nineteenth century, Freud began explaining abnormal behavior on the basis of the medical model. Retaining the idea of symptoms as reflections of deeper processes, he proposed that mental, not physiological, processes were the underlying causative factors of psychological problems. Abnormal behavior was only the external manifestation, or "symptom," of *unconscious* intrapsychic conflicts.

The psychodynamic approach rose to prominence in the 1920s and 1930s, and continues to dominate the conceptualization and treatment of psychological problems to the present time. Most contemporary mental health workers were trained in this view. The basic psychodynamic assumptions have permeated our society to such an extent that we all tend to look at behavior in these ways. If you hear that someone eats too much, your first response may be to wonder *why* he does so. The fact that you asked "Why?" and possibly generated some guesses about his state of anxiety or need for love, indicates that you think almost automatically in psychodynamic terms. You are looking for an underlying reason.

The psychodynamic orientation provides the labels for our current systems for categorizing abnormal behavior. The structure of this text, insofar as it follows the standard nomenclature of the field, is built upon the psychodynamic viewpoint. This approach has given birth to many offspring, with varying degrees of legitimacy, all of which have developed differently from the parent concepts of Freud. Self-actualization, existential approaches, and psychoanalysis are but a few of the better-known examples. We will discuss these and other related approaches in Chapter 3.

The Behavioral Viewpoint

The behavioral approach is a relatively recent development in general psychology, and has an even shorter history as a clinical method for the treatment of abnormal behavior. This viewpoint avoids reference to hypothetical internal states, and focuses primarily on overt and measurable phenomena. The observable behavior is the point of interest, not as a symptom of some other process, but as *the* central concern. Theoretical emphasis is placed on how the patient has learned maladaptive behaviors, rather than on his or her possible intrapsychic conflicts. The individual's environment is considered important in the initiation and maintenance of abnormal functioning. As with the psychodynamic viewpoint, there are also variations within the behavioral perspective, which will be discussed in Chapter 3.

The two viewpoints are basically irreconcilable, despite the attempts of some theoreticians to integrate them. The psychodynamic and the behavioral approaches ask different questions about human behavior, and consider different data to be relevant in providing the answers. At this point in our scientific development, neither view can be singled out as a sufficient explanation for all abnormal behavior. Both perspectives have made valuable contributions to our understanding, and will necessarily coexist and compete for some time to come.

It is important for the student of abnormal psychology to understand the hypotheses generated by both viewpoints. The field of study is not a static body of factual knowledge. There is no consistent theoretical base from which to generate quick and easy answers. You are learning about a developing and expanding field of knowledge recently dominated by one point of view (the psychodynamic) but currently being challenged by a very different approach (the behavioral). This will create problems for you in that the simplest proposition is always made more complex by the alternative view. But to present the field as fixed would be a distortion of the current state of things. It is our desire to have you share the excitement of the struggle and to be an active participant in the debate.

Within the next few years, developments are likely to occur that will radically alter our current viewpoints. Your knowledge of the present struggles in the field of abnormal psychology will better equip you to understand those developments.

Summary

In this chapter, we have discussed the popularly held views of abnormal behavior, especially the misconceptions and negative attitudes held by the general public. On the assumption that students enter the field with at least some of these preconceived ideas, we attempted to equip you with a more accurate picture of the problem of abnormal behavior in our society today. The vast number of persons affected, the enormous costs involved in their treatment, and the personal devastation that results have all been touched upon.

A brief historical overview was presented to show how we have arrived at our present conceptualizations of abnormal behavior. Sensitivity to the problem heightened in the Greek and Roman eras, but was effectively lost during the Middle Ages. A slow recovery began in the sixteenth century and culminated in the scientific approach of the late nineteenth and twentieth centuries. The organic and medical models of abnormal behavior developed along with the scientific approach. At present, of the variety of theoretical perspectives, two major viewpoints are vying for domination in the field of abnormal psychology: the psychodynamic approach and the behavioral approach.

2.

The designation and classification of abnormal behavior

Designating Behavior as Abnormal

The decision that a person's behavior is "abnormal" has far-reaching consequences for that individual. From the moment he is labeled "abnormal," every aspect of that individual's life is altered in rather dramatic—and often unpleasant—ways. In light of these powerful effects, it is important that we look closely at the manner in which such decisions are made.

The use of the word "abnormal" indicates that the action referred to is different from normal behavior. However, underlying our use of the word "abnormal" is the assumption that we know what normal behavior is and can recognize the deviations from it.

At first glance, the distinction between normal and abnormal seems to be an easy one to make. We all know the way normal people act. They act like us. Abnormal behavior is what the media depict as what goes on in state hospitals for the insane. There are obvious differences between everyday behavior and the bizarre, unusual, sometimes violent behavior that is associated with madness. But the ease in distinguishing between them diminishes when we realize that the very unusual behaviors are much more rare than we were led to believe and the great majority of people experiencing psychological difficulties do not look different from us. It is even more difficult to remain comfortable with our conception of normality when we begin to question just how normal *we* are. What about that nightmare last week? that unexplainable self-defeating pattern of studying (or not studying) that consistently leads to poor grades? that rush of unexplainable joy that left us laughing and not knowing why?

One author had this experience in New York's Times Square:

I wasn't paying much attention to any of these sights—I walk through them every day, thinking of other things. Then, as I was about to cross 45th Street, the strange thing happened: I couldn't figure out how to cross the street. I stood there at the curb in a state of bewilderment, unable at first even to realize what it was that I couldn't figure out. I carefully told myself that it would be all right to cross the street whenever the traffic stopped, but as I watched the trucks and taxis flowing south along Broadway, I couldn't determine which part of traffic was supposed to stop, or which street I was trying to cross. Then I thought, as one always does at moments of crisis, "This can't be happening." Then I felt a touch, just a touch, of fear—panic. Even while I kept reassuring myself that this couldn't be happening, I also saw myself standing utterly helpless in the middle of Times Square— intellectually incapable of finding out how to cross the street, but repeatedly warning myself that if I made a mistake, the oncoming traffic would kill me. (Friedrich, 1976, p. 1)

Friedrich was so intrigued by this experience that he went on to explore the whole issue of abnormality in a book titled *Going Crazy* (1976). He considers himself normal, as do most of us, despite the occasional experiences of something "not normal."

The normal-abnormal distinction appears to be far less clear than one would like it to be. This is an accurate reflection of where psychology as a field of study finds itself at present. However, the search for the concept of normality continues; it is the attempt to understand normality to which we now turn.

Criteria of Normality

The notion of a normal organism has its roots in medical tradition. If we wish to evaluate an individual's *physical* normality, medical science has provided us with reasonably objective methods. Bodily functions and properties, such as blood pressure, temperature, height, and weight, may be measured and compared to the "normal" readings. The designation of abnormal is made when one or more of these measures falls outside the accepted limits of normality for that measure.

To apply the same methodology to behavior, normal attributes must be specified and ways to measure these attributes developed. A person whose measurements fall outside the accepted limits of normality would be designated as abnormal. The major problem with this seemingly straightforward procedure is in deciding and agreeing upon what is normal.

There is little information and even less clarity about the nature of psychological normality. One proposed solution is to attempt to define normality in terms of the relative lack of deviant signs and symptoms. However, this results in a circular process of always defining one state by the absence of another. This certainly is not a useful approach to the problem.

Another trend tries to conceptualize the normal personality in terms of positive, progressive growth toward more productive and satisfying ways of life. This leads to the prob-

"Stop worrying. These days everything is normal." (*Sidney Harris*.)

lem of defining rather vague concepts concerned with positive development.

Shoben (1957) attempts to overcome these deficiencies by describing what he calls "a model of integrative adjustment" (p. 186). His model is based on considerations of the human being's unique potentialities, with specific emphasis on the person's ability to forego immediate pleasures for long-term gains. This approach, for example, allows for nonconformity to be classified as normal if it allows an individual, through self-control, to reach a higher level of gratification in the future. Shoben characterizes his model of integrative adjustment by criteria of "self-control, personal responsibility, social responsibility, democratic social interest and ideals" (p. 188). While he admits that this is not the ultimate definition, he makes the justifiable point that it does allow the normal person the possibility of being an independent individual who may be considered well adjusted even though he or she does not conform to the statistical average of his or her reference group.

Instead of delineating criteria for normal behavior, some investigators turn the problem around. They attempt to formulate theories of normal development from studies of abnormal patients. However, it makes more sense to acquire an understanding of normality from the study of normal individuals. But often it is difficult to find normal subjects to evaluate. Abnormal subjects (those in treatment) can be found in psychiatrists' offices and in hospitals. Reliably "normal" individuals or groups are not that easy to identify.

There are two problems in forming a structure for normality. The first is *normative ambiguity*, which refers to the use of the term "normal" at times in reference to facts and at other times in reference to subjective values. It is easy to mistake our own values for facts. Values must be validated empirically before being applied to a definitive structure of normality.

The second difficulty is the immense *diversity of behaviors*, all of which may be considered normal. With so many different behaviors, how do we determine what is normal? Some psychologists (e.g., Kaplan, 1967) feel that any concept of normality must provide for a wide range of behaviors, all related to normality, but not all of which are expected or required to be present in all individuals at all times. Certain of these traits, however, such as curiosity, spontaneity, realism, creativity, and confidence, should be present in various degrees at various times and in various situations.

Where does all this leave us in our attempt to define "normal" as a base for designating the "abnormal"? We must caution against the hasty formation of a poorly conceived construct of normality that has the potential for doing more harm than good. But the immediate outlook for a more satisfactory definition of normality is dim.

> Is a profile emerging that reliably describes the normal man or woman? Definitely not. The more one studies normal populations, the more one becomes aware that healthy functioning is as complex, and coping behavior as varied, as the psychopathological entities. Normality and health cannot be understood in the abstract. Rather, they depend on the cultural norms, society's expectations and values, professional biases, individual differences, and the political climate of the time, which sets the tolerance for deviance. (Offer and Sabshin, 1975, p. 463)

Given this pessimistic outlook, we have little choice but to follow the advice of Smith (1961), who concludes: "We can get about our business without wasting our effort on the search for consensus on a unified set of mental health criteria when consensus is not to be had" (p. 306).

Criteria of Abnormality

Although researchers have been unable to construct and agree upon formal definitions of "normal" and "abnormal," there is no lack of such classification in our society. Several dimensions or criteria have evolved by which individuals are designated as "abnormal." The relative effectiveness of those criteria is the subject of this section.

The accompanying clinical cases (Box 2-1) are presented as illustrations of three individuals who, while in varying circumstances, are all

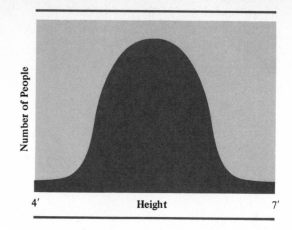

Figure 2-1 A curve representing the height of people in a normal group.

in the position of having decisions made about the normality or abnormality of their behavior. We will consider them in relation to the criteria systems that follow.

Statistical Criteria

Many measurable qualities of individuals, such as height and weight, can be arranged in a frequency distribution. Graphically, a bell-shaped curve results with most people falling at the center of the curve (see Figure 2-1). If a behavior can be measured and the value plotted in such a manner, an individual's position with regard to that behavior can be indicated statistically in relation to the total population measured. If the individual is unacceptably far from the central tendency of that population in either direction, he or she will be designated as "abnormal" for that behavior.

Problems of statistical criteria Since the determination is the *statistical* deviation, statistical criteria appear, at first, to be free of subjective value judgments. Consider our three cases. Miss C deviates statistically by cleaning too much. Mr. P qualifies as abnormal by marrying too much. But what of Mr. S? Even once is too much when it comes to attacking a police officer. Obviously, not all behaviors are clarified by arranging them in a frequency distribution.

Now consider Miss C again. How much is too much when it comes to cleaning? The cut-off point for normal cleaning is clearly arbitrary. This presents another problem for statistical criteria. Imagine how an individual would feel being hospitalized or designated abnormal because his or her frequency for some behavior falls one point outside a cut-off mark arbitrarily

designated as normal for that behavior.

A final problem with statistical criteria is that they are also a measure of *conformity* to the social context. If Mr. P, for example, lived in a society that permitted multiple marriages, his behavior might not be designated as abnormal. Statistical criteria are, then, social conformity approaches to abnormal behavior. They ask only how close an individual comes to the norm for that society.

Box 2-1 Three Cases of Abnormal Behavior

Mr. S

Mr. S, a 22-year-old college student, was brought by the police to a hospital emergency room after an incident on a subway train. He had been talking loudly and in a threatening manner, seemingly to himself. When approached by a transit police officer, Mr. S's only clear statement was, "So they finally sent you to get me." He then attacked the police officer and was subdued only after a lengthy struggle. In the emergency room, the psychiatric resident noted that Mr. S was very confused as to where he was and what had happened. He spoke about people being "out to get me" and plotting for some time in an attempt to control his mind. When that failed, they sent someone to get him, "once and for all."

Mr. P

Mr. P was a salesman for a national firm and was very successful at his job. Quite by accident, his wife of three years came across some papers indicating that he had been married before. When confronted with this fact, Mr. P shrugged it off as unimportant. His wife contacted a lawyer who found that Mr. P had indeed been married before. In fact, he had been married at least four times and none of these marriages had ever been dissolved. His wife brought both criminal and civil charges against him. Investigation revealed that Mr. P had left each marriage apparently on the spur of the moment. Although embezzlement did not seem to be a motive, he had, in each case, taken all available valuables with him. The court referred him for psychological evaluation. The psychologists found him cooperative and pleasant. He showed no empathy for the women he had deserted nor for his current wife, and no signs of remorse for what he had done. His only concern was what might happen to him as a result of the legal aspects of his case.

Miss C

Miss C presented herself to the mental health service at the university she was attending. She knew she was having trouble adjusting to the work at this large university and to living away from home. The therapist noted immediately that Miss C was dressed and groomed with exceptional care. Miss C told the therapist that she found herself forever cleaning up her room and arranging her work but never getting to it. She spoke of recently becoming interested in games she had played as a child, in which the object was to do things in a certain order or touch objects in a precise way. At first, she thought the games were fun, but found she was quite uncomfortable and greatly concerned when she didn't do the game correctly. Finally, she mentioned personal cleanliness as a growing problem. Miss C found that she was constantly washing her hands. Though this made her feel better at first, she almost immediately felt that she needed to wash her hands again as she must have gotten dirty. She showed the therapist her hands, which were badly irritated and sore from the continual washing. She was greatly concerned about all this. She didn't want to do the things she was doing, but she had strong feelings that something terrible would happen unless she did them. She felt she couldn't go on this way a minute longer.

Criteria of Personal Discomfort

Our society supports a complaint-response system of medical illness. Individuals go to a physician (i.e., classify themselves as ill) because they are aware of their pain or symptoms. The same approach can be applied to the designation of abnormality. The person's subjective assessment that he or she needs help would be the criterion.

Problems of personal discomfort criteria Of our three cases, only Miss C, who actually sought help, would thus be designated as abnormal. Consider Mr. S and Mr. P and the problem with this approach becomes apparent. Mr. S is obviously a danger to himself and others, yet he would not acknowledge any personal discomfort and would therefore be considered normal. Mr. P no doubt feels that he is doing just fine. His trail of emotional and legal disasters, however, clearly requires some response from society. Thus personal discomfort, while being an important criterion, has some obvious shortcomings when applied universally.

Criteria of Social Nonconformity

If an individual conforms to the cultural norms of a given society at a given time, he will not be designated as abnormal. If, on the other hand, he deviates from the social expectations, he will be designated abnormal.

These criteria would quickly identify Mr. S and Mr. P as abnormal. They have broken the social rules in no uncertain terms. Miss C, however, would be likely to be classified as normal since, if anything, she is inclined to overconform to social expectations of neatness and cleanliness.

Problems with social nonconformity criteria In a pluralistic society such as ours, which subsets of rules apply? How does the behavior of one subgroup look to someone not familiar with the social mores of that group? This problem becomes intensified by a clash of subcultures, when an individual finds himself in a different part of the culture from the one in which he has been functioning.

Even if all societies were homogeneous, all of them could not be considered as healthy. Could individuals who conformed to the social rules of Nazi Germany be considered normal? Could a deviant member of a psychologically disordered society be considered normal by other, more ideal criteria?

Another problem with social nonconformity criteria is that cultural conformity may limit cultural innovation. Creative advances in any society may be instigated by the nonconformist behavior of some of the society's members. If people exhibiting such behavior (wishing to improve society by changing it rather than adapting to it) run the risk of being labeled as deviant, their socially conscious activity will be severely curbed. The designation of abnormal behavior thus has the potential to become a political weapon. Many intellectuals in totalitarian societies have been incarcerated in mental institutions. Our own society condemns this practice of manipulation by negative labeling. The use of such labels, however, is not unknown in our society. Perhaps we merely find the instances of such labeling harder to recognize.

A final problem is that nonconformity is often used to justify hospitalization. Individuals displaying deviant behavior may be detained on the grounds that they are a danger to society. We will see in subsequent chapters how institutions evolved as places to "store" society's problems rather than as places to treat such individuals and return them to productive social functioning.

Legal Criteria of Abnormal Behavior

The interaction between a society's legal system and its mental health system is necessary. Unfortunately, this interaction is often a source of difficulty for both. The legal system is concerned with violations of the law, both actual and probable, and with the legal responsibilities of individuals. In Chapter 19, we will discuss in greater depth some of the issues of this relationship. For now, we need to be aware

This man spends most of his time campaigning for "husband liberation." Clearly, he is a social nonconformist, but is his behavior abnormal? (*Charles Gatewood, Magnum Photos.*)

that there are several terms used by the legal community to provide a legal designation of abnormal behavior. Some of the most important of these follow.

1. *Insanity.* The legal meaning of insanity has never been clearly stated. As a result, conflicts among members of the judiciary, the accused, the juries, and psychiatric witnesses are inevitable. The term "insanity" is usually employed to describe a type or degree of mental disturbance so severe that the individual suffering from it is not held accountable for certain legal responsibilities, such as specific violations of the law. Furthermore, the legally insane are not eligible to undertake other responsibilities such as business commitments or marriage.

Box 2-2 Criteria of Abnormality

Statistical	Anything that deviates from the central tendency of the population.
Personal discomfort	An individual's subjective assessment that he needs help.
Social nonconformity	Any behavior that deviates from social expectations.
Legal insanity	Inability to distinguish right from wrong.
Research definitions	Most often defined by the fact that a person is under treatment in a mental institution, but this definition is inadequate.

When used as a legal defense, "insanity" usually involves a question of the capacity to distinguish right from wrong, or good from evil.

2. *Irresistible impulse.* A defense of insanity may also be based on the fact that the defendant's mental state made it impossible for the defendant to control the urge to commit the crime. This "irresistible impulse" test was added by some states where it was argued that the right-from-wrong criterion, that is, knowing the nature and consequences of one's acts, placed too much emphasis on cognition or thought (Watson, 1975).

3. *Civil competence.* Civil competence refers to the mental soundness of an individual to carry out certain civil acts such as entering into a marriage or signing a business contract. A common example of a dispute over civil competence is the challenge of a will by disgruntled heirs on the grounds that it was not written while the person who made the will was "of sound mind, memory, and understanding." Since the individual whose competence is being challenged is usually no longer available for examination, the difficulties encountered can be extreme.

4. *Voluntary hospitalization.* Individuals who enter a mental hospital through their own volition or agreement have theoretically the same legal standing as they would have in a medical hospital. Patients are often required to agree to stay for a specified minimum time period or give a specified notice before leaving. This practice has questionable legal validity.

5. *Commitment and involuntary hospitalization.* Psychiatry and the law are basically in agreement that commitment refers to a legal procedure designed to permit involuntary hospitalization of a person suffering from or thought to be suffering from a severe mental disorder (Freedman, 1967). Involuntary "commitment" to a mental hospital requires court procedures in which the individuals are proven to be "mentally ill," a danger to themselves, a danger to others, or some combination of the three. Petitions to have a person committed may be filed by immediate family members, by the police, or by physicians who are not engaged in the ongoing treatment of the patients. To the lawyer, "commitment" is likely to be considered as a form of imprisonment. The psychiatrist considers it a procedure instigated to help the patient. In view of these differing opinions, it should not be surprising that conflicts arise frequently.

The danger with involuntary hospitalization is that the person may be committed for an indefinite period after a court hearing that had not allowed either enough time for the hearing or a thorough professional examination as warranted before a serious decision is made. In addition, the committed run the risk of receiving inadequate treatment that, combined with the psychological effects of being hospitalized, may do them more harm than good.

6. *Criminal responsibility.* The ability to control one's behavior is a crucial factor in deciding criminal responsibility. Throughout history, legal decisions provide a picture of the changing views of both abnormality and criminality. The varied approaches in this country are coalescing around a unified body of laws. Several states have adopted the following rule, known as the ALI (American Law Institute) rule in the determination of criminal responsibility:

(1) A person is not responsible for criminal conduct if at the time of such conduct as a result of mental disease or defect he lacks adequate capacity either to appreciate the criminality of his conduct or to conform his conduct to the requirements of law. (2) The terms "mental disease or defect" do not include an abnormality manifested only by

repeated criminal or otherwise anti-social conduct. (Watson, 1975, p. 2423)

The actual nature of a particular offense, the personality of the defendant, the skill of the attorneys, and the emotional reaction of the jurors, however, will usually have more effect than the official legal definitions. The possible inequities are obvious.

It is important to realize that these are all primarily legal terms. Their psychological meaning and relevance are often a matter of considerable dispute. This accounts, in part, for the general confusion that usually arises when psychologists or psychiatrists are called in as expert witnesses.

However, psychology is not interested in being a sparring partner for lawyers. Rather, it is concerned with the psychological state of individuals who have, through their behavior, come into conflict with society's laws and legal expectations.

Use of Formal Assessment Instruments

Just as a thermometer is an instrument designed to assess the normality of body temperature by comparison with normative data, psychological tests have been developed as instruments to assess the normality of psychological symptoms. Psychological tests have been notably successful in some areas such as intellectual assessment and vocational guidance. More controversial are the gains achieved in the assessment of personality and abnormal behavior. This subject will be discussed in detail in Chapter 5.

Research Definitions of Abnormality

Research into abnormal behavior is severely hampered by the lack of a clear definition of the phenomenon being studied (Scott, 1958). Often researchers have used deliberately limited but more objective definitions of abnormal behavior. The most frequently used definition is simply the fact that a person is under treatment in a mental institution. While totally objective, this definition has many limitations. Standards of psychiatric diagnosis—on which

admissions to the hospital depend—are by no means consistent. In addition, criteria for admission vary from region to region and from hospital to hospital.

The variety of criteria currently employed in the designation of abnormality reflects the complexity and confusion of the problem. None of the approaches stand out as obviously superior. All have defects seriously limiting the value of their use. As we have noted, there will be profound effects on a person's life from being labeled "abnormal." Can we afford to risk such potentially tragic consequences resulting from the use of such questionable criteria?

Sociopsychological Factors in the Designation of Abnormal Behavior

So far, we have been examining different theories for the designation of abnormality. What occurs in the so-called "real" world is often quite different from what the theories specify. In actual practice, there are crucial sociopsychological factors that also must be considered. Ullmann and Krasner (1969) have outlined the sociopsychological steps leading to the designation of abnormality:

> An individual may do something . . . under a set of circumstances . . . which upsets, annoys, angers, worries, or strongly disturbs somebody . . . sufficiently that some action results . . . so that the society's professional labellers . . . come into contact with the individual and determine which of the current set of labels . . . is most appropriate. . . . Finally there follow attempts to change the emission of the offending behavior. (pp. 21–23)

Note that the professional mental health worker does not enter into the decision-making process until after an individual's behavior is labeled as abnormal. The *initial* distinction between normal and abnormal is made at the *nonprofessional* level.

Considering this phenomenon in relation to the complaint-response medical system noted earlier, in which the individual initiates contact and is then responded to, we discover that people are initially labeled as "abnormal" by people close to them. They become psychological problems to themselves, their families, their friends, and to the authorities and other power figures in their environment. In other words, the decision of abnormality is made at the "civilian" level. The mental health professional is asked only to label the *type* of abnormality, not to decide if an abnormality exists. This puts a great deal of pressure on the professional to support the initial judgment of "abnormality." The professional will most likely make a conservative judgment and agree with the "civilian" assessment for fear of inadvertently turning away someone who might hurt himself or others. As we shall see, this conservative judgment often results in pain for the subject of that decision.

Diagnostic Classification

Classification in Science, Medicine, and Psychiatry

"Whenever man is confronted with a variety of phenomena, he is compelled to order them in some way or other" (Robbins, 1966, p. 3). This is nowhere more true—or more important—than in the field of science. Classification is used to reduce the complexity of describing and identifying phenomena by placing them into categories on the basis of similarity, or shared attributes.

In medicine, the grouping of similar physical signs or symptoms is a necessary step toward gaining knowledge about the diagnosis, treatment, and prevention of disease. The extension of the medical illness model to abnormal behavior brought diagnostic classification to this area as well.

A medical example of the advantage of categorizing symptoms was seen when individual physicians reported the occurrence of a particular type of cough—shallow, dry, painful—accompanied by some weakness and general malaise. Investigators noted that the dis-

order followed a similar course in many of the patients—deepening feelings of fatigue, painful coughing, loss of weight, production of blood in the sputum, and increasing disability, leading to death at a relatively young age. The initial categorizations and the procedure described below eventually led to the cure of tuberculosis. How this was accomplished will help us understand the value of the diagnostic approach to medicine.

Symptoms and Syndromes

Grouping together individual cases leads to putting together signs, or *symptoms*, into a general category with several common features (dry cough, loss of weight, blood in the sputum, etc.). The larger, general category is now called a *syndrome*. In the example of tuberculosis, the label applied to the syndrome was "consumption," which referred to the characteristic wasting away of the body. The label is often descriptive, as in this case. Occasionally, the name of the physician first indicating the category is used as the syndrome label.

Diagnosis, Prognosis, Etiology, and Treatment

Making a *diagnosis* may be described as judging an illness to belong to a particular category on the basis of the similarity of its symptoms to those of the category. This process became such an important aspect of mid-nineteenth-century medicine that some physicians specialized in it and became primarily diagnosticians.

The direction in which the disorder will progress also becomes predictable by assembling data from patients with similar symptoms and following the progress of the disorder. The common *course* of the disorder thus becomes clear. This is called the *prognosis*. It permits the physician to predict what will happen to the individual patient, including the chances of recovery, on the basis of what has happened to others with the same illness.

The next stage involves two different procedures, often carried out at the same time—

treatment and investigation of the cause of the illness. First, as the course of a disorder becomes more predictable, the physician can try to alter that course by employing various treatments that, on the basis of experience, speculation, or trial and error, are believed to be beneficial. At this point, the physician does not know the cause of the disorder. His treatments are determined empirically. In the case of consumption, the treatment included a variety of procedures aimed at building the general physical strength of the patient. Some were palliative measures such as nutritious food, rest, and sanitarium treatment in mountain resorts. Other approaches were more direct, even extending to surgically collapsing a lung to allow it to recover through rest.

Thus as a result of classification, diagnosis, and prognosis, treatments emerge. And the physicians' body of knowledge is increased, since generalizations about the effects of experimental treatments may be assembled and shared in the medical literature. Without the common labels, this would be impossible.

The other procedure that can follow from the categorization of similar symptom patterns is basic research on the cause of the disorder. In this example, examination of the products of the lungs, through the use of newly developed medical techniques, permitted the identification of an organism in the lungs of consumptives that was not present in the lungs of nonconsumptives. This organism was called the tubercle bacillis. It was soon recognized as the causal agent of consumption, that is, the *etiological* agent. The disorder thus became known as "tuberculosis." Once the etiological agent was known, it was possible to attack the cause directly, making treatment more specific and successful. In addition, preventive programs could be initiated.

This account of the approach to one disorder shows how the model met with such great success in nineteenth-century medi-

The work of Emil Kraepelin (1856–1926) (left) and Eugen Bleuler (1857–1939) (right) laid the foundation for our current diagnostic system for abnormal behavior. (*National Library of Medicine.*)

cine. Through the process of classification, diagnosis, prognosis, treatment, and the search for the etiological agent, age-old problems were either totally removed or ameliorated to the point of insignificance. Due to the development of these procedures, a highly productive stage in the history of medicine unfolded.

The Medical Model

How did abnormal behavior come to be explored through this medical approach? As described in Chapter 1, the connection between physical illness and abnormal behavior can be traced as far back as Hippocrates. Dramatic support for the organic viewpoint was heightened with the discovery that the behavioral manifestations of general paresis were due to a syphilitic infection. It was easy to generalize that all abnormal behavior was due to physical illness.

The next step was logical enough. Since abnormal behaviors are illnesses, the medical model will lead to their treatment and control.

Table 2-1 DSM-II Major Classifications of Mental Disorders

1. Neuroses
2. Personality disorders and certain other nonpsychotic mental disorders.
   A. Personality disorders
   B. Sexual deviation
   C. Alcoholism
   D. Drug dependence
3. Transient situational disturbances
4. Special symptoms
5. Psychophysiologic disorders
6. Psychoses not attributed to physical conditions listed previously
   A. Schizophrenia
   B. Major affective disorders
   C. Paranoid states
7. Behavior disorders of childhood and adolescence
8. Mental retardation
9. Organic brain syndromes
10. Conditions without manifest psychiatric disorder and nonspecific conditions

---

Kraepelin (1889/1937) employed a medical model to provide a comprehensive system of classification for disease—or nosology (from *nosos*, disease, and *logia*, study). He looked for the combination of symptoms that would best describe and predict the outcome of an affliction, thus creating terms such as "manic-depressive psychosis" and "dementia praecox" (precocious deterioration). Bleuler (1911/1950) went beyond the symptoms to the *process* of the pathological stages and produced a nosology that included terms referring to the process, such as "schizophrenia" (literally, the splitting of the mind).

Freud added significantly to the scope of existing terms by classifying the less severe reactions of the neuroses. In fact, our current diagnostic system is made up largely from the contributions of Kraepelin, Bleuler, and Freud.

The Current Classification System: American Psychiatric Association (APA) DSM-II

The U.S. federal government first began collecting statistical data on the mentally disturbed in 1840, although no attempt was made to classify types of disorder until 1880. These early attempts were primarily for census purposes and were discontinued thereafter.

In 1923, a special census was carried out that classified the hospitalized mentally disturbed, or inpatients. It was revised and formalized in 1934 as the American Medical Association's *Standard Classification Nomenclature of Disease*. This was the accepted standard until its inadequacies as a diagnostic aid to psychiatric discharge in World War II became apparent. In 1952, the U.S. Public Health Service sponsored, and the American Psychiatric Association published, the *Diagnostic and Statistical Manual of Mental Disorder*, known as the DSM-I.

The World Health Organization already had its own system of classification, which it found difficult to relate to the DSM-I. A committee was appointed in 1966 to reconcile the differences, resulting in the *International Classification of Diseases,* the ICD-8.

In 1968, another attempt was made to resolve the differences between the two systems and to correct criticisms made of the DSM-I. The result was the DSM-II, which in 1977 was the standard nosological system in the United States.

One interesting change made in the DSM-II was to replace the term "reactions," used in the DSM-I, with the earlier term, "diseases." As one observer put it, this represented a giant leap backward to the nineteenth-century viewpoint in its implication of disease processes rather than psychological reaction patterns.

The major classifications of disorders used by the DSM-II are shown in Table 2-1. Most of these disorders, along with their subgroups, are examined in later chapters of this book. At this point, we will outline each disorder briefly. The order chosen, not that of the DSM-II, is in accord with the text's discussion.

1. *Neuroses.* According to the DSM-II, the chief characteristic of the neurosis is anxiety, whether expressed by the person directly or unconsciously. Although neuroses do not cause distortion of the individual's contact with reality, they do result in distressing symptoms from which the patient wants relief. The DSM-II describes *anxiety neurosis,* characterized by strong feelings of impending disaster and panic, and *hysterical neurosis,* involving involuntary loss of function. Hysterical neurosis is subdivided into the conversion type, in which the individual may be affected with symptoms such as blindness or deafness, and the dissociative type, in which the state of consciousness may be affected, producing such symptoms as amnesia and multiple personality.

Another subgroup, *phobic neurosis,* describes feelings of intense fear of an object or situation, although those affected know intellectually that they are in no danger. The symptoms may include faintness, fatigue, nausea, or even panic.

Obsessive-compulsive neurosis is characterized by "the persistent intrusion of unwanted thoughts, urges, or actions that the patient is unable to stop" (DSM-II, p. 40). The thoughts may range from one word to trains of thought that often make no sense to the person. Actions may vary from simple movements to complex rituals. When the person is prevented from completing the ritual or feels unable to complete it, anxiety and distress usually result.

Other types of neuroses and their symptoms outlined by DSM-II are: *depressive neurosis*—excessively low mood in reaction to life events; *neurasthenic neurosis*—chronic weakness, easy fatigability, and exhaustion; *depersonalization neurosis*—feelings of unreality and estrangement from the self, body, or surroundings; *hypochondriacal neurosis*—preoccupation with the body and fear of presumed disease.

2. *Personality disorders.* These are long-term, generally lifelong, patterns of maladaptive behavior. The patterns are usually recognizable by adolescence or even earlier and are perceptibly different in quality from neurotic symptoms.

The types of personality disorders listed in the DSM-II are paranoid, schizoid, explosive, obsessive-compulsive, hysterical, asthenic, antisocial, passive-aggressive, and inadequate personalities.

Also included in personality disorders are *alcoholism, drug dependence,* and *sexual deviations,* such as fetishism, pedophilia, transvestism, transsexualism, exhibitionism, voyeurism, sadism, and masochism.

3. *Transient situational disturbances.* This category includes more or less temporary disorders that result from a severe reaction to overwhelming environmental stress rather than from an underlying mental disorder. Examples are attention-getting behavior resulting from sibling rivalry or "shell shock," which removes the individual from a life-threatening situation. Transient disorders may be of varying severity. The causes and manifestations of the disturbances are important in a diagnosis in this category.

4. *Special symptoms.* This category covers special disturbances, such as speech or sleep problems, that are not the result of an organic illness or other mental disorder.

5. *Psychophysiologic disorders.* These are physical symptoms, such as skin rashes or headaches, that are presumed to result from psychological factors. They involve a single organ system (e.g., respiratory,

gastrointestinal) that is usually under the control of the autonomic nervous system. The individuals are not always aware of their psychological state. Their physiological reactions, however, are stronger and last longer than normal.

6. *Psychoses.* In both social and medical terminology, the word "psychosis" has become associated with several meanings. The DSM-II definition is as follows:

> Patients are described as psychotic when their mental functioning is sufficiently impaired to interfere grossly with their capacity to meet the ordinary demands of life. The impairment may result from a serious distortion in their capacity to recognize reality. Hallucinations and delusions, for example, may distort their perceptions. Alterations of mood may be so profound that the patient's capacity to respond appropriately is grossly impaired. Deficits in perception, language and memory may be so severe that the patient's capacity for mental grasp of his situation is effectively lost. (American Psychiatric Association, 1968, p. 23)

Schizophrenia is the largest category included under psychoses. It includes a group of disorders that are characterized by marked disturbances in thinking, often leading to distortions of reality. Delusions and hallucinations may also occur. There are several subtypes of schizophrenia listed in the DSM-II. These will be discussed in Chapter 10.

The DSM-II makes a careful distinction between the schizophrenias, which are dominated by a thought disorder, and the *major affective disorders*, which are dominated by a mood disorder. Mood changes are, however, an accompanying symptom of schizophrenia and may include ambivalence, inappropriate emotional responses, and loss of empathy with others. Behavior may be withdrawn, regressive, and bizarre.

Major affective disorders dominate the mental life of the patient. They may take the form of depression or elation, or periods of depression may alternate with periods of elation. Regardless of type, the effect is extreme enough to cause the patients to lose some contact with their environment. The main types of affective disorders will be discussed in Chapter 12.

Paranoid states are a third main category under psychoses. These states are characterized by delusions, either of grandeur or persecution. Paranoid states can be distinguished from the other psychoses by the prominence of the delusion.

7. *Behavior disorders of childhood and adolescence.* This is an intermediate DSM-II category intended to cover childhood problems that are deeper and more resistant to treatment than transient situational disturbances, but less serious or internalized than psychoses, neuroses, and personality disorders. These disorders are characterized by symptoms such as overactivity, inattentiveness, shyness, over-aggressiveness, timidity, and delinquency. In actual practice, more severe childhood disorders, such as autism and childhood schizophrenia, are also classified in this category.

8. *Mental retardation.* This category refers to "subnormal general intellectual functioning which originates during the developmental period and is associated with impairment of either learning and social adjustment or maturation, or both" (DSM-II, p. 14). The five diagnostic categories related to intellectual functioning listed by DSM-II are (from least to most severe) borderline, mild, moderate, severe, and profound mental retardation.

In determining the severity of retardation, one must evaluate the patient's developmental history and present functioning, including intelligence test scores, academic and vocational achievement, motor skills, and social and emotional maturity.

9. *Organic brain syndromes.* These are disorders associated with impairment of the function of the brain tissue. Symptoms listed by DSM-II are impairment of orientation; of memory; of all intellectual functions such as comprehension, calculation, knowledge, learning; and of judgment. Lability (drastic mood swings) and shallowness of affect are also symptoms of the organic brain syndromes.

Whether a brain syndrome is regarded as psychotic or nonpsychotic depends on the severity of the impairment of the brain function. The cause of the impairment is not a deciding factor.

Whether the disorder is labeled "acute" (short-term) or "chronic" (long-term) depends primarily on whether the organic brain syndrome is reversible. The distinction is important because of essential differences in the prognosis and treatment.

10. *Conditions without manifest psychiatric disorders.* This category covers individuals who, though basically normal, nevertheless have severe enough problems to need professional mental health attention. Examples of these disorders are marital maladjustment, social maladjustment, occupational maladjustment, and asocial behavior (racketeers, dope peddlers, prostitutes, etc.). These maladjustments may develop into or bring on a diagnosable mental disorder.

Issues and Problems in the Use of DSM-II

The Medical Model—How Appropriate Is It?

At the beginning of the chapter, we questioned the concept of normality. In a classic paper, Szasz (1960) raises the question, "Is there such a thing as mental illness?" He argues that there is not. However, he does not claim that we are all happy, well-balanced, "normal" human beings. Rather, his argument is against the use of a medical model to describe and treat what he refers to as "problems in living."

Szasz contends that the myth that abnormal behavior is a "mental illness" is a result of the discovery that disorders of thinking and behavior can be caused by organic conditions such as syphilis of the brain. As we noted above and in Chapter 1, this discovery has led to schools of thought that believe *all* so-called "mental illness" results from some organic defect. We have suggested that this organic view of abnormal behavior as a sign of physical disease is misleading.

Szasz argues that the human body has a structural and functional integrity. Physical illness represents a deviation from the norm. To apply the medical model to mental processes requires a clearly defined mental norm. Such a norm, says Szasz, must be stated in psychosocial, ethical, and legal terms. Deviation from these norms is defined not by medical examination but by the patient himself (seeking help), by a legal expert such as a judge, or by a psychological professional such as a psychiatrist. Psychotherapy, however, traditionally follows the medical model in attempts to "cure" the patient's mental problem that was not medical in the first place.

Any science needs a classification system. The study of abnormal behavior is in an ambiguous position, however. Is it a branch of medicine related to chemistry and physics, or is it the study of human behavior and therefore related to psychology? Since "nosology" means the classification of *diseases*, a psychiatric nosology places the subject in the medical model. Differing views of psychological problems as brain disorders, mind disorders, or behavior disorders create separate nosologies.

Szasz goes so far as to postulate that this ambiguity, resulting in the use of terms such as "schizophrenia" that are meant to explain certain disorders, in fact, hinders understanding. Once something is labeled, the implication usually is that understanding exists (e.g., the label "tuberculosis"). He calls for the development of separate, more limited classifications that will create better-defined approaches to specific problems.

The failure to clarify the distinction between organic physical illnesses and functional psychological problems has had unfortunate consequences. Even though many attempts have been made by the mental health movement to convince the public that "mental illness" is no more stigmatizing than physical illness, this effort has been generally unsuccessful (Sarbin and Mancuso, 1970). Unfortunately, persons labeled as mentally ill are regarded as not merely sick, but as a special class of human beings to be feared, scorned, or pitied and nearly always to be degraded. And even when the symptoms disappear, the unfortunate individual usually remains stigmatized because the public is reluctant to accept "cures" as permanent. Since the source of the illness is the "dark, inner regions of the mind," experts can draw conclusions only by inference. The general public assumes that the source of the problem may still be in the ex-patient's mind, and so places limitations of social and occupational opportunity on the ex-patient (Sarbin, 1969).

Issues of the Reliability of the Diagnostic System

Criticisms of conventional psychiatric diagnosis range from demands for further refinement of the present system to arguments in favor of completely abolishing all labeling (Zigler and Phillips, 1961). Central to both arguments is the considerable lack of reliability of the present diagnostic system. Since diagnosis involves the occurrence of symptoms in particular combinations, the reliability of the system depends on the accuracy with which the symptoms have been described and the degree of certainty with which they may be ordered into classes. We have previously questioned the *validity* of these classes, that is, the extent to which these categories represent "real" or true categories of disorder. But even assuming their validity, there are wide differences among judges on the decision of whether a particular individual should be placed in that category, that is, the *reliability*. The symptoms do not always lead to reliable categorization of the individual.

In a study comparing the independent diagnoses of two pairs of psychiatrists, Ward and his co-workers (1962) found that two-thirds of the diagnostic disagreements between psychiatrists were based on the classification system itself. They found the system inadequate in three important respects. In 7.5 percent of the cases, disagreements in diagnoses were attributed to the diagnostician's having to make too fine distinctions. In other words, broader categories might have eliminated the disagreement. In another 30 percent of the cases, the disagreement was attributed to the need to classify a patient based on the "relative predominance of neurotic symptoms and personality disorders when both entities were present." Finally, in 25 percent of the cases, the disagreement was a result of unclear criteria. The study was done before the DSM-II was developed, but other studies have demonstrated similar problems in reliability.[1]

Sociopsychological Issues Involved in Labeling

When mental health professionals are confronted with abnormal behavior, they consider labeling the behavior to be part of their role. The label selected must be chosen from those available (Ullmann and Krasner, 1969). The DSM-II, by its very existence and authority, determines the labels available.

But, Ullmann and Krasner note, although the label may refer to the behavior, the people themselves now become connected to the label. From a distortion in their behavior, *they* come to be labeled as being *personally* distorted. From engaging in an "obsessive-compulsive" *act* such as excessive hand-washing, the people become labeled as "obsessive-compulsive neurotics." The distinction between labeling the *act* versus labeling the *actor* is important, since the procedure that follows this labeling centers not on reducing the hand-washing but on "curing" the neurosis. New interest and research by sociologists and social psychologists are emerging on this issue.

Labels are powerful. Once applied, they can have a devastating effect on individuals' attempts to show that they are normal. A study conducted by Rosenhan (1973) gave a dramatic indication of the negative influence of labeling. Several subjects, all of them considered "normal," gained easy admission to mental hospitals simply by applying on the grounds that they were hearing voices. Once admitted, the pseudopatients stopped simulating abnormal symptoms and acted normally. The object of

[1]Further aspects of the reliability issue may be found in Gauren and Dickenson (1966); Schmidtz and Fonda (1956); Blashfield and Draguns (1976).

this study was to see whether, and how quickly, they would be discovered as not being mentally ill.

The disturbing result was that they were *never* detected. Each was discharged with a diagnosis of schizophrenia "in remission." As Rosenhan put it, "The evidence is strong that, once labeled schizophrenic, the pseudopatient was stuck with that label. If the pseudopatient was to be discharged, he must naturally be 'in remission'; but he was not sane, nor, in the institution's view, had he ever been sane" (p. 252).

Rosenhan's study also showed the tendency of psychiatric experts to attribute abnormal behavior to the patients' mental disorder and to ignore any environmental causes. Outbursts by patients were invariably attributed to their mental condition. No consideration was given to the effect of being in a hospital environment or to reactions to mistreatment by the staff. Note-taking by the pseudopatients was seen as an aspect of their pathology ("patient engages in writing behavior") although the pseudopatients themselves were never questioned as to the reason for it.

In a further study, Rosenhan informed the staff of a psychiatric hospital that one or more pseudopatients would be attempting to gain admission during the next three months. Out of 193 patients admitted, 41 were alleged by at least one staff member to be pseudopatients. Since Rosenhan had not, in fact, sent any pseudopatients at all, the results are startling.

Rosenhan could hardly be accused of exaggeration when he concludes that "one thing is certain: any diagnostic process that lends itself so readily to massive errors of this sort cannot be a very reliable one" (p. 252).

Another aspect of labeling is that, once labeled, people find it very difficult or even impossible to get rid of the labels. The social environment will react to the label. Even more, the individuals themselves begin to accept the labels and act accordingly. Thus labels can become self-fulfilling prophecies (Rosenthal and Jacobson, 1968).

Labeling has a vicious circle aspect. Since the individuals are convinced that they are disturbed in a particular way, they may now engage in self-labeling. The individuals expect themselves to behave in a disturbed way, which may produce further undesirable consequences, which, in turn, may lead to further labels.

Summary

The problems of designating abnormal behavior would be simplified if agreement could be reached on acceptable criteria for judging *normal* behavior. Such agreement is, however, nonexistent. Social criteria, often applied recklessly, have serious defects. The problems of legal criteria are seen in the continual courtroom struggles between the legal and the psychiatric fields.

Some form of classification of abnormal behavior is necessary to a systematic study of behavior. The most commonly used method is the medical model, as exemplified by the definition of the DSM-II.

But the medical model has come under serious attack. "Mental illness," as a term and as a concept, has been charged with being an inaccurate metaphor at best, and a complete myth at worst. Psychiatric diagnoses, using the medical model, have been shown to be highly unreliable, yet labels continue to be applied. These labels, once applied, and the social stigma and negative influence that too often go with them, are very difficult to get rid of.

Psychodynamic and behavioral views of abnormal behavior

Currently, there are two dominant approaches to the study and treatment of abnormal behavior. They are not necessarily the "right" views, or even the "best" ones, but they do lead the field at the present time. Between them, these two approaches have provided the theoretical basis for most of the recent conceptualization, research, and therapeutic work in abnormal behavior. It is essential, therefore, to have a somewhat detailed understanding of each position, including its history, present state, and probable future directions.

Since concepts and terms drawn from the psychodynamic and behavioral views will be used throughout this textbook, it is crucial to understand them thoroughly before going any further in our study of abnormal psychology. You are probably already somewhat acquainted with these concepts, but the depth of knowledge necessary here resembles more of a lasting friendship with the information than a passing acquaintance with it.

Psychodynamic Approaches

As we noted in Chapter 1, the *medical model* of mental illness was at its peak in the second half of the nineteenth century. The most influential work of that period was Griesinger's *Pathology and Therapy of Mental Disease* (1845). For Griesinger, mental illness could be explained only in terms of physical changes in the brain and nervous system. Investigation of psychopathology was conducted entirely in the laboratory, where autopsies on deceased mental patients sought those "twisted molecules" that were supposedly responsible for the twisted thoughts.

Freud's training and background were in the mainstream of this medical model, yet he almost single-handedly advanced the model from a purely physical framework to a psychological version of the model—the psychodynamic model. Freud continued to believe in the symptom-etiology (or cause) relationship. But in his psychodynamic model, the causes of the symptoms were psychological forces rather than physical changes. The factors that led Freud to alter the model in this way will be considered shortly.

The basic assumptions of a psychodynamic system are (1) that causal factors are internal, and thus unobservable; (2) that intrapsychic forces are of a potentially conflicting nature; and (3) that the interaction of these forces determines observable behavior. In particular, the conflict of opposing intrapsychic forces may appear as the symptoms of mental disturbance.

These assumptions are the basis for numerous theoretical positions that all share the general label of "psychodynamic systems." Within this broad scope, there are two major categories. First, there is the classic view of *psychoanalysis*, built directly upon Freud's original assumptions. Other psychoanalytic approaches, for example, neo-Freudianism, have modified or added to these views, but they are still closely related to psychoanalysis. The more recent group of *humanistic* approaches are built upon the Freudian idea of psychological conflict, but these approaches focus not on purely internal forces but on the interrelationship of the individual with the forces of the external environment. Examples of this tradition are the existential and self-actualization schools of psychology.

Psychoanalysis

Historical Antecedents

The historical and cultural antecedents of psychoanalysis are found in late eighteenth-century Paris. It was there, during the same period that Pinel unfettered the mentally ill, that the curious phenomenon of "animal magnetism" developed. Amid much publicity, Anton Mesmer claimed to have discovered a process by which he could treat symptoms and "diseases" that did not conform to known medical syndromes, or respond to purely medical treatments. Today, we realize that he was dealing with neurotic disorders of a hysterical nature, that is, bizarre physical symptoms that could not be true physical disorders.

In 1774, Mesmer treated a young woman with an extensive array of symptoms including convulsions, vomiting, toothaches, fainting spells, and bowel disorders. Based on a vague theory combining astrology, gravitation, and magnetism, Mesmer applied magnets to parts of her body. He reported complete success in alleviating her symptoms after several treatments. Equal publicity was given to his results in a subsequent case of hysterical blindness (Fancher, 1973). Gaining a large following, Mesmer devised a method of mass treatment.

Anton Mesmer (1734–1815) developed the technique of "animal magnetism." Used in the treatment of hysteria, it was an early forerunner of hypnosis. (*National Library of Medicine.*)

These escapades into mass treatment were no doubt the beginning of his loss of credibility and eventual downfall.

> Mesmer built a contraption called the *baquet*, a sort of troughlike arrangement of mirrors and iron rods which could be placed in various directions by manipulation. People would surround the *baquet*, forming a closed chain by holding hands; Mesmer would appear, magnetic wand in hand, and the treatment would be carried out under his direction, the patients being touched, stroked, closely apposed to the magnetizer in the initial stages of the seance. (Zilboorg and Henry, 1941, p. 344)

Usually patients responded by falling into an excited, twitching trance, called a "crisis state" by Mesmer, after which they reported relief of their symptoms.

Commissions appointed to investigate Mesmer found his theories to be groundless, and he was dismissed by the medical profession as a charlatan. The importance of his actual "cures" was overlooked, tarnished by association with his fraudulent theories. Only later did it become evident that Mesmer's successes hinged on the usefulness of hypnosis and suggestion in the treatment of what came to be known as "hysteria."

Mesmerism, the popular name for "animal magnetism," became widely known through stage performances and demonstrations. Its theatrical potential was undeniable, since suggestions made to people in trancelike states could induce paralyses, anesthesias, hallucinations, amnesias, and posthypnotic suggestions. Many skeptics ridiculed the procedure, but the few physicians who studied it closely came to be impressed by the technique and its strange results. The British physician Braid proposed that the phenomenon was not a mysterious power, as the Mesmerists claimed. Rather, it was a function of the suggestibility of the subject. Braid preferred to call the state "neurohypnotism" (nervous sleep), which later usage shortened to *hypnotism*.

Jean Charcot, a French neurologist and important influence on Freud, was convinced that hypnosis and hysteria were closely related. He followed the medical model precisely in formulating the theory that hysteria was caused by physical degeneration of the nervous system. Charcot proposed that only hysterics could be hypnotized, since only they had the prerequisite neural damage.

This view was challenged by Charcot's fellow physicians Liebeault and Bernheim. They were convinced that individuals without hysteria or nervous system impairment could be hypnotized. The controversy continued for years, until Charcot finally came to agree with their position. Liebeault and Bernheim dispensed with all the stage dramatics that had surrounded hypnotism since the time of Mesmer, and began to use it as a scientific procedure in their clinic at Nancy. Their method involved suggesting to the hypnotized patient that the hysterical symptoms would disappear. Although relief was often obtained, the effects of the suggestion were frequently short-lived, and occasionally the technique did not work at all.

Jean Charcot (1825–1893), pictured here demonstrating hypnosis, theorized that only hysterics could be hypnotized. (*Culver Pictures, Inc.*)

The first steps toward an alternative treatment for hysteria were taken by Josef Breuer, a respected Viennese physician and elder colleague of Freud. During the 1880s, Breuer observed that better results in relieving hysteria could be obtained by the "talking cure" than by direct suggestion. Breuer's technique involved allowing hypnotized patients to discuss the anxieties, disturbed thoughts, and past events that concerned them. Hypnosis was used only to induce a state in which the patients would speak freely to the therapist. Breuer explained that the hysterical symptoms could be removed by the recollection of previously forgotten unpleasant events and the emotions that had been associated with them. This new therapeutic technique was called the method of *catharsis*, that is, discharge of strong emotions upon recall of traumatic past events.

We can trace the inheritance of Freud in a continuous chain beginning with Mesmer, through Charcot, Liebeault, and Bernheim, and finally to Breuer. The concept of the *unconscious* was developing during this time, both as an explanation for the phenomenon of hypno-sis, and as a repository for the forgotten material uncovered by Breuer's "talking cure."

Sigmund Freud

Little is known of the early life of Freud other than his birth in Freiburg, Austria in 1856. At the age of 4, he moved to Vienna with his family, where he lived until the year that preceded his death in 1939. In his medical career, Freud specialized in neuroanatomy and neurophysiology. His scientific training and many years of work in physiological laboratories taught him the value of the empirical approach. The scientific developments of this time seemed to have a formative influence on his thinking; for example, the Darwinian views of evolution emphasized the defensive and adaptive nature of an organism, a theme later repeated in Freud's theories. Traces of the new thermodynamic concepts in physics, such as the conservation of energy, are also found in Freud's conceptualization of psychic energy.

In 1885, Freud received a training grant that allowed him to go to France to study with

Charcot. In the summer of 1889, he went to Liebeault's clinic in Nancy, where he was moved to comment, "I received the profoundest impression of the possibility that there could be powerful mental processes which nevertheless remained hidden from the consciousness of men" (Freud, 1935/1952, p. 29).

When Freud returned to Vienna, he opened a private practice, married, completed a brief military obligation, and began to publish scientific articles. In his struggle to build up a medical practice, Freud was aided financially and intellectually by Josef Breuer. Although Freud was practicing primarily neurological medicine, many of the patients referred to him had symptoms of hysteria. When standard medical treatments failed in these cases, Freud adopted Breuer's method of catharsis. The two physicians collaborated on several cases, resulting in a publication entitled *Studies on Hysteria* (Breuer and Freud, 1895/1962). Many of the basic psychoanalytic hypotheses were presented in that text.

The Interweaving
of Therapy and Theory

Freud combined his scientific background and research interests with his everyday practice of medicine. In so doing, he became an example of the *scientist-practitioner*. Freud's theory emerged as a result of what he observed in the consulting room. It was constantly being modified in light of new insights gained from his patient population. The raw data for his theory were the actual material presented by patients as they went through the process of therapy.

Freud began his investigative/therapeutic work with hysteria by using Breuer's method of catharsis. This involved hypnotizing the patients and requesting that they explore the past for critical events and previously blocked emotions. Unlike Breuer, Freud was not completely comfortable in the role of hypnotist. He found that the results he obtained were often temporary, and were always dependent upon the very intense, personal feelings that developed in the patient toward the hypnotist. And there was the additional problem of the large number of patients who could not be hypnotized.

Freud evolved a different technique that seemed to lead in the same direction without formal hypnosis. He called it the method of *free association*. In this process, the patient is told to report everything that comes to mind, associating one thought to another with no editing or censorship. This absolute freedom from censorship was to continue as the basic rule of psychoanalysis.

The method of free association generally worked well in helping patients to remember early and difficult experiences. However, Freud discovered that there were some areas that were particularly difficult to reveal. He referred to these thoughts as "resisting" emergence into consciousness. When this occurred, patients would exhibit blocking, forgetting, evasiveness, and other similar reactions. Freud posited that an active process called *resistance* was keeping such material from becoming conscious. Freud would point out and interpret instances of this resistance to help the patient achieve *insight* into his or her difficulties with that particular area.

Employing these procedures, Freud found that he was dealing with very basic material in his patients' lives. A surprising amount of this material had to do with early sexual feelings and experiences. Three important formulations arose from his work at this point.

1. The cause of neurosis was often a traumatic sexual event in childhood. Unconscious memories, when revealed, frequently pertained to sexual advances or encounters by adults in the patient's family.

2. An active process exists to keep such unpleasant memories from consciousness, and is responsible for the resistance encountered in recalling these memories. Freud called this process *repression* and emphasized its role in the production of neurosis.

3. The client's development of intense feelings toward the therapist continues even without hypnosis. Freud labeled this *transference*, and considered it to be a powerful tool when used correctly by the therapist.

Psychoanalytic Theory

Basic concepts The psychoanalytic view maintains that all behavior is caused, or determined, by internal factors. Therefore, all behavior is meaningful, even if the meaning is not apparent to the conscious mind. Freud believed that our actions, our dreams, our errors, even our slips of the tongue, all have meaning and are determined largely by unconscious processes. Therefore, the first general feature of psychoanalytic theory is that it is based on the principle of *psychic determinism*.

Closely related to this is a second characteristic, the emphasis given to *unconscious processes*. Unconscious thoughts and motives cannot be observed directly. They can be inferred, however, from the patient's dreams and free associations, which are less subject to conscious control. Freud believed that most of our actions and mental functioning are determined by unconscious forces, particularly those portions of behavior regarded as "abnormal" or irrational.

A third characteristic of the theory is the central role played by *drives* or *instincts*. (Freud uses the two terms almost interchangeably.) The theory proposes that we are all born with instinctual needs that provide energy for the operation of the psychic system. This energy is called *libido*, and the instincts contributing to it are (1) self-preservative, (2) sexual, and (3) aggressive. Freud later abandoned the idea of a drive for self-preservation, and came to place major emphasis on the sexual drives or instincts.

Freud perceived the instincts as genetically determined biological needs. Unsatisfied instincts were said to create tensions within the individual. Reduction of these tensions (by satisfying the instinctual demands) was experienced as pleasurable.

A fourth characteristic of psychoanalysis is its *dynamic* nature. The individual expends energy in the pursuit of his or her goals. This psychic energy is channeled by conscious and unconscious forces that operate in a purposeful fashion to achieve their aims. Although the dynamic forces are not always in harmony with each other, the opposition of these forces and the compromise achieved are the basis of behavior. Some conflicts are of a more complex nature, and their solutions, as we will see, can result in emotional or neurotic disturbances.

Psychosexual development As the person grows from infancy to adulthood, the energy of the libido progressively centers on different parts of the body. The stages of development are indicated by these various areas, called *erotogenic (erogenous) zones* by Freud. Conflicts at each psychosexual stage must be resolved before the individual passes on to the next stage. Freud likened this process to the marching of military troops from battle to battle. For example, if the troops (the libido) are successful in winning the encounter, virtually all of them will move on to the next battle (the next psychosexual stage). The greater the difficulty of the conflict, the more troops that will be left behind on the battlefield, unable to advance to the next skirmish (Liebert and Spiegler, 1974). When a substantial part of the libido is left behind, or *fixated*, the individual's personality may become dominated by less mature modes of obtaining gratification or tension reduction. The stages in psychosexual development are:

1. *The oral stage.* During the first year of the child's life, satisfaction is obtained primarily through the erogenous zone of the mouth. Pleasure seeking, through eating and sucking, as well as aggressive instincts, shown by biting and chewing, are all expressed by oral behaviors. Weaning is the crucial conflict of this period. Great difficulty in parting with the breast or bottle may cause fixation at the oral stage.

2. *The anal stage.* For the second and third years of life, the anus is the site of tension and sensual gratification. Excretory processes are experienced as a source of pleasure, particularly as these functions come to be under the control of the child. The child can use his new skill to please or to annoy adults, especially the mother. Praise or punishment can befall the child depending on his or her anal behavior. Both retentive (holding back) and expulsive (forcing out) behaviors are pleasurable to the child, and fixation in either of these modes may

Box 3-1 Adult Personality Types Based on Fixation in Psychosexual Development

The Oral Personality. Individuals who are fixated at the early oral stage may hold an optimistic view of the world. They are likely to develop dependent relationships in adulthood, recreating the dependency and immaturity of the earlier stage. This may be unusually friendly and generous, with a childish belief that the world will "mother them" and that the world owes them a living. They are gullible and "will swallow anything." People fixated in the later *aggressive* oral stage may be pessimistic, cynical, competitive, and highly aggressive in adult life. These individuals use oral approaches to hurt, for example, "biting sarcasm."

The Anal Personality. Characteristics of the adult personality depend on whether fixation at the anal stage centers on the *retentive* or the *expulsive* mode. The anal-retentive personality shows the traits of obstinacy, parsimony, and orderliness. The adult is likely to be a stingy, hoarding, and stubborn individual, who is compulsively neat. On the other hand, the anal-expulsive personality shows traits of generosity and an outgoing nature. The adult fixated at this stage with expulsive tendencies may be highly creative, expressive, and artistically inclined.

Phallic or Genital Personality. Adult character will reflect any partial resolution of the Oedipal complex. Overinvolvement with sexual attractiveness and flirtatiousness will result. The person may appear self-centered and narcissistic, with women showing seductiveness and men adopting a "ladies' man" role. The "Don Juan" stereotype may appear. This results in conquests with little depth of affection. One female pattern Freud noted is what he called the "masculinity complex," (sometimes referred to as the "castrating woman") in which a woman does not accept a nonpenis model, and in "masculine" pursuits stresses competitive relationships with men.

---

be associated with subsequent patterns of adult behavior.

3. *The phallic stage.* The fourth and fifth years represent the time when the libido is centered in the genital region. Masturbation, experimentation with peers, and questioning of adults are indicative behaviors. This stage is labeled "phallic" because the penis is presumed to be the object of main interest to children of either sex. The little girl is envious, according to Freud, while the little boy is constantly fearing castration for his unconscious desire to experience sexual gratification with his mother. This represents the major conflict of the phallic stage, and has been termed the *Oedipal complex.*[1] Resolution hinges on the child's identification with the parent of the same sex. The girl assumes a female role, rather than desiring to become a boy. The male child relinquishes the desire to possess his mother and begins to emulate the traits of his father. In Freud's view, failure to resolve

the Oedipal conflict is "one of the most important sources of the sense of guilt which so often torments neurotic people" (Freud, 1935, p. 291).

4. *The latency period.* Freud felt that after about the sixth year, the child's sexual urges were dormant until their reawakening at puberty. During this period, the libido is channeled into school activities, relationships with peers, hobbies, etc.

5. *The genital stage.* At puberty, the adolescent becomes sexually mature and the libido is centered again on the genital area. The chances for nonneurotic heterosexual adjustment at this stage are increased if the individual has passed through the pregenital stages without major fixation of libido.

Intrapsychic structure and conflict The well-known concepts of *id, ego,* and *superego* resulted from Freud's efforts to group together mental processes and thoughts that had certain common properties. These divisions were never considered by Freud to be actual physical structures with boundaries or locations in the brain. Rather, they are descriptive labels for three kinds of mental functioning. In brief, we can say that the *id* consists of processes related

---

[1] This complex was named after Oedipus Rex, a figure from classic Greek drama, who murdered his father and married his mother.

directly to the instincts and drives and, as such, is the source of libidinal energy. The *ego* is the "executive" of the libido, seeking to channel the id's energy in accord with a realistic appraisal of the environment. The *superego* comprises the moralistic processes (the "conscience") as well as aspirations toward perfection (the "ideal" person we wish to be).

Characteristic of the id is that it operates on the *pleasure principle*, a hedonistic and totally selfish mode of functioning. It seeks immediate gratification of the uncensored instinctual demands. Freud spoke of the investment of emotional energy as *cathexis*, and of the desired source of satisfaction as the "object" of cathexis. Id processes are highly mobile in that the object of cathexis may quickly change if the primary goal is not accessible. If the discharge of libido cannot be effected by sucking the bottle, for example, the object of cathexis easily shifts to the thumb, which is available. This mode of discharging libidinal energy, by going to the most readily available source of pleasure, is referred to as the *primary process*, and describes an immature level of functioning.

Ego processes begin to appear around the time of the anal stage, when children must adjust their behavior according to environmental pressures. Ego processes are said to operate on the *reality principle*, taking external conditions into consideration. Delay of gratification, selection of more socially acceptable objects, and finding pleasure in ways that the ego feels are safer now dominate. This mode of channeling the libido is referred to as the *secondary process*, and is typical of the mature ego.

The ego begins merely as a mediator between the id and reality. Gradually, the ego starts to exercise an increasing degree of control over the id, and eventually comes to be in opposition—even direct conflict—with some of the id's strivings. The mature ego must become the master of the id; it must be able to short-circuit some of the instinctual demands of the id by fantasizing or some other method, rather than allow the individual to act out the impulses of the id in reality. By redirecting the libidinal energy into fantasies and dreams, the individual is saved from behaving in potentially embarrassing or inappropriate ways.

The superego makes its appearance as the Oedipal conflict of the phallic stage is being resolved. Identification with the parents also includes the process of incorporating (or *introjecting*) parental values and moral precepts. The children, who previously "behaved" out of fear of punishment, now come to distinguish good from evil on the basis of their own conscience. They truly "become" the parents in terms of accepting their stated moral position, their values, and their ideals.

Neither the id nor the superego is willing to compromise. The id demands total and immediate satisfaction. The superego insists upon self-control to the point of total suppression of many sexual and aggressive drives. It punishes thoughts and actions it considers unacceptable by creating strong feelings of guilt and shame. Intrapsychic *conflict* occurs when the direction and discharge of energy demanded by the id (or the ego or superego) are at odds with the requirements of one or both of the other aspects. For example, if instinctual id impulses are repugnant to the ego and superego, energy may be expended to keep the impulses deep in the unconscious, or *repressed*. The continual output of energy required to maintain repression is known as *countercathexis*—it represents a drain on the psychic system. Since current demands also require the use of the energy of the ego and superego, there is a potential for the stores to be depleted. If this occurs, one of two things may happen: the repressed impulses may break through, or the person may show great difficulty in day-to-day functioning.

Anxiety and defense   The warning signal of the psyche is the subjective feeling of *anxiety*. Anxiety indicates impending danger, either from internal or external sources. It may be a sign that an intense id impulse is about to break through, and that the ego is unable to restrain it. For example, unrefined sexual and aggressive instincts may press so strongly for gratification that the ego is challenged to resist. Anxiety signaling the id-ego conflict was termed *neurotic anxiety* by Freud. It is characterized as a sense of impending doom with no

Box 3-2 Ego Defense Mechanisms

Repression—the main defense mechanism used to keep threatening impulses at a totally unconscious level. Repression is silent. It is seen only through the absence of feelings or impulses that would otherwise be present.

Reaction-formation—the transformation of an impulse into its opposite. For instance, unconscious unacceptable sexual, loving impulses become conscious feelings of hate and disgust. The resulting opposite behaviors are often excessive and overstated.

Undoing—a thought or motor act that cancels the significance of an unconscious previous thought or act. For example, the unconscious thought about hurting one's children is followed by extreme overconcern for their well-being.

Regression—a return of the libido to earlier stages, particularly the recurrence of immature sexual impulses in relation to now "outgrown" sexual objects. In general, the adoption of any behavior pattern less mature than the behavior pattern it replaces.

Displacement—the transference of impulses from their original object to another object, usually with some similar properties. For example, aggressive impulses toward an employer are discharged instead on a spouse or child for some trivial annoyance.

Projection—the assignment of one's own impulse to another person. Attributing undesirable motivations found in oneself to others, often to the objects of the impulse. For example, "I hate him" becomes "He hates me."

Sublimation—the substitution of a socially acceptable impulse for an unacceptable one. This often entails creative or scientific endeavor, for example, painting or sculpturing nudes, studying reproductive systems, etc.

Rationalization—the justification of one's behavior in terms of acceptable motivations rather than the "real" motivations. Individuals explain their behavior in terms of their "good intentions." Their true motives remain unknown, even to themselves.

Denial—the conscious refusal to acknowledge unacceptable impulses, unpleasant facts, or undesirable behaviors. Consciously, the person ignores the existence of facts, for example, "I couldn't have done that" or "It just didn't happen."

Compensation—the ability of the ego to make up for a lack in one area with overachievement in some other area. The poor student becomes a more than adequate athlete.

Compartmentalization—the separation of two incompatible aspects of the psyche from one another to prevent the anxiety and disruption of their clashing. An example is the religious man who believes totally in the "golden rule" but who, as owner of a used-car lot, sells defective cars to poor people.

---

clear cause. He distinguished it from *moral anxiety*, which is generated by an id-superego conflict, where the anxiety is experienced as guilt or shame.

Objective anxiety is produced when an actual threat exists in the environment and must be dealt with by the ego. When the danger is real, anxiety can be reduced by acting upon the environment to minimize or avoid the conflict. In contrast, neurotic and moral anxiety signal *internal* danger, and must be dealt with by internal means, namely, the defense mechanisms of the ego.

Defense mechanisms are unconscious ego processes used to control the demands of the id and superego. The various defense mechanisms are defined and described in Box 3-2. Although they can be distinguished individually, usually more than one defense mechanism is necessary to prevent anxiety. Typically, an individual will employ a combination of defense mechanisms that is characteristic of that person's mode of response to anxiety.

The psychoanalytic conceptualization of abnormal behavior Anxiety and defense mechanisms are parts of normal behavior. The processes discussed are components of the everyday lives of all of us. Many of them, like the defenses, are there to help us cope with the constant compromises we must make between ourselves and the environment. The psychoanalytic view of *abnormal* behavior starts where these systems fail to maintain the delicate balance between these forces.

From his early work with Breuer on hysteria, Freud was convinced that neurotic symptoms had their origins in repressed traumatic past events. The emotions corresponding to these events had never been adequately expressed. Freud later added the condition that for any event or experience to be considered abnormal, it must be so unacceptable to the ego that defenses are brought into play against it.

You will remember that one of Freud's early hypotheses traced neurosis back to an event of a sexual nature in the patient's childhood. He was surprised to find later that the experiences his patients described were often fantasies rather than real memories. Nevertheless, the patients themselves believed them to be true. Freud soon recognized that sexual interests and activities in childhood were a pervasive and normal part of psychic life. He came to place less emphasis on bizarre traumatic experiences, and paid more attention to the development of normal sexual feelings.

Freud hypothesized that during development of the normal individual, some aspects of infantile sexuality must be repressed. Other sexual components are integrated in adulthood, and are expressed through acceptable sexual behavior. Freud proposed that repression went to an extreme in the neurotic person. Too

"When Jud accuses Zack, here, of hostility toward his daughter, like he seems to every session, why, it's plain to me he's only rationalizing his own lack of gumption in standing up to a stepson who's usurping the loyalty of his second wife. The way he lit into him just now shows he's got this here guilt identification with Zack's present family constellation. Calling Zack egotistical ain't nothing but a disguise mechanism for concealing his secret envy of Zack's grit and all-around starch, and shows mighty poor ego boundaries of his own, it appears to me." (*Drawing by Whitney Darrow, Jr.,* © *1976, The New Yorker Magazine, Inc.*)

Sigmund Freud (1856–1939), whose theories laid the foundation for the modern psychodynamic viewpoint. (*National Library of Medicine.*)

much energy was expended in keeping id impulses repressed. When pushed to extremes, the repression failed and anxiety-producing infantile sexual impulses escaped from the unconscious, giving rise to neurotic symptoms.

Freud described a symptom as a compromise between the id impulses and the ego (or superego) forces opposing entrance of the impulses into conscious thought and behavior. In many cases, Freud was able to show that neurotic symptoms express the unconscious sexual desires as well as the ego's defensive reaction against them. In this sense, Freud saw all symptoms as having meaning, much like the content of dreams. An example will clarify the compromise nature and the dual function of the neurotic symptom. The psychoanalytic literature describes the case of vomiting in a young woman:

On analysis, it developed that the patient had an unconscious, repressed wish to be impregnated by her father. The wish and the countercathexis against it originated during the oedipal period of the patient's life. . . . [She] functioned satisfactorily until her parents divorced and her father remarried when she was in her twenties. These events reactivated her oedipal conflicts and disturbed the intrapsychic equilibrium which had been established years before, with the result that the forces of her ego could no longer control her oedipal wishes adequately. In this case, one of the compromise formations that resulted was the symptom of vomiting. The symptom represented unconsciously the gratification of the repressed oedipal wish to be impregnated by father, as though the patient were demonstrating by her vomiting, "See, I'm a pregnant woman with morning sickness." At the same time the suffering caused by the vomiting and the anxiety which accompanied it— were the expression of the ego's unconscious fear and guilt which were associated with the wish in question. (Brenner, 1955, p. 204)

Freud proposed that the *primary gain* of a neurotic symptom resulted from the success of the ego in keeping the impulse from becoming fully conscious. By permitting only a distorted or disguised discharge of energy, the ego prevents the emergence of the full infantile impulse. Once a symptom develops, the ego may exploit other advantages that it brings with it, such as the sympathy of other people, special attention, relief from usual duties or from work. Freud felt that such *secondary gain* often accounted for the fact that many patients unconsciously prefer to keep their neurosis rather than lose the benefits.

As described in this section, psychoanalytic theory clearly adheres to the medical model by stressing that behavior can be traced to underlying psychological drives. Understanding the external symptom or behavior requires a careful study of unconscious processes in order to assess the internal motives represented by the symptom. In treatment, the emphasis is placed on discovering these underlying processes, rather than on dealing with the external behavior per se. Treating only the symptom is presumed to be both futile and potentially dangerous. It is futile in the sense that if the symptom is alleviated without resolution of the underlying conflicts, a new symptom may be generated by the unconscious processes. Freud referred to this occurrence as *symptom substitution.*

Treating only the symptom may be dangerous because the symptom represents a delicate balance of compromise in the psychic system. Upsetting this balance by relying on a temporary solution may cause more drastic disintegration of the personality, and make therapy even more difficult. The psychodynamic cure must therefore always be directed at the historical development of the conflict, rather than at the symptom that actually causes the patient to seek treatment or be institutionalized.

Other psychoanalytic theorists have added to or modified some of Freud's original propositions, but their basic approach is in keeping with this medical model. They all share the view of intrapsychic determinism as the basis for external behavior. The most important theorists joining Freud in this tradition are Carl Jung (1927), Alfred Adler (1923), Karen Horney (1937), Harry Stack Sullivan (1953), Heinz Hartmann, and Erik Erikson (1950).

The Humanistic Approach

In the same tradition, yet standing somewhat apart from the strict psychoanalytic approach, is the humanistic viewpoint, which includes the self-actualization and existential theories. The humanistic school of thought acknowledges the role of dynamic intrapsychic forces. Conflicts are seen to occur both *within* the individual and *between* the individual and his environment. Conflicts from both sources may result in a disturbance of the psychological "growth" of the person, a major focus of the humanistic theories. The concepts of anxiety, defense, insight, and personality development are found in the humanistic approaches, but a somewhat greater emphasis is given to the role of the external environment than is found in the classic psychoanalytic position.

Self-Actualization Views

The names of Carl Rogers and Abraham Maslow stand out in the field of contemporary clinical psychology. Going well beyond Freud's theory of the role of sexual and aggressive instincts, Abraham Maslow provided us with a more complete conceptual hierarchy of human needs and motivations. Maslow (1954, 1971) proposed a pyramidlike system in which higher-level needs are built upon more basic ones (Figure 3-1). We become conscious of the higher motives (or "being"-needs) only when the more fundamental needs are satisfied.

Maslow's sequence suggests that when the primary needs for food, clothing, shelter, and safety are fulfilled, the need for love and belonging emerges. Only when this need is adequately met does the person experience the need for esteem from others as well as from the self. The being-needs emerge next, with the drive for *self-actualization* having the greatest theoretical importance. Maslow defines self-actualization as "experiencing fully, vividly,

Figure 3-1 Maslow's hierarchy of needs. (*Adapted from Maslow, A. H., Motivation and Personality (2nd ed.). New York: Harper, 1954.* © *1970 by Abraham H. Maslow. Reproduced by permission of Harper & Row, Inc.*)

Abraham Maslow (1908–1970) studied human potential and the road to self-actualization, the ability to fully experience life. (*The Bettmann Archive, Inc.*)

Carl Rogers (b. 1902), a major contributor to the humanistic viewpoint, was instrumental in developing techniques of client-centered therapy. (*The Bettmann Archive, Inc.*)

selflessly, with full concentration and total absorption. It means experiencing without the self-consciousness of the adolescent" (Maslow, 1971, p. 45). Maslow suggests that we are all open to "peak experiences" that are transient moments of self-actualization. If lower needs remain unmet, our capacity for experiencing such moments is diminished. Deprivation of the being-need of self-actualization may result in feelings of despair and a sense that life is meaningless.

Self-actualization is also the key concept in the theory of Carl Rogers. He (1959, 1973) proposes that people develop a self-concept based on experience and interaction with the environment. Individuals also have an "ideal" self, an idea of the person they wish to be, which may or may not be congruent with the "real" self. When a discrepancy develops between the "ideal" self and "real" self, a state of tension and confusion results. For example, interactions with the environment may present an unfavorable picture of the self, which will result in internal conflict within the person. Feelings of unworthiness may produce anxiety and defensive psychological reactions. Rogers' technique of *client-centered* therapy brings

about change by providing complete acceptance and respect for the client. The client is given *unconditional positive regard* by the therapist. Rogers postulates that this positive regard is a basic need that should have been met in childhood by the significant people in the client's life. Providing this high degree of acceptance allows the individual to incorporate into the self-structure threatening feelings that were previously excluded. The person may then continue the self-actualizing process, becoming creative, spontaneous, adaptable, and open to new experiences.

The Existential View

In general, both Rogers and Maslow present very hopeful, optimistic schemes for personal growth and development of the full human potential. A contrasting view is based on the philosophical study of people's existence in the world, or *existentialism*. Theorists in this tradition include Laing (1965), May (1958), Binswanger (1963), and Boss (1963). Again the focus is on inner experience and internal conflicts, particularly those of a crisis nature. In contrast to the self-actualization approach, however, the framework of existentialism is rather gloomy and pessimistic. The crises that are considered most important are those having to do with such issues as despair, anxiety, dread, aloneness, death, and meaninglessness.

Existential theory holds that internal conflicts result when people feel too separate from the world in which they exist. R. D. Laing, a contemporary existential psychologist, gives us the following picture of the anxious and insecure person:

> The individual . . . may feel more unreal than real; in a literal sense, more dead than alive; precariously differentiated from the rest of the world, so that his identity and autonomy are always in question. . . . He may feel more insubstantial than substantial, and unable to assume that the stuff he is made of is genuine, good, valuable. And he may feel his self as partially divorced from his body. (Laing, 1965, p. 42)

Such people actually experience the outer world differently from the way others experience it, and must find ways of proving that they are "real," of preserving a sense of identity, and of preventing themselves from losing their "self" (Laing, 1965).

As in other theories, the goal is for people to come to know themselves, but the existential approach stresses that patients must really do this on their own. The emphasis in therapy is on the *choices* people must make in the *present*. Like the self-actualization approach, it stresses the "here-and-now" decisions rather than historical events or psychosexual development in childhood.

Laing has taken the unorthodox position that "madness" is in fact an attempt by people to solve an existential crisis. The symptoms are seen as a healing reaction to the problems being experienced, and in keeping with the medical model, Laing suggests that these symptoms must be allowed to run their course. Laing deviates from the Freudian approach, however, by not only insisting that we should not treat the symptoms, but also that we must not treat even the underlying disorder. He assumes that

what we call mental disturbance is an existential way of being in the world from which the patients will emerge healthier and better integrated than they were previously.

Critique of Psychodynamic Approaches

We are about to take psychodynamic theories to task for a variety of shortcomings. Before we begin, it might be wise to remind ourselves that the psychodynamic approaches, particularly psychoanalysis, have had great scientific and social impact on the psychological sciences. The applications in mental health of parts of the theory have resulted in substantial contributions that are now and will continue to be cornerstones of our view of humanity. It is generally conceded that Freud's intellectual impact was as important to changing our view

R. D. Laing (b. 1927), a chief exponent of the existentialist view, takes the unorthodox position that "madness" is an attempt to solve an existential crisis, such as loneliness, meaninglessness, or death. (*United Press International.*)

of ourselves as were the impacts of Copernicus and Darwin. Science advances by constantly challenging its theories, discarding what does not pass scrutiny, and building on the valid parts of the previous formulations. We must be careful, then, to preserve what is of value as we extend our contemporary view of people. With that warning, we must now go on to cast the scientist's skeptical eye on the psychodynamic viewpoint.

The criticisms that have been directed at the theoretical and therapeutic aspects of the psychodynamic approach have focused on several aspects (e.g., Skinner, 1954; Lehrman, 1960; Ellis, 1950). Points of contention include the following:

1. The psychodynamic approach is basically one of observation and description. It makes assumptions about underlying processes on the basis of manifest behaviors, but rarely offers predictions about future behaviors. It does not generate many testable hypotheses. In cases where predictions might be made, the theory can "explain" even opposite outcomes by supposing the presence of reaction-formation, denial, etc.

2. The basic concepts of the theory are vague and poorly defined. Often Freud is metaphorical rather than literal in his descriptions, for instance, of the Oedipal conflict. Most of the concepts cannot be measured or quantified. Thus another investigator could not concur on such issues as the *amount* of libido fixated at a particular stage, or the *degree* of cathexis, resistance, regression, transference, etc.

3. Some abstract concepts, particularly the id, ego, superego, "real" self, and "ideal" self, have become almost real things, or been "reified," in the theory. These intrapsychic structures tend to take on an independent, even demonological existence of their own. In psychoanalytic descriptions, the id and superego are portrayed as human forces able to demand and command the individual's performance.

4. The psychoanalytic approach (more than the other dynamic views) is not open enough to new ideas. It tends to be a closed philosophical system. In this regard, it has been accused of being unscientific since it is unwilling to search continually for new facts and to change hypotheses in the light of new data. The response to this criticism has been that psychoanalysis cannot really be understood as a system unless one has actually undergone analysis. Only its own adherents are seen as qualified to judge or to contribute to the system.

5. Another criticism deals with the origins of the theory. Freud based his ideas of normal personality development on data acquired during the therapy of abnormal individuals. Subsequent theorists, particularly those in the humanistic tradition, have attempted to remedy this shortcoming by gathering information from normal individuals as a basis for theoretical speculations.

6. Concerning the psychoanalytic technique itself, the charge has been made that psychoanalysts bias the outcome of therapy by "leading" the patient to conclusions that fit with Freudian theory. The efficacy of psychoanalysis, in comparison to other treatments, or even no treatment, continues to be debated.

7. The primary emphasis of the psychodynamic approaches on dynamic forces and inner, unobservable events has been questioned by behaviorists. B. F. Skinner (1954) charges that the theory deals with abstract and high-level hypothetical constructs. He argues that considering the present state of our knowledge, or lack of knowledge, about abnormal psychology, we should be dealing with more observable and controllable phenomena. This behavioral method of approaching abnormal behavior will now be considered.

Behavioral Approaches

Abnormal behavior is, first and foremost, *behavior*. The laws and principles that govern behavior in general must be assumed to govern abnormal behavior as well. This line of reasoning has profound consequences for the way we view abnormal behavior, and for the methods of treatment we choose to employ. The theories and therapies of specific kinds of abnormal behavior will be given in more detail in subsequent chapters. We will review here the behavioral principles that form the basis for the initiation, maintenance, and change of human behavior.

Behavior is defined as any observable activity of an organism. What we call *learning* refers to the relationship of behavior to events in the environment. Learning may be defined as "the acquisition of a functional connection between an environmental stimulus and some subject response" (Ullmann and Krasner, 1965, p. 16).[2]

It is assumed that all behavior is lawful (i.e., predictable and controllable) in that it must follow the principles of learning. Thus,

[2] The scientific analysis of behavior is based upon the study of learning, but includes contributions from other areas of psychology as well. This chapter cannot present a comprehensive coverage of all the material from either learning theory or the general approaches to behavior analyses. Space limitations require selectivity in the concepts to be discussed, focusing primarily on those that are relevant to the study of abnormal behavior. The student who seeks greater depth in any of these aspects might read other sources, for example, Kimble's *Foundations of Conditioning and Learning* (1967).

technically, there can be no such thing as "abnormal" behavior. *All* behavior is normal given the conditions under which it is learned. Certain learned behaviors may be detrimental to the individual, or undesirable to society, or both. Thus the term "maladaptive" behavior has generally been preferred by those employing a behavioral approach.

Historical Antecedents

The behavioral view grew out of a variety of scientific and philosophical trends during the early twentieth century. Its development paralleled the development of the psychoanalytic approach. The behavioral method, however, had its origins in the scientific laboratories rather than in the clinical consulting rooms associated with psychoanalysis.

Ivan Pavlov, working in Russia at the turn of the century, was interested in studying the attachment of responses to environmental

Ivan Pavlov (1846–1936) was the first to demonstrate that learning can occur through the association of a stimulus with a response. His work is the basis for theories of classical conditioning. (*The Bettmann Archive, Inc.*)

stimuli. While working on the physiology of the salivary glands in dogs, he was often hampered by the dog's salivation to numerous stimuli, including the sight of the experimenter (who brought food). At first an annoyance, this habit came to be of special interest to Pavlov. In his now classic study, Pavlov (1927) demonstrated that learning can occur through the association of a stimulus with a response. Pavlov called this learned response a *conditioned reflex*. He spent the remainder of his career in elaborating his theory of conditioning, and in extending his model to many areas of animal and human behavior. These laws of learning were formulated on the basis of observable behavior, without recourse to introspection or inference. For instance, Pavlov observed the conditions under which a behavior—salivation—occurred but did not explain away the phenomenon by inferring that the dog salivated because he was "hungry," an internal and unobservable state. This objective nature of observation is basic to all of the behavioral approaches.

During the same period in America, Edward L. Thorndike (1905) was experimenting with animals that were *actively* engaged in manipulating their environment, unlike the dogs that were the passive recipients of Pavlov's conditioning experiments. Thorndike placed his animals in a box from which they were required to escape in order to obtain a reward of food. He derived several principles of learning based on the "instrumental" nature of this behavior, that is, the responses are instrumental in creating change in the environment. Thorndike contributed the *law of effect* to psychology, stating the simple but important observation that behavior is controlled by its consequences. Behavior that is followed by a satisfying state of affairs is strengthened (i.e., made to happen more often), while unpleasant consequences cause a weakening of prior responses.

Applications of these two models of learning to abnormal behavior came slowly. The earliest demonstration of the Pavlovian model in the creation of maladaptive human behavior was achieved by Watson and Rayner (1920).

J. B. Watson (1878–1958), the father of American behavioral psychology, was the first to demonstrate the conditioning of maladaptive behavior. (*Culver Pictures, Inc.*)

Knowing that loud noises naturally produced a response of fear in a young child, Watson proceeded to condition a child to associate that fear with an object (a white rat) that previously had elicited no response (i.e., a neutral stimulus). Little Albert was unafraid of the rat until it had been presented several times in conjunction with a sudden, frightening noise. Albert then began to show a learned, or *conditioned*, response of fear when the white rat was presented without the accompanying noise.

Jones (1924) provided a sequel to this study with her demonstration that fears of young children can also be *eliminated* by behavioral means. In her research, fear-producing objects were presented in pleasant situations, or in conjunction with positive stimuli, such as food. Historically, Jones was the first to apply "behavior therapy" to instances of maladaptive behavior.

From the 1920s to the 1940s, many examples of behavioral manipulation were performed and published without the development of a formal model but with a general acceptance of the budding theory of "behaviorism." One of the most notable contributions was Dunlap's book *Habits: Their Making and Unmaking* (1932).

Skinner's publication of *Science and Human Behavior* (1953) marks the beginning of the systematic approach to behavioral analysis of both normal and abnormal behavior. His model emphasized changes in the *frequency* of behaviors. By noting increases or decreases in relation to previous frequencies, Skinner provided records of behavior in measurable terms. Given this method of quantification, we are now able to measure and evaluate behavioral change.

Clinical experience also contributed to the behavioral model through the efforts of Wolpe (1958). As a private practitioner, Wolpe employed clinical procedures based on behavior theory. As Dunlap (1932) had suggested previously, inhibition (prevention) proved to be useful in clinical situations as a method of dealing with maladaptive behaviors.

This sequence of historical developments produced two separate lines of investigation with regard to learning theory and behavior therapy. One line runs from Pavlov through Watson to Wolpe. These investigators have been concerned with the activities of the autonomic nervous system and have employed Pavlov's conditioning model as the basic paradigm of learning. The various terms applied to this model are *Pavlovian*, or *classical*, *conditioning*. More recently, this type of learning has been called *respondent* behavior, in light of the fact that the organism's behavior responds to stimuli that can elicit or call out that response. Learning occurs when the response thus elicited is associated with new stimuli.

The other line of investigation runs from Thorndike through Skinner to many current behavioral scientists who focus their attention on the voluntary muscles, and the actively behaving organism. The appropriate labels for this type of learning are *operant*, *instrumental*, or *Skinnerian conditioning*. The model emphasizes *operant* behavior, referring to the fact that the organism "operates" on its environment. Responses are emitted in the presence of stimuli, rather than elicited by stimuli as in the classical conditioning model.

The distinction between operant and respondent behavior is a distinction of convenience based on viewing one type of behavior in isolation from the other. In fact, it is rare for naturally occurring behavior to be purely of one type or the other. Behavior is usually a complexly intertwined combination of the two kinds of learning. This is particularly true of the behavioral events that concern clinicians. Maladaptive behaviors are often mixtures of conditioned emotional responses and operant behaviors learned in response to the environment. While these two lines of investigation will now be discussed separately, we must constantly remember that they are not truly separable in the real world.

Respondent Behavior

The theory of respondent conditioning is built upon the fact that certain stimuli automatically elicit responses from the organism. For example, in Pavlov's classic experiment, meat powder would always cause the dog to salivate. This response of salivation could be *conditioned* to a stimulus that did not previously elicit the salivation, for instance, a ringing bell. After pairing several presentations of the meat powder with the bell, the dog came to salivate whenever the bell rang, even without the presence of the meat powder. Pavlov called the bell the *conditioned stimulus* (CS) and salivation *to it alone* was the *conditioned response* (CR). Since salivation was an already built-in response to the meat powder, it did not have to be learned, or conditioned. Therefore, Pavlov termed the meat powder the *unconditioned stimulus* (UCS) and salivation, the *unconditioned response* (UCR). Box 3-3 depicts the Pavlovian design using the abbreviations

Box 3-3 The Classical Conditioning or (Pavlovian) Model

Pavlov's original design

paired
- UCS (meat powder) ⟶ UCR (salivation)
- CS (bell) ⇢ CR (salivation to the bell)

Watson and Rayner, 1920—"Little Albert"

paired
- UCS (loud noise) ⟶ UCR (fear, crying)
- CS (white rat) ⇢ CR (fear of rat)

Rachman, 1966—"sexual fetishism"

paired
- UCS (nude pictures) ⟶ UCR (penile volume increase)
- CS (black boots) ⇢ CR (penile volume increase)

Jones, 1924—elimination of conditioned fear

paired
- UCS (food) ⟶ UCR (pleasurable response)
- ⇢ CR (fear)
- CS ⇢ CR (pleasurable response)

UCS = unconditioned stimulus
UCR = unconditioned response
CS = conditioned stimulus
CR = conditioned response

given above. The solid line represents the built-in, and therefore, unlearned response; the dotted line represents the new stimulus-response connection, that is, the learned response.

If the *unconditioned stimulus* (UCS) is repeatedly left out (i.e., the meat powder is not presented for several trials), the conditioned response (CR) will decrease and eventually disappear (i.e., the animal will no longer salivate to the bell alone). This is termed *extinction* of the conditioned response.

Generalization is said to occur when a stimulus that is similar to the CS is able to elicit the CR. The degree of generalization increases as a function of the similarity to the CS. A corresponding task is for the organism to discriminate between what is and what is not the CS. Responses to the similar stimuli will eventually extinguish, leaving only the original CS capable of producing the CR. This process is known as *discrimination*.

The CR in respondent conditioning can represent a complex sequence of behaviors rather than a discrete response. Conditioned responses of distress, fear, and rage may involve many bodily systems, but all are basically of a respondent nature. Such patterns of complex responses are termed *emotional behavior* in respondent learning, and are of great importance in the field of abnormal psychology.

Maladaptive Behavior from Respondent Learning

If relevant stimuli can be attached to autonomic processes, so can irrelevant stimuli. In the respondent model, abnormality can result from the unusual or inappropriate connections between the real environment and the individual's responses. Watson and Rayner's classic study of Little Albert (1920) demonstrates how maladaptive conditioning might occur.

At approximately 9 months of age, Albert was tested with a variety of stimuli to see if he exhibited responses of fear to such items as a burning newspaper, a mask, a dog, a rabbit, a monkey, or a white rat. Prior to conditioning, Albert showed no fear in relation to these stimuli. He did, however, show a startled reaction and much crying when a steel bar was struck hard with a hammer, creating a sudden and loud noise. This fearful response is considered a normal reaction, since infants from the time of birth are generally frightened by loud noises.

Watson and Rayner attempted to establish a *conditioned* fear response to a neutral object, a white rat, by presenting it visually and simultaneously striking the steel bar. In this case, the loud noise represents the UCS, and the white rat, the CS. The natural fear response to the noise is the UCR, and fear of the white rat is the CR. (See Box 3-3.)

When the rat and the noise had been paired for a few presentations, Albert began to withdraw from the animal. After seven presentations of the rat with the noise, Albert cried immediately upon the sight of the white rat, and continued to exhibit fear of the rat even when no noise occurred. Up to a month later, Albert still showed the effects of this conditioning. In addition, he exhibited *generalization* of the conditioned emotional response of fear. When presented with similar-looking objects—a rabbit, a dog, a fur coat, and some cotton wool—Albert showed fearful responses and hesitancy that had not been present upon initial testing with these stimuli. Watson's view was that the conditioning and generalization would persist over time, and could possibly modify behavior throughout life. "Emotional disturbances in adults cannot be traced back to sex alone," Watson said, challenging the Freudians. "It is possible that many of the phobias in psychopathology are true conditioned emotional responses either of the direct or transferred [generalized] type" (Watson and Rayner, 1920, p. 14).

A similar demonstration of the learning of maladaptive emotional responses has been provided by Rachman (1966). This investigator attempted to demonstrate the male acquisition of a sexual fetish by the classical conditioning paradigm. The UCS in Rachman's study consisted of photographs of female nudes, while the CS was a picture of a pair of black, knee-high woman's boots, a common object of sexual fetishism. The response measured was the change in penis volume. The CS (black boots) did not originally elicit any change in penis volume, but after a number of pairings with the UCS (nude pictures), a picture of the boots alone produced a conditioned response. The number of CS-UCS pairings necessary to achieve this conditioning varied from 24 trials for one subject to 65 trials for another subject. Generalization to similar stimuli was also noted, for example, boots of different colors and shapes. Rachman points out that there seems to be little question that sexual arousal can be conditioned to previously neutral stimuli (Rachman, 1966).

By the same conditioning processes, appropriate sexual responses may be inhibited or prevented from occurring. If unpleasant consequences (e.g., failure and embarrassment) have been associated with sexual arousal, the individual may experience anxiety as a conditioned response to sexual stimuli, even in situations where the original threat is no longer present. The inhibition of normal responses may result in impotence or frigidity.

Pavlov realized that neurosis could be learned through classical conditioning, and proposed that one way neurosis could come about was from a breakdown of *discrimination*. This was shown in an experiment at Pavlov's laboratory by Shenger-Krestovnikova (1921) in which dogs were conditioned to respond to a CS that was a circle of light. They received the UCS (meat powder) only in the presence of this circle, and never when the light was presented in the shape of an ellipse. After this discrimination had been acquired, the shape of the ellipse was gradually altered until it was almost equivalent to the circular CS. After three weeks of such training, the animal was no longer able to distinguish the CS from the "ellipse," and would salivate to the wrong stimulus, or to neither. At the same time, the behavior of the dog altered radically. Pavlov observed that "the hitherto quiet dog began to squeal in its stand, kept wriggling about, tore off with its teeth the apparatus. . . . On being taken into the experimental room, the dog now barked violently. . . . In short, it presented all the symptoms of a condition of acute neurosis" (Pavlov, 1927, p. 29).

Pavlov emphasized that the temperaments, or constitutions, of his animals differed markedly. Dogs with certain kinds of temperaments would show breakdown of discrimination and abnormal behavior more quickly than others. Pavlov was later to relate an excitable temperament in humans to a predisposition toward manic-depressive psychoses, and an inhibitory temperament to schizophrenia and certain neurotic disorders. This line of clinical research was later pursued by Eysenck (1961), who is noted for his elaboration of the *intro-version-extroversion* continuum. Eysenck also proposed dimensions of *psychoticism* and *neuroticism* that interact with other tendencies of the individual, particularly the individual's capacity to be conditioned. For example, people high in introversion and high in neuroticism quickly develop conditioned fear responses. As a consequence, Eysenck felt that these people were constitutionally predisposed to develop anxiety states, phobias, obsessions, and compulsions. On the other hand, people high in extroversion and high in neuroticism are unable to form quick and strong conditioned responses. These individuals are seen as predisposed toward destructive and hysterical reactions. Eysenck's clinical research and theory have provided an abundant source of hypotheses about abnormal behavior and continue to hold a position of importance.

In contrast to Pavlov and Eysenck, the clinically based views of Wolpe (1958) do not consider constitutional factors to be critical in predisposing individuals toward abnormal behavior. Within a classical conditioning framework, Wolpe sees environmental events as the essential determinants of behavior. He maintains that "all human neuroses are produced, as animal neuroses are, by situations which evoke high intensities of anxiety" (Wolpe, 1958, p. 78), that is, the situations evoke conditioned fear responses. Wolpe's theory is concerned most directly with the development of *phobias*, specific and intense fears that may incapacitate the individual. Within the classical conditioning model, Wolpe proposes that phobias may result when the organism is exposed to noxious, unpleasant stimuli (UCS) and is prevented, either physically or psychologically, from escaping from the situation. The anxiety level and reactions of the autonomic nervous system are increased to such an extent that the fear reactions can be conditioned to any and all stimuli that happen to be present in the situation. Although some of these conditioned responses may be adaptive in preventing future unpleasant encounters, others may be irrelevant and "irrational" fears, resulting in maladaptive patterns of behavior.

Modifying Maladaptive Respondent Behavior

In the Pavlovian conditioning model, "therapy" for maladaptive behavior can take several forms, depending on the nature of the maladaptive response. Where an inappropriate learned relationship has occurred, the procedure is to break the inappropriate stimulus-response connection. This is achieved by the process of *counterconditioning*, which entails the introduction of a new connection in which the new conditioned response is incompatible with the old conditioned response. The basic design of this procedure is exemplified by Jones's experiments (1924) on the fears of young children. Seventy children were observed, ranging in age from 3 months to 7 years. They were tested in a wide variety of situations to determine whether they showed fearful responses to objects (snake, rat, rabbit, frog, mask, etc.) or to conditions (being left alone, being in darkness, etc.). When the children demonstrated specific fears, various methods were used in attempts to remove or lessen the conditioned fear responses.

The least effective methods were verbal appeals, or the simple passage of time before retesting. Repeated presentations of the feared objects or situations did not seem to minimize the fears at all, and distractions by other non-feared objects had only a temporary effect. The technique that most reliably and rapidly eliminated the conditioned fear response was associating the feared object or state with *another stimulus capable of arousing a positive, pleasant reaction*. The situation found to be most effective for children was the following:

> During a period of craving for food, the child is placed in a high chair and given something to eat. The fear-object is brought in, starting a negative response. It is then moved away gradually until it is at a sufficient distance not to interfere with the child's eating. . . . While the child is eating, the object is slowly brought nearer to the table, then placed upon the table, and finally as the tolerance in-

creases it is brought close enough to be touched. (Jones, 1924, p. 388)

This counterconditioning model is used to substitute a response that is incompatible with, and stronger than, the undesirable response to the same stimulus. If a stimulus can be made to elicit a pleasure response, it cannot elicit a fear response simultaneously. A diagrammatic presentation of the Jones experiment is shown in Box 3-3. It can be seen that previously conditioned fear, for example, of a white rat, is incompatible with the pleasurable CR that develops in association with the act of eating. The old link is broken and replaced by a newly conditioned response that is more appropriate or adaptive. Such procedures were to be employed by Wolpe and many other investigators working in the respondent model. The development of treatment approaches based on the respondent learning model will be discussed in Chapter 7.

Operant Behavior

The central concept of operant learning is that responses of the organism are influenced by the environmental events that precede them (antecedents) and follow them (consequences). *Antecedent* events are important in that they serve as signals for responses. Their presence may "set the occasion" for behavior, or may indicate that a behavior is inappropriate at a given time.

Consequent events are *contingent* (dependent) upon a particular response when they occur after that response is performed. Consequences are stimuli that affect behavior by increasing or decreasing the probability that a given response will occur again in that situation.

An event that increases the probability that a response will occur again is said to be a *reinforcer* of that behavior. *Positive* reinforcement refers to the situation in which a pleasurable consequence occurs. In experimental work, the reinforcer is often something administered by the investigator that is of a "positive" nature, such as food or water given to an organism that has been deprived of either stimulus. *Negative* reinforcement describes the situation in which an unpleasant consequence is *removed* following a given response. The experimenter may, for instance, turn off an electric shock after the appropriate response is made. This will have the effect of increasing the probability that the same response will be made in the future, since avoiding or escaping the shock is reinforcing.

The negative reinforcement situation must not be confused with *punishment*, in which an unpleasant consequence is *presented* following a given behavior. The desired result here is to *decrease* the probability that the behavior that just occurred will occur again, as when a child is spanked for lying to a parent. But since punishment brings with it many problems that interfere with learning (e.g., accompanying emotional behavior, reactions to the person who administers the punishment, response suppression in which the punished behavior returns very rapidly to its full strength when punishment is withdrawn), it is not considered the most effective or permanent solution to changing behavior.

A preferable method for decreasing the probability that a response will occur again is *extinction.* In this situation, the positive consequence is taken away or withdrawn when the behavior occurs. A clinical use of the extinction method is seen in the "time-out" situation. For example, a disruptive child may be removed from the classroom (where presumably some reinforcement is maintaining his disruptive behavior) to a separate "time-out" room, where he must stay for a specified period of time. Now that his disruptive behavior is no longer followed by the reinforcement of attention from the other children, it will decrease, that is, extinguish. This procedure is generally used in behavior modification settings in preference to punishment. Box 3-4 has a schematic representation of reinforcement, punishment, and extinction.

Basically, there are two kinds of reinforcing stimuli, *primary* and *secondary* reinforcers. Primary reinforcers are biological necessities

B. F. Skinner (b. 1904) was instrumental in the development of theories of operant behavior. (*Joel Stern.*)

and their reinforcing properties do not have to be learned. For example, food is automatically perceived as pleasurable; shock is automatically perceived as painful. Secondary reinforcers, however, must acquire their reinforcing value through association with primary reinforcers. For example, social reinforcers (praise, attention, disapproving looks) acquire their reinforcing power by early association with primary reinforcers (food, cuddling, slaps). When a conditioned reinforcer has been paired with *many* other reinforcers, it is termed a *generalized* reinforcer, and it has great effectiveness in controlling behavior. Money is the typical example of a generalized reinforcer. In behavior modification programs, "tokens" (poker chips, stars, checkmarks) acquire equally strong generalized reinforcing properties. Money and tokens are both backed up by a number of commodities for which they may be ex-

Box 3-4 The Operant (Skinnerian, Instrumental Conditioning) Model

Skinner's original design

S^D ————————————————→ R ————————————————→ S^R

(discriminative stimulus)   (response)   (reinforcing stimulus)

Effects of administering or withdrawing pleasant and unpleasant consequences (S^R)

S^R	given	taken away
pleasant consequence	positive reinforcement	extinction
unpleasant consequence	punishment	negative reinforcement

Punishment and extinction *decrease* the probability of response. Reinforcement, both positive and negative, *increases* the probability of response.

Other operant procedures

1. Provide *immediate* rather than delayed reinforcement.

2. Reinforce on an *intermittent* rather than a continuous schedule (the "partial reinforcement effect").

3. *Successive approximations*, or *shaping*, are methods used to bring about the desired behavior by selective reinforcement of responses already occurring in the direction of the final performance. Later, these responses are extinguished when responses more closely approximating the desired behavior appear, and so on until the desired behavior appears.

4. *Chaining* is a procedure used to establish an increasingly long set of responses prior to reinforcement of the entire sequence as a whole.

5. Allowing an individual to engage in certain *responses* can be used as a reinforcement. Premack (1959) noted that more frequent, or more probable, responses could be used to reinforce less frequent responses. This method, known as the *Premack principle*, requires observation of the organism when it is left to perform freely.

6. *Prompting* is a procedure used to direct the learner's attention to the stimuli and responses required to be learned, for example, physically guiding the respondent through the task. The term *priming* is sometimes used to describe these activities. The analogy is to priming a pump, that is, putting the response in to get the response out.

7. *Fading* is related to prompting in that it entails the gradual removal of guidance or additional aids to learning other than the specific S^D and S^R.

8. *Superstitious conditioning* (or *surreptitious conditioning*) is the accidental connection of a response to a reinforcement in the environment; the reinforcement is not actually contingent upon that response. Once the connection is made, it is probable that further connections will be made; thus a cycle of superstitious behaviors occurs. This cycle can become a *self-fulfilling prophecy*. For example, anxiety is decreasing while you are washing your hands. You connect hand-washing to the reduction of anxiety. You do that more and more until it makes you feel better to wash your hands.

changed. Thus they have greater flexibility and more power than most reinforcers.

Having discussed the consequences of behavior, let us return briefly to the antecedent conditions. An event that signals to the organism that reinforcement can be obtained (if a response is made) has been termed a *discriminative stimulus*, or S^D. Technically, a discriminative stimulus is a stimulus whose presence marks the time and place for reinforcement to occur. Other terms describing the same stimulus function include antecedent conditions, cues, and setting conditions. A simple example is the red light on the corner. It is a signal telling you of the increased probability of getting hit by a car if you cross. It in itself is obviously not a reinforcer, and it certainly does not *make* you stop (a UCS). At a more subtle level, social cues serve as discriminative stimuli. For example, you assess the mood of your friend to be positive before you request a loan, that is, you look for cues that give you some idea of the likelihood of reinforcement for your loan-requesting behavior. As another example, you engage in interpersonal verbal behavior only in the presence of other people. It is only then that it can be reinforced. This last example hints at how S^Ds might relate to abnormal behavior. Suppose you always engage in interpersonal verbal behavior in the presence of mailboxes rather than people. The behavior is deviant only because the antecedent condition is inappropriate.

Another feature of S^Ds is that their continual pairing with a reinforcer will lead to their acquiring reinforcing properties. A pigeon whose pecking behavior is always reinforced with food in the presence of the S^D red light, will eventually peck to produce the red light even without receiving food. This is important in understanding human behavior, which is often based on producing or removing S^Ds rather than on primary reinforcers. Without such a principle, how would we explain people being reinforced by getting someone else to smile?

Maladaptive Behavior in Operant Learning

Within the operant conditioning model, abnormal behavior is explained in terms of the general principles just discussed. Abnormal behavior is assumed to be no different in quality or origin from "normal" learned behavior. "Abnormal" responses are defined as those responses that are perceived as maladaptive in the individual's current situation, although they developed as a result of antecedents and consequences that did exist at a certain point in the individual's environmental situation.

Maladaptive behavior might develop along several lines. Bandura (1969) has presented a useful way of categorizing maladaptive behavior. The categories are as follows:

1. *Behavioral excess.* In this situation, responses are made with too high a frequency, or too great an intensity, for example, too much talking in the classroom, overeating, constant hand-washing.

2. *Behavioral deficit.* Responses that should occur do not, or are infrequent and weak. Lack of social behavior, hysterical paralysis, and unassertiveness are examples of such deficits. Perhaps the responses in question have never been learned. In some cases of bed-wetting, for example, it has been suggested that the child has simply never learned the association between a full bladder and wakefulness (Mowrer and Mowrer, 1938). In other instances of behavioral deficit, a once-learned response may have decreased in frequency due to subsequent punishment or extinction. For example, once patients are hospitalized for a long time, they sometimes stop talking. In all probability, this occurs because they received little or no reinforcement from the hospital staff for talking.

3. *Distortions in reinforcing stimuli (S^R).* It is possible that stimuli that are normally reinforcing do not act as reinforcers for a particular individual. For example, verbal praise may not control the behavior of autistic or retarded children. In other cases, inappropriate stimuli may be reinforcing. For some children, scolding may act as positive reinforcement (attention), thereby strengthening rather than weakening undesirable behaviors.

4. *Distortions in discriminative stimulus (S^D) control.* Antecedent events that normally control behavior do not do so in some situations, for example, not discriminating that you are with your parent, not your friend, and using language offensive to your parent. Behavior may be overcontrolled by S^Ds, leading to rigid behavior, or responses may be made to inappropriate S^Ds, e.g., eating anytime food is available or eating when the cue is a failed exam.

5. *Aversive behavior repertoire.* The individual may use aversive behavior to control others. For example, a child may use tantrums to control his parents.

These examples represent only a small sampling of the ways in which abnormal behavior can be developed. Systems that attempt to categorize abnormal behavior from an operant point of view are arbitrary in separating one aspect of behavior from its context. There are usually too many interrelated variables to categorize the behavior easily. For example, what is maladaptive for the particular individual; what is unusual about the specific behavior; what is appropriate within the social network; what labels are being employed. The classification systems have been unable to accommodate simultaneously so many variables.

The best approach to understanding maladaptive behavior is not by categorizing it, but by performing a *functional analysis* of the behavior in question. Such an analysis attempts to describe the relationship of a particular behavior to the antecedent and consequent environmental events that interact with it. Although this will be discussed in detail in Chapter 5, the following section describes an elementary functional analysis of maladaptive behavior, as used in the design of a program of behavior modification.

Modifying Maladaptive Operant Behavior

When using operant techniques to change existing behavior, the matters of concern are the overt maladaptive response and the way it can be changed using principles of learning.

Before beginning a modification program, a complete functional analysis is made of the maladaptive behavior. Briefly stated, the questions that are asked fall into three categories (Ullmann and Krasner, 1965):

1. *What behavior is maladaptive?* This involves the determination of the precise behavior to be increased or decreased.
2. *What environmental contingencies currently support the behavior?* This includes contingencies that maintain the present behavior as well as those that reduce the likelihood that more adaptive responses will occur. Stated another way, the difficulty may be not only that the "wrong" response has been learned, but also that the "right" response

has *not* been learned. This question is very important, for it emphasizes that the behavior is *currently* being maintained by the environment.
3. *What environmental stimuli may be manipulated to change behavior?* What environmental events that are reinforcing the maladaptive behavior can the behavior modifier control in such a way that they can be presented or withheld contingently upon the response to be modified?

Operant techniques for behavior change will be discussed in Chapter 7.

Broadening the Behavioral Viewpoint

Research on operant and respondent conditioning has helped to define the basic principles of both types of learning. We have noted how these principles can be employed to describe and understand abnormal behavior, and to create a theoretical basis for therapeutic intervention. Other investigators have elaborated upon the basic laws of conditioning in order to account for the extreme complexity of human behavior.

The operant-respondent dichotomy has proven useful at the theoretical level, but several experimenters have indicated that this separation may be artificial. For example, autonomic responses can be classically conditioned. It had been thought that because these responses are not under the direct voluntary control of the individual, they were not subject to operant conditioning. Miller (1969), however, demonstrated operant conditioning of intestinal contractions and heart rate in rats. Since that time, many other "involuntary" response systems have been found to be modifiable through reinforcement. This raises the possibility that contingencies that reinforce observable operant behavior may at the same time be strengthening unobservable "emotional responses." The formation of complex *operant-respondent chains* of behavior has been shown to occur in many situations when an environmental event acts as both a conditioned and a discriminative stimulus, that is, the CS and the S^D are the same event.

Giving a speech in class, for example, involves both respondent and operant behaviors. On the respondent side, there is the excitement, nervousness, and anxiety and the accompanying physical sensations (cold sweat, knees shaking, upset stomach, dry mouth, etc.). On the operant side are all the responses learned toward giving the speech (the speech itself, the instructions about how to stand, speak, move, etc.). The intertwining of the respondent and operant behaviors forms the total behavior chain for giving the speech. The teacher's introduction of the student can then become an S^D for the speech-giving operant behaviors and a CS for the respondent feelings and physical reactions. Depending upon the prior learning experiences, the next occasion of speech giving will include the intermixed chain.

Thus far, we have stayed within the boundaries of the two conditioning models, but many theorists have found it necessary to add to them in order to account for phenomena such as learning without reinforcement, or the appearance of complex, novel responses without a history of conditioning. Bandura (1969) has proposed that learning may occur by *imitation*, or modeling, of behaviors observed in others. This "learning-by-observation" does not fit totally into either an operant or a respondent model. Bandura argues that imitation learning may occur in the absence of reinforcement and without overt responding. When the imitative behavior is performed, however, reinforcement contingencies will then have an effect upon it.

Maladaptive behavior from modeling can occur in several ways. Simple modeling of maladaptive behavior might include the situation where a child raised by maladjusted parents imitates their abnormal behavior. Somewhat more complex modeling involves a response learned in one situation that is then emitted in a new situation. For example, a child observing an aggressive act toward a dog in a cartoon may exhibit already-learned aggressive responses to his own pet, although he had not done so previously. The imitation model may also create an inhibitory effect in which the individual

Albert Bandura (b. 1925) has proposed that learning may occur by imitation, or modeling, of behaviors observed in others. (*News and Publications Service, Stanford University.*)

does not make a response that would otherwise have been made. Bandura (1969) speculates that many phobic behaviors "arise not from injurious experiences with the phobic objects, but rather from witnessing others respond fearfully toward, or be hurt by, certain things" (p. 167). According to the imitation model, any analysis of maladaptive behavior should include the study of significant adults in the child's life. It is important to determine the models the adults might have provided for deviant behavior, either in exhibiting maladaptive responses or in inhibiting adaptive behavior.

Ullmann and Krasner (1975) give even greater emphasis to the social context in which behavior is learned. They propose a "sociopsychological" model in which a person's social environment influences the emission of complex patterns of responses identified as *social roles*. A role is a sequence of interrelated behaviors (a chain) that is learned by past experience and maintained by reinforcement. Based on previously experienced reinforcing contingencies, we form social *expectancies* of reinforcement for that role in particular situations, even though the original contingencies may not always be present.

Roles, as complex behavioral chains, can be reinforced as whole units and can be attached to antecedent cues in the same way we have been discussing individual responses. Emitting date-getting behavior in the presence of a girl that results in getting a date reinforces the whole chain of responses leading to that result in the presence of those cues.

If a role is viewed in the same way we have been discussing individual behaviors, then we can see the potential for abnormal behavior occurring in role-related behavior. Not having the appropriate role, emitting it in the presence of the wrong S^Ds, not emitting the appropriate role behavior where it is expected are just some of the ways in which problems can occur. In sociological terms, inappropriate role behavior leads to "rule breaking" that makes the individual appear deviant.

Another aspect of roles is that they are S^Ds to other people's role behavior, that it, they are complementary to the behavior of others. Smooth interpersonal functioning requires the smooth meshing of roles. Breaking interpersonal role-behavior rules is thus particularly uncomfortable, since it breaks the complementary aspect and disrupts the other person's behavior as well.

Ullmann and Krasner argue that the principal difference between normal and abnormal behavior lies in the societal reaction to the two kinds of behavior. For behavior to be considered appropriate, it must meet social expectancies as to correctness of time and place. "Inappropriate" behavior is frowned upon by society precisely because it is unexpected, unpredictable, and seemingly ineffective to the observer.

Ullmann and Krasner (1969) explain this social reaction:

> The person whose behavior is called maladaptive is probably acting in a manner unexpected by his immediate observers. The abnormal person's behavior is not disturbed; it is disturbing. The person seems to be disregarding important cues in his environment or attending to cues that are idiosyncratic or trivial or that he seems to misinterpret "irrationally." To the observer, the act may be particularly hard to understand because the person does not seem to be obtaining benefits that are routinely and currently available to a person of his social status. (p. 93)

There is another aspect to role behavior noted by Ullmann and Krasner that is of great importance in abnormal psychology. Once individuals are labeled as abnormal in any society, a new set of social expectancies and reinforcement contingencies come into play. The "sick" role exempts the individuals from performance of their normal duties and from responsibility for their condition; it obligates them to cooperate with persons society designates to "help" them. Even within a mental institution, the individuals are reinforced for playing the role of a mental patient. The staff may in fact contribute to the maintenance of maladaptive behavior by "expecting" it from the patients. We will discuss some of the far-reaching effects of these expectancies when we discuss institutionalization in Chapters 10 and 11.

In addition to adding social factors to learning theory, some psychologists also propose the addition of internal *cognitive* factors. In Bandura's model of imitation learning (1969), he suggested that the gap between observation and performance might be mediated by cognitive processes such as imagery and verbal symbolic activities. Other theorists who regard *cognitive mediation* as important in the derivation of abnormal behavior are Homme (1965), Cautela (1967), and Wisocki (1972). Homme has suggested that thoughts could be worked with like any other operant response, and he contributed the term "coverants"—operants of the mind—to learning theory. We will discuss this approach in greater depth when we review behavioral treatments in Chapter 7.

Behavior-Shaping Environments: How Environments Create and Support Maladaptive Behavior

In our investigation of the formation of abnormal behavior, we have considered the basic explanations of the operant and respondent conditioning models. The broadening of these models by the addition of social and cognitive factors has been discussed. The following vignette is presented here to illustrate several principles of conditioning as well as to underscore the importance of the environment in the development of maladaptive behavior.

Seal tanks are often used in resort areas as tourist attractions. The reason these are attractions is the fact that the seals engage in entertaining behavior, both comical and unusual. It was at such a seal tank that this author had the opportunity to observe a remarkable variety of abnormal or "bizarre" behavior. For example, one seal was racing up and down in the front of the tank trying to splash the visitors, making them run back from the railing. Another seal was perched statute-like on a rock toward the back of the tank, seemingly immobile until food came within his reach, which he would grab and eat, and then resume his pose. Still another seal screamed at very shrill levels, constantly charging up to the front of the tank and then swimming back again. Another seal appeared deeply depressed, head down and barely out of the water. He remained alone in the far corner, looking very sad and unhappy. He appeared to have no interest in the environment until food came within his reach at which time he charged to retrieve it only to return to his sad vigil in the corner. Still another seal engaged in a furious level of spinning, diving, and jumping, then stopping for a short period of time and finally began the whole cycle again.

After you've been entertained by all this, you may ask questions as to the nature of these responses. Are they natural to seals? How did they develop? Could we ask the three questions of functional analysis to help us understand this behavior? Applying our behavioral principles, we certainly can see *what* behavior is maladaptive in human terms, thus answering our first behavioral question. For the second behavioral question, observation would lead us to some of the environmental contingencies that might be maintaining such unusual and bizarre responses. We would note that the visitors are throwing food to the seals. This, in fact, appears to be the only environmental change that could be associated with their behavior. A tenable proposition is, then, that the behavior is maintained by the visitors' reinforcing those behaviors. That leaves open, though, the question of how these particular abnormal behaviors came to be. Applying our functional analysis, we should note the particular *ecology* of this seal tank. The only source of food for these seals is from the visitors. The seals are under high deprivation conditions, especially when there are few people feeding the relatively large number of seals. These events have all made for a situation in which a rather large number of deprived organisms exist in an environment where there are very few reinforcers and those are being dispensed by other organisms. To combat this, the seals must somehow emerge from the background in order to be noticed. Any particular seal must make his "impact" very quickly on the visitor passing through if he is to be fed some food. The more unusual behaviors are certainly more likely to be noticed and therefore to be reinforced.

Many other learning principles are useful here also. Since the organisms are on a rather "lean" *schedule of reinforcement*, their behavior would become very strong and stereotyped as demonstrated by the work on schedules of reinforcement. The particular behavior may have been strengthened through *superstitious* or *surreptitious conditioning*. Once a behavior occurs and is accidentally reinforced, that behavior has an increased probabiliy of occurrence. This further heightens the likelihood of its being reinforced in a cycle leading to more and more of the now stereotyped behavior.

From this example, we see how a number of events can come together to create a situation in which the environment not only develops, but also supports, extremely maladaptive behavior. Of course, we mean maladaptive with regard to some more "normal" environment—a judgment we make. Actually, the behavior should be thought of as quite "adaptive" to the environment in which the seals find themselves. After all, they do survive in that environment.

There is an obvious parallel here to the patients in a psychiatric ward. Note the "catatonic" seal upon the rock, the "depressed" seal in the corner of the tank, the "manic excitement" of the furious activity of two of the seals, and finally the "aggressive," "acting-out" behavior of the seal trying to splash the visitors. All of these behaviors have their parallels on the psychiatric ward. We can see that bizarre behavior, because of its very demanding nature, could develop in environments that have the features we noted in the seal tank. Some of these features are clear: the high levels of deprivation on the part of the organism, the small number of reinforcers available, and the "noncontingent" or arbitrary delivery of those reinforcers by other organisms. In our parallel situation, the psychiatric ward, attention (already noted to be an important reinforcer) is in very short supply. The staff who can administer that reinforcer do so in arbitrary, noncontingent ways, or, if contingent, often to the more bizarre or destructive behavior. The major point is that the parallels of these two environments, while not necessarily explaining each other, do supply a model for our understanding of how environments can create and maintain maladaptive behavior. Later in the text, we will also explore how, by using this understanding and some of the behavioral procedures we are exploring, environments can be used to create and support more adaptive behavior.

Critique of the Behavioral Viewpoint

Approaches to abnormal behavior based on operant and classical conditioning have proliferated in recent years. As we did with the psychodynamic approaches, we will take a deliberately critical look at the behavioral perspective. One criticism directed at behavioral therapies is that the learning theories upon which they are based are really not up to date. Researchers working in the area of learning are much less secure about the basic principles than are researchers who are willing to apply those "laws" in the clinical situation. In addition, behavior therapists sometimes ignore the finer points of learning theory. In their desire to find a procedure to apply to abnormal behavior, they occasionally create what amounts to caricatures of laboratory experiments and use the mantle of science to mask highly questionable procedures.

Adherents of the psychodynamic school criticize the behavioral perspective with regard to the "symptom" issue. They feel that behavior therapists place total emphasis on the peripheral responses, rather than on what for psychodynamic therapists is the central problem. The theme that "the symptom is the neurosis" is not easily accepted by those raised on psychodynamic principles. The existence of a group of related disturbances, or even an underlying problem causing the symptoms, is not easily disproven (Buchwald and Young, 1969).

Another set of questions concerns the generality of certain types of abnormal behavior. Why do individuals classed as "paranoid schizophrenics" show similar patterns of behavior if each behavior developed out of idiosyncratic conditioning experiences? By and large, the behaviorists have been accused of avoiding this problem by dealing only with abnormal behaviors that can be described in terms of specific symptoms. They have tended to avoid conditions that are characterized by several related behaviors (syndromes), such as depression, general unhappiness, and disturbed interpersonal relationships (Breger and McGaugh 1965).

The behaviorists claim to have greater scientific respectability than the psychoanalytic school, but it appears that the behaviorists are sometimes subject to the same criticisms. Their scientific-sounding terminology often obscures the fact that some of the terms may be no more objective than the terms used in other approaches. Using the words "stimulus," "response," and "reinforcement" is insufficient unless they are defined in such a way that they can be measured. One central and continuing problem is the circularity of the definition of reinforcement. Any increase in the probability of a response is attributed to reinforcement, yet the only definition given of reinforcement is "that which increases the probability of a response." While this circular definition allows a certain freedom in studying behavioral phenomena, it is a problem in our quest for objective designations.

The efficacy of behavioral methods is not as totally obvious as some of the claims of success might lead one to believe. Clearly, the numbers favor the behavioral approaches. However, the research on outcomes is not always as well designed as it should be. Criticisms have centered on three areas:

1. *Sampling bias.* As previously suggested, patients are chosen who are likely to benefit from behavioral procedures, that is, those with discrete symptoms rather than global disorders.

2. *Observer bias.* The patient reports his progress directly to the therapist rather than to an independent evaluator.

3. *Experimental control.* Clinical applications of behavioral principles are often not restricted to the manipulation of one variable at a time. In hopes of achieving a "cure," many things are tried at once, often including a large dose of something that resembles psychoanalysis itself (Breger and McGaugh, 1965).

Postscript: Psychodynamic and Behavioral Models Compared and Contrasted

There is no question that the first major breakthrough in abnormal psychology occurred with Freud. He provided a radical departure from previous emphasis on the biological aspects of mental illness, and is to be praised for liberating us from both the organic and the demonological points of view. The psychodynamic models built on Freud's approach fall short of perfection, however, in their reliance on unobservable mental constructs, in their perpetuation of the medical model, and in their practitioners' clannish refusal to accept new ideas or new scientific data.

The most directly testable hypothesis of psychodynamic theory has to do with *symptom substitution.* If the symptoms are eliminated without resolution of the underlying psychological disturbance, the psychodynamic schools propose that new symptoms will be produced. This prediction was based on clinical observation, but has not generally been supported in experimental situations. In a study of bed-wetting, 30 elementary school children were treated by behavioral techniques with a significant degree of success in removing the bed-wetting symptom (Baker, 1969). Teachers, unaware of who had been treated, rated general adjustment. Only three of the treated children developed anything that could be interpreted as new symptoms. Their teacher reported that the rest of the children were not only symptom-free but showed advances in other areas as well. The bulk of the research evidence is on the side of the behaviorists, indicating that such responses as tics and phobias can be treated successfully without the substitution of new symptoms. The behaviorists' point is well taken that at the present state of our knowledge, we might do better to deal with things that we can control (i.e., environmental contingencies) than to ask unanswerable questions about the etiology of abnormal behavior. The intrapsychic views have their greatest shortcoming in focusing on internal, inaccessible processes while ignoring the more potent and useful environmental stimuli. Occasionally, the behavioral views invoke complex social situations and numerous cognitive mediators to describe a particular behavior. At this extreme, little is gained over the inference of psychodynamic forces (Mischel, 1973).

It should not be assumed that there is a "correct" model as yet in the field of abnormal psychology. If the two dominant models are good in parts, why not combine the best of each? That would be equally inappropriate. As discussed in Chapter 1, competing viewpoints encourage further inquiry and the development of new ideas. Therefore, we should not seek premature reconciliation of the opposing views. Models of abnormal behavior will continue to develop. The psychodynamic and behavioral models currently lead the field, but several new, intriguing, and valuable viewpoints are on the horizon. The final section of the text will deal with these emerging views and future directions of the field of abnormal psychology.

Summary

Chapter 3 has been concerned with the two major views of abnormal psychology: the psychodynamic approaches and the behavioral approaches. Within the former, we have noted the contributions of Freud and the development of psychoanalysis. The offspring of this tradition is the humanistic school of thought, including the self-actualization approach and the existential point of view.

Within the behavioral approach, two lines are separable in theory, but in actual practice, they are shown to be closely interrelated. Respondent (Pavlovian, classical) conditioning provides the basis for current applications of behavior therapy. Operant (Skinnerian, instrumental) conditioning has led to the use of behavior modification techniques. In both conditioning designs, the environmental stimuli are manipulated to produce behavior change in the form of more adaptive responses. The behavioral viewpoint has been broadened by the addition of such concepts as operant-respondent chains, imitation, social roles, and cognitive processes. Both the behavioral and the psychodynamic approaches provide important, if differing, perspectives on maladaptive behavior.

Causal, contributing, and maintaining factors of abnormal behavior

Overview of Causal Factors of Abnormal Behavior

The Search for Etiological Factors

Throughout the history of abnormal psychology, investigators have searched for the all-important *etiological* factor, the elusive event or substance that *causes* abnormal behavior. In our medical example in Chapter 2, we described the search for the cause of tuberculosis, culminating in the discovery of the tubercle bacillus. Curative treatment was quickly devised, and this was followed, eventually, by prevention programs that have brought the disease under almost total control.

Table 4-1 Some Proposed Causal Factors of Abnormal Behavior

Biological Factors
Genetic structure
Biochemical factors
Neurochemical factors
Hormonal factors
Serum factors
Neurophysiological factors
Biological stresses and deprivations
Nutritional and vitamin deficiencies
Sensory deprivation and isolation
Sleep and dream deprivation

Psychological Factors
The developing organism
Infant reaction patterns
Early attachment—security
Maternal deprivation
Parent and family factors
Ordinal position of children in family
Child-rearing practices
Disturbed communication styles
Conflict, stress, and coping in the adult

Sociocultural Factors
Sociological variables
Age, sex, marital status, occupation, education, religion, economic status, social class, race
Cross-cultural studies
Ecological factors

Applying the disease model to examples of abnormal behavior gave no such easy success. Usually, direct causal factors for abnormal behavior could not be found. Therefore, the pure disease model gave way to a broader scope of possible causal events. Numerous specialized fields of the basic medical, psychological, and social sciences searched for causal explanations from their own perspectives.

Today, each specialized model of abnormal behavior proposes its own specialized causal factors. For example, the neurochemists propose a neurochemical cause and a drug "cure" for abnormal behavior. The socioculturalists place the cause and the cure in the effects of society. Causal theories are almost as numerous as symptoms, each theory suggested and supported by a separate area of investigation.

Much of the confusion in the field of abnormal psychology can be attributed to this chain of vigorous proposal of a hypothesis, rebuttal, and proposal of alternate causal hypotheses, each supported by its own evidence. The problem becomes even more perplexing—and, from an investigator's viewpoint, more fascinating—when we discover that each proposal has some reasonable claim to being the basic causal factor for abnormal behavior.

Proposed Causal Factors of Abnormal Behavior

Listed in Table 4-1 are some of the more prominent factors that have been proposed as *the* cause of abnormal behavior. In spite of its length, this list is by no means exhaustive. It is, in fact, limited to factors having a reasonable level of scientific support backed by a current, active group of investigators. We have also excluded the psychodynamic and behavioral views in this list, since they have already been presented in Chapter 3.

We will discuss each of the factors in the list and how it relates to our current attempts to understand abnormal behavior.

Multiple Routes to Abnormal Behavior and Functional Autonomy

How can such a wide range of factors all find scientific support among the highly critical investigators of abnormal behavior? If, for example, you inherit schizophrenia, how can you also get it by being traumatized during your early psychosexual development? Are these causes not mutually exclusive? Perhaps not, as we shall see.

Let us start by questioning the basic assumption that a simple linear cause-to-effect relationship exists in behavior. Assume, instead, a more complex relationship in which various environmental events act upon a developing organism, which also has a special genetic makeup. Assume, also, that the effects of those environmental events on the behavior of the organism are directly related to the way certain factors interact as well as to the presence or absence of other factors. Thus occupational stress (environmental events) could lead to schizophrenic behavior when this stress interacts with other factors, such as sleep deprivation or early childhood trauma, in a person with a possible genetic predisposition to overactivity.

This provides a model that can accept the possibility that there are *multiple routes* to abnormal behavior. It proposes that there are many events and conditions that shape and guide our lives and our behavior at various times.

This more complex view of causality also involves the concept of *functional autonomy*. The traditional medical model views causality in a simple direct way: A causes B; if A is not present, B does not occur. The tubercle bacilli cause the symptoms of tuberculosis; if we kill them, the symptoms are no longer present and the patient is cured. Applying this medical model to psychodynamics, we have intrapsychic conflicts causing the symptoms. When the conflicts are removed, the symptoms no longer occur. The continued existence of an early psychic conflict in the present personality structure of the individual provides a constant source of potential anxiety and, consequently, a constant influence on adult behavior. For example, an individual's unresolved Oedipal complex creates potential anxiety in his heterosexual relationships. This causes the development of behaviors designed to defend the individual against the anxiety, such as failing to relate to women in an adult manner. If the individual then undergoes psychoanalysis and resolves the early conflict, he is able to relate to women at an adult level and is "cured." Figure

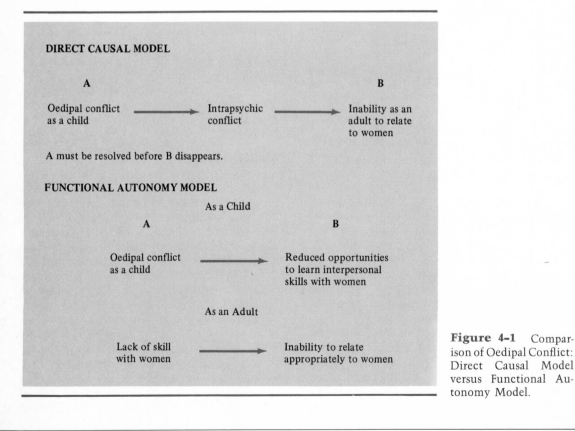

Figure 4-1 Comparison of Oedipal Conflict: Direct Causal Model versus Functional Autonomy Model.

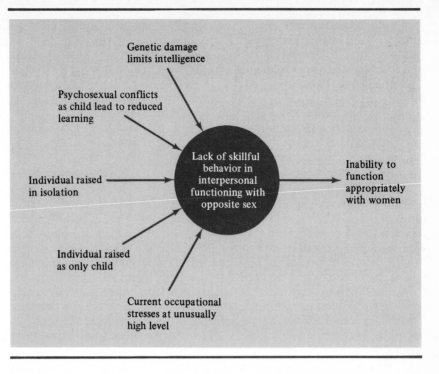

Figure 4-2 Multiple Causal Possibilities in the Functional Autonomy Model.

4-1 illustrates this approach as the direct causal model.

In our multiple routes model, an initiating event can cause a deficit in the person's functioning, but that deficit then becomes *functionally autonomous* from the original cause. It is separated from the causal factor but maintained by other factors in the person's present environment.

In the Oedipal conflict, for example, the early difficulty in relating to the mother is the original causal factor of the individual's problems in relating to women. The resulting behavior problem is that during the period when the individual would normally be developing interpersonal skills toward women, he is shy, awkward, and embarrassed. This creates the potential for continued inability to function skillfully in this area, even though he may have resolved the conflict of his original feelings toward his mother. The problem has become functionally autonomous from the original cause. In other words, the result of the original cause—inability to relate to women, which is a learning deficit—now becomes the *cause* of his present behavior. This model clearly supports the behavioral approaches that argue that behavior is maintained by the current environment rather than by historical, causal mechanisms.

Note the major difference between the two models in Figure 4-1. In the functional autonomy model, resolving conflict A will have no effect on behavior B. In order to change B, we do not even need to know A. In other words, working on interpersonal skills with women will remove B even though A has not even been discussed.

In addition, the functional autonomy model works independently of the exact nature of the original cause. Lack of skill in interpersonal behavior can be caused by any number of different factors, not just an Oedipal conflict. This expanded model is shown in Figure 4-2.

We now begin to understand how such a long list of causal factors can find simultaneous support. All of the factors indeed either cause direct symptomatic behavior or, more likely, contribute to behavioral deficits or distortions that are maintained by the ongoing interactions between the individual and his or her environment.

Where does this conceptual system lead us? It could bring us to the point where the proponents of the various factors in Table 4-1 could discover peaceful coexistence, since the multiple routes model permits each causal explanation to exist without negating all the others. The result, we hope would be greater rationality in the debate over these factors.

Causal, Contributing, and Maintaining Factors

The example shown in Figure 4-2 demonstrates how any number of factors can play a *causal* role in starting a process that then forms its own functional relationship to the environment. These same factors can also play a *contributory* role by complicating or amplifying an existing problem. A third role of these factors may be to *maintain* a deficit behavior. Maternal deprivation, for example, could cause deficits in learning. The disturbed interaction that results may then continue through the person's adult life, contributing to and maintaining those abnormal behaviors originally caused by the learning deficit. At still another, perhaps more complex, level, some psychological variables, for example, parental behavior, appear to *cause* some types of psychological problems, *contribute* to other types of psychological problems, and *maintain* still other types. The obvious complexities of the model are necessitated by the complexities of the problems they are meant to explain.

In the past, the tendency has been to reject any factor, regardless of the strength of evidence for it, unless it could provide a uniform explanation for a wide variety of abnormal behaviors and overcome all competing factors. The multiple routes model shows how inappropriate this is as a test of a variable. And

many important variables may have been prematurely rejected because of it.

At this point, we will examine some of the factors themselves. Because of the large number of factors involved, this will often take the form of a somewhat brief overview. Many of these factors will also be covered in greater detail wherever they relate to a particular disorder in later chapters.

Biological Factors of Abnormal Behavior

To many students without a strong background in biology, the terms "neurochemical influences" and "chromosomal variation" may sound incomprehensible. However, biological factors are undeniably important in the study of abnormal behavior. And although they are also undeniably complex, an effort has been made to present them here in as nontechnical a form as possible while still providing a framework for understanding the role of biological factors in behavior determination.

Genetic Factors

The science of psychological genetics is concerned with the relationship between an organism's genetic endowment and its behavioral interaction with the environment. In other words, it examines the way a person's *genotype* (total genetic composition) interacts with the environment to produce the person's *phenotype* (total observable composition, including appearance, physiology, and behavior).

Your genotype results from the pairing of your father's and your mother's genes at conception. The information carried in those genes will govern what species you belong to, what racial characteristics you show within that species, and what your individual differences are. It is this last type of information that we are concerned with here.

Some of your behavioral characteristics or predispositions are inherited through your genetic structure. The individual characteristics may come from one parent alone or from both parents. When the inherited gene pair includes two like genes you are said to be *homozygous* for that particular gene. The opposite is *heterozygous*, which means that the gene pair includes two unlike genes.

If one or both of your parents have a genotype that is, in effect, "programmed" for a specific behavioral disorder, what are the chances that you will show characteristics of the same disorder? This is the subject of Mendel's laws of inheritance. The answer is related to whether we are talking about a *dominant* or a *recessive* gene.

If a disorder is attributed to a dominant gene, at least one parent, by definition, has been afflicted with the disorder. In this case, one half of the children will, on the average, inherit the disorder. If both parents have the dominant gene (a homozygous situation), the probability is that three-quarters of the children will inherit the disorder.

When the disorder is attributed to a recessive gene, you are not liable to inherit the disorder unless you are homozygous (received the gene in question from both parents). If you are heterozygous (you received the recessive gene from only one parent), you will not be affected with the disorder yourself, but you will probably pass the gene on to half of your children (who may or may not inherit the disorder, depending on which gene they receive from their other parent). If your spouse is also heterozygous, the probability is that only one-fourth of your children will be affected with the disorder. If both parents are homozygous, all children will be liable to inherit the disorder. If one parent does not carry the recessive gene at all, none of the children will be affected.

Unfortunately, for geneticists, the simple cause-and-effect relationship between one gene and one definable disorder is the exception rather than the rule and its contribution to behavioral disorder is totally conjectural. Geneticists themselves feel that if behavioral effects occur, such traits would depend on a *polygenic* combination of many genes acting together to produce a particular behavioral characteristic.

The problem with genetic behavioral research lies in isolating environmental effects from genetic effects. To accomplish this, a number of methodological designs have been employed. The most common approaches are the family resemblance method, the twin-study method, and a combination of the two. The family resemblance method basically looks for *concordance* (similarity) between a chosen subject (the proband) with a particular disorder and the subject's relatives.

The twin-study method relies on the difference between *monozygotic* and *dizygotic* twins. Monozygotic (MZ) twins come from a single ovum and are therefore identical genetically. Dizygotic (DZ) twins result from two ova being fertilized by two sperm and are therefore no more alike genetically than two siblings of any age would be. This means that differences in MZ twins must be environmental. The differences between DZ twins are either environmental or hereditary. Thus if a particular trait shows a significantly greater concordance between MZ twins than between DZ twins, the conclusion is that the influence is genetic in nature.

Another research approach involving twins is the twins-reared-apart method. The theory is that differences in concordance rates between twins reared together and twins reared apart can be ascribed to the influence of the environment. A difficulty with the method is in finding twins who are not only reared apart but reared in significantly different environments.

Although the methodologies and interpretations of individual researchers have produced an expected degree of controversy, there is reasonable support for the belief that there is a genetic contribution to some behavioral disorders. Schizophrenia, for example, shows significant evidence for such a genetic theory (Böök, 1960). Some view the evidence as indicating a direct causal relationship. Others take a more moderate view of the relative effects of environment and inheritance. Rainer (1966),

(United Press International.)   (Florence Greenwald.)

Twins are often used in studying genetic involvement in the causation of abnormal behavior. Pictured here are monozygotic twins (left) and dizygotic twins (right).

for example, stated, "It should be understood, of course, that genes actually determine only a norm of reaction, the exact expression of which depends on many prenatal, paranatal, and postnatal interactions" (p. 284).

Genetic research in recent years has discovered a number of specific chromosomal aberrations. One of these, the presence of an extra chromosome, has been shown to be directly linked to mongolism, although there has been some recent evidence to the contrary. Other genetic-behavioral findings with regard to specific behaviors will be discussed later in the book.

The role of genetics in behavior determination is complex. The genetic view in extreme is summarized by the following statement: "All bodily structures and functions, without exception, are products of heredity realized in some sequence of environments. So also are all forms of behavior, also without exception. Nothing can arise in any organism unless its potentiality is within the realm of possibilities of the genetic endowment" (Dobzhansky, 1972, p. 530). Note the similarities here to the physiologist's statement during the organic period, which we discussed in Chapter 1—"no twisted

thought without a twisted molecule." Such simplistic pronouncements tend to obscure more than they clarify.

Biochemical Factors

Not surprisingly, the study of biochemical factors in abnormal behavior is based on the supposition that an interaction exists between these factors and the behavior. One of the methodological problems, however, has been in providing workable hypotheses for testing. Most attention has been concentrated on the biochemical events of the nervous system and the endocrine system. It is, consequently, in these areas that the most success—and most controversy—has been recorded.

Neurochemical Factors

There are two major approaches to the study of the relationship between biochemical factors and behavior. The first is to examine the neurochemical properties of organisms exhibiting abnormal behavior and look for distinctive neurochemical factors. The second method is to introduce chemical abnormalities or variations into the nervous system of the organism and look for any resulting behavioral changes.

One promising area of research is in the role played by *biogenic amines* (in particular *neurotransmitters*, chemicals involved in the transfer or modulation of nerve impulses from one cell to another). Recent evidence suggests their involvement in mood and affective (emotional) disorders (Miller, 1965). Experiments have shown what appears to be a direct relationship between the amount of these chemicals, particularly *norepinephrine*, at certain areas of the brain and some moods of depression or mania. Although a deficiency of norepinephrine seems to be a causal factor in depression, the evidence is, as yet, inconclusive. Nor can it be concluded that norepinephrine is the only transmitter involved. Significant effects have been found with other neurotransmitters, notably, *serotonin*. A deficiency of serotonin in the brain has been found in both depressives and manics. Further exploration of this and other neurochemical mechanisms is an active and promising field of research.

Hormonal Factors

Changes in the endocrine system during psychological stress are another promising area of research. For example, through blood samples taken from patients, relationships have been shown to exist between the production of steroid hormones and manic-depressive moods. Although, at present, these results may be interpreted as hormonal activity *accompanying* mood and stress behavior, there is at least the possibility that a causal relationship may also exist.

Serum Factors

The role of blood factors in behavior disorders is receiving attention. For example, one investigator has discovered a unique protein known as *taraxein*, in the blood of schizophrenics (Heath, 1959, 1961). But there has been difficulty in replicating this finding. There

has been evidence of the retention of sodium ions during depression and also during mania (Kety, 1975). On the other hand, comparisons of cerebral blood flow have shown no difference between schizophrenic patients and normal subjects (Kety et al., 1948).

In areas of biochemical research, the emphasis has switched from the search for one all-embracing solution to behavioral relationships to more specific, empirically resolvable hypotheses. The result has been a slow but steadily growing body of more reliable and complex knowledge.

Neurophysiological Factors: The Central Nervous System

To understand how behavior, both normal and abnormal, interacts with the body's response mechanisms, we will start with a brief (and overly simplified) review of the functions of the central nervous system.

The central nervous system is made up of the brain and the spinal cord. The functions of the spinal cord are, first, to pass nerve impulses to the brain and back to the muscles or glands and, second, to govern certain instantaneous reflexes such as withdrawing your hand from a hot stove or blinking your eye to avoid injury.

The brain is, of course, much more complex. Basically, its function is to identify, interpret, and respond to messages it receives from the sensory receptors. The three main divisions of the brain are the hindbrain, the midbrain, and the forebrain.

The *cerebrum*, which is part of the forebrain, is responsible for most of the higher cognitive processes such as learning, thinking, and remembering. It is made up of two hemispheres: the *right hemisphere*, which controls the left side of the body, and the *left hemisphere*, which controls the right side of the body. Verbal skills are also largely localized in the left hemisphere, while spatial abilities are localized in the right hemisphere. Joining the two halves is a connector called the *corpus callosum*. Much of the research on the brain has been centered around the surgical cutting of this connection in animals so that activity in each half of the brain can be studied separately.

Surrounding the cerebrum is the *cerebral cortex*, or "gray matter," as it is popularly known. Science has neatly divided the cortex into four regions: frontal lobe, temporal lobe, occipital lobe, and parietal lobe. Even within these lobes, specific functions are localized. Thus there are precise areas in the cortex where sensations from different parts of the body (right thigh, left ear, etc.) can be identified and "mapped."

Since all behavior is mediated by the nervous system, neurological changes often bring about abnormal behavior. Some disorders, in fact, are primarily due to malfunction of the nervous system. This does not mean, however, that *all* abnormal behavior is caused in this way. The evidence, at this point, is the reverse: most types of abnormal behavior are not due to malfunction of the nervous system. As we have been discussing, the human body is a very complex system that can interact with other complex factors in many causal, contributing, and maintaining ways.

Biological Stresses and Deprivations

Nutrition and Vitamin Deficiencies

Protein and calorie malnutrition in developing children has been shown to result not only in physical deficiencies but in behavioral manifestations as well. In severe cases of malnutrition involving infants less than 6 months old, there is a strong possibility of permanent damage to intellectual capacity even if the diet is corrected. In older children suffering from malnutrition, it is possible that when the diet is corrected, the behavioral problems resulting from that deficiency will disappear, provided that environmental factors do not interfere.

There are also several theories that name vitamin deficiencies in adults as a central and even major factor in the cause of psychological difficulties (Hawkins and Pauling, 1973; Ross, 1974). Starvation and undernutrition have often been noted as direct causes of disturbed

Box 4-1 Biological Rhythms and Abnormal Behavior

The study of biological rhythms is receiving increased attention, both in the popular press where it is known as "body time," and in the laboratory where it goes under the new label "chronopsychophysiology."

Rhythms being explored range from our biological reactions to day and night ("circadian" rhythms) to recurring cycles lasting a year or longer. Some relationships have been established, for example, between adrenal hormone level, which varies throughout the day, and some types of behavior such as emotional learning.

Since persons under stress often change their living rhythms and such changes, in turn, seem to cause stress, a compounding relationship is a possibility. Whether such changes of biological rhythm have a place in the role of cause, or of effect, or are part of a complex interaction, however, is not yet clear.

behavior, ranging from mild emotional symptoms to reactions bordering on psychosis (Schiele and Brozek, 1948).

Some nutritional effects, such as too much or too little sugar, have a very rapid effect on behavior. Other nutritional effects are more difficult to detect and may lead to a vicious circle situation: people under stress lose interest in a proper diet, which leads to malnutrition, which leads to greater stress, and so on (Fredricks and Goodman, 1969).

Sensory Deprivation and Isolation

Studies of prisoners' reports of brainwashing and biographical accounts of extreme isolation led to the hypothesis that reduced sensory input might be an important factor in the reported results. Investigators at D. O. Hebb's laboratory at McGill University were the first to study these experiences and their effects (Bexton, Heron, and Scott, 1954). Several other investigators have followed and, while reports have not been consistent, some abnormal behavior was usually the outcome of sensory deprivation and isolation (Zubek, 1969). Some clear findings have emerged amid the confusion. Sensory deprivation experiments do lead to perceptual and motor changes in the subjects, and to cognitive effects on reasoning, problem solving, and learning. Hallucinations were reported by subjects in the early studies, but in later studies hallucinations have been an inconsistent finding. So this phenomenon is open to question such as the possibility that they may have been suggested inadvertently in the instructions of the experimenters (Zuckerman and Coan, 1964).

That sensory deprivation does have profound psychological effects, however, seems clear. Changes in mood may be pleasant or unpleasant, mild or severe, with violent swings between a pleasant mood and an unpleasant one reported in some cases.

The actual conditions of the test, including experimenter's instructions, type of isolation, and subject characteristics seem to be important variables. More research is necessary to fully understand the effects of sensory deprivation and isolation.

Sleep and Dream Deprivation

A great deal of research has been directed at defining the functions of various sleep patterns. As yet, there are few conclusive results. Sleep deprivation studies have shown that after 40 sleepless hours, irritability, lack of perseverance, and distortions in perception increase. After 100 hours without sleep, psychotic-like symptoms in thinking, mood, and motor activity, often resembling the symptoms of schizophrenia, occur (Luby and Gottlieb, 1966).

Some studies suggest that sleep disturbance is a symptom of general psychological disruption rather than a symptom of a specific malfunction (Hawkins, 1970). One benefit of discovering which stages of sleep are most important would be that physicians would be able to prescribe sedatives or hypnotic drugs that least interfere with those particular phases. A question that remains to be answered is whether sleep is the critical factor, or is it dreaming that is really essential?

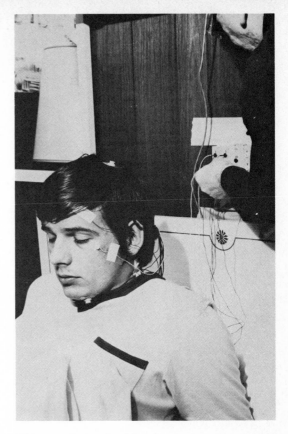

This experimental subject is wired up for a test to determine his sleep patterns. A new technology for sleep research has opened up many new directions for the investigator. (*United Press International.*)

Psychological Factors of Abnormal Behavior

Table 4-1 shows several of the important variables that come under the heading of psychological factors. In the most general sense, these variables may be described as individual-environment interactions. These interactions shape all of our lives, usually in a positive manner but sometimes in the direction of abnormal behavior. The following section explores some of the more important of these psychological variables.

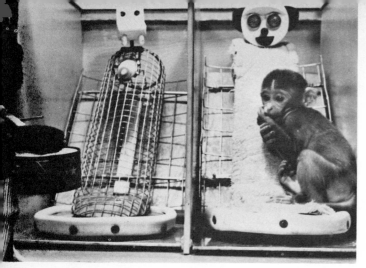

After separating infant monkeys from their natural mothers, Harlow found that they preferred the security of a surrogate mother covered in soft cloth to one made of wire mesh. When the monkeys were frightened, they scurried to the soft cloth "mother." (*Harry F. Harlow, University of Wisconsin Primate Laboratory.*)

The Developing Organism

Ever since Freud, psychological theories have investigated, emphasized, and, in some cases, denounced the role of early experience in the later development of normal or abnormal behavior. Specific childhood problems of abnormal behavior will be covered in depth in Chapter 15. At this point, we will discuss the factors in the development of the child that have been highlighted as possible contributors to psychological problems.

Infant Reaction Patterns

New realizations that babies are born with their own set of reaction patterns, such as activity and excitability levels, should help in the understanding of individual differences and parent-child interactions. The tendency to blame the mother for poor mother-infant relationships must be modified by the knowledge that some infants are born so reactive that they are a management problem for even the most ideal mother. These realizations may also help us to understand why individual children react differently to similar environmental stresses.

Early Attachment—Security

A classic study with baby monkeys altered the then current belief that infant-mother attachment was a learned response reinforced by feeding (Harlow, 1959; Harlow and Zimmermann, 1959). Newborn monkeys were separated from their biological mothers and placed in a cage where they had a choice of two surrogate (substitute) mothers—one constructed from wire mesh and the other from wire mesh covered with soft cloth. Not surprisingly, the monkeys clung mostly to the cloth mother. What made the experiment remarkable, however, is that even when the monkeys were "fed" by the wire mother (by a baby bottle attached to the breast area), they preferred the cloth mother for cuddling and security. In other words, their affectionate responses were largely independent of food supply and reinforcement.

When a frightening object was introduced into the monkeys' environment, they also scurried onto the cloth mother for protection. This action usually provided them with enough security to venture forth and inspect the frightening object.

These results indicate that affection and need for bodily contact are innate and not learned in monkeys. Is this also true for human infants? Both experimental evidence and theoretical deduction seem to indicate that it could be.

The problems with raising human infants with cloth or wire mothers are obvious. However, it may be safely assumed that maternal or other caretaker contact is an important aspect. In addition, the experiment provides us with still another contributing factor for abnormality: both wire-raised and cloth-raised monkeys exhibited disturbed behavior when placed in stressful situations without the support of their surrogate mothers.

Maternal Deprivation

Maternal *separation* is the break in the mother-child relationship—the event itself. Maternal *deprivation* is the situation the child is in after the break occurs. The difficulties of drawing concrete conclusions of the effect of deprivation on permanent behavior or personality are many. Variables involved are considerable: age at separation, length of deprivation, type of substitute environment, relationship with mother. (Children having poor relationships with their mothers may even show significant improvement after separation.)

Studies of children under 2 years of age following maternal separation (Spitz and Wolf, 1946; Robertson and Bowlby, 1952), however, did show a typical response pattern (Yarrow, 1964). The immediate reaction is one of protest, namely, crying and motor indications of unhappiness. This is followed by a passive period of withdrawal, characterized by signs of despair and apathy. If a substitute mother is available, some children will form an anxious, possessive attachment. If, however, no substitute is available, the children form a superficially happy response best described as "detachment," as though close human contact was not important for them. This attitude is shown even when the missing mother visits.

Does this experience have any permanent personality effects? Goldfarb (1945) concludes that early deprivation tends to lead to defects of both an emotional and an intellectual nature, including indiscriminate need for affection, difficulties in learning, disorganized aggressiveness, and a general lack of emotional maturity and self-insight.

But according to Yarrow (1964), it may not be that simple. While there does seem to be some evidence of long-term adverse influence on children subject to early deprivation, few comparative data are available on children who have had successful development in a positive environment. Also, what about father separation? Little research has been done in this area. Obviously, more research is needed on the many variables mentioned earlier before reliable conclusions can be drawn.

Parent and Family Factors

The family context is an important and powerful factor in the shaping and maintenance of a child's behavior. This section explores some of the ways in which the interactions between children and their parents and siblings may relate to abnormal behavior.

Parental Behavior

The most direct influence parents may have on their children's behavior is through modeling. The parent's behavior, whether normal or abnormal, is seen in the family context as the right way to act, and is imitated by the children. In some cases, the parents see their abnormal behavior as "normal," and they teach it to the children directly as the proper way to behave.

Other influences may take place on a more complex psychological level. Parents may react to their children in abnormal ways, often in reaction to their own childhood problems (Sperling, 1951; Hilgard, 1951). Children have been shown to be extremely sensitive in picking up and reflecting these psychological motives and conflicts from their parents. In cases of what is known as a *schizophrenogenic* parent (a parent who presumably causes schizophrenia in the child), the conditions are created for instigation of abnormality in the children even though the parents do not show a high degree of abnormal behavior.

While there may be less acceptance today of the psychoanalytic view of the extremely potent effect of parental behavior on children, the position of parents as a focal point in the

(Sylvia Johnson, Woodfin Camp & Associates.)

(Department of Housing and Urban Development.)

(Linda Rogers, Woodfin Camp & Associates.)

(Sylvia Johnson, Woodfin Camp & Associates.)

(David Austen, Woodfin Camp & Associates.)

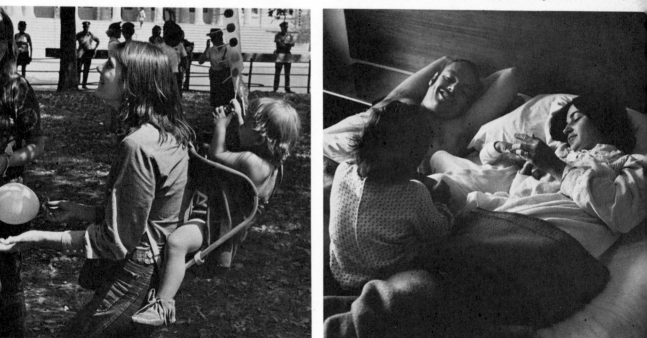

(Leonard Freed, Magnum Photos.)

(Joanne Leonard, Woodfin Camp & Associates.)

The family context is an important and powerful factor in the shaping and maintenance of a child's behavior.

way normal or abnormal behavior is transmitted to the child is obvious.

The Ordinal Position of Children in the Family

The position of a child in the family can have an important bearing on the child's behavior and on his or her later interpersonal relationships. Considerable research has been done on the difference between first-born and later-born individuals. First-born and only children, for example, have been shown to seek the company of others in anxiety-producing situations, while later-born children tend to avoid social interaction (Schachter, 1959).

Child-Rearing Practices

The way we rear children governs the kind of behavior we pass on from one generation to the next. One of the major issues involved in this psychological evolution is discipline.

Interesting and informative data on the consequences of parental discipline were collected by one investigator studying the interactions of restrictiveness versus permissiveness with warmth versus hostility (Becker, 1964). A hostile-restrictive attitude on the part of the parents tends to create in the children neurotic problems, social withdrawal, and an incapacity to assume adult roles. A hostile-permissive attitude may lead to maximal aggression and possible delinquency. A warm-restrictive approach may result in submissive, obedient children who are dependent and not overly friendly or creative. A warm-permissive approach tends to lead to children who are active, creative, socially outgoing, and willing to take on adult roles.

Also important are the consequences of *inconsistent* discipline. Several studies have shown that inconsistencies in discipline lead to antisocial behavior in children. McCord and his associates (1961), for example, studied a group of average, permissive, and restrictive working-class mothers and their sons. They found that the most assertive boys had mothers who used average amounts of discipline. The most restrictive mothers generally had the least aggressive sons. Perhaps the most interesting finding, however, was that the most aggressive boys had mothers who disciplined them inconsistently, being permissive at some times and restrictive at others.

Becker et al. (1959) also found that parental conflict, either between the parents in general or in approach to discipline, may lead to aggressive behavior on the part of the child. Figure 4-3 depicts what can happen to a child when both parents are poorly adjusted.

These findings are, of course, stated in extremely general terms with no indication of the role of factors such as relative influence of father and mother, age, methods of reward or punishment, and personality characteristics of the children.

In families with unresolved conflict between the parents, the child may be assigned the role of "family scapegoat" (Vogel and Bell, 1968). The function of the scapegoat is to provide the parents with a target and outlet for their own tensions, thus putting the child at the center in an uneasy family balance. To satisfy this role, the child must exhibit emotional problems for the parents to focus on. In other words, the child is the "symptom" of pathological family processes and his problems maintain the balance of that system.

Disturbed Communication Styles

An important concept of the relationship between family communication problems and abnormal behavior is contained in the *double-bind* theory (Bateson et al., 1963). The theory states that the child continually receives conflicting messages from one, usually his mother, or both of his parents. Both messages, given in one parental utterance, threaten him with punishment by withdrawal of love. Yet responding to one of the messages requires negating the other. In addition, it is made clear that the conflict is inescapable. An example might be the adolescent boy who is told by his mother to "be a man." If he complies, he is being unmanly because he is doing what his mother

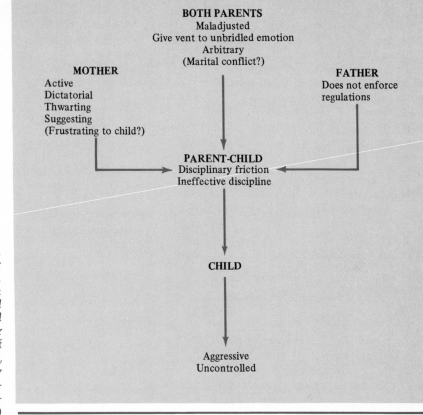

Figure 4-3 One Path to Aggressive Behavior in Children. (*Becker, W. C., et al. Factors in parental behavior and personality as related to problem behavior in children.* Journal of Consulting Psychology, 1959, 23, 113. © 1959 by *the American Psychological Association. Reprinted by permission.*)

BOTH PARENTS
Maladjusted
Give vent to unbridled emotion
Arbitrary
(Marital conflict?)

MOTHER
Active
Dictatorial
Thwarting
Suggesting
(Frustrating to child?)

FATHER
Does not enforce
regulations

PARENT-CHILD
Disciplinary friction
Ineffective discipline

CHILD

Aggressive
Uncontrolled

tells him to do; if he resists, he must act childish. He is effectively "double-binded." He is unable to go in either direction without arousing tension, nor can he leave the situation. The classic double-bind model also includes the "push-pull" of the double-binding parent. The mother, for example, will draw the child in with love until he comes too close, arousing her anxiety, at which point she rejects the child by psychologically pushing him away. To the child, a response to love-messages must eventually result in hurt and rejection. Yet moving away results in guilt and the anxiety of abandonment. The child's emotions are thus played with "yo-yo" style by the mother. Note that it is not out of any sadistic tendencies on the part of the mother, but her own disturbances about her attachment to her child.

When the double bind is applied continually (an important ingredient in the theory), the child finally learns to perceive his life in double-bind terms, and the complete pattern is no longer necessary to produce symptoms of disturbances in his or her behavior.

Many theoretical links have been made between the double bind and schizophrenia (Watzlawick, 1963). From constantly being placed in a double-bind position, the schizophrenic develops defense mechanisms that lead to questioning the metaphorical meaning behind every communication. The simple question, "Are you having a good time?" is taken as a possible invitation to illicit undertakings, an accusation of selfishness, or a condemnation for not being able to enjoy oneself. It should be noted that the soundness of the double-bind hypothesis has not yet been proven experimentally.

Conflict, Stress, and Coping in the Adult

Any adult who denies the existence of potential conflict and stress is, for the denial alone, classifiable as abnormal. All of us have to cope with a variety of stresses. They vary from interpersonal relationships (social interactions, marital stress, and occupational challenge) to internal feelings of loneliness, insecurity, and guilt.

Most of us deal with these potential conflicts in a satisfactory way that provides us with not only a tolerable level of stress in our environment but with an opportunity to profit psychically from the experience of meeting and overcoming each challenge.

Such challenges do come, however. Under most conditions, they are accepted as necessary features of life. Under other conditions, they are factors for the potential production of abnormal behavior. The line between achieving a functional solution and experiencing an insoluble dysfunction is often hard to discern. It is this line that we will search for in several of the chapters to follow.

Sociocultural Factors of Abnormal Behavior

Examination of the influence of a particular society on the individual and comparison of the characteristics of that society with other societies can lead us to new insights into the formation of human behavior. This is a comparatively new direction of exploration for psychology so that, even with the added contributions of sociologists and anthropologists, the foundations are anything but firmly established. To the many dedicated investigators, however, this lack of an established body of data serves only to increase the investigators' interest and involvement in the exploration of the social context of abnormal behavior.

Sociological Variables

Almost all societies have some concept of social class. Classification may be drawn along economic lines, prestige through birth, political power, or along some other lines. In American society, occupation and education are the main criteria. With regard to social class, statistics show that abnormal behavior is found more frequently "(1) in the lower class than in the upper and middle classes, (2) among persons who are not incorporated in meaningful social ties, (3) among those who do not have useful social roles, and (4) among those who have suffered traumatic loss of significant social ties" (Clausen, 1975, p. 375).

Causal relationships are, of course, harder to determine, particularly in light of the many variables present in a social context. A disproportionate number of schizophrenics, for instance, have been found to be from the lower classes. The question remains, however, whether they are schizophrenics because of the pressures of being lower class or they have fallen into the lower class because they are schizophrenics. There is evidence that direction of social mobility is related to the prevalence of abnormal behavior (Srole et al., 1962). Those who have gone up the social ladder exhibit fewer symptoms than those who remain in the class or go down. But again, the causal relationship is not clear.

The route a person with abnormal behavior takes in arriving at an institution is also influenced by social class (Hollingshead and Redlich, 1958). Lower-class patients tend to arrive by way of the courts or welfare agencies, upper- and middle-class patients through referrals by physicians, therapists, or family mem-

Individuals whose social dimensions have been disrupted by loss of employment may be more susceptible to abnormal behavior. (*Wide World Photos.*)

bers. The full effect of this variable, in terms of the treatment received and the attitude of peers, is not yet clearly defined.

As previously discussed, social response to behavioral deviance is basically negative (Scheff, 1963). Persons labeled as deviant not only find it difficult to return to society and rid themselves of the label but also tend to adopt the behavioral aspects of the label themselves. They are often aided in this by mental health professionals who "reward" them for discovering and acknowledging signs of abnormality in their behavior. ("Now that you *know* you are sick, you must be getting better.") In fact, one of the features that the DSM-II uses to differentiate neurotics from psychotics is that neurotics realize they have problems.

While there is evidence that *recent* migration to an urban environment is related to abnormal behavior (Faris and Dunham, 1939), there is little evidence for the belief that the trend toward urbanization, with greater social pressure and decreased feelings of belonging to an integrated society, leads inevitably to a greater incidence of mental breakdown (Eaton

and Weil, 1955). Individuals whose social dimensions have been disrupted by a change of environment or by loss of employment may be more susceptible to abnormal behavior, but whether this disruption occurs in an urban or rural setting seems to be inconsequential.

Other social factors in need of investigation are the effects of age, sex, marital status, and religion. Available statistical data in these areas show some differences but little in the way of useful cause-and-effect relationships.

Racial Issues

Minority groups are of special interest in the study of sociological variables because of the possibility that their unique social pressures may produce quantitative or qualitative differences in abnormal behavior. Many studies have attempted to investigate this phenomenon, resulting in more controversy than conclusions.

Some investigators claim, with good reason, that comparison between blacks and whites is basically invalid because of the extra stresses faced by the black population through discrimination, social change, reduced opportunities, and new emphasis on achievement criteria (Kiev, 1973).

Certainly, there is less of a difference between races in susceptibility to abnormal behavior than early reports would have us believe. What differences there are may be due to a form of racial discrimination as to who gets labeled and hospitalized. Clearly, differential rates of abnormal behavior in different races may be misleading, at the most, and insignificant, at the least.

Cross-Cultural Studies of Abnormal Behavior

If research discovers, for example, that depression is relatively rare among African natives (which seems to be true), and we can discover the reason why this is so, we may be able to reduce the incidence of depression in other cultures. As Wittkower and Fried (1959) put it, "The aims of [cross-cultural] research are to arrive at conclusions regarding which cultural norms make for mental health and which foster the development of mental illness; and by isolating and defining modifiable sociocultural variables, to work towards prevention, or at least reduction, of mental illness" (p. 423).

The authors cite many examples of cross-cultural similarities and differences:

Sexual perversions are common in Iran, rare in Russia.

Senile psychosis is rare in Hong Kong.

Japanese schizophrenics are less aggressive than their Western counterparts.

Suicide is high among white South Africans, virtually nonexistent among the Bantu.

In addition to differences of prevalence and degree, Wittkower and Fried (1959) found some "psychiatric syndromes" that were specific to certain geographical areas. An example is *Hseih-Ping*, a trancelike state known only in Taiwan. Symptoms include tremor, delirium,

disorientation, and identification with an ancestor.

This last symptom is obviously a culturally influenced phenomenon. Another example is provided by Laubscher (1937), who found that typical symptoms among schizophrenic African natives included delusions of being bewitched or poisoned, and delusions of grandeur involving being a chief or witch doctor.

These variations in what might be termed "symptomatic style" add to the difficulty of making cross-cultural comparisons. Establishing what is normal for a particular culture can provide further complications. In spite of the difficulties, however, there are indications that cross-cultural studies can contribute significant knowledge to our understanding of the sociocultural factors in abnormal behavior.

Ecological Factors

Although ecology, so far, has concentrated on the physical environment, there is also a significant role to be explored in the relationship of ecology to abnormal behavior. There are several fields already involved in the study of ecology, including community mental health, social ecology, and environmental ecology. In addition, there are a variety of other fields such as natural, technical, and social sciences concerned with both the physical environment and the organisms living in that environment. Together they form the *ecosystem*.[1] This growing field will be discussed in greater detail in the final section of the book.

Summary

Each specialized model of abnormal behavior proposes its own specialized causal factors. Since scientific support can be found for a wide range of factors, a *multiple routes* model is proposed. This provides for many different pathways and interactions rather than a

[1] The interested student may refer to Craik, 1970; Ittelson et al., 1970; and Calhoun, 1967.

straightforward cause-and-effect relationship. Abnormal behavior is the result of any number of causal, contributing, and maintaining factors. Many behavioral characteristics, including some disorders, are inherited through the genes. Another active area of research is in the field of biochemistry, including the role of neurochemical, hormonal, and serum factors.

Since all behavior is mediated by the nervous system, neurological changes can also bring about abnormal behavior.

In addition, there are many biological-environmental, psychological, and sociocultural factors, all of which can cause, contribute to, or maintain abnormal behavior. Research in the area is widespread and dynamic. Many old ideas are being replaced by new discoveries, with many more promised for the future.

Clinical and research methods of inquiry about abnormal behavior

Percy Knauth was a successful writer, editor, and foreign correspondent. Yet, slowly, painfully, he was nearing a crisis that would threaten his career, his family, his very existence.

As I awoke on an April morning in this little attic room in New York City, it hit me. I had been living in this world for nearly 57 years and at this mo-ment I wanted above anything else to get out of it. Quietly, peacefully, if possible painlessly, with no fuss to anyone.

The world, I was sure, had no further use for me and I had nothing to offer it. My life lay like a broken ruin around me, bits and pieces of remem-bered experiences which flashed into focus and out again; I could not concentrate on anything long enough to make any coherence out of it. . . .

Perhaps the worst thing about depression is the way it paralyzes the man in a man. The smallest decision, for example, absolutely floored me; I could not make my mind up about anything. Every morning I lay helpless, endlessly debating the pros and cons of arising. . . .

Sexually I was impotent. I lay awake nights thinking desolately, never again, never again, while my wife breathed quietly beside me. The thought haunted me; it made me feel old. (Knauth, 1972, pp. 74 ff)

Knauth's despair, indecision, impotence, and anxiety marked the beginning of a deep depression. As a writer, he wanted to share this painful experience with others. His story is interesting not only from a literary standpoint, but from a psychological standpoint as well.

One may wonder how the human condition could become so painful to an intelligent, successful individual or, for that matter, to any individual. As students of abnormal psychology, we must translate such musings into more formal questions: What is happening to this man? What caused this extreme reaction at this particular time in his life? What can be done to help him as an individual? How is his experience similar to what many other people go through at various stages in their lives?

Formulation of such specific questions is known as scientific *inquiry*. Such inquiry is central to the field of abnormal psychology, where both clinical treatment and experimental research are, at their most basic level, question-asking and -answering operations. This chapter focuses on the way psychologists formulate questions and the methods they employ to answer them.

Inquiry: Learning about Abnormal Behavior

Formulating and Answering Questions

The number of hypotheses in any field of inquiry is often greater than the number of facts. As we have seen, this is particularly true of abnormal psychology, where opinions, rather than facts, too often form the basis for labeling and treatment. Through the inquiry process, subjective opinion is transformed into objective fact.

Formal inquiry is distinguished from natural curiosity or casual observation by its systematic, step-by-step approach. In the case of Percy Knauth, the inquiry process may lead us from diagnosis to treatment of his problem. Choosing the basic questions is the first step. To make that choice, we must first determine the *purpose* of asking the question. In abnormal psychology, our purpose often centers on the treatment of specific clients or on determining the causes of their disturbed functioning. Some inquiries, however, may serve a more basic purpose, that is, the furthering of knowledge in a chosen area. The varied purposes of inquiry can be summarized by three questions basic to abnormal psychology (Holt, 1973, p. 2):

1. What are the phenomena studied in clinical psychology? (*descriptive* research questions)
2. What are the causes of these phenomena? (*dynamic* research questions)
3. What can be done to alter these phenomena? (*therapeutic* research questions)

The next crucial step is formulation of a hypothesis for testing. A *hypothesis* is a scientifically formulated guess about the question under investigation. The guess may arise from past experiments, observations, or even from skepticism over conclusions reached by other scientists. We may, for example, hypothesize that Knauth's depression can be alleviated by psychoactive drugs.

Whatever our hypothesis arises from, it must be capable of being tested objectively. Such testing may involve analysis of past case histories, observation of current patients, or design of formal experiments. Once again, a systematic approach is essential. Methods must be based on objective techniques that can be repeated by other investigators. In addition, the methods must produce answers that are both conclusive and understandable. This may not be an easy task.

Clinical and Research Approaches to Inquiry

Clinical practitioners have a unique place in the inquiry process. Most often, their primary role is as therapists, helping individual clients. In contrast to the objective observation and minimal personal intervention of researchers, whose job is to add to our general knowledge and understanding of abnormal psychology, clinicians include subjective observation and intuition among their legitimate tools (Lazarus and Davison, 1971). Nevertheless, clinicians play an important research role. This combined clinical-research orientation was formally endorsed at the Conference of the American Psychological Association Committee on Training in Clinical Psychology held in 1949 at Boulder, Colorado (Raimy, 1950). What has come to be called the "Boulder model" clinician represents the idealized notion that a clinical psychologist can, and indeed should, perform the dual role of research scientist *and* professional practitioner.

The unique position of the clinician—between the research situation and the individual in need of help—permits interaction in both directions. Ideas formulated for research may be put to the practical test and modified by the clinician. Their individual clinical cases may be viewed as mini-experiments that contribute to the basic understanding of problems in the general population. In this way, observations made by the clinician in treating individual clients may stimulate new avenues of basic research.

Kinds of Inquiry

Whether we favor clinical intervention, basic research, or a Boulder-model combination, our inquiry process can progress along many distinct lines. In the Percy Knauth case, for example, a behaviorist would concentrate on the external reinforcers for Knauth's depression. A psychodynamic theorist would seek the intrapsychic causes and implications of his behavior. Each of these approaches has much

potential value, and there is no inherent reason for pursuing one rather than another. In practice, choice of the kind of inquiry usually follows the investigator's particular research orientation.

Investigations of abnormal behavior generally follow one of five basic lines of inquiry: statistical, psychodynamic, behavioral, biological, and phenomenological. Table 5-1 summarizes these approaches.

Statistical inquiries provide a mathematical comparison between the individual or group being studied and some broader-based group or population. Percy Knauth's depression might be rated on a scale measuring depression. Comparison of his rating with ratings for a normal population would provide a statistical measure of the degree of his depression. Statistical inquiry provides nothing more than this mathematical analysis; it makes no attempt to pinpoint the *cause* of the problem under study.

Psychodynamic inquiries ask the "why" questions. They probe the nonobservable dynamic processes that underlie abnormal behavior. To do this, psychodynamic investigators employ techniques such as free association, dream analysis, hypnosis, projective tests, and the other psychodynamic routes to the unconscious that were discussed in Chapter 3. The emphasis on unobservable intervening variables and hypothetical constructs inherent in these techniques places severe limitations on their utility in systematic research. Data from psychodynamic inquiries are difficult to translate into purely objective, quantitative terms. As a result, inquiries at this level are frequently controversial. However, psychodynamic research often generates important hypotheses that can be tested further with better-controlled experimental techniques.

Behavioral approaches, you will recall from Chapter 3, emphasize three fundamental questions to the understanding of behavior: (1) What behavior is maladaptive? (2) What environmental contingencies currently maintain that behavior? (3) What environmental events can be manipulated to change the behavior? These questions focus on the person's current problems, not the historical events leading up to the problems. Behavioral inquiry, similarly, stresses external environmental variables, not unconscious internal events.

Behavioral inquiry of Percy Knauth might begin with careful specification of the behaviors involved. Next, the investigator would attempt to understand the consequences of these behaviors in the current situation, that is, what reinforcers (positive or negative, being presented or removed) occur contingently with his specific actions. Finally, an attempt would be made to manipulate these reinforcers and thereby modify Percy's undesirable behavior.

The inquiry process thus focuses on objective observation of the behavior and external events, on analysis of the function of the behavior in the environment (functional analysis), and on experimental manipulation. As we will discuss in the research section at the end of this chapter, these behavioral methods satisfy the requirements of formal experimental research. Thus behavioral inquiry is valuable from both the clinical and experimental standpoints.

Biological inquiry approaches the individual as a living organism, whose behavior is directly related to internal, physiological processes. Percy Knauth could be examined with an eye toward his biological functioning. Measures of physiological activity, biochemical changes, and bioelectrical discharges would be used to determine possible causes and cures for his abnormal behavior. Biofeedback and psychoactive drugs are but two examples of biological applications in clinical practice.

Phenomenological studies involve the person in the inquiry process. Knauth would be asked how he views his situation. What is his subjective evaluation of the events he has experienced? These are the questions central to phenomenological inquiry. Self-report data, however, are by definition subjective, rather than objective. Yet these data are still valuable for both research and clinical purposes. Historically, psychology has alternated between accepting and rejecting such introspective material. Recent attempts at standardization of

interview techniques and self-report inventories have added greater control to this subjectivity, and thus there is renewed interest in the phenomenological approach.

Table 5-1 Methods of Inquiry About Abnormal Behavior

Kind of Inquiry	Focus	Analytical Techniques
Statistical	Mathematical comparison of individual to general population	Objective tests providing numerical scores
Psychodynamic	Intrapsychic causes underlying abnormal behavior	Psychoanalysis, free association, dream analysis, hypnosis, projective tests
Behavioral	Environmental reinforcers for current behavior patterns	Objective observation, functional analyses, behavior inventories, rating scales
Biological	Physiological processes underlying behavior	Measures of biochemical and physiological activity, blood chemistries, electroencephalograms, electromyograms
Phenomenological	Patient's introspective analysis of his or her past and present behavior patterns	Interviews, self-report measures, archival records, biographical studies

Important Considerations for All Approaches to Inquiry

Whatever kind of inquiry is chosen, the investigator must be alert for many common pitfalls of scientific investigation. Some margin of error is inevitable in any study. The observer, the technical tools of measurement, and the subjects being studied all contribute to this error factor. This section discusses several important considerations in assessing, and reducing, the amount of error in scientific inquiries.

Consensual Validation

In evaluating study data the most important factor to consider is whether the data are consensually validatable. To put it in nonscientific terms, others must be able to "see" what you see. That "seeing," of course, refers to measurements obtained with one or several of the many scientific tools available. For example, biological data, such as body temperature, becomes visible and measurable when a thermometer is used. In order to meet the criterion of consensual validation, some invisible psychological data, such as thoughts, must be translated into a "harder" form by their verbal representation on psychological tests.

While the basic requirements of consensual validation must be satisfied in both clinical and experimental research, the meeting of these requirements is often put off during the preliminary stages of research. Hypotheses are commonly proposed to explain phenomena that have not been measured yet. Sooner or later, however, these hypotheses must be tested. Researchers must find or design some measurement technique that can provide this consensual validation. In the end, other nonbiased observers must be able to examine and verify the data used by the researchers to support their hypotheses.

Reliability-Replicability

Research is said to be reliable when it can be repeated by the original investigator and by others, with similar results occurring each time. Important in meeting this goal is the choice of measuring instruments: they must be accurate, dependable, and appropriate to the task at hand.

The nature of the events studied is also a crucial factor in providing reliable results. While rigidly controlled laboratory experiments usually meet the most demanding criteria of reliability, clinical observations are less likely to meet such stringent requirements. The abnormal behavior of Percy Knauth, for example, is likely to fluctuate from day to day. Repeated tests of his performance would be expected to show some variability.

Two measures of reliability are test-retest reliability and interrater reliability. *Test-retest* reliability measures assess agreement between two or more repetitions of the same procedure. *Interrater* reliability is a measure of the agreement between observations made by two or more investigators independently assessing the same event. Agreement is not expected to be 100 percent with test-retest reliability and interrater reliability. Rather, the investigator must determine what *degree* of reliability is necessary to support the findings of any particular study.

Validity

The results of an experiment may be reliable, but this does not ensure that they are valid. The validity of an inquiry process refers to the extent to which the process is *relevant* to what the inquiry is intended to measure. In other words, does the chosen method or measuring instrument actually answer the questions being asked by the inquiry? Results of a study designed to assess the amount of salt in water would be invalid if a thermometer were used as the measuring tool—no matter how accurate the thermometer—because temperature measures do not tell us anything about salinity. Similarly, the results of an investigation of the cause, extent, or type of Percy Knauth's depression would be valid only if the instruments used produced measures related to depression.

The four most commonly employed methods of assessing validity are face validity, predictive validity, concurrent validity, and construct validity.

Face validity is a straightforward, subjective evaluation of whether a measuring tool *looks* like it is measuring what you want it to measure. A questionnaire asking Knauth to rate his mood, eating habits, sleep, etc., would *appear* to be a good measure of depression. In other words, it has obvious face validity.

Predictive validity is the assessment of the measure's ability to predict other measures of the same problem. For example, if Knauth measured high on a new depression scale, this result should be *predictive* of high scores on other indicators of depression such as lack of appetite, difficulty in sleeping, or sexual impotence. Conversely, if another individual measured low on our new depression scale this result should be predictive of a lack of such signs of depression. If this individual turned out to show numerous signs of depression, we would

conclude that our new measure lacks predictive validity.

Concurrent validity is the accuracy with which one test relates to the results of another, already validated test. For example, to save time or money, valid short forms of personality or intelligence tests may be substituted for the longer, more complicated forms. A short form that produces results similar to the results obtained by the same subjects on the longer form is said to have concurrent validity.

Construct validity is the relation of the observed finding to some hypothesized attribute that *cannot* be observed. Such hypothesized constructs as anxiety, impulsiveness, or aggressiveness may be supported by observable measurements of galvanic skin response, speed of decision making, and frequency of hostile outbursts, respectively. These observed measures are said to have construct validity to the extent that they predict the occurrence of the hypothesized construct. For example, galvanic skin response (GSR) has construct validity for anxiety, since high GSRs are almost always seen in subjects suffering from severe anxiety.

Idiographic versus Nomothetic Levels of Analysis

As we have stated, clinical inquiry encompasses two parallel levels. These are (1) the particular case under study, and (2) the general population as a whole. The word *idiographic* is used to describe knowledge of the first level, the specific event or individual; *nomothetic* refers to the second, more general level. Theoretically, conclusions based on nomothetic observations apply to all individuals, while idiographic observations are true for one individual but not necessarily for others. It is important to distinguish between these two levels in evaluating the results of any particular inquiry.

To take a specific case, suppose we wanted to treat Percy Knauth's depression using psychoactive drugs. We might choose an agent that has proven effective for other depressed patients. That is, we have *nomothetic* knowledge of its general effects. Knauth's individual reaction to the drug provides us with the *idiographic* knowledge we need to adjust his dosage or to switch to a more effective drug.

Although these two levels may complement each other, their individual merits are frequently questioned. Critics of the nomothetic approach argue that extreme differences among patients make group averaging of results misleading. Nomothetic knowledge of the "average patient," they feel, is not useful in selecting treatment for any one individual. On the other hand, idiographic information about individual patients tells us little about the general population. This objection can be overcome, at least in part, by systematically applying successful elements of individual treatment to subsequent cases with similar characteristics. It should be recognized, however, that the nomothetic-idiographic debate is a continuing one, reflecting issues basic to psychological inquiry.

The Clinical Approach to Inquiry

Our review of the inquiry process has, so far, focused on general rules for asking the right questions and obtaining valid answers. Now we must put these rules into practice to help Percy Knauth. The decisions we are asked to make at this level will be of great consequence to his future. Thus our inquiry process must provide an understanding equal to the task of furnishing appropriate recommendations at this time of psychological description.

General Issues of Clinical Inquiry

The types of clinical questions asked and the clinical methods of investigation used to answer them are referred to as the *clinical assessment process*. The most significant difference between this and other inquiry processes, Korchin (1976) notes, is that "the unique purpose of *clinical* assessment [is] to gain [an] understanding of an individual *in order to act on his behalf*" (p. 124). Korchin's explanation emphasizes the purpose for acquiring this knowledge: its usefulness in determining the most effective recommendations for each patient. This goal-directed approach is significant in our evaluation of the clinical inquiry process.

Formulating Clinical Questions

Gertrude Stein, on her deathbed, was reputed to have suddenly opened her eyes and asked her visitors, "What is the question?" seeming then to fall asleep. After some moments, her eyes suddenly popped open again and she asked, "If there is no question then there is no answer." This insightful philosophical inquiry applies equally well to the clinical setting. The greater the clinicians' perception of the crucial questions to ask, the greater the utility of the answers they will obtain.

As we have emphasized, clinical questions lead to decisions about individuals' lives. The initial questions raised in a clinical inquiry are based on the kind of knowledge needed to meet the needs of the individual. The goals of these initial formulations, better known as *referral questions*, are fivefold (Korchin, 1976):

1. *To provide baseline information.* This part of the inquiry process seeks "before" data, useful in posttreatment comparisons.
2. *To evaluate patients' status after treatment.* This is the posttreatment analysis noted above.
3. *To plan and guide therapeutic intervention.* This is the major purpose of clinical inquiry. Planning is usually completed before treatment begins.
4. *To diagnose patients' problems.* Diagnostic inquiry may be necessary for administrative, record-keeping purposes, or for defining and categorizing unclear, borderline symptoms such as distinguishing organic brain damage from mental retardation.
5. *To predict future behavior.* Risks such as suicide must be recognized. In addition, analysis of patients' personality characteristics in relation to their psychosocial environment may provide a predictive basis for their future adjustment.

These referral questions may be answered along any of the lines of inquiry we listed previously: statistical, psychodynamic, behavioral, biological, or phenomenological. Whichever line he or she chooses, the clinician will then begin the process of "assessment." Assessment covers the broad scope of "knowing" the client as a whole person. It is different from the narrower category of testing, which involves measurement of the client's performance in certain structured situations. Although testing is an important *part* of the assessment process, test scores by themselves are not sufficient for full assessment. The clinician must fit each score into a general interpretation of the client's problem, and then tackle the job of planning appropriate therapy.

The Problem of the "Participant Observer"

The effect of an observer on the phenomena being observed is a problem in all sciences, but more so in psychology, and most particularly in clinical assessment. Interaction between therapist (the observer) and client is, in fact, an unavoidable part of the assessment process. The patients may be altering their behavior to meet what they believe are the expectations of the observer. The clinician's observations also may be influenced by his or her hopes and expectations that the patient's behavior will follow anticipated patterns. The successful clinician constantly must be aware of these possibilities and attempt to establish controls for them. From the design of testing instruments to the structuring of the clinical situation, the psychologist must recognize factors that can contribute to these possible sources of error.

In contrast, however, the sensitive clinician is also aware that the interaction process itself can be a source of knowledge about the client. In part, the interrelation of the observer and the observed may become even more important than the test data itself.

Clinical Methods of Inquiry

The varied procedures and instruments generally employed in clinical assessment have evolved from a long history of attempts to eval-

uate human behavior. Deciding which of these methods to use is part of the "creative art" of clinicians. Their choices are guided by the referral questions, the referral source, and by numerous client characteristics such as age, sex, and intellectual level. Basically, however, their decisions rest on their faith, comfort, and experience with particular techniques.

Our aim in this section is to describe these techniques and their applications in the clinical assessment process.

Clinical Observation

Observation generally refers to the assessment of a subject's visible behavior as it occurs in formal and informal situations. By *formal observation*, we mean deliberate, planned gathering of data on specific behavior patterns, most frequently in an interview situation. However, to the sensitive clinician, every patient encounter is an opportunity for observation, "looking with a third eye as he listens with the third ear" (Sundberg, Tyler, and Taplin, 1973, p. 200). Thus clinicians make important *informal observations* during therapy and testing sessions, and during home, school, or ward visits.

The setting, the observer, and the type of data gathered are important variables in the observation process.

1. *Setting.* The difficulties involved in assessing behavior in the unstructured settings of a subject's social environment have led to increased dependence on controlled settings such as the clinicians' offices. With the growing recognition of important subject-environment interactions, however, there has been a movement to observe behavior in unstructured, natural settings. Consequently, new methods for systematic recording of environmental observations are now being developed.

2. *Observer.* Although the clinician takes primary responsibility for making clinical observations, useful data can also be gathered by the patient's parents, teachers, hospital attendants, physicians, and other contacts. Ratings of the patient's peers may also serve the data-gathering process. The peer approach is often used in industrial and military settings as a basis for evaluation and

Box 5-2 Clinical Methods of Inquiry

Clinical observation	Assessment of a subject's visible behavior in formal and informal settings.
Interviewing	Assessment of a subject based on what he has to say and the manner in which he says it.
Case study	Integration of case history, observation, testing, and interview data.
Psychological testing	Structured instruments such as IQ test, MMPI, or TAT, used to evaluate subjects on the basis of scores they obtain or responses they give.

promotion. Since peers observe each other over a long period of time and in varied situations, they may provide significant insights that would be missed in the limited time available to a professional observer. However, peer ratings must be used with caution, especially for school children, to avoid making the people being observed feel anxious and insecure in the social setting. One increasingly popular alternative to these methods of observation is the client's use of patients as their own observers. With home-scoring systems, for example, the person can monitor his or her own environmental interactions.

3. *Kinds of data.* The type of data gathered in any particular setting, by any chosen observer, corresponds closely to the five kinds of inquiry discussed earlier. Depending upon the instrument or procedure employed, data can be obtained on observable behavior patterns, hypothesized internal states, physiological functions, or phenomenological insights. The form of the data may vary from gross judgments to precise scaled ratings of specific behavioral variables.

Problems of clinical observation While clinical observation is an important tool in assessment, it does not have the ability to provide a completely accurate picture of behavior and personality. Several factors contribute to this imprecision. First, peoples' behavior is often affected by the simple awareness that they are being observed. This is known as the *Hawthorne effect.* In addition, observers' expectations may lead them to exaggerate or overemphasize factors consistent with these expectations. Psychodynamic investigators, for example, may be very attentive to defense mechanisms used by their patients. Yet at the same time, they may be overlooking environmental reinforcers that may be responsible for the supposedly defensive behavior.

Observer bias is often apparent in the tendency to give higher ratings on specific traits to individuals whom observers feel are personally attractive or generally capable. This is known as the *halo effect.* Teachers, for instance, often grade their best students more leniently than their poor students. The halo effect may also work in reverse. Thus unpopular individuals may be criticized by their peers on specific traits not at all related to popularity. Or a poor person may be rated as less honest or capable than a wealthy person.

As we mentioned previously, *interobserver reliability*, or lack of it, may also present a problem. Different observers may make widely varying assessments of the same subject because of personal biases or viewing only limited aspects of the subject's behavior repertoire. The guidance counselor and the football coach, for example, may have quite different impressions of the same student.

Awareness of these observational pitfalls should produce improvements in the clinical assessment process. Observers may be given special training to overcome predispositions and to limit their own influence on what or who is being observed. The structure and control of the testing environment also may be changed to achieve these goals. In addition, components of behaviors under observation can be specified more clearly.

Behavioral approaches to clinical assessment meet many of these goals. Their concentration only on observable behavior has made these behavioral methods increasingly popular in clinical work.

Interviewing

Observation is one basic approach to clinical inquiry. Interviewing is another. In short, "We either 'ask 'em' or 'watch 'em'" (Sundberg and Tyler, 1962, p. 102).

The person-to-person interview is part of almost all assessment approaches. Its use reflects the basic belief that what individuals have to say is clinically important information, perhaps the *most* important information we can obtain. The interview emphasizes not only *what* clients say, but how they say it, how they relate to interviewers, and how interviewers relate to them. Clients' responses to the real or imagined pressures of the interview situation also can provide important clues about their adaptation to stress in their everyday lives.

A client's attitude has an obvious influence on what he or she will say. Is this the client's first visit to a psychologist? Is the client hoping for immediate and miraculous insight? Or has the client come to a psychologist under the duress of a spouse's urging, or even a court order?

Whether clients' motivations are positive or negative, the interview is likely to be an emotionally charged, difficult encounter for them. The very fact that the interview is taking place signifies that they are experiencing burdensome problems. Fear of ominous revelations may prevent clients from speaking honestly. Thus one of the clinician's first interview objectives is to discover the patient's motivations and, if they are negative or obstructive, to help him or her develop a more positive attitude. This requires great skill. With the aid of an understanding interviewer, however, the client's wish to obtain relief from his problems can lead to openness and cooperation.

As with other forms of clinical inquiry, the *purpose* of the interview determines both the type of information sought by clinicians and the kind of inquiry chosen. Some interviews are performed primarily to obtain a client's history. Standardized checklists have been designed to outline the type of data required. They include reasons for coming for the interview, present problems, early recollections, past and present health record, recreational interests, sexual development, self-descriptions, and important turning points in life (Sundberg, Tyler, and Taplin, 1973).

Interviews may be guided by statistical, psychodynamic, behavioral, biological, or phenomenological viewpoints, parallel to the kinds of inquiry we have mentioned so often. Thus a behavioral investigator might stress the client's current life problems, while a psychodynamically oriented investigator would explore early childhood experiences. Whatever the client's motivation, or the clinician's psychological orientation, however, skill and compassion are the most important ingredients in making the interview situation a fruitful one.

Case Study Method

This chapter began with a vivid recounting of part of Percy Knauth's *case history*, a biographical description of current and past events. The examining clinician would integrate this kind of material with observation, testing, and interview data in a report known as a *case study*. Included in the study are hypotheses relevant to causes and remedies for the patient's problems.

There are no rigid scientific guidelines for assembling a case study. The data summarized are "characteristically communications or observations of events which were not planned or intentionally altered by the investigator for the purpose of research" (Bolgar, 1965, p. 32). In other words, case study data are "naturalistic." They may include formally elicited interview and testing analyses, as well as autobiographical diaries and letters, dream descriptions, third-person accounts, and reminiscences—just about *any* material clinicians can find that will provide insights into their clients' behavior. Of course, much of this documentary material must be evaluated for accuracy, authenticity, and relevancy.

Basically, this extensive information gathering is intended to immerse investigators in the total past and present life situation of clients. At one time, this was considered routine in all cases. Now, although the practice is less common, its potential utility is still significant. The case of Percy Knauth is a good example. Many details of his background are important in understanding his depression: he spent his youth at a boarding school, where he longed for the warmth of the home he had left behind; wartime exposure to combat left him panic-stricken; his first wife had abandoned him and their children to marry another man; after 28 years as a writer and editor for the same company, he failed when he went out on his own. Now, at age 57, he felt isolated and fearful. He was paralyzed by "the horror of being alone in the world without a job, without a monthly salary, dependent entirely on my wits to keep myself and my family going" (Knauth, 1972, p. 76).

Merely assembling this vivid case history is not enough to solve Knauth's problems. The final step is organization and interpretation of the information and formulation of a course of therapy. Here, clinicians are guided more by inference and insight than by scientific methodology. This is the cause of much controversy over the merits of the case study method. Most clinicians and researchers agree on the need for more accurate and standardized techniques, such as those found in the psychological testing regimens we will discuss next.

Psychological Testing

In general, psychological tests are structured instruments used to evaluate subjects on the basis of the scores they obtain or the responses they give. Tests have the potential to furnish samples of behavior. Individual subjects can then be compared to average or "normative" standards for the behavior. While the actual form of the normative data varies from one test to another, in all cases the subject's characteristics or scores are measured against those of a broad sample of the population. Which test or tests are administered depends largely on the type of information the investigator needs for the assessment. The requirements often change during the assessment process, as the client's problems become more clearly de-fined. Thus additional testing is frequently necessary.

The usual procedure entails assembly by the clinician of a *test battery*, a collection of several instruments, each instrument designed to evaluate a specific area of functioning. As we will discuss next, test areas may include intelligence, personality traits, motor development, spatial ability, adaptability, and social competence. In cases where brain damage is suspected, specialized neurological tests may also be used. We will describe some of these instruments in the chapter on organic brain syndromes (Chapter 17).

Intelligence testing Piotrowski (1967) defines intelligence as:

> the capacity to solve new problems by means of reasoning. It involves an understanding of the relevant issues in new tasks and thinking of successful or satisfactory solutions to the tasks. The emphasis on novelty of the tasks serves the purpose of differentiating acts of intelligence from memory feats, although it is realized that memory has a role in reasoning. (pp. 509–510)

From this definition, it follows that measures of intelligence concentrate on reasoning ability rather than learned skills.

The first intelligence test was developed in the late nineteenth century by the French psychologist Alfred Binet. His goal was to sort out slow learners who then could be placed in remedial classes. Binet's test was designed to eliminate the effects of training and experience, by emphasizing reasoning ability and by including problems of such a diverse nature that individual training advantages would usually average out. In other words, Binet sampled so many different skills that a child's particular instructional background would be unlikely to affect his or her total score. Thus Binet's evaluation would represent the child's overall intellectual ability rather than his or her learned or practiced skills.

Binet introduced the concept of mental age (MA), a measure not necessarily identical

Intelligence testing overwhelmingly ranks number one over other psychological tests in administration and usage. Here, the subject is being given part of the Wechsler Adult Intelligence Scale (WAIS). (*Good Samaritan Hospital.*)

to the subject's chronological age (CA). Mental age divided by chronological age, and multiplied by 100, yields the intelligence quotient, better known as IQ. When MA and CA are the same, the IQ is 100, the average intelligence level for that particular age group.

Revised versions of the Binet test are still used today, although most assessment in recent years has employed the Wechsler Adult Intelligence Scale (WAIS) or the Wechsler Intelligence Scale for Children (WISC).

The diagnostic purposes of intelligence testing have evolved from Binet's classification goals to today's sophisticated analyses of organic brain damage, psychosis, neurosis, schizophrenia, and other psychological disturbances. Although these new uses are not widely accepted, intelligence testing still ranks first among all other assessment techniques in frequency of usage. In our competitive society, intelligence tests fulfill the need to compare ourselves and our children to the general population. To psychologists, on the other hand, the supposedly high predictive value of IQ for success in school, occupation, and everyday life situations is its drawing power.

It can be predicted that individuals with substantially below-average scores on intelligence tests will experience failure and frustration in a culture geared for high levels of attainment. Similarly, people of superior intellectual ability may become frustrated and

alienated by a society operating at a mental pace too slow for their needs. Psychological problems are a possibility in both groups. Thus IQ scores significantly different from the norm provide useful information in the investigation of abnormal behavior.

Objective assessment Standardized measuring instruments that minimize the effects of the tester on the administration, scoring, and interpretation are classified as *objective tests*. These tests are given under carefully prescribed conditions that attempt to eliminate any chance of subjective analysis.

Objective tests usually take the form of self-explanatory written questionnaires that subjects complete by themselves. True-false or multiple-choice answers are favored in these tests because they facilitate objective scoring. At one time or another, you probably have completed objective tests in popular magazines or newspapers. By adding up your checks on perhaps 20 "yes-no" or "always-sometimes-never" questions, you immediately learned your "Dating Rating," "Open-mindedness Quotient," or other behavior rating.

Professionally administered objective tests are quite similar to the popularized versions. Their most common psychological focus is personality assessment. However, there is much disagreement about what is really being assessed by these tests. As Butcher explains, "In actuality, personality theory as a discipline has not had much influence on the development of personality tests and vice versa" (Butcher, 1974, p. 2). Thus most personality tests cannot reveal *how* particular behavior patterns evolved. Rather, they measure the strength of selected characteristics or forces already present within the personality. These characteristics are known as *traits*.

The most comprehensive measure of personality traits in use today is the Minnesota Multiphasic Personality Inventory (MMPI). The MMPI was introduced by Hathaway and McKinley in 1942 as an improvement over the instruments in existence at that time. It is a paper-and-pencil test consisting of 550 true-or-false questions covering family relationships, personal health, sexual attitudes, religious orientation, and political preferences, among others. All items on the MMPI are written in the first person to encourage self-reference:

I find it hard to keep my mind on a task or job.

I am happy most of the time.

I refuse to play some games because I am not good at them.

One reason for the popularity of the MMPI is its ease of administration and scoring. A subject's answers on the test are tallied on ten personality trait scales such as anxiety, depression, masculinity-femininity, schizophrenia, and emotional excitability. Four other scales measure test-taking problems such as carelessness, or faking. The subject's scores on each scale are grouped together in a *personality profile*, a graphic representation of how he or she compares to average subjects in each trait category.

It was originally hypothesized that a high MMPI score in any scale would correlate with pronounced evidence of that particular trait in the individual. For example, the higher the score on the schizophrenia scale, the more likely the patient was to be schizophrenic. It was found, however, that the subject's *profile configuration*, a selected combination of scores, was more predictive. A client scoring high on depression and schizophrenia, for example, is likely to be clinically different from a client scoring high on depression and hysteria.

Proponents of the MMPI maintain that its results are more accurate than those obtained by experienced clinicians using interview, observation, and other traditional techniques. It is not surprising that these claims are hotly contested by many clinical investigators. These investigators' common criticism of trait measures attacks the assumption that behavior is consistent, and that resultant personality characteristics are stable (Cronbach, 1970). They argue that trait descriptions are only statistical summaries or averages of behavior tendencies seen in a wide range of situations. Calling a person "highly anxious" or "fairly honest" does not answer the question, "Anxious (or honest) in what situation?" This controversy has become known as the "state versus trait" debate. Still another argument revolved around the relative value of these cold, objective measures compared to the sensitivity of the clinician in leading the patient to understanding. This is referred to as the "clinical versus statistical prediction" debate.

Despite these arguments, the use of personality profiles has become increasingly common in clinical practice, schools, government, and industry. Although many of these measures have questionable validity, they are often employed in making decisions that seriously affect human lives. Classroom assignments, employment and promotion opportunities, among others, are frequently based on personality assessment measures. The seeming irrelevance of so many of these instruments to job requirements or other life situations is underlined in a personality measure created by humorist Art Buchwald (1965). Buchwald's test, the North Dakota Null-Hypothesis Brain Inventory (NDNHBI), contains such revealing items as:

I salivate at the sight of mittens

Some people never look at me

I am never startled by a fish

A wide necktie is a sign of disease

My eyes are always cold

Anyone familiar with the numerous items in personality inventories administered so relentlessly in schools, boardrooms, and factories will realize that Buchwald's satirical items are, unfortunately, not unlike many of the items on the real personality inventories.

There are many other objective tests and inventories being used, abused, abandoned, sworn by, criticized, developed, and redeveloped. They measure everything from maturity to test anxiety. All of them employ the type of self-report characteristic of objective testing.

Projective assessment   Percy Knauth, in his desperation, may be quite able and willing to complete the self-report items in an objective test. These responses may help the therapist to diagnose Knauth's problems and to design therapeutic strategies that will return him to more normal functioning. There may be areas, however, about which Knauth, or any individual cannot, or will not, respond constructively. Certainly, psychodynamic theory would predict that much important information exists only at the *unconscious* level, where it is not directly

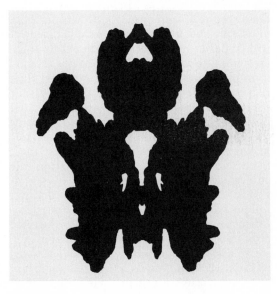

Figure 5-1   An inkblot resembling those used by Rorschach.

available to the patient. Exploration of personality at this level employs a group of instruments known as *projective techniques.*

In contrast to the standardization and explicitness of objective measures, projective techniques use the subject's response to an unstructured, ambiguous situation, and the clinician's subjective interpretation of that response. Most tests present the subject with a vague stimulus. A minimum of instruction is given to elicit the subject's interpretation of the situation.

Underlying this approach is the hypothesis that "the way in which the individual perceives and interprets the test material or 'structures' the situation, will reflect fundamental aspects of his psychological functioning" (Anastasi, 1968, p. 494). Subjects' projective test responses are viewed as significant expressions of deep-seated emotional fears, anxiety, and mental strengths (Piotrowski, 1967). The ambiguity of the stimulus materials is presumed to minimize defense reactions, and thus permit expression of hidden emotions.

Since each subject's responses are unique, standardized scoring of this type of test, while possible, is quite difficult. In direct contrast to the objective approach, projective test scoring is left to the skill and experience of the individual clinician. Obvious problems of reliability and validity result. To some investigators, this is a crucial drawback of such tests. To others, particularly those who value their own intuition and interpretive ability, it is insignificant.

The *Rorschach* inkblot test is the most widely known and used of the projective techniques. It employs ten symmetrical inkblots of various shapes and colors (Figure 5-1). Subjects are asked to describe "what they see" in each blot. The examiner notes the content of the subject's responses, the part(s) of the stimulus that are used, the way in which the picture cards are held, the time taken to answer, and emotional or other behavioral attitudes of the subject. Rorschach hypothesized that his highly ambiguous visual stimuli would elicit responses revealing an "individual's idiosyncratic ways of perceiving his world, and thus provide a sort of x-ray of his personality structure"

(Shneidman, 1965, p. 508). Not surprisingly, the almost limitless combination of responses by subjects and interpretations by clinical investigators has made validation of the Rorschach test a source of continuing frustration and controversy.

The *Thematic Apperception Test* (TAT) is another frequently used projective instrument. Created by Murray and Morgan at Harvard in 1935, the TAT consists of 30 pictures, typically portraying one or two individuals in an ambiguous situation. Subjects are told to make up stories about each picture (Box 5-3). Murray explains that "the test is based on the well-recognized fact that when a person interprets an ambiguous social situation, he is apt to expose his own personality as much as the phenomena to which he is attending" (Murray, 1938, p. 531).

As with the Rorschach, many interpretation and scoring schemes have been devised for the TAT. The most popular approach focuses on needs, such as security, affiliation, or achievement, that subjects express in their TAT stories. Environmental forces that interfere with attainment of these needs are often portrayed in descriptions of domination or attack by another person, or of withdrawal of affection or public ridicule. Repetition of common themes in many stories indicates to the investigator which life problems are most troublesome to the patient.

The *Children's Apperception Test* (CAT), which features picture situations with animals, is a variation of the TAT, designed especially for young patients.

The *Bender-Gestalt Visual Motor Test* consists of nine geometrical figures that the subject is asked to copy. Because it is a good measure of visual-motor coordination, the test is used principally in the diagnosis of brain damage. However, interpretations of the subject's drawing style, strength of line, copying precision, and other features have been used as personality assessment measures. Validity of this technique is highly dependent on the ability of the individual examiner.

In *word-association tests*, first introduced by Jung, the subject is asked to respond spontaneously to each of a long list of stimulus words.

Although these tests are easy to administer, the scope of information they produce is quite limited.

Sentence-completion tests follow the format of word-association tests, except that the subject is asked to complete sentences rather than to respond to single words. The test sentences are designed to elicit expressions of interpersonal attitudes, occupational problems, anxieties, and other feelings.

The Research Approach to Inquiry

General Issues of Research Inquiry

The questions of *clinical* inquiry explore the world of the individual client: What is his or her problem? What can be done to help him or her? The *research* approach asks a different set of questions: How does this client compare with other clients previously studied? What can understanding of his or her problem contribute to general knowledge about all individuals?

As we mentioned earlier, idealized "Boulder model" clinical psychologists pursue both these avenues. Their clinical role permits them to observe and treat the abnormal behavior of widely differing patients. The scientific training central to their research role helps them to formulate experimental hypotheses from their rich source of material. At the same time, they study hypotheses and research findings of other investigators that they can apply in treating their own clients. In addition, their clinical role makes them uniquely qualified to test these hypotheses in the most appropriate setting, the clinical situation itself.

Scientist-practitioners obviously have a unique and complex position. They are generators of researchable questions, integrators and appliers of basic scientific information, and active researchers testing hypotheses generated by themselves and others. While the number of people they can see personally in their clinical work may be small, the number potentially aided by their research contributions may be immeasurable. Thus it is in the role of re-

Box 5-3 Three Tales from the TAT

This drawing of a young boy and violin elicited the following stories from three subjects of comparable intelligence and educational level. (*Reprinted by exclusive permission of McBer and Company, Boston, not to be reproduced.*)

A 40-year-old man responded:

This is a picture of a young boy contemplating a violin. It is difficult to know where to start to pick out the best relevant details. The boy is certainly concerned with some problem about the violin, but does not seem to be greatly disturbed. Possibly he has wanted to go out and play but has been told that he must spend so much time practicing his violin lesson. He is not interested, however, and is sulking.

A 22-year-old woman responded:

A young boy looking at the violin on the table. His expression is one of tiredness and not much interest. It seems to me that he is too young to be forced to take violin lessons, at an age that he would have no love of the instrument or music. It is possible that his mother either believes that it is good to have a child "play something," or has visions of his becoming a great violinist. All this might lead to the child's dislike of the whole thing.

A 33-year-old woman responded:

First impression is the staged effect—child does not look at an unfamiliar object so quiescently. The child's facial expression is one of melancholy. The appearance somewhat—remark about questions—the bow is not clear-cut. Emotions as strong as this probably meant to be indicated here not in context with quietness of subject-coloring and delineation of individual and violin.

Interpretation of these responses by an experienced clinician (Henry, 1956) classified the first man's story as fairly standard. He observed all major details of the picture (boy and violin) and clearly related them. Although he identified the basic stimuli, at the same time, he hedged by insisting that it was only a picture, not a real boy. ". . . His approach bespeaks a caution and a hesitancy quite unlike the 22-year-old woman who moves directly into action. . . . He is more cautious and pedantic, and she is more active and direct. . . . Her story is well marked with motive and feeling, her plot lively and showing time sequences. Her basic idea is not too different from the man's, but the enthusiasm, vigor, and personal identification which she puts into it distinguish her clearly. . ." (Henry, 1956, pp. 40–44).

According to Henry, the response of the last woman was quite clearly that of a disturbed personality. Her firm, but logically unconnected associations seem out of touch with reality (a "staged effect"; appearance not "clear-cut"), and reflective of confused emotions (emotions are "strong," yet child looks "quiescently"). At the time of this test, the subject's behavior was socially acceptable. The following week, however, she suffered a schizophrenic breakdown, necessitating hospitalization and psychotherapy.

From Henry, W. E. *The analysis of fantasy.* New York: Wiley, 1956, pp. 40–44.

searcher that clinicians can make their most significant contributions.

Our look at research issues and procedures in this section will help us evaluate experimental contributions to our knowledge of abnormal behavior. In addition, it will provide us with the background to understand, in later chapters, how other research questions are formulated and how particular strategies are chosen to respond to those questions.

Exploratory Research and Hypothesis Testing

The clinical practitioner's routine interaction with clients often suggests potential research hypotheses. This informal data gathering is known as *exploratory research*. Before such informal data can be accepted as scientific knowledge, they must be subjected to the controlled, formal experimentation known as *hypothesis testing*.

Population and Sample

Usually, researchers cannot test their hypotheses on vast populations. Even if they could locate every depressed individual, or every normal individual in their locale, the time, expense, and effort of evaluating so many subjects would be prohibitive. It is more productive to draw *samples* representative of the general population.

Investigators must carefully specify the variables that define the population under study, and draw their study sample accordingly. They must make a compromise between a sample size small enough to be economically and practically feasible, and one large enough to provide good representation of the population as a whole.

Percy Knauth may be considered as a sample of the population of depressed individuals. We would expect that our findings in his case would generalize to this whole population. The extent to which this expectation is justified, however, depends upon how well Knauth represents that entire group of depressed people.

Control Groups and Single-Subject Designs

Testing a hypothesis implies the need for comparison. The basic method for achieving such comparison involves selection of a *control group* carefully matched to the experimental group on every dimension except the one under investigation. In other words, we might compare Percy Knauth and other depressives to subjects similar in age, sex, and socioeconomic states who are not suffering from depression. This comparison should indicate specific characteristics or experiences that differentiate the two groups. Control groups matched for all factors *including* the one under investigation, are commonly used in evaluating experimental treatments. In these studies, the experimental group receiving the particular treatment is compared to a matched control group that does not receive the treatment. For example, to evaluate a drug for depression, two groups of depressed people would be used—the drug is given to one group and not to the other.

The *single-subject design* compares subjects to themselves rather than to control groups. Comparison between pretreatment and posttreatment scores is the most common application of this design. As the example in Box 5-4 illustrates, groups of individuals receiving the same treatment are frequently evaluated in this manner.

Single-subject studies are particularly important in clinical research. Their prime advantage to the investigator is elimination of the need for selecting and testing separate control groups. Contrasted to this saving of time and effort is the difficulty in controlling variables such as chance fluctuations in a subject's mood or life experiences that may occur between the pretreatment and posttreatment tests. Control group studies lessen these confounding influences. They also eliminate the possibility that factors in the testing situation rather than the experimental manipulations themselves may account for posttreatment changes. Many researchers believe, however, that the confounding variables are themselves worthy of investigation (Shapiro, 1966).

Box 5-4 Single-Subject Design to Measure the Effect of Reinforcement

Single-subject design may refer not only to individual cases but also to any number of subjects examined as a group. Ayllon and Azrin (1965) used this design in a study of the effect of reinforcement on performance of ward job activities. During the *first 20 days* of the experiment, 44 chronic schizophrenic patients were rewarded for carrying out their work assignments. Positive reinforcement took the form of tokens that could be exchanged for privileges or for items from the commissary.

In the *second 20 days*, the reinforcements were given on a noncontingent basis; patients were reinforced whether they completed their tasks or not. This new nonrelationship was clearly explained to the patients.

The *final 20 days* of the study reinstated the original reinforcement system. Figure 5-2 illustrates the results. Work performance dropped dramatically during the period when tokens did not have to be earned. However, performance returned almost immediately to previous high levels when the reinforcement system was reinstated, thus demonstrating a strong relationship between work performance and reinforcement in this particular group of patients.

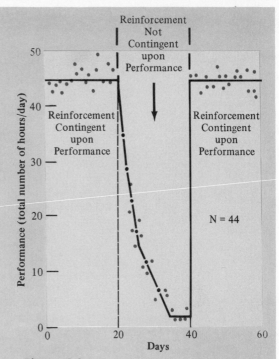

Figure 5-2   Total number of hours of work by a group of patients as a function of reinforcement contingencies: (*Reprinted with permission of Ayllon, T., and Azrin, N. H. The measurement and reinforcement of behavior of psychotics.* Journal of the Experimental Analysis of Behavior, 1965, 8, 357–383. © 1965 by the Society for the Experimental Analysis of Behavior, Inc.)

Research Methods of Inquiry

Because every experiment differs in its objectives and in the particular methods employed for achieving them, it is difficult to categorize research approaches into groups or types. The variations are almost infinite. However, it is possible to find studies that share some characteristics. Sundberg and Tyler (1962) have done this in their classification of research inquiries as descriptive, relational, or experimental.

Descriptive Research

The outstanding characteristic of descriptive research is its focus on phenomena *as they are*. Descriptive studies usually do not manipulate or control events. Rather, they attempt to define and identify important factors. This type of investigation covers a wide spectrum, from broad surveys of public opinion to behavioral studies of specific hospital, school, or other populations. Interviews, questionnaires, and natural-environment observation are commonly used in these studies. Data obtained with these instruments are then translated into the *descriptive statistics* of frequency counts, averages, and standard deviations.

Descriptive research may seem elementary in comparison to sophisticated experimental treatments. However, descriptive instruments are far from elementary in design and usage. The complexity of census-taking or political-polling operations bears out this point. It is important to remember, as well, that "description is not an end in itself. . . . All sciences started out with simple description, but they began to make real progress when they contributed to our understanding of nature by putting the observations into coherent patterns" (Holt, 1973, p. 7). Thus elementary descriptive research may be seen as a means to a more complex end. Description reflects the desire to understand basic phenomena. This desire leads to formulation of cause-and-effect inferences, which produce the testable predictions and hypotheses so basic to scientific inquiry.

Observational studies make up one class of descriptive research. Like the clinical observation we discussed in the previous section, research observation does not intrude on the environment under study. Frequency of conversational interchanges between residents of a hospital ward, average sleep time of depressed subjects, comparison of years in therapy of depressed versus schizophrenic patients—these are subjects representative of observational research. To take a specific example, Harmatz, Mendelsohn, and Glassman (1975) observed the time hospitalized schizophrenics spent in 13 behaviors, such as pacing, reinforcement seeking, passive entertainment, and verbal behavior directed toward another patient. To eliminate problems of observer fatigue and loss of visual contact while writing, a system of push-button recording was devised. This system permitted an operator to record the occurrence and duration of all activities, even when several occurred simultaneously. These observations were used to draw behavior profiles of institutionalized schizophrenics, who were "typified by a lack of adaptive behavior, a blankness and a failure to get involved with their environment" (p. 86). This recording procedure might also be applied in behavior diagnosis and in the evaluation of various therapies. We can see, then, how descriptive research can become the basis for later experimental design.

Epidemiological studies are another type of descriptive research. They provide statistical descriptions of the occurrence and distribution of particular problems in a chosen population. Epidemiological research identifies risk groups that can then be studied by other methods to develop treatment and control measures. Medical investigation often relies on epidemiological techniques. For example, the study of goiter incidence in areas low in natural iodine was instrumental in the development of therapeutic diet supplements. In the field of abnormal psychology, epidemiological studies of the incidence of problems among inner-city dwellers provided support for the view that environmental factors may be related to behavioral problems.

Relational Research

Like descriptive research, relational research does not manipulate the variables that it examines. Rather, this approach takes description of events or individuals one step further, to evaluate relationships between existing variables.

Correlation is the analysis of how variables interrelate and influence each other. This is the prime concern of relational research. What is the relationship between parental divorce and children's aggressive behavior? Is there a correlation between overcrowded living conditions and the incidence of neurotic behavior? These questions typify the relational approach. It is important to note that correlation indicates nothing about cause and effect. A correlation between parental divorce and childhood aggression does not mean the divorce caused the aggression—only that they tend to occur together.

Frequently, many factors contribute to an interaction between variables, setting up complicated crosscurrents of relationships. A sophisticated statistical procedure known as *factor analysis* permits us to measure the relative contribution of each of the factors, and, to some degree, to specify the nature of their interaction.

Experimental Research

Experimental research is the process of hypothesis testing in which investigators manipulate variables and make objective observations of the effects of the variables on specified behaviors.

As you may remember from an introductory psychology course, a *variable* is "any factor, event, or phenomenon that may assume different values, i.e., that may have *variable magnitudes*" (Maher, 1970, p. 14). Variables can be environmental factors (heat, light, sound), physiological factors (fatigue, body injury), or psychological factors (attitudes, learned behaviors). In research, we divide our attention between those variables that experimenters manipulate (the *independent* variables) and those they measure or observe (*dependent* variables).

Although many factors may be present in research studies, it is important to recognize that not all of them are experimental variables. If, for example, we control light and room temperature so that they are the same for all subjects at all times during the experiment, they are not considered as variables in that particular study. Other factors that may vary, without affecting the experimental situation, are also not included as experimental variables. Hair-color or eye-color variables, for example, would be unlikely to influence a test of reaction time.

Such irrelevant factors are easily ignored in most experiments. But sometimes, the process of elimination is not so easy. Is eye color, for example, a variable to be considered in visual perception? Does age influence aggressive behavior? Findings from previous research may guide investigators in their decisions to control or ignore such variables. However, researchers must be exceedingly alert to the possibility of unexpected variables that may confound their results. The more complex the behavior under investigation, the more critical this scrutiny must be.

Strict control of experimental variables increases the probability that predictions based on the research findings will prove correct. Since such predictions always have some element of uncertainty, researchers must work hard to ensure their accuracy. As Bachrach (1962) states, "This is essentially what we mean when we talk about controlling events" (p. 43).

Suppose we wish to test the effects of a new drug on Percy Knauth's depression. Administration of the drug, under control of the experimenter, is the *independent* variable. Knauth's response or lack of response to the drug is the *dependent* variable. The simplest manipulation of the independent variable would be a drug versus no-drug study, asking how Knauth's behavior differs before and after taking the drug. Or different drug doses could be tested for their effects. The purpose of the experiment will determine which independent variable is chosen. Drug versus no-drug studies detect whether the drug has any effect on subjects' symptoms; varied doses provide information about the relationship between strength of the drug and the subject's response.

In some experiments, the independent variable may be controlled but not manipulated. Suppose we administer an equal dosage of the drug to depressives and to nondepressives. Since the dosage is constant, the drug is not a variable in this study; the subjects become the independent variable. Obviously, the experimenter cannot control depression by "administering" it to one group and not to the other. Control of the variable is thus achieved by *selection of subjects* rather than by manipulation. The dependent variable is the effect of the drug on depressed versus nondepressed subjects.

Recognition and control of variables in experimental research are essential for the establishment of internal and external validity. *Internal validity* implies that results of the experiment can be confidently attributed to the independent variable manipulated by the investigator. This assumes that experimental and control groups have been treated identically in all significant respects, except for the independent variable. If this condition of internal validity is met, the results obtained can be accepted as proving or disproving the experimental hypothesis.

External validity may be more difficult to establish. An experiment is externally valid when the findings from the specific, internally valid situation can be confidently *generalized* and applied to other, related situations. If Percy Knauth reacts favorably to a particular drug or treatment in a laboratory experiment, can we expect the same positive results for him and other depressives in natural environments?

Much experimental research takes place in controlled laboratory settings, simply because control is easier to achieve in the laboratory. But many researchers argue that lack of external validity is an inherent weakness in this approach. They contend that the gap between the experimental situation and the "real world" is too great. One answer to this challenge that is finding increasing support is the *field experiment*, in which the independent variable is controlled or manipulated in the natural environment rather than in a laboratory. Subjects are observed and their reactions to experimental manipulations recorded, sometimes without the subjects' awareness that they are being tested.

In many cases, particularly the testing of clinical hypotheses, field situations are either unavailable or impractical. One solution to this problem is the use of *experimental analogue research*. Analogues are essentially laboratory experiments modeled from comparable real-life situations that are impractical to observe directly. Suppose, for example, the clinical researcher wishes to assess the effectiveness of a particular therapy in reducing stress in Percy Knauth's usual environment. A controlled stress situation could be set up in the laboratory and experiments constructed to measure Knauth's reaction to the stress, before and after administration of the therapy. The results could then be used as the basis for a therapy program.

Unfortunately, analogues suffer from the same external validity problem they were designed to avoid. Conclusions drawn from these simplified experiments, which isolate and control one variable at a time, do not always apply to complex situations of everyday life. In addition, subjects often view analogue experiments as artificial contrivances and find it impossible to react spontaneously.

The analogue, nevertheless, has an important place in experimental research. In one sense, any research study may be classified as an analogue, since all experimental manipulations mimic real-life situations, at least to some degree. And all investigators hope that their findings will generalize to similar situations in the natural environment.

Evaluating Research Approaches

Reading this chapter cannot miraculously transform you into an expert clinical researcher. Obviously, that would take more time and experience than we could possibly provide in one short section, or even in an entire book. Your reading should, however, make you a knowledgeable consumer of the research we will be presenting in subsequent chapters. We hope you now have some understanding of why inquiries are made, how they are formulated, and which tools may be employed to answer them. Box 5-6 provides a useful checklist of these important inquiry questions.

Basically, all scientific inquiry is a process

of asking and answering questions. You should now be aware of how the process of research and clinical inquiry are related and of some of the approaches each takes toward its own type of inquiry. You should also be better equipped to evaluate the findings presented in this book by determining whether they adequately meet the criteria discussed in this chapter.

Summary

The role of scientific inquiry is to transform hypotheses into objective knowledge, through observation and evaluation. This involves the formulation of questions or hypotheses and the development of research processes to justify or disprove the hypotheses.

Clinical psychologists have the dual role of research scientist and professional practitioner. Ideas formulated in the laboratory may be put to practical use in treating clients. Conversely, observations of clients may suggest hypotheses for testing in the laboratory.

Investigations of abnormal behavior may be categorized into five basic kinds of inquiry: statistical, psychodynamic, behavioral, biological, and phenomenological. The reliability and validity of these approaches are limited by the efficiency of the measuring instrument used and by the expertise of the investigator making the measurements.

The significance of any experiment may be evaluated by (1) consensual validation, the examination of methods and results by other investigators; (2) reliability-replicability, the degree to which the same results may be reached repeatedly; and (3) validity, the demonstration that obtained results are actually relevant to the stated purpose of the inquiry.

The major purpose of clinical inquiry is to gain understanding of individual clients in order to act on their behalf. Clinical methods of inquiry include observation of the subjects' behavior, interviews, and construction of case histories. Psychological testing of intelligence and personality is also important in clinical assessment.

The research approach to inquiry concentrates more on the pursuit of general knowledge of abnormal behavior than on understanding of specific individuals. To test their hypotheses, researchers must take representative samples of the population they are studying. Control group and single-subject designs are typical research inquiry approaches. Research inquiries have been classified as descriptive, relational, or experimental. All three approaches attempt to identify the important variables that control human behavior in the laboratory and in natural environments.

Psychotherapeutic Intervention

PART TWO

Psychotherapy:
General issues and
traditional approaches

Despite the obvious and subtle distinctions among the various forms of abnormal behavior that were described in Part I, it is clear that they all have one property in common. Such behaviors create great difficulty for the individual experiencing them and for those around them. We noted in Chapter 2 that these difficulties may become the impetus for seeking help in changing the behavior. It is at this point that professional help to deal with the problem may be sought out. Depending on what source of help is sought, different methods may be applied. This broad variety of psychological helping procedures may be described under the general label of *psychotherapy*, the topic of study in Part II.

What is psychotherapy? Box 6-1 presents some actual examples of psychotherapeutic approaches in action. Is it possible that these very different approaches can all be considered part of the same process? There do not seem to be any common features that would include all of these procedures. Perhaps a definition of psychotherapy will be helpful in our attempts to organize the discussion. Box 6-2 presents several definitions.

The variety of definitions also makes it clear that psychotherapeutic approaches are as varied as the theoretical perspectives upon which they are based. Psychotherapy is not a single procedure, yet there are a number of qualities that are present in all psychotherapeutic situations and that have meaning for all workers in the field of abnormal behavior. Although we cannot present a unitary view of all psychotherapeutic procedures, an examination of these common features may yield insight into the methods themselves and the abnormal behaviors with which they deal.

General Issues of All Psychotherapies

Basic to all types of psychotherapy are the issues of *inquiry* and *behavior change*. From the actual examples given in Box 6-1, it is obvious that all the therapeutic procedures involve the generation and evaluation of *hypotheses*, either explicit or implicit, about the person's behavior. This holds true whether the therapist and client together explore some facet of interpersonal conflict, or whether the therapist acts alone to design a behavior change procedure. The scientific inquiry—the act of formulating and answering questions—is the essential quality that sets the psychotherapist apart from other "advice givers." After all, "Miss Lonelyhearts" columns deal with many of the same issues in people's lives as the psychotherapist does. What makes therapy different from newspaper columnists' answers? It is the fact that therapists refrain from giving glib answers to the complex problems faced by their clients. Although quick and easy solutions may be requested, the therapist knows that they will rarely be useful.

In the therapeutic relationship, formulating the appropriate questions is usually more important than providing quick answers. This is often as difficult for beginning therapists to learn as it is for the confused clients who are seeking a rapid solution to their problems. When you begin to understand why the therapist doesn't just *tell* the impotent man that he loved his mother too much, or tell the neurotic woman that she should stop being afraid of elevators, then you have begun to understand psychotherapy. It is a special process of inquiry where therapist and client together explore the life situation.

The second issue common to most psychotherapies is that they seek to eventually produce *behavior change*. Clients most often present their problems in terms of a need to *change* something—to stop having a symptom, to start being assertive, to start or stop thinking or feeling a particular way. The individuals often know what is wrong with their behavior, but have been unable to find any way of changing the situation.

In all societies, there are numerous agents for behavior change. Parents, teachers, clergy, prison wardens—all are agents of socialization and behavior shaping. Some patterns of behavior, however, are resistant to the ordinary socializing techniques, and have become the domain of psychotherapy. Despite the sometimes confusing ways of stating them, the goals of all psychotherapies are changes in behavior. This includes not only overt actions and verbalizations, but also what the clients think, how they perceive their world, and how they react emotionally. All psychotherapies share the view that people are *capable* of changing or being changed. Our actions are not seen as hopelessly predetermined, but capable of change at any

Box 6-1 Examples of Psychotherapeutic Encounter

Psychoanalysis

Therapist: What do you think this is all about?
  Patient: I don't know.
Therapist: Here you meet this man and then you get this attack.
  Patient: Yes, it sounds funny.
Therapist: Do you think there is any connection between seeing this man and your attack?
  Patient: There must be, but what?
Therapist: Well, what? (*pause*) What do you think?
  Patient: I . . . I don't know, doctor, I really don't.
Therapist: Well, perhaps the man stirred up feelings in you, upset you, scared you?
  Patient: (*blushes, stammers, pauses*) Yes, I feel upset. This kind of man makes me feel funny.
Therapist: What kind of a man is he?
  Patient: Well, his eyes and build. He reminds me of my father when he was drinking, which was most of the time.

From Wolberg, L. R. *The technique of psychotherapy* (Part 1, 2nd ed.). New York: Grune & Stratton, 1967. Reprinted by permission.

Desensitization

One patient was unable to talk with other people. When confronted with the prospect of conversation, he would tremble, smoke numerous cigarettes, and become tearful. . . . The patient and the therapist worked out a hierarchy dealing with anxiety provoked by social conversations. At first the patient imagined himself talking freely about a film he had seen, then progressed to talking about future plans with close relatives. He was also trained to relax. Throughout the therapy, both the patient and ward personnel stated that he became more friendly and relaxed. He was more talkative, and reported a reduction in unusual thoughts and vivid dreams. After desensitization, he communicated in regular therapy sessions and brought in material which he had not talked about in years. [This was considered] a successful demonstration of the usefulness of desensitization with psychotic patients.

From Schaefer, H. H., and Martin, P. L. *Behavioral therapy.* New York: McGraw-Hill, 1969, p. 59.

Behavior Satiation

During nine years of hospitalization, a female patient had continually hoarded large numbers of towels in her room. This behavior continued despite numerous efforts to discourage it, and the nurses were forced to remove the towels routinely about twice a week. When a program of stimulus satiation was initiated, the nurses, rather than removing the towels, gave them to her throughout the day. When the patient was in her room, the nurses would simply hand her a towel without comment. The first week, she was given an average of seven towels a day, and by the third week this number was increased to 60 towels a day. When the number of towels in her room totaled over 600, she started taking a few of them out. The patient continued to rid herself of towels until she had virtually none.

In the early stages of the satiation procedure, the patient spent much time folding and stacking the hundreds of towels in her room. She appeared pleased and grateful for the towels, thanking the nurses for finding them for her. Later she told the nurses, "take them towels away. . . . I can't sit here all night and fold towels." Typical remarks made later in the satiation procedure were, "Get these dirty towels out of here. . . . I can't drag any more of these towels, I just can't do it." The patient was under observation for over a year after termination of the satiation program. No further hoarding of towels was observed, nor did any other behavior problem appear to replace the hoarding.

From Ayllon, T. Intensive treatment of psychiatric behavior by stimulus control. *Behaviour Research and Therapy.* 1963, 1, 382–385.

Direct Analysis

Patient: Out, out. He says to take the thumb out. Take it out.

Therapist: You have me mixed up with your mother. Did she tell you not to put your thumb in your mouth? (Patient nods.) Were you a thumb sucker as a baby? (Patient nods.) I don't mind if you suck your thumb.

Patient: Thank goodness.

Therapist: That's all right. Don't bite it. You can keep it there as long as you want. It's all right. It's all right. Do you get pleasure from it?

Patient: Yes.

Therapist: Is it very exciting?

Patient: Yes. Yes. Hard. Hard. I love them. . . . I love cigarettes. Why doesn't someone give me a taste. I want my thumb. I can't have my thumb. It's nice to suck a thumb. A baby can certainly suck a thumb with its mother.

Therapist: I am your mother now, and I will permit you to do whatever you want.

Patient: (Sucks thumb vigorously, breathing deeply and regularly.)

From Rosen, J. N. *Direct Analysis: Selected Papers.* New York: Grune & Stratton, 1953, p. 113.

Group Approach

Hi, I'm Dave, the trainer for our group. We'll be meeting together, and I figured I'd just say a couple of words about how I see our time together. The group time is designed to allow flexibility and freedom in relating to one another. There are a number of things we can do together. We could see how we get to be a "group," how we create ways of working together, deciding things, and develop our relationships. We could also get a line on how we really see each other—the feelings evoked in us by each one of us and how we respond to each other. Finally, maybe we can even try out ways of behaving that are a little different and more satisfying than those we are accustomed to. I'm the trainer, and you must be wondering what that means. To me it means that you, not me, decide what to do in here, such as the topics you want to talk about or the activities you want to try, but that I can be counted on to ask, "What's going on?" The idea is to try to understand not only what we do or say—the content level—but also the feeling underneath, the processes going on. Well, let's see, did I leave anything important out? Oh, yeah, here's a thought—the participation of each one here determines what we'll get out of this. I'm going to stop talking now, so we can get on with it. (Pause.) Unless you have something you want to ask me at this point. (Pause.) O.K., that's it. . . .

From Lakin, M. *Experiential groups: The uses of interpersonal encounter, psychotherapy groups, and sensitivity training.* Morristown, N.J.: General Learning Press, 1972, p. 20. © 1972 General Learning Corporation. Reprinted by permission of Silver Burdett Company.

stage of life. Without this basic assumption, psychotherapy would be useless.

Common Features of the Psychotherapies

In addition to the general issues presented thus far, all therapeutic methods have some specific features in common. Some of these are due to the shared historical heritage of psychotherapy. They may also reflect something even more basic in terms of our accumulated wisdom of how to help each other. The ancient qualities of sharing, cooperation, and support are deeply rooted in the human's individual and social nature. They form the basis for all therapeutic relationships.

The Therapeutic Relationship

The "helper" role has existed in all societies in one form or another. It can be on an informal basis (a parent or friend, a "natural" helper), or on more formalized terms (a therapist, counselor, or advisor). In most cases, the therapeutic relationship involves direct contact between the helper and the "help-ee." Occasionally, a therapist may deal with behavior change indirectly (i.e., via parents or teachers) and may never meet face-to-face with the person in the "client" role. Although there are many unusual forms of therapy, and we will explore some of them, the great majority of therapeutic interactions are carried out in a verbal manner with both the therapist and client present. Most research and discussion of psychotherapy are based on this traditional view of the client-therapist relationship.

There is general agreement that a client's progress in therapy depends on having a good relationship with the therapist. There is less agreement as to exactly what constitutes a "good" relationship. It seems to depend on characteristics of the therapist, characteristics of the client, and elements of the therapeutic interaction itself. In general, all one-to-one helping relationships, whether or not they are termed "psychotherapy," follow a similar pattern. An individual places his trust and reliance upon a person he perceives as an authority with the expectation that this person possesses the skill and desire to help him overcome a particular problem. The more confused and helpless the individual is, the greater his dependency upon the "expert."

The psychotherapeutic relationship is a particularly interesting kind of helping relationship because of its many facets. The therapist may function somewhat in the role of a parent, yet he or she also relates as a friend. Throughout, however, it remains a professional relationship with qualities of authority and detachment. Perhaps its unique, multilevel qualities have contributed to the success of the psychotherapeutic process. It may be the tapping of all these potentially powerful relationships that enables changes in behavior to occur (Wolman, 1976a).

Basic Elements of Therapy

As suggested above, clients come to the treatment situation with certain expectations. Once in therapy, they find there are additional ground rules, "norms," or ways of behaving in this particular relationship. They are reassured that they will find complete *confidentiality* in regard to communications with the therapist. This element of confidentiality provides the essential basis for the growth of trust in the therapist.

In addition, the clients find that their communications to the therapist are accepted in a nonjudgmental fashion. This unconditional *acceptance* of the clients' behavior, thoughts, and feelings is a second essential feature of the therapeutic situation. The non-critical, nonpunitive attitude of the therapist represents a very special—perhaps ideal—form of friendship. It has been suggested that the increasing demand for therapy in today's society may be due in part to the rewarding effects of receiving such unconditional positive regard (Schofield, 1964). Along with this acceptance, the quality of *empathy* must be present in the therapeutic relationship. Empathy has been defined as the ability "to sense the client's private world as if it were your own, but with-

Box 6-2 Definitions of Psychotherapy

1. [Psychotherapy endeavors] to alter the behavior and change the attitudes of a maladjusted person toward a more constructive outcome.

2. [Psychotherapy alludes] to the entire collection of approaches attempting to influence or assist a patient toward more desirable ways of thinking, feeling, and behaving.

3. [Psychotherapy] is a method of treatment which aims to help the impaired individual by influencing his emotional processes, his evaluation of himself and of others, his evaluation of and his manner of coping with the problems of life. It may also include, if need be, influencing and changing his environment and thus altering the problems he has to deal with and simultaneously increasing his potentialities of mastery and integration.

4. Psychotherapy is a certain kind of social relationship between two persons who hold periodic conversations in pursuit of certain goals; namely, the lessening of emotional discomfort and the alteration of various other aspects of client behavior.

5. Psychotherapy is a process in which changes in an individual's behavior are achieved as a result of experiences in a relationship with a person trained in understanding behavior.

6. In its classic sense, psychotherapy is defined as the restructuring of the malfunctioning personality.

7. Psychotherapy is a form of help-giving in which a trained, socially sanctioned healer tries to relieve a sufferer's distress by facilitating certain changes in his feelings, attitudes, and behavior through the performance of certain activities with him, often with the participation of a group.

8. Psychotherapy can be defined as a psychological process occurring between two (or more) individuals in which one (the therapist), by virtue of his position and training, seeks systematically to apply psychological knowledge and interventions in an attempt to understand, influence and ultimately modify the psychic experience, mental function and behaviour of the other (the patient). This form of interaction is distinguished from other relationships between two people by the formality of a therapeutic agreement (whether explicit of implicit), the specific training, skill and experience of the therapist, and the fact that the patient (either voluntarily or by coercion) has come to the therapist seeking professional therapeutic help.

9. Psychotherapy is the treatment, by psychological means, of problems of an emotional nature in which a trained person deliberately establishes a professional relationship with the patient with the object (1) of removing, modifying or retarding existing symptoms, (2) of mediating disturbed patterns of behavior, and (3) of promoting positive personality growth and development.

Collected by Wolberg, L. R. *The technique of psychotherapy* (Part 1, 2nd ed.). New York: Grune & Stratton, 1967. Reprinted by permission.

out ever losing the 'as if' quality'' (Rogers, 1957, p. 99).

Given confidentiality, acceptance, and empathy, the patient truly is free to respond in the therapeutic situation. Indeed, the situation is such that one might never want to leave it. This brings us to a fourth critical feature, which is the limited nature of the therapeutic situation. It is a *limited* relationship in that the therapist's involvement is restricted to certain time periods. This structures the relationship so that the client cannot become excessively dependent on the therapist, and so that their time together can be used most effectively. It is also assumed that at some point, the client and therapist will agree that the client is ready to terminate therapy.

Given these general features of the situation, we will now turn to specific client and therapist variables. Can we predict what kind of client will derive the greatest benefit from psychotherapy? Or what kind of therapist is

Box 6-3 Professions Involved in Psychotherapy

Many different kinds of people are involved in the administration of psychotherapy. Persons known as "therapists" may come from diverse backgrounds with large differences in education and experience. First, there is the *psychiatrist* who has spent four years in medical school, one year of internship, and probably three years of residency training in his psychiatric specialty.

A psychiatrist may take further training after his residency and focus on the dynamic, Freudian approach. Training to become a *psychoanalyst* is offered primarily in the analytically oriented institutes. It is a lengthy process, entailing the student's own psychoanalysis and indoctrination in Freudian theory.

Instead of pursuing the medical route, the *clinical psychologist* first obtains a doctoral degree in psychology (Ph.D. or Psy.D.) at an accredited graduate school. After the three to five years of course work required for this degree, including research training and supervised clinical experiences, the clinical psychologist must then complete an internship. In this profession, as in psychiatry, continuing education is stressed, even after the fulfillment of all requirements for certification and licensure.

A *psychiatric social worker* has obtained a degree from a school of social work. Usually this is a master's degree in social work (M.S.W.), but some institutions offer a doctoral degree. The role of the psychiatric social worker involves helping clients with adjustments to social agencies, particularly in vocational and educational situations. Psychiatric social work also involves a great deal of individual counseling and therapy in the traditional manner.

Psychiatric nurses may or may not have college or graduate-level backgrounds. Usually, they possess a nursing degree with specialized training in the psychiatric field. They deal with hospitalized patients or those related in some way to the hospital setting (e.g., day care, outpatient care). The nurses dispense medications and deal with other physical aspects of treatment. They have primary responsibility for the day-to-day existence of the psychiatric patients on the ward, and render both individual and group therapy as time allows. *Psychiatric aides* may work in close cooperation with these nurses. No academic training is necessary, although many junior colleges have begun offering an associate arts (A.A.) degree in mental

---

most effective with his or her clients? Studies of clients who have made substantial progress in changing their behavior show that numerous variables are associated with success in therapy. Clients who eventually do well in therapy are more likely to indicate that they *respect, trust,* and *like* their therapist, even at early stages in treatment.

The patient's *motivation to change* is also a crucial factor. The prognosis is best for a client with a great deal of anxiety about his situation, and a strong desire to make changes in it (Frank, 1961). A high degree of emotional arousal may also be conducive to the client's active exploration of his feelings, fears, values, turmoils, and life choices. The amount of constructive personality change that results has been found to be proportional to the depth of this *intrapersonal exploration* during therapy.

Other patient characteristics that are associated with success in therapy are *friendliness,* *high intelligence, verbal fluency, dependency on the therapist, middle- or upper-class status, and only a moderate degree of pathology.* This description of the "good" patient might lead one to suspect that from the beginning a person with these qualities would elicit greater interest and effort on the therapist's part. The "likability" of the client has itself been associated with the results of therapy; significantly greater success in therapy has been found for likable clients than for less likable ones (Stoler, 1963).

Clearly, "good" relationships are more easily established with "good" patients, but what about the more difficult patients? Clients who do not possess all the above attributes can be and are helped in therapy. This is perhaps where the therapist variables—training, experience, and personality—make the difference in achieving success in treatment.

It has been argued that specific methods or techniques are not as important as the actual

health. The aides have the most direct contact with the hospitalized patients, and may participate in therapy sessions, yet therapy is not considered part of their job specifications.

In a growing number of situations, *lay* therapists, or paraprofessionals, are being trained to do specific kinds of counseling or behavioral interventions. Homemakers, college students, parents, and other "non-professionals" have proven to be effective as therapists when provided with some basic knowledge and skills. The success of any lay therapist training program appears to depend on three factors: (1) the selection of mature, well-adjusted, socially skilled, and successful people; (2) programs designed to teach a specific role by means of appropriate practice; and (3) a minimum of unrelated material or requirements (Matarazzo, 1971).

It seems evident that some psychotherapy skills can be taught, learned, and practiced. It is equally obvious that other qualities that make a psychotherapist successful are more difficult to specify, and impossible to "teach" through academic methods. The qualities of warmth, empathy, positive regard, self-adjustment, and maturity seem essential, but they are not learned through graduate study.

Many of the current training programs emphasize actual experience in the arts and skills of psychotherapy. Hence, students must undergo lengthy internships, postdoctoral studies, intensive supervision, videotaped sessions, and so on—all oriented toward the shaping of effective therapist behaviors. The training process is expensive in terms of time and money.

Despite differences in approach, educational background, or any of the numerous other variables we have seen to be important, there is one unifying fact. All psychotherapy is geared toward helping people at times of enormous personal difficulty. All psychotherapists, though their individual motivations may vary, must share a large investment in the desire to help others. As we have seen, that personal investment is in itself a very important factor in the interaction that results. Psychotherapy is an exhausting activity, with great strains and frustrations. It is also an uplifting and rewarding activity accompanied by intense joy and satisfaction.

experience of the therapist. Professional training is clearly essential, but the argument is that in actual practice, experienced therapists are much alike. There is research evidence suggesting that, in techniques and concepts, the experts do not differ greatly from each other despite their different theoretical schools of thought (Fiedler, 1950a, 1950b). Indeed, the same study showed that the various experts were more alike than were novices within the same school. This gives some indication that therapy is an art as well as a science. It is a skill and a talent that must be nurtured through practice.

Nevertheless, *training* is critical in establishing the status and authority of therapists. Their professional status is conveyed through such symbols as their title (often "doctor"), certificates and diplomas, memberships in organizations, their clinical office setting, and their "tools" of the trade (psychological tests, tape recorders, etc.). Although some therapists will themselves ignore the status differential and treat the patient as an equal, the existence of the status differential allows many of the therapeutic processes to operate.

Perhaps even more important than training and experience are the *personality* variables. "Ideal" therapists (as described by various investigators) are sincere, are totally accepting of the patient, and have a great degree of personal warmth. They are "permissive" in allowing the client complete freedom to respond in the therapy session, but retain something of the role of a teacher, guide, model, and source of reward. They must be expert conversationalists, specialists in verbal *and* nonverbal communications. The requisite skills have been described as "sensitivity to the emotional nuances of the patient's communication . . . deftness in leading the patient to particular topics, capacity both to tolerate the patient's silences and to use his own silence in communicating" (Schofield, 1964, p. 106).

The therapists' *empathy* must be *accurate*, that is, their interpretations should coincide with the clients' experience. The goal, according to Rogers (1957), is "to sense the client's anger, fear, or confusion as if it were your own, but without your own anger, fear, or confusion getting bound up in it" (p. 99). The therapist should be interested in, respect, and like the client as a person, not as a "case," or bundle of symptoms. A sense of personal commitment to the relationship may be of greater importance than the experience or training of the therapist.

Of all these qualities, we may perhaps single out *warmth* as a critical dimension. If the therapist is genuine, this warmth will signify a personal interest and commitment to the client. Warmth will be demonstrated further by the spontaneity of the therapist's behavior and his or her efforts to understand the patient. Raush and Bordin (1957) see these expressions of warmth as filling patients' needs that stem from early childhood. Communication of warmth is therapeutic in itself, and also acts to strengthen the bond between therapist and client.

We have discussed some of the basic elements of the therapy situation, including client and therapist variables. Yet there are probably other factors involved that elude our attempts to label, quantify, and study them. The relationship is a subtle one. Someday we may be able to specify the most effective combination of therapist, method, and client—based perhaps on the nature of the problem and the personality of the client. At present, however, we cannot even say that there is a "best" way to go about training a psychotherapist.

Issues Involved in Therapeutic Change

We have stated that *change* is the goal of psychotherapy. There are several factors that enter into the potential for change, regardless of the nature of the change, or the particular techniques employed to achieve it. These factors involved in change are related to the interpersonal nature of the therapeutic process.

First, we must again consider the client's *expectancies* for change. The client comes into the therapeutic situation with anticipations that may range from optimism to pessimism about the likelihood of his or her improvement. These expectancies have an effect on the outcome of treatment. The relationship does not seem to be a direct linear one, since patients with either extremely high *or* extremely low expectancies both show little therapeutic benefit. It is the patients with *moderate* prognostic expectations that evidence the greatest amount of change for the better (Goldstein, 1962).

The prognostic expectations of the therapist have also been shown to be related to actual progress in treatment. Through various channels, these therapist expectations may be communicated to the patient. Accordingly, research on expectancy is divided into two areas: studies of the expectancy *trait* (what the patient brings with him or her to therapy) and studies of the expectancy *state* (what is explicitly or implicitly conveyed to the client by the therapist). A crucial point to note is that while expectancies of success in therapy may *correlate* with actual success, there is no evidence that the expectancies are *causal* factors. At this stage, although we cannot rule out the importance of expectancies, we can't rely upon them as explanations for the results of therapy.

Often mentioned in the same context as expectancy is the *placebo effect*. A placebo is a "pharmacologically inert substance that the doctor administers to a patient to relieve his distress when, for one reason or another, he does not wish to use an active medication" (Frank, 1961, p. 66). Formerly, this indicated a medicine given simply "to please" patients, hence the term "placebo"—Latin for "I shall please." Today, the usage is extended to research situations involving non-drug treatments as well. Current use employs a refinement of the technique in which even the person who administers the treatment may not know that it is inactive, for example, in the "double-blind" study (see Chapter 5).

Patients who respond favorably to a placebo seem to believe that the treatment can and will help them. They are more trusting of others (including their doctor), are better integrated socially, are more emotionally reactive, more dependent, and more conventional than nonreactors (patients who don't respond favorably to a placebo) (Frank, 1961). A common characteristic of the placebo reactor is a very high level of anxiety (Shapiro, 1971). From this information, we can see great similarity between the placebo reactor and the "good patient" in psychotherapy. In both cases, the healing power may stem in part from mobilization of the patient's trust and hope of relief. The patient's trait and state expectancies, the therapist's interest—all these factors combine to raise the hopes of the patient for relief. In this climate, there may be an increase in the expression of emotions (catharsis) and an increase in suggestibility on the part of the patient.

As patients are more able to discuss their feelings with their therapists, they are increasingly able to relinquish some degree of control. They are more easily influenced and persuaded—more highly *suggestible*. There is some evidence that people who are more suggestible to begin with derive greater benefits from psychotherapy. As Frank (1961) observes, this may be due to the fact that suggestible clients tend to stay in therapy longer than nonsuggestible ones. Furthermore, high levels of anxiety will increase both dependency and suggestibility. Thus a client with this combination of characteristics has a much better prognostic outlook than a nonanxious, withdrawn, and mistrustful patient. The psychopath (like Mr. P in Chapter 2), an extreme example of the nonanxious, withdrawn, and mistrustful patient, is one of the most difficult clients to help. "Individuals who fear submitting themselves to others, who retreat from domination, who are reluctant to yield to their dependency drives, who are compulsively independent, who preserve a defensive detachment, or who are fiercely competitive may resist suggestions, even those that can be helpful to them, no matter how convincingly they are phrased" (Wolberg, 1967, p. 31). On the other hand, clients who first accept therapeutic suggestion more or less "on faith" will eventually come to their own conclusions based on logic and intellectual understanding.[1]

Another general factor that enhances the probability of change in psychotherapy is the process of *catharsis*. Freud and Breuer were the first to note the psychological importance of the emotional release accompanying the "talking cure." In most current therapeutic approaches, this fact is still acknowledged and catharsis is encouraged.

> The sheer act of talking can provide an individual with considerable emotional palliation. It furnishes a motor outlet for the release of tension. It softens inhibitions and liberates conscious and unconscious conflicts that have been held in check. It exposes suppressed attitudes and ideas that the person has been keeping from himself, and it encourages him to subject these to the light of critical reasoning. It brings to the surface repudiated and fearsome impulses, with their attendant feelings of shame. In this way it takes the strain off autonomic channels which have been used to unload accumulated neurotic energy. (Wolberg, 1967, p. 29)

Through this ventilation process, clients can relieve their bottled-up feelings without fear of rejection or misunderstanding.

Basic to all therapies is the idea that clients will change the ways they think about things. This includes restructuring thoughts about themselves as well as the world around them (Kelly, 1955). The process of *cognitive restructuring* may be related to other factors leading to change in the following way. Clients come into therapy with expectations of being helped to resolve their emotional pain. The therapists' interest and optimism act to increase the clients' hope. Increasing rapport and trust lead to heightened suggestibility and greater expression of emotions. The emotional catharsis, when received in a nonpunitive manner, reduces the clients' negative feelings of guilt and shame. In feeling better about themselves, they begin to think differently about the world and their place in it.

[1]For further discussion of suggestibility in therapy, see Abroms, 1968; Orne, 1962.

The Therapeutic Contract

All therapies, regardless of their methods or goals, should have explicit statements and agreements between the parties involved. It is crucial to spell out what is to be done, and exactly how it is to be accomplished. This agreement is necessary to prevent any misconceptions on the part of either the client or the therapist. Frank (1961) refers to this process as the "convergence of expectancies" between the two partners in the therapeutic relationship. Throughout the text we will use the term *therapeutic contract* to refer to this agreement.

Goals, Strategies, and Formats of the Psychotherapies

Psychotherapies vary along a number of dimensions that reflect their particular conceptions of abnormal behavior and the process of behavior change. The three broad dimensions we will use in discussing the various therapeutic systems in this chapter are (1) the *goals* of treatment, (2) the *strategies* employed, and (3) the *format* in which the strategies operate.

Goals are the aims and objectives of therapy. While therapies ultimately aim for some form of behavior change, one therapy might get to that point through retraining of a specific behavior, while another therapy assumes that a great restructuring of personality is necessary. Various systems have been proposed for categorizing therapies according to their stated goals. In the next section, we will discuss some of these individual systems in detail. It should be evident that in addition to *overall* goals, each treatment may also have *specific* goals for particular clients at certain points in their treatment.

Strategies refer to the actual techniques employed to reach the goals. These also vary greatly and are related to the particular view of behavior formation and maintenance. The *format* aspects deal with some of the important physical, spatial, and temporal variables of treatment. The traditional verbal, one-to-one format is only one possibility. Numerous other approaches include group treatment, therapy done outside the office in the "real world" ("in

vivo"), little or no contact between therapist and client, automated procedures employing tape recorders and videotapes, family therapy, marital therapy, variations in the length or number of sessions, and so on. Recently, there has been an increase in the variety of formats considered acceptable. While the "consulting room" model still dominates, the view is weakening that it is somehow more "correct."

Varieties of Treatment Approaches and Some Attempts at Organization

There are so many different types of psychotherapy that it is difficult to keep track of them. Not all are of equal importance, and many have only the most meager (if any) support for their effectiveness. The field of psychotherapy has become a marketplace for ideas about what might help people. Like any marketplace, it has its charlatans and fly-by-night outfits along with the highly reputable dealers. "Consumers" are presented with a bewildering array of merchandise. In their extreme need and confusion, they often have to make some very difficult choices. To get some idea of the number of treatment approaches that are currently available, see Table 6-1. Extensive as this list is, it does not exhaust the field. One study (Brown, 1976) says that there are 130 varieties of therapy cited in the literature!

Dimensions for Categorizing Treatment Approaches

There have been several attempts to bring order to the chaos by grouping the treatment approaches along unifying dimensions. London (1964) organizes the various therapies on a continuum with *insight* at one end and *action* at the other. He separates the various therapies according to the amount of emphasis each places on either pure understanding or overt motor acts. Although such a differentiation is possible, many therapies do not clearly fall on one end of the continuum or the other. There is considerable "blending" in the middle ground. In fact, in actual practice, even the methods of the purists at both ends often overlap (London, 1964).

Table 6-1 Examples of Current Types of Psychotherapy

psychoanalysis	implosive therapy	occupational therapy
analytic therapy	social learning theory	art therapy
individual psychology	reality therapy	poetry therapy
will psychology	radical therapy	conjoint therapy
character analysis	primal therapy	multiple impact therapy
interpersonal psychiatry	psychodrama	social network intervention
direct analysis	T-groups	crisis intervention
client-centered therapy	encounter groups	sex therapy
existential psychotherapy	sensitivity groups	autogenic therapy
logo therapy	Esalen groups	psychosynthesis
Gestalt therapy	Adlerian therapy	experiential therapy
fixed-role therapy	Jungian therapy	conditioned reflex therapy
rational-emotive therapy	Morita therapy	general semantics
transactional analysis	biofeedback	learning theory therapy
bioenergetics	meditation	assertion structured therapy
reciprocal inhibition	dance therapy	

In line with the major theoretical approaches discussed in Chapter 3, we can also classify therapies in terms of whether they are *psychodynamic* or *behavioral.* Though similar to the insight-action dimension just discussed, this classification focuses more on the *goal* or aim of the approach. London's dimension is based more on the strategies and formats employed. The psychodynamic goal is to effect *intrapsychic* change. This is very different from the behaviorist's aim of changing *observable behavior.* Although "blending" may be a little less likely here, there have been attempts to integrate the two theories (Lazarus, 1971).

Therapies can also be characterized by the degree to which they intervene on the *psychological* versus the *biological* level. In the biological approach, the strategies include the use of drugs, chemicals, electroshock, psychosurgery, biofeedback, etc. Again, a blending of techniques is the rule rather than the exception. A specific therapy can be basically psychological in approach with biological supports, or the other way around.

Wolberg (1967) divides existing therapies into three major categories: *supportive, reeducative,* and *reconstructive* (Table 6-2). The goals of supportive therapies are to strengthen the existing systems of adaptation, control, and defense. Guidance, reassurance, and inspirational group therapy might all be included as examples of *supportive* systems for personal growth. At a deeper level, *reeducative* therapies aim for readjustment of behavior and modification of existing systems. Behavior therapies and conditioning, family therapy, psychodrama, rational-emotive therapy, and directive therapy are a few examples of attempts to change the person's functioning in some way, with or without insight into unconscious conflicts. The goal of *reconstructive* therapies, such as Freudian psychoanalysis, transactional analysis, or existential therapy, is the probing of unconscious conflicts. Extensive alterations of the personality structure are sought through the client's achievement of insight. Although Wolberg first proposed this classification in 1954 when many of the current therapies were undreamed of, even the most recent developments can be described by one or another of his categories. Again, mixtures or blending of categories is frequent.

Issues of Research and Evaluation of Psychotherapy

After the development and flowering of the practice itself, scientific research on psychotherapy was delayed for many years. Until the late 1950s, the treatment room maintained an

Table 6-2 Varieties of Psychotherapy

Type of Treatment	Objectives	Approaches
Supportive Therapy	Strengthening of existing defenses. Elaboration of new and better mechanisms of maintaining control. Restoration to an adaptive equilibrium.	Guidance; environmental manipulation; externalization of interests; reassurance; pressure and coercion; persuasion; emotional catharsis and desensitization; prestige suggestion; suggestive hypnosis; inspirational group therapy; supportive adjuncts (somatic theory, muscular relaxation, hydrotherapy).
Reeducative Therapy	Deliberate efforts at readjustment of behavior and the living up to existing creative potentialities, with or without insight into conscious conflicts.	Behavior and conditioning therapy; "relationship therapy"; "attitude therapy"; interview psychotherapy; client-centered therapy; directive therapy; distributive analysis and synthesis (psychobiologic therapy); therapeutic counseling; casework therapy; "rational therapy"; reeducative group therapy; family therapy; psychodrama; semantic therapy; philosophic approaches (existential, Zen Buddhist).
Reconstructive Therapy	Insight into unconscious conflicts, with efforts to achieve extensive alterations of character structure. Expansion of personality growth with development of new adaptive potentialities.	Freudian psychoanalysis; Kleinian analysis; neo-Freudian psychoanalysis (Adler, Jung, Stekel, Rank, Ferenczi, Reich, Fromm, Sullivan, Horney, Rado); psychoanalytically oriented psychotherapy; transactional approaches; existential analysis; adjunctive therapies (hypnoanalysis, narcotherapy, play therapy, art therapy, analytic group therapy).

Adapted from Wolberg, L. R. *The technique of psychotherapy* (Part 1, 2nd ed.). New York: Grune & Stratton, 1967. Reprinted by permission.

aura of mystery and privacy. It was closed to the researcher's probing questions. The effectiveness of therapy was proclaimed universally by the therapists, but scientifically it was unsubstantiated.

The initial impetus to change this state of affairs came from the challenge of a British psychologist, H. J. Eysenck. Based on statistics from large populations, Eysenck (1952) concluded that the data

fail to prove that psychotherapy, Freudian or otherwise, facilitates the recovery of neurotic patients. They show that roughly two-thirds of a group of neurotic patients will recover or improve to a marked extent within about two years after the onset of their illness, whether they are treated by means of psychotherapy or not. This figure appears to be remarkably stable from one investigation to another, regardless of type of patient treated, standard of recovery employed, or method of therapy used. From the point of view of the neurotic, these figures are encouraging; from the point of view of the psychotherapist, they can hardly be called very favorable to his claims. (pp. 322–323)

Eysenck's assertions forced psychotherapists to look more critically at the outcome of their procedures. The research activity that followed uncovered another major criticism of psychotherapy. Bergin (1966) hypothesized a possible "deterioration effect." He found that some patients were unquestionably left in worse condition after therapy than they were in prior to therapy. This prompted Eysenck (1967) to compare recommending therapy to advocating "a cure of the common cold on the ground that, while it kills some of the patients, others get well more quickly than they would have" (p. 150).

A flurry of research activity followed all of these charges (see Martin, 1971; Malan, 1973; Kiesler, 1971). More objective guidelines have been established for the evaluation of the outcome of psychotherapy (e.g., Stieper and Wiener, 1965), and beneficial results of certain kinds of therapy for certain types of patients have been documented.

Psychodynamic Psychotherapy—Insight, Personality Change, and Growth Therapies

The psychodynamic view of abnormal behavior has many variations that are consistent with the basic Freudian approach. (See Chapter 3 for a review of the theoretical position.) Therapies based on these variations can appear quite different, especially in their strategies and formats. Their common feature, however, is a belief that there is a dynamic interaction of the components of the psyche (the mind) with each other and with the external environment. When these interactions cause conflicts that the person cannot resolve alone, abnormal behavior may develop.

"Gee! Wow! Like I'd really *love* to Barney, but monday night is my rap group, tuesday is my sensitivity training evening, wednesday night is my identity study group meeting, thursday night I have my Gestalt-encounter, friday, it's my group therapy night, saturday night I go to my consciousness raising session and sunday night I have to wash my hair and watch Kojak." (*Henry Martin.*)

The basic approach to treatment of such abnormal behaviors follows the theory of their origin. First, the therapist must understand the dynamic interactions that are causing the conflict in the patient. Then he must move the patient in the direction of being able to understand them. This is the first step in resolving the conflict, and thereby removing the abnormal behavior. The variations on this basic theme can best be described by employing the three dimensions mentioned previously: (1) the *goals* or aims of treatment; (2) the *strategies* or techniques employed to achieve these goals; and (3) the *format* they work in.

Individual Psychodynamic Therapies

Most psychodynamic therapies deal with clients or patients in a one-to-one manner, as distinguished from group treatments. This reflects the office model adopted from medicine by Sigmund Freud. The doctor-patient format is so much a part of our conception of therapy that it somehow seems more "correct" than other arrangements. Very clearly, it is a talking therapy rather than an action-oriented process. In a sense, the one-to-one format may have prescribed the strategy and, in fact, may have reflected back upon the goals of therapy.

Orthodox Psychoanalysis

Goals As stated by Freud, the primary aim of psychoanalysis is to render the unconscious conscious. By way of accomplishing this, analysts must overcome the resistances and defenses of their patients. They must also deal with transference and countertransference reactions that appear during the course of therapy. The ultimate goal, however, is to allow unconscious impulses and repressed emotions to become accessible to the patients' conscious processes. When the patient is able to evaluate his or her unconscious motivations, changes of personality and behavior may result. Ego and superego processes may be restructured as a consequence of the insight achieved in therapy. The overall aims of orthodox psychoanalysis may be summarized as follows:

1. allowing unconscious material to become conscious
2. lifting of repression
3. overcoming resistance
4. dealing with transference
5. restructuring ego and superego
6. restoring mental health

Freud questioned whether the goals of total awareness of the unconscious or total restructuring of the personality were ever fully achieved. One of his final papers (Freud, 1937/1964) seems to indicate that he doubted that there was ever an end to the process, although there might be significant relief from particular symptoms or problems.

Strategies Three interrelated processes are at work in the psychoanalytic method: emotional abreaction or catharsis, intellectual insight, and the recall of repressed memories. Although different writers emphasize one or the other of these processes, they are all necessary and interdependent parts of the treatment. Functionally, all three often occur together in time.

Freud and Breuer originally attributed the major curative effect to abreaction, or discharge and relief through talking out pent-up emotions. They labeled this process *catharsis*, and for a time made it both their goal and sole technique. Catharsis usually involved the recall of forgotten memories that formed the basis for hysterical symptoms. Today, catharsis is still considered valuable in providing the patient with a sense of conviction about the existence of unconscious processes. This expression of emotion may bring with it a temporary sense of relief, but it is not an end in itself. In fact, it may become a source of delay in the psychoanalytic process. For example, "a patient may confess some guilt-evoking event to the analyst. Then, feeling relieved, he may avoid the subject instead of analyzing its cause, history, meaning, etc." (Greenson, 1967, p. 48).

The therapist encourages catharsis in hopes of eventually increasing the patient's intellectual understanding of, or *insight* into, his symptoms. Insight-furthering techniques

"Your treatment will be quite simple; I help you to become aware that you hate your mother—I present you with my bill—You no longer hate your mother, you hate me!" (*Marvin Tannenberg.*)

used in analysis include confrontation, clarification, interpretation, and working through. *Confrontation* and *clarification* bring into sharp focus the psychological events being analyzed. The patient must face what is bothering him and define it specifically. The most important analytic procedure is *interpretation*. This is the precise strategy by which the unconscious is made conscious. It is the psychoanalyst's responsibility to deduce the true meaning of the patient's utterances and then, at the appropriate time, tell the patient what he is *really* saying.

Through interpretation, the patient and analyst go beyond what is readily observable, to assign meaning and causality to psychological events. The timing of interpretations is crucial. Freud recommended against communicating interpretations to patients as soon as the interpretations are formulated by the analyst. Even in the later stages of therapy, it is wise not to tell patients the true meaning until they are on the verge of discovering it themselves. Interpretative skills are applied to many routes to the patient's unconscious. These routes include (1) dreams, (2) free associations, (3) symptoms and symptomatic acts, (4) behavior within the session, (5) behavior outside of the session, (6) behavior in the past, (7) the relationship to the analyst, (8) other interpersonal relationships, and (9) life style and character (Bernstein, 1965).

Following interpretations by the therapist, the process of *working through* is required. Working through the resistances and the transference reactions of the patient must be accomplished before interpretations can be truly effective. Until this is done, the interpretations will not really be heard by the patient. Evidence of resistance is seen in any unwillingness or inability of the patient to cooperate with the analyst. Silence, lateness, missing appointments, defense mechanisms (projection, denial, rationalization), acting out, and so on, are all indications of resistance.

Resistances are not always resolved merely by calling them to the patient's attention. "Only when a resistance has reached its height, when its manifestations are clear and unmistakable, and only by living through it, will a patient finally be convinced of its existence and power" (Bernstein, 1965, p. 1182). The analyst must encourage the patient to work through the resistance—to overcome it by continuing analysis in spite of it—and in so doing, to free the unconscious, repressed memories and thoughts.

Working through the *transference reaction* is likewise a difficult process for both patient and therapist. Often called the "transference neurosis," it consists of the patient's emotional reaction to the analyst in which past impulses and attitudes are directed toward the analyst. Transference "refers to the fact that patients must inevitably transfer and repeat in the treatment relationship the characteristic attitudes and expectations which they have developed in the course of their lives and which operate in the present to interfere with their capacity to live a normal and satisfactory life" (Bernstein, 1965, p. 1181). By this repetition or reenactment, the patient's neurotic functioning is clearly demonstrated to the analyst. It is, in fact, directed *at* the analyst, but it mirrors old conflicts and dependencies from the patient's past. Again, direct or premature interpretation will fall upon deaf ears. The transference must be allowed to develop so that it can be used by the analyst for therapeutic purposes. Distinction between past and present circumstances will be facilitated as the patient perceives that the therapist is not acting like other authority figures in his past. He is not a threatening or hostile father, or a domineering mother. The patient is thus enabled to work through the transference, resolving old conflicts as he also deals with his present dependence on the analyst.

Aside from this neurotic transference reaction, the patient-analyst relationship has another quality that has been described as a "working alliance." This working alliance has been defined as "the relatively nonneurotic, rational relationship between patient and analyst which makes it possible for the patient to work purposefully in the analytic situation" (Greenson, 1967 p. 46). It is marked by the mature cooperation of the patient's "reasonable ego" with the therapist's "analyzing ego." A necessity for successful therapy is the patient's ability to move back and forth between the neurotic transference reaction (where he brings repressed, irrational, and infantile behavior into the therapeutic situation) and the working alliance (where he and the analyst apply their rationality to this material and achieve insight into its meaning).

Perhaps the most important strategy in psychoanalysis, at least its characteristic feature, is the use of the *free association* technique. The patient is required to say everything and anything that comes into his mind. This is the so-called "fundamental rule" of psychoanalysis. The patient is told to avoid all planning and censorship in putting his thoughts into words; thus he is to speak about whatever comes to him, even if it makes no sense.

Format The use of the couch in psychoanalysis can be seen as a direct consequence of the free association technique. Although originally employed for relaxation prior to hypnosis, Freud continued to use the couch even after he stopped using hypnosis. He observed that with the analyst out of sight, the patients were thrown entirely upon their own inner resources for free association material. Their thoughts were not shaped by the therapist's facial expressions, and their verbalizations were freed from any feedback on the analyst's part. At the same time, the analyst did not have to guard his own facial expressions and reactions, which could ultimately restrict the patient's free association.

Analysts assume a passive role in orthodox psychoanalysis. They maintain a constant, calm attentiveness to everything the patient says and does. Freud stressed the importance of avoiding suggestion or suggestive influence on patients. He also emphasized the importance of not making any negative judgments about the patients' behaviors, thoughts, or wishes. In this sense, analysts are supportive rather than absolutely neutral. They do not condemn any deviancy from "normal" or socially acceptable impulses. Therapists must also put aside their personal involvements in order to be effective as analysts. This includes their emotional reactions to the patient, or *countertransference*. Countertransference is an "unavoidable impurity" in therapy (Patterson, 1973). The analyst, no matter how carefully trained, will have emotional reactions that are inappropriate, that cannot be avoided, and that interfere with therapeutic progress. Recognizing and controlling these feelings is considered essential in orthodox psychoanalysis.

Psychoanalysis is a long-term treatment, usually requiring from three to five years, but often taking much longer. It is also an intensive form of therapy with as many as five hourly sessions per week being the usual treatment. During the time that patients are undergoing analysis, they are cautioned to refrain from making major changes or decisions affecting their lives. They are exhorted to postpone any such actions at least until they are discussed with their analyst. The patients are also instructed not to carry any impulses into immediate action. In other words, "acting out" is prohibited by the ground rules of psychoanalysis. This serves a number of purposes. First, it protects emotionally unstable people from undertaking dangerous or self-destructive actions. Second, it makes them conscious of their impulses, and more likely to verbalize about emotions that would ordinarily remain unconsciously expressed through behavior. Third, the rule against acting out provides the therapist with an instrument to measure the degree and direction of the patients' resistances. Each defiance of the acting-out prohibition is in itself significant for the therapeutic process.

Psychoanalytic Psychotherapy

The extreme duration, expense, and general format of orthodox psychoanalysis have made it a procedure that is beyond the resources of most people. A version has evolved that shares the general theoretical background, but is more accepting of limited gains in symptom reduction. This version is known as psychoanalytically oriented psychotherapy. Areas of divergence from the orthodox position are noted below.

Goals Psychoanalytic psychotherapy focuses attention on real present-day problems rather than past conflicts. It deals more with conscious perceptions, emotions, and relationships. The emphasis is on emotional experiencing rather than intellectual insight. A stated goal of psychoanalytic psychotherapy is the "emotional re-education" of the client (Alexander and French, 1946).

Strategies The primary difference in strategy from traditional psychoanalysis can be summed up in one word: *flexibility*. Psychoanalytic psychotherapy is tailored to meet the needs of the individual client. In addition, adherents to the newer approach assert that they "seldom use one and the same method from the first to the last day of treatment" (Alexander and French, 1946, p. 25). Perhaps most important, these therapists have experimented with the transference relationship so as to use it most effectively, given the particular psychodynamics of each case.

Format Patients either lie on a couch or sit facing the therapist. Free association is employed, but often gives way to direct conversation between patient and therapist. In this relationship, the therapist is not expected to be a "blank screen" as is the ideal orthodox psychoanalyst. Rather, the therapist is encouraged to present himself or herself as a "real" person. He or she behaves normally, rather than in a reserved fashion. The therapist attempts to put the patient at ease, and will often initiate topics of conversation rather than await the patient's free associations. Drugs and environmental manipulations may be used in combination with psychotherapy. The therapist takes an active, directive role in treatment, as opposed to the totally passive role of the psychoanalyst, who is limited to carefully timed interpretations.

Based on the hypothesis that daily sessions might overly gratify the patient's dependency needs, the frequency of sessions is considerably lessened. One or two hourly meetings per week are usually arranged. Length of treatment depends on the patient's capacity to function. Rather than being open-ended and indefinite, this method of psychotherapy recommends testing the patient's ability to function without therapy by frequent interruptions and gradual phasing out of sessions. Interruptions pave the way for termination, but leave open the possibility of continuing support for the patient, should it be required (Patterson, 1973).

Client-Centered Therapy

Goals The aim of Rogers' client-centered approach to psychotherapy is personality change in the direction of growth and self-actualization. Neurotic patterns are seen as thwarting the normal strivings to reach one's potential. The overall goal for each of us, as described by Rogers, is

> to live in increasing harmony with himself and with others. . . . This process of living in the good life involves a wider range, a greater richness, than the constricted living in which most of us find ourselves. . . . It seems to me that clients who have moved significantly in therapy live more intimately with their feelings of pain but also more vividly with their feelings of ecstasy; that anger is more clearly felt but so is love; that fear is an experience they know more deeply, but so is courage. And the reason that they can thus live fully in a wider range is that they have this underlying confidence in themselves as trustworthy instruments for encountering life. (Rogers, 1961, p. 194)

The goal of therapy is growth, change, and flexibility in the person, as opposed to the fixed, limited, and rigid range of experience of the neurotic. As discussed earlier, Rogers proposes that neurosis results from a conflict between the "perceived self" and the actual self experienced. People suffer from not knowing who they really are, and not acknowledging the full range of their own feelings, some of which are "incongruent" with who they think they ought to be. The subgoal of therapy, then, must be to increase individuals' sense of "congruence" within themselves. Clients must experience the feelings that have not been admitted into their concept of self. Once this occurs in

an accepting climate, the feelings can be incorporated without guilt, which results in unity and integration in the self-concept (Rogers, 1966). The individuals must also come to set fewer conditions for their sense of worth, and they must increase their positive self-regard.

Strategies The therapist employs several specific techniques to assist the client in achieving these goals. The most characteristic method of the Rogerian school is the nondirective *reflection of feeling*. Therapists provide a mirror for their clients, putting into words the emotions that the clients are experiencing. They also restate the content of the communication, but, most important, point out the underlying feelings as they are exhibited by the clients.

Rogers has emphasized that the therapist must work from within the client's private world.

> Many therapeutic systems consider the achievement of an empathetic grasp of the client's private world only as a preliminary to the real work of the therapist. . . . The client-centered therapist aims to remain within this phenomenal universe throughout the entire course of therapy and holds that stepping outside of it—to offer external interpretations, to give advice, to suggest, to judge— only retards therapeutic gain. (Rogers, 1966, p. 190)

It is also essential for the therapist to provide the patient with *unconditional positive regard*. The therapist's way of being with the client must convey a genuine and accurate empathy—an understanding and sharing of the patient's problems and his or her situation. Rogers (1957, p. 96) has summed up these goals and strategies neatly into his statement of six "necessary and sufficient conditions" for constructive personality change:

1. Two persons are in psychological contact.
2. The first, whom we shall term the client, is in a state of incongruence, being vulnerable or anxious.

Client-centered therapy is informal, unstructured, and always face-to-face. (*Charles Harbutt, Magnum Photos.*)

3. The second person, whom we shall term the therapist, is congruent or integrated in the relationship.

4. The therapist experiences unconditional positive regard for the client.

5. The therapist experiences an empathetic understanding of the client's internal frame of reference and endeavors to communicate this experience to the client.

6. The communication to the client of the therapist's empathetic understanding and unconditional positive regard is to a minimal degree achieved.

Format Client-centered therapy is always face to face. It is informal and unstructured. The therapist, however, maintains the position of a knowledgeable authority. Therapy sessions typically are held for one hour at a time on a weekly basis, but other arrangements are possible. Client-centered therapists, as we have indicated, are not entirely passive, but are extremely nondirective. Their communications deal mainly with restating, rephrasing, and reflecting the words and feelings of their clients. The clients must take the initiative in directing and maintaining the therapy process.

Gestalt Therapy

Goals The aim of Gestalt therapy is the *reintegration of attention and awareness* that have been blocked or fragmented in the individual. When this psychological malfunctioning occurs, the person needs to be put back together again, to be made "whole," and to function in an integrated manner. Like the other schools of thought we have discussed, the goal of Gestalt therapy is the reintegration of conscious and unconscious processes.

In the Gestalt view, awareness is blocked by *projecting* aspects of the self onto others, by *retroflecting* or negating impulses (holding them back), by *desensitization* (loss of sensory awareness, "not hearing," "not seeing"), and by *introjecting* or adopting patterns from others without really assimilating them within the self. Such blocking leaves people with great areas of inaccessibility. They are alienated and divided within themselves. A consequence of blocking is the accumulation of "unfinished business"—undischarged tensions, unexpressed emotions, and unfulfilled needs. The therapeutic goal is directed not at solving these problems, but rather at pointing out and eliminating the blocking, so that the patients can solve their own problems. Once the patients are "in touch with their own concerns," they are left to their own resources (Perls, 1970).

Strategies   There are several characteristics of Gestalt interventions during therapy. First, the intervention builds on present behavior, the *"now"* feelings and actions of the person. Second, the intervention is usually *noninterpretative*. Patients are asked what they are doing, or what is going on. They are asked, not told, *"how"* they are acting. Finally, the intervention is meant to expand the patients' sense of *responsibility* for their own behavior. The point is made that their behavior is under their control, and, when they become aware of how they are behaving, they can choose to change or not to change. Note the emphasis on the client's responsibility to decide.

In other aspects of therapeutic technique, the patient is requested to refrain from talking about his or her own body as an *"it"* ("What is your hand doing?" "It is trembling") and to acknowledge the *"I"* ("I am trembling"). Patients in a group are asked to be aware of the difference between talking *to* and talking *at* a listener. They may be asked to whom they are saying something, and whether this communication is really reaching its intended receiver.

Patients must talk to each other directly, rather than talking about a person in general. The therapist will frequently stop the patient who asks a question, and ask him to turn it into a statement instead. Often the question is really not necessary; it may be a defensive maneuver by the patient, or an attempt to hook the therapist into providing support.[2]

Format   Procedural operations of Gestalt therapy vary tremendously as to time, place, number of persons involved, duration, etc. Adherents of this school actually seek out unusual environments for therapeutic sessions. Often meetings are scheduled for special locations such as retreats, motels, and camps. Gestalt therapists are more active and dynamic than in any of the previously discussed therapies. They are insistent on the client's responding, and reacting in the desired "here-and-now" framework. The therapists may badger their patients, becoming almost unbearably intrusive, but this is accepted as standard therapeutic practice. On the other hand, the therapists may drop communication with their patients until they respond in the desired fashion.

Existential Therapy and Humanistic Therapy

Goals   The primary goal of existential and humanistic therapies is to help the individual experience his or her existence as *real* and *meaningful*. Patients who seek treatment are regarded as having lost the sense of meaningfulness in their lives, particularly in the existential approach. The goal of therapy, then, becomes that "the patient encounter his own experience with full awareness and immediacy" (Martin, 1971, p. 69).

In the humanistic view, the goal of therapy, and of life, is the process of self-realization, growth, or self-actualization. In this respect, there is great similarity to the goals of client-

[2]For further discussion of these techniques, see Perls, 1970; Levitsky and Perls, 1970.

centered therapy. It is parallel to Gestalt therapy in that both approaches stress that the individual must come to function as an integrated "whole" (Buhler, 1971).

Strategies Like the client-centered approach, these therapies are concerned with the phenomenal world of the client. Like Gestalt therapy, they emphasize here-and-now-interactions. Yet the humanistic and existential traditions also have ties to the orthodox psychoanalytic methods, especially in their frequent emphasis on transference, repression, and resistance. Although some existentialists and humanists are more psychoanalytically oriented than others, they always emphasize the meaning and reality of existence at the present moment, rarely delving into past, historical complexities.

There is a wide variability of therapeutic techniques among the adherents of the existential and humanistic schools. In fact, the only unifying factor may be that they shun the standard techniques. The "encounter" is the important aspect of the therapeutic relationship. Getting to know the client's phenomenological existence is of primary concern. Understanding his sense of unreality or of meaninglessness must be accomplished first; the specific therapeutic techniques will follow as a consequence of this "experiencing" with the client (May, 1969).

Format Existential psychotherapists tend to be more formal than Gestalt therapists. They prefer office locations and standard appointment hours. During the sessions, they are generally traditional in approach, but there is a great deal of variability in style among therapists. Some have their patients recline on a couch, others prefer to have their patients face to face with them.

Humanistic psychotherapists tend to be looser in style, with therapy sessions designated whenever and wherever it seems appropriate. The more traditional of the humanists follow closely along the lines of Carl Rogers' client-centered approach.

Group Psychodynamic Therapies

Goals Although originated as early as 1905, the group technique did not come into widespread use until clinicians were faced with a vastly increased pressure for psychological services during and after World War II. Therapists trained in individual methods were forced to adapt their techniques to treat several patients simultaneously. Group methods were viewed as a necessary, perhaps inferior, substitute for one-to-one psychotherapy.

Led by Kurt Lewin and his early colleagues and students, interest soon shifted from the individual to the whole group as the "unit" for treatment. In 1946, Lewin organized a workshop for community leaders that was designed to train them to work with intergroup tensions, particularly interracial tensions. Work on small-group sociology advanced with the establishment of conferences at Bethel, Maine. These conferences were the origin of the National Training Laboratory (NTL). The training groups, or T-groups, were designed to examine the dynamics of group interaction, particularly the processes of democratic and cooperative achievement of group goals. The original goals of the T-groups did not include dealing with individual emotional problems, but it was soon evident that increased awareness and sensitivity were found to be closely associated with the group experience. Eventually these became goals in themselves for other groups aimed at "personal growth" and "human relations training."

The current increase of small-group situations can be classified according to the groups' goals of effecting change within the individual (the *intrapersonalist* approach); between individuals, dyads (pairs of individuals) or subgroups (the *interpersonalist* or *transactionalist* approach); or within the group as a social entity (the *integralist* approach) (Parloff, 1968). The goals can range from alleviation of the person's emotional pain, in the intrapersonalist approach, to the enhancement of organizational effectiveness in business, educational, or military settings. The latter has come to be known as organizational development, or "OD," and is representative of the integralistic type of goals. The vast majority of groups, however, focus on interpersonal functioning of the normal individual, stressing his or her personal style of interaction in dyads and very small groups.

Strategies The techniques used in group situations are as varied as the goals of the groups. The strategies can originate from any of the theoretical orientations we have already described, including the Gestalt, psychoanalytic, client-centered, existential, and humanistic approaches. In style, the therapist may be directive or extremely nondirective. In the nondirective case, the therapist's role may be described as that of a "facilitator" rather than a therapist or leader. In all types of groups, the group members help each other to understand and solve personal and interpersonal problems. Interpretive comments are made not only by the therapist, but may come from all group participants. Some of the currently available types of group therapy are listed in Table 6-3 to give you an idea of their variety.

Format The way the group is actually run depends on its goals and strategies, with a wide range of variation possible. The location of a particular group can be anywhere from a traditional office to a retreat swimming pool. The duration of a group session can range from the standard 50-minute therapy hour to marathons lasting for several days of around-the-clock participation. The T-group experience is usually short-term, meeting for several hours daily for a week or two. In some cases, this may be increased to a month or more, or shortened to as little as two days. This is in definite contrast to the group designed to provide individual therapy for psychological problems. This therapy group would typically meet for shorter intervals—one to two hours—over a longer period of time, even as many as four or five years (Gottschalk and Pattison, 1969). Groups can be composed of completely unrelated people, or of people with certain common characteristics, such as people who work together within the

same organization, members of a family, or other related patients, or couples . Groups may be composed of members of both sexes, or of only one.

We can see that groups can be formed for any reason, under any circumstances, by any particular group of individuals. While there are some very important and helpful kinds of groups being offered, many groups are of questionable benefit. Some evidence indicates that certain groups may indeed be harmful to some individuals. After surveying reports and evaluations in the press and professional journals, Parloff (1970) has concluded that "participation in most encounter groups is likely to be more dangerous than attending an office Christmas party and somewhat less dangerous than skiing" (p. 289).

Critique of Psychodynamic Approaches to Therapy

In Chapter 3, general criticisms of psychodynamic theory were presented. These criticisms also apply to the psychodynamic therapies, particularly those related to the basic issue of internal, intrapsychic conflict.

Psychodynamic therapies, when aiming for a total reconstruction of the personality, can become a lengthy and expensive endeavor. The patient is required to possess a high degree of verbal skill and the ability to deal at an abstract conceptual level with complex psychological relationships. While this is most noticeable in the psychoanalytic school, it is also true of the client-centered and other growth-oriented therapies. All of these therapies basically require that the client be highly self-motivated. In short, given the necessary time, money, educational level, and verbal skills, one could argue that the person would have to be healthy enough to have achieved a great amount of success at life just to undertake these therapies.

The basic question to be asked of all therapies is, do they really work? While this issue has generated much research, the question remains unanswered. In light of the Eysenck (1952) and Bergin (1966) data, we cannot easily report that they always work better than no

Table 6-3 Varieties of Group Experiences

Psychoanalytic groups	Primal therapy groups	Couples' groups and marital
Existential groups	Network therapy	therapy (see Chapter 15)
Psychodrama	Consciousness-raising groups	Psychosynthesis
Sensitivity groups	Transactional analysis	Theater of encounter
Gestalt therapy groups	(see Chapter 20)	Group games
Bioenergetics	Interactional analysis	Rolfing
Family therapy (see Chapter 15)	Multiple impact therapy	Personal growth groups
T-groups, or training groups	Synanon groups (see Chapter 14)	Sensory awareness groups
Esalen groups		Fantasy groups

treatment—but neither can we assert that they do not work at all.

Despite the eventual answer to the question of the efficacy of psychodynamic therapies, we must remember the overall needs of society for psychological services. Even if the psychodynamic approaches were 100-percent effective, the time, expense, necessary verbal skill, etc. prelude most people from this type of treatment. Thus we would still need to develop other techniques to meet the current demands. There are also large classes of prospective patients who cannot be helped by the psychodynamic therapies, for instance, young children, severely incapacitated or retarded patients, etc. Behavioral therapies have begun to provide some relief of psychological distress in these areas.

Summary

Although there are many different approaches to psychotherapy, and many definitions of it, there are several features common to all therapeutic procedures. Foremost is that they all make hypotheses about the factors behind a client's abnormal behavior and seek to change that behavior.

The therapeutic relationship is based on the client's trust of his or her therapist and the therapist's warmth, unconditional acceptance of, and empathy with his or her client's behavior, thoughts, and feelings. Both the therapist's and client's expectations of the likelihood of change are important factors in the degree of success of the therapy. Other important factors are the client's suggestibility and ability to talk out his or her problems.

Psychodynamic therapies, although diverse in their strategies and formats, are based on the common belief that abnormal behavior is the result of unresolved intrapsychic conflict. In order for behavior change to occur, the therapist must understand the dynamic interactions of the mind that are causing the conflict in the patient, and then lead the patient to an understanding of these interactions.

Foremost among the individual psychodynamic therapies is orthodox psychoanalysis, in which the primary aim is to render the unconscious conscious. Among the psychoanalyst's strategies are catharsis, insight, confrontation, interpretation, and working through resistances and transference reactions. Other individual psychodynamic psychotherapies include psychoanalytic-type psychotherapy, which focuses on present-day problems; client-centered therapy, which aims at personality growth and self-actualization; Gestalt therapy, which tries to reintegrate attention and awareness that has been blocked or fragmented; and existential therapy, which attempts to help the individual experience his or her existence as real and meaningful.

The goals, strategies, and formats of the various group psychodynamic therapies are extremely diverse, but can be classified as to whether the therapy seeks change within the individual, between individuals, or within a group as a social entity.

7.

Psychotherapy: Contemporary approaches to behavior change

The psychodynamic approaches to psychotherapy have dominated clinical practice for much of the twentieth century. While they are still important, the disadvantages discussed in Chapter 6 have led to the development of a variety of competing approaches. Three approaches to treatment that have found particularly strong support among current practitioners are the behavioral approaches, the community mental health movement, and the somatic therapies.

These three contemporary approaches represent the changing conceptualizations about abnormal behavior. They all reject the psychodynamic proposition that abnormal behavior is a "symptom" of some intrapsychic conflict. However, they move away from the psychodynamic model in quite diverse directions. Each of these three approaches has its own response to the traditional views as well as its individual orientation to treatment. The discussion to follow will compare and contrast these viewpoints and note the strengths and weaknesses of each. Their differences from the traditional approach and from one another provide the contemporary clash of viewpoints and methods from which still further advances will certainly follow.

One common feature of these three diverse approaches is their view that the resulting behavior changes are the product of the *active intervention* of the therapist. This is in contrast to the psychodynamic schools, which hold to a *passive intervention* model, in which intrapsychic conflicts interfere with normal psychological functioning. It is the removal of those conflicts that returns the person to his or her normal state. This is the direct causality model described in Chapter 4 and represented by the "illness" view that when the "germ" is removed, normality returns. The psychodynamic therapist takes no responsibility for the behavior in that presumably normal state. The *active* therapies take the contrasting view that the nature of the change is very dependent on the operations of the therapy itself. Therefore, the practitioners of these approaches recognize the importance of how therapists should see their role, what responsibility they should take for the changes that occur, and the way they must deal with clients on these issues. Ethical issues about freedom of choice, informed consent, and societal manipulation are seen as much more important in such approaches.

These therapies do share one important quality with each other and the psychodynamic approaches—they are all based in the "helping relationship" model discussed at the beginning of Chapter 6. No matter how mechanistic or "direct" the intervention, they are sensitive to the problems of relationship, empathy, and caring that are the hallmark of all psychotherapies.

Behavioral Approaches to Psychotherapy

Behavioral approaches to treatment present an interesting turn in our inquiry process. Examination reveals that each case report, if it meets the ideals of behavior theory, is actually a mini-experiment in which therapist and client together conduct a functional analysis of the problem situation, generate hypotheses about the way the current behavior is maintained, and design procedures to modify that behavior. The ultimate test of significance is production of the desired change in the client's behavior. The beauty of this behavior change model lies in its emphasis on proper control. In contrast to subtle patient-therapist interactions of psychodynamic models, behavior therapy rests on objective methods that may be replicated by any other investigator or practitioner. Thus each "experiment" not only produces therapeutic gains for the client, but also serves to advance scientific knowledge. This exemplifies the true integration of the scientist-practitioner model discussed throughout this text.

Basic Principles

Work by Pavlov, Thorndike, Watson, Wolpe, Eysenck, and Skinner, among others, as discussed in Chapter 3, laid the basis for psychotherapeutic applications of learning theory. Behavior change techniques can be traced directly to their theoretical models of operant and respondent conditioning. Learning theory focuses, of course, on *behavior*—"those activities of an organism that can be observed by another organism or by an experimenter's instruments" (Hilgard, 1962, p. 614). Behavior therapies concentrate on *maladaptive* behavior and, in particular, on its modification by *expe-*

rience, "the process by which new or altered behavior comes about as a result of prior response" (Hilgard, 1962, p. 623).

Applying these learning theory definitions to actual practice, behavior therapists must ask themselves the same procedural questions we listed in Chapter 3 (Ullmann and Krasner, 1965):

1. What behavior is maladaptive?
2. What environmental contingencies currently support the maladaptive behavior?
3. What environmental manipulations might alter the subject's behavior?

While both psychodynamic and behavioral therapies answer question 1, questions 2 and 3 are addressed only by behavioral techniques. Unlike the search in psychodynamic therapies for internal, unobservable causes of conflict, the behavior therapies insist on observable responses, explicit specification of treatment conditions, and the objective evaluation of therapeutic outcome. Behavioral approaches further distinguish themselves from the psychodynamic approaches in their basic assumptions about maladaptive behavior (see Box 7-1).

Our discussion of behavior change techniques is divided into three sections. The first covers procedures based on the *respondent* learning model, centering on Pavlovian, or classical, conditioning. The next section describes procedures based on the *operant* learning model or instrumental conditioning. The third section describes new and different treatments that may be viewed simply as variations of the above themes.

Despite the many differences in the large assortment of behavior change techniques, it has been said that all behavioral methods reduce to either extinction or conditioning (Mowrer, 1965). One other similarity shared by all behavior change techniques is the *systematic* use of environmental contingencies to alter the subject's response to stimuli (Ullmann and Krasner, 1965). As you read about each behavioral approach, concentrate on two crucial points. First, observe the orderly, program-

Box 7-1 Some Behavioral Assumptions About Maladaptive Behavior

1. Behavior therapy concentrates on maladaptive behavior itself, not on presumed underlying causes.

2. Behavior therapy assumes that maladaptive behaviors are, to a considerable degree, acquired through learning, in the same way that any behavior is learned.

3. Behavior therapy assumes that psychological principles, especially learning principles, can be extremely effective in modifying maladaptive behavior.

4. Behavior therapy involves setting specific, clearly defined treatment goals.

5. The behavior therapist adapts his method of treatment to the client's problem, rather than specifying one prescribed method to be used for all patients.

6. Behavior therapy concentrates on the "here and now," not on minute explorations of early childhood experiences.

7. Behavior therapy employs only those techniques that have been subjected to empirical test and have been found to be relatively effective.

From Rimm, D. C., and Masters, J. C. *Behavior therapy: Technique and empirical findings.* New York: Academic Press, 1974.

matic manner in which the therapist manipulates the stimulus environment. Then, note the replacement of maladaptive responses by more adjustive behavior.

Procedures Based on the Respondent Learning Model

As defined in Chapter 3, *respondent* behavior is involuntary behavior controlled by stimuli that elicit the particular behavior, for example, the startle response. The respondent learning model specifies that such involuntary nervous system responses (UCRs) normally elicited by specific stimuli (UCSs) can be *conditioned* to be elicited by other stimuli (CSs)

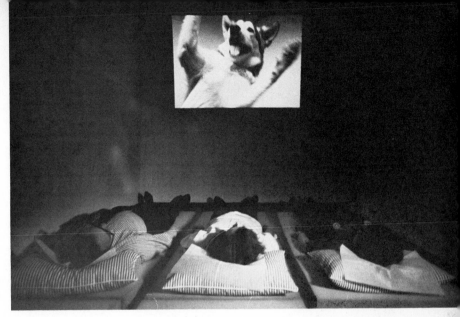

Systematic desensitization is based on the premise that relaxation and fear are incompatible responses. The subjects in this photograph, who were all afraid of dogs, were first taught to relax their muscles, and were then exposed to increasingly frightening pictures of dogs. The ability to view without fear the complete succession of pictures should generalize to the real world and real dogs. (*The New York Times.*)

through learning. Respondent learning is further elaborated by processes such as extinction, generalization, and discrimination. Typical examples of abnormal behavior as a result of respondent conditioning are maladaptive reactions to unusual situations (such as fear of elevators or airplanes) or maladaptive reactions to too many stimuli (as with the overgeneralization of fear in the anxiety reaction) or the overreactivity of physiological response systems (as in psychophysiologic disorders). Behavior therapies are also useful when conditioned responses *fail* to occur as they should, as in sexual impotence, for example.

In this section, we will discuss five different respondent techniques: systematic desensitization, flooding, assertion training, aversive conditioning, and covert sensitization. Each is particularly suited to special problem situations. In actual practice, however, these methods are flexible and complementary. Respondent techniques may be used together, or even in combination with operant methods, as dictated by each individual case.

Systematic Desensitization

Chapter 3 described Mary Cover Jones's pioneering application (1924) of behavior ther-

apy to eliminate fears in young children. Jones found that repeated presentations of fear-producing stimuli in association with those producing pleasure would rapidly eliminate the conditioned fear responses. Individuals *learn* to fear certain stimuli in their environment that are not in themselves threatening. The result is phobias, anxiety reactions, and behavioral problems, such as impotence, which stem from the interference of anxiety mechanisms. In Jones's study, rabbits were the conditioned fear-producing stimuli. To counter that conditioned fear, Jones frequently presented rabbits during pleasurable mealtimes. This inhibited, and finally extinguished, the fear response.

Years later, Wolpe (1958) reanalyzed and extended Jones's work. Borrowing a term from the neurophysiologist Sherrington, Wolpe gave the name *reciprocal inhibition* to the blocking of fear by a competing response. The term *counterconditioning* is applied to such procedures. Therapy based on reciprocal inhibition later became known as *systematic desensitization.*

Systematic desensitization entails substitution of a response that is incompatible with the undesirable response (substitution of pleasurable eating, to use Jones's example, in place of fear or anxiety). Contemporary desensitization procedures have generally used *relaxation* as the anxiety-inhibiting response. The rationale is that muscle tension is directly related to anxiety. Thus if tense muscles can be relaxed, the individual will also experience a reduction in anxiety. To obtain such muscle relaxation, therapists train patients to tense and then relax separate groups of voluntary muscles slowly, one after the other, in an orderly sequence, until the main muscle systems throughout the body have been relaxed. The procedure employed by Wolpe was designed by Jacobson (1938), who called it progressive relaxation. Once the procedure is learned and practiced by the patient, he can achieve deep relaxation in a relatively short period of time.

The crucial second aspect of the treatment is the individual's ability to create vivid, detailed mental scenes involving his phobia or problem. During therapy, the client is asked to imagine ten or more of these scenes, one by one, in a *hierarchy* of increasing anxiety-production. Box 7-2 contains a hierarchy developed by a 24-year-old female student suffering from incapacitating test anxiety. Note that items 1 through 5 present an identifiable temporal pattern of increasing anxiety as the day of the examination nears. Items 6 through 10 reflect situations the patient herself has identified as significant to her anxiety. A similar hierarchy could be constructed for fear of heights, fear of social situations, or other maladjustments. Clients also specify one or two additional scenes, these to be of relaxing, pleasant situations.

Armed with the hierarchy and the relaxing scenes, the client begins systematic desensitization. First, he induces deep self-relaxation. Then the therapist instructs him to imagine the first scene in his hierarchy, as clearly as possible, in as great detail as possible, as he would perceive it if he were right there. If seven to ten seconds pass with no indication of anxiety, the next scene in the hierarchy is imagined, and so on up the list until the patient signals his anxiety. Immediately, the therapist reinstitutes relaxation procedures while the client imagines the agreed-upon pleasant scene. Soon he is relaxed enough to reenter the hierarchy at the previously reached point. After perhaps ten sessions, repeating the same fear-producing images, alternated with periods of relaxation, the client can proceed through the complete hierarchy without once signaling anxiety.

The value of this clear-cut technique lies in its speed and proven effectiveness. In a review of 75 published papers summarizing data from 90 therapists treating nearly 1,000 different clients, Paul (1969b) reported a median range of between 16 to 23 sessions required to achieve systematic desensitization, with "relapse" and "symptom substitution" notably absent. This is significantly quicker than traditional methods of psychotherapy.

Research is the hallmark of behavior therapy, and systematic desensitization procedures are continually refined on the basis of new research. You will find further discussion of this research in the section "Research and Evalution of Behavioral Approaches." It should be mentioned here, however, that *every* aspect of the treatment paradigm—the steps in relaxation training, the use of items in a hierarchy, the completion of anxiety rating scales—is subject to experimentally tested changes. Such changes go from use of simple hierarchies to use of 20 or more items, to major shifts of the therapy environment out of the therapist's office and into real-life "in vivo" situations.

Flooding or Implosion

The implosive technique combines principles of respondent learning with traditional concepts of defense mechanisms from psychodynamic theory. This approach has proven attractive to dynamically oriented practitioners seeking the speed and objectivity of behavioral methods (Stampfl and Levis, 1967).

The flooding procedure resembles a dramatic performance, with the therapist as the featured actor. He narrates vivid, anxiety-provoking scenarios that incorporate specific cues from the patient's history. Again and again, the therapist describes these unpleasant scenes, encouraging the patient to reenact past traumas. Unlike desensitization, the goal is not to remove this anxiety through relaxing the patient, but to flood the patient with the most intense anxiety possible, until spontaneous reduction occurs.

Remember our usual conditioning paradigm. Pairing a neutral stimulus (CS) with a fear-producing stimulus (UCS) will create an anxiety response (CR) to the neutral stimulus whenever it is presented in the future. Thus any place, person, or situational stimulus may become the object of fear if it is associated with some fearful stimulus. Furthermore, such fearful stimuli will continue to reactivate the original feelings of anxiety. According to psychodynamic principles, individuals employ defense mechanisms as a means of avoiding these frightening associations. These defenses are an integral part of the maladaptive syndrome. By recreating the original trauma (CS) or something closely approximating it, in the *absence* of any fear-producing stimuli (UCS), the learned defense responses are extinguished and the maladaptive behavior ceases.

An example will clarify the actual procedure. Hogan (1968) described the following treatment of a severely depressed woman who had gained over 70 pounds from compulsive eating and who exhibited generalized hypochondriacal symptoms, hatred, and aggression toward her family, and morbid fears of death and of her own impulsiveness. She could not talk, work, or sleep. Hogan led her through scenes symbolically dramatizing her fears of rejection and death as punishment for her behavior:

Outside of the therapy room during one session, a caretaker was using a high-powered lawnmower. We had the subject imagine that she was being punished by having the mower cut her to bits as it passed back and forth over her body. The accompanying auditory stimulus heightened the anxiety arousal in the situation, making it more realistic and terrifying for the patient. (Hogan, 1968, p. 425)

Nothing is too anxiety-provoking for this technique. In fact, the worst procedural mistake is exposing the client to anxiety and then stopping because he is too distressed. This will only recondition his anxiety rather than permit extinction to occur.

The implosive technique has been questioned by many practitioners for its unusual mixture of psychodynamic and behavioral principles. Because of this and the very unpleasant nature of the therapy for both patient and therapist, it has not received widespread clinical use, or extensive enough experimental validation. It remains for future investigators to establish its value, or discount it, as a clinical technique.

Assertion Training

Assertion training is also similar to Wolpe's counterconditioning methodology, except that assertion rather than relaxation is the response incompatible with anxiety. Assertive behavior is defined as the expression of honest and straightforward feelings in an interpersonal situation. Assertion training aims to increase the client's ability to engage in such behavior in a "socially appropriate manner."

Assertiveness produces a feeling of well-being, and leads to significant social rewards. Thus any deficiency in assertiveness is hypothesized as the source of a client's anxiety and maladaptive behavior. Therapists employ detailed interviews and questionnaires to support this hypothesis and to specify areas of deficient functioning. It should be remembered, however, that just as desensitization therapists focus not on whether their clients are fearful or fearless, but on their specific fears, so assertion trainers focus only on specific situations in which assertion is a problem. They are not trying to create unselectively assertive, i.e., aggressive people; rather, they are trying to help their clients become people who can express feelings in a manner "both personally satisfying and socially effective" (Rimm and Masters, 1974).

Interpersonal problems and social anxieties are areas best suited for this therapeutic approach. Typically, treatment begins with the therapist and client play-acting significant social scenarios, such as the one described in Box 7-3. This technique is called *behavior rehearsal*. The therapist directs the client to "stand up for his rights," while carefully avoiding the "overkill" of an unnecessarily angry response. The goal is a "minimal effective response" that will accomplish the client's aims with the least possible effort and apparent negative emotion, and a very small likelihood of negative consequences.

Aversive Conditioning

Associating painful stimuli with the behavior to be discouraged is an idea probably as old as civilization itself. We know it best as *punishment*, the operant procedure in which an unpleasant stimulus *follows* undesirable behavior. The respondent form, known as *aversive conditioning*, involves counterconditioning an undesirable CS-CR connection. The model for this is as follows: The attractive stimulus (CS) must be paired with an unpleasant stimulus (UCS) that produces some auto-

---

Box 7-3 Behavior Rehearsal in Assertion Training

A male college student is working with the therapist on assertive approaches in rehearsing how to ask for a date over the telephone. The student pretends he has engaged a girl in preliminary small talk and is now ready to ask for the date.

Client: By the way (pause) I don't suppose you want to go out Saturday night?

Therapist: Up to actually asking for the date you were very good. However, if I were the girl, I think I might have been a bit offended when you said, "By the way." It's like your asking her out is pretty casual. Also, the way you phrased the question, you are kind of suggesting to her that she doesn't want to go out with you. Pretend for a moment I'm you. Now, how does this sound: "There is a movie at the Varsity Theatre this Saturday night that I want to see. If you don't have other plans, I'd very much like to take you."

Client: That sounded good. Like you were sure of yourself and liked the girl, too.

Therapist: Why don't you try it.

Client: You know that movie at the Varsity? Well, I'd like to go, and I'd like to take you Saturday, if you don't have anything better to do.

Therapist: Well, that certainly was better. Your tone of voice was especially good. But the last line, "if you don't have anything better to do," sounds like you don't think you have too much to offer. Why not run through it one more time.

Client: I'd like to see the show at the Varsity, Saturday, and, if you haven't made other plans, I'd like to take you.

Therapist: Much better. Excellent, in fact. You were confident, forceful, and sincere.

From Rimm, D.C., and Masters, J.C. *Behavior therapy: Technique and empirical findings.* New York: Academic Press, 1974, p. 94.

matic fear or anxiety response (UCR). As Watson and Rayner (1920) noted in Little Albert, the neutral stimulus then comes to elicit fear (the CR).

A wide variety of behavior problems has been treated with aversive conditioning, for example, alcoholism, sexual deviations, overeating, smoking, and various drug addictions. The treatment of alcoholism is the most frequently mentioned. Typically, alcoholics are given medications that produce vomiting. Subjects then drink their favorite alcoholic beverages, so that the sick feelings and vomiting become paired with their usually pleasant feeling. Painful shocks have also been used in place of chemical aversion therapy.

Investigators must be alert, however, to more serious risks of aversive conditioning. Some, like pain and frustration, are short-lived. Others, such as generalized anxiety or gastric ulcers, may be long-lasting or even permanent. These unexpected and undesired extratherapeutic reactions are further disadvantages of aversive conditioning.

Covert Sensitization

Aversive conditioning, without a physical unpleasant stimulus, is the hallmark of covert sensitization. The client is trained to imagine that he has received the noxious stimuli during his pleasurable, but maladaptive, behavior. It is similar to systematic desensitization and flooding in that the client most often visualizes the undesirable behavior, but it can also be accomplished with the undesirable activity actually occurring. For example, the client can actually take a drink and then vividly imagine getting sick and vomiting. The final step of the procedure is to imagine great relief or very pleasant scenes when the undesirable behavior stops.

Cautela (1967) presents the example of an obese client imagining eating his favorite dessert, apple pie:

As you are about to reach for the fork," the therapist tells him, "you get a funny feeling in the pit of your stomach. You start to feel queasy, nauseous, and sick all over. . . . You bring the piece of pie to your mouth. As you're about to open your mouth,

you puke; you vomit all over your hands, the fork, over the pie. . . . As you look at this mess you just can't help but vomit again and again. . . . Everybody is looking at you with shocked expressions. You turn away from the food and immediately start to feel better. You run out of the room, and as you run out, you feel better and better. You wash and clean yourself up, and it feels wonderful. (p. 462)

About ten of these scenes are presented in each session. The client is also asked to practice imagining similar scenes at home and during his everyday activities.

In respondent conditioning terms, maladaptive behavior paired with aversive consequences leads to escape from the situation and reinforcement by a feeling of relief—all this, within the confines of the client's imagination.

Covert sensitization has proven successful with problems of alcohol and drug addiction, homosexuality, and juvenile delinquency, in addition to obesity. Relying on no special equipment, and easily practiced outside the therapy setting, this technique is quite attractive to the clinician. Its methodology lacks scientific sophistication, however. Much is left uncontrolled and unobjective. It is impossible to measure or control the stimulus, a thought image in the subject's mind. Nor can the therapist standardize his narratives. They must be tailored to suit each client's specific fantasies. What can be controlled experimentally are the therapist's instructions to the client. This factor may then serve as a variable in outcome studies of the covert sensitization procedure.

Procedures Based on the Operant Learning Model

In contrast to the respondent approach, which emphasizes immediately preceding stimuli, and to the Freudian approach, which stresses stimuli from the distant past, the operant model studies not the precedents, but the consequences, of freely emitted learned behaviors. Pleasing consequences (positive reinforcers) maintain or increase the probability that the response will occur again in the future. Aversive consequences (negative reinforcers) make it less likely that the response will be repeated.

The operant model represents a multifaceted approach to the science of behavior in its emphasis on objective observation and empirical recording of events in a controlled experimental environment (Krasner, 1971). Not surprisingly, operant therapies are also multifaceted, focusing on three goals of behavior change: (1) establishment or increase of desirable responses, (2) elimination of undesirable behaviors that compete with the acquisition or use of acceptable responses, and (3) arrangement for the stimulus control or eventual generalization of newly acquired habits to ensure maintenance of the therapeutic gain (Karoly, 1975).

Positive Reinforcement

Any stimulus that increases the frequency of the response it follows qualifies as a positive reinforcer. The response may range from a simple motor act such as eating or running to complex "higher-level" responses such as attitudes or opinions.

Although the controlling principle remains constant, the actual reinforcer may take numerous forms: food or drink (*primary*, unlearned reinforcers); cigarettes or gum (*conditioned* reinforcers); money, tokens, or poker chips (*generalized* reinforcers, effective for their "exchange value"); smiles, praise, or pats on the head (*social* reinforcers).

One problem with preselecting reinforcers is that their value and strength vary from individual to individual. Nonsmokers do not find cigarettes reinforcing. A dollar bill might be an effective reinforcer for an unemployed teenager but not for a retired millionaire. Premack (1965) solved this problem by observing what subjects do most. Given the opportunity to engage in many activities, individuals who most often choose to watch television probably find television reinforcing. If they most frequently choose to eat, then eating is probably reinforcing to them. According to this *Premack principle*, any such *high-probability* behavior can be used to reinforce a *low-probability* be-

Box 7-4 Behavioral Approaches to Psychotherapy	
Positive reinforcement	The increase of desirable behavior through use of positive reinforcers such as food, gum, money, or praise.
Shaping	Reinforcement of successive approximations of the target response.
Contingency contracting	Specification of goals and methods of treatment.
Self-control procedures	Self-monitoring, self-evaluation, and self-reinforcement.
Token economy	Use of tokens as positive reinforcers. These tokens can be exchanged for items desired by the patient.
Extinction	Withdrawal of reinforcing stimuli that maintain undesirable behaviors.
Punishment	Any stimulus that decreases the frequency of the response it follows.
Time-out	Removal of the person emitting undesirable responses from problem-enhancing situation.
Coverant procedures	Use of mental images, daydreams, or fantasies as self-reinforcement of desired behaviors.

havior. Thus by making TV-watching or eating contingent upon some nonpreferred activity like doing homework, the frequency of the low-probability behavior will increase. This principle has been applied to a wide variety of experimental situations. When swimming was used to reinforce toothbrushing at a boys' summer camp, everyone remembered to brush. Free-time periods reinforced periods of staying seated for a class of deaf girls (Kazdin, 1975).

Since activities and privileges that could be used as reinforcers may be identified in almost any situation, the Premack technique has had wide application. One drawback, however, is that some reinforcing activities—a trip to the zoo, for example—cannot be presented immediately after the desired behavior occurs, or repeated frequently. Generalized reinforcers are useful to bridge this time-delay gap. Some examples are tickets, coins, or poker chips that can be exchanged later for specific reinforcers. Such "token economies" will be discussed later in the chapter.

The way the reinforcer is employed is as important as the choice of the reinforcer. Immediacy of delivery, schedules, chains—in fact, all of the dimensions of reinforcement discussed in Chapter 3—must be considered in the therapeutic use of operant reinforcements.

In many instances, it is not even necessary to introduce a material reinforcer. Often just providing *feedback* can serve to improve performance. Handicapped workers on an assembly line, for example, increased their production when they were told how many assembly units they completed each day, and how many points toward a reward they would have earned. In fact, they knew that no points were actually to be distributed. Feedback alone increased performance (Zimmerman et al., 1969).

Shaping

The process of reinforcement of successive approximations of the target response is known as *shaping*. Especially with children, new and complex behaviors cannot be expected to arise spontaneously. The therapist must first select some initial criterion response that already exists in the subject's behavior repertoire, and use this response as a starting point in the approximation process. Responses most like the desired end response are strongly reinforced, while those incompatible with the final goal receive no reinforcement. As the behavior shifts closer to the goal, new criteria are established for obtaining reinforcement.

Isaacs, Thomas, and Goldiamond (1960) reported a striking example of the shaping process in their therapy of a catatonic schizophrenic patient who had been mute for the full 19 years of his hospital stay. He was withdrawn

and exhibited so little psychomotor activity that the investigators searched in vain for even one ongoing behavior pattern to use as the first criterion in a shaping procedure. The patient (*S*) remained impassive, staring straight ahead, no matter what attempts were made to interest him. At one session when the experimenter (*E*) removed a cigarette package from his pocket, some chewing gum fell out with it. *S*'s eyes moved toward the gum for an instant. This small response provided a starting point for conditioning. During beginning trials, *E* held a stick of gum in front of *S*'s face and waited for eye movement in the direction of the gum. When this response occurred, *E* gave him the gum. After two weeks, the response probability had increased such that *S*'s eyes moved toward the gum as soon as it was held up. The next criterion was lip movement. An extra session passed before spontaneous lip movement occurred and could be reinforced. Next, *E* withheld the gum until *S* simultaneously made some type of vocalization. By the end of a week, holding up the gum quickly produced eye movement, lip movement, and a croaklike vocalization. During the next two weeks, *E* held up the gum and prompted *S*, "Say gum, gum." Repeating the prompt following each of *S*'s vocalizations, *E* gradually made reinforcement contingent upon closer and closer approximations of the word. During a session at the end of the sixth week, *E* prompted, "Say gum, gum," and *S* suddenly replied, "Gum, please." Reinstatement of other words soon followed. After 19 years of not speaking, *S* had finally reentered the vocal world. Without this very gradual shaping process, the end result probably never would have occurred.

Contingency Contracting

With subjects capable of intellectual reasoning and complex social interactions, specifying the goals and methods of a treatment course can produce immediate behavior change. Behavior *contracting* achieves this goal.

Box 7-5 presents a sample contract between

a 12-year-old boy and his father, who was concerned about the son's ability to accept responsibility. As with most contracts, the son played a major role in planning the program agreed upon. Important elements included in this model contract are: (1) detailed descriptions of the privileges each party expects from the contract, (2) the sanctions for failure to comply, and (3) specification of observable, easily monitored target behavior. Similar contracts have been used to control drug and alcohol abuse, to decrease weight of obese patients, and to limit absenteeism of high school students. Contingency contracting appears to focus on the restructuring of previously troublesome social relationships. Both the favorably changed relationship and the contract itself seem to produce resolution of problems (Kazdin, 1975).

Self-Control Procedures

In the therapies described thus far, reinforcers are administered by *external* sources, such as therapists or parents. In most real-life situations, however, the individual acts as his own monitor, selecting a plan of action, following rules and prohibitions, refraining from excesses. Often when this self-control and self-reinforcement break down, behavior problems develop.

Self-control procedures aim for *immediate* internalization of techniques usually associated with the therapeutic process itself. In actuality, clients becomes their own therapists. Considering the shortage of professional personnel so often noted, this has an added benefit.

Although the therapist is still an important factor in producing behavior change, his services are required for only a short time. He guides the client in the three aspects of self-regulation: self-monitoring, self-evaluation, and self-reinforcement. The *self-monitoring*, or observation stage, alerts the client to the almost automatic aspects of his own behavior that may be maintaining his maladaptive behavior and guides him to adopt *stimulus control* methods. For example, smokers who light up when coffee is served must first recognize that the coffee

may trigger their desire to smoke. They then have two choices: removing the stimulus (they might leave the table before the coffee arrives) or negating the triggering power of the stimulus through self-generated verbal responses ("If I drink this coffee, I will not smoke"). Self-monitoring by itself is often therapeutic. Just by keeping records of their undesirable behavior, smokers (McFall, 1970) and obese patients (Stuart, 1971) reported progress in reducing their problems. The *self-evaluation* stage directs clients to compare the information obtained from self-monitoring what they are *now* doing with the criteria for what they *should* be doing. Therapy helps them to reduce the discrepancy between present behavior and desired behavior. The *self-reinforcement* stage is motivational. Achieving a close match between performance and self-evaluation criteria produces reinforcing satisfaction. A large discrepancy yields negatively reinforcing dissatisfaction. The clients may also reward themselves with attendance at a ball game or the theater, some luxury article of clothing, or just the self-praise of thinking "I did well" (Kanfer, 1975).

Bootzin (1972) reports an interesting case study in the self-control training of an insomniac, who never went to a therapist's office. The client's wife was instructed in the self-control procedures. She explained them to her husband and reported the results. The client usually retired at midnight, but could not fall asleep until 3 or 4 A.M. He would worry about everyday problems and often turned on the television. Finally, he would fall asleep while watching TV. Self-evaluation revealed that bedroom stimuli usually associated with sleeping had become associated with behaviors incompatible with sleeping, such as worrying. Treatment focused on stimulus control. The client was instructed to use his bed only for sleeping, not for worrying, reading, or watching television. If he could not sleep, he was instructed to leave the bedroom. Only when he felt sleepy could he return to bed. If still unable to sleep, he was instructed to arise again and repeat the procedure, until he finally fell asleep in the bedroom. At first, the client got up four or five times each night before going to sleep.

Box 7-5   Contract between a Son and his Father

Son agrees to:

1. Carry out garbage pail each day.

2. Work six hours on Saturday every week. Work will consist of anything that he is capable of doing, such as hoeing, weeding, washing the car, or helping father, and so forth.

Father agrees to:

1. Pay $4 per week for above work each week (Saturday).

Both parties agree to the following conditions:

1. Penalty for failing to carry out garbage after being reminded will be reduction of 25¢ for each failure.

2. Penalty for not working on Saturday when work is available will be 40¢ per hour unless condition is covered by another condition.

3. When no work is available due to bad weather or father unable to supervise, $1 per Saturday will be paid.

4. Reevaluation after a trial period of three weeks.

5. If son is sick, there will be no penalty reduction on garbage detail, and $1 will be paid for Saturday. A total of $2 will be paid under this condition.

Signed: _____   Signed: _____
           (Father)   (Son)

From Dinoff, M., and Richard, H. D. Learning that privileges entail responsibility. In J. D. Krumbaltz and C. E. Thoresen (Eds.), *Behavior counseling: Cases and techniques.* New York: Holt, Rinehart and Winston, 1969.

After two weeks, however, he no longer got up. He went to bed, stayed there, and fell asleep.

Token Economies

Operant conditioning principles of reinforcement have recently been applied to entire communities, in the form of *token economies*. Just as money has become the token of choice in our economic system, any other token may be used as the medium of exchange in an experimental situation. Of course, tokens like coins, poker chips, or trading stamps in themselves have no reinforcing properties. They must be established as *generalized conditioned reinforcers* (see Chapter 3) by pairing them with backup reinforcers, the actual items desired by the participants. Ayllon and his colleagues, who pioneered the token system, found that even severely retarded children quickly learned the reinforcing value of tokens when tokens were given to them before meal-

time and then taken by attendants at the door of the dining room (Ayllon and Azrin, 1968).

Nonretarded schizophrenics and other problem patients have been introduced to similar programs through verbal and written instructions. Atthowe and Krasner (1968), for example, distributed a manual to male V.A. hospital patients before instituting a token economy. Their token economy was developed to cover all phases of the patient's life. Each patient was reinforced with a set number of tokens and verbal praise immediately after the completion of some "therapeutic" activity. This could be getting out of bed in the morning, taking showers, interacting with other patients, or attending ward activities. Tokens could be exchanged for cigarettes, money, watching television, and other basic items, or in greater amounts, for ground privileges and weekend passes. The token program had a significant effect on the patients and on the staff. Patients who had previously settled into the compliant and apa-

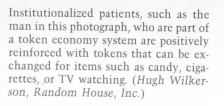

Institutionalized patients, such as the man in this photograph, who are part of a token economy system are positively reinforced with tokens that can be exchanged for items such as candy, cigarettes, or TV watching. (*Hugh Wilkerson, Random House, Inc.*)

thetic behavior typical of institutions now took an active interest in maintaining themselves and their ward. In return, staff morale increased as aides realized that their socially reinforcing behavior was producing a therapeutic effect on patient behavior.[1]

Making behavior contingent upon its consequences is the prime feature of token economies. In institutional settings, daily events in the ward go on unchanged by patients' behavior, be it constructive or destructive. What results is behavioral extinction of almost *all* responses, characterized by the vacant stare and random activity of many institutionalized patients. Noncontingent relationships in home or classroom environments also produce characteristic nonproductive behavior. In all situations, token economies make the world "pay off" again. They provide a powerful force to modify behavior to fit socially approved models. Their success has generated applications in a wide range of settings, which we will discuss in detail in Chapter 11.

Approaches to Weakening Behavior— Extinction, Punishment, Time-Out

The three procedures discussed in this section have a common goal: decreasing the frequency of undesirable behavior. *Extinction* entails withdrawal of reinforcing stimuli that

have been maintaining high-probability behaviors. Learning theory predicts that responses not followed by reinforcing consequences will decrease in frequency and finally disappear. The principles involved should be familiar from our discussion in Chapter 3. If, for example, a child's tantrums are reinforced by parental attention—even the negative attention of scolding or spanking—the tantrum behavior will continue. By walking away during a child's tantrum, the parent withdraws his or her attention and reduces the likelihood of the repetition of the outburst.

The extinction process is not always smooth, however. It is often difficult to identify the maintaining reinforcer. Some reinforcers may be difficult to withhold. A teacher may not be able to just ignore disruptive classroom behavior; parents may be unable to extinguish delinquent behavior reinforced by a child's peers. Furthermore, because the child may try ever harder to get attention, response frequency may increase before decreasing during extinction. Frustration produced by lack of accustomed reinforcement may cause side effects such as crying or aggression. In short, persistence is necessary for extinction to succeed.

It is also necessary to substitute an acceptable alternative behavior, usually one that is incompatible with the one being extinguished. Reinforcement that previously maintained the nondesirable behavior is now made contingent on the alternative behavior. For instance, a mother may ignore bedtime tantrums, but at-

---

[1]See Kazdin and Bootzin (1972) for an excellent review of work in this area.

tend to appropriate bedtime preparations. Without this planned substitution, a string of undesirable substitutions may result. As the individual searches for responses that will produce reinforcement, the crying and kicking of a tantrum may be replaced by head banging, then by somatic complaints of stomachache or headache, then by fears, or even bed-wetting. These "symptom substitutions" can be avoided by pinpointing desirable behavior that will produce the usual amount of attention and thereby alleviate frustration (Tharp and Wetzel, 1969).

In everyday situations, *punishment* is employed more frequently than is extinction. From our personal experience of spankings and deprivation, we all know how punishment works. Technically, however, punishment refers to *any* stimulus that decreases the frequency of the response it follows. It is not always clear beforehand what will be punishing. Some unpleasant stimuli may actually be positive reinforcers rather than punishments. Recall the parent's scolding of tantrum behavior, which increased the probability that tantrum behavior would be repeated. Conversely, any seemingly neutral event, such as self-monitoring of smoking behavior, may be viewed as punishment since it decreases the frequency of problem behavior.

As we noted in our discussion of aversive conditioning, therapists and parents find it difficult to administer "bad" stimuli in the name of "doing good." They dislike becoming targets for frustration and, possibly, aggression. Thus positive reinforcement is used wherever possible, with punishment employed only as a last resort.

One behavior-weakening technique that avoids the direct application of painful stimuli is *time-out* from reinforcement. Time-out removes the person emitting the undesirable responses from the problem-enhancing setting. It is effective with high-frequency disruptive behaviors that are cued and reinforced by observers and co-performers. In group situations, such as classrooms and institutions, this technique focuses on the disruptive individual without penalizing the entire group. For exam-ple, one recreation program for delinquent boys employed an isolation room in which offenders were confined for a set time interval. Fighting and rule breaking were significantly decreased without evoking fear and hostility (Taylor and Brown, 1967).

Obvious advantages of this procedure are its short duration and absence of painful stimuli. On the other hand, socially withdrawn individuals may not benefit from what for them may be a positively reinforcing removal from a group situation. Also, disruptive students taken from the classroom may welcome the opportunity to escape confinement in the classroom. The most effective time-out, therefore, is one that removes situational reinforcers without introducing additional reinforcers to take their place (Kazdin, 1975).

Coverant Procedures

Earlier, we described the internalized images and instructions used in covert sensitization and in self-control procedures. In this section, we will discuss covert operants, also known as *coverants*. Coverants are freely occurring mental images, daydreams, or fantasies that may be "harnessed" to provide self-reinforcement of desired behaviors. Such nonobservable experiences may seem quite out of place in behavioral models. Theorists explain that coverants *are* observable, although only by the individual to whom they occur.

Homme's application (1965) of coverant control to giving up cigarette smoking provides a good illustration of this procedure. Homme first identified coverant images of events incompatible with smoking, for example, thoughts about cancer, early death, or susceptibility to heart disease. These incompatible images are strengthened by making one high-probability behavior—perhaps having a cup of coffee, or walking around the room—contingent on their occurrence. Homme's coverant method follows a precise sequence of events:

Stimuli compatible with smoking   (1)

Are followed by an anti-smoking coverant   (2)

Often followed by a related pro-non-smoking coverant such as "I will feel better" or "My food will taste better" (3)

Finally, the high-probability behavior (HPB) removes the subject from the smoking stimuli (4).

Similar strategies have been developed for *coverant extinction* of an undesirable behavior. With this approach, the client is asked to imagine a target response, followed by imagined *neutral* effects rather than the usual pleasant consequences. The smokers of our previous example would picture themselves smoking, but experiencing none of the expected relaxing or satisfying effects.

As we mentioned in our section on covert sensitization, it is impossible to control coverant imagery. The therapist can rehearse scenes with his or her clients, but can never evaluate whether the stimuli and responses the clients present to themselves are following the prescribed patterns. Nonetheless, as a *self-use* procedure, coverant conditioning has definite advantages over traditional office-bound therapies.

Variations of the Behavioral Approaches

In this section, we will discuss other behavior change procedures that have generated much attention and experimentation. Each emphasizes *active* intervention to resolve behavioral problems.

Group Applications

Many behavioral one-to-one, client-therapist techniques are also employed with groups of clients. Group applications, as we noted in Chapter 6, have the clear advantage of extending therapeutic services simultaneously to more than one individual.

Lazarus (1961) was the first investigator to use desensitization with groups of phobic patients. His hierarchies were based on elements of the particular phobia that were shared by the members of each group. With an acrophobic (fear of heights) group, for example, the anxiety hierarchy contained situations such as looking down from a height of 80 to 100 feet, and sitting high up on a grandstand during a football game. In the first session, the patients received relaxation training. Following sessions covered items in the hierarchy. Subjects were told to raise their left hands if any scene proved upsetting. When any client in the group signaled anxiety, the scene was interrupted and the relaxation procedure was employed. Lazarus (1961) reported that "apart from occasional restlessness in those who were ready for more 'difficult' anxiety items but who were constantly reexposed to stimuli which they had long since mastered, no harm seemed to ensue from proceeding at a pace that was obviously too slow for part of the group" (p. 509). Subjects receiving this group desensitization showed greater improvement than subjects in traditional therapy groups that stressed "insight" and reeducation. Similarly promising results have been demonstrated with group assertiveness training (Rimm and Masters, 1974).

Interest in group applications of the behavioral approaches centers on more than just economy and efficiency of the treatments. For many problems, especially those involving interpersonal functioning, the group approach seems particularly suitable, since the interpersonal components (i.e., other people) are there to be used in the modification program.

Automated Applications

Automation techniques can also extend the limited supply of professional contact hours. Tape-recorded therapy is a good example. The therapist and patient meet together in the initial screening and instructional phases. Then the therapist prepares a recording tailored to the client's needs, and permits him or her to work at home. This approach has proven particularly successful for desensitization therapy. In one study (Morris and Thomas, 1973), college students with various incapacitating phobic reactions were given tape recordings of deep muscle relaxation training. They practiced relaxation at home twice daily for one week. The following week, the subjects met with their experimenter to construct individual anxiety hierarchies. They returned home with another tape containing step-by-step procedures of systematic desensitization, and with scoring forms to indicate their daily progress. Subjects took from three to ten weeks to complete their hierarchies successfully. Posttreatment anxiety inventories revealed significant decreases in both specific anxiety toward phobic objects and in general anxiety levels.

The positive findings of this study and other similar experiments are important demonstrations that behavioral improvements from desensitization therapy reflect more than a simple desire to please the therapist. With automated procedures, and no therapist present, objective benefits directly related to the treatment are apparent.

Rational-Emotive Psychotherapy

Ellis (1962) has devised another systematic combination of office therapy and "homework." His system of rational-emotive therapy (RET) is based on the assumption that what an individual says to himself determines the way he feels and acts. When irrational beliefs produce erroneous or damaging self-appraisals, the RET practitioner steps in to correct the client's mistakes.

The RET paradigm has been summarized in an *A-B-C-D-E* outline: *A* refers to a real external event that the individual experiences; *B* represents the chain of self-verbalized thoughts produced by *A*; *C* refers to the emotions and behaviors caused by *B*; *D* represents the therapist's reinterpretation of the *B* chain of thoughts; and *E* stands for the beneficial emotional and behavioral consequences of the procedure.

To give you an example, a depressed client complains that no one respects him and "proves" it by recounting a conversation with his employer, who criticized him for a report. The therapist identifies this as the precipitating external event *A*. He now must discover the client's internal thoughts, *B*. Through probing

questions, the therapist discovers that, "He has no respect for my work" has been verbalized by the client as, "Nobody respects me. I'm a worthless being." This produces *C*, feelings and expressions of depression, anxiety, and anger. The RET practitioner now helps his client to point *D*, a reexamination of his conclusions, and discovery that being criticized does *not* mean being worthless. Which brings the client to the more positive consequences emotionally and behaviorally, or point *E*.

Such oversimplification of the RET technique should not minimize the proven value of expert help in reexamining damaging self-appraisals. Ellis's emphasis on conscious thinking contrasts strongly with traditional analytic emphasis on the unconscious. Its ease of application and clarity of presentation have made RET an attractive alternative to psychodynamic therapy.

Biofeedback

As noted in Chapter 3, involuntary nervous system responses traditionally were viewed as pure respondents, that is, not subject to operant conditioning. With the demonstration that many autonomic responses are sensitive to positive and negative reinforcement, new techniques of behavior modification have arisen. *Biofeedback training* is the prime example. Although we will discuss this method in more detail in Chapter 9, our present review of relaxation and self-control procedures is incomplete without some mention of biofeedback methods.

Knowledge about the ongoing functioning of one's own physiological systems can be reinforcing, in the strict sense of increasing the probability that a certain response will occur. A typical example is muscle relaxation training. Muscle tension is monitored by recording electrical signals, called electromyograms (EMGs), directly from the muscle. These signals are transmitted to a subject in the form of visual or auditory stimuli. High tones, for example, can represent high tension, and low tones, low tension. Subjects learn to reduce muscle tension by trial-and-error attempts to

The subject of this photograph is receiving biofeedback training, that is, information about her autonomic responses that will help her control those responses. Biofeedback programs have been used to reduce muscle tension and eliminate tension headaches. (*Michal Heron.*)

keep the tone low. No one teaches them how; they simply pay attention and react to the stimuli their responses produce.

Biofeedback programs have been used to reduce muscle tension and eliminate tension headaches. Other claims for biofeedback cures of cardiac arrhythmias, high blood pressure, and seizures have not been substantiated (Blanchard and Young, 1974). The news media have given biofeedback the "hard sell" as a *cure* for many other ailments, and these conclusions, too, must await experimental validation. Nevertheless, biofeedback promises new behavior modification techniques combining both respondent and operant learning paradigms.

Modeling

Observation of behavioral models is an important part of the assertion training techniques described in our respondent-learning therapy section. Modeling methods have been applied to other behavior modification techniques, and have proven particularly useful with children.

Modeling refers to the process of observational learning in which the behavior of one individual or group, the *model*, acts as a stimulus for the thoughts, attitudes, or behavior of another individual, who observes the model's performance (Marlatt and Perry, 1975). The process occurs in stages: *acquisition*, in which the observer simply views the actions of the model, without receiving reinforcement or engaging in any practice; and *performance*, in which the observer actually makes the response he has observed, and receives reinforcement or punishment. Three important effects are found. First, the *observational learning effect*, in which observers learn new or novel responses that they have not previously attempted. Learning to drive by watching instructional movies is one illustration. Second, the *disinhibitory/inhibitory effect*, in which performance of a previously learned behavior is increased (disinhibited) or decreased (inhibited). Watching people cross thin ice is an example of this effect. If they fall in, an observer will be inhibited from taking the same risk and experiencing the same negative consequences. Last, the *response facilitation effect*, in which performance of an already-learned behavior, not under an existing constraint or inhibition, is increased.

Albert Bandura is well known for his investigations of modeling. His research has pinpointed several important variables in the application of modeling procedures, such as *choice of model* (a live person versus symbolic written material or prerecorded presentations), *presentation* of the model (to maximize observer attention and retention of the modeled behavior), *incentives* to perform the modeled behavior (such as vicarious reinforcement obtained by watching the model receive reinforcement), and *prompting* or *coaching* by the therapist following the modeling. Recall how some of these factors aided assertion training. Bandura and his associates (Bandura and Barab, 1973; Bandura, Blanchard, and Ritter, 1969) found that observational experiences produce significant reduction in fear and phobic behavior. In simple terms, watching others doing something fearful without getting hurt can lower the phobic individual's anxiety so that he can do it himself. When fearful consequences do not result, the avoidance behavior is extinguished.

Research and Evaluation of Behavioral Approaches

Behavior therapy owes its fast-growing popularity to claims of superior effectiveness and rapid results. Experimental outcome research has, in fact, supported these claims. Lang and Lazovik (1963) were among the first investigators to examine a behavior therapy (desensitization) in a controlled laboratory setting. They evaluated two groups of snake phobic patients, one simply tested, then twice retested, for phobic behavior, and the other tested, trained in relaxation methods, tested again, desensitized, and then retested. *Control* subjects showed no appreciable improvement on their three tests. Similarly, no improvement was seen for *experimental* subjects following just pretherapy relaxation training. Thus simple relaxation did not account for the therapeutic results. After desensitization, however, significant reduction in phobic behavior was demonstrated, proving the effectiveness of desensitization therapy.

In his previously mentioned review of systematic desensitization therapy of nearly 1,000 different patients treated by more than 90 therapists, Paul (1969b) supports Lang and Lazovik's contention (1963) that this behavior therapy technique "reliably produces measurable benefits for clients across a broad range of distressing problems in which anxiety was of fundamental importance" (p. 159). Thus psychodynamic explorations of the unconscious seem unnecessary for relief of anxiety.

We have already noted how each behavioral approach is like a mini-experiment, incorporating testing of treatment hypotheses and effectiveness. Clearly, this experimental paradigm lends itself to outcome studies better than traditional psychodynamic methods. Critics (e.g., Martin, 1971), on the other hand, express concern about the seeming overemphasis on such experimental evidence. Where, they ask, are large-scale studies in clinic settings, or even smaller, well-controlled studies of groups of self-referred patients with neurotic complaints? Overreliance on case histories of uncontrollable but successful treatments, and on laboratory studies of carefully screened subjects represents science more in name than in fact. This is a valid criticism of behavior therapy.

Success in treating well-specified fears and anxieties with *identifiable* causes has been well demonstrated. Hospital programs using operant conditioning paradigms have also produced impressive results. Psychodynamic therapists now challenge their behaviorist colleagues to prove their methods on the "central life problems" they feel are more typical of the outpatient.

Evaluation

The use of behavioral approaches to treatment is increasing dramatically. These techniques avoid the length and expense of psychodynamic approaches and extend treatment to severely disturbed or retarded subjects not considered treatable by traditional therapies. Despite unresolved theoretical issues, behavioral techniques have taken a respected place in the psychotherapeutic armament.

Community Mental Health

Community involvement in treating abnormal behavior was termed "a bold new approach" by President John F. Kennedy in a special message to Congress in 1963. Congress responded with funds for construction of comprehensive community mental health facilities. These governmental actions formally instituted the *community mental health movement.*

Basic Concerns

As a field, community mental health (CMH) is not tightly defined by any one viewpoint. If there is a central theme, it is that *social contexts* are important for the develop-ment and change of behavior patterns. Some important principles are outlined in Box 7-6. The CMH approach is oriented to providing services that promote the general well-being of an entire population group. These services are particularly valuable to the poor and uneducated, who normally would not receive attention.

Prevention

Inherent in the idea of promoting general well-being is an emphasis on prevention. Typi-

---

Box 7-6 Principles Underlying the Community Mental Health Approach

1. The environmental context is always relevant, and social realities are often prepotent [superior] in determining and changing behavior.

2. Mental health professionals are accountable to the communities they serve.

3. Social approaches to amelioration can be effective.

4. Prevention is the most valued answer to the mass problem of mental disorder.

5. Help for a problem is best offered in close proximity to where the problem became visible, and through indigenous resources.

6. Optimal programming requires community participation, if not control.

7. The more urgent needs of local populations or groups should order program priorities and determine the characteristics of facilities.

8. Regaining or enhancing competence are important objectives of treatment.

9. Since milieu can be structured to facilitate mental health, intervening at the level of social system is a preferred strategy.

10. Services should reach out to recalcitrant high-risk groups and be rendered parsimoniously, efficiently, and equitably.

11. The accidental or developmental stresses and strains of life are strategic points of entry for preventive intervention.

12. Since the causative chain in mental disorder seems linked to the stresses of debilitating social problems, social reform is an important professional goal.

13. Professionals can be better deployed and the manpower pool effectively enhanced by training nonprofessionals to perform helping tasks.

14. Careful planning, innovative programming, and the formulation of new conceptual models are to be encouraged.

15. Since psychological disorder is practically legion, public education about mental health should be a high priority activity.

From Roen, S. R. Evaluative research and community mental health. In A. E. Bergin and S. L. Garfield (Eds.), *Handbook of psychotherapy and behavior change: An empirical analysis.* New York: Wiley, 1971, p. 777.

cal public health parlance divides prevention into three categories targeted at (1) reducing the incidence of mental disorders and promoting psychological well-being in the community (*primary* prevention); (2) preventing minor disorders from becoming prolonged and severe (*secondary* prevention); and (3) minimizing the impairment that may result from these disorders (*tertiary* prevention) (Cowen, 1973). This three-pronged approach concentrates on active prevention rather than after-the-fact treatment.

Systems

The community approach has often been called systems-centered in contrast to the person-centered focus of most other therapies (Cowen, 1973). By systems, we mean the key social institutions and settings such as family and school that shape human development. Systems-oriented research stresses "environmental engineering" of factors relating to mental functioning. The findings of the research have been applied to classroom design, teacher training, and lesson planning, among others.

Another tool of the systems approach is *epidemiology*, the study of incidence. The epidemiological method tries to match frequency of occurrence of disease states in certain populations with distinguishing characteristics of their environment. When the hazardous characteristics are identified, programs can be generated to remove similar hazards in other populations. Roen (1971) discusses the Stirling County (Nova Scotia) Study of economically depressed communities as an example of the ambitious epidemiological approach. The study mapped interconnections between abnormal behavior and community "disintegration," which was defined as a community's failure to perform traditional functions of protection against dangers, promotion of harmony, and division of labor. Comparisons were made between matched deprived communities that differed only in their degree of social disintegration. More cases of abnormal behavior were found in disintegrated communities than in integrated communities, suggesting that the

"whole tenor of community life is the important force in mental health, and not poverty or low socioeconomic status *per se*" (Roen, 1971, p. 780).

Emphasis on ecology has also filtered into community mental health approaches. *Ecological methods*, which will be discussed in detail in Chapter 19, focus on mutual relationships between organisms and their environments. In particular, ecological psychology studies people as they are, in the settings to which they have become accustomed. The operational premise is that the environment is not passive, but actively causes certain behavior patterns to develop.

Methods of Intervention

Crisis Intervention

CMH resources are especially relevant in times of crises. Crises, by definition, are brief, concentrated periods of disturbance. Normal, predictable crises, such as starting school, getting married, or nonemergency surgery, are amenable to preventive therapy. However, death of a family member, loss of a job, or serious accident cannot be anticipated. Such disruptions in a person's life necessitate crisis intervention, that is, professional attention at a time of great emotional unrest. Immediate psychological care has been shown to forestall later serious problems. Thus a small investment of time during a crisis may have a high "payoff" in averting disastrous consequences and building new strengths.

Community Consultation

Although crises are sometimes predictable, the mental health expert may be the last to know of their impending threat. Often teachers, physicians, clergy, and other community workers are more likely to recognize significant trends. For this reason, another important emphasis of the community approach is direct consultation with agencies, social groups, and individuals who have basic, regular contacts with community members. These individuals are often drawn into the therapeutic effort as nonprofessional assistants.

Nonprofessional Assistants

Increased contact between maladjusted persons and normal members of the community who become nonprofessional assistants benefits both groups. The maladjusted individuals have more helping agents available, and the well-adjusted individuals, through exposure to behavior problems, become more tolerant and caring toward those in need of help. Students living in "college towns" or unemployed homemakers, for example, have proven to be enthusiastic and sometimes even more effective than the trained mental health professionals they are assisting. Parents and siblings have been trained to act as therapists in the home environment. In addition, the massive "ex" movement demonstrates the effectiveness of ex-patients, ex-addicts, ex-alcoholics, and many other "ex-es" in helping those with similar problems.

Evaluation of Community Mental Health

The community approach is an exciting development in the mental health field. It has broadened the base of available services and increased general awareness of the nature and scope of psychological problems.

Scientific evaluation of community efforts is difficult, if not impossible. How, for example, does a suicide prevention center know if it has prevented suicides? Experimentally oriented community therapists take the statistical approach to such questions. Yearly decreases in suicide, crime, or truancy provide support for their mental health programs. But statistics miss the "human" aspects of a more satisfying outlook on life, or better adjustment in family, school, and work situations that CMH programs feel they facilitate.

Frequently, the community psychologist can more easily identify the causes of abnormal behavior than he or she can act to change them. Lack of jobs, poor housing, crowded classrooms are obvious precipitants of anxiety and frustration. The corrective "prescriptions" the therapist might wish for are often better filled by politicians or economists. Thus the community therapist must often choose between *opening* an office and *running for* office.

The need for defending the "good works" of programs often hampers objective evaluation of their efficacy. Science and advocacy (social supportiveness) are uncomfortable partners. The ability to separate these two issues will do much to determine whether community mental health becomes a social movement or a scientific approach to the study of people. Other issues of community psychology and community mental health will be discussed in Chapters 19 and 20.

Somatic Therapies

Physical and chemical efforts to change abnormal behavior have a long history. In Chapter 1, we discussed the ancient skulls bearing evidence of trephine holes presumed to be evidence of primitive attempts to release "evil spirits." Chemotherapy goes back to the early days of folk medicine, when roots and herbs were used as "cures." Despite the proposals of other approaches, there is an abiding belief in the organic model of abnormal behavior. As a result "dramatic cures" for abnormal behavior get top billing in the news media, although most soon fade from attention.

What we will discuss in this section are not miracle panaceas, but specific *somatic treatments* that help to stabilize problem behavior. Such treatments are by no means "curative," in the sense of modifying central *processes* that may be causing abnormalities. This does not reduce their significance, however. Somatic therapies are an important source of help for many types of abnormal behavior. For some, they are critical.

Pharmacological Therapy (Drug Treatment)

Introduction of effective psychopharma-

Table 7-1 Classes of Psychopharmacological Agents (Generic and Brand Names)

Sedatives	Minor Tranquilizers
amobarbital (Amytal)	chlordiazepoxide (Librium)
pentobarbital (Nembutal)	diazepam (Valium)
phenobarbital (Luminal)	meprobamate (Equanil, Miltown)

Major Tranquilizers

Phenothiazines	Butyrophenones	Rauwolfia Alkaloids
chlorpromazine (Thorazine)	haloperidol (Haldol)	reserpine (Serpasil)
trifluoperazine (Stelazine)		Rauwolfia serpentia (Raudixin)
thiondazine (Mellaril)		(whole root)

Antidepressants

Monoamine Oxidase Inhibitors	Tricyclics
isocarboxazid (Marplan)	imipramine (Tofranil)
phenelzine (Nardil)	amitriptyline (Elavil)
tranylcypromine (Parnate)	nortryptyline (Aventyl)
lithium carbonate	

Stimulants

amphetamine	(Benzedrine)
dextroamphetamine	(Dexedrine)
methylphenidate	(Ritalin)

Adapted from Byck, R. Drugs and the treatment of psychiatric disorders. In L. S. Goodman and A. Gilman (Eds.), *The pharmocological basis of therapeutics* (5th ed.). New York: Macmillan, 1975. © 1975 by Macmillan.

cological agents (drugs) in the early 1950s created a sudden and dramatic transformation in the field of psychotherapy. Clinicians plagued by unresponsive cases of long standing could now produce immediate, if not permanent, behavior changes with drugs. Mental hospital wards, once places of chaotic terrors for inmates and professionals, took on an unheard-of calm as medicated patients became manageable and occasionally more rational. It seemed, at last, that the magic cure had been found (McNeil, 1970).

Research and clinical analysis tempered this original excitement, of course. It soon became clear that the drugs did not cure. They merely reduced and flattened symptoms that previously prevented patients from being treated by other methods.

Psychoactive substances are usually classi-fied as sedatives, tranquilizers, or antidepressants (see Table 7-1).

Sedatives, for example, the barbiturates pentobarbital and phenobarbital, are used in low doses to decrease the restlessness and instability of rage, anxiety, and emotional stress of crisis situations. In high doses, their main effect is sleep. Ideally, a dosage balance is reached that calms the patient without putting him to sleep. Sedatives lessen agitated activity, but they cannot actually free the patient from his maladaptive symptoms.

Tranquilizers have the remarkable ability to modify *affective* (emotional) states without seriously impairing *cognitive* (intellectual) functions. Their usefulness extends to almost all types of abnormal behavior. Symptom reduction through the use of tranquilizers has been demonstrated with tension, anxiety, hyperactivity, agitation, impulsiveness, aggressiveness, and hallucinations.

Tranquilizers are usually subdivided into two categories: *minor* (weak) and *major* (strong). The minor tranquilizers, known by such brand names as Librium, Valium, and Miltown, are used as antianxiety agents in the treatment of neuroses. These agents are the *most frequently prescribed* drugs in the United States (Byck, 1975).

Major tranquilizers are usually reserved for patients suffering from psychoses, agitated depressions, and organic brain disorders. When chlorpromazine, the most popular major tranquilizer, was introduced in 1952, it was hailed as a "wonder drug" and quickly adopted as a cornerstone of psychiatric treatment. Chlorpromazine calms agitated patients and produces progressive disappearance of acute and chronic psychotic symptoms. Many patients previously uninterested in or hostile to therapy can enter treatment while taking chlorpromazine. An unfortunate side effect, however, is marked indifference to what goes on in therapy and in everday life as well.

Antidepressants were discovered serendipitously in the 1950s during experimentation on improving tranquilizers. Surprisingly, these agents produce no significant effect on normal subjects, but do produce relief from depression and euphoria in manic-depressive patients.

Before the discovery of these agents, stimulants had been used as mood elevators. But they were short-acting and caused severe side effects such as insomnia, loss of appetite, and jumpiness. In addition, patients felt even more deeply depressed when drug action wore off than before they had treatment (a *rebound effect*). Modern antidepressants, such as Tofranil and Elavil, avoid these side effects. They act to "trigger a chemical state of alertness in the brain that is reflected in the patient's behavior and rouses him from his inattention to the outside world" (McNeil, 1970, p. 147).

The salts of the element *lithium* have also become recognized as effective antidepressants, particularly in the treatment of manic-depressive psychosis. In contrast to chlorpromazine and the other phenothiazines, which dull af-

fect, it is claimed that lithium "puts a brake" on the uncontrolled manic behavior of this syndrome without impairing the range or quality of a patient's emotional life. Although careless overdosage may result in death, lithium has been administered safely, often over a period of many years, with few serious complications.

Another class of antidepressants, the monoamine oxidase (MAO) inhibitors, were originally used in the treatment of tuberculosis. However, euphoria was so often produced as a side effect that MAO inhibitors were added to the psychotherapeutic drug arsenal. Their action in the brain to inhibit the activity of the enzyme monoamine oxidase produces a rise in important neural transmitter agents. This often enhances the effects of other psychoactive drugs. Thus MAO inhibitors, such as Marsilid, Nardil, and Parnate, are often administered in carefully controlled combination with other agents to enhance their therapeutic effectiveness.

Evaluation

Psychoactive agents have proven to be such an "easy" solution to so many behavioral problems that careful scientific evaluation has been notably lacking in this field. Of almost 1,000 studies published during the mid-1950s on the introduction of chlorpromazine, only 10 met the criteria for scientific control (Peterson, 1966). Often there is no reliable evidence that psychoactive drugs are any better than pharmacologically inert sugar-coated placebos. Physicians have employed such harmless "sugar pills" for decades, with marked success. In scientifically rigorous studies, placebos have relieved neuroses, colds, coughs, headaches, gastrointestinal disorders, and a long list of other illnesses. If just taking a pill, *any* pill, can produce dramatic cures, obviously claims for specific tranquilizers and antidepressants must be supported by controlled experimental study. The greatest need is for *double-blind* studies (see Chapter 5) in which neither the physician nor the patient is aware of what agent is being administered, the active drug or a placebo.

Despite these scientific objections, the

merits of pharmacological therapy are apparent in savings of time, effort, and money. Drugs also provide measurable controls on the intensity and duration of treatment. In addition, long-term studies consistently report marked reduction in rehospitalization among drug-maintained patients as compared to nonmedicated patients (Gittelman, Klein, and Pollack, 1964).

Electroshock Therapy

When psychotherapeutic and pharmacotherapeutic approaches fail, or when serious psychoses demand immediate intervention, therapists fall back on powerful, but occasionally irreversible treatments. Of these, electroconvulsive (ECT), or electroshock (EST), therapy is probably the best known.

Modern ECT was developed by Cerletti and Bini in Italy in 1938. Their procedure entails placing electrodes at each side of the patient's forehead and then applying from 70 to 130 volts of electricity for about 0.5 second. Epileptic-like seizures lasting less than one minute then occur. Depending on the results obtained, treatments are repeated two or three times a week for a total of 5 to 30 applications.

How or why shock treatments work is completely unknown. Nevertheless, they sometimes provide dramatic, rapid improvement particularly in depressed patients and, more specifically, in depressives with self-blame as the major element in their symptom picture. Although impairment of memory and learning ability follow ECT, these side effects are temporary.

In practice, both drugs and ECT are interdependent. Improvement obtained with ECT reduces patients' anxiety levels to the point where pharmacotherapy and psychotherapy can be more effective.

Psychosurgery

Apart from ancient skull trephinings, direct physical treatment of the brain was not popularized until this century. In 1936, Egas Moniz, a Portuguese neurologist, described his surgical *lobotomy* for severing the connection between the thalamus and the frontal lobe of the brain. The procedure acquired a reputation for producing thousands of human "vegetables" relieved in anxiety but also without ambition, imagination, or consciousness of self. This "nightmare of psychosurgery" should be modified by the fact that more refined techniques that have improved the treatment outcome are now available. Psychosurgery continues to be a tool (although a hotly debated one) in the treatment of abnormal behavior (Kalinowsky, 1975).

It must be emphasized that psychosurgery is still limited to those patients who have not responded to traditional techniques. Psychoactive drugs are the therapy of choice today. However, there are some studies that support psychosurgical procedures, especially considering the extremely severe and otherwise unresponsive conditions of the patients treated. In one review (Post, Rees, and Schurr, 1968) of 52 patients with long-standing, disabling illnesses, surgery left 14 symptom-free, 14 "moderately" benefited, 15 "marginally" benefited, and only 9 unimproved. These changes were maintained or enhanced over a three-year observation period. Unfortunately, two-thirds of the patients

Box 7-7 Somatic Therapies	
Pharma-cological therapy	Use of sedatives, tranquilizers, and antidepressants to decrease undesirable behaviors and increase desirable behaviors.
Electroshock therapy	Use of electroshock to reduce anxiety levels. Particularly effective in depressives whose major symptom is self-blame.
Psychosurgery	The severing of the connection between the thalamus and the frontal lobe of the brain. Generally used only for otherwise unmanageable cases.

suffered from the adverse affective changes so frequently associated with psychosurgery before the 1970s. These changes include impairment of a sense of responsibility, and reduction in sensitivity and depth of feeling for others.

Evaluation

Psychosurgery is still a very controversial treatment procedure. At present, probably no more than 500 psychosurgeries are performed annually in this country, and these by perhaps a dozen neurosurgeons (Holden, 1973). The legal and moral aspects of this treatment are crucial issues to civil rights advocates. They point out that the vast majority of psychosurgeries are performed on institutionalized mental health patients and prisoners who cannot give free and informed consent.

The greatest benefit of this ongoing controversy is renewed attention to what we don't know about brain functioning. On a very basic level, there is still no conclusive evidence in human subjects that specific areas of the cortex control specific patterns of behavior. Future research on brain-behavior relationships will guide the use of psychosurgery techniques. Considering what we still don't know about the brain, it is hard to defend so radical and irreversible a procedure as psychosurgery.

Other Somatic Therapies

In addition to psychoactive drug, electroconvulsive, and surgical therapies, other electrical and chemical therapies are currently being tried in the treatment of mental disorders. Many have been tested successfully in preliminary trials. Others have not withstood experimental trial, but are nevertheless regularly employed by individual treatment centers.

Niacin (vitamin B_3) therapy in the treatment of schizophrenia is one example of a nonproven method. It has been hypothesized that excesses of methyl compounds in the brains of schizophrenics would be taken up by niacin, a methyl acceptor. The large ("mega") doses of niacin used in this therapy give it the label "megavitamin therapy." Similar therapies

directed at correcting molecular abnormalities in the brain have been classified as "orthomolecular" psychiatry. Although controlled studies by the Canadian Mental Health Association discouraged use of niacin therapy, this has not prevented orthomolecular psychiatrists, especially in Canada, from continuing to treat schizophrenic patients with niacin alone, and in combination with vitamin C, special diets, drugs, and convulsive therapy. What positive results are obtained may be due more to the accompanying therapies than to the niacin (Abrams, 1975).

Beneficial effects have also been claimed for drug-induced *sleep therapies* in which patients spend up to 20 hours per day sleeping, for ten or more days. The 70-percent recovery or improvement rate claimed for patients with chronic anxiety states is overshadowed by reports of death and serious complications.

Another so-called "sleep therapy" uses low-level electrical currents passed through the skull to relieve anxiety, insomnia, and depression. These *electrosleep* currents actually produce only tingling sensations, usually without sleep. Although double-blind studies of real versus sham electrosleep currents have supported the efficacy of this technique, there is still no proof that the currents ever reach the brain, or any explanation of how they act to produce benefits (Rosenthal, 1972).

Evaluation of Somatic Therapies

Somatic therapies are, for the most part, designed to reduce incapacitating behavior patterns. These procedures make patients more manageable and amenable to concurrent treatment with other psychological techniques. Although they cannot promise to "cure," neither can dynamic, behavioral, or community approaches. It is, of course, very easy for psychoanalytic practitioners to dismiss drugs and physical treatments for their bad side effects or potential dehumanization. The fact is, however, that somatic therapies have produced dramatic benefits. Before the advent of psychopharmacology, for example, mental hospitals were extremely unpleasant places, whose net effect on patients was further disruption and deterioration of their behavior.

What is still lacking, however, is clear demonstration of when drugs and physical treatments help, and when they present more of a potential danger than can be justified. Such findings will guide the judicious application of somatic therapies, both alone and in conjunction with other psychological treatments.

Summary

Contemporary treatments of abnormal behavior fall into three major classifications: behavior change techniques, community mental health approaches, and somatic therapies. Different as these three approaches are, they have the common orientation of *active intervention* to produce behavior change.

Behavior change techniques fall into two categories: (1) those based on the respondent learning model, including systematic desensitization, flooding, assertion training, aversive conditioning, and covert sensitization; and (2) those based on the operant learning model, including positive reinforcement, shaping, contingency contracting, self-control training, token economies, extinction, time-out, punishment, and coverant control. Respondent and operant approaches are often used together or adapted for group and automated applications.

Community mental health approaches emphasize the social context in which behavior patterns develop and change. Techniques focus on prevention, crisis intervention, and consultation with local resource people. Nonprofessionals from the community are often trained for active participation in the mental health care program.

Somatic therapies include physical and chemical treatments with drugs, electroshock, and psychosurgery. The most important psychoactive drugs are classed as sedatives, tranquilizers, and antidepressants. These drugs have largely supplanted older procedures such as electroshock and surgery as the treatment of choice, although the latter techniques have their adherents as well.

Controlled studies of all the behavior change approaches, while greater in number than traditional approaches, are still fewer than ideal. Claims of success often rest on anecdotal rather than scientific evidence. Additional research is needed to guide the development and application of new psychotherapeutic methods.

Overview of Psychotherapy

In the two chapters that make up Part II of this text, we have presented considerable information about psychotherapy. As we have seen, it is a very special type of inquiry, comprising many different conceptualizations of the nature of abnormal behavior, but focusing on the singular goal of helping people with psychological difficulties.

Therapeutic procedures are, as we have noted, often controversial. Reports of their effectiveness are frequently more anecdotal than scientific. Research on psychotherapies has emerged as a field of study in its own right. Still, no easy answers have developed as to the best therapy or, for that matter, the best outcome for patients in therapy. What research does indicate is that human aspects of the psychotherapeutic encounter may indeed be the critical element.

We are left, then, with a picture of psychotherapies as a unique mixture of art and science, with one unifying theme: the helping relationship and its overriding goal of treating those with abnormal behavior with the best techniques possible.

Types of
Abnormal Behavior

PART THREE

8.

The Neuroses

The Nature of Neurotic Behavior

The *neuroses* are the most common examples of what we call abnormal behaviors. We tend to think that almost everyone has some kind of neurosis, and some of us seem to have a whole collection of them. One reason they are so commonplace is that we have given this label to so many different behaviors. What began as a formal concept in abnormal psychology has spilled over into our culture, and now we freely describe all manner of odd responses as "neurotic."

In this chapter, we will describe these behaviors and show how the process of inquiry is demonstrated in the study of neurosis. We will consider some intriguing new and emerging conceptions of this age-old problem.

The "Neuroses"—Definition and Orientation

DSM-II defines the neuroses in these terms: "Anxiety is the chief characteristic of the neuroses. It may be felt and expressed directly, or it may be controlled unconsciously and automatically by conversion, displacement, and various other psychological mechanisms. Generally, these mechanisms produce symptoms experienced as subjective distress" (American Psychiatric Association, 1968, p. 39).

The concept of "anxiety...felt...directly or...controlled unconsciously" is taken directly from psychodynamic theory. As we have noted, such terms do not lend themselves to behavioral description, which requires objective constructs. In fact, psychodynamic thinking pervades the whole conception of neurosis, including the description, formation, and treatment of the presumed syndrome.

Is neurosis, therefore, a purely psychodynamic invention? We know its various forms exist when we see people (sometimes ourselves) wrestling with their troublesome effects: depression, compulsions, phobias. What we question, however, is the way the psychodynamic conceptual system has evolved a common etiology with a single explanatory model for all of the neurotic behavior patterns. This consolidation is the source of our problem. In an attempt to separate out the behavioral (objective) and the psychodynamic (subjective) aspects, we will present descriptions of the behaviors and look at them from the two viewpoints. We will appeal to psychological research to help us in evaluating the differences.

To begin our study of the neuroses, we need first to examine their presumed central motivator, as DSM-II describes it—anxiety.

The Concept of Anxiety

Laughlin (1956) defines anxiety as "the apprehensive tension of uneasiness which stems from the anticipation of imminent danger, in which the source is largely unknown or unrecognized" (p. 8). He contrasts this anxiety response to an internal threat with *fear*, which is an "emotional response to an . . . external threat or danger." Whereas fear is useful in mobilizing our resources to meet the known threat, anxiety is an excessive reaction to a hidden danger, without focus or direction. Our major problem in studying anxiety, however, is that we cannot directly specify, elicit, and observe its elements, as good research demands.

Psychodynamic View of the Neuroses

Most likely, when you think of neuroses, you think first of defense mechanisms. In fact, this popular notion of the neuroses as "defense mechanisms" sums up their causes and their overall function in the psychodynamic view. Defense against what? Anxiety, says DSM-II. But where does the anxiety come from? Psychodynamic analysts suggest we look at people's earliest years for unresolved problems in the process of their development: disruptions in relations with parents or siblings, disturbing treatment by parents and peers, frustrating experiences in expressing and satisfying impulses and desires, and so on. In short, they theorize that the developing personality is unable to deal effectively with the problems that it meets at certain stages. In each instance, it makes some limited adjustment, a partial solution in order to protect itself from injury.

Note that the neurosis itself does not necessarily emerge at the point where the conflict occurred. The conflicts that are provoked during the early stages of sexual and social development are, as we pointed out, partially repressed. This incomplete repression sets the scene for the subsequent emergence of the neurosis when the adult can no longer tolerate the still unresolved impulses and frustrations. In some cases, disturbing events in adult life precipitate the neurosis. A broken romance, sexual problems, loss of a job, aging, death of a loved one—all are examples of life stresses that can provoke neurotic behavior in the person who harbors unresolved conflicts from childhood.

Some psychodynamic theorists consider neurosis and psychosis as states in a continuous process. Kubie (1958) proposes a chain model in which frustrated drives lead to neurosis. The process builds up as the disturbances become aggravated, causing psychosis in the vulnerable personality.

One clear distinction frequently made between neurotics and psychotics relates to their awareness and discomfort about what is happening to them. Neurotics are presumed to be aware of their problems to the point where they show great concern over them. They are anxious about their troubles, dissatisfied with their lives, always trying to do better. On the other hand, psychotics are thought to be unaware of their problems, detached from reality except for tangential, distorted relationships, and pose a potential danger to themselves and to others. Psychotics have escaped from their torments; neurotics are obsessed with theirs.

Behavioral View of Neurotic Behavior

In Chapter 3, we considered both respondent and operant behavioral approaches and some principles common to both. The respondent theorists find the concept of anxiety a useful one. They view anxiety as an autonomic response of the organism. In contrast, the operant theorists consider the concept of anxiety so confusing that they tend to avoid its use whenever possible. While they agree that anxiety definitely occurs, they think of it as a "package," or system, too all-encompassing to be usable in their treatment techniques. This group finds it difficult to deal with a complex autonomic response common to all sufferers. They prefer to specify a particular complex of observable components that can be treated individually.

In a report of a series of experiments with animals Wolpe (1952) describes the *respondent* behavior position. Wolpe maintains that anxiety is a learned behavior that can be relieved by conditioning procedures. He reviews experiments by Pavlov (1927) and others, who induced severe anxiety behaviors in dogs and cats by compelling the animals to make increasingly difficult discriminations of shapes, tones, and other indicators as conditioned stimuli for eating. When the animals became confused by the similar stimuli, they developed neurotic behaviors.

Wolpe also describes the effects of noxious stimuli—noise, pain, and electric shock—in producing neuroses. He conditioned cats to eat at a food box when a buzzer (conditioned response) sounded. After a number of training trials, the cats responding to the buzzer received strong shocks as they approached the food box. This treatment caused the cats to howl, tremble, spit, and claw the cage. Wolpe identifies these behaviors as neurotic. Even when the cats were not shocked, they continued to show these behaviors inside the cage. Furthermore, they refused to eat, even when deprived of food for several days. The sound of the buzzer intensified the neurotic behaviors. When the experimenter presented the food in his hand away from the shock cage, the cats gradually overcame their inhibition and began to eat, with decreasing signs of anxiety. Eventually, they were returned to the cage, where they continued to eat freely at the food box. Wolpe considers the persistence of the inhibition without the noxious stimuli as evidence of a learning process. Learning is indicated further by the extinction of the inhibition by hand feeding. Wolpe concludes that the anxiety response can be learned through exposure to noxious stimuli while in a confined situation.

The *operant* theorists shy away from the use of the term "neurosis" for the same reason they avoid "anxiety." Because they view each individual's behavior patterns as the result of his or her unique social reinforcement (Bandura, 1969), they are unable to lump behaviors into a syndrome that forms an illness category. They reason that a unique pattern emerges from each combination of learning events. To understand such a behavior pattern, we must make a *functional analysis* of the person's behavior. It would be helpful if we could know the historical learning events that created the abnormal behavior, but this is often difficult or even impossible. At any rate, these events are primarily of theoretical interest, since operant behaviorists address their modification therapy exclusively to the present, observable behaviors and the stimuli maintaining those behaviors.

Types of Neurotic Reactions

Although we are uncomfortable with the DSM-II listing of the neuroses, it does provide a convenient structure for a discussion of the various behavior patterns that are of interest in the study of abnormal psychology.

We will first give a description of each of the more important behaviors, and then examine them from the psychodynamic perspective on etiology and treatment and from the behavioral viewpoint on analysis and treatment. Finally, we will survey pertinent research on the behavior. In so doing, we will see the traditional formulations, the emerging approaches, and the future prospects visible in current research. The research examples will give us both a better insight into the problems and a look at research methods in the field of abnormal psychology.

Anxiety Reaction

Behavioral Description

Anxiety is a pervasive, persistently recurring sense of dread and unrelieved apprehension. Sometimes the anxiety is related to a particular life situation—unsatisfactory performance on the job, a shaky marriage, financial burdens. More often, however, it has no specific reference. We call this condition "free-floating" anxiety. Visible behaviors include jumpiness, irritability, sweaty forehead and palms, a flushed face, pacing about, nervous twitching, and a generally troubled expression. The victim may feel muscular tension, throbbing headache, stomach sensitivity ("butterflies"), heartburn, "gas" pressure, neck and back pain, mouth dryness, difficulty in breathing, nervous tremors, and heart palpitation.

Rapid, deep breathing may cause hyperventilation, with associated dizziness, tingling sensations, and contraction of the fingers. Each sufferer will have his or her own array of symptoms and mode of onset.

William James, the eminent psychologist, described his walking nightmare of anxiety in these vivid phrases:

The universe was changed for me altogether. I awoke morning after morning with a horrible dread in the pit of my stomach, and with a sense of the insecurity of life that I never knew before, and that I have never felt since. It was like a revelation; and although the immediate feelings passed away, the experience has made me sympathetic with the morbid feelings of others ever since. It gradually faded, but for months, I was unable to go out into the dark alone.

In general I dreaded to be left alone. I remember wondering how other people could live, how I myself had ever lived, so unconscious of that pit of insecurity beneath the surface of my life. (James, 1920)

The above is a description of *chronic anxiety*. Chronic anxiety is usually punctuated by attacks of acute anxiety (Box 8-1).

Acute anxiety sometimes occurs as a sudden, isolated event, but is more often experienced as a series of intense, periodic attacks in a setting of chronic anxiety. Most of the behaviors of acute anxiety are the same as those we have described for the chronic condition, although the acute reactions are usually more severe. In addition, the suddenness of the onset is so frightening that it may cause sheer panic, which intensifies the behaviors, especially the autonomic reactions—fast, pounding heartbeat; sweating and flushing; gastric disturbance.

Aside from the specific physical symptoms, clients report an overwhelming sense of impending doom, a nameless dread that is perhaps the most distressing part of the attack.

Psychodynamic Approach

The *psychodynamic etiology* of anxiety neurosis is traced to problems of inadequate ego

Box 8-1 Will This Happen to Your Professor Tomorrow?

A Case of Acute Anxiety

I was about half an hour into giving a lecture when it suddenly came over me. I had been perfectly well up until that time. There was nothing unusual about the situation, the lecture was the fourth or fifth in a series I was giving to a class I knew, and I had not been worried or concerned about anything before I began. All at once, without any warning, I felt something start up in me. It was as if a sudden, slight impulsion had simultaneously hit my upper chest and head. I was momentarily thrown off balance and felt I was swaying to the left (although I am sure my body did not really move), and I experienced a mild fullness in my throat. I kept on talking, following the text of my lecture, but automatically, without really being aware of what I was saying, since my attention was now focused on what was happening within me. Almost immediately my heart began to race, I broke into a sweat, especially across my forehead, around my eyes and upper lip, and felt flushed in the face and fullness in the front of my head that seemed almost to be an inner confusion. Central to this was a feeling of what I would almost call panic, which seemed to fill my whole awareness. Despite the fact that this was intensely vivid and real, I find it almost impossible to describe it in words. It was a kind of dire apprehension of I know not what, and I felt almost overwhelmingly moved to run, to get away, to escape, lest I collapse then and there.

Cited in Nemiah, J. C. Anxiety: Signal, symptom and syndrome. In S. Arieti and E. B. Brody (Eds.). *The American handbook of psychiatry* (Vol. 3, 2nd ed.) New York: Basic Books, 1974, p. 95. © 1974 by Basic Books.

functioning in dealing with threats from the superego. When driven to express some unacceptable wish—sexual or aggressive—the ego is likely to develop a sense of guilt and a fear of the consequences of expressing the impulse. The threat of punishment by the superego (or by society) causes the ego to repress the impulse. If the repression is not complete, there is danger that the impulse may escape its bounds and expose the ego to shame. The conflict itself is a consequence of unresolved problems in childhood—sexual urges toward parents, etc. In this circumstance, the anxiety warns the ego of the threat posed by the inner conflict.

In addition to the anxieties aroused by the superego threat and the id impulse, there are castration (mutilation or loss of genitals) anxiety and separation anxiety (dating back to childhood fears of parental loss). The following report describes an anxiety reaction precipitated by the recollection of a childhood shock.

A 27-year-old woman entered the hospital complaining of multiple fears. She was too frightened to get on streetcars or buses, to go to the movies, and to go out to supper. She was also afraid that she would not live up to the expectations of her mother, was dubious about her own capabilities, and indicated that her marriage was in difficult straits and that she had previously been separated from her husband for 18 months. She stated that their only son was a bed wetter. In addition, she presented the symptoms of acute anxiety with palpitation, perspiration, dizziness, and shortness of breath caused by the hyperventilation syndrome.

Brief questioning elicited the information that her mother had been a nagging, sadistic person, who unmercifully switched the patient and her brother whenever they failed to obey her command. The father, a mild, subservient individual, had seldom been at home. The patient was a quiet and obedient, though fearful, child, usually timid and retiring, who felt that she must always acquiesce to the wishes of others or be subject to their criticism and withdrawal of affection.

The diagnosis in this case was long-standing anxiety neurosis, associated with the hyperventilation syndrome and a phobic state. The anxiety attacks occurred regularly in situations in which the pa-

tient's husband, mother, or even the doctor did something or said something to arouse in her a fear of separation associated with a wish to retaliate angrily. She could not allow herself to express further criticism and rejections. Although the majority of anxiety attacks were relieved after several months of psychiatric treatment, she was not entirely free of her symptoms until a year of regular visits had elapsed. (Kolb, 1973, p. 407)

Psychodynamic treatment, as described in Chapter 6, seeks the underlying psychodynamic factors in the patient's personality. Throughout the therapy, there is no attempt to treat the symptoms per se, for, according to Freud, why try to eliminate a symptom when the patient will replace it through a process of *symptom substitution*? The personality itself must be analyzed and historic conflicts resolved, thereby removing the roots of the neurotic responses.

Behavioral Approach

As we mentioned earlier, behaviorists see the psychodynamic view of anxiety as misconceived as a bundle of related behaviors emerging from a common origin of psychic conflict. They appeal, instead, to learning models for both the analysis and the treatment of the behaviors themselves.

The initiating factor in the process of developing anxiety behavior is an aversive, or noxious, stimulus. This may be anything from a loud noise in the nursery or an adolescent's sexual embarrassment to a business failure or social rejection.

In addition to such noxious events, Wolpe (1958) suggests that "conflicting action tendencies" may provoke anxiety responses. An aversive event becomes associated with objects or actions that are part of the experience. If the event is sufficiently painful, only one such occurrence may be necessary to establish the response. Thus the unpleasant reaction is learned in a perfectly natural way through association with the aversive event. Notice how the behaviorists externalize the cause. In the psychodynamic model, the cause is internal.

The rest of the process involves generalization of the response to other objects and events ("cues") that bear some similarity to the original stimulus. Thus a child who had been punished for some sex play might generalize the anxiety response to all sex-related acts, however innocuous (like holding hands), and eventually to the word "sex" itself. Direct experience with the negative stimulus is not necessary. Repeated warnings of attack by animals may cause a child to react with anxiety to the sight of a dog or other animal, without ever having been bitten.

Operant conditioning requires that the subject initiate the response, which is then reinforced. Miller (1973) describes the reinforcement of an anxiety response that operates to avoid contact with an aversive stimulus. For example, not attending social events because of embarrassment in public eliminates such embarrassment, reinforcing the social avoidance behavior.

Behavioral treatment aims at modifying the learned behaviors. A supportive client-therapist relationship may sometimes be all that is needed to allay anxieties. Where possible, modification of conditions that provoke anxiety reactions accomplishes the avoidance benefit that Miller demonstrated—with the result that the person no longer feels the need to avoid the particular situation entirely. Suggestion and relaxation exercises are effective measures in many cases.

Direct application of learning theory involves modification of the symptomatic behaviors. Several techniques have been used with success. As we described in Chapter 7, *deconditioning*, or *desensitization*, is a procedure in which clients work their way up through a hierarchy of environmental stimuli of increasing anxiety-producing potential. At each level, they learn to associate the noxious stimulus with a nonanxious reaction, until they have been desensitized to the entire hierarchy, which loses its power to provoke anxiety reactions. Because of the complex of behaviors in an anxiety neurosis, several hierarchies have to be negotiated in this way in order to reduce the general response.

Another promising method is *anxiety management training* (AMT) (Suinn and Richardson, 1971). Like desensitization, the AMT client is conditioned to link anxiety-producing cues with new responses that inhibit the former anxiety responses. But the AMT client is *made* anxious and then relaxed, as opposed to desensitization, which avoids the anxiety by means of gradual exposure.

Unlike desensitization and AMT, which use relaxation as the incompatible response, *assertion training* uses a bold, confident attitude as the response that is incompatible with anxiety. The method, which we outlined in Chapter 7, assumes that a deficiency in assertiveness is the maladaptive behavior that must be corrected. Unlike AMT, assertion training deals with the specific behavior involved in the anxiety.

Research

Marks and Lader (1973) did a statistical study of prevalence, comparative frequency of behavior, and outcome of anxiety states. They estimated that anxiety states occur in between 2 and 4.7 percent of the normal population in the United States and Britain. The proportion is substantially higher among psychiatric outpatients—between 6 and 27 percent of all cases.

In general, two-thirds of clients with anxiety states are women, but there is no way to know if they experience more anxiety or simply admit it more readily. Among clients in therapy, the gender distribution is equal (which may indicate that men tend to acknowledge anxiety only when it is severe enough to need treatment).

Marks and Lader also found certain abnormal physiological reactions associated with anxiety (Table 8–1). Pain, cold, muscular effort, noise, and anticipation are among the stimuli that produce abnormal reactions in anxiety patients. These reactions include significant changes in pulse rate, respiration volume, work performance, skin conductance, oxygen consumption, and withdrawal reactions. The reasons for these exceptional physiological responses are not known.

Table 8-1 Percentage of Patients with Anxiety Neurosis Who Showed Particular Symptoms[1]

Symptom	Patients	Controls
Palpitation	97 (90)	9
Tires easily	95 (78)	19
Breathlessness	90 (75)	13
Nervousness	88 (99)	27
Chest pain	85 (—)[2]	10
Sighing	79 (20)	16
Dizziness	78 (55)	16
Faintness	70 (20)	12
Apprehension	61 (80)	3
Headache	58 (65)	26
Paresthesia (tingling)	58 (25)	7
Weakness	56 (65)	3
Trembling	54 (70)	17
Breath unsatisfactory	53 (75)	4
Insomnia	53 (48)	4
Unhappiness	50 (—)	2
Shakiness	47 (70)	16
Fatigue	45 (76)	6
Sweating	45 (62)	33
Fear of death	42 (—)	2
Smothering	40 (28)	4
Syncope	37 (—)	11
Flushes	36 (—)	—
Yawning	35 (—)	14
Pain radiating to left arm	30 (—)	2
Vascular throbbing	29 (—)	1
Dry mouth	25 (—)	1
Nervous chill	24 (—)	—
Nightmares	18 (40)	9
Vomiting and diarrhoea	14 (—)	0
Anorexia	12 (28)	3
Panting	8 (—)	—

[1] All figures refer to patients of Wheeler et al. (1950) except figures in parentheses which refer to 50 patients of Miles et al. (1951).
[2] (—), Not cited.

Adapted from Marks, I., and Lader, M. Anxiety states (anxiety neuroses): A review. *The Journal of Nervous and Mental Disease*, 1973, 156, 3–18. © 1973 by Williams & Wilkins.

Beck, Laude, and Bohnert (1974) investigated the ideation (thoughts and visualizations) of a number of acute and chronic anxiety neurotics. Using a structured interview technique, they found a consistent pattern of visualizing personal danger just before an anxiety attack occurs. In a majority of cases, the anxiety reaction was brought on by a specific event (social confrontations, physical distress, being alone at night). Many of the subjects habitually fantasized themselves in perilous, frightening, or humiliating situations. The common practice of visualizing themselves in danger suggests a therapeutic procedure for anxiety-prone clients: desensitization of the clients to the situations they visualize by means of the conditioning techniques we have discussed.

Phobic Reactions

Behavioral Description

Phobias are manifestations of anxiety. Unlike general anxiety, however, phobias focus on a particular object, situation, or body function. The phobic response is intense and acute—it surges to panic level as soon as the object is sighted or experienced. Box 8–2 presents a partial list of the principal phobias.

While mild phobias are probably common, especially among children (remember your fear of the dark?), the severe phobic neuroses that seriously interfere with normal living make up only a small proportion of the abnormal behaviors treated. Their effects can be crippling, as we see in this case of agoraphobia (fear of open spaces), reported by Janet, the famous nineteenth-century French psychiatrist:

He was about 25, when there started what he himself called "the trouble with spaces." He was crossing the Place de la Concorde (alone, it should be noted) when he felt a strange sensation of dread. His breathing became rapid and he felt as if he were suffocating; his heart was beating violently and his legs were limp as if half-paralyzed. He could go neither forwards nor backwards, and he had to exert a tremendous effort, bathed in sweat, to reach the other side of the square. From the time of that first episode on he took a great dislike to the Place de la Concorde and decided that he would not risk going there again alone. However, a short while after the same sensation of anxiety recurred on the Invalides Bridge, and then in a street, which though it was narrow, seemed long and was quite steep. . . .

After this unpleasant experience, he was not allowed to go out alone, which was exactly what he wanted, since his attacks could thus be controlled. Whenever he came to a square, he would begin to tremble and breathe heavily, develop tics and repeat the following absurd phrase: "Mama, Rata, bibi, bitaquo, I'm going to die." His wife had to hold him tightly by his arm, and then he would calm down and cross the square without further incident. His wife has to accompany him absolutely everywhere now, even when he goes to the toilet. (Janet, 1903)

Notice how the phobia spreads, characteristically, from the particular open space to all spaces. Of course, the fear of the object or situation can be allayed by avoidance. The avoidance of the feared object is central in the psychodynamic interpretation of phobic reactions in general.

Psychodynamic Approach

The *psychodynamic etiology* of phobic neurosis owes much to Freud's interpretation (1909/1955) of the case of Little Hans, a 5-year-old boy who had an inordinate fear of horses. Freud hypothesized that the boy had displaced his fear of his father, against whom he had Oedipal and resulting aggressive impulses. He was afraid of retaliative punishment from his father. This was unacceptable to the ego and therefore repressed and then displaced onto horses.

In the story of Little Hans, we can see the phobia from the psychodynamic viewpoint. There is a failure to fully repress the unacceptable impulse. The patient detaches the anxiety from the threatening object or situation, and attaches it to some other symbolic object or situation that is avoidable. This act of displace-

Box 8-2 The More Common Phobias

By Their Technical Names, with Their Objects and Derivations Indicated:

1. Acrophobia: Height (Gr., *acra*, heights or summits)
2. Agoraphobia: Open spaces (Gr., *agora*, marketplace, the place of assembly)
3. Ailurophobia: Cats (Gr., *ailouros*, cat)
4. Anthophobia: Flowers (Gr., *anthos*, flower)
5. Anthropophobia: People (Gr., *anthropos*, man, generically)
6. Aquaphobia: Water (Lat., *aqua*, water)
7. Astraphobia: Lightning (Gr., *asterope*, lightning)
8. Brontophobia: Thunder (Gr., *bronte*, thunder)
9. Claustrophobia: Closed spaces (Lat., *claustrum*, bar, bolt, or lock)
10. Cynophobia: Dogs (Gr., *cynas*, dog)
11. Equinophobia: Horses (Lat., *equinis*, horse)
12. Herpetophobia: Lizards or reptiles (Gr., *herpetos*, a creeping or crawling thing)
13. Keraunophobia: Thunder (Gr., *keraunos*, thunderbolt)
14. Mysophobia: Dirt, germs, contamination (Gr., *mysos*, uncleanliness of body or mind; abomination or defilement)
15. Numerophobia: A number or numbers (Lat., *numero*, number)
16. Nyctophobia: Darkness or night (Gr., *nyx*, night)
17. Ophidiophobia: Snakes (Gr., *ophis*, snake or serpent)
18. Pyrophobia: Fire (Gr., *pyr*, fire)
19. Self-confining phobia. Phobically imposed area or spatial restrictions.
20. Zoophobia: Animals (Gr., *zoos*, animal)

Most Commonly Feared Objects:

Airplanes	Dark	Insects	Senility
Aloneness	Death	Knives	Sex
Anger	Dirt	Lightning	Sharp objects
Animals	Disease	Lizards	Snakes
Arguments	Doctors	Medicine	Solitude
Atomic explosions	Dogs	Men	Spiders
Birds	Fights	Mice	Strangers
Blood	Fire	Night	Syphilis
Boats	Flowers	Occupations	Thunderstorms
Cancer	Genitals	Old age	Trains
Cats	Germs	Open spaces	Travel
Childbirth	Heights	People	Venereal disease
Closed spaces, confinement	Horses	Poison	Vermin
Cosmic phenomena	Hospitals	Poliomyelitis	War
(Planetary collision, etc.)	Illness	Rats	Water
Crowds	Insanity	Rodents	Women

From Laughlin, H. P. *The neuroses in clinical practice.* Philadelphia: Saunders, 1956. © 1956, W. B. Saunders Company.

ment presents some curious relationships between the phobia and its source. Fenichel (1954) offers some symbolic interpretations of phobic masking of threatening impulses. For example, street phobia is related to exhibitionistic urges, acrophobia (fear of heights) to fantasies of erection, claustrophobia (fear of closed spaces) to a desire to return to the womb.

Psychodynamic treatment is based on this concept of symbolic displacement. The first step is to trace the phobic symbolism to its neurotic origin—the intrapsychic conflict between the impulse of the libido and the ego defenses. This turns out to be a baffling search that may not yield to analytic techniques. In order to gain direct insight into the source of the phobia, the patient is sometimes induced to enter the phobic situation. A further objective of the "immersion" process is quite similar to behavior relaxation therapy, although without the formal procedures. By experiencing the phobic sensation repeatedly, with support from the analyst, the patient gains confidence from successfully passing the test without harm. Muscular relaxation is encouraged, by hypnosis in some difficult cases, to reduce the anxiety to a manageable level.

Behavioral Approach

Behavioral analysis of phobic neuroses takes its cues from both classical and operant conditioning theories. You will remember from Chapter 3 the case of Little Albert described by Watson and Rayner (1920). Instead of attributing phobias to some internal conflict, as Freud did in the case of Little Hans, they demonstrated that fear could be a conditioned response. Little Albert's phobia lasted long after it had been conditioned. According to respondent theories, however, it should have become extinguished over time.

Operant conditioning explains the persistence of the phobia by reference to avoidance behavior. The phobic anxiety motivates the subject to avoid the aversive, fear-inducing stimulus. This reduces the anxiety, as we indicated earlier. The removal of the fear-inducing aversive stimulus, which acts as a negative

reinforcer, continues to reinforce the phobic behavior by relieving the anxiety.

Still another behavioral route to phobia, also mentioned earlier, is the acquisition of phobias by children through modeling adult phobic behaviors (Bandura, 1969). Seeing a model (such as a parent) react to a stimulus with fear induces fear toward that stimulus in the child. That fear is then maintained by the avoidance procedures just described.

Behavioral treatment is based on principles we have discussed in Chapter 7. Two prominent behavioral techniques are desensitization and flooding implosion. We have described the desensitization procedure earlier in this chapter as a treatment for general anxiety, but it is more directly applied to phobias. Geer (1964) reports the successful treatment of a 17-year-old girl's excessive fear of lice, which was interfering with her family relations and her social life. The experimenter used the technique of *reciprocal inhibition*, in which relaxation, both muscular and mental, is set up as the incompatible response competing with the phobic reaction. First, the patient was trained in initiating deep relaxation at will. Then she was trained in generating clear visualizations of offensive scenes. During the conditioning process, she visualized a sequence of situations, starting with the relatively mild "writing the words bug and lice" and progressing through a hierarchy of increasingly distressing situations, until she was able to visualize a stranger combing the patient's hair with the stranger's comb. In each situation, the patient visualized the scene several times until she could do so without anxiety during three successive presentations. A three-month follow-up study showed that the lice phobia did not recur even on occasions when the patient was exposed to possible infestation.

The *flooding* technique exposes the patient to the actual phobic object or experience for periods of up to several hours at a time. *Implosion* is basically the same as flooding, except that visualization of the situation is used, not the actual object or experience. The therapist gives the patient support during the sessions. Good results with these two techniques have been reported. While the psychodynamic approach of immersion is meant to relieve some internal conflict, flooding and implosion are simply meant to relieve phobic behavior.

We noted how children sometimes acquire phobias by modeling adult phobic behaviors. Bandura, Blanchard, and Ritter (1969) describe the procedure of modeling and guided participation in the treatment of phobias. The client watches the model go through the steps of desensitization, and then the client is conducted through the sequence by the therapist.[1]

Research

There is some evidence that most phobias will "go away" without therapeutic intervention. Agras, Chapin, and Oliveau (1972) followed 30 untreated phobic subjects for five years. The study was conducted initially by questionnaire, then by psychiatric interview. At the end of five years, all of the subjects under 20 were either symptom-free (40% of total) or significantly improved (60% of total), while of those over 20, only 6 percent were symptom-free and 37 percent improved. Other findings indicated that generalized phobias had a poorer prognosis than specific phobias. The degree of fearfulness was also a good predictor of outcome; those low in fear showed substantially greater improvement than those high in fear. Perhaps the most impressive conclusion of the study is that the rate of improvement for untreated adult phobics (43%) fell between the corresponding rates for treated patients in two other studies (37% and 55%).

A counterexample to the finding of negligible effect of treatment is provided by Razani (1974), who compared drug therapy with standard desensitization procedure. He divided a sample of five people suffering a variety of phobias into groups of three and two. The first received drug treatment for five sessions, followed by standard desensitization for five more

sessions. The sequence was reversed for the other group. (This technique is called a "crossover" experiment.) The patients were rated by themselves and by the therapist for phobic severity before treatment and after the fifth and tenth sessions. The result was that both kinds of treatment were effective in reducing phobic reactions from panic level to a tendency to avoid the phobic situation. The drug treatment appeared to be somewhat more effective than the standard desensitization. However, neither method reduced the phobic response to a point where the subjects could approach the phobic situation without uneasiness. More sessions might have effected greater improvement. Clearly, enough benefit from the treatments was realized to make a big difference to phobics whose lives are seriously hampered by their fear.

Hypochondriacal Reaction

Behavioral Description

Most of us can give a pretty good description of a hypochondriac's behavior. There seems to be one in almost every family, and the behavior is quite explicit and audible. The common manifestation is a morbid and absorbing concern over one's physical health. Hypochondriacs are often hypersensitive to certain body functions and signs, such as pulse rate. In their single-minded attention to body functions and disorders, hypochondriacs withdraw from the problems of the external world. While hypochondriacs seem to have an exaggerated fear of disease, they seldom actually have a serious illness.

Some authorities question whether hypochondriacal behavior is neurosis. One authority (Kenyon, 1965) reports a study in which only 3 out of 255 patients with hypochondriacal behaviors had no other, broader syndrome. Some investigators, however, have found the condition diagnosable as a separate entity. In studies using the hypochondria scale of the MMPI, there was a significant discrimination between hypochondriacs and normals. There is a question, however, about the involvement of

---

[1] For those who wish more information, the Bandura et al. report presents a detailed description and evaluation of the modeling procedure.

"The undertaker wants to know when you'll sign the certificate on that hypochondriac?" (*Ed Arno.*)

other traits (e.g., hysteria, depression) that seem to parallel and, possibly, include hypochondria.

Psychodynamic Approach

Fenichel (1945) offers an exposition of the *psychodynamic etiology* of hypochondria. He followed Freud's formulation of the patient's withdrawal of the libido from the outside world. The limited libido energy is used in the patient's hypochondriacal defenses against the anxiety-provoking threat. Fenichel saw the behavior as an intermediate stage between hysterical and psychotic reactions.

Psychodynamic treatment of hypochondria takes the characteristic course of seeking the source of the problem in some early conflict. This unresolved conflict has left the individual less able to cope with current life stresses and thus tempted by neurotic solutions to current conflict. Since hypochondriacs have attached their reactions to such explicit, physical ailments, they often resist efforts to uncover more remote, psychological causes.

Behavioral Approach

Behavioral analysis focuses more on the hypochondriac's behavior rather than on its symbolic meaning. The most obvious observation, from the behavioral standpoint, is that the attention gained by hypochondriacs in the course of their continual complaints and displays of suffering reinforces the behavior. Hypochondriacal behavior can also be seen as the result of deficits in other spheres of life. Focusing on the operation of one's body can be one result of a lack of interest in other external stimuli. This process suggests previous extinction of outer-directed behavior, leaving the individuals with only the internal feedback to respond to. Behavioral treatment would therefore try to reestablish external sources of reinforcement.

Research

Kenyon (1965) reviews a number of psychological, personality, and clinical studies of hypochondria. One study using the MMPI (McKinley and Hathaway, 1940), found that while there is substantial overlap between hypochondriacs and normal subjects, the two groups are significantly different. Interestingly, they discovered a similarity between the psychological traits of hypochondriacs and hysterics, who will be discussed in the next section.

One of the more systematic and sophisticated studies of "hypochondriasis" used factor analysis of principal components to develop a definition of the neurosis (Bianchi, 1973). The findings indicated that the chief components are: (1) inhibition of anger, with maternal over-solicitude, (2) anxiety leading to a disease phobia, (3) psychogenic pain, especially in sensitive women who are subject to much "unnecessary" surgery, (4) somatic preoccupation, generally more evident in men, who play the role of "self-medicating physician," and (5) a disease conviction component, demonstrated by a certainty of disease in the face of contrary evidence.

Hysterical Reaction—Conversion Type

Behavioral Description

Hysteria is classified into two types: *conversion* and *dissociative*. We will discuss conversion hysteria in this section, and dissociative hysteria in the next.

The conversion hysteric has actual physical symptoms, but without any organic explanation for the symptoms. DSM-II defines the conversion type as a disorder in which "the special senses or voluntary system are affected, causing such symptoms as blindness, deafness, esthesias, . . . paralyses. . . . Often the patient shows an inappropriate lack of concern or *la belle indifférence* about these symptoms" (American Psychiatirc Association, pp. 39–40).

Conversion hysteria occurs mostly among females. It manifests itself as motor or sensory disturbances, and it may simulate or complicate most of the physical diseases. In Chapter 9, we will discuss psychophysiologic disorders, which are physical problems resulting from psychological stresses. In psychophysiologic disorders, there is usually tissue change representing the damaged system. In hysteria, there is loss of function but no physical change to the organ system. The hysterically paralyzed individual's legs are perfectly normal, and he or she can eventually walk again.

The motor disturbances of conversion hysteria are seen in abnormal movements and comprise a variety of tremors, tics, jerks, convulsive writhing and thrashing of the limbs, and a walk resembling a drunken stagger. Paralysis can affect all of the extremities, singly or in combination, but again there is no muscle degeneration or nervous disorder. In fact, the pattern of the paralysis does not follow the effects of damage to the nervous system. Rather, it mimics the way nonmedically trained individuals think paralysis would affect the involved member. Often, patients appear to be completely unconcerned with the paralysis or numbness. This is referred to as "la belle indifférence." Janet (1907) described the case of a young girl who, some days after a serious accident in which she badly cut her right hand, began to complain of numbness in it. The doctors examined her and found that there was indeed a physical reason for the numbness. In examining her, however, they also discovered that she was hysterically numb on her entire left side, a fact that she never even mentioned!

Anesthesia (numbness) is the most common sensory disturbance in the conversion reaction. "Stocking and glove anesthesias" are examples of the localization of the condition according to personal notions instead of neural patterns. In such cases, the lack of feeling is in an area approximating a glove on the hand or a stocking on the foot. However, there is no such pattern to the nerves and anesthesia would never form that pattern naturally.

Inga S., a thirty-four-year-old married mother of four, was brought to the outpatient clinic of a large eastern hospital by her husband. They had been living in a small home in a lower middle class neighborhood. . . .

All of her pregnancies were painful and difficult, and two unplanned children served to reduce Inga's faith in contraceptive devices. In recent years she had acceded to having intercourse only to please her husband, and from the onset of her symptoms had not had relations with him at all.

Inga's symptoms dated back to eight weeks prior to her hospitalization. Her husband was out late playing cards that night. Soon after retiring, she noted the onset of a numbing sensation in her feet which gradually rose up both legs as far as her stomach. This was accompanied by heart palpitation and difficulty getting her breath. Her mouth felt dry and she became nauseated. Very quickly after the numbness began, it changed to stiffness of her lower extremities. Inga awoke one of her children who summoned a neighbor, and the latter called an ambulance, which took her to the local hospital. Here she found it difficult to talk because of the dryness of the mouth, and was again nauseated. She remained overnight and returned home the following morning. At this time she felt nauseated and her legs were stiff and weak. She was referred to a private psychiatrist, but couldn't see him because of the expense involved. (Zax and Stricker, 1963, p. 160)

Instead of becoming numb, some conversion hysterics experience a heightened sense of pain. Abdominal pain is a frequent symptom. Sometimes it is reported to be so excruciating that patients become the object of excessive surgery, since the physicians regularly consulted are not oriented toward making a psychological diagnosis. In addition to pain, patients frequently project a full spectrum of physical ailments that are remarkably similar to the real thing. The simulated disorder may be "borrowed" from someone who has a close emotional relationship with the patient. For example, patients might imitate the symptoms of a parent who has recently died or the pains of a wife in labor.

Deafness and blindness are exhibited by some patients, but with peculiar aspects that indicate retention of some of the "lost" function. For example, patients with hysterical blindness in both eyes manage to walk about without aid or accident, and can reach for objects without groping.

Psychodynamic Approach

Typical of the psychodynamic view of the *etiology* of conversion hysteria is Laughlin's definition (1956) of the disorder. He defines conversion as "the unconscious process by which intrapsychic conflicts, which would otherwise give rise to anxiety, instead secure symbolic external expression" (p. 241). He says that individuals transform the ideas that they do not want to think about and their defenses into physical symptoms.

Note that the anxiety-producing ideas are *consciously* put aside, while the process of converting them into physical symptoms is *unconscious*. In other words, the patients are aware of the nature of the undesirable impulses but do not recognize the way in which the internal conflict between the impulses and the superego is worked out in production of physical symptoms.

According to psychoanalysts, repression occurs as a result of misdirected sexual urges in the Oedipal period. The resulting undischarged libidinal energy forces an outlet through another channel. In this case, the outlet is hysteria, which protects the individuals against the discovery of the rejected impulse. In addition, it provides symbolic representations (the physical symptoms) that effectively mask the sexual urge and thus relieve the anxiety by maintaining the repression. We see a clear picture of this process in the case of the mother who feared she would murder her child.

A twenty-six-year-old married mother sought treatment because of a tremendous dragging weakness of her right arm. This was severe enough to result in an inability to do her housework or to care for her eight-month-old daughter. She also reported being so anxious when in the kitchen that she could not remain there. The clinical picture was of the patient as an immature mother. She had been so deprived of love and affection herself that the needs of her child in this direction had become an intolerable burden to her. This resulted in a rejecting attitude toward the child which was communicated to the child intuitively, empathically, and directly.

The response of the child in turn was to become restless, tense, and anxious, and to develop poor sleeping habits and digestive upsets. All of this resulted in an added drain on the mother. Her resentment and hostility toward her child was increased, setting up a vicious circle. The weak arm developed as a final safeguard to awareness of her overwhelming rage. As a result a nurse was hired for the child which helped her avoid the child (and her "murderous" feelings). This arrangement also helped satisfy dependency needs on the part of the mother, who was unable to function on a more mature level because of her own early deprivations of love and affection.

The mother was hostile to the child because she herself never got any real warmth. Her own great need for affection made it less possible for her to tolerate demands on her by another person. The anxiety about the kitchen was found to relate to kitchen knives (potential murder weapons) which were kept there. One cannot easily wield a knife with a paralyzed arm! The symptom symbolically served to reinforce the inhibition of any possible overt physical act in response to her consciously disowned hostile thoughts. (Laughlin, 1956, pp. 255–256)

Laughlin and others speak of conversion hysteria as a kind of "body language" with which the patients communicate their deeper needs. In effect, the patients are calling for attention and, at the same time, expressing their dependence on those around them. Since their pseudo-disabilities are physical, they ex-

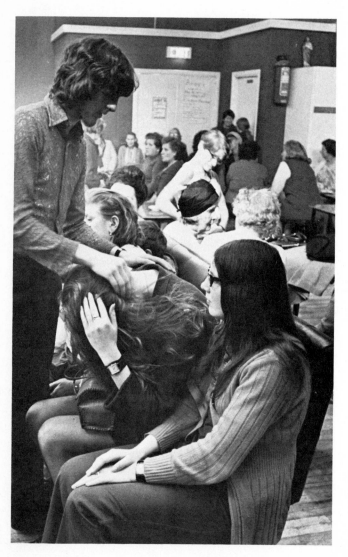

Because it is the ultimate in suggestion, faith healing sometimes demonstrates dramatic effects with conversion hysterics. Unfortunately, such miracle cures are most often transitory. (*Daily Telegraph, Woodfin Camp & Associates.*)

plain and justify themselves to society: the disabilities cannot be brushed aside or treated with contempt. The attention and concern the patients evoke serve to reinforce the symptoms, leading to chronic behavior.

There are other aspects to the etiology of conversion hysteria that are not compatible with the strictly psychoanalytic explanation based on Oedipal conflict. Some cases seem to be direct reactions to environmental stress or a frightful accident (with no physical injury) or an unsympathetic family—none of which is clearly a result of the Oedipal situation or involves symbolism.

The *psychodynamic treatment* of conversion hysteria evolved from Freud's early cases of hysteria. Indeed, psychoanalysis was first developed to deal with the hysterical neuroses. Only later did Freud and others deal with the whole neurotic spectrum. The procedure is aimed at uncovering the psychic problems underlying the conversion reaction.

Suggestion, hypnotism, and faith healing (which is, of course, the ultimate in suggestion) sometimes demonstrate dramatic effects with conversion hysterics. Miracle "cures" are usually transitory, however. Symptoms may return or be replaced by other symptoms.

The psychotherapist's problem here is that, unlike other neuroses, the symptoms are physical conditions that the patients believe are genuine; they are not vague anxieties whose causes need to be investigated.

Behavioral Approach

The *behavioral analysis* of conversion hysteria attaches great importance to the uses and advantages of the "symptoms" to the patients. Practitioners frequently refer to the "secondary gain" that the patient realizes, namely, the direct advantage in punishing an antagonist or in escaping from some distressing situation. The following case presents an explicit example of the use of conversion to resolve an impossible dilemma:

M., a young man who had been a dancer and an acrobat in a circus, enlisted in the army during peace time. Here he found the discipline rigid, his duties irksome, and his experiences monotonous. He longed for travel, excitement, attention, and the opportunity for exhibition enjoyed in his former life. The situation became quite intolerable, but to leave meant that he would be treated as a deserter. A hysterical conversion reaction, induced by two conflicting motives, the one to conform to the requirements of military life, the other to secure escape from a hated situation, provided a solution that permitted him to gain his own end, i.e., to obtain immunity from unpleasant experiences and tasks, and at the same time alleviated his anxiety and enabled him to maintain his self-respect. On arrival at the mental hospital to which he was transferred, he could neither walk nor stand, and his legs were anesthetic to even vigorous prickings by a pin. At the same time, he displayed a significant attitude of unconcern (la belle indifférence) as to his disabilities, although, as far as he was consciously aware, they were complete and incurable. His absence of concern is to be explained by the fact that the penalty was less than the gain, although one must not conclude that this weighing of advantages and disadvantages was at all a matter of conscious reflection. A few months later, the man was discharged from the army on a surgeon's certificate of disability. Soon the suspended motor and sensory functions began to return. Persistent efforts to walk met gradually with success, and in another three months he left the hospital practically well. (Kolb, 1973, p. 418)

Ziegler and Imboden (1962) view conversion hysterics' "body language" as a somatic, symbolic code that the patients employ in enacting a social role. The social role of individuals with an "organic" illness enables them to send out messages of emotional distress. The selection of behaviors reflects the patients' previous experience with illnesses and their relationship with others who have had such illnesses. The "sick" role is an important one in our society, for it allows the individuals certain privileges in not meeting the usual social requirements. Being physically sick can thus become a solution for some individuals caught in what are to them insurmountable conflicts.

The *behavioral treatment* of conversion

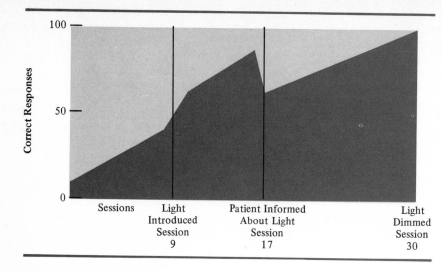

Figure 8-1 Experimental analysis of hysterical blindness. (*Adapted from Parry-Jones, W., Santer-Weststrate, H. C., and Crawley, R. C. Behaviour therapy in a case of hysterical blindness.* Behaviour Research and Therapy, *1970, 8, 79–85.*)

hysteria sometimes demands ingenuity in designing an appropriate technique. Parry-Jones, Santer-Westrate, and Crawley (1970) treated a poorly educated 47-year-old woman. She progressively lost her vision, although no physical or neural injury could be found. Her family claimed she could see, yet she walked with a white cane and tried to learn Braille. In her treatment, she was started on a time-judgment task in which she was to press a button at what she thought were 20-second intervals. She found counting helped her keep track of the time. After some trials, during which a buzzer reinforced correct judgments, a cuing light was lit at intervals of 18 to 21 seconds. Although she said she could not see the bulb, she abandoned the counting and her performance improved markedly (Figure 8–1). Subsequent changes in the task included increasingly difficult discriminations of lighted shapes and then rapidly presented letters, numbers, and simple drawings. At this point, she remarked on the marvel of her returning vision. However, she did not generalize her visual ability outside the laboratory.

The treatment continued, with the requirement that she describe objects in the room, including magazine pictures and Ror-schach shapes. She was given strong reinforcement by the hospital staff for her miraculous recovery. A two-year follow-up found her fully sighted and employed. The experimenters themselves raise the question of how much of the recovery may be due to the special attention the patient received. They point to the gradual improvement in her visual performance as evidence of the effect of the behavioral treatment.

Assuming that "secondary gain" reinforcement was a motive, Liebson (1969) undertook to modify conversion behavior by applying operant learning techniques in the case of a 47-year-old man who had experienced pain and weakness in his legs, accompanied by attacks of giddiness. His condition had forced him to give up his job. Psychotherapy, milieu treatment, and drugs all had failed to improve the behavior. Liebson set up a program of monetary rewards as reinforcers for performance of specific tasks, which were organized in a pattern designed to shape the patient's behavior by successive approximations (see Chapter 3). Seven months later, the patient had progressed from a two-day-a-week work schedule to five days, and was still performing satisfactorily six months later.

Research

There has been a persistent effort among practitioners and researchers to identify and describe the "hysterical personality," that is, the combination of traits that predispose people to hysterical behavior when life gets too difficult.

Slavney and McHugh (1974) conducted a controlled study of psychiatric inpatients with "hysterical personality" diagnoses, rating them on various factors against a control group of patients not diagnosed as hysterical personalities. They quote the DSM-II diagnosis of hysterical personality: "These behavior patterns are characterized by excitability, emotional instability, overreactivity, and self-dramatization. The self-dramatization is always attention-seeking and often seductive. . . . These personalities are also immature, self-centered, often vain, and usually dependent on others" (p. 43).

The researchers studied two groups of patients, each consisting of 28 women and 4 men. The mean age of subjects was 27 years. The experimental group was formed of patients who were diagnosed as conversion hysterics. The demographic and family history data were similar for the experimental and control groups. There was no difference between the groups in frequency of serious illness or surgery. The record of suicide attempts was more heavily weighted for the experimental patients (52%) than for the controls (16%). Fewer experimental patients had been prescribed antidepressant drugs than the control group. In short, the principal differences between the hysterical and control groups were the hysterical group's higher frequency of suicide attempts and overly dramatic manner. No other differences were significant. Slavney and McHugh conclude that the hysterical personality is not well defined in actual fact. This compromises the diagnosis and treatment of such patients.

An interesting extension of the hysterical phenomenon is reported by Kerckhoff and Back (1968). They reviewed and analyzed the behavior of a large number of female factory workers who were frightened into a state of *mass hysteria* by the information that an infestation of June bugs was causing sickness among the workers. The news had the effect of an epidemic as the hysteria spread through the factory. Instead of germs, the agent of contagion was a cognitive belief. Kerckhoff and Back set forth a number of postulates for conditions and relationships affecting the speed and pervasiveness of the spread of contagion in such situations. Individual characteristics, like suggestibility and social needs, determine the victims, while the urgent need for action coupled with the demonstrated action (hysteria) of others facilitates the response of becoming "sick from the bug infection." It would be unwise to draw conclusions about hysterical personality from this mass experience, since the common reaction and the relationships with co-workers introduce factors not ordinarily present in the individual hysterical situation.

Hysterical Reaction—Dissociative Type

Behavioral Description

Dissociative reactions are psychologically caused disturbances of memory and consciousness. Although most of them are relatively rare, the dissociative hysteria states provide some of the most fascinating cases in the psychiatric literature. The examples are so intriguing that they have been the subjects of newspaper articles, popular books, and motion pictures. As a consequence, most of the public is familiar with such terms as somnambulism, amnesia, and multiple personality, which are among the diverse manifestations of dissociative reactions.

Somnambulism literally means sleepwalking, but as a term from abnormal psychology it should not be confused with the simple act of walking in one's sleep. Somnambulism episodes may occur during either waking or sleeping states. They are observed as a detachment from the immediate situation and a total preoccupation with some private matter. In a sense, they are a form of hallucinatory experience. Recovery of consciousness is usually sudden and spontaneous.

Amnesia is the general label for "loss of memory," which may result from brain damage or psychological repression. The memory loss varies in scope from the selective forgetting of certain life events or subjects to the blanking out of extended periods or the total erasure of the entire past life of the patient. We will not spend time on organic amnesia, since it can be explained fully in neurophysiological terms as the consequence of physical shock or brain tissue deterioration (from aging, alcoholism, etc.). The emotional, or psychological, types of amnesia are properly called "dissociative." Although amnesics suffer memory loss, they are usually aware of some missing segment in their memory, the contents of which are effectively blocked from recall.

Lest we consider amnesia a completely pathological process, it must be noted that selective forgetting is a useful and even necessary ability for normal living. Certain painful experiences can interfere with appropriate attitudes and behavior, and are best dismissed from consciousness. In this connection, many women report an inability to recall the agony of a previous, difficult childbirth when they contemplate another pregnancy. Sleep is seen as a kind of temporary amnesia that gives respite from what could otherwise become an overpowering pile-up of stressful events.

Stories of *multiple personalities* existing in the same body invariably excite the imagination. A number of classic cases are cited in the psychiatric literature. The concept of "alternating personality" was first identified by a Boston physician (later, psychiatrist), Morton Prince (1906), who described a patient who he called "Sally Beauchamp," a woman with three characters: "the saint, the devil, the woman." Each of the conflicting personalities is insulated from the others, although one of them—in Sally's case, the "devil"—may be aware of the existence of the other personalities, while the latter are unaware of the former. Transitions between the personalities are sudden and dramatic. When one of the personalities is domi-

nant, the person pursues a career and a life style appropriate to that character. Occasionally when an abrupt transition occurs, the person finds himself in a strange situation. For example, Sally's impish personality did not emerge spontaneously. Rather, it was discovered by Prince when Sally was under hypnosis. We will shortly look at another of these famous cases in which spontaneous transition occurred: *The Three Faces of Eve*.

There are other variations of dissociation, and amnesia plays some part in all of them. The *fugue state* is the label for behavior with amnesic aspects, in which people lose all consciousness of their lives and identities and are often found wandering in a daze far from their usual haunts. In some cases, they disappear completely, adopt a new identity, and take up a new life in some distant community, engaging in an occupation in which they had no previous experience.

Trance states of spirit mediums, "visions" of religious mystics, and automatic writing (apparently not under the writer's control) are signs of dissociation. In Chapter 10, we will see that dissociation is involved in schizophrenia. In psychotic disorders, however, the dissociative reaction is no longer at the level of a neurotic response to difficult circumstances. Instead it is associated with a more profound level of abnormal functioning.

Psychodynamic Approach

By now, you have received enough clues from the descriptions of the various hysterias and know enough of Freudian models to anticipate the psychodynamic etiology of dissociative hysteria. Repression is the force behind the various hysterical behaviors. It is easy to understand how repression would account for amnesia and, in turn, how threatening impulses and consequent internal conflicts could motivate repression.

The variations in hysterical manifestations seem to be traceable to personality differences that have developed at Oedipal and pregenital stages. Pregenital maladaptations are reflected in hysterics' dependency needs. Oedipal problems show themselves in guilt reactions, brought on by conflicts between the ego and the libido. We see evidence of guilt reactions in the transformation of "immoral" sexual drives into religious experiences—the exalted sensation of divine love expressed in sexual terms (ecstasy, delights, passion, and the like). The earlier sexual conflicts also set the stage for the multiple personality, in which the repressed "devil" emerges occasionally. Where the forbidden drive cannot be tolerated at all, patients flee the menace by going into a fugue state. This blocks all consciousness of the repression when some shocking or disastrous event stirs the deeply rooted anxieties.

Initially, *psychodynamic treatment* deals with individuals' coping mechanisms, attempting to strengthen their ability to meet stressful problems with constructive measures. Most psychoanalysts advise against treating the amnesia immediately, preferring to allow lost memories to return naturally when the underlying disorder has been cleared up. In the event of severe disability, they recommend the use of hypnotic suggestion to break through the fugue or the alternate personality. Under hypnosis, patients may be made to relive the events preceding the onset of the amnesia. Conservative treatment follows conventional psychotherapy procedures, with the objective of discovering and removing the basic conflicts responsible for the dissociation.

Behavioral Approach

The concept of "dissociative reaction" rejects a behavioral approach since it implies a splitting of the psyche, a phenomenon that is not open to observation by the behaviorist. Because this type of disorder is uncommon, there is little opportunity to study or treat it from the behavioral viewpoint.

In constructing a theory of dissociation, the behaviorist would focus on the behaviors themselves (amnesia, fugue, hallucination) and functionally analyze them as particular responses to life events. When this is done, it is apparent that the dissociative response is a way of resolving life conflicts that are otherwise

unresolvable. Like conversion hysterics' use of the sick role, dissociative hysterics use psychic events outside their control as the solution to their problems.

Research

Since the various kinds of dissociative reactions are rare, there is not a large volume of research literature on the subject. But in spite of the fact that there are only about 100 cases of multiple personality documented in the literature, the phenomenon has been given much attention in several detailed reports. The most famous is the "Three Faces of Eve." This case has been so widely publicized in a book, a motion picture, and countless newspaper reviews that we will only summarize it here from the account by Thigpen and Cleckley (1954).

Eve White, a married woman of 25 and mother of a 4-year-old girl, was a patient of the authors of the report. She suffered "blackouts" following headaches and had difficult family problems. Her manner was demure, sweetly dignified, and somewhat restrained. In the course of therapy, a second personality suddenly emerged after a blackout: Eve Black, a boisterous, frivolous, "unmarried" woman, who held Eve White in contempt, and since childhood, had willfully caused Eve White great suffering. Eventually, a third personality, Jane, appeared. Jane was mature, sensible, self-possessed, apparently better balanced than Eve White. The psychiatrists found themselves in a dilemma, favoring Jane as the personality with the best adjustment and most competent personal resources. Which of the personalities should they try to preserve and which should they abolish? The question is left unsettled among some philosophical doubts about the validity of psychodynamics and the role of the psychiatrist.

Prince's and Thigpen and Cleckley's accounts of their multiple personality cases have encountered some professional challenges regarding possible deception or role-playing by the patients. Ludwig and his co-workers (1972) undertook a systematic analysis of the four personalities presented by Jonah, a 27-year-old male. Their object was to determine how much transfer of intellectual information and similarity of affect responses there was among the different personalities. Jonah, the central figure, was shy, passive, and conformist, designated by the authors as "the square." Sammy was coolly rational and legalistic—"the lawyer." King Young was a pleasure-seeking, sexually aggressive type—"the lover." Usoffa Abdulla was an angry, powerful, protective deity—"the warrior." A fifth personality dubbed "De Novo" was in the process of developing.

The investigators administered a series of tests to the separate personalities. We will report the most significant ones here. (1) The MMPI showed an internal consistency of the individual personalities and a clear distinction among them. The personality of Jonah was especially distinct. (2) The Adjective Check List (ACL) test, on which the subject indicates agreement or disagreement with favorable or unfavorable self-descriptive adjectives, showed some cross-similarities, but the three adjunct personalities showed no desire to change. (3) All of the personalities had roughly similar IQs in the low-normal range.

Several learning and memory tasks were administered to determine transfer of learning from one personality to another. (4) In the paired-associates test, each personality was trained to perform three perfect trials in one of four lists of ten pairings. Each list was then presented to the others. There was almost total failure of the other personalities to present correct associations for each original list of stem words, indicating no transfer of information. (5) A variation of the paired-association task in which mistakes are corrected as they occur, to improve learning, showed that the practice effect on the trained personality facilitated learning by the others. (6) An objective GSR test of words rated high in affect by each personality showed that the other three personalities all reacted emotionally to Jonah's high-affect

The Three Faces of Eve is the dramatic story of a woman with three distinct personalities. Here Joanne Woodward portrays Eve Black (left), a boisterous woman whose personality was diametrically opposed to Eve White (right), the personality who originally presented herself for therapy. (*Museum of Modern Art, Film Stills Archive.*)

words and to their own, but not to each other's. This finding is consistent with their roles in serving Jonah's special needs in various crisis situations. (7) Neurological examinations showed "normal" results in the various, standard reflexes and coordination movements, except for Usoffa, who exhibited immunity to pain in many normally sensitive areas.

The main conclusion was that the personalities were independent in their affect responses. This would be expected in an amnesic condition. A certain degree of "personality leakage" was noted in the learning tasks, where affect is not involved. Each identity has its specialized function in coming to Jonah's aid when he is overwhelmed by interpersonal conflicts or sexual frustrations. The crisis serves as an "automatic switch-over mechanism."

As an addendum to this study, note the creative use of the inquiry process. This example makes clear how such an orientation expands our knowledge about abnormal behavior.

Depersonalization Neurosis

Depersonalization neurosis, rarely found as a separate entity, was first given status in the 1968 DSM-II revision. The manual describes it as a dominant "feeling of unreality and of estrangement from the self, body, or surroundings" (p. 41). A brief self-report makes the sensation of depersonalization clear:

An eighteen-year-old girl gave birth to an illegitimate child. Her parents gave her very little support in this difficult position. Instead they upbraided her as a loose and depraved woman. They refused to allow her to keep the baby or even to marry the child's father. In the course of this experience she became ill with symptoms of fever and pleural effusion, and she was hospitalized for pulmonary tuberculosis. As a result, she was able to get away from her parents and their intolerable control at least for a time.

Her respite from her mother, however, was brief. Soon the mother was herself hospitalized for tuberculosis. The authorities thought they were doing mother and daughter a favor by placing the mother in the same room with the patient! Directly the

patient developed strong feelings of unreality. She felt that there was an invisible wall separating her from the rest of the world, a wall which came down so that it also separated her mother's bed from hers. She developed vertigo, and felt that she could stand aside and watch her head swirling round and round. When she washed, she noticed that her hands did not seem to belong to her. In treatment, these symptoms recurred whenever she discussed her mother. (Laughlin, 1956, pp. 327–328)

Psychodynamic theorists are, of course, at home in finding explanations for such a phenomenon as a psychological defense. Federn (1952) sees the sensation as a loss of the sense of self as energy is withdrawn from the ego boundaries to respond to pressing conflicts elsewhere in the psychic structure. Since depersonalization is more commonly associated with other disorders—notably, schizophrenia and depression—diagnosticians should look closely for other behaviors, possibly in their onset stage (Nemiah, 1975). In this connection, the patient's previous use of drugs that produce psychotic-like symptoms (psychotomimetic drugs) should be investigated.

Obsessive-Compulsive Reaction

Behavioral Description

Obsessions are thoughts that invade a person's consciousness and take root, resisting the most strenuous efforts to expel them. Compulsions are irrational impulses to perform acts that the person rejects as absurd or against his or her sense of propriety. DSM-II describes the disorder as characterized by

the persistent intrusion of unwanted thoughts, urges, or actions that the patient is unable to stop. The thoughts may consist of single words or ideas, ruminations, or trains of thought often perceived by the patient as nonsensical. The actions vary from simple movements to complex rituals such as repeated handwashing. Anxiety and distress are often present either if the patient is prevented from completing his compulsive ritual or if he is concerned about being able to control it himself. (American Psychiatric Association, p. 40)

Although obsessive-compulsive neurosis as just described is rare, the individual behaviors are common. How many children always avoid walking on the cracks in sidewalks? Most of us have fixed procedures for grooming and dressing in the morning that amount to a ritual we repeat throughout our lives. Such behavior, however, is usually limited to small segments of our daily activity, and does not qualify as a true neurosis unless it spills over and pervades one's whole waking life. We see such a spreading effect in the development of a compulsive pattern that was so pervasive the individual had to be hospitalized.

A 40-year-old male inpatient in a Veteran's Administration Hospital lived a highly constricted and ultraregimented life. Upon awakening in the morning he neatly rolled the blanket and top sheet (one at a time) toward the foot of the bed. He then got dressed, following a specific order from which he never deviated, then made up the bed by reversing the sequence of rolling the blanket and sheet. The entire sequence took about two hours.

His meals were approached in a similar manner: before sitting he went through a lengthy procedure of aligning his silverware and removing food from the tray in the "correct" order. The cafeteria was usually empty before he was satisfied that everything was arranged properly.

Much of his daytime activity involved traveling to and from meals and to bed. He was extremely cautious in where and how he walked. In walking down a hall, he had to reach various points in a determined amount of steps; if it did not work out, he became quite anxious and backed up to his original position and started over.

He spent a great deal of time waiting for elevators. There were four elevators in operation, and the wait was usually brief; however, the "right" elevator had to come at the "right" time or he did not feel secure in getting aboard. He continually punched the button in various sequences while awaiting the "safe" combination of elevators.

During his waking hours, his gestures and facial expressions were puppetlike and highly ritualized.

Each grimace and movement was calculated to ward off danger and prevent panic. (Butcher, 1971, p. 34)

Some compulsions seem to be motivated by a feeling of guilt and are related to things that demand rigorous dedication in our society: parents, children, religious institutions, for example. The anxieties evoked by these demands and the guilt of not being able to meet them may be momentarily relieved by compulsive behaviors, as in this example:

Mrs. B., a thirty-three-year-old housewife, consulted a psychiatrist complaining of fear of germs and dirt, obsessions about religious ideas, and obsessions about the number 3. These symptoms had begun about three months earlier, following the birth of her second child. She had had a similar episode five years earlier after her first child was born. This lasted about six months and finally cleared up under counselling with her pastor. She was a bright person who was always orderly, methodical, conscientious, and dependable. As a child she was overly concerned with the "normal" compulsions that children have, such as counting the pickets in fences, avoiding the cracks in sidewalks, etc. At age ten she became obsessed with the idea that she would die on a certain Tuesday in October.

With her present episode she had developed a number of compulsions in response to her fears and obsessions. For example: She washed her hands repeatedly and relaundered clothes because of her fear of germs and dirt, and she avoided reading automobile license plates and house numbers because she wished to avoid the number 3. After several weeks in the hospital she improved enough so that she was able to carry on with her housework, although she was still troubled somewhat by her symptoms. (Rowe, 1975, pp. 78–79)

Religious compulsion may also be motivated by guilt. Many cases of demonic "possession" in the Middle Ages were probably examples of compulsive behavior directed toward religious objects. A number of such cases are reported in the *Malleus Maleficarum* ("Evildoer's Hammer") by Kramer and Sprenger, who were official inquisitors. Their volume, de-

"Ah, Mr. Pyle . . . Right on time as usual."
(*Don Orehek.*)

scribed in Chapter 1, presents the case of a man who felt compelled (by the devil, he claimed) to stick out his tongue whenever he passed a church or genuflected.

As we have seen, poorly repressed hostility can produce conversion hysteria in some patients. In others, it may result in severe anxieties over the possibility of causing injury or death to relatives or even to strangers.

Marcia C., a thirty-nine-year-old married mother of two, entered the psychiatric wing of a local hospital shortly after her husband had begun an extended business trip which was to keep him away for several weeks. The family had been living in a middle-class neighborhood of a medium-sized New England town.

Marcia's symptoms dated to two years prior to her admission when at a family Christmas celebration, she began to doubt whether she had correctly made the dessert being served. This doubt was accompanied by extreme anxiety, and fear that she might have harmed the children and guests, and soon spread into other areas. She had belonged to a few community groups, and resigned from them, feeling that she could no longer discharge her responsibilities adequately. Marcia became unable to give her children even vitamins for fear of making a mistake and injuring them, and could not cook for fear that she would poison someone through an incorrect preparation. She gave up driving the family car, plagued by the thought that she might kill someone, and at times had to look under the car to assure herself that there was nobody there. She repeatedly checked locks, faucets, the fireplace, and her husband's tools as possible sources of danger to the household. She began to bathe as often as six times daily, doing so particularly if she happened to brush against something that carried germs—like the garage door—before she would touch things in the house. Her hands became swollen from repeated washings, but she continued such practices. After a year of these symptoms she went to the family physician, who prescribed tranquilizers, which lessened the intensity of the symptoms, but did not relieve them entirely. (Zax and Stricker, 1963, pp. 170–171)

The obsessive fear of contaminating others is responsible for repeated washing of the hands (until they become raw and swollen), taking baths, and scrubbing the whole bathroom after each use. Although the performance of the compulsive act is presumed to reduce the anxiety over the poorly repressed hostility, the exaggerated concern seems to surge up almost immediately after the action, which becomes the event that triggers successive repetitions. ("Did I really clean up *all* the dirt?")

Psychodynamic Approach

Clues to the *psychodynamic etiology* of the obsessive-compulsive neurosis are provided by the defense mechanisms that make up the patient's behavior repertoire. They are undoing, displacement, and reaction formation. You may refer to Chapter 3 (Box 3-2) for a discussion of neurotic defenses. When someone compulsively "takes back" an ill wish, he or she is *undoing* the "curse." The undoing is necessitated by leakage of anxiety from incomplete repression of the unacceptable wish. Thus the unacceptable desire to be rid of the responsibility of the children is undone by obsessive overconcern for their well-being. *Displacement* is a further defense mechanism that transfers the hostile thought to a suitable substitute, preferably inanimate, by means of a touching or foot-stamping maneuver. Other obsessions or compulsions may be used as distractions. That melody running through your head may be the ego's way of avoiding some unpleasant thought. A ritual may keep you so busy that you won't perform the unacceptable behavior motivated by the unconscious. *Reaction formation* is another form of undoing. In this the person under stress does exactly the opposite of what his or her undesirable wish is, to counter the anxiety-producing feelings. A person's compulsive hand-washing and floor-scrubbing may represent opposite behaviors to mask an impulse to make things dirty and cause (possibly fatal) infection to hated people.

Psychodynamic treatment has had mixed results with this neurosis. In some cases, all that is needed is the therapist's volunteering to take full responsibility for the consequences of the patient's impulses. Unfortunately, the patient's day-to-day and minute-to-minute rehearsal of the obsessive thoughts and repetition of the compulsive actions engrave them so deeply on his or her mind that they have become irresistible reflexes. Moreover, the narrow, fixed attitude of the anal-compulsive individual militates against the employment of psychoanalytic techniques. The open attitude required for free association and the discussion of sexual issues, and the willingness to give oneself to the therapeutic process are not among the characteristic traits of the obsessive-compulsive neurotic. Hence, as might be expected, prognosis is poor. In one study, only 38 percent of the treated patients were rated as improved, and these still had residual symptoms.

Behavioral Approach

The *behavioral analysis* focuses on what are called "reparative responses" that children acquire as a result of parental discipline. Through a process of operant conditioning, children learn to meet the threat of punishment for some infraction by making amends ("Do it for mother") or by an act of atonement ("Say you're sorry"). Often the threatened punishment is vague, opening the way to a generalized reparative response to almost any threatening event. Furthermore, inconsistent discipline results in an intermittent reinforcement schedule (see Chapter 3). Such a variable schedule is the best way to prevent extinction. Thus the reparative responses continue. The reduction of anxiety by reparation of the offense enhances the reinforcement. Repetition of the *threat of punishment* is not necessary, since children will anticipate it (i.e., supply their own threat) as a result of guilt feelings, and will perform the reparative response with the reinforcement provided by the parent's failure to apply punishment on every occasion.

Direct, reality-based behaviors also occur. People who have had, or have witnessed, traumatic illness may seek to control such unpredictable dangers in the environment by engaging in rigid patterns of behavior, especially those designed to reduce dirt and germs by repeated hand-washing and exhaustive house-cleaning.

There is bound to be chance reinforcement of some rituals. This, as we know, promotes superstitious behavior, which would account for many of the seemingly pointless, irrational compulsions.

Evidence for the conditioned learning hypothesis for obsessive-compulsive behavior comes from animal learning experiments. Mather (1970) reviews a large number of laboratory studies of fixation induced in animals by generating conflict situations to disrupt stimulus discrimination. When shock, a blast of air, or other aversive stimuli are applied at the point of presentation of the discriminative stimulus, that is, the cue that marks the time and place of the reinforcement, the animal's response becomes fixated at that point. Fixation is the repetition of the response in spite of the fact that it is not producing reinforcement. The critical factor in creating the fixation is not the frequency of repetition of the response or the frustration produced by the experimenter's preventing access to the reward, but the conflict set up by the aversive stimulus.

Similar fixating responses have been obtained with human subjects who were presented with insoluble choice problems coupled with distracting noise or mild electric shock. The shock caused the subjects to persist in their erroneous choice regardless of its failure to yield a positive reinforcement. The emotional reaction brought on by the shock and by the conflict created by the impossible discrimination task combines to induce a fixating effect.

Mather proposes the theory that conflicts inherent in the uncontrollable nature of life events (disease, accidents, death) induce fixations, just as similar conditions did in the laboratory. The partial reinforcement (variable contingency schedule) that occurs under ordinary conditions—as when steps taken to guard against infection are occasionally "successful" (i.e., sickness did not ensue)—is ideal for developing compulsive behaviors. Motivation conflicts can be experienced when behavior patterns that satisfy personal needs meet with punishment by others, provoking guilt-based anxiety. When the punishing person changes to a favorable attitude, even if it is for reasons unrelated to the reparative behaviors under-

taken by the offender, the irrelevant behaviors are likely to become fixed under the stress inherent in the situation, and reinforced by the emotional relief resulting from the offender's return to favor. The relaxation of anxiety achieved in these situations makes the behaviors particularly resistant to therapeutic extinction.

Behavioral treatment of compulsive habits operates on two levels: (1) prevention of the behavior and (2) relief of the anxiety aroused by the provocative stimuli. After desensitization procedures had failed to demonstrate reasonable effectiveness, Meyer (1966) introduced the technique of preventing the obsessional behavior in order to demonstrate to the patient that failure to perform the actions would have no fearful consequences. The desired cessation of the behavior was achieved by "modification of expectations." In other words, he eliminated the expectation of disaster. In the case of obsessive thoughts, the prevention is accomplished by "thought stopping" (Wolpe, 1958). The stopping is done simply by allowing the patient to ruminate for short intervals and periodically disrupting the repetition of the obsessional thought by shouting "Stop!" Eventually, the patient interrupts his own ruminations by shouting "Stop!" to himself.

Analogous to thought-stopping is response prevention. For example, faucet handles are removed to prevent hand-washing. Eysenck and Rachman (1965) have put forth a possible explanation for the effectiveness of such direct techniques. They theorize that guilt and anxiety may follow as well as precede the compulsive action. Preventing the action thus relieves the emotional motivation.

Flooding and participant modeling therapies operate on the principle of anxiety reduction through familiarization. Rachman, Hodgson, and Marks (1971) compared the effectiveness of flooding with participant modeling therapy on ten cases that had been resistant to other forms of therapy. Flooding involved procedures such as the handling of animals by a patient who dreaded contamination. Participant modeling led the patients through a hierarchy of increasingly threatening behaviors first modeled by the therapist and then imitated by the patient. Both techniques were equally successful, and both surpassed ordinary relaxation training in effectiveness. A subsequent experiment in which both flooding and modeling were combined showed better results than were obtained with either method alone.

Research

We have already referred to Mather's summary of research designed to determine how compulsive behaviors are acquired, as an aid in the development of therapeutic techniques. Most of the experiments in this research dealt with the conditions required for inducing fixation of behavior, which seems to be the central feature of the neurosis.

Other experimentation in this area is directed toward the testing of different therapeutic techniques. We will review a typical study of a behavioral method and one of insight therapy.

Mills et al. (1973) conducted a series of experiments in which response prevention was the main technique. Their objective was to separate the effects of the technique from other treatment variables. Each experiment was run with a single patient, which limits our ability to generalize the results.

Their first case was a 31-year-old, female, compulsive hand-washer. They established a 7-day baseline of free hand-washing at about eight times a day (not really excessive). Then they instructed her on the necessity of preventing her from washing her hands—and did in fact prevent her—for about 14 days. Next she was permitted free washing for 14 days. During this period she averaged one washing and 3.6 urges to wash per day. The results were ambiguous, however, since the experimenters could not separate the effect of the actual prevention of hand-washing from the effects of the instructions the patient was given. Was the decline in hand-washing in the third period (14 days of free washing) simply a result of the patient's acting on previous instructions?

To separate the two variables, the next patient (also a female hand-washer) was given instructions to decrease hand-washing for 14 days, but was not prevented from so doing. She was then subjected to response prevention for 14 days. This was followed by free washing for 3 days, 7 more days of prevention, 11 days of free washing, and, finally, 7 days of instruction with a rationale for not washing, but no prevention. There was a progressive decline in hand-washing, although frequency of urges increased during the intervals of prevention.

Two more experiments were performed to test the effects of the patient's expectancy of improvement. The experimenters found that the use of a placebo alone, when the patient was told the drug would relax her and thus decrease hand-washing, was not enough to curb the behavior permanently. Response prevention combined with a placebo (and thus increased expectancy of improvement) was found to be the most successful procedure.

Gullick and Blanchard (1973) treated an obsessional patient with a combination of insight and behavior therapies. The 33-year-old male (with a Ph.D. in plant physiology) was obsessed by the nagging thought that he had blasphemed God. The experimental variable was the number of obsessional thoughts counted by the patient each day. (Remember that obsessives are fully—and uncomfortably—aware of every irrational thought.) He was initially required to participate in group therapy sessions for three days. Daily psychotherapy sessions followed for nine days, in which the patient was given insight into the nature of his problem.

Five days of thought-stopping included, first, the therapist's giving interrupting commands, then self-interruption by the patient. Next, three days of no treatment, followed by three more days of treatment, another suspension of treatment, and then resumption of therapy. The reduction in obsessional thoughts during each of the therapy periods was significant, while there was an increase during the first suspension of treatment and a sharp decrease during the second suspension. At that point, *attribution therapy* was introduced. This procedure is designed to change the patient's assumptions about the "location" of the cause for his anxiety—from internal obsessional thoughts to environmental stresses. In other words, he was persuaded that the problem was not in him but in the outside world. He was thus instructed in reinterpreting his reactions. In addition, he was given a course in assertion training, modeling his responses on the therapist's performance. The obsessional count thereupon dropped to zero.

After 33 days of hospital treatment, the patient was involved in a program of weekly group therapy sessions and private visits with the therapist. A nine-month follow-up found the ex-patient free of obsessive behaviors.

Depressive Reactions

While depression often accompanies the psychoses, this emotional disturbance stands alone as a common neurosis, sometimes referred to as "situational" or "reactive," since it is frequently precipitated by a tragic event: a death, a divorce, loss of a job, or some frustrating disappointment. We will discuss it at length in Chapter 12 in the context of related affective disorders. It is included here among the neuroses in recognition of its role as a defense against anxiety.

The name is descriptive of the low state into which the victims sink, tormented by self-doubt and awash with self-pity. They are racked with guilt over intolerable rage toward the person or thing they have lost, or they may be oppressed by a sense of failure to achieve meaningful success in life. On the other hand, the elation at attaining a cherished goal after a long struggle at the cost of friends or family may turn to ashes when the gain is measured against the loss. Remorse over pain inflicted on others may start the downward plunge into sadness, loss of interest in their work, and vague feelings of hostility. Guilt confused with self-pity may lead to excessive mourning of a departed relative (who was abused by the mourner) or to exaggerated self-indulgence in promiscuous behavior or heavy drinking. Other aspects of depressive neurosis will be examined in Chapter 12.

Neurasthenic Reaction and Existential Neurosis

Behavioral Description

The category of abnormal behavior labeled neurasthenia has had a spotty career. It was the subject of controversy and reshaping at the hands of virtually every psychiatric diagnostician, including Freud, who spared its existence but constricted its broad scope. Later it disappeared into oblivion when DSM-I gave it no mention, only to be resurrected in DSM-II:

> Neurasthenic neurosis (neurasthenia) is characterized by complaints of chronic weakness, easy fatigability, and sometimes exhaustion. Unlike hysterical neurosis, the patient's complaints are genuinely distressing to him, and there is no evidence of secondary gain. It differs from anxiety neurosis and from the psychophysiologic disorders in the nature of the predominant complaint. It differs from the depressive neurosis in the moderateness of the depression and in the chronicity of its course. (American Psychiatric Association, pp. 40–41)

The definition sums up the symptoms: weakness, fatigue, lack of stamina, exhaustion. Since it often attacks the young (people in their twenties and thirties), the lack of energy and will is quite noticeable. Every task, even mere movement itself, is beyond the capability of the sufferers. Other symptoms include insomnia or restless sleep from which neurasthenics wake with a sense of fatigue that lasts through the morning, impaired memory and concentration, irritability, headaches, hypochondriacal tendencies, and exaggerated dependency needs.

It is not uncommon for neurasthenics to be diagnosed by the physician for some physical dysfunction, and to be treated, usually with drugs, for some glandular or nutritional deficiency. The medication fixes the individual's view of their ailment as a physical disorder, blinding them to any consideration of the emotional factors that may motivate the reac-

Box 8-3 The Neuroses

Anxiety reaction	A pervasive, persistently recurring sense of dread and unrelieved apprehension, often punctuated by severe attacks of anxiety.
Phobic reaction	Anxiety focused on a particular object, situation, or body function that is so severe it interferes with normal living.
Hypochondriacal reaction	A morbid and absorbing concern over one's physical health and body functions.
Hysterical reaction—conversion type	The impairment without organic explanation of the organs of special sense or a voluntary system.
Hysterical reaction—dissociative type	Psychologically-caused disturbances of memory and consciousness, such as somnambulism, amnesia, and multiple personality.
Depersonalization neurosis	A dominant feeling of unreality and estrangement from the self, body, or surroundings.
Obsessive-compulsive reaction	The persistent intrusion of unwanted thoughts, urges, or actions that the patient is unable to stop.
Depressive reaction	Characterized by self-doubt, self-pity, and guilt. Often occurs in reaction to a tragic event.
Neurasthenic reaction	Chronic weakness, fatigue, and exhaustion.
Existential neurosis	Boredom, indifference to alternative activities, and a sense that life is meaningless.

Maddi (1967) describes a neurotic condition that bears a strong resemblance to neurasthenia with depressive qualities. He calls it *existential neurosis*—"the sickness of our times." It has cognitive, affective, and activity components. These are, respectively, a sense of the meaninglessness and triviality of life; blandness and boredom; indifference to alternative activities. Prior to onset of the neurotic phase, neurasthenics do only what is necessary to satisfy basic biological and social requirements for mere survival. They have no feeling for the needs or sensitivities of others. Alienation characterizes their mode of existence. In fact, about all they manage to do is exist—in a constant state of unfocused fear and nameless anxiety. Only the threat of imminent death can rouse them from their apathy and sting them into an awareness of the superficiality and barrenness of their life style, at which point the "existential neurosis" may be diagnosed.

The fact that existential neurosis is deemed a product of our times distinguishes it from neurasthenia, which has a long history, as we pointed out earlier. However, we also noted neurasthenia's changing diagnostic status. It may be that once again, neurasthenia has taken on attributes relevant to the problems of our age, and has thus emerged—at least in some cases—as existential neurosis.

Psychodynamic Approach

Attempts to account for the *psychodynamic etiology* of neurasthenia have taken two directions. In one, the symptomatic fatigue and lack of energy have been traced to sheer physical exhaustion, with possibly some undiagnosed somatic illness. Freud rejected that explanation and ascribed neurasthenia instead to an inadequate discharge of psychic tension as a result of abnormal sexual functioning (e.g., masturbation instead of conventional intercourse). The sexual behavior generates intrapsychic conflicts between the ego and the unacceptable impulses. Contemporary psychoanalysts feel that the neurasthenics' numerous unresolved conflicts require so much of their

tions. Despite the DSM-II definition, the physical symptoms are the ideal secondary defense for the neurotic.

sexual energy that there is little left for ordinary, day-to-day functioning. Put another way, the struggle to maintain the ego boundaries depletes their energy resources, leaving them barely enough energy to tie their shoelaces.

Psychodynamic treatment of neurasthenia consists largely of conventional psychotherapy. At the outset, the therapist may recommend change of occupation, diet, or social activities. Such measures are, of course, designed to break habituated patterns and result in only temporary relief.

Insight therapy is sometimes effective with rational patients. Seeing their problem as a consequence of internal conflicts may open their vision to various interpersonal hostilities that may set up such conflicts. Intensive psychotherapy can then probe for evidence of such deep-seated conflicts, leading to an emotional release that relieves the energy-draining anxiety.

Intensive psychotherapy also explores the personality of patients to learn the motivation for their goals, satisfactions, attitudes, and relationships. Most suitable for exploration is the patient-therapist relationship, since its ongoing development can be observed. The course of the analysis proceeds through a close scrutiny of current, daily reactions, which provides clues to guide a probing examination of patients' early childhood experiences and relationships. Laughlin (1956) presents a neurasthenic case in which intensive psychotherapy succeeded after treatment of organic symptoms had failed.

A thirty-six-year-old research chemist was referred for analytic treatment because of complaints of severe chronic fatigue, excruciating, nearly constant headaches, weakness, sexual maladjustment, and various minor somatic complaints. By chance, he was on the tall and thin side, with a typical asthenic [nonathletic] build and imperfect posture.

His fatigability was such that the slightest exertion was completely exhausting. He had gradually reduced his working time to a total of only four hours per day. When I first saw him, he was on the point of giving it up entirely. During the remainder of his time, which was spent strictly at home, he

carefully alternated each fifteen to thirty minutes of activity with one half-hour of reclining.

These measures were totally ineffective in reducing his fatigue. He had experienced progressive difficulty in concentration. Together with his severe headaches, these symptoms had resulted in an increasingly restricted social life, a situation foreign to his previous nature. Life had become so intolerable that he had been on the point of suicide. He chose psychiatric treatment in what amounted to a last desperate resort, having visited half a dozen physicians in various fields in his search for an organic basis and cure of his terrible symptoms.

This case is clinically rather typical of very severe Neurasthenia. This patient, however, proved an apt candidate for intensive treatment and eventually, during the course of more than four years of treatment—on a three-times, and later two-times a week basis—he stopped having his headaches entirely. His fatigue also completely subsided. For more than two years he has worked full-time and has been able to resume his former level of social activity. (p. 486)

But psychoanalysis is an extremely lengthy process, and the neurasthenic sometimes needs immediate relief just to carry on. In view of this, it is no wonder that so many sufferers choose the fast, if temporary, relief of "pep" pills.

Behavioral Approach

The *behavioral analysis* of neurasthenia parallels that of depression, since the two are similar in many basic respects. As in the case of depression, the onset of neurasthenia is precipitated by a change in social roles or relationships (loss of a job, death of a loved one), which causes a corresponding change in reinforcement schedules. For this reason, we find the heaviest incidence of the disorder in the middle years when the most drastic disruptions take place in the course of living: grown-up children leaving home, sudden attainment of a long-sought goal (high position, degree, wealth), sexual dysfunction, existential crises ("what does it all mean?"), divorce, deaths of relatives and friends. Such life-changing events change the pattern and type of reinforcements to which the individuals have become accustomed. Suddenly, current behaviors lose their relevance. They elicit neither positive nor negative reinforcement from the environment, and noncontingent behaviors become extinguished in clusters, gradually reducing the individuals to minimal responses and the characteristic apathy of the washed-out neurasthenic.

Behavioral treatment takes its cue from what we have just observed as the central motivation for neurasthenic behavior: absence of familiar reinforcements. Logically, we would look for new sources of reinforcement. We will discuss the procedure by which this is accomplished—along with pertinent research on the problem—in Chapter 12, as part of our consideration of depression.

Traumatic and Occupational Reactions

Traumatic neurosis (psychodynamic name) or traumatic reaction (behavioral name) generally occurs immediately after a catastrophic event. The main symptoms are severe, persistent anxiety and amnesia limited to the traumatizing event. Examples of such events are major automobile or train accidents, battlefield crises, devastating civilian bombardment during wartime, near-drowning episodes, natural disasters, explosions, and airplane crashes. In *psychological trauma*, victims suffer a variety of emotional and physiological reactions, which may clear up in a short time as they recover their equanimity. However, in the case of *traumatic neurosis*, the effects are so severe as to incapacitate the victims and cause personality changes. Traumatic neurosis is experienced either as an *acute* episode that soon dissipates or as a *chronic* neurosis that persists and may even result in additional abnormal behaviors.

The acute traumatic neurosis is marked by (1) spells of uncontrollable emotion, (2) insomnia or disturbed sleep (sometimes nightmares of the event), and (3) loss of memory of the event (Janis, 1971). The behavioral effects of these symptoms include lethargy, depression, and irritability.

Several factors determine the degree, duration, and depth of the traumatic reaction. Certain personality characteristics may predispose the victim to traumatic neurosis. Being the survivor of a near-miss event, especially if friends or relatives succumbed in the disaster, accentuates the emotional effects. The severity and duration of the event correlate with the intensity and duration of the reaction. Front-line soldiers under fire for extended periods suffer more intense and longer-lasting anxiety than those behind the lines who were exposed to sporadic shelling in air raids.

Not all traumatic reactions are caused by exposure to catastrophe. Sleep deprivation over long periods of time produces disordered thinking that approximates psychosis. Such loss of sleep can occur as a result of a distressing experience, such as failure in a love relationship, threat of job loss, or pressure to perform on a task that exceeds one's capabilities. A satisfactory resolution of the panic, loss, or threat permits resumption of regular sleeping habits, which, in most cases, restores emotional equilibrium.

When recovery does not occur within a few days or weeks after the event, the traumatic reaction settles into a chronic neurosis. Patients deteriorate into invalidism, depending on others to take care of them. This situation relieves patients of burdensome responsibility for themselves, providing secondary gains that reinforce their helpless behavior. Their irritability and impatience with those who serve them reflect their underlying guilt over their helplessness, coupled with their anxiety over their helpers' possible refusal to continue caring for their needs. Pervasive, new, chronic behaviors join the acute syndrome. These include generalized apprehensiveness toward every aspect of the patients' world—nothing is safe any longer. Not only is their self-confidence lost, but with it goes their trust in others. Their withdrawal and resentment are often expressed in rude, selfish conduct.

In spite of the grip the chronic neurosis has on patients, improvement and even full recovery are possible with insightful treatment.

Occupational neurosis is a common, special case of traumatic neurosis. Intense stress, fear of failure, a demoralizing embarrassment on the job (as when a worker is given a dressing-down by his or her boss in front of co-workers) are among the possible precipitating events. The traumatic reaction may manifest itself in the individuals' developing a crippling impediment that prevents performance of their jobs (the writer gets a muscle spasm or cramp that makes writing impossible; the laborer develops an excruciating backache that prevents bending or lifting; and so on). Inability to perform the job removes the workers from the scene of the trauma and thereby provides them with the secondary gains that perpetuate the neurotic condition. While recovery is possible in many cases, the promise of full and perma-nent cure must be qualified by the tendency of extremely traumatic experiences to stubbornly resist extinction. Even when there seems to be recovery after highly traumatic events, the symptoms tend to recur—occasionally years later. It is suspected that some traumatic experiences result in a hypersensitivity to stress in the victims, rendering them subject to a revival of the earlier reaction when some stressful situation is encountered at a later date.

Personality Disorders

Behavioral Description

When we approach the subject of personality disorders, we enter an area whose boundaries are only vaguely defined. In this category, we will find descriptions that echo those by which we have learned to distinguish the neu-

A traumatizing event, such as a train wreck, can lead to severe, persistent anxiety and even personality change. (*Wide World Photos.*)

Box 8-4 Types of Personality Disorders

Paranoid personalities are characterized by hypersensitivity, rigidity, suspiciousness, morbid jealousy, and an inclination to blame others for their failures. They examine "evidence" repeatedly to find justification for their suspicions of mistreatment and plotting against them by others. Paranoid personality may be a progressive condition culminating in schizophrenia.

Schizoid personalities are withdrawn, apathetic to conflicts, "loners" with few friends. They are given to fantasizing and are unable to focus and express their stressful emotions. Schizoid personality may lead to schizophrenic psychosis, depending on environmental and genetic factors.

Cyclothymic personalities resemble manic-depressives in mood swings between elation and depression. They are often found in families of manic-depressive patients. Cyclothymic personalities are likely to be egocentric and unreliable. Prognosis points to eventual manic-depressive psychosis.

Obsessive-compulsive personalities are fastidious perfectionists in their concern for conformity, with excessively high standards. They are inclined to be extremely conscientious, yet riddled with doubt about their inadequate performance. The personality provides an ideal matrix for development of the corresponding neurosis.

Hysterical personalities are emotionally unstable, histrionic types. They are sexually seductive, with strong dependency needs based on immature attitudes. The typical distribution of those in treatment is 90 percent female, 10 percent male.

Explosive personalities vent their rage and frustration in outbursts of temper and verbal or physical abuse. The tantrums are grossly out of proportion to provocations. These people may often come from families with a history of violent behavior and alcoholism.

Passive-aggressive personalities passively express their hostility through "obstructionism . . . stubbornness and intentional inefficiency" (Winokur and Crowe, 1975). They are resentful of the failure of others to meet their needs. The symptoms are to be interpreted in terms of patients' motivation, since their behaviors may be the result of other disorders, such as depression or neurasthenia.

Asthenic personalities are associated with low energy, fatigability, inability to experience pleasure, and sensitivity to stress. This type may be confused with symptoms of anxiety neurosis or neurasthenia.

Inadequate personalities are the chronic "losers," described in DSM-II as accustomed to making "ineffectual responses to social, psychological, and physical demands" (p. 44), although they are not incapacitated or handicapped. The chief attribute of this personality type is poor judgment. This category comprises incompetent, indifferent, stereotyped, unemotional people, resentful of the success of others, unwilling to face their own shortcomings (Winokur and Crowe, 1972).

roses, and others that echo descriptions given in later chapters on the psychoses. Mental health workers proceed with caution in dealing with these conditions.

The criteria that determine the designation of "personality disorders" are simply stated by Salzman (1974). They are "maladaptive patterns of behavior that are not sufficiently definite or severe to be considered neurotic or psychotic syndromes" (p. 231). The line that separates the "personality disorder" from its corresponding neurosis or psychosis is defined

more by the judgment of the particular diagnostician than by formal specifications. However, Box 8-4 briefly describes the features that identify a number of such disorders.

Psychodynamic Approach

As we noted in Chapter 3, personality problems such as the ones described in Box 8-4 emerge from a disturbance in psychological development at one of the genital or pregenital stages. The adult personality pattern reflects the psychosexual dynamics operating at the stage in which psychic conflicts were not appropriately resolved.

Traditional psychotherapy addresses the underlying source of the dysfunction. The patient is confronted with the irrationality of his present behavior and the difficulties it creates. He is then taken on an exploratory journey back to the childhood period in order to trace the present behavior to its origins in the developmental stages. The analyst seeks clues to the attributes that make up the patient's present personality and determine his reactions by probing the childhood experiences for poorly resolved psychosexual conflicts.

By means of transference, the therapist actually participates in the patient's dynamic interaction with his environment. The attitudes of the patient toward the therapist reveal the patient's underlying motivations and guide the therapist in determining the critical psychic areas for investigation. Through the interaction, the therapist can help the patient discover both the origins of his disturbances and the effect of the disturbances on his present behavior. The primary objective of the psychotherapeutic method is not the elimination of symptoms of anxiety but the improvement of personality function, thereby correcting the disorder and releasing the energy previously used in maintaining a precarious psychological balance. The sense of well-being and hopefulness emerges when that energy works to gain real satisfactions for the individual.

Behavioral Approach

In Chapter 3, we commented on the vigorous debate between the behaviorists, who uphold the importance of *situational* variables, and the psychodynamicists, who maintain that the *personality* variables are the determinants of behavior—the so-called "state-trait" controversy.[2]

---

[2] Mischel (1968) has presented persuasive evidence for the dominant effect of situational factors, crediting them with greater influence than previous interpretations have suggested. We can present no final verdict here on that debate.

Indeed, as individuals we show consistency in our response style in many situations. Do these patterns represent our personality? Is our rigid, stereotyped behavior, which we manifest in inflexible responses, the result of conflict-motivated personality defects, or of disordered reinforcement contingencies? These are unsettled questions, and it is clear that they are pivotal in the psychodynamic versus behavioral contest.

In looking at the deviant patterns characteristic of the personality disorders, the behaviorists are most inclined to adopt a functional analysis approach. They want to identify the situational determinants of the behavior and the reinforcing consequences that maintain it. Taking this tack, behaviorists underemphasize the inner, motivating factors of the personality disorder and focus on the regularities of the behavior that result from learning.

The Borderline Patient

A new category of dysfunction has emerged recently to provide a diagnostic refuge for those whose problem falls between the neuroses and the psychoses. Implicit in this accommodation is the acknowledgment of a continuum of behavior rather than a clear division between the psychotic and the neurotic. So appealing is the conception that there is talk that it should be a formal category. Many fear, however, that the category would be used as a wastebasket diagnosis for all doubtful conditions. Indeed, there is evidence that diagnoses of patients as borderline depend more on the diagnostician than on the patient.

The borderline patient is distinguished by two predominant modes of reaction: anger and depression. Unlike the expression of these behaviors in the neuroses or psychoses, however, anger in the borderline case is usually defensive rather than aggressive, and depression has the quality of loneliness rather than guilt or remorse.

Two subsidiary affect conditions color the borderline picture: anxiety and the inability to experience pleasure (anhedonia). This should not be confused with the "flat affect" characteristic of certain psychoses.

In contrast to the crippling effects of neurosis and psychosis, the borderline state generally does not interfere with performance on the job. Borderline patients are frequently gainfully employed, although their careers tend to be blocked at a low level.

The most serious behaviors of the borderline patient include drug and alcohol abuse, self-mutilation and other self-destructive acts (which may not be intentional), and sexual excesses. There is a suspicion that confusion of sexual identity sets the stage for the sexual deviances.

When borderline patients cross the border into psychosis, often in response to stress, they develop only a few new behaviors, and do not stay for long. They suffer no delusions or hallucinations, they have no loose associations, they do not accept their psychotic reactions as "right" or compatible with their ego, and the psychotic episodes are short-term. The question of thought disorder in these psychotic episodes is a matter of disagreement, probably because of the lack of consensus about what thought disorder really is.

Gunderson and Singer (1975) spell out six diagnostic characteristics for identifying the borderline patient. We merely list them here: (1) intense affect in the form of anger or depression; (2) impulsive behavior, including self-mutilation; (3) social adaptiveness, shown in satisfactory job performance and good appearance; (4) brief psychotic episodes; (5) good performance on structured tests like the WAIS and bizarre responses on unstructured tests like the Rorschach; and (6) superficial, transient interpersonal relationships alternating with intense, dependent relationships.

Gruenewald (1970) divides the borderline category into four groups: (1) bordering on the psychoses; (2) bordering on the neuroses; (3) the core syndrome—lonely, depressed, confused, and angry; and (4) "as if"—devoid of affect, socially functional but with diffused identity. She presents the following case as an example of the fourth, "as if," category:

This 28-year-old man looks younger than his stated age. There is something of the "dead end kid" about him. His facial expression is bland. Though he laughs occasionally, he presents himself as even-tempered. He is subservient, arrogant, and covertly derogatory.

In the interview, he was constantly alert to cues from the examiner to guide his attitudes and behavior. He spoke of the desirability of further schooling to obtain a college degree which would enable him to have a white collar or professional job instead of the manual labor he now performs, but he also was at pains to differentiate between education and intelligence. He emphasized his intellectual capacity and artistic talent, both of which are less than he likes to believe, and he projected his inability to implement his fantasies on external factors. He minimized a record of juvenile delinquency and berated the army psychiatrist who rejected him as unfit for military service, and he suspected that the interview was for the purpose of checking up on him.

He was reluctant to engage himself in the tests for fear of exposing partly realized deficiencies. His intelligence level is slightly above average, but his often incorrect use of highflown expressions is designed to make himself appear very intellectual. The record indicates little capacity for empathic identification and a general depreciation of interpersonal relationships. Humor is put in the service of manipulating the environment. He knows what one is expected to feel guilty for but does not experience a sense of guilt. Violence is taken lightly without appreciation of its meaning. The protocol is pervaded by psychopathic elements. Fantasy is used for withdrawal and wish-gratification as well as a preconscious planning device for manipulation. The life he leads is one of isolation and lacks meaningful relationships. (pp. 182–183)

We note in this case the characteristics of borderline patients: blandness, overestimation of their own skills and intelligence, fantasizing of success, unwillingness or inability to face their shortcomings, lack of identification with others, manipulative style, and, finally, isolation and futility.

Summary

The neuroses comprise a wide spectrum of behaviors, with anxiety as the common denominator. In the psychodynamic view, the anxiety arises from inadequate repression of internal conflicts. Defective or displaced ego boundaries are thought to be responsible for the intrusion of unacceptable urges from the libido or threats from the environment. The behavioral analysis concerns itself with the overt behaviors and the environment's reinforcement of them. In this view, phobias, obsessions, compulsions, and the hysterias are learned responses to life stresses. Experimental demonstrations of the way "neurotic"-type behaviors are learned, maintained, and modified give evidence favoring the behavioral interpretation of neurosis.

Psychodynamic treatment seeks the sources of conflict in developmental periods and, by insight therapy, releases the energy tied up in the mechanisms of repression. There are a variety of behavioral procedures for changing the maladaptive behaviors and initiating and maintaining appropriate behaviors.

Other neurotic and pseudo-neurotic categories provide additional diagnostic classifications. These are needed for reactions that do not properly qualify as either psychoses or neuroses. These are traumatic reactions, personality disorders, and borderline syndromes. Their characteristic behaviors are more vaguely defined than the psychotic or neurotic syndromes.

Psychophysiologic disorders

The Body-Mind Issue

Can purely psychological, nonphysical events cause medical problems? This question touches upon the same mind-body dichotomy we discussed in Chapter 1, that is, the belief that the mind or psychological side of an individual is somehow separated from his or her physical or somatic side. During the era of "organic models" of mental illness, practitioners believed there could be "no twisted thought without a twisted molecule." While most medical scientists have abandoned that extreme position, contemporary researchers now search for "twisted thoughts *causing* twisted molecules."

This chapter is concerned with physical disorders arising from the psychological state of an organism. We are not asking *whether* the mind can affect the body, but *how* and *why* psychological variables affect physiological functioning.

How can we demonstrate the nature and extent of the connection between psychological factors and physical disorders? Subjectively, we have come to accept the idea that people are more likely to have physical problems during times of psychological stress. We are concerned that friends and relatives who are going through a difficult time may be "getting sick over their problems." In an attempt to demonstrate the connection, however, no ethical investigator would experimentally induce the kinds of stress that might produce physical breakdown. One approach that psychophysiological research has taken is to do "natural experiments" using subjects going through times of psychological crisis as a means of testing the relationship between psychological events and physical disorder. Three events that have been studied through such natural experiments are bereavement, cumulative life-change events, and sudden death.

Bereavement Studies

The death of someone close to a person provides one kind of "natural experiment" in which the psychological event is clear and changes in the physical status of the survivor can be evaluated. Numerous studies of bereaved men and women present a consistent picture of disturbances in physical functioning, more frequent doctor's visits, and more frequent hospital admissions. The physical effects of bereavement are so profound that significant changes in life expectancy often result.

To cite a representative report, Rees and Lutkins (1967) compared 903 close relatives of recently deceased residents of Llandiloes, a small Welsh town, with 878 matched control subjects from the same community who had not experienced bereavement. During the first year following bereavement, the death rate was seven times greater for the bereaved group than for their matched controls. In a similar study of widowers in England and Wales, investigators reported that the death rate during the first six months of bereavement was 40 percent above expected levels for married men of the same age range (Young, Benjamin, and Wallis, 1963; Parkes, Benjamin, and Fitzgerald, 1969). Increased incidence of heart disease accounted for much of this dramatic rise in the death rate.

In another study from Harvard University (Parkes and Brown, 1972), 68 widows and widowers under the age of 45 were compared with a control group of 68 married women and men matched by sex, social class, nationality, family size, and other relevant factors. The bereaved subjects used significantly more alcohol, tobacco, and tranquilizers, and had a greater incidence of appetite and sleep problems than did controls. Only 4 members of the control group had been hospitalized during the previous year, as compared to 12 from the bereaved group, a strikingly significant difference.

Life-Stress Research

The most salient feature of bereavement is its representation of a great change in the survivor's way of life. Researchers have found that the death of a spouse is, in fact, the most "impactful" change that can occur in a person's lifetime (Toffler, 1970). Therefore, it is not surprising that stress of bereavement produces so many physiological problems. What is surprising is the finding that other much less momentous events may also threaten an individual's health.

Investigators led by Thomas Holmes at the University of Washington School of Medicine (Holmes and Rahe, 1967) compiled a list of significant life changes. They interviewed thousands of men and women from many countries, representing diverse life styles, and found surprising agreement in the way all these respondents rated the "impactfulness" of various positive and negative life events. What emerged from this survey is the Life-Change Units Scale shown in Table 9-1. Notice that each life event is assigned a specific point value, based on the top rank of 100 for death of a

Table 9-1 Life-Change Units Scale

Life Event	Value	Life Event	Value
Death of spouse	100	Foreclosure of mortgage or loan	30
Divorce	73	Change in responsibilities at work	29
Marital separation	65	Son or daughter leaving home	29
Jail term	63	Trouble with in-laws	29
Death of a close family member	63	Outstanding personal achievement	28
Personal injury or illness	53	Wife beginning or stopping work	26
Marriage	50	Beginning or ending school	26
Fired at work	47	Revision of personal habits	24
Marital reconciliation	45	Trouble with boss	23
Retirement	45	Change in work hours or conditions	20
Change in health of family member	44	Change in residence	20
Pregnancy	40	Change in schools	20
Sex difficulties	39	Change in recreation	19
Gain of new family member	39	Change in social activities	18
Change in financial state	38	Mortgage or loan less than $10,000	17
Death of close friend	37	Change in sleeping habits	16
Change to different line of work	36	Change in number of family get-togethers	15
Change in number of arguments		Change in eating habits	15
with spouse	35	Vacation	13
Mortgage over $10,000	31	Minor violations of the law	11

From Holmes, T. H., and Rahe, R. H. The social readjustment rating scale. *Journal of Psychosomatic Research*, 1967, 11, 213–218.

spouse. Thus getting married, with a score of 50, may be considered 50 percent as impactful as the death of a spouse. Change in school rates at 20, vacation at 13. Holmes and his colleagues administered a Schedule of Recent Events (SRE) questionnaire to thousands of subjects. Questionnaire responses were then scored on the Life-Change Units Scale, and compared with each individual's subsequent medical history. An astonishing correlation was found between high life-change scores and risk of medical illness. Eighty percent of the subjects scoring over 300 developed serious ailments during the following year. Major illness occurred in 53 percent of those with scores from 150 to 300, and 33 percent of those with scores below 150.

Holmes' colleagues (Arthur and Rahe, 1967) selected sailors on six-month assignments at sea, where their medical records could be closely observed. Before departure, each sailor was questioned carefully about the events of the previous year. Had he married, taken vacations, or even received traffic summonses? Reports were tallied and life-change scores computed for all subjects. Analysis of medical records following the tours of duty revealed that men scoring in the upper 10 percent suffered $1\frac{1}{2}$ to 2 times as many illnesses as those in the lowest 10 percent. Even more significant, life-change scores were directly related to the severity of the illness: the higher the life-change score, the more severe the illness that occurred. These findings indicate that changes, per se, be they pleasant or unpleasant, can endanger an individual's health. Toffler, in summarizing the psychological literature on the subject, notes that there is a "physiological price tag" carried by all significant life events.

As Toffler (1970) states, "The more radical the change, the steeper the price" (p. 296).

Sudden Death

Our examples thus far have emphasized the predictive value of stress measures. Given stressful life events, medical problems may develop. These studies are essentially correlative, in that they show a relation between stress and illness, but cannot prove that stress *causes* illness.

Anecdotal reports of sudden death following psychological stress do provide more of a causal demonstration of the mind's control over the physical body (Richter, 1957). Many of these reports mention "voodoo"-type curses in primitive societies. After learning of a curse put upon themselves, previously healthy individuals suddenly grow pale, weak, and tremulous. Their death within hours or days confirms the "voodoo" prophecy. Physiologist W. B. Cannon (1942) explained this phenomenon as an extreme case of the fight-or-flight reaction in the autonomic nervous system. The body responds to stress or anxiety with activation of the sympathetic nervous system and an outpouring of adrenaline. One action of sympathetic activation is to increase the heart rate. Thus too much stress may cause the heart to beat so fast that it goes into constant contraction, causing death.

Other researchers have postulated that some stressful situations are perceived as so hopeless that the organism responds in exactly the opposite way. The *para*sympathetic nervous system becomes overstimulated, resulting in such slow breathing and heart rate that death can occur. Researchers studying endurance in rats found that their extremely careful methods of handling even the fiercest of wild rats so thoroughly eliminated all hopes of escape that the animals never even attempted to bite the researcher handling them, and drowned immediately when dropped into water for a swimming test. Heart-rate measurements showed slowing of the heart, rather than the acceleration that might have been expected with the usual fight-or-flight reaction (Richter, 1957).

The scientific literature contains anecdotal records of similar sudden deaths in humans encountering hopeless situations. Engel (1971) has collected 170 cases of sudden death seemingly due to helplessness and hopelessness. He tells of a previously healthy 43-year-old man who died four hours after receiving what turned out to be a false call that his son had been kidnapped. Another middle-aged man unable to face returning to troubles in his home town, but prevented by circumstances from relocating in another area, died suddenly during a rest stop on a train trip between the two communities.

These informal observations of sudden cardiac malfunction are supported by findings of predeath stress build-up in 39 Swedish men listed as sudden victims of heart disease (Rahe and Lind, 1971). Based on the Schedule of Recent Events questionnaires completed by close survivors of the deceased, researchers calculated Life-Change Units (LCU) totals for each quarter of a year, starting three years prior to death. As illustrated in Figure 9-1, both victims without a history of cardiac trouble and those with a prior history showed a significant increase in life-change intensity during the six months before death. The LCU score peaks in quarters 1 and 2 of the top graph represent a threefold increase in LCU magnitude, as compared to two and three years prior to death. In contrast, the bottom graph shows that the LCU elevation for previously symptomatic subjects occurred during quarter 5 in the second year prior to sudden death. This elevation was maintained over the entire period before death. Of 15 who had predeath episodes of heart trouble, 13 of these episodes occurred during this final $1\frac{1}{4}$-year period. The authors compared their findings to those in another study of survivors of heart attacks. The survivors experienced much lower LCU levels.

General Overview

The previous examples make it very clear that physical problems, illness, and even death can be related to psychological factors. At one time, it was thought that only a small class

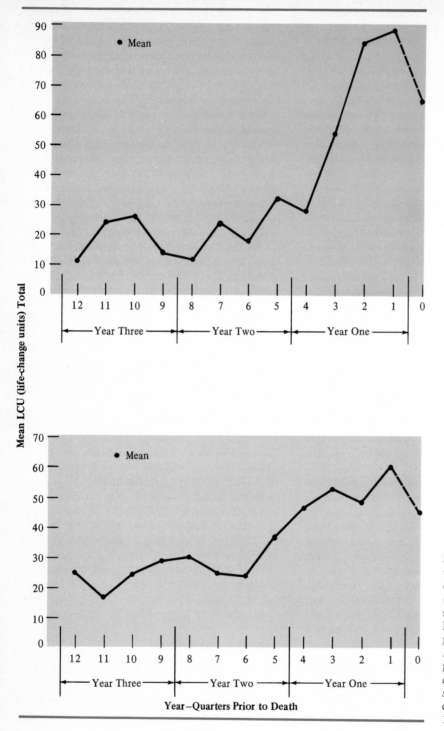

Figure 9-1 (Top) Sudden-death subjects without a history of coronary heart disease. (Bottom) Sudden-death subjects with a prior heart disease. (*Adapted from Rahe, R. H., and Lind, E. Psychosocial factors and sudden cardiac death: A pilot study.* Journal of Psychosomatic Research, *1971, 15, 21.*)

of illnesses was related to life stresses. Ulcers and asthma are the best known of these "psychosomatic" ailments. It should be clear from the evidence presented in this section that psychological factors enter into far more illnesses than had previously been suspected. Some investigators even suggest that all physical illnesses may be psychologically determined. More likely, psychological variables may contribute in some way to the development and maintenance of physical problems. The more we learn of the complex interactions of mind and body, the more important they appear in the study of the health sciences. As neuroanatomist C. J. Herrick emphasizes:

> Our civilization and all its accumulated wealth and values are in dire peril just because people have not recognized that the criteria of fitness (the biologist survival value) have shifted from the psychological level of bodily security and comfort to the psychological and moral levels. (Herrick, 1956)

Types of Psychophysiologic Disorders

The DSM-II contains a listing of physical disorders of presumably psychogenic origin. It states:

> This group of disorders is characterized by physical symptoms that are caused by emotional factors and involve a single organ system, usually under autonomic nervous system innervation. The physiological changes involved are those that normally accompany certain emotional states, but in these disorders the changes are more intense and sustained. The individual may not be consciously aware of his emotional state. (American Psychiatric Association, 1968, pp. 3–4)

This definition, of course, emphasizes the traditional notion that psychological stress affects specific body functions rather than predisposing the body to many, nonspecific disorders.

Despite this limitation, the DSM-II listing presents a useful division of psychophysiologic disorders into ten body-system categories. The remainder of this section follows the DSM-II guidelines with brief descriptions of each system and its related psychophysiologic disorders.

Psychophysiologic Skin Disorders

The diagnosis of psychophysiologic skin disorder applies to a variety of skin irritations and eruptions and other conditions in which psychological factors may be implicated. The skin is subject to direct autonomic nervous system control, and to indirect control by endocrine systems. Thus it is not surprising that investigators find psychiatric causality in over 75 percent of their dermatology patients (Kolb, 1973).

Psychophysiologic Skeletal Muscle Disorders

Muscles tense for a variety of reasons. It is understandable how psychological tensions can be expressed in this way. Muscles under tension are also more likely to be strained and go into spasm. Thus we can see that even sudden muscle reactions can be the result of long periods of psychological stress. Backache, muscle cramps, and even the syndrome of rheumatoid arthritis all have been associated with psychological causes. With rheumatoid arthritis, for example, onset or worsening is often related to emotional stress.

Psychophysiologic Respiratory Disorders

The respiratory system is directly involved in many overt expressions of emotion, the most obvious being speaking, laughing, and crying. Thus it is not unusual to find respiratory problems associated with psychological difficulties.

The most frequently encountered psychophysiological respiratory problem is hyperventilation, or overbreathing. As we noted previously, autonomic responses to stress include an increase in respiratory rate. In anxious individuals, this fast breathing is prolonged. This produces changes in the balance of the body's carbon dioxide ratio that are accompanied by feelings of light-headedness or faintness, perspiration, unsteady gait, heart palpitations, and tingling sensations in the fingertips, toes, and mouth region.

Bronchial asthma is perhaps the best known of the respiratory syndromes. Although a physiological sensitivity to antigens is thought to be necessary to predispose individuals to asthma, psychological factors have been identified as the cause in as many as 75 percent of attacks in susceptible individuals (Kolb, 1973). Some patients experience attacks at regular times of day, or under specific circumstances. One often-cited example is the "rose asthma" associated with real flowers, which also occurs at the sight of papier-mache roses. This type of attack is viewed as a conditioned response to an environmental cue.

Psychophysiologic Cardiovascular Disorders

As we noted in our section on sudden death, stress can produce the powerful fight-or-flight syndrome of increased heart rate, increased blood pressure, and changes in cardiac rhythm. On the other hand, feelings of despair and helplessness may produce slowed heart rate and lowered blood pressure. Such physiological factors may play a causative role in the cardiovascular complaints of susceptible individuals. These patients have been called "labiles" (i.e., liable to change) because of their sensitivity to environmental cues that produce cardiovascular changes. Psychophysiologic cardiovascular disorders include heart attack, stroke, hypertension, migraine headache, and other ailments. We will discuss this important syndrome picture in greater detail in the final section of this chapter.

Psychophysiologic Hemic and Lymphatic Disorders

Though less often implicated, psychological factors have been found to influence the body's blood and lymphatic systems. Psychogenic anemia is one example of this category of disorders.

Psychophysiologic Gastrointestinal Disorders

The diagnosis of psychophysiologic gastrointestinal disorders applies to conditions such as peptic ulcer, chronic gastritis, ulcerative or mucous colitis, constipation, hyperacidity, "heartburn," and irritable colon. These disorders are the most frequently reported of all psychophysiological complaints. Our section on peptic ulcers at the end of this chapter discusses the genesis and treatment of this representative gastrointestinal disorder.

Psychophysiologic Genito-Urinary Disorders

Although the relationship is unclear, some genito-urinary disorders are thought to be psychologically determined. Among these in women are disturbances in menstruation, pos-

Box 9-1 Types of Psychophysiologic Disorders

Type	Example
Psychophysiologic skin disorder	acne, eczema, hives
Psychophysiologic muscular-skeletal disorder	backache, muscle cramps
Psychophysiologic respiratory disorder	bronchial asthma, hyperventilation
Psychophysiologic cardiovascular disorder	heart attack, stroke, hypertension, migraine headaches
Psychophysiologic hemic and lymphatic disorder	anemia
Psychophysiologic gastrointestinal disorder	ulcers, colitis, heartburn
Psychophysiologic genito-urinary disorder	disturbances in menstruation, impotence
Psychophysiologic endocrine disorder	diabetes, weight problems
Psychophysiologic disorder of an organ of special sense	vertigo

sibly including infertility, difficulty in urination, and frigidity and, in men, urination difficulties, impotence, and premature ejaculation. While we list the problems of frigidity, impotence, and premature ejaculation here, they are no longer viewed as physical disorders per se. They will be discussed in Chapter 18.

Psychophysiologic Endocrine Disorders

The endocrine glands secrete hormones that control many aspects of body function. Since endocrine activity can be affected by psychological factors, physiologic disorders of the endocrine system frequently follow psychological stress. Diabetes, for example, is a deficiency in pancreatic secretion of insulin, the hormone that controls glucose levels in the blood. Although this is a biological problem, it has been demonstrated that glucose levels are elevated during periods of psychological stress. Thus these psychologically caused changes can aggravate the metabolic problem.

Similarly, thyroid gland disorders may produce weight problems, cardiac malfunctions, and general nervousness. All can be exacerbated by psychological stress.

Psychophysiologic Disorders of an Organ of Special Sense

This diagnosis applies to stress-related disturbances in specialized body organs. Vertigo, or dizziness, due to inner-ear malfunction is one example of this category.

Other Psychophysiologic Disorders

This collective category describes disturbances related to a variety of problems not located in the above systems. One such problem relates to sensory information coming from all the various body parts. These sensory messages can be tempered by psychological messages relating to the same body areas. For example, when disability or amputation of any body part occurs, these combined psychological and physiological messages may still continue, with a resultant "phantom limb phenomenon," in which pain is experienced in the disabled or missing limb. This is especially common among amputees. Stimulation in the nerve endings of the stump accounts for some phantom feelings. These same feelings, however, can be caused by psychologically disturbing thoughts or events, even in the absence of physiological stimuli.

It is important to note for each of these formal categories that observable, physiological proof of tissue damage is present. Thus psychophysiological complaints cannot be dismissed as imaginary. They are, rather, biological indications (results) of psychological disturbances. There are so many psychophysiologic disorders that it is not practical to describe all of them in depth in a textbook of this length. Instead, we will save for the end of this chapter an analysis of two representative disorders—heart attack and stomach ulcers—which may serve as diagnosis and treatment models for the entire class of psychophysiological complaints.

Theoretical Aspects

We have observed thus far that psychological stress can produce biological disorders in numerous body systems. Two major questions now arise: (1) Why do such disorders occur? and (2) What determines which disorder does occur? In other words, what causes biological systems to break down under psychological stress, and why does one system break down as opposed to some other system?

Why Psychophysiologic Disorders at All?

W. B. Cannon, whose research we mentioned earlier, proposed the theory that living organisms operate on a principle of *homeostasis*, the tendency to maintain internal functioning within certain constant limits (1929). A rise in body temperature, for example, signals the need for sweating, which cools the body down to normal levels. A fall in blood calcium leads to transfer of stored calcium in bone tissue to the blood, until there is a return to normal levels. This striving for equilibrium occurs in systems throughout the body.

Psychological cues can also signal equilibrium-producing changes. Situations causing psychological stress switch on what Cannon labeled the *emergency reaction*, a "fight-or-flight arousal" pattern. This reaction pattern serves a protective, adaptive function. It prepares the organism to handle dangerous situations, such as escape from predators, thus ensuring survival. In addition, it promises a quick resolution of the emergency, so that the body can immediately revert to equilibrium levels.

Hans Selye (1946, 1956) expanded Cannon's principles of emergency reaction and homeostasis into a three-part *stress reaction theory*. Selye's explanation centers on a three-stage *general adaptation syndrome* exhibited almost stereotypically whenever the body is threatened by stressors. All stressful stimuli, from emotional reactions to bacterial infections, from fatigue to body injury, produce the same response pattern. The first stage, the *alarm reaction*, corresponds to Cannon's fight-or-flight pattern. The goal is quick mobilization against stress and an immediate return to body equilibrium levels. When continued defense against generalized or specific stressors is necessary, the body enters the second or *resistance stage*. Here a new level of physiological balance is maintained, replacing accustomed equilibrium stages. This resistance, however, cannot be maintained indefinitely. Prolonged exposure to stressors brings the body to the third point, the *exhaustion stage*. At this stage, the body resources are so depleted that further stress may produce collapse or even death.

The theories of Cannon and Selye represent "nonspecific" models of psychophysiological illness. These models describe psychophysiologic disorders as *generalized* stress responses, rather than specific systemic reactions to specific psychological pressures (Kaplan and Kaplan, 1967). In this viewpoint, specific symptoms such as gastric or cardiovascular hyperactivity merely reflect the body's general emergency response to any noxious stimuli, from bodily injury to death of a spouse. These theorists find it impossible to predict which symptoms or disorder will be correlated with any one psychological stress.

What Determines the Type of Disorder?

In contrast to nonspecific models, much psychophysiological research focuses on relationships between specific psychological stresses and predictable somatic complaints. The collection of clinical and experimental literature in this area reflects the diversity of contemporary theories. We will focus on five of the most representative viewpoints.

Somatic Weakness Theory

According to this model, effects of stressful stimulation are seen first in "weak links" in the body chain, that is, in organs vulnerable because of genetic weakness, prior illness, or injury. Findings of a higher incidence of certain psychophysiologic disorders within blood relatives support this view (Kaplan and Kaplan, 1967). Research on newborns also implicates genetic predispositions. In one study, for example, some infants showed gastric hypersecretion, leading to the inference of genetic susceptibility to peptic ulcer (Mirsky, 1958).

Psychodynamic Theories

Unresolved conflicts, according to psychodynamically oriented researchers, may be expressed in specific predictable disorders related to (1) the age in infancy when particular stressful events occurred; (2) the stressed problem area, such as feeding or bowel control; (3) the kind of psychological reaction involved, such as fear, hostility, or dependence-independence; (4) the event that originally precipitated the psychophysiological reaction (Lachman, 1972).

Franz Alexander (1950) and his associates proposed the original psychodynamic theories of specific psychological response patterns. They studied numerous patients suffering from various organic problems. Each problem area appeared to reflect specific chronically repressed emotional conflicts. In ulcer patients, for example, he supposed that there existed a chronic wish to be fed, opposed by feelings of shame and guilt. With hypertension, it was chronic tension from incompletely repressed aggressive tendencies. In addition, Alexander postulated two related, and necessary, factors for illness to actually occur. First, there must be some constitutional weakness in the target organ system; then, a specific "onset situation" must occur, some life event that would activate old conflicts.

In actuality, Alexander combined the weak-link model with psychodynamic theory, adding an awareness of the effect of life stresses. Thus an individual exhibiting some genetic organ weakness, and history of psychodynamic conflict, will develop psychophysiological symptoms only if external life events activate the conflict area (Reiser, 1975).

Personality Types

Just as Alexander identified specific elements in the psychological history of various patient groups, other researchers emphasized specific elements in personality makeup. Using objective personality profiles obtained through interviews or questionnaires, these investigators found that patients with certain somatic illnesses did indeed share similar personality traits.

Most notable among these clinical researchers was Flanders Dunbar, who hypothesized that competitive, "executive" personality types were most vulnerable to coronary artery disease (1943). While this correlation was accurate, its theoretical usefulness was limited without some demonstration of causality. In fact, Dunbar could not rule out the possibility that common personality factors arose as a result of the disease.

Other personality researchers focused on more demonstrable causes. Grace and Graham (1952) found that specific attitudes toward events were related to the onset and occurrences of specific psychophysiologic disorders. By attitudes, they meant an individual's perception of various situations and of the actions he or she might choose to take in these situations. The examples in Table 9-2 illustrate particular attitudes associated with various symptom pictures.

Life-Stress Events

As we mentioned at the beginning of the chapter, life stresses such as death of a spouse, marriage, salary increases, and many other changes may foreshadow major health problems, and even sudden death. Although generalized symptoms of anxiety, sleep disturbances, and loss of appetite were noted, coronary artery disease was the specific diagnosis in a large proportion of these deaths (Parkes, 1972). In addition, diseases present before the period of life stress either recurred or got worse. These findings tend to support somatic weakness theories, as opposed to psychodynamic and personality models.

Marriage is one life-stress event that can lead to psychophysiologic disorders. (*Martine Franck, VIVA, Woodfin Camp & Associates.*)

Table 9-2 Relationship of Patient Attitudes to Psychophysiological Symptoms

Symptom	Number of Patients	Attitude
Eczema	27	Feels that he is being interfered with or prevented from doing something and cannot overcome frustration; is concerned with the obstacle rather than the goal. Ex: "I want to make my mother understand, but I can't."
Cold, moist hands (Raynaud's disease)	10 (4)	Feels need to undertake some activity but may not know what to do. Ex: "Something had to be done." (Included in previous group.) The contemplated action was hostile. Ex: "I wanted to put a knife through him."
Asthma	7	Facing a situation that he would rather avoid or escape. Essential feature was desire to have nothing to do with it. Ex: "I wanted to go to bed and pull the sheets over my head."
Diarrhea	27	Desired to get a situation over with, to get rid of something or somebody. Ex: (Patient had bought a defective car.) "If only I could get rid of it."
Constipation	17	Individual grimly determined to carry on with a situation but with no expectation of improvement or success. Ex: "It's a lousy job, but it's the best I can do."
Nausea and vomiting	11	Preoccupied with a past mistake, something he wished he hadn't done or that hadn't happened. Ex: "I wish things were the way they were before."
Duodenal ulcer	9	Individual seeking revenge, wishing to injure a person or thing that had injured him. Ex: "He hurt me, so I wanted to hurt him."
Migraine headache	14	When individual had been making an intense effort to carry out a planned program and was now relaxing. It made no difference whether or not the project had succeeded. Ex: "I had to meet a deadline."
High blood pressure	7	Individual feels that he must be constantly prepared for threat. Ex: "Nobody is ever going to beat me. I'm ready for anything."
Low back pain	11	Individual thinking of walking or running away from something. Ex: "I just wanted to walk out of the house."

Maher, B. *Principles of psychopathology*. New York: McGraw-Hill, 1966, p. 245; based on Grace and Graham, 1952.

Individual Response Specificity

Researchers have noted the tendency of many individuals to exhibit consistent response patterns to a wide range of stressful stimuli. "Cardiovascular reactors" characteristically ex- perience chest pain and palpitations, "muscle reactors" have headaches, and "gastric reactors" get stomach pains (Malmo, 1967). Such characteristic patterns may reflect inheritance of somatic responsiveness. It is common, in fact, for family members to exhibit similar responses during crisis situations. In some families, everyone breaks out in hives; in others, everyone converges on the bathroom.

In short, heredity determines which system will be most reactive in a given individual. If the individual is put under stress for extended periods of time, we can expect that system to be overtaxed and susceptible to damage. You can actually predict right now the type of psychophysiologic disorder you might eventually have by noting what systems react to current stresses. If before exams your stomach is upset or you break out with acne, you know that those systems are reactive. This information could be used preventively to reduce stress when the reaction starts or to initiate early treatment if the stress must continue.

Learning Models

Research in the fields of respondent and operant conditioning strongly suggests that learning of involuntary, visceral responses can play a significant role in the development of psychophysiologic disorders (Knapp, 1975). What this means, in essence, is that an individual's conditioning history determines what psychophysiologic disorders he or she will develop, and what environmental stimuli will elicit them.

To take an example of respondent conditioning, investigators had asthmatic patients repeatedly inhale an allergen, producing an attack of asthma (Dekker, Pelser, and Groen, 1957). Later, they found that inhalation of a nonallergenic substance also elicited asthmatic attacks. An association had been conditioned between the act of inhaling a substance and the onset of an attack. Further testing showed generalization of the asthmatic response to the inhalation of pure oxygen, and even to the presentation of the inhalation mouthpiece itself.

Respondent conditioning explanations of psychophysiologic disorders cannot, however, account for chronic conditions that seem unrelated to specific environmental events. Recent findings in the field of operant learning, on the other hand, do account for long-term and multifaceted psychophysiologic disorders. Neal Miller has been at the forefront of research in this field. He and his co-workers have demonstrated, usually in lower animals, that organisms can learn to control visceral responses that are usually considered to be purely involuntary. Miller's group has produced consistent and reversible changes in heart rate, blood pressure, intestinal activity, urine production, and brain-wave activity (Miller, 1969). We will discuss these studies later in this chapter in the section on biofeedback. It may be noted here that similar conditioning in human beings may be responsible for individual differences in visceral responses to stress. Miller proposes the example of a child who doesn't want to go to school. His anxiety elicits a wide variety of generalized autonomic symptoms, perhaps upset stomach, diarrhea, and headache one day, pallor and dizziness on another. The child's mother may notice frequent trips to the bathroom and conclude that he is sick enough to stay home. The relief from fear the child experiences reinforces the intestinal response and makes it more likely to recur in the future. The headaches, pallor, and other symptoms, which did not gain attention (reinforcement) will be less likely to recur (Miller, 1969).

Miller is not alone in his attention to autonomic conditioning. Lachman (1972), for example, has developed a complete "autonomic reaction learning theory of psychosomatic phenomena." Basically, Lachman hypothesizes that psychophysiologic disorders result from a vicious circle effect. The process begins with external stresses. Inherited and learned differences in sensitivity to these stresses make each individual susceptible to particular "implicit reactions" (changes in blood pressure, heart rate, intestinal motility, hormonal secretion, etc.). These physiological changes then produce stressful internal stimuli, which exacerbate the implicit reaction. As an example, consider the cycle for ulcer development diagrammed in Figure 9-2. The initial external stimulus may have been work pressures. The implicit predisposed response in this subject is stomach hy-

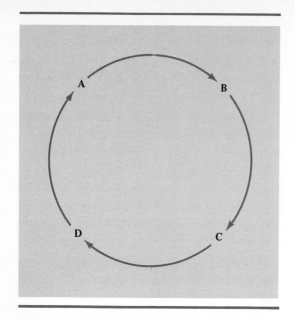

Figure 9-2 Vicious circle for ulcer development. A = noxious stimulation from area of ulcer; B = perceptual effect of noxious stimulation; C = emotional reaction, including hyperactivity; D = further inflammation of ulcer. (*Lachman, S. J. Psychosomatic disorders: A behavioristic interpretation. New York: Wiley, 1972.*)

peracidity. Repetition of the external stress intensifies hyperacidity, creating a mild ulcer. The ulcer itself is an implicit internal stimulus; the discomfort it causes is stressful. The emotional reaction to this added stress is exacerbation of the ulcer. The chronic repetition of this syndrome increases physiological damage, creating a recognizable psychophysiologic disorder, in this case severe peptic ulcer.

Treatment Approaches

As the previous section indicated, psychophysiological syndromes are complex responses to a complex assortment of stimuli. The major stumbling block in choosing a treatment for such disorders is deciding which variables merit the most attention. The problem boils down to two central issues: modification of the patient's particular personality pattern versus modification of the way the patient reacts to stress and conflict. Therapists tend to take sides on this matter according to their basic orientation. Psychodynamic practitioners opt for personality changes, while behaviorists emphasize changes in response patterns to characteristic stimuli.

Regardless of the ultimate choice of psychological therapy, somatic therapy takes first priority. In many cases, life-threatening medical problems are evident in patients with psychophysiologic disorders. The bronchospasms of asthma, the mineral depletion of anorexia nervosa (loss of appetite that results in extreme weight loss), the bloody diarrhea of ulcer conditions—all require immediate medical attention.

Unfortunately, the urgency of these medical problems often jeopardizes the patient's chances for psychological assistance. The medical doctor who first sees the patient may note predisposing elements of stress. In general, however, these variables usually do not receive sufficient attention to ensure treatment of them. Thus medication such as steroids for asthmatics, or surgery such as colectomy (removal of all or part of the colon) for severe ulcerative colitis, may end the patient's treatment. When psychological problems are recognized, management may be achieved with one of the vastly popular drugs (that induce psychological changes). These surgical and pharmacological treatments, in themselves, may eliminate the symptoms of psychophysiologic disorders. Symptom substitution is rare in these cases (Ramsay, Witkower, and Warnes, 1976).

For the patient whose difficulties persist, specialized treatment is the next step. This may include psychoanalysis and psychotherapy, behavior therapy, group therapy, family therapy, and hypnosis. Each of these categories includes many therapeutic approaches. Since we cannot describe all of them in detail, we will instead summarize three representative techniques—

psychodynamic approaches, behavioral approaches, and hypnosis.

Psychodynamic Approaches

You will recall from Chapter 6 that psychodynamic therapies focus on a patient's inability to handle intrapsychic conflicts that stem from his or her developmental history. As applied to psychophysiologic disorders, these methods concentrate on stressful events that cause physical symptoms, and on characteristic defense mechanisms used by the patient in dealing with such stresses.

Most often cited is the prevalence of oral-anal fixation from disturbances of the mother-child relationship in the early preverbal period. Despite evidence of psychodynamic involvement, most patients insist that their problems are purely medical. This makes these individuals poor candidates for psychotherapy. Some investigators feel, in fact, that the majority of patients with psychophysiologic disorders are unsuitable for analysis, and often deteriorate under such treatment (Stokvis, 1960; Sifneos, 1972).

In their review of outcome studies of psychodynamic psychotherapy, particularly for ulcerative colitis and peptic ulcer, however, Ramsay et al. (1976) found improvement in a significant number of cases. They noted several important factors in successful treatment. For example, one study indicated that the longer the duration of treatment, the better were the results (Karush et al., 1969). Of 18 patients treated for a year or less, only 10 (56%) showed improvement. Of 12 patients treated for one to three years or more, 10 (83%) were physically improved. Of 4 patients treated for less than six months, 3 showed no improvement. Another study (Weinstock, 1962) indicated that patients who did best with psychotherapy came to treatment after hospitalization, and with only mild symptoms. Investigations also emphasized the importance of completion of the analytic course (Orgel, 1958). Out of 15 gastric and duodenal ulcer patients, 5 who dropped out of treatment continued to experience problems, while the 10 who completed analysis

were symptom-free on follow-up 10 to 22 years later.

Even considering such positive results, the extensive expenditure of time and money involved with psychoanalysis makes it less popular than other therapies. Nevertheless, Ramsay et al. (1976) emphasize that for certain patients it may be dramatically, and quickly, effective. They describe the case of a 50-year-old executive suffering from severe angina pectoris (recurrent chest pain) that forced him to give up his professional position, and to change his entire life style. He even relinquished his mistress. Three years of psychopharmacological therapy and attention to environmental stresses did not relieve his symptoms. Psychoanalytically oriented therapy focused the patient on his self-directed aggression, and after eight months' treatment he was symptom-free.

Behavioral Approaches

While several years is not considered a long time for psychodynamic therapy, you will remember from Chapter 7 that behavioral approaches often produce results quite rapidly. In recent years, the behavioral approach has proven particularly effective in the treatment of psychophysiological problems. As we discussed earlier in this chapter, respondent and operant conditioning have been indicated as playing a significant role in the development of psychophysiologic disorders. Thus it is not surprising that conditioning-oriented therapies are proposed as ways of eliminating these disorders.

In the area of autonomic, *involuntary* muscle functioning, behavior therapy helps patients to become aware of, and to control, internal body processes. *Biofeedback* is the most popular approach to autonomic conditioning. A detailed description of this technique is presented in the next section.

Operant techniques are used to establish control of *voluntary* muscle responses. With anorexia nervosa patients, for example, selective positive reinforcement of desired eating patterns leads to significant weight gain

(Bachrach, Erwin, and Mohr, 1965; Leitenberg, Agras, and Thomson, 1968).

Behavioral approaches have also been employed to treat muscle spasms, skin eruptions, diarrhea, vomiting, epileptic seizures, and many other psychophysiologic disorders (Ramsay et al., 1976). Migraine headaches, which tend to be difficult to treat, respond particularly well to behavioral approaches. A combination of desensitization and assertion training resulted in an impressive 89.5 percent reduction in the number of migraine attacks in experimental patients as compared to controls who did not receive treatment (Mitchell, 1969, 1971).

Asthma has also been treated successfully with the behavioral approach. As we discussed previously, the asthma syndrome begins with unconditioned responses to allergens; these responses then become conditioned to neutral stimuli. *Shaping* may also produce asthma-like responses. When a crying child does not receive attention and comfort, he or she may alter the crying response until a variant that *does* produce reinforcement is hit upon. Labored breathing, an effective attention-getter, is the likely result. This shaping explanation could account for the development of asthma even in patients who are not sensitive to allergens (Turnbull, 1962). Behavioral treatments attempt to extinguish the conditioned asthmatic response. One study reported the effectiveness of conditioning an incompatible response of relaxation to relevant environmental stimuli that previously produced asthmatic attacks (Walton, 1960).

Despite the apparent effectiveness of behavioral techniques, it should be remembered that this is a relatively new treatment approach. Long-term follow-ups have not yet been done.

Hypnosis

Hypnosis is a relatively old and still controversial approach to the treatment of psychophysiologic disorders. By definition, hypnosis implies a temporary alteration in attention, induced by another person, that produces susceptibility to suggestion particularly of ideas and responses previously unknown to the sub-ject in his or her usual state of consciousness. Although anesthesia, muscle paralysis, and other changes have been reported during hypnosis, scientific analysis of this technique has been attempted only recently.

At present, there is still much disagreement on the usefulness of hypnosis for the treatment of psychophysiologic disorders, or of any disorders for that matter. On the positive side, however, hypnosis has been reported effective in cases of duodenal ulcer, irritable bowel syndrome, migraine headache, and even warts. For example, hypnotic suggestion produced greater clinical improvement than did conventional therapy in a study of matched groups of duodenal ulcer patients (Moody, 1953). Of 90 patients suffering from migraine headaches, hypnotherapy produced complete relief of up to 8 years' duration in 34 individuals, and a 25 to 75 percent reduction in migraine episodes in 29 other individuals. Investigators emphasize, however, that cure is often dependent on susceptibility to hypnosis. For example, wart sufferers capable of "deep trance" showed a 65 percent cure rate, while not one unsusceptible subject was cured (Asher, 1956).

Of the three techniques covered in this section—psychodynamic approaches, behavioral approaches, and hypnosis—behavioral approaches are currently the most popular. For this reason, we will present next a detailed analysis of biofeedback as an example of one promising behavioral approach in the field of psychophysiologic disorders.

Biofeedback

For autonomically mediated behavior, the evidence points unequivocally to the conclusion that such responses can be modified by classical, but not instrumental, training methods. (Kimble, 1961, p. 100)

This was the prevailing view, as stated in a respected learning text, at the time Miller first began his studies of autonomic conditioning.

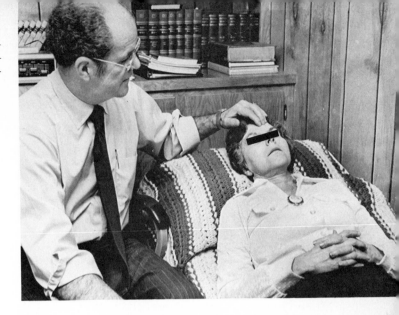

Hypnosis is a relatively old and still controversial approach to the treatment of psychophysiologic disorders. (*United Press International.*)

Observations from as far back as Plato's time supported this view that presumably involuntary visceral responses obeyed different laws of responding than did voluntary skeletal muscle responses. Plato referred to "inferior souls" governing visceral behavior, as opposed to the superior rational soul in the head. This ancient view was echoed in the nineteenth century by the French neuroanatomist Bichat, who compared the "great brain" and spinal cord controlling skeletal responses to the "little brains" of the lowly "vegetative" chain of spinal ganglia that presumably controlled emotional and visceral responses. Cannon's more sophisticated twentieth-century descriptions still retained the idea of an autonomic nervous system incapable of the finely differentiated individual responses characteristic of higher neural centers. Contemporary investigators also followed this two-part explanation in their focus on hysterical disorders, which were controlled by "higher" symbolic centers. They classified psychophysiologic disorders as autonomic, involuntary responses to emotional arousal (Miller, 1969).

Despite this discouraging historical perspective, Miller persisted in their belief in only one kind of learning, identical for both autonomic and voluntary responses. If they could demonstrate operant control of visceral responses, the historical picture of a separate and inferior, totally involuntary nervous system would at last be disproved. With it, the treatment approach to psychophysiologic disorders would be radically altered.

Miller used water-deprived dogs in his early experiments. The animals were reinforced with water whenever they showed spontaneous bursts of salivation. These dogs learned to *increase* salivation. Dogs in a comparison group received water only when there were long intervals between bursts of salivation. These dogs learned to decrease salivation. The classical learning model would have predicted that only one response—either increase or decrease in salivation—could be conditioned. This follows the reasoning that salivation and other autonomic responses are reflexes that can occur only in one fixed pattern. The operant model, on the other hand, stresses the role of reinforcement in determining the probability of recurrence of any response that immediately precedes the reinforcement. In these dog studies, both increases and decreases in salivation were seen, thus illustrating principles of operant learning in a supposedly involuntary system.

These early studies were not definitive. They had not controlled for the possibility that changes in visceral responses such as salivation might actually be caused by subtle adjustments in skeletal muscles. In other words, Miller had to make sure that the animals learned to produce visceral changes using a *visceral* response, not a *skeletal* response.

Miller attempted to control the heart rate of rats. Miller's associates chose direct electrical stimulation of "reward centers" in the brain as their reinforcing stimulus. Using this approach, they were able to demonstrate small, but statistically reliable, changes in heart rate. Rats rewarded for rate decreases learned to lower their heart rate; rats rewarded for rate increases speeded up their heart rate. When preliminary shaping procedures were added, larger rate changes were produced, with 20 percent heart-rate changes in either direction seen after just 90 minutes of training.

Encouraged by these results, Miller and his associates went on to condition intestinal contractions, peripheral vasodilation (expansion of blood vessels in fingers, toes, skin, etc.), blood pressure, and brain-wave activity. Many scientists are still not convinced that these experiments are valid. Miller himself has had some difficulty repeating his original findings (*Medical World News*, 1973). Nevertheless, this preliminary work has produced a dramatic shift in attitudes toward autonomic functioning. Miller originally had great difficulty in persuading his graduate assistants to challenge accepted theories with such unconventional experimentation. In contrast, this field of research is now a burgeoning center of activity, with over 250 papers published.

Experimental Verification in Human Subjects

Miller's work revealed new treatment possibilities for psychophysiologic disorders. Many technical problems had to be resolved, however, to make his procedures applicable to human subjects. First, a system was needed to provide subjects with continuous information about shifts in the autonomic activity being

measured. This would let them know when they were making the desired adjustments. This knowledge, or *biofeedback*, would help subjects learn to control processes that, before, had been totally unconscious.

Many of the earliest biofeedback studies were performed by researchers at Harvard University (Shapiro et al., 1969). They monitored systolic blood pressure in normal male college students. If biofeedback could help normal individuals to lower their blood pressure, then this technique might also help patients with high blood pressure. In a typical study, ten subjects were used in a blood pressure "up" group and ten in a "down" group. Following a signal, subjects attempted to raise or lower their blood pressure. A pressure change in the desired direction produced a short flash of red light, coupled with a tone. Every 20 flashes of light earned the reinforcement of a different *Playboy* magazine picture projected for several seconds on a screen in front of the subject. The slides provided incentive for subjects to keep the light flashing and the tone beeping as often as possible.

The results of this study are shown in Figure 9-3. You can see that "up" group subjects tended to maintain or slightly decrease their blood pressure during the sessions, as compared with the "down" group, which showed a significantly greater and more consistent decrease in pressure readings. Despite this clear change in the "down" group, the success of the opposite group is not so readily apparent. Their pattern, however, does follow that seen in many other studies of autonomic functioning. Typically, an initial increase is produced, followed by return to baseline levels or slightly below.

This study definitely indicates that systolic blood pressure can be modified by the use of biofeedback and operant reinforcement. Interestingly, most subjects said they had felt no control over their physiological responses. Although they were able to produce the desired effects, they had no idea of which specific body function was actually being conditioned.

Later studies (Schwartz, Shapiro, and

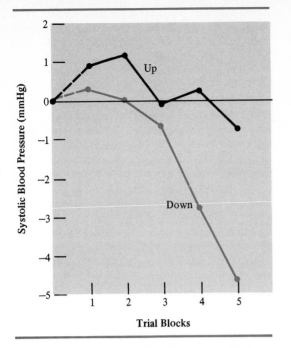

Figure 9-3 Average approximate systolic pressures in groups reinforced for increasing (*up*) and decreasing (*down*) blood pressure. Each point is the mean of ten subjects, five trials each. (*Shapiro, D., et al. Effects of feedback and reinforcement on the control of human systolic blood pressure.* Science, 1969, 163, 589. © 1969 by the American Association for the Advancement of Science.)

of both responses was obtained in just a single training session. As in Figure 9-3, conditioned heart rate and blood pressure increases were much smaller than conditioned decreases. However, both effects were statistically significant at high levels of confidence.

Biofeedback as Therapy

Recent reviews cite biofeedback successes in controlling blood pressure, relieving muscle tension associated with headaches, restoring muscle function following stroke and spinal injury, and regulating electroencephalograph (EEG) rhythms in epileptics and in children with attention disorders. One research group even reported the unusual finding that biofeedback could help men to raise their scrotal temperature, as a possible birth control method.

In contrast to these exciting and dramatic demonstrations are previously mentioned reports of difficulty in replicating the original animal findings of Miller's group. In addition, the Harvard researchers whose pioneering techniques spawned interest in biofeedback now take a cautious, conservative stand on current claims for their methods (Medical World News, 1973). They emphasize that laboratory studies with normal subjects do not necessarily generalize to patients in the outside world. These investigators even go so far as to question whether feedback is the crucial requirement for success in autonomic conditioning studies. Cognitive or somatic "strategies" may also underlie supposed biofeedback effects. In one study, for example, a patient treated for Raynaud's disease, a problem of reduced blood flow producing cold and pain in the extremities, found that free association of sun, warmth, and other "hot" thoughts would control his symptoms as well as biofeedback did (Schwartz, 1973). In other patients, it is possible that motivation, or positive expectation of gain, is the real conditioning factor.

Taken together, these reminders of environmental, cognitive, and biological factors impinging on the biofeedback process dampen

Tursky, 1971) attempted more complex feats, for example, conditioning of two autonomic responses, heart rate and blood pressure. Conditioning was accomplished by presenting a short light and tone feedback to some subjects for *integrating* heart rate and blood pressure (both increasing or both decreasing), and to other subjects for *differentiating* the responses (one increasing and one decreasing). For every 12 correct heart rate–blood pressure combinations, subjects earned a three-second showing of an interesting slide and a monetary reward. As illustrated in Figure 9-4, significant control

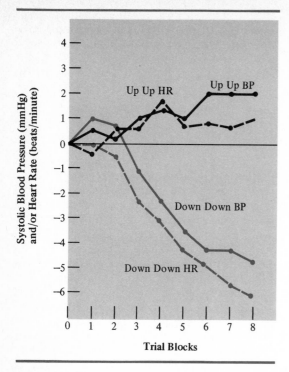

Figure 9-4 Average heart rate (HR) and systolic blood pressure (BP) in subjects rewarded for simultaneously increasing both HR and BP (*up-up* integration) and for simultaneously decreasing both HR and BP (*down-down* integration). Each point is the mean of five subjects, five trials each. (*Schwartz, G. E., Shapiro, D., and Tursky, B. Learned control of cardiovascular integration in man through operant conditioning.* Psychosomatic Medicine, *1971, 33, 61.*)

enthusiasm for many apparent treatment successes. A recent review article by Blanchard and Young (1974) described the very few biofeedback studies employing strong experimental design. Blanchard and Young found strong support only for electromyogram (EMG) feedback. This technique involves recording electrical activity of various muscles while providing feedback to patients on their success in controlling this activity. EMG training produced dramatic return of muscle function in patients suffering from paralysis, neuromus-

cular disorders, and motor nerve injuries. The technique was also successful for eliminating subvocal speech during reading and for preventing tension headaches.

EMG biofeedback actually conditions striate muscle responses, already assumed to be under voluntary control. Thus convincing EMG studies do not demonstrate anything really new or surprising. Unfortunately, autonomic response control studies, which would be revolutionary, are often unconvincing. For example, studies of cardiovascular control have produced positive results. Yet Blanchard and Young fault these studies for their lack of adequate controls.

Electroencephalographic conditioning, especially of alpha brain waves, has received much public attention. Again, Blanchard and Young find little scientific support for clinical benefits of this treatment. They hypothesize that biofeedback training merely conditions subjects to disregard alpha-blocking environmental cues, without actually raising their baseline alpha wave production level.

Claims for miraculous biofeedback cures are, as we have seen, quite misleading. The current status of biofeedback therapy is promising, but unproven. Well-controlled research is necessary before this approach can be accepted as a primary treatment for psychophysiologic disorders.

Two Specific Psychophysiologic Disorders

Peptic Ulcers

One of the most frequently diagnosed psychophysiologic disorders is gastrointestinal ulcer, a localized erosion of the mucous membrane, usually of the stomach or small intestine. Pain, ranging from mild to severe, is the major symptom. Medical control is achieved with a combination of bland diet, preventive use of antacid preparations, and, in serious cases, surgery.

From a psychological standpoint, pro-

"One businessman's lunch. Will that be ulcer or hypertension?" (*Sidney Harris,* © *1972 Medical Tribune.*)

longed emotional stress triggers ulcer-producing events. Emotional arousal of the autonomic nervous system activates the vagus nerve, which stimulates intestinal contractions and secretion of gastric juices. Prolonged periods of such activation increase the probability of damage to mucous membranes, and of subsequent exposure of sensitive underlying tissue to attack by stomach acids.

Traditional Views and Treatment Approaches

Ulcer patients have been thought to share a similar psychological makeup, centering "around strong needs to be taken care of, to lean on others, to be fed, and to be nurtured" (Engel, 1975, p. 671). Although developmental influences determine the precise expression of these personality characteristics, they usually fall into one of three basic patterns:

1. *Pseudo-independent.* These individuals hide their dependency under a facade of aggressive, controlling self-reliance. In marriage and work relationships, they show contempt and coldness toward those they force to obey their domineering commands. Pseudo-independents fit the stereotype of successful business or professional people who overwork themselves and their associates in a perpetual frenzy of ambitious ventures.

2. *Passive-dependent.* In this personality group, dependency needs are both conscious and overtly expressed. These individuals appear passive, compliant, and eager to please. They seek supportive, nurturing relationships in which they are openly clinging and dependent.

3. *Acting-out.* The infantile personalities of this group are marked by insistent and demanding attitudes, often expressed in antisocial or even criminal acts. Such irresponsible and inconsiderate individuals are typically drifters, frequently unemployed, and dependent on drugs or alcohol.

Although these three personality types differ in their outward demeanor, and in the effectiveness of their psychological defense mechanisms, they all share the common denominator of dependency needs. Frustration of these needs produces activation of the ulcer syndrome. Such frustration typically involves threats of loss of love or security, which the patient feels helpless to counteract. Zax and Stricker (1963) cite a typical case illustrating the dependency need of an individual.

Aaron V. was a shy, quiet garage mechanic in his early thirties. Aaron's young, socially oriented wife frequently argued with him about his desire to spend quiet evenings at home in front of the television set. The arrival of children lessened her pressures on him for a more active social life. At the same time, however, he began to complain that she was not giving him the attention he felt he deserved. These complaints were accompanied by his first signs of stomach pain. Following the birth of his second child, Aaron experienced frequent headaches as well. The birth of his fourth child signaled worsening of his stomach pains, especially during times of stress. Aaron's physician diagnosed the abdominal problem as a duodenal ulcer. However, the strict diet he ordered did not reduce Aaron's symptoms. Instead, it produced continuous, unbearable feelings of hunger. In despair over his worsening condition, Aaron sought psychiatric treatment. He was seen in weekly sessions extending over a period of nine months. He voiced the need to express his feelings to someone who would be concerned about his physical problems and his family relationships. In lengthy discussions, he revealed irritation at his wife's disrespectful attitude toward him, and impatience with her handling of their children. She was eventually requested to join in the therapy sessions. This course of treatment produced marked relief of Aaron's symptoms, but did not change his immature, dependent personality.

Research Approaches

Development of gastric ulcers appears to be dependent upon three factors: physiological susceptibility, a history of psychological conflict, and environmental events.

One of the classic studies of *physiological factors* in ulcer development was reported in 1947 by Wolf and Wolff. They were acquainted with a 56-year-old man who, due to a childhood accident and resulting surgery, had a plastic window over his stomach that permitted visual observation of his gastric functioning. This unusual and, for the investigators, fortuitous phenomenon, permitted revolutionary research on ulcer-related events. Wolf and Wolff found that emotions such as anger, resentment, or anxiety were accompanied by increased motion in his gastric secretions and swelling of the stomach lining with blood. This condition produced complaints of heartburn and abdominal pain. During sustained periods of such stress-produced activity, the investigators observed frequent erosions and bleeding points on the mucosa. Most of these injuries healed spontaneously in only a few hours. However, when the investigators artificially kept one area of erosion moist with gastric juices for four days, the injury grew in size and presented the appearance of a chronic peptic ulcer. Pressure applied at the site caused pain. When the ulcerated area was protected from gastric juices by a petrolatum dressing, the area healed promptly.

This demonstration of prolonged acid secretion and gastric motion associated with stressful events provided the physiological explanation of ulcer production. A later supporting study (Dragstedt, 1956) did, in fact, show that ulcer patients secrete 4 to 20 times as much stomach acid as normal subjects, particularly at night when the empty stomach is most susceptible to damage.

As we mentioned earlier, studies concerning *psychological, personality factors* in ulcer patients have suggested a syndrome of dependence, hostility, anger, and familial or work pressure. Psychodynamic theorists trace the development of these problems to the oral stage of infancy. In particular, frustration of intense cravings for passive oral gratification is presumed to create defense mechanisms that play a significant role in the development of ulcers. One frequent criticism of such psychodynamic theorizing is a lack of scientific validation. To counteract this problem, researchers (Wolowitz and Wagonfeld, 1968) developed an experimental paradigm to measure passive oral traits in ulcer patients. They chose a food-preference inventory that differentiated between passive oral preferences for sucking, as opposed to aggressive oral, biting needs. The inventory presented choices between soft versus hard, liquid versus solid, wet versus dry, bland versus seasoned foods, for example, peanut butter versus peanut brittle, and mashed potatoes versus french fried potatoes. As predicted, ulcer patients had a significantly greater preference than matched controls for passive foods characteristic of the early diet of infants. You should be asking yourself, however, is this cause or effect, that is, do they prefer such foods because they are less irritating to the ulcer?

Environmental stresses are well-known, accepted precursors of ulcer conditions. Experimental validation of this idea has, for obvious ethical reasons, centered on animal studies. Sawrey and his co-workers (1956, 1958), for example, exposed rats to shock whenever they approached food or water. By the end of two weeks of this approach-avoidance conflict situation, many rats had developed ulcers or died from gastrointestinal hemorrhages. Food and water deprived, but unshocked, control rats did not exhibit ulcers. In a similar series of stress studies, Brady (1958) trained pairs of monkeys, seated in adjacent chairs, to avoid electric shocks by pressing a lever every 20 seconds. Both animals received shocks in this avoidance test, but only one, the "executive" monkey, could actually control the shocks. The other monkey's lever was a dummy. Both animals experienced the same physical stress, since both received the same number of shocks, at the same time. However, only the "executive" experienced the psychological stress of deciding when to press the avoidance lever. Brady's executive monkeys developed ulcers; the control monkeys did not.

Brady's findings have not gone unchallenged, however. Weiss (1968) noted that Brady's monkeys were not randomly chosen as executives or controls. In actuality, Brady trained eight monkeys together. The first four to learn the bar-pressing avoidance task were assigned to the executive positions. Weiss proposed that these animals' quick learning indicated greater emotionality or lower pain tolerance, which might have predisposed them to ulcers. To test this, he ran three groups of rats

In his classic "executive" monkey study, Brady demonstrated that psychological stress can lead to ulcers. (*U.S. Army Photo, Walter Reed Army Institute.*)

randomly assigned to executive, helpless, or no-shock conditions. Contrary to Brady's findings, Weiss's helpless animals developed the most ulcers. This supports the traditional belief that unpredictable, helpless situations are more stressful than predictable situations in which an individual can act to prevent disaster.

Multifactor Research

The studies discussed so far focus on *correlations* between single factors—physiological, psychological, or environmental—and incidence of ulcer development. Analysis of complex interactions of all three factors has the advantage of *predicting* which individuals may develop ulcers. In one such report by Weiner et al. (1957), blood pepsinogen levels of 2,073 army inductees provided the *physiological* measure. Subjects with the highest values were judged to be gastric hypersecretors, as compared to hyposecretors, those with the lowest observed values. Subjects representing these two extremes were then rated on *psychological* functioning as measured in projective tests such as the Rorschach. The 16 weeks of basic training that followed these tests provided the *environmental* stress factor. Weiss found strong correlation between pepsinogen levels and personality test results. Hypersecretors showed intense "oral" needs relating to wishes for physical closeness and dependency on others. Frustration of these needs resulted in suppressed anger—suppressed for fear of jeopardizing the dependency relationships. Hyposecretors, on the other hand, were less dependent and more self-centered. They freely expressed hostility toward sources of frustration.

Examinations at the outset of the study revealed evidence of healed duodenal ulcers in three subjects, and of an active ulcer in one. After 8 to 16 weeks of training five additional men showed active ulcers. All nine of them were hypersecretors and eight of them were in the upper 5 percent of the blood pepsinogen distribution. All of these ulcer patients displayed evidence of the oral gratification conflicts common to the hypersecretory group.

This study, like other studies we have discussed, emphasizes the complex interdependence of many factors in the genesis of peptic ulcer. Here, neither high gastric secretory levels nor specific psychodynamic conflicts were independently responsible for the psychophysiological ailment. Instead, these factors acted together, under the stimulus of environmental stress. As we will see in our next section on coronary disorders, such stimulus interaction is common in the development of most psychophysiologic disorders.

Heart Disease

Coronary heart disease (CHD) is the leading cause of death in the United States today.

While there is no definitive evidence that psychological factors in themselves cause CHD, there is substantial evidence that personality characteristics and psychological stress interact with biological predispositions to produce coronary symptoms (Lipowski, 1975).

Heart problems may express themselves through changes in cardiac rate, rhythm, output, or stroke volume. These changes may affect arterial blood pressure and, in turn, produce effects in other body systems dependent upon optimal blood supply. Explanation of the complex physiological relationship between the heart and total body functioning is beyond the scope of this book. From a psychological viewpoint, however, the heart is clearly regarded as the center of body activity, the center of life support. Thus it is not surprising for anxiety and tension to be expressed by life-threatening coronary symptoms.

Coronary artery disease is the classification applied to numerous disorders so common in our modern world. Perhaps the best known of these is the "heart attack," in which a blood clot that forms within a major blood vessel blocks blood supply to a portion of the heart muscles. An area of dead tissue, a myocardial infarction, results. Another common cardiac problem is the angina pectoris syndrome of recurring radiating chest pain. It is caused by insufficient oxygenated blood supply to the heart muscle. Narrowing of the coronary arteries due to lipid deposits (atherosclerosis) is a common precipitant of the angina syndrome.

Traditional Views and Treatment Approaches

It was not much more than ten years ago that investigators were still reluctant to list psychological factors in the traditional etiological picture of age, sex, arteriosclerosis and atherosclerosis, hypertension, diabetes, diet, blood cholesterol level, lack of exercise, and heavy smoking (van der Valk and Groen, 1967). This hesitancy was not supported by scientific evidence. Cannon's studies of autonomic functioning indicated that increased speed of blood clotting was part of the fight-or-flight arousal

A common precipitant of heart disease is a narrowing of the coronary arteries due to lipid deposits. (Top) A cross section of a normal coronary artery. (Bottom) A cross section of a coronary artery, narrowed by lipid deposits and blocked by a blood clot. (*American Heart Association.*)

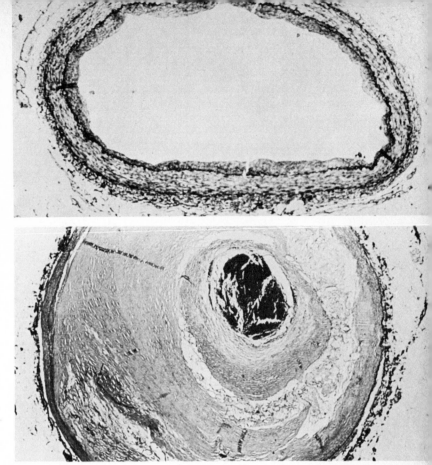

pattern (Cannon, 1942). Later studies supported this contention. Thus a possible relationship between stress, clotting, and heart attack may be hypothesized. Similarly, autonomic arousal effects on the cardiovascular system may play a role in angina attacks (Lachman, 1972).

Psychodynamic investigations focus on common personality factors in coronary patients, and in their response to certain conflict situations. Similar to the ulcer-prone individuals we discussed in the previous section, most coronary-prone subjects do not express their frustrations with overt aggressive outbursts of anger, complaining, or depression (van der Valk and Groen, 1967). Their common response to conflict is increased hard work or pretended indifference to setbacks. Again like ulcer patients, these people tend to suppress their wishes for love and attention. In contrast, however, ulcer-prone individuals shun competition in favor of acceptance by colleagues. The potential heart patients are strivers, intent on outdoing all others. Potential heart patients present an exaggerated expression of qualities considered socially desirable for men in our contemporary world. The coronary-prone man is often a "pillar of society," a hard-working "solid citizen" committed to high standards. He exercises control over his behavior, drives, and impulses, governing his behavior rationally rather than emotionally. What this means, of course, is that our Western culture predisposes men toward the development of coronary heart disease. In physiological terms, the non-emotional, controlled life style of such individuals may not provide sufficient arousal of the autonomic nervous system responses to maintain optimal cardiac performance in stressful situations. This possibility is supported by the finding of less efficient cardiac adaptation to exercise in Western man (Minc, 1965).

Research Approaches

Current research on psychophysiologic cardiac disorders has focused on life-style analysis. One of the best-known investigations in this area was conducted by Friedman et al. (1968). These researchers identified two basic behavior profiles: *Type A*—coronary-prone individuals whose life style is marked by extreme competitiveness, impatience, restlessness, and an excessive sense of time urgency relating to commitments and responsibilities; and *Type B*—individuals notably lacking in these behavior characteristics, and relatively immune to coronary heart disease. Prospective studies confirmed that the Type A behavior pattern exists *before* the onset of heart disease symptoms, thus ruling out disease-related causes of life-style differences. In a follow-up of their original screening of 3,295 men, Friedman's group found six times as many deaths from coronary heart disease among Type A individuals as in subjects classified as Type B.

Friedman's findings have been criticized from a psychological standpoint (Mai, 1968). Specifically, no established psychological tests were employed to identify individuals as Type A or Type B. When scientific rating scales were used to compare 46 myocardial infarction patients with 49 controls, few basic differences were observed. Although coronary patients were significantly more unreflective and less able to handle aggression, the groups were essentially similar in all other attributes (Miles et al., 1954).

In contrast, an experimental study aimed at verifying Friedman's concept of "time urgency" in Type A subjects did support the Type A–Type B dichotomy (Glass, Snyder, and Hollis, 1974). The experiment tested subjects' ability to perform time-estimation tasks requir-

ing a low rate of response for reinforcement. Type A subjects not only performed poorly in this time-related task, they also showed greater signs of tension than did Type B subjects. There is, therefore, some support that the behavioral style of coronary-prone individuals does indeed fit a distinctive pattern. While some of these characteristics have been demonstrated scientifically, other factors await experimental validation.

Behavioral Control of Heart Function

Identification of illness-prone individuals is the goal of most studies mentioned in this section. Treatment to prevent or delay the expected problem would be the desired next step. To date, however, efforts in this direction have not yielded fruitful results (Blanchard and Young, 1973).

From studies performed recently, it would appear that biofeedback treatments hold the greatest promise for coronary heart disease patients. As we discussed earlier, however, many biofeedback experiments employed normal subjects, not actual coronary cases. More important, the degree of reported cardiovascular changes, while statistically significant from an experimental viewpoint, is rarely clinically significant. A recent review of numerous operant conditioning studies (Blanchard and Young, 1973) indicates that promising findings with biofeedback control of cardiovascular responses are now being extended and strengthened. At present, traditional pharmacological and psychodynamic approaches directed at minimizing stress reactions are still the best preventive measures for coronary-prone individuals.

Summary

Studies on bereavement and other life stresses have demonstrated a convincing relationship between psychological events and physiologic disorders. The body's autonomic reaction to emotional stress produces a generalized physiological arousal that may, in turn, put strain on specific body systems. The determination of which system will be most affected varies with the theoretical perspective. An individual's prevailing somatic weaknesses, unresolved psychodynamic conflicts, characteristic response tendencies, and conditioning history or some combination of these are among the currently favored views.

Therapeutic intervention in the illness process can follow either psychodynamic or behavioral models. Psychodynamic therapies focus on developmental conflicts and defense mechanisms that shape the personality pattern of the psychophysiological patient. Behavioral techniques employ the principles of respondent and operant conditioning to modify a patient's learned somatic responses to specific stressful stimuli. Of the behavioral approaches, biofeedback training has proven particularly promising in its emphasis on voluntary control of what had been thought to be purely involuntary functions.

Research on two of the most prevalent psychophysiologic disorders, peptic ulcer and coronary heart disease, has implicated biological, psychological, and environmental stress factors in the total disorder process. Current investigations emphasize the complex interrelationship of all three of these factors in the development and treatment of psychologically caused physical complaints.

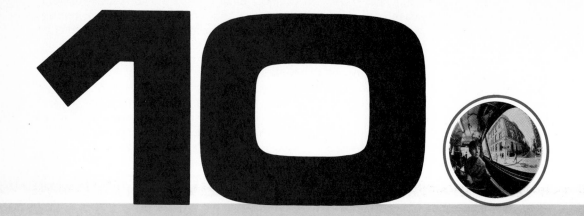

Schizophrenia: Background, classification, and description

The Concept of Schizophrenia

A medical student with a Ph.D. in psychology gives the following account of the beginning of a major psychological crisis in his life.

I got up at 7 A.M., dressed, and drove to the hospital. I felt my breathing trouble might be due to an

old heart lesion. I had been told when I was young that I had a small ventricular septal defect. I decided that I was in heart failure and that people felt I wasn't strong enough to accept this, so they weren't telling me. I thought about all the things that had happened recently that could be interpreted in that light. I looked up heart failure in a textbook and found that the section had been removed, so I concluded someone had removed it to protect me. I remembered other comments. A friend had talked about a "walkie talkie," and the thought occurred to me that I might be getting medicine without my knowledge, perhaps by radio. I remembered someone talking about a one-way plane ticket; to me that meant a trip to Houston and a heart operation. I remembered an unusual smell in the lab and thought that might be due to the medicine they were giving me in secret. I began to think I might have a machine inside of me which secreted medicine into my blood stream. Again I reasoned that I had a disease no one could tell me about and was getting medicine for it secretly. At this point I panicked and tried to run away, but the attendant in the parking lot seemed to be making a sign to motion me back. I thought I caught brief glimpses of a friend and my wife so I decided to go back into the hospital. A custodian's eyes attracted my attention, they were especially large and piercing. He looked very powerful. He seemed to be "in on it," maybe he was giving medicine in some way. Then I began to have the feeling that other people were watching me. And, as periodically happened throughout the early stages, I said to myself that the whole thing was absurd, but when I looked again the people really were watching me. One patient said, "They have the full strength medicine around here." I thought maybe the heart medicine I was being given was morphine and that I might be addicted. When I was in pediatric clinic there was a conversation between the pediatric social worker and a surgeon. He said that an operation had been planned but the equipment was all smashed. I thought this supported the idea that there was a machine inside of me, and the amphetamines I had taken messed it up. All of a sudden I felt a warm glow. I felt these people were trying to help me. They seemed to be giving me helpful hints. I thought that all the doctors in a meeting I went to were psychiatrists and that they were trying to help me. Conversations had hidden meanings. When someone told me later that I was delusional, though, I seemed to know it. But I was really groping to understand what was going on. There was a sequence with my delusions; first panic, then groping, then elation of having found out. Involvement with the delusions would fade in and out. One moment I would feel I certainly didn't believe these things; then, without realizing it, I would be caught up in them again. When reality started coming back, when I realized where I was and what had happened, I became depressed. There were times when I was aware, in a sense, that I was acting on a delusion. One part of me seemed to say, "Keep your mouth shut, you know this is a delusion and it will pass." But the other side of me wanted the delusion, preferred to have things this way. The experience was a passive one; that is, I just sat back as these things happened to me. Getting better was passive too; it just happened, so to speak, as I watched. (cited in Bowers, 1968, p. 353)

This student's account helps us share in the inner experience of someone feeling distortion in every aspect of his life. His perceptions of what is happening around him are "crazy." His world has turned topsy-turvy. What seems to make sense to him is nonsense to us. But the fact that his impressions are false does not reduce what is obviously very profound anxiety, nor does it lessen the sense of desperation that engulfs him.

This "madness" has concerned people in all cultures, through all the ages of recorded history. In our time and society, the young man is called a "schizophrenic" and is generally hospitalized for that "illness." The symptoms seem clear and the label has the definitive, diagnostic solidity of the Greek nomenclature that makes up the language of medical science. Indeed, our present concept of schizophrenia is largely based on the medical model of abnormal behavior that we outlined in Chapter 1.

The behaviors and the label, however, give a deceptive image of certainty to our understanding of schizophrenia. While hundreds of thousands of patients diagnosed as schizophrenic populate our hospitals, continuing controversy raises troubling questions about the way this disorder is viewed and treated. We will explore these psychological issues, focusing on the particular disorder called schizophrenia.

The Development of the Concept of Schizophrenia

In the early 1800s, Pinel, Esquirol, and other French psychiatrists described the behavior of patients whom we would now characterize as schizophrenic. Morel, in 1856, labeled as *demence precoce* (dementia praecox) the condition of a bright adolescent who withdrew into gloomy silence, occasionally uttering threats of killing his father (Lehmann, 1975).

In a desire to bring some order to the proliferation of descriptions of various forms of abnormal behavior, psychiatrists of the mid-nineteenth century argued over a workable nosology (system for classification of diseases). The two alternatives were classification according to causes and classification according to symptoms. Since the causes were (and still are) obscure and hypothetical, the "symptomologists" prevailed, but the debate continues.

At the end of the nineteenth century, Kraepelin, a German psychiatrist, made a major contribution by organizing the various psychiatric syndromes into useful categories. He amplified the simple cause-versus-symptom choice by considering the prognosis (course and outcome) of the disease as a further means of discriminating among similar syndromes. For example, he distinguished between dementia praecox and manic-depressive psychosis. Dementia praecox ends in deterioration; in manic-depressive psychosis, Kraepelin felt the "personality structure" is preserved. He divided the dementia category into three groups: the hebephrenic, the catatonic, and the paranoid. We will consider these later in more detail.

Kraepelin's nosology, while an advance over previous, rather primitive schemes, was the object of immediate and continuing challenges. First, dementia praecox did not always lead to complete deterioration. Kraepelin acknowledged that about 13 percent of dementia patients recovered with no sign of deterioration. Second, in the face of a large array of symptoms, confirmation of a diagnosis would have to wait, possibly for years, until the outcome could be observed. Physicians were not happy with a nosology that required waiting until the patient became incapacitated or died before they could decide what ailed him or her. Furthermore, a fixed prognosis denied the possibility of discovering effective therapies.

Taking Kraepelin's syndrome classification and Freud's new psychodynamic concept of abnormal behavior, Eugen Bleuler made the first significant attempt to determine the mechanisms that would account for bizarre behavior patterns labeled as dementia praecox (Bleuler, 1911/1950). He based his explanation of hallucinations and delusions on Freud's concepts of unconscious motivation, repression, and fantasy symbolism (Arieti, 1974b). Contrary to Kraepelin's emphasis on outcome, Bleuler saw the dissociation, or splitting, of the mind between emotion and intellect as the principal clinical aspect; so he gave it the name it still bears: *schizophrenia* ("split mind"). This must be distinguished from multiple or split personality, which is a dissociative neurosis.

Bleuler introduced the concepts of association of ideas, affective disturbance, ambivalence, and autism into the study of schizophrenia. These were applications of Freudian ideas. Another of Bleuler's innovations involved the ranking of behaviors in a hierarchy of primary and secondary significance.

While he made a strong case for the effect of intrapersonal conflict, Bleuler acknowledged the likelihood of an underlying organic disease, possibly caused by some toxin. He also recognized the probability that the various schizophrenic processes might ultimately be revealed as a family of related disorders (like the various cancer types), and so he pluralized "the schizophrenias" in the title of his first text in 1911.

Adolph Meyer (1957), a contemporary of Bleuler, introduced a humanistic view of schizophrenia. Meyer theorized that it was the result of the accumulation of "faulty habits." The patient's conflicts of instincts evoke what Meyer called substitutive reactions—inappropriate responses to the problems of daily living. Therefore, we must consider each patient's personal experience if we are to explain his or her schizophrenic behavior. Meyer discounted organic and psychic causes, preferring to treat schizophrenia in terms of behavior reactions.

Since 1930, some attempts have been made to refine the nosologies proposed by Kraepelin and Bleuler. Langfeldt (1939), for example, distinguished between schizophrenic *process* (gradual deterioration) and schizophrenic *reaction* (sudden onset) in his concept of "schizophreniform" psychoses. We will take a closer look at this distinction shortly.

In the next chapter, we will discuss current theoretical approaches to schizophrenia. It is clear, however, that a century of study by the greatest minds in the field has produced neither a definitive picture of the behavior nor a unified theory of the causes of that behavior. In fact, we are still debating the very existence of a disease-like syndrome called schizophrenia.

Greenberg (1975) denies that we have any objective evidence of a *disease* called schizophrenia. She sees the whole conception of schizophrenic disease as a play on words, in which vocabulary has replaced measurable fact. Since there are no consistent definitions of schizophrenia, we infer the "disease" from descriptions of various behaviors, and so the behaviors become the disease, which must then be defined in terms of the named behaviors. According to Greenberg (and others, including Szasz and Laing), we have made the conglomeration of concepts into a real thing, and have built a huge institutional system in which patients and practitioners are compelled to act out their respective roles.

Current Definition of Schizophrenia

The following is an excerpt from the DSM-II definition of schizophrenia:

> [Schizophrenia is characterized by] disturbances in thinking, mood, and behavior. Disturbances in thinking are marked by alterations of concept formation which may lead to misinterpretation of reality and sometimes to delusions and hallucinations, which frequently appear psychologically self-protective. . . . Mood changes include ambivalent, constricted, and inappropriate emotional responsiveness and loss of empathy with others. Behavior may be withdrawn, regressive, and

bizarre. . . . The mental status is attributable primarily to a thought disorder. (p. 33)

The manual describes the various types of schizophrenia, which are simple, hebephrenic, catatonic, paranoid, acute undifferentiated, latent, residual, schizoaffective, childhood, chronic undifferentiated, and other. We list them here, without description, as a framework for our more detailed examination in following sections.

Epidemiology of Schizophrenia

In Chapter 1, we pointed to the appallingly large number of mental patients in our hospitals. Now we will see that the largest category of mental illness among those patients is schizophrenia.

Incidence rates for treated cases range from 0.5 per 1,000 population to a high of 1.0 (per 1,000) in the United States, although studies of selected communities show incidence rates from 0.43 to 0.69. Prevalence rates indicate that between 0.23 and 0.47 *percent* of the population will be treated for schizophrenia in one year. That is, between 460,000 and 940,000 people will need treatment. Extending those figures in terms of bed-days of hospital care, we find that half of the beds in mental hospitals are occupied by patients diagnosed as schizophrenic. They represent a large part of the estimated $14-billion-a-year burden of direct and indirect costs of schizophrenia.

Other indicators of the magnitude of the problem include the count of almost two million first admissions to all U.S. facilities in 1970 (9.52 per 1,000) and the estimate that one million more schizophrenics annually would require treatment if suitable facilities were available throughout the country.

Behavioral Description

In this section, we will review the behaviors of schizophrenia and see how they are grouped to form the currently recognized diagnostic types.

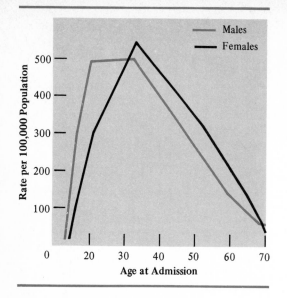

Figure 10-1 Rate per 100,000 population of schizophrenic admissions to all types of mental health services, by age and sex, United States, 1969. (Mental health statistics: Utilization of mental health resources by persons diagnosed with schizophrenia, Series B, No. 3. *Rockville, Md.: National Institute of Mental Health, 1973.*)

Clinical Manifestations

Since schizophrenia is defined by its behaviors, we can gain an understanding of present nosology by looking at the large variety of behaviors and the combinations, or systems, in which they occur.

Disturbance of Social Relationships

One of the most common features of schizophrenia is social withdrawal. What schizophrenics experience as extremely painful contact with a real world full of frightening enemies repels them, driving them into their own fantasy world of comforting delusions. The medical student's account presented at the beginning of this chapter portrays this vividly.

From the very outset, schizophrenics become totally absorbed in their own disturbed perceptions and feelings. They are overwhelmed by an unending flood of excruciating sensations over which they have no control. The peculiar behavior that they manifest in acting out their fantasies repels those around them, provoking their rejection; and thus those around them confirm the schizophrenics' fears and suspicions. The separation from their society is now virtually complete and self-perpetuating.

Perceptual Distortion

Considerable research has been addressed to the general hypothesis that the schizophrenic suffers from perceptual defects. Some patients report that noises all seem louder, colors brighter and almost luminous (McGhie and Chapman, 1961). Other patients say they cannot tell where sounds are coming from.

Dizziness and momentary paralysis are frequently cited reactions to a sudden sound or the turning on of a bright light. This interruption of action may be related to patient's commonly expressed problem in paying attention to what he or she is hearing, saying, or doing. The schizophrenic's easy distractibility may be related to his or her hypersensitivity to every incoming stimulus, which some have argued is a consequence of some neurological disorder.

Defective perception of size constancy is further evidence of visual dysfunction in schizophrenics. This shows itself in two ways. First, some schizophrenics tend to underestimate the size of distant objects. Weckowicz (1957) had patients repeatedly adjust the length of a rod to match the apparent length of another rod placed at varying distances. Where normal people use spatial cues in judging that an object has the same size at different distances, schizophrenics are somewhat deficient in this ability. The second kind of disturbance in size constancy is best described as size fluctuation (metamorphosis). A patient reports, "Suddenly the other person became smaller and then larger and then . . . smaller again" (Chapman, 1966, p. 229).

Schizophrenics often give signs of *fragmented perception*. They cannot seem to evaluate and select important details, and screen out non-essentials, in order to form a whole image. Bemporad (1967) demonstrated this in an experiment in which subjects were presented with cards on which numbers composed of dots of various sizes and colors were printed on backgrounds of contrasting color. Schizophrenics did more poorly than the control group in reporting the numerals.

The disruption of the schizophrenic's ability to perceive gestalt (whole image) forms readily, as normal people do, could account for a wide variety of problems. Among these problems are the inefficient perception of speech as word fragments ("When people are talking, I just get scraps of it") and the faulty comprehension of scenes in daily life ("Everything is in bits. You put the picture up bit by bit into your head"). The mental overload imposed by such piecemeal stimulus processing plays an important part in some theories of schizophrenic behavior.

Schizophrenic patients also report a lack of depth perception ("I see things flat . . . as if there were a wall there and I would walk into it"), cross-modal stimulation (e.g., visualizing colors when hearing tones), and runaway acceleration of events ("Things happen too quickly. . . . They get blurred"). The schizophrenic's impression of motion speed-up is also evidence of a defective sense of time. A high degree of variability has been found in the accuracy of schizophrenics' estimates of the length of short and long time intervals (Dobson, 1954; Rabin, 1957).

To our list of perceptual disruptions, we can add periodic deafness, peculiar smells and tastes, and *déjà vu* (a strange feeling of having viewed the same scene on a previous occasion).

Disturbance of Thought (Cognitive) Processes

For many investigators the primary feature of schizophrenia is a disturbance of thought processes. Thought processes, however, must always be inferred from behavioral events. This section deals with some of the behaviors presumed to reflect the disturbances of thinking ascribed to schizophrenia and some of the theoretical explanations that have been proposed based on those behaviors.

Schizophrenic communication gives the impression of disconnected sequences of ideas instead of logical chains of thought. It seems that the fragmentation seen in the schizophrenic's perceptions affects his or her thinking as well. The breaks may come between sentences, where the speaker shifts from one context to another, or between words, or even syllables, reducing the communication to incoherent chatter. Such behavior suggests faulty associations, and, indeed, that was Bleuler's primary symptom in his conception of the schizophrenic mind. He proposed the loosening of associations, using the analogy of "broken threads," as an explanation of the schizophrenic's illogical mode of expression.

While Bleuler's "broken threads" hypothesis implies some organic disorder, others see the deviant associations as the product of schizophrenics' total preoccupation with their emotional responses. Their logic serves their emotional needs instead of conforming with the laws of reason (Chapman, 1966). Under intense emotional pressure, schizophrenics abandon the logic of reality and retreat into a world of delusions. Here, words lose their normal associations and become symbols to be interpreted according to one's idiosyncratic desires. Objects, too, no longer have their ordinary function but are treated as tokens that signify whatever suits one's fantasies. This transformation of symbols resembles the magical thinking of early childhood, which we referred to in Chapter 3 as "primary process." We must, however, note that the similarities are not a clear indication of regression. Cameron (1946) gave schizophrenics and children a sentence-completion test, and found significant differences between the logic of the two groups' responses.

The nature of schizophrenic logic has been analyzed by von Domarus (1964) in an attempt to find some specific pattern of error in deductive reasoning. This pattern may lead schizophrenics to reason as follows: (major premise)

All frogs have warts; (minor premise) *some people have warts;* (conclusion) *therefore, some people are frogs.* Von Domarus found that schizophrenics made such errors with high consistency. He concluded that schizophrenics judge objects as identical on the basis of any specified common property (warts, in the example above). The von Domarus principle would account for many reported examples of schizophrenic identifications, including Arieti's classic example (1955) by a female patient: "The Virgin Mary is a virgin; I am a virgin; therefore, I am the Virgin Mary."

The von Domarus principle has not withstood experimental testing, however. One researcher (Williams, 1964) tested groups of schizophrenics and normal controls on various types of deductive reasoning and found that the schizophrenics performed as well as the controls. It seems that the von Domarus principle of errors in deductive reasoning applies to normal people as well as to schizophrenics. Others have theorized that normal people make the same kinds of logical errors as schizophrenics do, but schizophrenics grasp at more bizarre conclusions in a compulsive effort to reshape the real world into a delusional sanctuary (Henle, 1962).

One thing that can be salvaged from the failure of the von Domarus principle is the concept of *overgeneralization* of responses. Treating objects with limited or minor similarities as identical is a form of overgeneralization. This concept can also be viewed as *overinclusion* of unrelated objects in a given set. Cameron (1946) gave patients sentence-completion and object-sorting tasks (objects to be grouped into categories). He found that schizophrenics were unable to exclude irrelevant objects. One patient included the blotter, the desk, and the examiner in one category in an object-sorting task. He explained, "I've got to pick it out of the whole room. I can't confine myself to this game."

Chapman (1956a, 1956b) found, however, that when schizophrenics overincluded, the extraneous objects did have certain similarities to the correct ones. In many cases, the similarities were related to a patient's idiosyncratic criteria for sorting (such as shadows cast by objects, personal associations to objects, etc.). This effect seems to be associated with the schizophrenic's indiscriminate attention to irrelevant details.

An alternative hypothesis is that the schizophrenic's problem in sorting tasks is a result of an impaired ability to use abstract concepts in finding common properties. Thus, as a consequence of excessive concreteness, we would expect schizophrenics to be deficient in the ability to generalize.

In a more refined object-sorting task, which allowed patients to use personalized criteria in sorting, McGaughran (1957) found that chronic paranoids gave as many abstract responses as the control group, although the control group used more conventional sorting criteria. The problem, then, does not lie in ability to abstract, but in the preference for private meanings of objects. This preoccupation with private ideas is one of the most generally observed characteristics of the symptom we call autism, an escape from reality.

Schizophrenics frequently report a frustrating phenomenon called *blocking*, in which, as one patient describes it, "I may be thinking quite clearly and telling someone something and suddenly I get stuck. . . . What happens is that I suddenly stick on a word or an idea . . . and I just can't move past it" (McGhie and Chapman, 1961, p. 109). While blocking seems to occur quite often in schizophrenic speech, we all experience it at times. The disturbed and idiosyncratic emotional behaviors of schizophrenics might account for their higher frequency of blocking.

Mednick (1958) has proposed a learning theory model to explain schizophrenic thought disorder. Heightened anxiety, or drive, causes stimulus generalization, increasing the probability of occurrence of competing responses (including remote, weak associates). Broen and Storm (1966) add that the high drive raises the probability for all responses, improving the likelihood of unusual, bizarre responses.

Mednick's theory collides head-on with Chapman's hypothesis that schizophrenics favor the most likely connections in making responses. For example, in a word association test, schizophrenics would invariably give the most probable associate, for example, salt-pepper. While Chapman's hypothesis has found more experimental support than Mednick's or Broen and Storm's interpretations, drive theory still has considerable appeal on the basis of the powerful effects of anxiety in schizophrenic behavior.

There is certainly an abundance of behaviors relating to thought disorder, enough to differentiate schizophrenia from other psychoses. However, distinguishing among causes, effects, and interactions remains a problem for ongoing research. A major complication is the variability of schizophrenics, with regard to both the changing behaviors within individuals and the inconsistencies of behaviors within types. Such variability tends to "wipe out" distinctive performance characteristics in experiments, leaving experimenters with no proof of their hypothesis about abnormal behavior. We are then moved to reflect on Adolph Meyer's statement that each schizophrenic must be looked at separately in the light of his unique, personal experiences if we are to find "method in his madness."

Disruptions in Verbal Behavior, Language, and Speech

We would, of course, expect that a thought disorder would cause abnormalities in speaking and writing. However, since a patient's utterances are the principal means by which we discover what his or her thought processes are, we must distinguish between thought disorder and the language through which the disorder manifests itself. For example, slips of the tongue are a form of verbal disturbance that we do not attribute to the thought disorder associated with schizophrenia. To approach the problem, let us first review the verbal behaviors that schizophrenics exhibit.

Symbolism is often the vehicle for schizophrenic expression. Patients construct elaborate concepts around references to religious, occult, esoteric, and other symbols.

Incoherence describes the chaotic result of faulty associations, inability to filter out irrelevant details, and a preoccupation with private conceptions. "Word salad" is one typical form of incoherence, in which the patient utters a string of unrelated words that make no sense to the listener.

Schizophrenic *neologisms* (literally, new words) are usually combinations of ordinary words and loosely related syllables. Although they seem to be meaningless, patients often are able to explain their significance. Occasionally an extensive complex of objects and feelings relevant to the schizophrenic's experience is compressed into a neologism like "polamolalittersjitterstittersleelitla."

The repetition, in conversation, of part of what the previous speaker has just said is called *echolalia.* While this is part of the normal development of language, and occasionally part of normal speech, some schizophrenics do it persistently. *Verbigeration* is similar to echolalia in the repetition of previous words or phrases, but here schizophrenics repeat their own words senselessly and endlessly. The difference is that with echolalia, patients seem to be trying to hold onto some meaningful link of communication with the other speaker, and they use the single repetition to help themselves in forming an appropriate reply. *Perseveration* is another excess of repetition in which patients cannot seem to let go of an idea or a combination of words. Sometimes schizophrenics give the same response to a series of different questions.

Schizophrenics often associate unrelated words because they sound alike ("steeple people"). In free association tests, we all might respond with such a *clang* (sound) association when we cannot think of a more meaningful word. Schizophrenics respond this way for the same reason, only much more frequently, perhaps because they have fewer associations.

Mutism (a refusal to speak), a characteristic of autistic children, occurs among schizophrenics. The reason for it may differ from case to case. Recall that the medical student in his delusion heard part of himself say, "Keep your mouth shut." McNeil (1970) describes the case of a 12-year-old boy who "had not spoken one intelligible word for the last three years. He could communicate but he would not speak. . . . Peers and adults . . . learned to understand the needs reflected in the look in his eyes and the posture of his body and would respond with the appropriate actions designed to satisfy his needs and wishes" (p. 31).[1]

Motor Behavior

The odd postures and mannerisms of schizophrenics are indicative of their disturbed condition. The most noticeable are *catatonic* behaviors such as distorted mannerisms, for

[1]The interested student should consult Maher (1966) for an extensive review of research in this area.

example, facial grimacing and stereotyped movement (inflexible rituals in performing various actions).

Another motor symptom is *echopraxia*— the imitation of movements of others. Another is *negativism*, a refusal to cooperate with requests for motor activity, although there is no sign of hostility.

At the opposite extreme to abnormal motor activities are the stuporous states, including *catalepsy*, in which the patient remains in a fixed position until someone changes it. Catalepsy is a pliant state, often called "waxy flexibility," since the patient's arms and legs can be placed easily in any position and will remain in that position for hours.

Gestures may be purposeful and logical. In the case cited above of the 12-year-old who chose to remain mute, his gestures were a body language that effectively substituted for speech.

Extensive investigations have been made of psychomotor functioning of schizophrenics (Winder, 1960). In general, these studies show that schizophrenics react substantially more slowly than normal people do in a variety of motor tasks. However, cooperative patients equaled normals on manual skill and steadiness tests. This raises some question about the validity of motor response tests, since many schizophrenics are generally uncooperative. The effects of medication also complicate the findings in psychomotor research.

Problems in Emotional Behavior

Given schizophrenics' perceptual and cognitive disorders, which render them incapable of efficiently processing the information that comes at them, we can more readily understand some of their seemingly abnormal emotional responses to their difficult situation.

The most common characteristic is a general reduction in emotional response, a poverty of affect, which at its lowest point is referred to as *flat affect*. Patients are indifferent to what goes on around them. In some cases, patient apathy is marked by *anhedonia*, the total inability to feel any pleasure, no matter how delightful the experience would normally be.

Catalepsy, a stuporous state, is sometimes called "waxy flexibility" because patients' arms and legs can be placed easily in any position and will remain in that position for hours. (*Burk Uzzle, Magnum Photos.*)

A possible explanation for flatness of affect may be the efforts of patients to detach and insulate themselves from their painful perceptions. They sometimes engage in a process called *depersonalization*, which reduces them to the state of an unfeeling object. This would account for the blunting of affect.

Inappropriate responses are a more puzzling kind of emotional behavior. The patient's reactions are incompatible with the situation. Arnold G. is a representative case:

His conversation and behavior were childish and marked by foolish and inappropriate laughter. At first he thought it was awful to be among so many crazy people but shortly thereafter realized it was quite a joke, and laughed heartily about his fate. . . . He was childishly changeable in his behavior and affect. . . . Arnold underwent progressive deterioration . . . [becoming] generally indifferent to events around him. (Zax and Stricker, 1963, p. 102)

We can get more insight into possible underlying motivations for the inappropriate behavior in this report by a patient: "Half the time I am talking about one thing and thinking about a half a dozen other things at the same time. It must look queer to people when I laugh about something that has nothing to do with what I am talking about" (McGhie and Chapman, 1961, p. 109).

Wildly fluctuating emotional behavior of the manic-depressive type is observed in some patients. One interpretation suggests that such seesaw changes are uncontrollable responses to conflicting impulses, causing emotional turmoil in the patient.

Other Characteristics

The picture of schizophrenic dysfunction at the perceptual, cognitive, and emotional levels is blurred by factors that are only indirectly related to the essential disorder. Intellectual deficits among early-onset, chronic patients, resulting from inadequate education, lower their performance on cognitive tasks—as would be the case with similarly deprived nonschizophrenics. In like manner, the early curtailment of social relations causes arrested development of social maturity. The impoverished existence of schizophrenics, empty of any clear expectations for the future, cannot help but sap their motivation, which, in turn, weakens their powers of attention.

Behavior Patterns ("Types" of Schizophrenia)

In his organization of mental disease syndromes into a single diagnostic category, Kraepelin grouped three basic subtypes under the heading of dementia praecox: catatonic, hebephrenic, and paranoid. Bleuler added a type that he called simple schizophrenia. For reasons that we will discover, it has become increasingly hard to distinguish clearly among the types. Later, we will discuss the validity of the classic descriptions of types and consider the question of whether they really should be considered as separate entities. First, we will describe the types as they are presented in current textbooks of abnormal psychology and psychiatry.

Simple Schizophrenia

Simple schizophrenia is a curious example of an illness whose individual behaviors go unnoticed in people we meet every day. When clustered together in one person, these behaviors add up to a serious disturbance. The syndrome has a gradual onset, and does not become evident at least until adolescence.

Its principal behavioral features are a loss of drive and interest in all activities. While this may occur after the person has performed reasonably well in school and career, the ranks of simple schizophrenics also include high school and college dropouts, hobos, drifters, and prostitutes. Most of the behavioral symptoms are exemplified in the following case:

Billy was brought to the hospital by his mother because of his refusal to leave the house for any reason, his lack of motivation, and his numerous physical complaints. During the admission interview Billy avoided looking at the interviewer and mumbled rather incoherently when addressed. With encouragement he was able to answer questions, but his answers were sometimes odd and circumstantial.

Billy's mother reported that during high school he was a very quiet boy who had few friends. Although his school work was good in the primary grades, his work in high school progressively deteriorated to the point that his graduation was "a gift." He also showed a loss of interest in other things and had no friends. When Billy graduated his father insisted that he enlist in the army. (He believed that army life would "make a man out of

Billy.") Billy's experience in the army was highly traumatic and he was unable to adjust. He was discharged in three months. Since his return home he had shown no interest in anything—he stayed home alone (his parents both worked), watching TV and staying in bed. He went for several days without speaking to his parents.

In the hospital, Billy avoided others and spoke only if someone directly confronted him. His behavior was regressed and unusual; he stayed in bed with the covers over his head for hours at a time. Occasionally, he would strike out at fellow patients without provocation.

After a period of six months of hospitalization in which Billy received ECT, psychotherapy, and various medication regimes, he was discharged from the hospital essentially unimproved. Billy told his therapist that he wanted to begin college to study astronomy or military science. Billy's return home was marked with behavior identical to that which necessitated his first admission. (Butcher, 1971, p. 75)

Note that the behavior pattern lacks any outstanding or bizarre features, for example, hallucinations or delusions. Perhaps if Billy had not been forced to try to adjust to the army, he would not have been hospitalized at this time. He does show the slow progressive deterioration that had been described as "the withering of personality" (Kolb, 1973), which probably would have resulted in his eventually becoming identified as a problem.

There is a significant difference in the case of Lorraine N., who, in spite of her apparent indifference, manages to keep working at her gainful though illicit employment:

Lorraine has been a prostitute since she was 16. Although she is the virtual prisoner of her employer, she is no more distressed by her bondage than by her daily labors of love. Nothing much distresses her and very little interests her. She keeps pretty much to herself and rarely joins in the endless stream of gossip and small talk of the other girls. She plays her professional sexual role with well rehearsed gusto, but it is tedious make believe. As Lorraine reports, "I don't even think about it when I'm doing it. It's like he's doing it to some-

body else." Nothing seems to bother Lorraine. She feels nothing about her past life, accepts life day by day, and hardly thinks about tomorrow. She can not quite comprehend what life is all about but she doesn't worry about it. (McNeil, 1970, p. 96)

Hebephrenic Schizophrenia

The prominent features of the hebephrenic schizophrenic are delusions and hallucinations. Onset dates from the mid-teens to late adolescence, and is often marked by episodes of depression and other affective disturbances. The following case shows most of the clinical behaviors:

About six months before commitment to the hospital at age 32 she "began to grow thin and nervous" and became careless about her work, which deteriorated in quality and quantity. She believed that other girls at her place of employment were circulating slanderous stories concerning her. She complained so indignantly that X, an attractive young man employed in the same industrial plant, had put his arm around her and insulted her that her family demanded that the charge be investigated. This showed not only that the charge was without foundation but that the young man in question had not spoken to her for months. The family, however had not suspected mental disease until six days before her commitment, when she returned from her work. As she entered the house that evening, she laughed loudly, watched her sister-in-law suspiciously, refused to answer questions, and at sight of her brother began to cry. She refused to go to the bathroom, saying that X was looking in the windows at her. She ate no food and the next day declared that her sisters were "bad women," that everyone was talking about her, and that X had been having sexual relations with her, that although she could not see him he was "always around." In her hallucinatory experiences she heard X say, "Aren't you going to fire her? I've had her. She don't know it." The patient became resistive, was afraid of being killed, and at times said, "I'm dead." She stated that she was being poisoned, saw her dead mother, and heard her speak.

As the patient became noisy, did not sleep, and ate but little and then only when spoon-fed, she was committed to a private institution. Here she was uncooperative, silly, grimaced, and whiningly repeated, "Oh, mama! mama! I want to see my father before I die." She heard voices outside her window and at night would come to the door of the room several times saying, "What is it all about? Oh, mama!" Her associations became loose: she took no interest in the care of her person or in other patients but would stand for hours with her back against the wall, her head thrust forward, fingering her hair, and unobservant of her environment.

After a residence of four months in the private institution, the patient was transferred to a public hospital. As she entered the admitting office, she laughed loudly and repeatedly screamed in a loud tone, "She cannot stay here; she's got to go home!" She grimaced and performed various stereotyped movements of her hands. When seen on the ward an hour later, she paid no attention to questions, although she talked to herself in a childish tone. She moved about constantly, walking on her toes in a dancing manner, pointed aimlessly about, and put out her tongue and sucked her lips in the manner of an infant. At times she moaned and cried like a child but shed no tears. As the months passed, she remained silly, childish, preoccupied, inaccessible, grimacing, gesturing, pointing at objects in a stereotyped way, usually chattering to herself in a peculiar high-pitched voice, little of what she said being understood. At an interview 18 months after her hospitalization, she presented an unkempt appearance, was without shoes, sat stooped far over, smiled in a silly manner, and presented a picture of extreme introversion and regression. During the attempted interview, she rarely spoke, although she occasionally replied, "I don't know" in an entirely indifferent manner and apparently with no heed to the question. The nurse reported the patient as seclusive, resistive, idle, and with no interest either in the activities of the institution or in her relatives who visited her. (Kolb, 1973, p. 332)

The case recital constitutes a catalog of hebephrenic behaviors: severe depression (before the commitment), delusions of persecution, hallucinations (hearing voices), silliness (childish whining and chatter), gri-

macing and stereotyped movements, looseness of associations, loss of interest in herself and her environment, inappropriate laughter, and eventual deterioration into a completely introverted woman.

Catatonic Schizophrenia

Catatonia is the most clearly visible of the schizophrenic types. Its characteristic motor behaviors are obvious even to the naive observer: rigid immobility and wild excitement. These extremes of behavior usually alternate during the early stages, intense agitation subsiding into a stuporous trancelike state. In each case, one or the other of the two states eventually predominates.

Generally the onset is sudden, developing from excited ravings and hallucinations to apathetic withdrawal within a few days or weeks. In the excited state, patients describe delusions of cosmic proportions (conflicts with forces of evil, divine contacts, and the like). Their speech is often incomprehensible, exhibiting echolalia, neologisms, verbigeration, and word salad. Their movements are often stereotyped, and they often assume odd postures (*posturing*). Prior to the development of effective drugs, extreme cases of uncontrollable excitement occasionally ended in sudden death, either from sheer exhaustion or devastating fright.

In the stuporous state, patients are mute and apparently inattentive to what is happening around them. However, the disinterest is not a lack of contact, since on emerging from the stupor, patients have total recall of everything that they witnessed during their trance. Stuporous patients who refuse food will suddenly snatch some from a nearby plate and devour it ravenously. Such behavior leads to the hypothesis that the catatonic stupor is simply an *unwillingness*, rather than an inability, to move.

Some patients in stupor show the waxy flexibility of catalepsy. Although they can be induced to come out of their fixed posture to take walks or engage in other activity, they soon return to the catatonic pose. Others maintain a rigidly immobile, awkward posture for such long periods that circulatory, joint, and skin disorders develop. They behave in a negativistic manner—do not eat when observed, retain urine, defecate in bed, and resist change in position.

As in the case of other schizophrenic types, the sudden onset offers hope of recovery. However, some patients continue to deteriorate until a vegetative state is reached. The following case shows both the excited and stuporous features of catatonia.

Two months before commitment the patient began to talk about how he had failed, had "spoiled" his whole life, that it was now "too late." He spoke of hearing someone say, "You must submit." One night his wife was awakened by his talking. He told her of having several visions but refused to describe them. He stated that someone was after him and trying to blame him for the death of a certain man. He had been poisoned, he said. Whenever he saw a truck or a fire engine, the patient stated that someone in it was looking for him in order to claim his assistance to help save the world. He had periods of laughing and shouting and became so noisy and unmanageable that it was necessary to commit him.

On arrival at the hospital, the patient was noted to be an asthenic, poorly nourished man with dilated pupils, hyperactive tendon reflexes, and a pulse rate of 120 per minute. In the admission office he showed many mannerisms, lay down on the floor,

pulled at his foot, made undirected, violent striking movements, again struck attendants, grimaced, assumed rigid, attitudinized postures, refused to speak, and appeared to be having auditory hallucinations. Later in the day, he was found to be in a stuporous state. His face was without expression, he was mute and rigid, and paid no attention to those about him or to their questions. His eyes were closed and the lids could be separated only with effort. There was no response to pinpricks or other painful stimuli.

On the following morning an attempt was made to bring him before the medical staff for the routine admission interview. As he was brought into the room supported by two attendants, he struggled, grimaced, shouted incoherently, and was resistive. For five days he remained mute, negativistic, and inaccessible, at times staring vacantly into space, at times with his eyes tightly closed. He ate poorly and gave no response to questions but once was heard to mutter to himself in a greatly preoccupied manner, "I'm going to die—I know it—you know it." On the evening of the sixth day he looked about and asked where he was and how he came there. When asked to tell of his life, he related many known events and how he had once worked in an airplane factory, but added that he had invented an appliance pertaining to airplanes, that this had been stolen and patented through fraud and that as a result he had lost his position. He ate ravenously, then fell asleep, and on awaking was in a catatonic stupor, remaining in this state for several days. (Kolb, 1973, pp. 334–335)

Since most catatonic patients spend most of the time either in a state of excitation or stupor, there is a diagnostic question as to whether the patients merely differ in inclination toward one of the two states or the states are indeed examples of different syndromes. This issue was investigated by Morrison (1973) in a study that is a model of case study research. He methodically analyzed 250 case records of diagnosed catatonic patients, who belonged to either the predominantly excited group or the withdrawn (sometimes called "retarded") group. Tabulating symptoms, course, and outcomes, he found significant differences between the two groups, sufficient to warrant his suggestion that they are separate diagnostic syndromes with different prognoses (good for the excited, poor for the withdrawn).

Paranoid Schizophrenia

Paranoid schizophrenia comprises about half of the diagnosed cases of schizophrenia in the United States. Like catatonia, its course and behavioral features are clearly defined and consistent. Delusions and hallucinations of a particular character are usually the most notable behavior.

Paranoid schizophrenia is usually associated with middle age and the elderly. Slater and Roth (1969) report that the average age of paranoid onset is 35, while the average age of onset for the other types is 23. The late onset of paranoid schizophrenia allows more time for development of social maturity, which helps to account for the ability of many paranoids to maintain workable relationships in the community.

The primary sign of paranoid schizophrenia is delusional behavior. Paranoid delusions are generally of a persecutory and grandiose nature. Patients envision themselves as the new Messiah or Savior of the world, or some other historical or religious figure with a grandiose mission. They believe they are being persecuted by enemies bent on thwarting their mission. Their vivid hallucinations (mostly auditory) support their delusions, which often involve rather elaborate scenarios. Their delusions eventually disintegrate into confused and self-contradictory schemes if the condition persists for a long time.

An important feature of the thought disorder underlying the delusional behavior is a form of concept generalization called "spread of meaning." This refers to patients' disposition to extend their *ideas of reference* (they are the object of others' conversation and action) to include people with no apparent relationship to the theme of their delusions. In extreme cases, this can become dangerous, leading to senseless homicidal crimes.

Unlike the detached, withdrawn hebe-

phrenics and catatonics, paranoids are aggressively vocal and active on their own behalf. They join causes that are somehow compatible with their "mission." Since they are rather intelligent, and do not usually exhibit the verbal abnormalities characteristic of other types of schizophrenia, they may go unrecognized among members of the so-called "lunatic fringe."

About half of the paranoid schizophrenics have an acute onset that progresses into a chronic state marked by an alternating pattern of remissions and recurrences. The onset in some of these cases is gradual, permitting the people to integrate their paranoid attitude with their daily experiences. The following case excerpt illustrates some of the prominent features.

George is a 22-year-old male, the second of two siblings in a middle-class family. Although described as high-strung throughout his life, he never showed gross abnormalities of behavior. During college, however, he found the scholastic work increasingly hard. He finally decided to quit school and to accept a job as a salesman, but he found that this occupation too was not satisfactory. He appeared different to the members of his family, who thought he was probably worried about his working conditions. He appeared distressed and absent-minded and soon grew very peculiar. He became increasingly preoccupied with certain thoughts, which he revealed to his parents and sister. On hearing the word home, he understood homo; if he heard the word fair, he felt fairy was the word really meant. He became more and more convinced that people thought he was homosexual. When he saw groups of people in his neighborhood, he was sure that they were talking about him. He often "heard" them talking about him and making accusations. He became more and more preoccupied, upset, unable to attend to his work. He became somewhat neglectful of his appearance, oblivious of the many usual aspects of life, and more and more involved in thoughts of being accused, spied on, spoken of, ridiculed. In a few weeks, it became impossible for him to hold his job, and he quit voluntarily. A few days later he became increasingly restless and finally agitated. The psychiatrist who was consulted recommended hospitalization. (Arieti, 1974b, p. 37)

"I, Julius Caesar, Emperor of Rome, being of sound mind and body, do hereby . . ." (*Tom Stratton.*)

A second paranoid group is identified as "confabulatory": these patients invent an imaginary past life that gives substance to their delusions.

A third group is characterized by their ability to compartmentalize their delusions. Their real and delusional worlds are completely separate, allowing them to lead somewhat "normal" and productive lives until a crisis involving family or fellow workers triggers a paranoid outbreak.

An interesting phenomenon is the *folie á deux* or *folie á trois*, described by Arieti (1974b) as two or three concurrent cases of paranoid schizophrenia in the same household. The initial case is generally an aggressive, overbearing member who forces his or her own delusional system on the others. The others, usually passive and submissive, go along with the "donor" to avoid making things worse. Such induced cases are readily curable upon separation from the initiator.

Although paranoid schizophrenic behaviors are generally clear-cut, some patients exhibit thought behavior that approximates paranoid delusions but without such essential features as persecutory or grandiose themes. The medical student who led off this chapter presents us with delusions of implanted instruments, but instead of reacting to imagined persecution, he sees the others as friends trying to help him. We will discuss paranoid conditions with behaviors that differ in some aspects from the characteristics we have described.

Acute Undifferentiated

Acute undifferentiated schizophrenia is not so much a syndrome as a stop along the way to the development of a pattern of behavior for which a definite diagnosis can be applied.

As the label indicates, the onset is sudden, following an extended period of emotional stress and a sense of an inability to cope with life's demands. Social relationships are unsatisfactory and there are increasing conflicts with family and friends.

Patients display a mixed array of behaviors that, at first, do not quite add up to a major schizophrenic syndrome. They are likely to be emotional, depressed, with occasional evidences of excitement, and disturbed to the point of sleeplessness, with loss of appetite. After a few weeks of such distress, marked by occasional outbursts of bizarre behaviors, the behaviors either dissipate or resolve themselves into a clearer picture of one of the major types.

Because the undifferentiated type cannot be described by a clear-cut pattern of behavior, the best way to bring it into focus is to look at a case.

Gertrude W. was a 35-year-old, unmarried grocery clerk with an eighth-grade education when she was admitted for hospitalization. We see her social frictions, ideas of reference, anxiety, depression, sleeplessness, loss of appetite, vague auditory hallucinations, all yielding to treatment.

The onset of the symptoms leading to Gertrude's hospitalization occurred about six weeks before her admission. At that time she began feeling poorly and was disturbed at meeting a male acquaintance with whom she had quarreled a few weeks before. She also argued with one of her sisters, who declared, "If you keep running around the way you are, you'll go nuts." These events were followed by a dream in which she was falling from an airplane. She awoke terror-stricken from this dream and thereafter never quite felt herself. She felt that there was something between her and the others which prevented her from becoming close to people. As a result she stopped talking to those around her. Her sleep pattern became so disturbed that she slept only a few hours a night and even this interval would be disturbed by upsetting dreams (being pursued by a man with gun, being rejected by a beau). She began to have a feeling approximating the tightening of an iron band around her head. For most of this period she was unable to work and lost interest in her usual activities. Because she feared that people were staring at her, she refused to venture outdoors. Her anxiety mounted progressively, and she lost her appetite and suffered a weight loss of ten pounds. When she developed the idea that one of her breasts had been removed (a distant cousin had once had a mastectomy) and began reporting loud noises in her room which no one else heard, her family became alarmed and suggested she seek hospitalization. Gertrude concurred in this without much arguing.

When interviewed in the hospital, she was oriented but, despite good retention and recent memory, had no recollection of events prior to her symptom onset. She nevertheless knew some general facts. She spoke coherently but rapidly and seemed resigned to always feeling anxious and depressed. She complained that she felt distant from people and admitted to having heard her name called while alone and to a continual buzzing in her ears.

She remained a patient for three months, during which time she was treated with ataractic [tranquilizing] drugs. She responded well to this, as well as to the supportive milieu of the hospital. She was much improved on discharge and was advised to seek private follow-up treatment. (Zax and Stricker, 1963, pp. 95–97)

Box 10-2 Less Common Types of Schizophrenia

There are several types of schizophrenia, seen less frequently than the others, whose prominent symptoms are not essentially schizophrenic, but whose behavior is so bizarre that a diagnosis of schizophrenia is indicated.

Schizoaffective type: Patients exhibit fluctuation between manic elation and hopeless despair, with auditory hallucinations. In the depressed state, patients are overwhelmed by feelings of worthlessness and guilt, and may be suicidal.

Childhood schizophrenia: To be discussed in Chapter 15.

Residual schizophrenia: After years of illness, sometimes after long remission, the patient lapses into a state of fixed and constricted behavior. Common features are a lack of ideas; narrowed interest; minimal, ritualized activity; and bland attitude.

Latent schizophrenia: This is the label for "potential" schizophrenics or schizoid personalities. Latent schizophrenics occasionally exhibit abnormal behavior without psychotic episodes; therefore, they are not diagnosable as schizophrenic. When applied to those with gross and pervasive neuroses, this category is sometimes referred to as *pseudoneurotic schizophrenia.*

Chronic Undifferentiated

We saw that acute undifferentiated schizophrenia is a transitional label. In contrast, the chronic undifferentiated type is a dead-end category, where behaviors that were classified as catatonic, hebephrenic, or paranoid during the earlier phases of "illness" have now deteriorated to the point where the original behaviors are no longer distinguishable.

Chronic patients are generally long-term schizophrenics whose onset varied from childhood through middle age. Behavior in the later stages of chronic schizophrenia may include any or all of the schizophrenic signs, usually in an irregular or dulled way: thought disturbance, flat affect, disinterest in and unresponsiveness to environment, autistic preoccupation with one's own thoughts, fear of and unwillingness to engage in any but minimal routine activities, unkempt appearance, stereotyped movement with slow reaction time, and generalized intellectual deficit. The deterioration of intellectual skills and, indeed, of the chronic patient's whole personality may be the effect of a lifetime spent in a blank, depersonalizing institutional environment, as much as the by-product of schizophrenia. We will explore the effects of hospitalization at the end of this chapter.

Paranoia and Paranoid States

Sometimes a person is diagnosed as paranoid even though there are no schizophrenic behaviors per se (hallucinations, grandiosity, severe depression). The paranoid behaviors are associated with the "paranoid personality" (suspicions, hostility, sensitivity, rigidity, jealousy). These behaviors appear to permit such individuals to function, albeit belligerently, in the community.

Dimensions of Schizophrenic Behavior

Several dimensions have been proposed and found useful in the diagnosis and clinical appraisal of schizophrenia as a process. These dimensions have been particularly useful in research attempts at expanding our understanding of schizophrenic behavior.

Process-Reactive Dimension

In reactive patients, the onset is sudden after a symptom-free life, and the prognosis is good. In process patients, the onset is gradual and insidious, heralded by a previous history of emotional troubles and social problems; the prognosis is poor for this group. Box 10-3 shows the contrasting life patterns of the two groups. Although generally considered as two subgroups, *process* and *reactive* have been posited by Becker (1956, 1959) as the end points of a continuum representing levels of personality organization (perceptual, emotional, and adaptive functioning under stress). Herron

(1962) evaluated the various attempts to distinguish empirically between process and reactive patients, including responses to Rorschach tests, perceptual and cognitive tests, and certain drugs. He concluded that there was strong support for the distinction.

Acute-Chronic Dimension

This dimension is directly related to the process-reactive distinction, and the two are often used interchangeably. In simplest terms, *acute* designates sudden onset precipitated by a traumatic event; *chronic* identifies a long-term condition, marked by a history of abnormal behavior.

Premorbid Adjustment Dimension

This measure is based on the manner in which patients responded to their personal problems at various stages in their life before the onset of illness (premorbid adjustment). It cuts across all of the diagnostic categories in determining prognosis on a case-by-case basis, thereby contradicting Kraepelin's formulation of typical outcomes associated with distinct syndromes.

The concept of premorbid adjustment centers on the maturity of an individual's attitudes and actions in his or her social relations, expressed in measurable terms as "social competence." Phillips (1953) has designed a rating scale to evaluate a patient's premorbid adjustment and effectiveness in dealing with personal problems. The Phillips Premorbid Scale assigns differential values, or weights, to key factors in the patient's premorbid history. Among the areas of interest are sexual experiences, recent and earlier social aspects of life (marriage, etc.), and personal relations.

The Phillips method of evaluation relates normal behavior to adequate functioning at each level of development. Maturity determines social adequacy. If patients have, in the past, demonstrated such maturity in their social behavior, they should have a more favorable prognosis, since they have shown they have ways of resolving their behavior problems.

Box 10-3 Items Defining Frame of Reference for Case History Judgments

Process Schizophrenia	Reactive Schizophrenia

Birth to the Fifth Year

Process Schizophrenia	Reactive Schizophrenia
a. Early psychological trauma	a. Good psychological history
b. Physical illness—severe or long	b. Good physical health
c. Odd member of family	c. Normal member of family

Fifth Year to Adolescence

Process Schizophrenia	Reactive Schizophrenia
a. Difficulties at school	a. Well adjusted at school
b. Family troubles paralleled by sudden changes in patient's behavior	b. Domestic trouble unaccompanied by behavior disruptions; patient "had what it took"
c. Introverted behavior trends and interests	c. Extroverted behavior trends and interests
d. History of breakdown of social, physical, mental functioning	d. History of adequate social, physical, mental functioning
e. Pathological siblings	e. Normal siblings
f. Overprotective or rejecting mother, "momism"	f. Normally protective, accepting mother
g. Rejecting father	g. Accepting father

Adolescence to Adulthood

Process Schizophrenia	Reactive Schizophrenia
a. Lack of heterosexuality	a. Heterosexual behavior
b. Insidious, gradual onset of psychosis without pertinent stress	b. Sudden onset of psychosis; stress present and pertinent; later onset
c. Physical aggression	c. Verbal aggression
d. Poor response to treatment	d. Good response to treatment
e. Lengthy stay in hospital	e. Short course in hospital

Adulthood

Process Schizophrenia	Reactive Schizophrenia
a. Massive paranoia	a. Minor paranoid trends
b. Little capacity for alcohol	b. Much capacity for alcohol
c. No manic-depressive component	c. Presence of manic-depressive component
d. Failure under adversity	d. Success despite adversity
e. Discrepancy between ability and achievement	e. Harmony between ability and achievement
f. Awareness of change in self	f. No sensation of change
g. Somatic delusions	g. Absence of somatic delusions
h. Clash between culture and environment	h. Harmony between culture and environment
i. Loss of decency (nudity, public masturbation, etc.)	i. Retention of decency

From Kantor, R. E., Wallner, J. M., and Winder, C. L. Process and reactive schizophrenia. *Journal of Consulting Psychology*, 1953, 17, 158. © 1953 by the American Psychological Association. Reprinted by permission.

Zigler and Phillips (1960) have extended the method of rating social competence. They classified pathological behavior according to three descending levels of social competence: (1) turning against self, (2) turning against others, and (3) avoidance of others. Behaviors corresponding to the last category (avoidance of others) are identified with schizophrenia.

Phillips and Zigler (1961) have also devised another method of deriving predictions of outcome from premorbid behavior. They found evidence that patients who demonstrated *thought* distortion (suspiciousness, bias, obsessions, bizarre ideas, etc.) scored higher in social competence than those whose behavior consisted largely of disturbed *actions* (homicide, assault, rape, compulsions, etc.). The logic behind the *action-thought* dichotomy is that in the course of development, maturation progresses toward symbolic concept formation and higher order verbal thinking. Therefore, patients who are thought-oriented are likely to have reached higher levels of maturity and, hence, greater social competence.

Evaluation of Current Nosology

The cases we have described may give the impression that we are looking directly at the patient's symptoms, like a picture in a medical textbook. Actually, these case reports are descriptions taken from clinical records that were written by mental health professionals. In the process, they are subject to the biasing effects of the authors' points of view. One way to avoid the distortions of interpretation is to bypass the reporters and observe directly the behaviors of schizophrenic patients.

Lorr and his colleagues (1963), for example, have questioned the traditional categories of schizophrenia. Using their Inpatient Multidimensional Psychiatric Scale (IMPS), they have generated a view of patient behaviors on the ward that differs from textbook descriptions. Their IMPS appraisal indicates that the hospitalized schizophrenic is much less active and manifests fewer behavioral symptoms than the textbooks represent.

Harmatz, Mendelsohn, and Glassman (1975), employing naturalistic observation procedures described in Chapter 5, recorded frequency and duration of patient behaviors, which they classified into 12 categories on their Behavioral Observation Scale (BOS) (Box 10-4). They found much less bizarre behavior than might be expected. Instead, they noted that the typical hospitalized schizophrenic spends most of his or her time in a state of blankness and noninvolvement with his or her environment.

Blashfield (1973) undertook an ambitious study of the DSM-II categories to evaluate their

---

Box 10-4 Behavioral Observation Scale

Pacing: non-goal-oriented, repetitive walking.

Self-stimulatory behavior: continual handling, fondling, or touching of a particular part of the body.

Active entertainment: entertainment-producing behavior requiring some physical activity, such as playing pool or cards.

Passive entertainment: entertainment with minimal physical activity directly related to it, such as watching television or reading the paper.

Atavistic behavior: annoying or destructive behavior toward self or others, such as screaming, hitting, or breaking furniture.

Reinforcement-seeking: behaviors associated with the acquisition of tangible reinforcers such as soft drinks, candy, or cigarettes.

Nonverbal interpersonal behavior: social interaction without verbal behavior, such as nodding to another person.

Bizarre behavior: unusual or odd behavior, such as gesturing to oneself, talking while alone, or assuming odd postures.

Verbal behavior 1: social verbal behavior directed toward another patient.

Verbal behavior 2: social verbal behavior directed toward a nonpatient, such as a ward staff member or visitor.

Noninvolvement: no observable behavior, such as sitting without attention to surroundings or sleeping.

Nonclassificatory behavior: any observable behavior that cannot be subsumed under the other categories.

From Harmatz, M. G., Mendelsohn, R., and Glassman, M. L. Gathering naturalistic, objective data on the behavior of schizophrenic patients. *Hospital and Community Psychiatry*, 1975, 26, 84.

---

reliability, overlap, and coverage. His method was to submit symptom descriptions based on IMPS definitions for a number of "artificial patients" to a panel of 55 clinicians, who then diagnosed the cases according to the DSM-II categories. He found very low diagnostic correlation among the clinicians. Overlap between DSM-II concepts was shown to be high, indicating confusability of similar concepts in making diagnoses. On the basis of his findings, Blashfield proposed a new hierarchical classification of types of schizophrenia (Table 10-1). Note the separation of excited and withdrawn catatonia under two different hierarchies.

The recent trend in classifying schizophrenias has been away from the illness-disease designations toward designations that emphasize behavioral features. Again, we observe the signs of change as the practitioners in abnormal psychology move toward a different model. In no other clinical area does the abandonment of an illness-disease model seem more imperative than in our conceptualizations of schizophrenia.

The Course of Schizophrenia

As we have pointed out, schizophrenia is not a static condition; it is a condition that undergoes change. The process proceeds through a series of stages from onset to outcome. In this section, we will discuss the patient's experience during onset and hospitalization, and look at some studies of prognosis.

Onset Experiences

The initial events leading to what may eventually be labeled as "schizophrenia" represent a wide array of behaviors. Studies by McGie and Chapman (1961), Chapman (1966), and Bowers (1968), reviewing interviews with recent first-admission patients, have contributed some examples of the onset events as experienced and reported by the patients themselves. The following are some examples from these first-person accounts.

I have to put things together in my head. If I look at my watch I see the watch, watchstrap, face, hands and so on; then I have to put them together to get it into one piece." (Chapman, 1966, p. 229)

Table 10-1 Proposed Revision to the Hierarchy of the DSM-II Classification of Schizophrenia

Hierarchy
Schizophrenia: large concept types
Paranoid type
Undifferentiated types
Acute type
Chronic type
Schizophrenia: small concept types
Excited types
Catatonic excited type
Schizoaffective excited type
Depressed types
Catatonic withdrawn type
Schizoaffective depressed type
Other types
Hebephrenic type
Simple type
Latent type
Residual type

From Blashfield, R. An evaluation of the DSM-II classification of schizophrenia as a nomenclature. *Journal of Abnormal Psychology*, 1973, 82, 386. © 1973 by the American Psychological Association. Reprinted by permission.

My senses seemed alive; colors were very bright, they hit me harder. . . . I noticed things I had never noticed before. (Bowers, 1968, p. 350)

It's like a temporary blackout—with my brain not working properly—like being in a vacuum. I just get cut off from outside things and go into another world. This happens when tension starts to mount until it bursts in my brain . . . taking in too much of my surroundings. (Chapman, 1966, p. 231)

My mind goes blank when I listen to somebody speaking to me. . . . My concentration drifts away. . . . I go into a daze. (Chapman, 1966, p. 232)

The arms and legs are apart and away from me and they go on their own. That's when I feel I am the other person. (Chapman, 1966, p. 232)

I have to pick out thoughts and put them together. . . . I have an impression of what I wanted

to say, . . . but I couldn't get the words I needed—words that weren't correct came out. (Chapman, 1966, p. 236)

Big magnified thoughts come into my head when I am speaking and put away the words I wanted to say. . . . A barrier inside my head stops me from speaking properly and the mind goes blank. (Chapman, 1966, p. 236)

None of my movements come automatically to me now. I've been thinking too much about them, even walking properly, talking properly . . . doing anything. (Chapman, 1966, p. 239)

When I start walking I get a fast series of pictures in front of me. Everything seems to change and revolve around me. Something goes wrong with my eyes and I've got to stop and stand still. (Chapman, 1966, p. 243)

These experiences tend to be dramatic, bizarre, and disorienting events for those suffering them. Table 10-2 summarizes the three most important complaints for a group of 40 patients at the time they were admitted to the hospital. These presenting complaints, like the individual examples above, are pervaded by a sense of "something terribly wrong" and the resulting sensation of extreme anxiety and distress about what is happening. Even in cases where the onset has been more gradual, the incident that leads to hospitalization is often a sudden increase in the difficulty of the problem for the individuals or those around them.

The behaviors we described as typical of hospitalized schizophrenics contrast sharply with these presenting complaints. Withdrawal, noninvolvement, lack of activity, and so on, were the major behavioral features. Are the typical behaviors of hospitalized schizophrenics indicative of a different disorder? Are they the result of drug treatment? Are they part of the course of the illness—that is, the movement from an acute phase to a chronic phase? These have all been suggested and defended as the explanation for changes from the active onset picture to the "burnt-out schizophrenic."

The behaviorists suggest another possibility, that is, that the behavior is functionally related to the environment in which it occurs. The contrasting abnormal behaviors "make sense" given the situations in which they are found. Onset behaviors are responses to conditions prevailing at the time. The so-called "chronic" behaviors are appropriate to the hospital situation. The behaviorists might explain the course of the disorder as follows: individuals may show unusual behaviors as part of a behavioral reaction to a crisis situation or as a learned life-script. Action is called for to help both them and those around them to deal with these events. The individuals are labeled "schizophrenic" because of the easy availability of a label that categorizes these behaviors. Because it provides an immediate solution to the problem, hospitalization is likely. The hospital then trains the individuals to behave in ways that are appropriate to hospitals but that also have come to be defined as "schizophrenic." (After all, hospitalized schizophrenic patients show those behaviors, the reasoning goes.) Those are the behaviors of the withdrawn, apathetic, "chronic undifferentiated schizophrenic." The decision to hospitalize and the effects of hospitalization can thus be seen as important parts of the *process of schizophrenia.*

The Decision to Hospitalize

What is the decision incident that finally puts the individuals into the hospital? Who makes the decision, and how is it reached? These are crucial questions, since, as we shall see, it is at this point that patients' problems with institutional treatment begin.

Smith and his colleagues (1963) studied the "last straw" incidents in 100 cases. They classified the precipitating behaviors into three categories: (1) danger to self or others, (2) socially unacceptable behavior, (3) illness requiring treatment by patient, family, or doctor. While grossly unacceptable behavior (shouting, nudity, obscene language) was the decisive factor that impelled the community to seek commitment of the individuals, the family initiated the request after actual assault (including suicide attempts) or destruction of property. When fear of bodily injury was not the com-

Table 10-2 The Early Symptoms of Schizophrenia

Case Number	Presenting Complaints		
	One	Two	Three
1	Change in experience of self	Confusion of thought	Withdrawal
2	Concern with condition of feet	Loss of interest	Preoccupation with bodily functions
3	Aggressive behavior	Lassitude	Persecutory ideas
4	Anxiety	Grandiose preoccupation	Ideas of reference
5	Anxiety	Loss of concentration	Persecutory ideas
6	Marital problems	Suicidal ideas	Persecutory ideas
7	Ruminating about life	Withdrawal	Persecutory ideas
8	Religiosity	Loss of efficiency	Unable to concentrate
9	Restlessness	Preoccupied with bodily functions	Seclusiveness
10	Loss of concentration	Withdrawal	Religiosity
11	Backache	Religiosity	Ideas of reference
12	Concern about facial appearance	Aggressive behavior	Ideas of reference
13	Anxiety	Hypochondriacal ideas	Suicidal ideas
14	Sensations in chest and abdomen	Irritability	Lassitude
15	Philosophical ruminations	Fear of homosexuality	Lack of feeling for relatives
16	Truancy from school	Religiosity	Depression
17	Inability to mix with others	Ideas of reference	Persecutory ideas
18	Lack of interest	Attacks of limpness, trembling, and staggering	Ideas of reference
19	Hypochondriacal ideas concerning nose	Self-consciousness about speech	Feeling of deadness
20	Anxiety	Poor concentration	Perplexity
21	Moodiness	Solitariness	Religious preoccupations
22	Hypochondriacal preoccupations	Obsessional ideas	Ideas of reference
23	Self-consciousness of appearance of nose	Inability to enjoy anything	Ideas of reference
24	Anxiety	Dysphagia [difficulty in swallowing]	Inability to concentrate
25	Loss of efficiency	Loss of interest	Lassitude

Table 10-2 Continued

Case Number	Presenting Complaints		
	One	*Two*	*Three*
26	Headache	Poor memory	Fear of mixing with others
27	Self-consciousness	Listlessness	Depression
28	Feeling body is changed	Ideas of reference	Withdrawal
29	Hypochondriacal pre-occupations	Moodiness	Solitariness
30	Loss of feeling	Poor concentration	Moodiness
31	Poor sleep	Sexual preoccupations	Ideas of reference
32	Feeling separate from others	Fear of insanity	Unreality feelings
33	Feeling of inadequacy	Fear of homosexuality	Confusion of thoughts
34	Self-consciousness	Moodiness	Seclusiveness
35	Daydreaming	Loss of efficiency at work	Withdrawal
36	Self-consciousness	Inability to mix in company	Numb feeling in face
37	Aggressive impulses	Anxiety	Persecutory ideas
38	Various somatic complaints	Loss of concentration	Daydreaming
39	Infatuation with stranger	Moodiness	Ideas of reference
40	Loss of concentration	Daydreaming	Inability to think

From Chapman, J. The early symptoms of schizophrenia. *The British Journal of Psychiatry*, 1966, 112, 244.

pelling factor in family decisions, the action generally reflected the family's inner conflicts and sensitivity to community attitudes, as this case shows:

A male patient hit his mother periodically, talked in a loud and hostile manner . . . used profane language, and masturbated openly at home for one year. The decision to seek hospitalization occurred promptly when he carved obscenities on the new grand piano. The mother acted because she was afraid that her spouse, the patient's stepfather, would leave her, since the piano was a status symbol and the carvings would present tangible evidence to the neighbors that the family was indecent. (Smith et al., 1963, p. 76)

In only 4 out of the 100 instances did individuals themselves ask to be admitted to a hospital.

Since the patient is seldom the one who requests hospitalization, legal procedures are required before one person can be committed by another. This process is intended to protect the patient against unfair action. Typically, the hearings in such cases are held after an affidavit (formal complaint) is filed with a judge, who thereupon issues an order for a hearing before a commission. Miller and Schwartz (1966) observed the hearing procedures on 58 cases before a county commission that consisted of two local physicians (one a psychiatrist) and a Superior Court judge.

Three decisions were possible: dismissal, commitment, or an order for further psychiatric observation. The way in which the decisions were reached presents a disturbing view of the plight of people who violate the community's standards of acceptable behavior.

Miller and Schwartz found that although courtroom etiquette was relaxed, the proceedings seemed like a rehearsed, stylized ritual. Patients were seldom addressed directly, nor were they informed of their rights to counsel or jury trial. The doctors gave a brief report of the patient's condition, presumably based on an examination. Some resistant patients, however, protested that only a perfunctory examination, or none at all, had been given. Their protests seem justified, since the doctors recommended commitment in virtually all cases, thereby showing no discrimination among patients, and apparently accepting the complainants' "diagnosis" of mental illness.

Court proceedings were often as short as the psychiatric examinations. "The average length of the hearings was 4.1 minutes—the median length was less than three!" (Miller and Schwartz, 1966, p. 30). It seemed to Miller and Schwartz that the conclusions were predetermined, with a distinct bias against the defendants.

The defendants' deportment was either bewildered, mute, voluntary, or defiant. The passive ones were routinely committed, with only 4 exceptions in 24 cases. Only 2 of the 13 voluntaries were dismissed (for obvious alcoholism). However, one-third of the 21 resisters were dismissed. This group appeared to be younger, more alert and intelligent. When they directed their protest against the complainants (and not the doctors), and managed to keep their tempers under control, they evidently impressed the judge enough to rule in their favor.

The Miller and Schwartz sample of cases is typical of the hospital commitment process that prevails today. Whatever their real problems and needs, defendants have the deck stacked against them in a "Catch-22" dilemma: denial of sickness and resistance to authority are among the very "symptoms" that define their "mental illness." These individuals should be given the help they need, but the proper role of professionals in providing this treatment must be examined critically.

The Effects of Hospitalization

The nature and course of schizophrenia, as we have noted, are likely to lead to hospitalization. The patient's problematic life outside the institution is then replaced by a new kind of sheltered life inside the hospital designed to help him or her get better. How does the hospital actually work?

The best place to start this part of our inquiry is in the hospital itself. Perrucci (1974) gives us a detailed picture of life on the psychotic wards of a mental hospital. He takes us through a typical day in Ward X, which provides Intermediate Treatment Service. This service offers a diversified treatment program aimed at speeding progress toward convalescent leaves.

Fifty female patients (some wards have both sexes) are housed in the ward, two to seven per room in 18 bedrooms. The bedrooms are locked during the day so that withdrawn patients will not spend all their time in bed. There is a large dayroom in which chairs are arrayed in classroom style in front of a TV set. The nurses' office is off-limits for patients unless they are asked to enter. Outside the office, there is a desk where patients sign out and in when they leave and return to the ward. The ward is furnished with standard beds, chests, and chairs. It has a look of cold orderliness, with no privacy or personalization.

The staff includes a doctor, a ward nurse, attendants, a social worker, and a work therapist. Only the attendants work full time in the ward, although some hospitals have nurses constantly in each ward. The ward nurse supervises the attendants, who are at the bottom of the hospital hierarchy.

The doctor visits the ward about once a week to check staff problems and sign orders. Every second week he conducts "ward rounds," accompanied by the staff. He speaks briefly to each of the patients gathered in the dayroom, asking each about her condition. Most of the patients' contacts are with the ward attendants, who dispense medications and see that the patients proceed to their work assignments or medical appointments.

Here is a summary of the patients' daily routine, unvarying from day to day.

5:30 A.M. Patients who work in dining rooms are awakened and get dressed.

6:15 A.M. Other patients arise and wash up en masse in the lavatory.

6:30 A.M. Medication is dispensed at nurses' office.

6:45 A.M. Patients make beds and straighten up.

7:15 A.M. Patients go to breakfast in a group.

7:45 A.M. The roll is called in the dayroom. Patients bicker with each other during roll call.

8:00 A.M. Patients go out on work assignments.

11:00 A.M. Medication is dispensed.

12:15 P.M. Patients go to lunch as a group. Afternoon. Patients either continue their work, go to the beauty parlor, canteen, or recreation, or to art and typing classes.

4:00 P.M. Roll call. Evening shift comes on duty.

5:15 P.M. Dinner. Patients go as a group.

5:45 P.M. Medication is dispensed. Patients bathe and dress for evening activities: dancing, ping-pong, shuffleboard, weekly movies. Others watch TV, read, write letters, do their laundry, or go to bed.

9:00 P.M. Patients return from activities.

10:00 P.M. Lights out.

We get a depressing picture of hospital life that is routinized and completely controlled. Perrucci aptly characterizes it as "unfreedom."

What happens to the patient's sense of identity and personal worth? You will remember, from Chapter 2, Rosenhan's fascinating study (1975) in which he and seven other "sane" volunteers of varied backgrounds sought admission as psychiatric patients to 12 hospitals in five states. The only complaint they presented was of hearing voices whose words referred to the "meaninglessness of life." Besides these uncertain symptoms, they described their lives accurately to interviewers.

All but one of these "pseudopatients" were admitted as schizophrenic, and after from 7 to 52 days the other seven were discharged as schizophrenic "in remission." This label indicated the belief that the patients had been psychotic. Yet upon admission, all the pseudopatients abandoned their symptoms and resumed their normal behavior for the duration of their stay. While the professional staff failed to detect the deception, a number of fellow patients quickly recognized the pseudopatients as normal!

The normal behavior of a well-motivated person is misconstrued in the context of what Perrucci refers to as institutional "norms." When Rosenhan's pseudopatients made a practice of openly taking notes on their observations, several of the nurses recorded comments on the "writing behavior" as part of the patients' compulsive abnormal behavior.

Rosenhan sees part of the problem as an effect of the limited contact the professional staff has with patients. The degree of "staff segregation" is measured by the number of times per day the various staff members emerged on the ward.

Daytime nurses emerged briefly an average of 11.5 times, afternoon nurses emerged 9.4 times. Physicians emerged on the ward 6.7 times per day on the average (some only emerged once!). The lowest-level staff, the ward attendants, spent about 11 percent of their on-duty time among the patients, part of that doing maintenance chores.

When the pseudopatients managed to initiate a contact with the doctors, conversation was perfunctory and detached. Responses were curt, patronizing, and occasionally ignored the question that had been asked. In such situations, the patients are not treated as individuals but as faceless nonentities. Their efforts to command attention or engage in a dignified relationship with members of the staff are

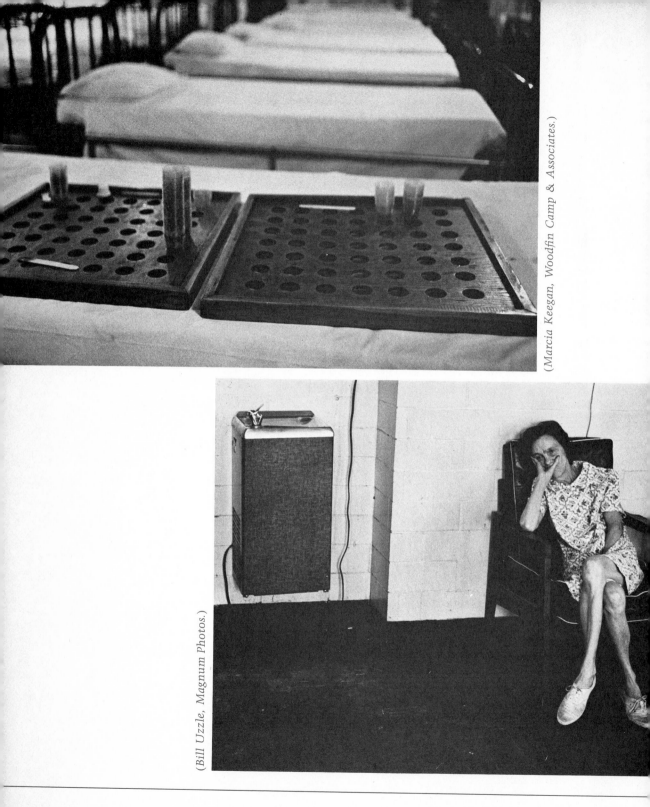

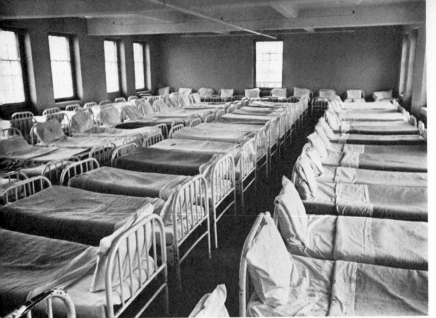

Many believe that the hospital environment—its total control, regimentation, impersonality, and depressing atmosphere—is responsible for cases of chronic schizophrenia.

(Marcia Keegan, Woodfin Camp & Associates.)

blocked by the authority structure that subordinates patients to staff. It is no wonder that they feel depersonalized and powerless.

Zusman (1966) reviews several theories of the effects of institutions on patient behavior. One theory (Barton, 1959) attached the label *institutional neurosis* to a syndrome comprising "apathy, lack of initiative, loss of interest, submissiveness, . . . deterioration of personal habits, loss of individuality" (Zusman, 1966, p. 293) as a result of isolation from the outside world, enforced idleness, and subordination to staff.

Another theory (Miller, 1961) goes one step further and traces paranoid, depressive, catatonic, psychopathic, and passive neurotic responses to the institutional environment.

Three factors have been proposed to account for this deterioration of behavior: the social pressures of an institution, the pattern of susceptibility or resistance to the pressures, and the length of exposure to them (Wing, 1962). Behaviors induced by the institutional milieu are hard to distinguish from symptoms of the illness.

Martin (1955) labels as *institutionalization* the process whereby patients surrender their independence to the authority of the institution as imposed and enforced by the staff at all levels. This inevitably results in patients' inability to function outside of the institution. This conditioning process is called *chronicity* (Sommer and Witney, 1961).

Gruenberg (1963) analyzed the motivating forces in chronicity in terms of seven factors: (1) susceptibility, (2) dependence on current cues, (3) labeling as incompetent and dangerous, (4) induction into the sick role, (5) learning the role, (6) loss of work and social skills, and (7) identification with the sick.

Eventually, the schizophrenic's personal identity is stripped away and replaced by the depersonalized role of patient. His transformation is brought about by the system of privileges and punishments that control his responses and enforce cooperation. According to Goffman (1957), this is the result of the control over the patient, which he summarized with the label "Total Institution."

Our scanning of these views of the damaging effects of hospitalization on susceptible patients brings us face to face with questions that are currently challenging what was considered, until recently, an enlightened advance over previous systems. The essential problem lies in the conditioning effect of institutional procedures. Remember from Chapter 3 how the seals in the tank acquired bizarre behaviors in responding "normally" to reinforcements. Patients can be just as easily conditioned by suitable reinforcements that teach them how to function effectively in the hospital environment. It is those very same behaviors, however, that make them incompetent to function in the outside world (Braginsky, Braginsky, and Ring, 1969).

What can we conclude from this discussion? One conclusion is that these data support our suggestion that people who experience traumatic events that provoke extremely disturbed behavior for a short time and who become patients and enter a hospital learn to become "schizophrenics" in the hospital.

Outcome Studies (Prognosis)

When we try to discover the likelihood of recovery from schizophrenia, we run into baffling difficulties. It is relatively easy to find out about hospital discharges and even hospital readmissions. But a discharge does not necessarily mean recovery, and a readmission (as we have seen in our discussion of commitment) does not always mean that the patient needs to be institutionalized.

What are the chances of various outcomes? Hogarty et al. (1973) indicated that only 10 to 15 percent of patients in remission (i.e., lessening or disappearance of symptoms) will relapse within a year. These are the current possibilities: (1) Degeneration into a terminal, vegetable state is unlikely. (2) Thirty to 40 percent of schizophrenics will attain a condition of stable chronicity; we see them walking the streets aimlessly, talking to themselves. (3) Some will attain full remission with occasional relapses. (4) A majority will experience some remission with personality impairment showing residual behaviors. (5) Some will gain full, permanent recovery.

A study of outcomes at 17 to 30 years after remission (Roff, 1974) found that 9 percent were fully recovered, 27 percent had settled into a neurotic kind of adjustment (that is, functioning with some problems), and 61 percent had unfavorable outcomes (incapacitated, rehospitalized, etc.). The number of functioning cases seems to be due, in part, to the community's increasing ability to maintain individuals who would formerly have been unable to get along. Simon et al. (1965) reviewed data from an earlier, long-term follow-up study (Wirt and Simon, 1959) that confirmed the good prognosis usually attached to rapid onset and maturity. They concluded that active intervention (outside treatment) was better than hospitalization. The 1959 eight-year study of 56 hospitalized patients, out of the 80 originally selected, found that only 20 percent had improved, 50 percent were worse, and 30 percent were unchanged, a rather discouraging outcome pattern.

Analyzing the data in terms of factors correlated with various outcomes, Schooler et al. (1967) offer a useful set of predictors.

1. The number of previous hospitalizations is unrelated to the rating of patients' adjustment outside.
2. More rapid onset leads to functioning at a higher level on return to the community.
3. Patients older at admission are more likely to be working regularly than younger ones, but at a lower-level job than before.
4. Placebo treatment is followed by fewer rehospitalizations than treatment with the phenothiazines.
5. Phenothiazines and psychotherapy after discharge reduce hospitalization. (The contradiction with Predictor 4 seems to be explained by the total treatment program after hospitalization that helps ex-patients work out their personal and social problems as well as reduce their tensions.)
6. Housewives' reentry into their neighborhoods is more successful following shorter hospitalization.
7. Ex-patients in conjugal homes are more likely to be self-supporting than those in parental homes.

We must conclude our review of prognoses on a somewhat pessimistic note. Schizophrenic patients have a minimal chance of complete recovery and only a fair chance of remission, with a strong likelihood of one or more relapses.

Summary

We have followed schizophrenic patients from the premorbid indications of illness, through diagnosis and hospitalization, and back into the community. The history of the schizophrenic model turns on the pivotal contributions of Kraepelin and Bleuler, who introduced methods of classifying behavior types according to signs of varying significance.

Ongoing efforts to establish well-defined nosological types are complicated by the wide spectrum of interactive behaviors that involve every aspect of patients' responses: perceptual, cognitive, speech, psychomotor, and emotional. The dimensional concepts relating to premorbid and onset characteristics (acute-chronic, process-reactive) offer the most reliable basis for prognosis with respect to particular types. Indications are that we are moving away from the disease model view of schizophrenia.

The effects of hospitalization on the course of the illness are evident. The susceptible patients respond to the overpowering forces of institutional structures and practices. Professional observers agree on the way the hospital regimen systematically depersonalizes patients, aggravating their problems and reinforcing behaviors that are the basic behaviors for what we now label as "schizophrenia."

Outcome studies offer minimal hope of full recovery, but the majority of patients gain remission, with residual problems that can be helped through intensive outpatient programs of drugs and psychotherapy.

11.

Schizophrenia: Causal, contributing, and maintaining factors and treatment approaches

Now that we have had a detailed look at the category of abnormal behavior called schizophrenia—the evolution of the concept, its behavioral manifestations, and the way our society reacts to people labeled as "schizophrenic"—we turn to the theory and research on the factors related to the abnormal behaviors and approaches to changing these behaviors.

Here again, as in other areas of abnormal psychology, we must carefully find a path through a thicket of conflicting views. As we saw in Chapter 10, many researchers and therapists still see schizophrenia as a clinical entity with a definable pattern of symptoms, the cause of which they hope to discover. Others find that each patient shows particular behaviors that are maintained by the patient's environment. These two extreme views compete vigorously in our literature and in our institutions. Out of this competition have come some major changes in our thinking about this complex behavioral problem.

Causal, Contributing, and Maintaining Factors

Through the years, the focus of the wide variety of approaches to schizophrenia has been on the medical model of "illness." This motivated the search for a set of direct causes. As we saw in Chapter 4, however, interactive factors may open up one or more routes to a functionally autonomous deficit. The proper search is for contributing factors rather than direct causes. We will, therefore, consider a variety of theoretical interpretations, none of which is exclusively "right" or "wrong" but all of which are illuminating.

Biological Factors

Genetic Factors

You will recall the presentation in Chapter 4 of the factors (zygosity, dominant and recessive genes, etc.) and the patterns (Mendelian distributions) that determine genetic effects. In accordance with genetic laws, a decision that genes are in some way responsible for schizophrenia requires three kinds of statistical evidence: "(1) The frequency of schizophrenia must be greater in families of schizophrenics than in families of nonschizophrenic controls. . . . (2) The frequency of schizophrenia in relatives of schizophrenics should be positively correlated with the degree of blood relationship . . . . (3) The concordance rate for schizophrenia must be higher in monozygotic (MZ) than in dizygotic (DZ) twins" (Rosenthal, 1974, p. 589).

The best available way to obtain such data is from *longitudinal* (i.e., long-term) studies of schizophrenic families and of their twin offspring. Since we are aware of environmental influences on those who have some predisposing characteristics, we would want one of the twins to be reared by an adoptive, nonschizophrenic family. A number of such studies have been made.

One study (Kety et al., 1968) was conducted in Denmark of two groups of adopted children, approximately half of whom came from schizophrenic families. There were more than four times as many diagnoses of schizophrenic-related disorders among the index cases (adults who, as children, had been adopted from the schizophrenic families). A similar Danish study (Rosenthal, 1971) found the rate of schizophrenia diagnosis almost twice as high among the index cases.

In the United States, a study was made of the children of hospitalized, schizophrenic mothers (Heston, 1966). Of those placed at birth in foster homes, 16.6 percent were eventually hospitalized for schizophrenia, a rate approximating that for children reared by schizophrenic parents.

The results from these and similar studies seem to support the theory that genetic influences play a significant role in the development of schizophrenia. We must note, however, that as many as half of the MZ pairs do *not* become schizophrenic. Moreover, most schizophrenics do not have schizophrenic parents. It seems, then, that we cannot settle for a totally genetic explanation.

Nevertheless, theorists who accept genetic involvement in schizophrenia have proposed several conceptions of the process by which genes contribute to the development of the pathology. The genetic theories can be put into two classes: monogenic-biochemical theories and diathesis-stress theories. *Monogenic-biochemical* theories assume that a single gene or a combination of two major genes is responsible for the "metabolic error" that produces a biochemical abnormality. *Diathesis-stress* theories assume that there is an inherited *predisposition* that causes an abnormal response to life stresses. The monogenic-biochemical theorists seek an essential biological defect as the direct cause, while the diathesis-stress theorists look for some abnormality in the central nervous system as a contributing factor.

Mednick and Schulsinger (1968) investigated the births of children of schizophrenic mothers and found that they were frequently reported as more difficult than the births of children of normal mothers. Tests of the children of schizophrenic mothers showed more deviant responses, poorer social adjustment, and withdrawal. The results, indirectly, suggest the possibility of brain damage, but do not exclude the effects of the psychotic mothers' behavior.

The most popular genetic theory is the *polygenic* hypothesis. It assumes that there are a large number of critical genes with additive effects (polygenes). Exposure to life stresses activates certain polygenes, which then release latent symptoms. Process schizophrenics are presumed to have an exceptionally high count of such polygenes.

The main arguments against genetic theories of schizophrenia are addressed to the fact that an alternative, environmental explanation can often account for the family incidence and twin-study correlations and the concordance rates. Twins reared in the same family would be subject to the same schizophrenogenic influences. The blame may be shared by intra-uterine, physiological, and environmental conditions.

Biophysical Factors

Biochemical Factors

There has been an upsurge of interest in the role of biochemical processes in generating psychoses, largely based on the effects of chemicals, such as LSD, that produce psychotic-like behavior (*psychotomimetic* drugs), and on the reduction of schizophrenic behaviors by antipsychotic medications. It is, of course, tempting to envision rapid cures by drugs, with little or no psychotherapy.

Neurotransmitter substances, secreted by the synapses (the nerve terminals), are chemicals that are involved in the transmission of signals from one nerve to another. As such, they are essential components in sensorimotor reaction connections. Interruption or overexcitation of any of these connections causes faulty response to the stimulus. There are various ways in which this can happen. The presence of certain chemical substances in the body fluids is often taken as evidence of defective function in the neurotransmitter chemistry.

Neurotransmitters, like serotonin and the catecholamines (epinephrine and norepinephrine), can be blocked or intensified by other chemicals. LSD, for example, causes hallucinations similar to those in schizophrenia. However, this hypothesis has been questioned as a result of data on nonschizophrenics who have taken LSD and whose experiences were significantly different from experiences observed in schizophrenics. Furthermore, attempts to establish the relationship between the level of catecholamines and schizophrenia have not been uniformly successful.

Abnormal antibodies have been indicated as primary causative agents. In a series of studies (Heath et al., 1958, 1967), a gamma globulin antibody called taraxein was administered to normal subjects and produced schizophrenic behavior. A number of other researchers have failed to duplicate these findings, however. While some studies have shown abnormal levels of various immunoglobulins in the blood of schizophrenics, the levels of the same globulin vary between studies.

Carbohydrate metabolism has long been suspected of involvement in schizophrenia. Patients show an abnormally high tolerance for glucose. However, feeding patients a high-carbohydrate diet for several days before testing virtually eliminates the tolerance difference. This points to the possibility of nutritional deficiency in hospital diets as the determinant of the high tolerance. Related to the metabolism issue is the characteristic lack of energy displayed by schizophrenic patients. Attempts to associate that phenomenon with a disorder in phosphate metabolism have, as in the case of glucose tolerance, yielded no positive results.

Hormone responses of schizophrenics have also been noted as abnormal. Since the schizophrenic's deviant behavior under stress is a central feature, researchers have postulated that abnormal hormone levels may indicate some biochemical defect underlying the stress-induced behavior. Among the candidates affecting the schizophrenic's stress responses are thyroid hormone, insulin, certain steroids, and adrenal substances. Hoskins (1946) reported a significant difference between schizophrenics and the normals in the amount of adrenal substances.

Hoskins subjected his patients to stressful motor tasks, and found them incapacitated as a result of deficient adrenal response. Once again, however, this seemingly definite result is compromised by the finding that removal of both adrenal glands (Apter, 1958) did not aggravate schizophrenic symptoms. It is likely that the hormonal abnormalities may be a result of some other defects in the biological systems of patients.

Vitamin deficiency may be expected among patients as a result of inadequate nutrition and the hospital regimen. Megavitamin therapy (enormous doses of vitamins) has acquired enthusiastic exponents. But there is little concrete evidence for its use.

It appears, then, that although there are tantalizing indications of biochemical effects in schizophrenia, there is no decisive evidence at this time.

Physiological Factors

Physiological factors, although closely associated with biochemical factors, are generally studied separately. We are concerned here with the physiological effects of stress and arousal.

Measurements of heart rate, skin resistance, and muscular tension are the principal means of evaluating arousal levels and stress reactions. In one experiment (Malmo and Shagass, 1949), early acute schizophrenics and patients suffering from clinical anxiety reacted similarly to pain. Note that high levels of anxiety are associated with high arousal, as are certain types of schizophrenia. Another study (Pfister, 1938) differentiated early stages of schizophrenia from later chronicity by a gradual decline from high to low heart rates, which fell below normal in late chronic stages.

Fenz and Velner (1970) performed a series of tests on heart and respiration rates, galvanic skin response, and muscle resistance on schizophrenic and normal subjects. Heart and respiration rates under stress were substantially higher for both process and reactive schizophrenics than for normal subjects. Muscle potential was also higher and skin conductance lower for the patients. Apparently, schizophrenic arousal levels vary under different tests. Venables and Wing (1962) found that the more socially withdrawn schizophrenics had higher skin potentials and, hence, were more highly aroused (Figure 11-1).

The attempt to correlate autonomic response consistently with arousal level has not been altogether successful. Researchers report contradictory results. Perhaps the clue can be found in the finding that schizophrenic responses are marked by sharp, sudden swings in arousal between high and low extremes (Epstein, 1967). On the basis of such evidence, it could be concluded that schizophrenics are unable to adjust their autonomic responses to variations in stimulation. Although the arousal variable plays a central role in many theories, researchers must find empirical ways of resolving the inconsistent results.

Psychological Factors

Psychodynamic Approaches

Psychodynamic interpretations of schizophrenia are founded on the Freudian concepts we discussed in Chapter 3. Freud himself saw schizophrenia as a psychosis that would not readily submit to psychotherapy. Schizophrenic patients are unable to cathect (invest psychic energy) in objects and cannot engage in transference with a therapist. In short, they are

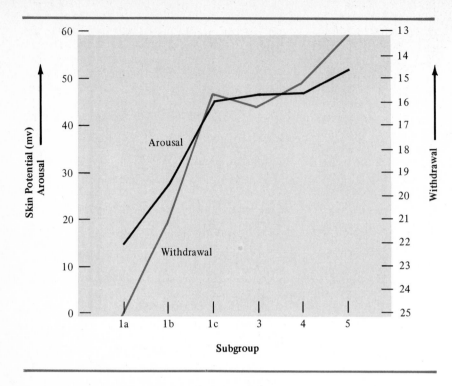

Figure 11-1 Skin potential and withdrawal measures of clinical subgroups of schizophrenics. The subgroups were formed from interview measures of withdrawal. They range from 1a, least withdrawn, to 5, most withdrawn. (*Venables, P. H., and Wing, J. K. Level of arousal and the subclassification of schizophrenia.* Archives of General Psychiatry, 1962, 7, 114–119. © 1962, American Medical Association.)

no longer in touch with the world. Psychotic defenses against anxiety correspond to the neuroses, but differ in intensity and in the schizophrenic's lack of awareness of them. Look back over Chapter 3 and you will recognize the psychodynamic origins of many of the schizophrenic behaviors we have seen in the cases presented in Chapter 10.

Essentially, Freud saw schizophrenic behavior as a regression of the libido back to a state of autoeroticism (self-initiated sexual excitement), accompanied by a loss of object relations. This return to infantile narcissism is graphically described by Fenichel:

The infant starts out in a state of "primary narcissism" in which the systems of the mental apparatus are not yet differentiated from each other, and in which no objects exist as yet. The differentiation of the ego coincides with the discovery of objects. An ego exists in so far as it is differentiated from objects that are not ego. . . . The schizophrenic has regressed to narcissism; the schizophrenic has lost his objects; the schizophrenic has parted with reality; the schizophrenic's ego has broken down. In schizophrenia the collapse of reality testing, the fundamental function of the ego, and the symptoms of "disintegration of the ego" which amount to a severe disruption of the continuity of the personality, likewise can be interpreted as a return to the time when the ego was not yet established or had just begun to be established. (1945, pp. 414–416)

Orthodox Freudians have variously traced schizophrenic behavior back to oral trauma, to the anal stage, and to a breakdown of ego boundaries. As a consequence of these disruptions, schizophrenics can no longer perceive or test reality.

Neo-Freudians have elaborated the psychodynamic analysis in terms of regression (Sullivan, 1962; Arieti, 1955; von Domarus, 1944) and of excessive, exhaustive emotional investment by a personality that is burdened with memories of an earlier period in the collective unconscious (Jung, 1936). Sullivan (1962) found the roots of the illness to be in "disastrous interpersonal relations" arising from severe childhood traumas.

Ego psychologists blame the breakdown of ego boundaries for the development of schizophrenia (Federn, 1952). In the healthy personality, the well-defined ego boundaries serve as a sensory organ to distinguish objects in the environment from the self. In the schizophrenic, it is the ego that is ill. The ego boundaries become blurred or nonexistent. Paranoids take

the false certainty of a false reality as the basis for their actual life. Their thoughts are their reality; there is no reality testing because the ego has lost the boundaries that provide the basis for such testing. In the struggle between the conscious and the unconscious, efforts to protect the ego from the hobgoblins of the unconscious fail, opening the gates to the intrusion of hateful products of the unconscious. This, according to Federn, accounts for the schizophrenic's heightened sensations, level of arousal, and aggressiveness.

Family Factors

Family factors are often credited with a major contribution to the making of a schizophrenic. Investigators have painted a picture of harmful patterns of interpersonal relations in so-called "schizophrenogenic" families: weak, passive father; dominant, complaining ("tyrant-martyr") mother; inconsistent discipline; cold, rejecting parents; general disharmony and lack of communication.

One of the conditions that is thought to be prevalent in schizophrenogenic families is called the "double-bind" situation. (This destructive "push-pull" game was described in Chapter 4.) However, one study (Ringuette and Kennedy, 1966) tested the hypothesis by submitting letters from mothers of schizophrenics and of normals to a panel of expert judges. There was no agreement among the judges on double-bind messages in the correspondence.

Frank (1965) looked for some consistent pattern of emotional behavior that distinguished schizophrenogenic families. Assembling data on broken homes, schizophrenic parents, inconsistent discipline, and other presumably causal factors, he found considerable overlap between schizophrenic and normal families. Families of schizophrenics do in fact tend to have domineering, overpossessive, rejecting mothers; passive fathers; discord; and lack of reality orientation. But so do many homes of normal children. Frank's conclusion is that there is no one discriminating schizophrenogenic factor, and, indeed, that is what

---

Box 11-1 A Contemporary Psychoanalytic View

One psychoanalytic theorist, Silvano Arieti (1974c, 1974d), divides the development of a psychosis into four periods.

1. *Early childhood.* Mistrust instilled by unstable parents causes child to reject them, especially the mother; consequently, child does not develop self-trust.

2. *Late childhood.* Secondary (verbal) process begins. Schizoid personality withdraws from unpleasant experiences with mother; stormy personality fights off intolerable fears and anxieties toward mother; senses own inadequacy.

3. *Puberty.* Higher cognitive processes and sexual urges develop. Schizoid cannot confront the world with inadequate defenses from earlier periods. "Psychotic panic" occurs.

4. *Psychosis.* Only escape is through change in thought processes—a reversion to primary process in which objects can be magically transformed. The paranoid externalizes his or her internal threats.

---

the evidence we have reviewed seems to indicate.

High Risk and Premorbid Adjustment

A research approach that has potential as a basis for clinical intervention is the detection and study of children who have a high risk of becoming schizophrenic. Current research is aimed at identifying factors in childhood that show high correlation with later onset.[1]

Garmezy is investigating the risks of four groups of children, age 9–13: (1) children with schizophrenic mothers, (2) children who "act out," (3) children of depressive, nonpsychotic mothers, and (4) overinhibited children. The first two groups are considered higher-risk candidates and the second two, lower-risk. The study is probing how well the children in each group adapt to the environment at each of the four stages of development.

Mednick and Schulsinger are working on three interrelated projects: (1) a longitudinal study of children of schizophrenic mothers, started more than a decade ago, (2) a follow-up study to the one mentioned earlier in the chapter of consequences of difficult births, and (3) an intervention program with high-risk preschoolers. Findings thus far indicate that high-risk children (identified by a battery of psychological tests) experienced longer and more difficult births, more family conflict, and poorer social adjustment. Mednick has advanced the theory that schizophrenia is the result of a learning process in response to environmental demands. His study has been challenged, however, on the basis of findings that some of the "well" fathers had records of psychiatric problems.

Rodnick and Goldstein are studying four groups of disturbed adolescents (antisocial, family conflict, passive, withdrawn) and their families. Batteries of psychological and psychophysiological tests are used to measure how well adjusted each group is. The object of the study is to identify the pathological consequences of family interactions, adolescent thought disturbance, and adolescent social problems. So far, the study has shown significant effects of family conflict on disturbed behavior in adolescents.

Manfred Bleuler (1974) conducted a 20-year study of 184 Swiss children of schizophrenic parents (Table 11-1). Of these children, ten became schizophrenics, but 5 of them recovered fully. This is a much lower net "yield" of psychotics than other studies have shown. Bleuler credits the difference to his more conservative diagnostic criteria. His conclusion is that about 10 percent of the children of schizophrenic parents become schizophrenic. A more unexpected and therefore more impressive statistic to Bleuler is that the great majority of children who grow up under extreme abuse in the most dismal environments develop strong resistance to the destructive forces and emerge to lead nearly normal lives.

There are many pitfalls in research on high risk populations, however. First, there is a difficulty in finding families that meet the study's specifications, in enlisting cooperation of all their members, and in following them for the extended duration of a longitudinal study. Once this is done care must be taken in determining that the "well" spouse in a schizophrenic family is indeed clinically evaluated as normal. The reliability of the researchers' diagnoses of parents is related to the desirability of running a "blind" study in which the investigators are not informed of the diagnoses so that their judgments will not be affected. The selection of the critical variables in the parents and children appropriate to each child's stage of development also poses complex problems. Finally, no valid scales are available yet to permit proper weighting and balancing of the importance of genetic and environmental factors.

One type of study that avoids some of these pitfalls is the retrospective, in which the researcher examines the early history of currently hospitalized schizophrenics in an attempt to predict future behavior. Watt (1972)

[1]A few studies are outlined here to show the scope and methods of current inquiry. More details of these and other studies can be found in the Garmezy paper (1974).

Table 11-1 Types and Frequencies of Mental Disorders Among the Children of Schizophrenics

	Under Age 20[1]	Age 20–29	Age 30–39	Age 40–59	Over Age 60	Total
Number of children	41	33	45	63	2	184
Schizophrenia		1	4	5		10
Epilepsy		1				1
Feeblemindedness		1	1			2
Schizoid psychopathy		1	1	1		3
Alcoholism			1			1
Other disorders or eccentricities	1	7	6	8		22
Suicide	1			1		2

[1]Subject child's age at death or at the conclusion of study.

Bleuler, M. The offspring of schizophrenics. *Schizophrenia Bulletin*, 1974, 8, 94.

obtained school records, including teachers' comments, of the patients. An analysis indicated: (1) the in-school behavior of preschizophrenic children was different from normal children's, (2) the behavioral difficulties became prominent in adolescence, (3) the preschizophrenic boys grew more aggressive and defiant, while the preschizophrenic girls grew more shy and submissive as they entered adolescence. Watt concludes that adolescent behavior is predictive of psychotic development.

We have discussed the greater likelihood of schizophrenia for the children of schizophrenic parents. The frightful ordeal these children suffer every day of their lives makes the large percentage of children who survive such environments with normal behavior add up to a miracle of human strength. These three accounts will give you a child's-eye view of what life is like with a schizophrenic parent (Garmezy, 1974, p. 115).

She is quite a nice mother, really. She doesn't do anything bad. She doesn't hit or anything. She just sits. She is like a kid, mostly. When I give her a lot of candy she just sucks it all up like a vacuum cleaner. She doesn't comb her hair and her dress has spots on it. Sometimes she laughs at me and I am not making any jokes. I say: "Mom, why are you laughing at me?" and she just laughs more. I don't like it when she laughs like that. It's not like real laughing. She never used to be like that when I was little. She was just ordinary.

. . .

You cannot believe what it's like to wake up one morning and find your mother talking gibberish.

. . .

I wake up dreaming or maybe just daydreaming. I don't know what, but her face is coming toward me and she looks good and then suddenly her face begins to change and look mean and horrible like a monster. (Anthony, 1969, p. 445)

Learning Approaches

Learning theorists have investigated factors in the thought disorders of schizophrenics that affect their learning rates on various tasks. Conditioning, of course, is one form of learning, and tests of response to reinforcement have been given. One experiment (Taylor and Spence, 1954) demonstrated that schizophrenics were more easily conditioned than either normal or neurotic subjects.

Another experiment (Lindsley, 1960) used operant conditioning techniques. Patients had to press a bar to receive a reward as reinforcement for their operant response. The results for the schizophrenics were disastrous—90 percent failed to develop stable response levels. Lindsley attributes this to competing psychotic responses.

Other explanations may be found in the schizophrenics' lack of motivation and distractible attention. These deficiencies show up in many experimental test results. Reread (in Chapter 10) the self-reports of schizophrenics who were deluged with stimuli they could not attend to selectively, and consider how such a patient would deal with a test situation.

Schizophrenics manifest an inability to inhibit (prevent) response. Failure to inhibit incorrect responses leads to poor performance. They also tend to generalize stimuli excessively, which may account for their "relative inability to make differential responses to different stimuli within the same class" (Maher, 1966, p. 384).

While the learning of schizophrenics is demonstrably deficient, it is impossible to draw definite conclusions about the nature of their problem because of the confounding effect of motivational, attentional, and general cognitive deficits.

Behavioral Approaches

Behavioral formulations have been based on variations of the learning concept that we have just discussed. Typical of these views is Ullmann and Krasner's proposal (1975) that schizophrenic behavior is learned because responses to normal social stimuli are not reinforced. Therefore, instead of attending to appropriate stimuli in the environment, schizophrenics react to internal cues that go unnoticed by normal people—hence, their idiosyncratic behavior. Because they are not positively reinforced for their responses to social stimuli, they hallucinate, that is, they react to internal stimuli instead. In effect, the "wrong" stimuli control their behavior.

The social breakdown process, which we observed in the hospital (in Chapter 10), continues the deterioration of response learning of schizophrenics by exposing them to institutional situations that reinforce responses to arbitrary and often absurd procedures and customs. This reminds us again of the example of the seals in Chapter 3.

Sociocultural Factors

Does schizophrenia occur in all societies? The question has significance since a negative answer would point to culture as an important determinant of schizophrenia. As so often happens in the literature of schizophrenia, two diametrically opposite opinions prevail.

Lehmann (1975) musters an array of studies that have found geographical concentration and historical changes in types of schizophrenia. The paranoid form is said to be most common in the United States; the hebephrenic most common in Brazil and Africa, where there is a low incidence of the paranoid type. Paranoid reactions are associated with more highly developed cultures, and catatonic reactions with more primitive societies. Lehmann also traces the trends in kinds of schizophrenic behavior through the last half of the nineteenth and the first half of the twentieth centuries. For example, studies have found a decrease in aggressiveness of patients during that period, although this may be an effect of changes in methods of treatment.

On the opposite side of the question, Torrey (1973) finds no valid evidence for the universality of schizophrenia. In his review of the literature, he raises questions about methodology and diagnosis in many studies. Margaret Mead (1949), for example, found cases of catatonic dementia praecox in Samoa, but the natives she studied had been exposed to Western missionary influences. Benedict and Jacks (1954) surveyed five studies of primitive societies where schizophrenia had been found, but Torrey argues that they were hospitalized cases and hospitalization indicates more highly developed groups. Lambo (1955, 1965) studied primitive Africans diagnosed as schizophrenics and concluded that the diagnoses of the more primitive patients may have mistaken other organic diseases for schizophrenia. Thus, according to Torrey, there is no clear case for the universality of schizophrenia, which seems to be a product of life in technologically advanced cultures.

In the search for causative or contributing factors in schizophrenia, data from sociological studies have provided strong evidence of correlation between incidence of psychosis and social class. One study (Hollingshead and Redlich, 1958), for example, found schizophrenia severity and prevalence inversely related to socioeconomic status (SES). In other words, the more severe cases of schizophrenia were found among the lower classes.

Another study (Faris and Dunham, 1939) found a higher concentration of schizophrenia in central Chicago than on the periphery of the city. In the same vein, yet another study (Lemkau and Crocetti, 1958) detected a relationship of uncertain nature between schizophrenia and urbanization.

Dunham (1964) made a careful study designed to establish possible correlations between incidence rate and social class. He selected two communities in Detroit based on their wide difference in rates of schizophrenic first admissions, one very high and the other very low. He then surveyed 178 psychiatric facilities in Michigan and found more than 3,000 cases of abnormal behavior from the two target communities. These cases were divided into five social classes according to SES. The findings showed no inverse relationship between incidence and SES. Although the highest concentration of cases was in the lowest social class, the remainder were about equally distributed among the other four classes. The substantial number of fathers who were in higher classes than their schizophrenic children strongly suggests a downward drift in the status of schizophrenics. Their condition impedes their attainment of occupational goals at their fathers' level. However, there was no clear pattern of upward or downward mobility among the schizophrenics themselves.

Kohn (1973) sums up the evidence for social class relationship to schizophrenia but rejects a simple formulation. He reviews the census-taking problems that we have already discussed. His major thesis is that the family is a structure within which the various forces are focused and caused to interact. Most of the factors that have been suspected of being implicated in the schizophrenogenic process are directly involved in the dynamics of low-SES families. The heritability of schizophrenia would be a natural result of the tendency for "bad genes" to concentrate in lower-class families as earlier generations of schizophrenics slipped down the social scale (what Kohn calls the "multigenerational drift").

While stress seems more evident in lower-class families, Kohn does not see it as a direct cause. Rather, he feels that the poorer conditions of life in such families make it difficult for the individual to adapt to stressful situations. Kohn also emphasizes the family's central function as interpreter of social values to its children. Their limited education, narrowness of experience, and subordination to the economic and political power wielded by others incline them toward conformity and rigid attitudes. The parents communicate their powerlessness and impose their constricted conceptions of reality on their genetically predisposed children—the so-called "high risk" candidates for schizophrenia. In short, all the forces that push the child toward psychosis are concentrated in and on the low-SES family.

Research on Etiology

One could be confused easily by the mixture of schizophrenic research results that differ in their variables and their data. Are there some common denominators in the competing theories that we may put together into a forecast of coming developments or, at least, an indicator of present directions? There seems to be some agreement on the influence, if not the relative importance, of certain factors (notably,

Poor living conditions make it difficult for individuals to adapt to stressful situations. (*Charles Gatewood.*)

genetic and social-familial) in the cause of schizophrenia. Let us see how they are handled by several researchers in their formulations.

Pollin (1972) finds empirical support for an integrative model with genetic, psychological, and environmental components. While genetic predisposition seems undeniable, he believes that the many instances of schizoid behavior in only one of a set of twins of schizophrenic parents rule against the possibility of a single dominant gene.

The fact that 50 to 75 percent of MZ twins are discordant for schizophrenia (only one twin affected) raises doubt that genetic defects are essential to the etiology of schizophrenia.

The psychological aspect is seen in the different treatment of "difficult" children by their parents. Once labeled, they are locked into their role by rigid family attitudes toward abnormal behavior and are thereby sensitized to stressful situations generated by the family.

Finally, the effect of the environment is demonstrated by the abnormal responses to life stresses. Stresses have been observed to increase the rate of metabolism of the catecholamines. Pollin theorizes that stress activates the biochemical mechanism.

Meehl (1962) brings genetic, biochemical, psychological, social, and learning theories together into a hypothetical scenario. His formulation is summed up in his definition of schizophrenia as "a neurological disease of learned origin." The definition is represented in this simplified formula:

Neural defect (*schizotaxia*) + aversive social learning = *schizotype.*

The schizotype (one predisposed to schizophrenia) becomes schizophrenic under life stresses if he or she cannot adapt effectively.

As outlined by Meehl, the learning process is motivated by the feedback of positive and negative reinforcement from limbic centers. An imbalance in their functioning, caused by what Meehl calls "synaptic slippage" (the schizotaxic neural defect), generally minimizes feedback from the pleasure center, thereby enhancing aversive responses. As a consequence, learning is disrupted, and the individual is unable to discriminate social cues. A further consequence is the inability to suppress wrong and inappropriate behavioral responses. Recall the patients who "couldn't stop the wrong words from coming out." The end result is the inability to control assaults on the ego, leading to its deterioration. The front line of the assaults is manned by the parents, whose behavior is open to question, even when they are not diagnosed as schizophrenic. One study (McConaghy, 1959) found that a number of nondiagnosed pairs of parents of schizophrenics had subclinical (below problem level) thought disorders—confirming the grim picture of family environment.

Zubin (1975) offers a *vulnerability* hypothesis. In his model, the predisposing factor is the vulnerability of the person at risk. When a vulnerable personality is under stress, a breakdown is threatened. Schizophrenic onset occurs when the stress exceeds the vulnerability threshold. To meet the threat, the person attempts to mobilize his *coping* skills, which are limited by his *competence* (especially deficient in lower-SES families). Unfortunately, Zubin does not define or trace the source of the vulnerability.

Much of the apparent confusion of theories of causality probably is due to the pervasive medical model and attempt to locate a single causal mechanism for abnormal behaviors, which inspired the hunt for a "magic bullet" cure. In Chapter 4, we suggested a complex process in which many variables interacted to generate and maintain deviant behavior, some entering the process at different stages. It was suggested at that point that the abnormal behavior might in fact be the result of many processes. The behaviors may be the end product of numerous variables that cause, contribute to, or maintain the behavior. Nowhere is this more likely than with the wide variety of behaviors we place under the umbrella of the label "schizophrenia." Some schizophrenic behaviors may be the result of genetics, others may be the result of chemical imbalances, while others are due to the modeling behavior of very disturbed parents. Perhaps most schizophrenic behaviors are created by the subtle interaction of many variables, for example, genetic vulnerability + chemical imbalances + life stresses + poor coping skills.

The fact that for every proposed causal relationship there are equally viable alternative causes should finally make us aware that in arguing about the truth of our individual experiences, we may be in a situation like the proverbial six blind men groping around an elephant who, by each touching a different part, end up describing it differently. Perhaps we are really six blind men groping around six *different* animals, wondering why none of our descriptions matches.

Treatment Approaches

One major goal of all of the studies, analyses, and theories about the nature and causes of schizophrenia is the development of the most effective treatments. Since, for most approaches, cure is related to cause, we would expect to find the same confusion in recommended therapeutic methods that we observed in proposed causal mechanisms.

The medical model presumes a cause that needs to be treated—preferably a single illness with a single cause, psychological or other. Remember again, however, our discussion in Chapter 4 of *functional autonomy*, which implies that certain events may initiate a process and other, completely separate, events may enter later to intensify and keep the process going.

Regardless of the special attractions of different theories, the best criterion for judging appropriate treatment is its effectiveness: Does it do the job? And does it do it without harmful effects? This leads to the concept of minimally effective treatment, that is, the treatments chosen should be those that present the least risk of severe and irreversible consequences. Conservative restraint is necessary, particularly with the psychoses, where the drastic nature of the behaviors may prompt the use of drastic measures of therapy.

Psychodynamic Approaches

Traditional Psychoanalytic Approaches

Psychoanalysts themselves do not consider Freudian techniques a treatment of choice for schizophrenia, and the discouraging results of outcome research bear them out. The analysts find it difficult to adapt their highly verbal and intellectual methods to the disrupted condition of schizophrenics.

Will (1975) spells out the arguments against psychodynamic psychotherapy for schizophrenia. He does not see how analysts can play an effective role, since schizophrenics are incapable of forming the close relationship with the analyst so necessary for the procedure. Undetermined causes and lack of a functional model of the variables frustrate analysts in their search for underlying factors to which they can direct their therapy. In fact, the possibility of organic, biochemical, or neurophysiological causes calls for nonpsychotherapeutic intervention (e.g., medication). The extended length of treatment on an individual basis is beyond the financial means of those patients who come from lower-SES groups. Schizophrenic patients generally do not have the necessary motivation and attention span to continue the long-term procedures, where progress proceeds at a painfully slow rate. Will also notes that psychoanalysts do not, as a rule, have the necessary tolerance for the unresponsiveness and hostility of schizophrenics. Despite these objections at the theoretical level, Will has become renowned for his successful work with schizophrenic patients.

Since Freud's time, there has been some modification of the psychoanalytic view of schizophrenic treatment. Contrary to Freud's pessimism about the patient-analyst relationship, Federn (1952), one of Freud's pupils, established successful transference with schizophrenic patients. He focused his efforts on strengthening ego boundaries. Sechehaye (1951, 1956) entered the patient's psychotic world by presenting him with symbols that gratified frustrated needs ("symbolic realization")—a technique that requires great insight into the psychotic's illusions. Instead of entering the psychotic's world, Fromm-Reichmann (1950) and Sullivan (1953, 1962) tried to bring the patient into the real world by showing him that only a few people were involved in his unhappy experiences. The success of these two analysts testifies to the predominant importance of the therapist's warmth, patience, and resourcefulness over and above the validity of his theoretical formulations.

Three therapists of the orthodox psychoanalytic tradition have undertaken to adapt Freudian principles to the treatment of schizophrenia.

Wolman (1976b) has set up a theoretical framework for his therapy: he refers to it as a "modified Freudian model." The key is Sullivan's concept of interpersonal relations. Wolman identifies the various parent-child relationships, classifying them into directional interactions: instrumental (the child *takes*), mutual (*give-and-take* between parent and child), vectorial (the parent *gives* to the child). In schizophrenogenic families, the relationships are reversed: the parent demands (takes) and the child protects (gives to) the parent. This reversal of roles upsets the cathexis (i.e., concentration of psychic energy) functions and affects the nervous system, leading to somatic symptoms. The therapist's objective is to redirect the reversed libidinal energy concentrations into normal interpersonal relationships.

A systematic but flexible procedure is followed, incorporated into a set of rules (Wolman, 1976b).

1. unconditional support to protect the patient's self-esteem;
2. ego therapy to reinforce the patient's collapsed ego;
3. one-step-at-a-time progress, supporting less dangerous behaviors along the way;
4. pragmatic flexibility to strengthen the superego in the face of uncontrollable impulses;
5. individualization—tailoring the rules to the individual as he or she interacts with the therapist;

6. reality testing—gradually helping the patient to "see the light";

7. parsimony of interpretation—keeping the explanations to a minimum;

8. realistic management of transference, to prevent excessive dependence or affection on the part of the patient;

9. control of countertransference, to prevent overinvolvement of the therapist;

10. rational handling of hostility—the banning of violent, acting-out behavior

Arieti (1974a) also has modified the practice of classical psychotherapy in treating schizophrenics. To Arieti, the therapist's first and most essential objective is to break through the patients' autistic and sometimes hostile barrier and establish a sincere, trustful relationship. The therapist's helpful role is defined clearly at the outset. Without asking provocative questions, the therapist gets patients to talk about their symptoms, gradually guiding the patients to a point where they can recognize how their expectations of events (e.g., hearing voices on regular occasions) cause the events to happen. Patients are further made aware of their habit of "concretizing" vague threats into delusions, hallucinations, and other behavior patterns. The actual psychoanalytic process centers around redirecting patients' hostilities and feelings of persecution away from outsiders and back into proper reference to their parents. The patients are made aware of their parents' influence on their condition when they were children. This stage in the treatment also includes further reinforcement of ego feelings and boundaries. Throughout the program, the therapist participates actively in the lives of the patients, with a trained psychiatric assistant to sustain some of the burden. As we saw in other techniques, Arieti's method demands a skillful, sensitive, yet firm and honest, approach.

Will (1975), despite his theoretical difficulties discussed earlier, brings exceptional understanding and tolerance to the therapeutic situation, and accomplishes impressive results. His principal thesis is the natural response of regressive behavior to intolerable threats to self-esteem and security. The following is Will's description of his first experience with a schizophrenic patient.

Circumstances then led to my having the opportunity to spend a great deal of time with a withdrawn, mute patient who had failed to respond to a variety of treatments. Of necessity I put aside the paraphernalia of my ordinary medical work and found that I must listen and observe but for the most part not to otherwise act. No miracles were achieved but the patient became a person to me, and he showed me aspects of myself that were discomforting. Through personal therapy I looked as best I could at my own background, motives, values, and goals, and realized that what I saw could be on occasion useful if not pleasing. The schizophrenic patient was of particular interest as he persistently challenged any tendency to feel that one had "found the answer." Of greatest importance to me was the idea that to be psychotic was not to be somehow inhuman. As I came to know the patient as a person he was found to be in significant ways like myself, a finding applicable to all "strangers" and of increasing value in a world of easily breached national boundaries. (Will, 1973, pp. 153–154)

Will eventually developed his individual style of psychoanalytic therapy with schizophrenics.

I am not so much concerned with the styles of psychotherapy as I am with aspects of the experience that can be less subject to fashionable variation. Among the principles of treatment are the following:

1. As the disorder itself is not meaningless and unrelated to human experience, it can be dealt with in ordinary terms.

2. Relational bonds will develop as the result of frequent meetings of patient and therapist, and these ties will be intensified if the meetings are accompanied by emotional arousal. The relationship can be useful or otherwise; the observable details of the involvement are what we know as technique.

3. The therapist need not be "perfect"; he will make mistakes and he will have exposed

in himself a wide range of feelings. None of these—mistakes and feelings—can he deny; he must be aware of them and use them wisely, but he will rarely be certain as to the rightness of his acts.

4. The therapist should have or acquire certain abilities, among which are taking pleasure in the growth of another person; tolerance of attachment, dependency, and the inevitable stress of separation; the strength to set limits and yet permit another person to live in a way of his own; and the capacity to cooperate with members of a team, enduring the accompanying envy, jealousy, competition, anger, and affection. Finally, he should be able to accept the often slow pace of growth. (Will, 1973, p. 155)

R. D. Laing

Laing (1964) takes a distinctly non-Freudian, existential view of the schizophrenic's condition and appropriate treatment for it. He sees schizophrenics in terms of their experiences and natural feelings. Schizophrenics are people driven into despair by a rejecting family and society. To Laing, patients' reactions to their world are logical and correct, and so they must be approached with full regard for the legitimacy of their status in a mad world. He suggests that therapists try to accompany patients on a journey through their disordered thoughts, to discover their true self. Laing, however, is not explicit about the proper techniques for effective therapy according to the existential model.

Rosen's Direct Analysis

Rosen (1947, 1953) practices a controversial method, which is said to be based on Freudian theory, but which uses few of the Freudian techniques. The method is referred to as "primary process" and "direct analysis" because it confronts the unconscious material directly and attempts to impose the patient's real world directly onto his consciousness. The patient spends virtually his entire waking time in the company of the therapist and his assis-

tants (who sometimes must be present and active for 16 hours at a stretch!). The therapy team reinforces suitable behaviors and constantly challenges the patient's bizarre or otherwise inappropriate responses. The patient is repeatedly made to face his deviant impulses and unreasonable fears, and is coaxed, harangued, and subjected to direct interpretations of his behavior. The duration and intensity of the daily treatment may qualify it as a form of shock therapy. Rosen's method has been criticized, and his claimed successes either doubted or attributed to his personal manner.

Evaluation of Psychodynamic Therapies

Although the individual analysts have achieved successful results with psychodynamic therapy, their effectiveness is frequently credited to the genius and manner of the therapists rather than to the intrinsic power of the methods employed. The evidence of effectiveness usually comes from individual case anecdotes and not from formal research. The sparse psychodynamic research on schizophrenia—an unfortunate shortcoming of the psychodynamic school in general—has yielded ambiguous results. This is largely a consequence of inadequate methods of handling the problems of doubtful diagnoses, unmatched controls, uncontrolled drug treatment, and other purely methodological weaknesses.

The general conclusion, drawn from the individual case reports and the unsatisfactory results of experimental studies, is that psychodynamic therapy offers some value for management of patients but little promise as a therapeutic method.

Somatic Therapies

As we might expect from our knowledge of the medical model, physical treatments have had a long and complex history in the search for a "cure" for abnormal—and especially, schizophrenic—behaviors. Somatic therapies have achieved an important position in the treatment of schizophrenia. We must remember, however, that the currently available somatic interventions are not cures, but aids in managing the problem behaviors.

Somatic interventions comprise three main lines of attack: (1) pharmacological therapy, (2) electrical or chemical convulsive therapy, and (3) psychosurgery.

Pharmacological Therapy

In Chapter 7, we surveyed the various drug categories and their development. In this chapter, we will review their use with schizophrenic behavior. The major tranquilizers are the drugs usually used in treating schizophrenia. They are referred to under these (largely synonymous) terms: *ataraxic, antipsychotic,* and *neuroleptic* drugs.

Although the mechanism of neuroleptic action is unknown, there is evidence that these drugs reduce the permeability of cell membranes, thus inhibiting the passage of transmitter substances at the synapses and blocking activation in the central nervous system (CNS).

Clinical applications of the neuroleptic drugs are grouped according to four main objectives. They are used as (1) principal therapeutic agents in the management of acute schizophrenic crises, (2) principal therapeutic treatment in the management of chronic schizophrenic conditions, (3)symptomatic treatment of acute psychomotor disorders, and (4) maintenance therapy for patients in remission (Lehmann, 1974).

Conventional maintenance therapy requires patients to take the drug indefinitely, even though they may, at some point, no longer need it. The psychiatrist has no way of knowing when that point might be reached. Some recent research (Hogarty et al., 1974) has shown relapse rates twice as high for patients on placebo as for those on *chlorpromazine.* The most conservative decision seems to be to maintain the medication indefinitely.

The drugs most commonly used in the treatment of schizophrenia are the *phenothiazines,* but all neuroleptic drugs have about the same therapeutic effects. The main differences are in their side effects. The number and severity of the side effects must be weighed against their advantages as a means of maintaining the patient.

Because of its simplicity, ease of administration, general effectiveness, and minimal involvement of irreversible side effects, drug treatment is the most popular form of therapeutic intervention for schizophrenia. The preponderance of research evidence favors the method, particularly when accompanied by some form of psychotherapy.

It would be reasonable to conclude that the widespread use of neuroleptic drugs has made it possible to maintain many patients in their own communities, thereby greatly reducing the schizophrenic hospital population. From the dual standpoint of the high cost and undesirable behavioral effects of hospitalization, maintenance pharmacotherapy has certainly demonstrated its value. Its most important benefits may be that it is making it possible to use social and psychological techniques with schizophrenics in the community.

To round out our pharmacological review, we mention the use of megavitamin therapy, consisting of massive daily doses of nicotinic acid and ascorbic acid (vitamin C). While there has been a flurry of interest in the scientific literature and some successes have been reported for this method, the number of studies is limited and observance of clinical research standards is lacking.

Electroconvulsive Therapy

We described electroconvulsive therapy (ECT) in Chapter 7 and will consider it further in Chapter 12 as a treatment for depression. Here we summarize the results of its use with schizophrenia.

It must be acknowledged that we know even less about how ECT works than we do about the action of drugs in relieving schizophrenic behaviors. There are few reliable studies of ECT in comparison with other therapies. May (1975) reviews the few available reports, which are mostly unreliable because of their loose methodology. The usual criteria are release and relapse rates. One study apparently found ECT better than insulin; another found it less effective than psychotherapy; still another found it more effective than psychotherapy. One researcher (Langsley, Enterline, and Hickerson, 1959) compared ECT with chlorpromazine for female schizophrenic and manic patients, and found ECT resulted in longer hospital stays. We must suspend judgment on the various findings, however, in view of the questionable methodology in most studies.

Psychosurgery

The use of surgical techniques in the treatment of schizophrenia emerged mainly from the calming effects of lobotomies on animals. The use of psychosurgery reached its peak in the 1950s, before the burgeoning of the drug alternatives. Because its mechanisms are not understood and its effects are irreversible, its use today is limited.

The sites of destruction of brain tissue include the frontal lobes, thalamus, and hypothalamus (Figure 11-2). Two examples: the *prefrontal leucotomy* cuts the neural pathways between frontal areas and the lower brain centers. The *prefrontal lobotomy* accomplishes a similar disconnection between the frontal areas and the thalamus. A follow-up study of 300 leucotomy patients showed that 19 died as a direct result of the surgery, but the outcomes of the other operations are clouded by the uncontrolled selection of patients and undefined criteria of improvement (Maher, 1966).

Given the ambiguous and even negative evidence on the effects of both ECT and psychosurgery, and noting that they violate our ideal of using the most effective treatment with the least destructive impact on the patient, there would seem to be little to support the current use of ECT and psychosurgery for schizophrenia.

Individual Behavioral Approaches

Behavior therapists offer no "cure" for schizophrenia since they see no organic disease entity. They do see learned abnormal behavior, which they attack directly in two ways: (1) modification of specific maladaptive behaviors in individuals by respondent and operant methods; and (2) design of ward programs in institutions, aimed at modification of the behavior of all the ward patients. The ward programs are called "token economies."

Respondent Approaches

Respondent techniques have not been used frequently in schizophrenic behavior therapy. Schizophrenics usually do not complain of the anxiety we associate with the neurotic patient. Therefore, techniques based on the reduction of anxiety (e.g., desensitization) generally are not useful. There have been some cases, however, of phobic behaviors in individuals classified as schizophrenic. Cowden and Ford (1962) cite such a case in which they desensitized two paranoid schizophrenics whose fears had inhibited their ability to speak. The treatment reduced the phobic reaction and generalized to the elimination of nightmares and persecutory delusions.

Meyer and Gelder (1963) describe the improvement through desensitization of three out of five cases of agoraphobia (fear of open public places) severe enough to result in schizophrenic behavior. A patient who complained of "pressure points" over his eye reacted to the sensations with delusions of hostile spirits and persecution. Mimicking the pressure sensations by simple muscular manipulation corrected the patient's interpretations. The sensations were relieved through relaxation exercises. The results were generalized to various tension-producing life situations (Davison, 1966).

Operant Approaches

Operant therapy, like respondent conditioning, focuses exclusively on overt behaviors, attempting to modify them by means of reinforcement techniques. In Chapter 5, we discussed single-subject research designs. These are particularly appropriate to the evaluation of clinical behavioral procedures. You may remember that some procedures use the subject as his or her own control by conditioning the new behavior, then comparing it with the pre-

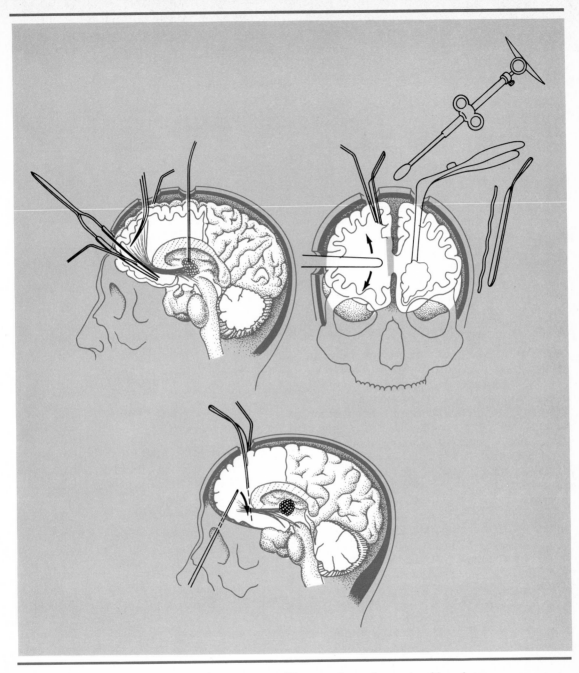

Figure 11-2 Psychosurgery is a drastic, irreversible procedure of questionable value. These drawings show a variety of techniques used to cut neural pathways between different areas of the brain.

viously observed *baseline* behavior (the A-B paradigm). In the A-B-A variation, the conditioned behavior is allowed to extinguish through nonreinforcement, and comparisons are drawn. The modified behavior may again be conditioned (A-B-A-B) to establish the change with respect to the original baseline behavior. A few case examples will describe the basic procedures and results in modification of several types of specific schizophrenic behaviors.

Thought disorder was modified by contingent social reinforcement in a series of experiments (Meichenbaum, 1966, 1969). By reinforcing appropriate interpretations of proverbs with encouraging words and smiles, significantly higher scores were obtained from the schizophrenic group than from the controls, who were not reinforced for their appropriate interpretations.

Verbal conditioning was applied to irrational speech (Rickard, Dignam, and Horner, 1960). The experimenters turned away after delusional speech but paid attention to rational statements. At a two-year follow-up session, the patient spoke rationally most of the time (although his continued residence in the hospital raises questions about the depth of the adjustment).

You will remember from Chapter 7 the case of *mutism* reported by Isaacs, Thomas, and Goldiamond (1960). They used chewing gum reinforcers to shape verbal behavior by the patient's successive approximations of speech (first lip movements, then grunts, then vocalization, etc.). At the same time, the patient's nonverbal requests were ignored. (Recall the young mute schizophrenic in Chapter 10 who satisfied his needs by using silent gestures.)

Social behavior was also controlled in an experiment (Ayllon and Haughton, 1962). A group of 32 chronic schizophrenics, who were regularly late and had to be coaxed into the dining room by attendants, were not allowed in the dining room unless they entered within a given period of time following the announcement of the meal. After several missed meals, most of the group entered the dining room within five minutes of the announcements.

Token Economies: Behavioral Approaches to the Institution as a Vehicle for Treatment

The Hospitalization Problem

The search for effective, large-scale therapeutic methods has been motivated by two major problems:

1. In 1971, there were 1,269,000 admissions to inpatient services in U.S. mental hospitals. You will recall a statistic cited earlier: about half of the beds in mental hospitals are occupied by schizophrenics. Since 27 percent of admissions each year are schizophrenic cases, you can see that this group of psychoses accounts for the largest share of long-term hospital residents.

2. We have already considered in Chapter 10 the second of the two problems at some length: the detrimental effects of hospitalization on schizophrenic patients. The discouragingly low, 6 percent chance of eventual discharge for patients who have been hospitalized for two years or more testifies to the disabling effects of the "social breakdown syndrome." We saw how this syndrome operates in the hospital setting to condition patients to become compliant, passive objects, rendered socially incompetent for community living. It is a study in learned helplessness. It is in this context that we now look at the successes, failures, and promise of the programmed environment referred to as token economy systems.

Mechanics of the Token Economy Approach

The basic procedures for token economies have been discussed in Chapter 7. The following are the essential ingredients in a token economy program.

1. *Specific target behaviors.* Some advocates prefer to focus on correcting small behavioral features, such as bizarre speech or movements. Others argue for reinforcement of large behaviors, such as social interaction on the ward.

2. *Back-up reinforcers.* These are "good life" re-wards—special foods, recreation privileges, candy, cigarettes, and unusual benefits.

3. *Tokens for the back-up reinforcers.* These make possible immediate reinforcement and ad-justments in incentives.

4. *Rules for token exchange for back-up reinforc-ers.* These refer to rates of and times for exchange.

The program concentrates on areas of so-cial development, aiming at returning patients to their community. These areas include:

1. *Resocialization*—self-care and interpersonal relations.

2. *Instrumental role performance*—occupational and household skills.

3. *Reduction of symptomatic behaviors.*

One of the chief advantages of the token economy is that it constitutes a microcosm of the outside world. It presents our society's val-ues—earned compensation, cooperative en-deavor, behavioral norms—in a simple, dy-namic situation. This contrasts, of course, with

the arbitrary dispensation of needed objects according to the staff's interest in keeping the patients docile. The artificial reinforcements in the nontoken ward encourage nonfunctional behaviors, minimal responsiveness, and super-stitious conditioning because they attend to the most grotesque responses. (Remember the seal tank example in Chapter 3.)

Basic Token Economy Systems

Ayllon and Azrin (1965) conducted a token economy experiment with eight female patients (five of whom were schizophrenics), using an A-B-A design. In the A-phases, contin-gent reinforcement was applied to ward jobs usually preferred by the patients. During the B-phase, the reinforcements were switched to the nonpreferred jobs. Figure 11-3 shows the flip-flop change in time spent on the two kinds of work. A control group was given reinforce-ment only during the A-phases, but none dur-ing the B-phase. Performance on nonpreferred jobs plunged during the B-phase, confirming the motivating effect of the reinforcement.

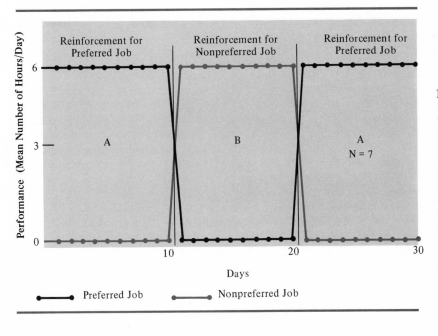

Figure 11-3 Mean number of hours patients worked per day when positive reinforcement was varied between pre-ferred and nonpreferred jobs. (*Ayllon, T., and Azrin, N. H. The meas-urement and reinforce-ment of behavior of psy-chotics.* Journal of the Experimental Analysis of Behavior, 1965, 8, 357–383. © 1965 by the Soci-ety for the Experimental Analysis of Behavior, Inc. Reprinted by permission.)

In a subsequent study, Ayllon and Azrin (1968) reinforced 45 females, averaging 16 years of hospitalization, for behaviors related to self-care and ward chores. Results were favorable. When the value of the tokens was increased, rewarded group behavior increased. At the same time, the establishment of functional behaviors eliminated the incompatible symptomatic behaviors. Of the 24 participating patients who were released, 11 returned to the hospital within nine months—a reflection on the limitation of long-term effects in such programs. Nevertheless, an encouraging change in staff attitudes occurred during the program. Working on the token ward became a status symbol, and staff members got much satisfaction from the visible improvement in the performance of supposedly untreatable patients.

Schaefer and Martin (1966) targeted for correction the apathetic behaviors of 40 female chronic patients. Personal hygiene, work activities, and social interaction were the specific behaviors that were reinforced. As a result, there was a reduction in observed apathy measured by an increase in the rewarded activities. A follow-up study (Schaefer and Martin, 1969) reported a recidivism (return to hospital) rate of 14 percent, compared to 28 percent for the entire hospital and 35 percent for all state facilities.

Apathetic behavior was also the target of Atthowe and Krasner's 1968 study of 86 patients, of whom one-third were over age 65. The objectives were patients' (1) becoming responsible for their own care, (2) planning for their future, and (3) making rational decisions. Specific reinforced behaviors included personal hygiene, help on the ward, attendance at ward activities, and social interactions. Positive results were seen in increased self-sufficiency in matters of personal care (more shaving, showering, and proper dressing), increased attendance at group events, and—most significant—more requests for weekend leaves.

Extensions of Token Economy Techniques

One of the principal objectives of token economy programs is to help the "hard core,"

long-term psychotic. McReynolds and Coleman (1972) set up a token economy for severely regressed patients who had spent an average of 13 years in the back ward. At the inception of the experiment, only 10 percent were capable of dressing themselves. Most were spoon-fed. They were given token reinforcement first for carrying their own food trays; next, for using eating utensils; then, for grooming. After one year, 30 of 47 were bathing and dressing themselves, and 12 had off-ward assignments, where none had performed such service before. There were also measurable improvements in staff attitudes. Before the program, the staff had considered none of the patients capable of discharge; after, 30 percent were considered releasable. The token ward staff came to judge 75 percent of their patients as aware and responsible, while the staff on other wards rated only 20 percent of their patients that highly.

Younger (average age 26) acutes (half were first admissions) were reinforced for work assignments, occupational therapy, responsibility, and personal hygiene in a study by Herson et al. (1972). Positive reinforcement included off-ward privileges and weekend passes; patients were given fines (paid by earned tokens) for disruptive behavior. An A-B-A design was applied. The patients responded well in the B-phase and reverted to their baseline passivity and disinterest when reinforcement was suspended during the second A-phase, indicating the effectiveness of the tokens.

Failure of many token economy "graduates" to make it in the community is a source of discouragement and concern for practitioners of token economy procedures. It would seem that token economy conditioning alone is not enough to maintain patients in the community. Recognition of this shortcoming has led to the extension of reinforcement therapy to patients' natural environment by training parents, teachers, etc., in reinforcement techniques.

To bridge the gap between ward and community, rehabilitation programs have been set up, incorporating sheltered workshops outside the hospital, with employment cooperation from establishments in the community,

Many hospitals set up token economy systems as a means of reinforcing behavior. The patient who occupies this room must exchange five of his earned tokens for rent, much as he would have to in the "real" world. *(John Oldenkamp/IBOL, Courtesy Random House, Inc.)*

involving municipal authorities and unions. One such program has maintained a very low, 12 percent recidivism rate!

Evaluation of Token Economy Programs

Results of the considerable number of token economy programs provide encouraging evidence of their effectiveness, but clearly they are not cure-alls. Their advantages are impressive: mass therapy by trained nonprofessionals, relatively low cost, no drastic or irreversible treatments. Liberman (1972) made a cost-benefit analysis of a token program involving 32 male chronic schizophrenics who averaged more than ten years of hospitalization. For an additional program cost of $424 above custodial care, 9 patients were discharged (none from the control group). At that 28 percent discharge rate, the state would save $380,000 if the discharged patients remained in the community for two years!

Some subjects are not affected by contingent reinforcement, however. Ayllon and Azrin (1965) reported 18 percent of subjects unaffected; Atthowe and Krasner (1968) reported 10 percent unaffected. Finally, some of the gravest psychotic behaviors do not respond to token economy methods. Hallucinations, disordered thinking, manic behaviors are a few

examples bypassed by token economy programs.

As we move away from the disease model, our institutional procedures must be transformed from mere holding stations into active treatment centers. Paul (1969a) warns that we cannot settle for drug maintenance without patient recovery. We must move patients out of institutions before they become trapped by the "institutionalization syndrome" and degenerate into manageable nonentities.

If there were no other motivation, the courts have now mandated the "right to treatment" for involuntary patients; custodial care is not legally adequate (Bazelon, 1969). The courts have even specified the size and qualifications of the professional staff.

The Therapeutic Community

Current progress in the treatment of psychosis points toward one form or another of "milieu therapy" (Schwartz and Swartzburg, 1976). The main objective is to prepare patients for their return to the community. Logically, the ward's basic operation must be modeled after the community. In milieu therapy, the central theme is the patient's assumption of responsibility for his or her own behavior and that of others in the ward. As in the community, the expectations of authorities (the staff) impose standards of behavior on each patient. Group activities are the focus of life in the ward milieu, and interested participation is reinforced.

As always, there are problems and criticisms:

1. Staff reluctance to share power with patients.
2. Individual problems not treated individually.
3. Role confusion as a result of patient's self-responsibility.
4. Loss of continuity as a result of staff and patient turnover.
5. Impact of failures on participants.

Looked at in a positive way, the problems are real-life opportunities for the development of problem-solving and decision-making skills, which are essential for successful adjustment in the community.

The final step is to generalize the positive results to the community situation. As we improve and advance today's hospital programs, we are trying to replace the hospital supports by alternatives that will help to maintain the new behaviors in the natural environment. In Chapter 20, we will look at recent developments in partial hospitalization, halfway houses, and aftercare procedures, in an appraisal of new directions in therapy.

Summary

We have found a number of culprits guilty of contributing to the onset of schizophrenia. Genetic effects can predispose high-risk children, making them vulnerable to life stresses generated in the schizophrenogenic family. Such children often exhibit abnormal behavior in adolescence.

Biochemical processes may also be accomplices. Abnormal action of neurotransmitter substances at the synapses has been proposed as a cause of psychotic reactions. These and other metabolic abnormalities may adversely affect arousal and attention-focusing mechanisms, causing schizophrenic behavior.

The psychodynamic interpretation is based on Freudian concepts of regression and diffusion of ego boundaries, leading to loss of object reality with consequent primary process thinking.

There is doubt that schizophrenia is universal. It appears to be associated with technologically developed, urbanized societies. Schizophrenia seems to be concentrated in low-SES classes, probably due to the downward economic slide initiated by earlier-generation schizophrenics, who also endow the family with unfavorable hereditary influences.

Psychodynamic treatment is not generally recommended, although some psychoanalysts have obtained successful results with modifications of Freudian techniques. Tranquilizing drugs reduce schizophrenic symptoms, permitting the use of psychological therapies. ECT and psychosurgery are drastic treatments of dubious effect.

A more promising therapeutic approach is operant conditioning, using reinforcement of desirable behaviors to eliminate bizarre responses. Token economy programs apply contingent reinforcement procedures to large groups of patients, rewarding target behaviors with tokens exchangeable for desired items and special privileges.

Affective disorders and suicide

Mood, emotion, affect, feeling state, frame of mind are just some of the words we use to label a set of sensations we all experience, yet find great difficulty in describing. These sensations are internal states whose nature can only be inferred from the way we act or from what we say. Difficult as they may be to define, they are central components in our psychological functioning.

People ask, "How do you feel?" They assume that the way you feel sums up the way things are going in your life at this point. Is your mood, then, the *result* of your experiences? To some extent, it is. Yet you know how your mood affects the things you do and colors your life. When you are sad, the world becomes dark. If you try to erase the gloom, nothing helps. The activities you usually enjoy lose their excitement, become boring and pointless. Jokes fall flat, cheerful friends irritate. Do your moods spring from some deeper source to determine your behavior? Again, we answer with a qualified "yes." In this apparent contradiction, mood is both a cause and an effect.

The complex nature of affect concerns all psychologists, even though they may approach the understanding of human behavior from different points of view. But no sector of psychology is more concerned with affect than abnormal psychology. We have seen how dramatic changes in the individual's affective state are a notable feature of many disorders. In some conditions, the various distortions of affect are the central features. Affective disturbances are among the most important in their impact on human behavior. Our state of mind determines our levels of action and our efficiency of performance. When we are feeling fine, we are ready to "lick the world." When we are down in the dumps, we lose all ambition to achieve and all capacity to enjoy the rewards of achievement. We can just about manage to exist. And when even that level of action becomes too burdensome, we may perform the ultimate act of ending existence itself.

Description of Affective Disorders

We all feel sad at times, weighed down by a sense of futility in coping with a life that demands too much and gives too little. We soon recover our normal spirit and drive ahead. But there is a sadness that goes too deep and lasts too long. It is the suffocating mood of severe depression that causes serious problems. More puzzling and less frequent are the manic states of heightened emotion. Feeling good can also create problems when we become too high and the feeling lasts too long—especially when it is

inappropriate to the circumstances. It is then that elation—the sense of unrestrained joy—becomes troublesome. Too high or too low, the mood state is the source of far-reaching distortions that upset most of our psychological and physiological functions.

First, we will take a descriptive look at depression, saving for later attempts to categorize, understand, and treat the problem. Then we will do the same for the manic states.

Depressive Reactions

Behavioral Description

We can consider the signs of depression under three types of functions: emotional, cognitive, and physical (or somatic). The *emotional* reaction is one of unrelieved misery. A cloud of gloom surrounds the victims. They are so full of sadness, they feel like crying and often complain that they cannot release the tears that are inside them. Humor leaves them cold and cheerless. They have lost their feelings for friends and family, as if a wall separated them from others.

Cognitive changes relate mainly to self-appraisal. Depressed people tend to think little of themselves. They see themselves as incompetent, unworthy of anything but pity. Their problems are monstrous. And if their real problems are not bad enough, they imagine problems that do not exist. They even blame themselves for other people's problems. The self-condemnation may extend beyond day-to-day failures to a conviction of moral guilt. It may even reach back to magnify childhood or adolescent misdeeds into cardinal sins. There is also a retardation or disruption of thinking that can seriously handicap their ability to perform their jobs or to participate in conversation.

Physical dysfunctions are a common feature of depression. They include slower movements, backache, headaches, heaviness in the chest, lack of energy, constipation, stomach upset, loss of appetite, and insomnia. In addition to the somatic disturbances, sexual drive drops, often to a condition of impotence or frigidity. Table 12-1 sums up the symptoms, which seem to affect almost every function. Note the reference to suicidal behavior, the final cry for help or surrender to despondency. We will discuss suicide separately in the last section of this chapter.

Depression takes two forms: retarded and agitated. *Retarded* depression is evidenced in slow, deliberate movements. Patients speak less and engage only in necessary activities. In contrast, *agitated* patients are highly animated and move about restlessly. It is almost as if they were trying to block out the anguish by building a wall of activity. This should not be confused with manic states, however, in which patients do not report feeling depressed.

Since some depression is a normal event in our lives, how can therapists tell when they are looking at a case of clinical depression? There are four criteria that differentiate normal depression from pathological depression: intensity, duration, precipitating event, and psychopathological features. Quantitative norms are not yet available for determining degrees of intensity or duration necessary for a positive diagnosis of clinical depression. Nor do life events always submit to objective measurement. These criteria are appraised by each diagnostician according to his or her professional judgment, experience, and bias. Psychopathological factors—hallucinations, delusional thinking, loss of weight, suicidal behavior—are more easily observed. Techniques are currently under study that provide scales to evaluate the severity of clinical symptoms and behaviors as a basis for operational definitions of various levels of depression.

One might ask why depressive behavior exists. We know that anxiety serves some adaptive purpose, but does depression serve any purpose? An interesting interpretation of depression as a manifestation of adaptive functions is presented by Klerman (1975). His is a Darwinian view of normal and clinical depression and their function in humans and animals. According to his thesis, affect serves the purpose of survival of the species by providing "signals" that warn protectors of a threat to weaker members. (Note how someone else's

Table 12-1 Signs and Symptoms of Depression

Emotional
  Sad, unhappy, blue
  Crying
Cognitive
  Pessimism
  Ideas of guilt
  Self-denigration
  Loss of interest and motivation
  Decrease in efficiency and concentration
Behavior and Appearance
  Neglect of personal appearance
  Psychomotor retardation
  Agitation
Physical
  Loss of appetite
  Loss of weight
  Constipation
  Poor sleep
  Aches and pains
  Menstrual changes
  Loss of libido
Anxiety Features
Suicidal Behavior
  Thoughts
  Threats
  Attempts

Adapted from Mendels, J. *Concepts of depression.* New York: Wiley, 1970, p. 7.

depression arouses our caretaking activity.) The adaptive functions of depression relate to:

1. social communication (anxiety over separation of mother and infant)
2. physiological arousal (depression increases the activity of the nervous system, elevating anxiety levels in preparation for the fight-or-flight response)
3. subjective awareness (affective transmission of information about physical sensations from the environment to the cognitive centers)
4. psychodynamic defense (depression serves adaptive functions of the ego)

Thus the adaptive functions of depression, and of the other affective conditions, are (like anxiety) essential mechanisms by which humans meet and survive crises presented by their environment.

Levels of Depression

There are three distinct levels of depression. In the *simple* state, the depression is mild and does not get in the way of productive activity. People in this state resist the effects and hold on to reality, although their interest in the outside world is decreased.

The *acute* stage may be a gradual deterioration in mood from the simple state or it may invade suddenly without a noticeable build-up. It is in this stage that individuals may break with reality. They may harshly accuse themselves of corruption and incompetence. These ideas and judgments are so exaggerated that they border on delusions. The depressed mood of these individuals is visible in their sullen expressions and dejected manner, slow movements, and crying spells. They complain of a multitude of bodily disorders: loss of appetite, loss of sexual drive, cessation of menstruation (in women), constipation, assorted aches and pains. Suicide becomes a frequent topic and is a real possibility for some.

Depressive stupor is the lowest point that anyone can reach. People in this stage have degenerated to a nonfunctioning state—mute, motionless, deaf to all communication. They are so indifferent to basic functions that they wet their beds and clothes and must be spoon-fed (sometimes they must be fed intravenously, when they will not even open their mouth or swallow food). Fortunately, since the introduction of drug and shock therapies, this hopeless state is rarely seen.

Manic Reactions

Behavioral Description

The general manifestations of a manic reaction (differing in degree, as we will soon observe) are listed in Table 12-2. The listing also shows the relative occurrence of the behaviors on the basis of observations of 20 manic

patients during a longitudinal study by Carlson and Goodwin (1973). We will review the study shortly.

Table 12-2 Classical and "Atypical" Symptoms in 20 Manic Patients

Symptoms	Patients Manifesting Symptoms (%)
Hyperactivity	100
Extreme verbosity	100
Pressure of speech	100
Grandiosity	100
Manipulativeness	100
Irritability	100
Euphoria	90
Mood lability	90
Hypersexuality	80
Flight of ideas	75
Delusions	75
Sexual	(25)
Persecutory	(65)
Passive	(20)
Religious	(15)
Assaultiveness or threatening behavior	75
Distractibility	70
Loosened associations	70
Fear of dying	70
Intrusiveness	60
Somatic complaints	55
Some depression	55
Religiosity	50
Telephone abuse	45
Regressive behavior (urinating or defecating inappropriately; exposing self)	45
Symbolization or gesturing	40
Hallucinations (auditory and visual)	40
Confused	35
Ideas of reference	20

From Carlson, G. A., and Goodwin, F. K. The stages of mania. *Archives of General Psychiatry,* 1973, 28, 226. © 1973, American Medical Association.

Manic behavior is characterized by frenzied activity. Manic patients chatter constantly. Much of the talk consists of grandiose plans for even more activity. Manic patients are untiring. They seem to have an endless supply of energy. As might be expected from such continuous activity, manics often suffer drastic weight loss. Even more significant is the impression one gets that the manic's torrent of physical and verbal activity is designed to shut out the imminent intrusion of some horrible anguish.

The meaninglessness of the activity is apparent in the easy distractibility of the person. Actions often consist of aimless moving about of objects, but these are abandoned in midcourse, as the individual responds to another flight of ideas and suddenly takes off on another "project."

When these defenses are frustrated or interrupted, manics react with irritability, profanity, or a brief crying spell. Almost at once, however, they regain their manic momentum and are off in a flurry of activity.

Levels of Mania

The manic mood rises and falls, from a fairly normal state, through several levels of increasing excitement, to a peak of uncontrolled mania, and then back down again. The "roller coaster" cycle may be completed within a few days or go on for a week or more until it runs its course. Since the patients in the Carlson and Goodwin study (1973) present a good description of manic cycles, we will examine them more closely to get a picture of the characteristic behaviors at each level. The patients were rated twice daily for degree of manic or depressive behavior by a team of nurses, who also made written observations of each patient's affect, psychomotor activity, and cognitive state. The daily observations of behavior sequences provided information for the construction of a chart of each patient's progress through the stages of a complete manic episode. Three stages were distinguished according to grossness and intensity of the behavioral clusters. Figure 12-1 graphs a typical episode, which started on the 94th day of residence, peaked on the 100th day, and gradually subsided to a normal level on about the 115th day.

Below the graph are brief listings of the behaviors characteristic of each of the three manic stages. Samples of the actual speech and accompanying motor activity of five of the patients are given in Table 12-3. You get a vivid picture of the wild thoughts, explosive changes, and uncontrolled movements of patients in the peak manic Stage III. At the same time, you can almost feel the helpless despair.

The three stages of escalating manic excitement correspond approximately to the three levels of mania conventionally identified as hypomania, acute mania, and delirious mania. Let us take another look at how the basic behaviors develop from a tolerable level to an extreme level.

At the *hypomanic* level, we meet the aggressive, dynamic "go-getters." Drawing on a seemingly endless supply of energy, they work, literally day and night. They are awesome human dynamos, never satisfied unless they are juggling four or five projects at the same time. Here is their prototype, Dave B.:

As Dave liked to say, "Sleeping is a bad habit; Thomas Edison never slept more than 42 minutes a night." Dave could never quite accomplish this, but he frequently worked through the night without tiring and a cat nap seemed to revitalize him completely. Dave's reputation for having a finger in 10 full scale projects at the same time was accurate. His secret was speed and organization wedded to a high energy level and an insatiable interest in whatever was new. Dave seldom finished what he began since the mundane details of execution bored him once he had generated the original idea. Dave had tried, briefly, all the usual hobbies and interests but abandoned each in turn once he had mastered its intricacies. He did everything so well and so vigorously that few of his friends were aware of how restless and depressed he became at those odd times when he found himself "between" projects. (McNeil, 1970, p. 111)

If we follow Dave's career round-the-clock, we find that he is not so much a driver as a

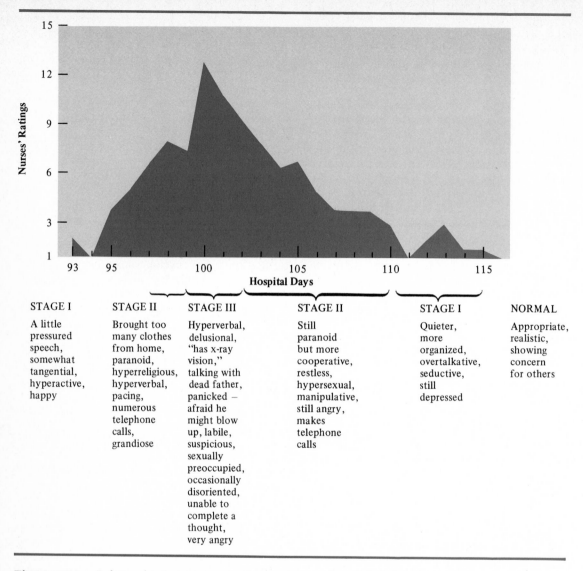

Figure 12-1 Relationship between stages of a manic episode and daily behavior ratings (patient 69). (*Carlson, G. A., and Goodwin, F. K. The stages of mania. Archives of General Psychiatry, 1973, 28, 223.* © 1973, American Medical Association.)

driven man, working at a fever pitch as if he were trying to escape a pursuing demon—and, indeed, this is just what he is doing. The pace is a killing one, and unless Dave can manage to stabilize his emotional stress, he will overshoot the hypomanic border and land in the acute stage. The warning signals are a growing impatience with questions and opposition, a rashness in taking greater and greater risks to set new records or recoup previous losses, a boiling excitement that often pushes the hypomanic into reckless actions, including sexual promiscuity and daredevil sporting feats.

Once over the line into the *acute* stage, the victims are menaces to themselves, their friends, and their families. Free of even the few restraints that kept their behavior within socially acceptable limits, the people in the grip of acute mania are obsessed with the need to prove that everything they do is absolutely

Table 12-3 Excerpts from Daily Nursing Notes on Manic Patients, Including Patient Verbalizations

Stage I	Stage II	Stage III
"Now I feel like talking" and does so, increasing intrusiveness and irritability, flight of ideas, restless; "I'm not feeling so depressed."	Hypersexual, bizarre (wearing 3 dresses at a time), screaming, angry, delusion; in control but frightened that other patients are against her; grandiose, incessant talking.	Very frightened, talking and crying constantly, pacing. "I'll never get out." "I have cat eyes. He crawls around inside me and he can't stand the light." Profane, hypersexual, uncooperative. "Oh, please let me die. I can't take it anymore." "National Institute of Hell."
"I'm going higher than a Georgia pine. I'm going to fly tonight. I could kill you."	Pacing, manipulative, religious; says he can't trust people; crude, hypersexual, assaultive; wants to be King Kong; grimaced and postured, as if anguished; felt "life on the unit is designed to test my tolerance."	Much pacing, grimacing, and bodily shaking; slaps self on arms; afraid of dying. "They're going to cut out my heart." Afraid of being given TNT; thought there was special meaning when his doctor pointed a finger at him; running up and down hall making animalistic noises.
Hyperactive, pressure of speech, sarcastic, playful; "I'm having a ball." Talks of spending $3,000,000.	Took bath in nightgown, yelling, crying, laughing, throwing food, threatening, combative.	Throwing things, exposing herself, trying to escape, parading around in flimsy pajamas crying, "even God has given up" and later, "I'm dying. The radioactivity has made my hair straight." Voided on the seclusion room floor.
"I'm excited but I don't think I'm worried about anything." Later, "You'd rather have me on top of the table than under it wouldn't you?"	Talking about big plans for Christmas party; very loud, profane, almost assaultive, slightly paranoid, very inappropriate telephone use (calling people to solicit money).	
Somewhat labile, good frame of mind, very busy.	Hypersexual, hyperverbal, hyperactive, suspicious; very angry, assaultive, obscene; banging on urinal door; wanting to use phone to buy stocks.	

From Carlson, G. A., and Goodwin, F. K. The stages of mania. *Archives of General Psychiatry*, 1973, 28, 222. © 1973, American Medical Association.

right, even if they must develop an elaborate delusional system to maintain their self-importance. In the following speech to two police officers bringing him to the hospital, Joe A. describes his inner turmoil most eloquently by the very incoherence of his frenzied speech.

I need guys that are loyal and enthusiastic about the great opportunities life offers on this planet! It's yours for the taking! Too many people pass opportunity by without hearing it knock because they don't know how to grasp the moment and strike while the iron is hot! You've got to grab it when it comes up for air; pick up the ball and run! You've got to be decisive! decisive! decisive! No shilly-shallying! Sweat! Yeah, sweat with a goal! Push, push, push, and you can push over a mountain! Two mountains, maybe. It's not luck! Hell, if it wasn't for bad luck I wouldn't have any luck at all! Be there firstest with the mostest! My guts and your blood! That's the system! I know, you know, he, she, or it knows it's the only way to travel! Get 'em off balance, baby, and the rest is leverage! Use your head and save your heels! What's this deal? Who are these guys? Have you got a telephone and a secretary I can have instanter if not sooner? What I need is office space and the old LDO [long-distance operator]. (McNeil, 1970, pp. 113–114)

Delirious mania is the end of the line if the victims have not been toned down by therapy or medication before they reach this critical point. Their thinking is disorganized, their behavior extremely excited, their perceptions hallucinatory. Their speech and actions are frantic, distorted, destructive.

Classification Approaches

The behavioral manifestations of disturbed mood, which we have just described, are the basic elements in the classification of affective disorders. Those behaviors are the signs, or symptoms, that differentiate various disorder groups. The mention of "symptoms" takes us back to the medical model that implies that there is a primary, central illness. According to this view, the mood changes are simply secondary symptoms or processes. We do not propose to repeat the medical model arguments again. All we need note at this point is that the behavioral manifestations are probably related to several events, including physical illnesses (e.g., manic behavior during feverish illness) and psychological stresses (manic behavior following a week of final exams).

The formal classification that we will now discuss groups the disorders according to the central, affective components of the syndrome. These include neurotic depression, psychotic depression, manic-depressive psychosis, and involutional melancholia.

In addition to the formal categories, we will review two other variables that may be useful for diagnostic discriminations: the endogenous-exogenous distinction and the unipolar-bipolar distinction.

Neurotic Depression

Since neurotic depression is not totally incapacitating, we have no way of estimating its prevalence. Aside from the many people who consult private therapists or go to their physician for antidepressant medication, there are undoubtedly many others who lead lives of quiet desperation. A profound sense of being alone is, indeed, one of the principal features of the reaction.

The onset may be rapid, such as an immediate reaction to a tragic event. For this reason, neurotic depression is sometimes called *reactive* depression. On the other hand, the condition may develop slowly as a result of long exposure to a continuing problem, such as an unhappy marriage or persistent financial worries.

We have already enumerated the symptomatic behaviors. In recalling them, note particularly the victims' overriding compulsion to criticize and castigate themselves for all manner of personal defects and inadequacies, both real and imagined. Also note the physical ailments that plague the sufferer: discomfort in the heart and stomach regions, gastric disturbances, widely distributed aches and pains, loss of appetite, insomnia, and a generally dejected demeanor in facial expression and posture.

There seems to be a close association between neurotic depression and certain personality dimensions. We are not surprised to find that the pessimist can also be a depressed neurotic; a dismal outlook is one of the main effects of the depression. Hysterical tendencies may also go with the dramatization of faults and complaints. People of this personality type are also predisposed to threats and superficial attempts at suicide in order to demonstrate their desperate need for help. The obsessional personality can also be developed against a background of depression, especially when the obsessive behaviors emerge soon after a deep, personal loss. Again we must ask which is the cause and which is the effect? Do these personality traits lead to depression or does depression lead to these traits?

An interesting variation of neurotic depression is "success depression" (Mendels, 1970). In an apparent contradiction, depression sets in upon the achievement of a long-strived-for goal. Several explanations are ventured: (1) overwhelming responsibilities of the new position, (2) loss of dependency status, (3) a sense of unworthiness, (4) abuse or destruction of a rival who was a friend, (5) the emptiness in the realization of "no more worlds to conquer."

Psychotic Depression

There is not yet a clear-cut basis for a differential diagnosis between neurotic and psychotic depression. Two principal features are ordinarily used to establish a diagnosis of neurotic depression: (1) The onset is associated with precipitating events, especially a deep, personal loss or tragedy, or a sudden, disastrous change in circumstances. (2) Manic swings are absent; in fact, there are no mood changes.

The greater severity of the depression is an indication of psychosis, as are hallucinations, delusions, and other evidences of distorted thinking. As with other neurotic-psychotic distinctions, it is the victim's relative contact with reality that becomes the main determinant of

the diagnosis. The following case presents the behaviors that are associated with psychotic depression.

Samuel E., a fifty-five-year-old married physician, voluntarily entered the psychiatric wing of a large private hospital in the northeast. . . .

[His wife] felt that Samuel was a moody, apprehensive man who was excessively and needlessly concerned with finances. She recognized that he always lacked real confidence in himself, and attempted to bolster him by constant praise. . . .

Six months prior to admission Samuel began to notice that his practice, which had previously grown enormously, began to taper off slightly. He began to engage in bouts of self-deprecation and experienced much depression over his "failure." His sleep was fitful and disturbed, and his appetite was greatly reduced. About three months prior to admission, when he began to cry for no apparent reason, he reluctantly saw a psychiatrist. However, he was resistant to hospitalization, which was immediately suggested. The psychiatrist was extremely concerned about the possibility of suicide and finally, with the aid of the family, succeeded in convincing Samuel that he should hospitalize himself.

When drug therapy failed, Samuel was given a series of seven electroconvulsive shock treatments, during a five-week hospital stay, and improved considerably, although some confusion remained. He was then discharged in the care of the psychiatrist who made the initial referral. After a short period of time, when the confusion lifted, the idea that he was a failure returned. He began to speak about this with the neighbors, and within three months began to have crying spells again. Although he had accumulated a considerable amount of money, his wife had to return to work in order to appease him, and reassure him that the family was not on the verge of poverty. One month prior to his second admission he began to have insomnia, lost his appetite and a considerable amount of weight, and, because he was now convinced that he was penniless, began crying with increasing frequency. (Zax and Stricker, 1963, pp. 44–46)

Even though professionals agree on some of the diagnostic signs, multivariate analyses (a method of determining the relative importance of certain combinations of factors in a particular condition) thus far have been unable to separate a neurotic group from a psychotic group (Klerman, 1975, p. 1010).

Manic-Depressive Psychosis

We have seen manic and depressive behaviors alternating in the same person. The contrast between elation and despondency, between retarded movement and furious activity, seems to distinguish two different disorders. Yet, on closer inspection, the two states have much in common: sleep disturbance, disordered thought, and sudden crying spells. It has been suggested that the manic frenzy is a panic-stricken effort to put off the impending depression.

A principal characteristic of the manic-depressive psychosis is the recurrence of the attacks. The circular sequence may start with either a manic or a depressive episode. In many cases, the manic stage may not occur regularly; the individual suffers a series of depressions before a manic state intervenes. (Some confusion arises from the occasional practice of classifying the person as "manic-depressive" when only one mood state—depression or elation—is observed. This will be discussed in more depth later in the chapter.) The following case is a classic example of the repetitive, circular pattern:

M.M. was first admitted to a state hospital at the age of 38, although since childhood she had been characterized by swings of mood, some of which had been so extreme that they had been psychotic in degree. At 17 she suffered from a depression that rendered her unable to work for several months, although she was not hospitalized. At 33, shortly before the birth of her first child, the patient was greatly depressed. For a period of four days she appeared in coma. About a month after the birth of

"He certainly is a good psychiatrist. My husband used to be depressed." (*Don Orehek.*)

the baby she "became excited" and was entered as a patient in an institution for neurotic and mildly psychotic patients. As she began to improve, she was sent to a shore hotel for a brief vacation. The patient remained at the hotel for one night and on the following day signed a year's lease on an apartment, bought furniture, and became heavily involved in debt. Shortly thereafter Mrs. M. became depressed and returned to the hospital in which she had previously been a patient. After several months she recovered and, except for relatively mild fluctuations of mood, remained well for approximately two years.

She then became overactive and exuberant in spirits and visited her friends, to whom she outlined her plans for reestablishing different forms of lucrative business. She purchased many clothes, bought furniture, pawned her rings, and wrote checks without funds. She was returned to the hospital. Gradually her manic symptoms subsided, and after four months she was discharged. For a period thereafter she was mildly depressed. In a little less than a year Mrs. M. again became overactive, played her radio until late in the night, smoked excessively, took out insurance on a car that she had not yet bought. Contrary to her usual habits, she swore frequently and loudly, created a disturbance in a club to which she did not belong, and instituted divorce proceedings. On the day prior to her second admission to the hospital, she purchased 57 hats.

During the past 18 years this patient has been admitted and dismissed from the hospital on many occasions. At times, with the onset of a depressed period, she had returned to the hospital seeking admission. At such times she complained that her "brain just won't work." She would say, "I have no energy, am unable to do my housework; I have let my family down; I am living from day to day. There is no one to blame but myself." (Kolb, 1973, p. 376)

Women comprise 70 percent of manic-depressive patients. About 6.5 percent of manic-depressives suffer more than three attacks; about 42 percent have more than one. Prognosis is good for single-attack victims but is uncertain as the number increases. Mrs. M., from our example, had a favorable outcome.

Involutional Melancholia

The DSM-II gives us a diagnostic description of a disorder that has been studied since the time of Hippocrates.

> This is a disorder occurring in the involutional period [when bodily changes result in a lessening of activity] and characterized by worry, anxiety, agitation, and severe insomnia. Feelings of guilt and somatic preoccupations are frequently present and may be of delusional proportions. This disorder is distinguishable from Manic-depressive illness . . . by the absence of previous episodes; it is distinguished from Schizophrenia . . . in that impaired [reality] testing is due to a disorder of mood; and it is distinguished from Psychotic depressive reaction . . . in that the depression is not due to some life experience. Opinion is divided as to whether this psychosis can be distinguished from other affective disorders. It is, therefore, recommended that involutional patients not be given this diagnosis unless all other affective disorders have been ruled out. (American Psychiatric Association, 1968, p. 36)

We see in this definition the distinguishing features of involutional melancholia: the absence of previous episodes, a primary mood disorder, and the absence of precipitating events. It is necessary to qualify the last of these features by acknowledging the circumstances that tend to occur during the involutional period and that contribute to, and may even trigger, the onset of the melancholia.

While time of life sets the bounds to the period of heaviest incidence—age 40–55 for women and 50–55 for men—age itself is not the decisive factor. The onset period tends to coincide with the menopause in women and the climacteric in men, when sexual drives often decline, accompanied by a loss of the sense of vital purpose. The children have left home and have established their own independent lives and families. Mother is no longer needed; Father is "over the hill." Retirement is in sight. The unhappy reactions are accentuated by the youth worship of a "with-it" society that denies the aged and aging a place of honor and a role of continuing influence.

As a consequence of the growing awareness of diminished usefulness, the older man and woman focus more and more on the mistakes of the past, blaming themselves for their lack of high attainment and for the personal problems of their adult children. A steady diet of self-accusation develops into pessimism, irritability, nervous agitation, insomnia, and a general withdrawal from active living. Interest narrows to the sensations of one's own body functions. This is the ideal setting for hypochondria, which provides physical problems to blame for the tension, the headaches, the sleeplessness, the loss of appetite and weight, the inability to concentrate and to remember. Judith B. is a typical example:

Judith's two children were grown and gone and, try as he would, her husband Ed seemed unable to fill the void they left. Judith always treated her children as her "light and life" during their growing years and this left little energy for her husband. Her overprotectiveness of the children had been suffocating to them and each had broken free of her meddling at an early age. Now they seldom visited her and the significance of their flimsy excuses was not lost on her. Judith was convinced that her children hated her because she had been an evil mother who had destroyed their chance for happiness. When both the son and daughter got divorced, Judith shouldered all the blame. She became irritable and depressed and this mood alternated with a hysterical agitation. After two dramatic but ineffectual attempts at suicide, Judith was hospitalized. She has a drugged calmness about her now, but she continues to have a worried and pained facial expression and is easily upset by even the most commonplace events. (McNeil, 1970, p. 119)

Endogenous-Exogenous Distinction

This frequently applied distinction provides the grounds for another of the debates that divide the field of abnormal psychology into opposing camps. The *endogenous* type of disorder is presumed to arise from within the individual and has no known external reference. By implication, this is a biochemically caused state. The *exogenous* type of disorder is presumed to be caused by external factors. Some investigators view the two conditions as a dichotomy; others consider them the end points on a continuum. The first group discriminates two distinct sets of symptoms. In this view, endogenous depression is marked by symptoms listed in Table 12-4. The exogenous type shows contrasting behaviors in greater response to life events (including recent loss or frustrating experience), less retardation, fewer somatic complaints, less profound depression. But we note that the exogenous behaviors correspond to endogenous behaviors; exogenous behaviors are simply less extreme. Even if the two kinds of behaviors can be separated into clusters at each extreme, there is no basis for assuming that they distinguish two different disorders. Patients' behavior patterns rarely fall entirely into one classification. It seems more likely that the behaviors can be evaluated along a continuum with "endogenous" and "exogenous" as the end points.

Unipolar-Bipolar Distinction

A few pages back we distinguished between psychotics who alternate between manic and depressive states (i.e., *bipolar*) and those who experience only one of the states (i.e., *unipolar*), usually depression. Theories have been proposed that separate the two groups into distinct types of disorder.

Perris (1966) has built a model on the unipolar-bipolar distinction. He supports the model with the results of a study in which he compared two such groups along a number of dimensions, including genetic background, precipitating factors, and personality traits. There were significant differences on several dimensions (more frequent somatic factors among unipolars, lower median age for bipolars, faster response to ECT by bipolars, longer episodes with less frequent relapses among unipolars).

Winokur (1973) has developed a more elaborate model, which divides the bipolar and unipolar types into two subtypes: bipolar I and II, and unipolar early onset and late onset. Bipolar I patients are classic manic-depressives; bipolar II patients may have had a single episode without previous mania. Table 12-5 shows the relative occurrence of Winokur's criteria among unipolar and bipolar patients. Notice again, as in Perris's tabulations, bipolars are younger and have more episodes than unipolars. Winokur attributes considerable predisposing influence to genetic factors.

Causal, Contributing, and Maintaining Factors

As with other disorders, investigators have taken a number of approaches to the study of etiological causes, contributing variables, and factors that determine the persistence of the problems.

Psychodynamic Factors

Abraham (1911/1960, 1916/1960), one of Freud's students, set the scene for the early psychoanalytic explanations of depressive psychosis. He saw the patients trapped in the oral period by lack of gratifications. As a result of these deprivations, the patients developed an ambivalent attitude toward people. In other words, depressed patients feel that their personal objects are either good or bad; they cannot accept the paradox that these objects alternate between two poles. Accordingly, they find it intolerable to hate a love object (parents, siblings, spouse, etc.), and so they repress their hostility toward others and direct it inward toward their own ego.

Freud (1917/1956) modified and amplified Abraham's hypothesis into a theory of "melancholia" based on a switch in the object of the libidinal energy. The libido first attaches itself to a love object. Loss of the object, through death or grave disappointment, causes with-

Table 12-4 Criteria for a Diagnosis of Endogenous Depression
1. Psychomotor retardation or agitation
2. Distinct quality to depressed mood (e.g., different from the feeling one has following the death of a loved one)
3. Lack of reactivity (response) to environmental changes
4. Loss of interest in usual activities or decreased sexual drive
5. Poor appetite
6. Weight loss
7. Sleep difficulty or sleeping too much
8. Loss of energy, fatigability or tiredness
9. Self-reproach or inappropriate guilt
10. Complaints of, or evidence of, diminished ability to think or concentrate, such as slow thinking or mixed-up thoughts
11. Recurrent thoughts of death or suicide, including thoughts of wishing to be dead
12. Suicidal thoughts or behavior

Based on Feighner, J., et al. Diagnostic criteria for use in psychiatric research. *Archives of General Psychiatry*, 1972, 26, 57–68; Mendels, J., and Cochrane, C. The nosology of depression: The endogenous-reactive concept. *American Journal of Psychiatry*, 1968, 124 (Supp.), 1–11. © 1968, American Medical Association.

drawal of the libido into the ego. By this process, the ego is identified with the lost object (introjection) and thereby becomes the target of the repressed hostility toward the love object. Thus, out of an ambivalence toward the love object comes a regressed, narcissistic identification of object with ego, which then serves as the scapegoat that is punished by the sadistic self-deprecation stirred up by the superego.

In mania, the ego has overcome the loss of the object, releasing large amounts of libidinal energy that seeks other objects in which to invest itself without superego censorship. From this comes the manic extroversion, the hearty manner, the promiscuous sexual adventures, and above all, the interest in immediate results and instantaneous gratifications.

The existentialists deal with the person's

Table 12-5 Differences Between Bipolar and Unipolar Depression

	Bipolar	Unipolar
Presence of mania in patient	yes	no
Median age of onset in patient	28	36
Six or more episodes	57%	18%
Affective disorder in parent	52%	26%
Families with two generations of affective disorder	54%	32%
Affective disorder in parents or extended family	63%	36%
Bipolar psychosis in first-degree	10.8%	0.35%

Modified from Winokur, G. The types of affective illness. *Journal of Nervous and Mental Diseases*, 1973, 156(2), 87. © 1973, The Williams & Wilkins Co. Reprinted by permission of author.

subjective experiences of mania and depression. The manic-depressive lives two lives, alternating between love and hate, between euphoric optimism and hopeless pessimism. In this, as in the other affective disorders, the existentialist school sees manic-depressives' modes of behavior as their way of living in a world in which the past haunts them with the constant reminder of their faults and failures. Their responses, in the existentialist view, are a composite of despair, surrender, self-punishment, and occasionally, an exaggerated joy in, and outpouring of, words and actions.

In psychoanalytic theory, *involutional psychotic melancholia* is distinguished from neurotic depression by the fact that the anxieties in neurotic depression relate more to the environmental conditions, while the anxiety in involutional psychosis is less specific, and more regressive toward early childhood helplessness and dependency. Psychotic depressives cling to impossible goals in a subborn effort to prove their worth, strength, and goodness in the face

of loss frustration, or inadequacy. They have not learned how to handle the emotional effects of loss or deprivation with mature responses; instead, they resort to the primitive infantile defenses.

The same immature and infantile defenses, with their overtones of helplessness and dependency, are raised in the depressive phase of manic-depressive psychosis. The behaviors that emerge from this helpless state are the characteristic anger, guilt, and feelings of unworthiness. In line with this formulation, we can see the manic stage as "a massive denial against the underlying depression" (Kolb, 1973, p. 378). Frustration of grandiose schemes provokes hostility that threatens the person's dependency role. This, in turn, may precipitate the depressive phase. Kolb (1973) further suggests that the person's cyclical behavior may reflect an identification with the indifferent paternal figure during the manic phase and with the submissive, self-abasing maternal figure during the depressive phase. Clearly, both of these internalized figures can be the object of the hostility that is considered the basic motivation in both phases of the cyclical psychosis.

Some attempt to scientifically study patients with affective disorders has been made by psychodynamic theorists. Cohen and his colleagues (1954), for example, studied 12 manic-depressive patients in an attempt to develop a profile of manic-depressives, their character and their interpersonal relations. They found these patients highly sensitive to, and dependent on, the regard and approval of others, locked into conventional values, very competitive and childishly envious, yet fearful of being envied, unfeeling of the needs of others, and manipulative in the pursuit of gratification of their own desires. Their families sought status in the community and readily used their children as instruments to attain that position (through scholastic achievement, etc.); parental discipline was sporadically and inconsistently applied.

In a study of the dream content of manic-depressives, Beck (1971b) sought support for the hypothesis of inverted hostility (self-hatred). He found that the dreams were composed of masochistic themes: deprivation, disappointment, frustration, rejection, punishment, physical discomfort or injury, being lost. They were the wish-fulfillment dreams of chronic "losers." Beck characterizes them as dominated by a "cognitive triad": a negative view of the world, of oneself, and of the future, with an overriding sense of loss rather than the commonly hypothesized feeling of hostility.

Behavioral Factors

Psychodynamic theories have dominated the treatment of the affective disorders for many years. Behavior theorists have labored under the criticism that while their explanations might account for individual or selected groups of depressive behaviors, they do not cover the extensive pattern of behaviors characteristic of such patients. Ferster (1973) has addressed the challenge of explaining the behavioral development of a pattern of depression.

According to Ferster, a behavioral explanation starts with a functional analysis of depressive responses relative to environmental reinforcements, that is, a quantitative study of contingency schedules (see Chapter 3 for a discussion of these concepts). Such an analysis shows that depressed people have a low frequency of behaviors most likely to elicit positive reinforcements. The low frequency of positive reinforcement, in turn, tends to extinguish the performance of the appropriate social behaviors. For example, depressed people don't engage others in conversation, do not maintain the conversations others initiate, do not smile, nod, emit social reinforcers, or show any of the numerous responses necessary for normal interaction. They soon stop interacting entirely and lapse into an impoverished pattern of alternately passive and complaining behavior. Studies confirm that depressives lack social skills, which further limits their repertoire of effective behaviors.

In an earlier study, Ferster (1966) offered an experiment using animals, showing how behavior responses are reduced by three kinds of events: (1) the requirement of long sequences of repetitive behavior before reinforcement is elicited, (2) the presentation of aversive stimuli to the subject, (3) a sudden environmental change involving separation or loss of an important source of reinforcement. Since the reinforcers in (1) and (3) control a large amount of a person's behavior, their reduction or withdrawal can lead to the extinction of a substantial segment of the repertoire. Ferster suggests that depressed people's failure to develop a rich repertoire of behaviors may start in infancy, when their mothers fail to respond to their needs. In these cases, the mothers may not have made appropriate responses to the infants' signs of tension and relaxation. As a result of the infants' continuing frustration, their perception is narrowed by their deprivations, and they do not learn to interact adequately with other people's behavior. This limits their view of the world and consequently their social repertoire. The flow diagram in Figure 12-2 illustrates the vicious circle in which a limited or reduced repertoire of social behaviors causes a reduction in reinforcement, leading to depressive responses—"the cry for help." These cries are often met with sympathy, which acts as positive reinforcement that serves to maintain the behavior.

Seligman (1975) and a number of other behavior researchers have proposed that depression is closely related to "learned helplessness." Experiments with animals and humans, in which the subjects were exposed to aversive situations where escape was not contingent upon avoidance behavior (i.e., the aversive situation would continue or end regardless of what the subject did), have demonstrated that both animals and humans developed a sense of utter helplessness. The subjects who had learned they could not control or avoid the unpleasant stimuli by any consistent behavior showed six kinds of responses: (1) fewer voluntary responses, (2) negative cognitive set—the anticipation of inevitable failure, (3) fading of helplessness after only one session of uncontrollable shock, but fixation of the attitude after a series of sessions, (4) lowered aggression and competition, (5) loss of appetite, (6) physiological changes. We are reminded by Seligman that

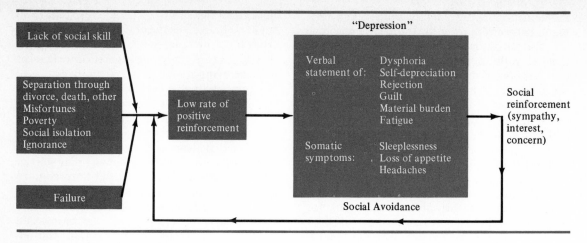

Figure 12-2 Schematic representation of the causation and maintenance of depressive behavior. (*Lewinsohn, P. M., and Shaffer, M. Use of home observations as an integral part of the treatment of depression: Preliminary report and case studies.* Journal of Consulting and Clinical Psychology, 1971, 37, 88. © 1971 by the American Psychological Association. Reprinted by permission.)

these responses of learned helplessness have their counterparts in depression. The proposed analogy is related to the operant theory of extinction. Those who support the learned helplessness conception argue that reinforcement that is independent of response (noncontingent) is equivalent to a total absence of reinforcement in its ability to extinguish behavior.

Hiroto and Seligman (1975) conducted a series of experiments with college students. They exposed one group of students to situations in which (1) they were unable to turn off an unpleasant noise by button pressing and (2) they were given insoluble visual discrimination problems. A control group of students experienced success in this pretraining phase. When the frustrated subjects were placed in situations in which they could control the aversive stimulus and solve the problems, they tended to fail with higher frequency than the control group. The researchers concluded that since the experimental subjects' expectation of failure generalized from the tasks in the first phase to the tasks in the second phase, the subjects had developed a *trait* rather than just a *state* of helplessness. This finding is significant

because it demonstrates that continued exposure to such situations can create a "depressed" style of reaction to many situations.

Other Psychological Factors

Cognitive views of depression center on the thought disorder manifested in the distorted attitudes expressed by depressed people. Beck's observations (1963, 1967, 1970, 1971a) are prominent among cognitive approaches. In his view, abnormal thinking patterns, or schemata, are responsible for depressive behavior. These schemata are idiosyncratic ways of looking at the world, the self, and the future. The world is lousy, the self is rotten, and the future is hopeless. Such faulty schemata arise from (1) biased conclusions drawn fron neutral situations, (2) selection of the wrong aspects of situations, (3) overgeneralization of single experiences to one's whole life, (4) distortion of the magnitude of events, (5) inexact labeling of experiences, leading to wrong implications. These twisted attitudes cause inappropriate responses in interpersonal interactions. The distorted feedback depressives receive from these interactions further distorts their schemata, perpetuating the cycle.

Family factors are blamed by some for the depressive psychoses. Loss of one or both parents has been found with greater frequency in the early lives of manic-depressives than of normals. Brown (1961) found that 41 percent of the depressed patients in his study had lost a parent before age 15, compared with a 12 percent loss during childhood for England's general population. On the other hand, Pitts et al. (1965) found no significant correlation between abnormal behavior and childhood loss of a parent. These studies have been questioned, however, on the grounds that the controls were medical inpatients who may have had psychological problems.

Family background characteristics have been examined in an effort to establish predisposing patterns of attitudes and behaviors. One study (Cohen et al., 1954) concluded that manic-depressives came from families belonging to racial minorities, striving for higher social status, suffering financial reverses, and having a history of abnormal behavior. However, Mendels (1970) questions the specific association of such family conditions with manic-depressives; he thinks these conditions may be generally predisposing factors for all forms of abnormal behavior.

We have discussed previously several other *psychological precipitants and stress factors* in connection with various affective disorders. Loss was one of the principal events that triggered the onset of a disorder. We see three kinds of loss: (1) the death of a loved one, (2) the breakdown of a relationship—spouse or dear friend, (3) a severe disappointment or failure. Depression ensues, possibly because the recent loss evokes memories of childhood loss (or threat of loss) of mother's love. Or the loss may reveal the dismal fact that life is a succession of losses and thus is a meaningless experience, a waste of time. Even a triumph does not assure happiness; it may expose the victor to envy (another separation with threat of loss of friends). The goal is reached and the competitive drive that gave life its exhilaration

is over. Everything loses its taste, goes flat and stale. So the saying goes, "The path of glory leads but to the grave." This is the middle-age depression, the time of involutional melancholia. The first signs of aging make real the latent threat of decline of vigor, attractiveness, sexual powers.

What makes some people more vulnerable or more subject to such severe emotional reactions? One factor that is suggested by many of the various theories is stress. Forrest, Fraser, and Priest (1965) found that 158 depressives had a three-year record of far more stress factors in their lives than 58 controls. Paykel et al. (1969) counted three times as many life stresses for depressives as for controls during the six months before onset. On the other hand, Hudgens, Morrison, and Barchha (1967) found few stressful events in the six months prior to onset. The contradictory indications are probably due to the sampling procedures (especially the difference between inpatient and outside control groups) and the definitions of stressful factors.

Sociocultural Factors

Studies designed to develop a demographic and sociocultural profile of the depressive psychotic have not produced a consistent, conclusive picture.

A national survey studying depression (Levitt and Lubin, 1975) showed a rising incidence with age, a negative correlation with level of education, no correlation with marital status, a tendency toward depression among black females but no significant association with other racial groups, a pattern of psychosis at the lowest income levels and neurosis at the upper levels, a negative relationship between depression and social class.

Another study aimed at involutional melancholia found the peak incidence among women in the 51–60 range and men in the 61–65 range (Ford, 1975). Women outnumber men three to one in the involutional group. Minority groups are not strongly represented in this middle-age disorder, which seems concen-

(Tim Eagan, Woodfin Camp & Associates.)

(Virginia Hamilto

(Tim Eagan, Woodfin Camp & Associates.)

trated among middle-class whites and those with strong religious commitment.

Biological Factors

Genetic factors, whose role we noted in schizophrenia, also serve a function in predisposing individuals to the affective disorders. One study found that 22 out of 23 identical twin brothers and sisters of manic-depressive patients were also diagnosed as manic-depressive, a concordance rate of 96 percent. The concordance rate is 20 to 25 percent between nonidentical twins and between siblings, substantially higher than the percentage of manic-depressives in the general population. However, the precise nature of the genetic inheritance is still unclear.

Biochemical factors also appear to be operative but of uncertain function (Mendels, 1970). Cortisol, a steroid hormone secreted by the adrenal cortex, is produced in increased quantity during depression and is reduced during the manic phase. Since the same increase in cortisol is observed in other agitated states, the relationship is probably a general response to stress. The change in hormone levels during menstruation and menopause is also related to depressive moods.

Sodium and potassium metabolism have also been implicated in depression. The balance between the concentrations of these electrolytes (substances capable of conducting electricity when in a liquid form) inside and outside the neuronal membrane has a critical effect on the excitability levels of the neurons. Manic patients tend to have a high concentration of intracellular sodium.

Amine level also seems to be related to mania and depression. High amine levels are associated with overactivity and alertness (as in manic elation), while a deficiency seems related to depression. These conclusions are derived from the indirect evidence of decreased amounts of the products of serotonin (a catecholamine) breakdown in the urine of depressives, and of the relief of depression provided by drugs that produce serotonin. We do not know about the possible functional interac-

tions between the amines, the steroid hormones, and the various electrolytes, but observed separately, their effects are significant.

Neurophysiological factors so far show little promise as correlates to the affective disorders. Studies of blood pressure show some relationship with depression, but without proper controls the results are not decisive. EMG studies show high levels of muscular activity in mute and retarded patients, and these levels are inversely correlated with severity of depression. But the samples tested thus far have been too small for generalization. EEGs of depressed patients indicated light, restless sleep over extended periods, with more sensitivity to noise, but these results can be matched in many so-called "light sleepers" who are emotionally normal.

Treatment Approaches

Manic-depressive patients in the acute stage are in an emergency state. Immediate hospitalization is often considered to be necessary for several urgent reasons: (1) Their involvement with well-meaning but indulgent family and associates may be deepening the problem. (2) They may be unable to care for themselves. (3) They may be suicidal and should be under protective observation.

Psychodynamic Approaches

The psychodynamic therapist's objective is to help patients with affective disorders to discover their underlying impulses (hostility, aggression) and gain an insight into the motivations for their feelings (loss, grief, guilt).

Daniels (1962) describes the psychodynamic therapeutic procedure in some detail. He first explores the patient's life situation and his or her psychological impulses and motivations. He then addresses himself to the three dominant feelings that afflict the patient: grief, guilt, and shame. The therapist joins the patient as a "mourning partner" in talking out the loss. Complete acceptance of the patient's reactions is the rule at this point. In dealing with the patient's guilt, the therapist assumes the role of the patient's conscience, presenting a mildly authoritarian attitude in directing a course of action to be followed rigorously. Gradually, the therapist eases the control and permits more indulgence in self-gratification by the patient. He clearly indicates that the patient need no longer feel guilty. The therapist counteracts the sense of shame by continuing to offer professional judgment of the patient's worth and competence. Throughout the procedure, the patient is guided to change his or her irrational thought patterns (remember Beck's faulty schema?), to break the habituated anxiety-depression sequence by confronting and dissipating the anxiety at its source.

The previous outline, of course, applies to the depressed stage of the cycle. In the manic stage, the therapist cannot establish contact. The indicated procedure here is to repeatedly stop the manic's detailed accounts, provoking anger and irritation, which brings on the treatable depression.

Behavioral Approaches

The variety of techniques used in the behavioral treatment of depression testifies to the ingenuity of the experimenters. No single procedure has attained general practice. Many of the programs seem to be built around manipulation of the particular subject's behaviors. Ferster (1973), for example, suggests working to increase the patient's verbal repertoire. Systematic desensitization, implosion therapy, group therapy, family therapy have all been tried in the treatment of depression.

We will survey a selection of different techniques that are directed mainly toward increasing the reinforcement of appropriate behavior.

Robinson and Lewinsohn (1973b) applied the "Premack principle," which states that high-frequency responses can reinforce adjacent low-frequency responses. (Low-frequency responses are characteristic of depressives.) In their experiment, depressed female college students in the Premack group had a light turned on when nondepressed talk occurred and were then allowed depressed talk while the light was on. Thus the depressed talk was contingent on nondepressed talk. A contingency control group had the light turned on under the same conditions but were allowed some low-frequency activity other than depressed talk while the light was on. In a deprivation control group, depressed talk was not permitted during no-light periods, but it was permitted during light-on periods. Light-on periods were not contingent on nondepressed talk. The Premack group's nondepressed talk increased significantly over its baseline and over the performance of the other contingency group but not over the deprivation group, indicating that restriction of depressed talk, rather than reinforcement of nondepressed talk, was the effective variable.

In another experiment, Robinson and Lewinsohn (1973a) made the amount of therapy time available to a male patient contingent on his rate of speech on any topic. A buzzer was sounded whenever the rate fell below the most recent upward change, thus pushing the rate steadily higher. A variation of this technique was applied to a patient whose therapy time depended on whether he made definite decisions and took action regarding career goals. This too resulted in improved performance.

Lazarus (1968) suggested three therapy techniques for reactive depression: time projection with positive reinforcement, affective expression, and behavior deprivation and retraining. The first technique, time projection with positive reinforcement, was tried on a female depressive. Under hypnosis, she visualized gratifying experiences in the future. The patient reported herself free of depression one week and one year after treatment. In the second technique, affective expression, Lazarus had his patient vent his anger, amusement, affection, and sexual excitement. Using the third technique, Lazarus subjected a patient to a period of sensory deprivation, then "retrained" him to environmental stimuli, to which he was presumably more sensitive. The second and third techniques have not been tested yet for continued beneficial effects.

Token economy systems, which we described in the treatment of schizophrenia in Chapter 11, have been studied by Reisinger (1972). Smiling was rewarded with tokens, crying was penalized by token fines. Later, crying was merely ignored. A female patient, hospitalized for 6 years, was discharged 20 weeks after the start of the program and was found to have maintained her gains 14 months later.

Twenty married patients incapacitated by depression were paired with their spouses in a joint therapy program set up by McLean, Ogston, and Graver (1973). The couples were first trained in the differential effects of positive and negative reinforcers. They were given "cue boxes," which had button-operated red and green lights. The couples used these boxes to inform their partners of when their (the partner's) statements were supportive (green light) or sarcastic, negative (red light). A counter on each box tallied the totals of red and green lights. Finally, the couples were trained in setting up agreements that would govern their mutual behaviors at home. Results showed improvement in problem behaviors during the eight-week program. There was no change on retest three months later.

In our discussion of the environmental feedback model of depressive behavior, earlier in the chapter, we noted how indiscriminate reinforcement of depressed behaviors serves to maintain them. Lewinsohn and Shaffer (1971) went into the homes of patients to record quantitatively the interpersonal behaviors and to suggest beneficial changes. In one case, they found a lack of interpersonal communication between the spouses, with the wife addressing most of her conversation to the child. In another home, the depressed husband was uniformly rewarding his wife's favorable and hostile expressions with appreciation and praise. In the first case, an increase in amount of intercommunication followed the couple's practice of observing each other's behavior and noting its effects on themselves. In the second case, the wife divorced the depressed husband, who was then encouraged to develop a wider range of social and academic activities.

Our review of cognitive theory of depression features the work of Beck (1967). His therapeutic procedure is designed to bring to patients an awareness of their negative "automatic thoughts" and to develop their ability to see objectively how these thoughts distort the real world. The individuals explicitly identify the distortion whenever it occurs in their automatic responses to situations. This leads to a reduction of such negative responses.

The most effective treatment for learned helplessness seems to be forcing the subject to experience success. Dogs are pushed back and forth in a shuttle box, learning that movement response produces escape reinforcement. Similarly, patients are exposed to success experiences in assertion training. A by-product of the change from helplessness to assertiveness is the relief of depression, since depression is probably the result of early experiences of failure to control one's environment.

Somatic Therapies

Electroconvulsive therapy (ECT), also referred to as electroshock therapy (EST), was described in Chapter 7. It has had dramatic success in many cases of depression and involutional melancholia. In one study of more than 500 patients (Bond, 1954), 72 percent of those who received ECT improved compared with 59 percent of the nontreated. (Depression is often a self-limited condition that gets better with time.) Other studies show improvement rates ranging from 40 percent to 100 percent of ECT patients. ECT is indicated especially in cases of severe, endogenous depression and conditions that stubbornly resist other forms of therapy. Undesirable aftereffects of ECT include temporary amnesia and confusion.

Psychoanalysts object to ECT because it gives patients a belief in a physical or even magical cure, making them resistant to the probing techniques of psychodynamic therapy. We do not know why ECT works. Theorists have speculated that it provides patients with a massive dose of the punishment that they feel

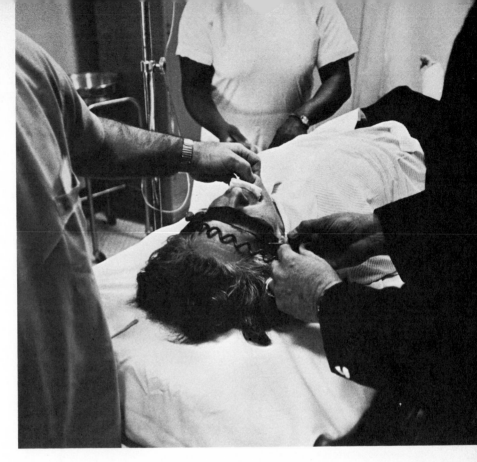

The patient in this photograph is being given electroconvulsive therapy. ECT has had dramatic success with many cases of depression and involutional melancholia. (*Paul Fusco, Magnum Photos.*)

they deserve. The ECT thus absolves patients of their sins, relieving the depression. Others feel that basic biochemical imbalances are reduced by the electrochemical effect on the brain. At present, all theories on ECT are highly speculative.

Drug therapy has met with success in the treatment of various types of depression, but the results are by no means general and some toxic side effects limit their use.

In acutely agitated, hostile cases, the major tranquilizers such as chlorpromazine are used. Among the anti-depressant drugs, the tricyclic compounds (e.g., imipramine) are more widely used than the monoamine oxidase (MAO) inhibitors. The tricyclics offer a selection of sedative and nonsedative properties to fit the specific requirements of the patient's life, and

have fewer side effects than the MAO compounds.

Lithium carbonate has become something of a "wonder" drug because of its impressive effects in cases of severe depression and acute manic states. However, its use as a "mood stabilizer" is still experimental. Other drugs, such as the less toxic imipramine, match its effectiveness in the treatment of unipolar depressives. Lithium has been found effective in less active manic cases, but chlorpromazine surpasses it in effectiveness in more highly active manic cases. In some studies, lithium has shown no effect in cases of severe depression. But in a number of other studies, lithium has demonstrated such dramatic improvement in severely depressed patients that it has been accepted as a primary medication. Lithium has some serious side effects: hand and mouth tremors, nausea, and when used to excess, drowsiness, confusion, seizures, and coma (Schuyler, 1976). Counteractive treatment is available for such reactions.

Suicide

We think of suicide as the final act of utter desperation, the response to intolerable suffering or deep depression. This seems to give suicide a kind of justification. After all, it does end the problem that motivated the act. Many, however, look at suicide as psychotic by definition, an abnormal behavior resulting from a distorted view of reality. The conceptions of suicide and of those who attempt it are varied and contain many unsupported generalizations. Fortunately, we have collected a great deal of hard information about suicide. Box 12-1 poses these data against prevailing myths.

Statistics on Suicide

As noted in Box 12-1, the U.S. suicide rate is 10 to 11 persons per 100,000 population and ranks among the top five causes of death for white males aged 10 to 55. It is the second-highest cause of death for white males between 15 and 19. Among European countries, Hungary for years has had the highest suicide rate (in 1969, 48.3 for males and 18.9 for females per

---

Box 12-1 Suicide: Fact versus Fiction

1. *People who talk about suicide won't commit suicide.* The fact is that 60 to 80 percent of those who commit suicide have threatened to do so.

2. *The suicide rate is rising.* With occasional fluctuation, the present rate of 10 to 11 suicides per 100,000 population is about the same as it was in 1900.

3. *Suicide and attempted suicide are the same class of behavior.* Ninety percent of those who attempt suicide never actually commit it. The two groups probably overlap in their psychological motivations, but they do show distinct differences.

4. *Suicides belong to certain classes.* All social and economic classes are well represented. People in good and bad circumstances do it—executives, children of the rich and the poor, college students and laborers.

5. *Causes of suicide are known and consistent.* Diagnosed depressed patients account for only 10 to 40 percent of suicides. Generally, an accumulation of health, financial, and other personal factors precedes the fatal act.

6. *Terminally ill people do not commit suicide.* They do—perhaps in order to take control over their fate rather than wait passively for it to overtake them.

7. *Suicide is a "crazy" act.* Schizophrenics usually do not commit suicide during their acute phase. When psychiatric patients commit suicide, they are usually in an improving stage. Suicide notes are often lucid, rational documents, with no indications of psychosis.

8. *Suicide is an inherited behavior.* There is no reported concordance of suicide among dizygotic or monozygotic twins.

9. *Suicide is related to weather or cosmic phenomena.* There are no correlations at all.

10. *Improvement in a suicidal patient means the danger is over.* This is not so. Most psychiatric patients who commit suicide do so within 90 days of hospital discharge.

11. *Patients in hospitals are not a risk.* The suicide rate in psychiatric hospitals is three to five times that in the general population.

From Pokorny, A. D. Myths about suicide. In H. L. P. Resnik (Ed.), *Suicidal behaviors.* Boston: Little, Brown, 1968.

100,000). Other high rates are found in Finland, Austria, Germany, Czechoslovakia, Denmark, Switzerland; countries with low rates include Scotland, Italy, Ireland, Greece. Malta is at the bottom of the list with a rate of about 1 per 100,000. Interestingly, the high-rate countries have shown increases over time, while the low-rate countries have tended to decrease.

The ratio of male to female suicides ranges from about 1.5–4.5 males to 1 female for the European countries. In the United States, the male-female suicide ratio is about 3:1, but for *attempted* suicides the ratio is reversed at 1:3. While currently more males commit suicide than females, the sex ratio is moving toward equality. Likewise, the disparity between white and black suicides is equalizing as the rate for blacks increases. Under age 35, more single women commit suicide, while over that age, males predominate. In the over-35 group, the rate for single men is double that for married men (Weissman, 1974).

In a study of 2,769 male suicides over a 7-year period in North Carolina, Zung and Green (1974) found that the number of suicides peaked in May (not during the holiday seasons, as is usually believed), but were not significantly lower during the other 11 months; the monthly tally is quite stable. Monday is the peak day of the week for suicides, but this, too, is not drastically different from the Saturday low point. There was no statistically significant seasonal variation.

Methods of committing suicide have changed over the years. In all parts of the world, drugs have become the most widely used method for suicides. These are generally prescribed drugs, like the barbiturates. The barbiturates, of course, are prescribed for the very disorders that account for a large proportion of suicides.

Psychological Characteristics

Shneidman (1969) speaks of the patient's "lethality" and "perturbation" as the two key factors in determining the level of psychological distress that can lead to suicide. One can be highly perturbed, yet not suicidal. The distress is a consequence of the operation of many emotions: hostility, guilt, dependency, hopelessness, despair, any of which may play the decisive role in suicide.

It has been observed that events that precipitate suicide are frequently dyadic, that is, between two people. Often, the dyadic interpersonal tensions—between man and wife, parent and child, two lovers—power the drive toward self-destruction. The complex interactions between these two may determine both the suicidal impulse and the forces that work to prevent it. The suicide note often throws some light on the dyadic relationship.

Although we have pointed out that diagnosed depressed patients make up only 10 to 40 percent of all suicides, their suicide rate is far higher than the rate for the general population. In the 45–64 age group, where depression falls heaviest, the rate is double the national rate. The suicide rates for schizophrenics and alcoholics are also well above the national rate, leading to the suggestion that the individuals with the most suicidal tendencies are schizophrenic depressives. Clearly, however, no single type of problem dominates the suicide statistics.

The suicide note is one of the most fascinating of documents. The fact that we are reading the thoughts of a person who, at the moment of writing, had resigned himself or herself to imminent death gives the note an almost mystical significance. Yet the content of most of the notes on the occasion of self-inflicted death is often not exciting or even informative.

Shneidman (1973) analyzes and classifies suicide notes written by historical figures and unknowns. He finds a variety of reasons for writing them: confession, removal of guilt, a plea for understanding, a demand for action. The following are some examples of suicide notes from Shneidman's work:

Dearest darling i want you to know that you are the only one in my life i love you so much i could not do without you please forgive me i drove myself sick honey don't be mean with me please I have lived fifty years since i met you, I love you—I love you. Dearest darling i love you i love you. Please don't discriminat me darling i know that i will die dont be mean with me please i love you more than you will every know darling please an honey Tom i know don't tell Tom why his dady said good by honey. can't stand it any more. Darling i love you. Darling i love you. (pp. 389–390)

To my wife Mary: As you know, like we've talked over before our situation, I'll always love you with all my heart and soul. It could have been so simple if you had have given me the help that you alone knew I needed.

This is not an easy thing I'm about to do, but when a person makes a few mistakes and later tried to say in his own small way with a small vocabulary that he is sorry for what has happened and promises to remember what has happened and will try to make the old Bill come home again, and do his best to start all over again and make things at home much better for all concerned, you still refuse to have me when you as well as I know that I can't do it by myself, then there's only one thing to do. . . . (pp. 389–390)

The following suicide note, abbreviated from the original, is a discourse on this individual's life situation and the reasons for his actions. It exemplifies the rational suicide and supports our previous point that suicide is not necessarily a psychotic act.

In November 1966, I discovered that I had acute myelogenous leukemia. My initial reactions are difficult to describe and still more difficult to recall accurately. However, I do remember feeling that somehow the doctor's remarks could not be directed to me but must be about some other person. Of course, I shook off that feeling very soon during this conversation and the full realization of the import of the diagnosis struck me. I was steeped in a pervasive sense of deep and bitter disappointment. I thought that I had been maliciously cheated out of the realization of all the hopes and aims that I had accrued during my professional career. . . . The next subjective feeling I can clearly identify is that I was increasingly apprehensive following the diagnosis about my inevitable decreasing body efficiency and thus very likely my decreasing efficiency and interest in my work. . . .

This engendered some little guilt over my anticipating not being able to do the job I had been doing. . . . Nonetheless, I did have pangs of remorse when I finally had to stop seeing long-term patients because my physical symptoms interfered too much with appointments. Surprisingly, I did not feel consciously angry or frightened by the knowledge that I had a life-threatening illness.

I was gravely disappointed and terribly annoyed that this thing inside my body would interfere with my life, but at no time did I really feel, as one might put it, "angered at the gods" for having such sport with me. Nor did I find that I used denial as a defense to any extent early in the course of the illness, as I did later on when it appeared that some of the chemotherapeutic measures were having considerably good effect and I began to feel that I could go on interminably from drug to drug and not die of my disease. . . .

People wrongly assume that a sick person should be "protected" from strong, and particularly negative feelings. The truth is that there is probably no more crucial time in a person's life when he needs to know what's going on with those who are important to him.

In the several months since the inception of my illness I became increasingly aware of a new sensitivity that had gradually but progressively developed in my interpersonal relationships, both with patients and with all my acquaintances. . . . One thing I noticed most pointedly was that I was very much more tolerant of the vagaries and inconsistencies of other people's attitudes and behavior than I had ever been before. . . .

It would appear that the peace I made with myself during my illness and the maturing ability that I was developing to cope with life crises like this one, arose from several dynamic factors. One was the increasing capacity to sublimate the rage and aggression engendered by the impotency I felt regarding this invasion from within. . . . It was very seldom that I was conscious of any feelings of despair or depression. . . . (pp. 391–392)

Introspective notes like this one appear to be the exception. We do not wonder that most suicide notes do not explore the inner perplexities of the writers' minds at the moment of death, since the individuals have cut themselves off from their attachment to life and have focused, with tunnel vision, on the immediate moment and the pressing problems that have pushed them to this crisis. Perhaps the potential suicides write a final call for help, a hopeless illusion of talking with the real person whom they feel might have saved them with understanding and tolerance.

The Campus Suicide— A Special Concern

Suicide on the college campus has become a sufficiently significant topic to warrant separate study (see Box 12-2), since a surprising number of students take their lives (it is the second-highest cause of death at Yale, for example). Knight (1968) speculates on likely reasons for this phenomenon. The campus is a world of change and contradictions. Here students are expected to exercise the conventional achievement drive in a setting of casual in-difference to the values esteemed in the "real" world outside. They have left the bosom of their families, given up childhood friends, abandoned their formal religion (if not their belief in God), and yet they have not found their own identity. Without a well-defined identity, they face grave problems in establishing relationships in the academic milieu. This *identity diffusion* leads to experiments with *negative identity:* the denial of the values and a scorn for the roles that are esteemed by their families. The identity crisis may reflect *separation anxiety*, the loss of their dependency status before they are ready to assume their adult roles. Curiously, the separation anxiety may not reach a critical state until the senior year, when the students are about to embark on their careers.

Depression haunts the campus. Under the stresses imposed by heavy workloads, self-monitoring responsibility, and fear of the consequences of academic failure, the students may feel rejected by parents or parent surrogates (the faculty). Fatigued by their continu-

Box 12-2 The Typical Suicidal Student

Is there a set of characteristics that describe the suicidal college student? Seiden (1966) compared 23 student suicides with the rest of the population at a large university. While 70 percent of the students were under 25 years of age, 60 percent of the suicides were over 25. The incongruity is more pronounced at the 30-year boundary: 6 percent of the student body was over 30, but 26 percent of the suicides were over 30. Seniors and graduate students were disproportionately represented among the suicides in terms of their distribution in the whole student population. The male-female sex ratio was 3:1 (similar to the national ratio). Of the 23 suicides, 20 were white, 3 were of Chinese descent; only 4 of the 23 were foreign. The student suicides were not having academic problems: two-thirds had above-average grades, 10 undergraduate suicides had above-average grades, but only 4 of 10 graduate students who had completed a semester had grades that were above average. Eight of the students had presented themselves to the mental health service at the university, seeking psychological treatment. An unexpected discovery was that the peak season for suicide on campus occurred in February and October, at the beginning of the semester, not during final exam week.

The psychological factors in these cases give meaning to the suicide data. The 23 students provided plenty of clues and signs of their mental condition before the final act. At least 5 had attempted suicide previously. Others had given warnings in morbid conversations about death. Their symptoms of insomnia, anorexia, and dependency presented a clear picture of agitated depression. Their psychological problems were of three kinds: (1) concern over studies—pushed themselves too hard, worried over grades; (2) unusual physical complaints—inability to eat and sleep, failing sight, violent stomachaches without physical cause; (3) interpersonal difficulties—stormy love affairs, withdrawal from society. One of the suicides had isolated himself so completely, he had been dead in his room for 18 days, unmissed, before he was found.

ous exposure to difficult, new material and doubts about their ability to meet the standards, they are vulnerable to feelings of inadequacy and unworthiness. Aggressive impulses may be translated into daredevil exploits—Russian roulette, dangerous driving, violent sports—which can be destructive.

"Therapy" for Suicide—Prevention and Management of Attempters

While there is obviously no treatment for suicide, there are measures calculated to reduce the likelihood of the event. As we discussed in Chapter 7, there are three levels of prevention: (1) identification of people at risk, (2) obtaining information from unsuccessful attempters as a basis for prediction, and (3) saving attempters who are found alive (McCulloch and Philip, 1972).

Preventive intervention must be applied at several levels; it cannot be directed toward individual symptomatic behaviors. The typical attempter has limited social skills and generally poor interpersonal relations. The therapist, social worker, family, and neighbors must establish continuing contact with the patient, to strengthen interpersonal ties and provide readily available, receptive, interactive people to relate to and communicate with.

Recognizing the danger signals in the potential suicide's communication of intent is perhaps the most critical function in prevention. Robins et al. (1959) interviewed family, friends, job associates, and others who had regular contact with 119 suicides, to find out the ways in which the deceased had signaled their intention. Two-thirds of the group had clearly communicated their purpose, 41 percent by direct announcement or threat. Others stated that they would be "better off dead," "wouldn't be missed," "can't take it any longer." Some made dire predictions: "Someday you'll find me dead," "I won't be here tomorrow." Some started putting their affairs in order, called old friends not contacted for years, talked about suicides of other people, speculated aloud about how it would feel to cut one's throat or hang oneself. The majority had clini-

This man is answering calls on a suicide hot line. His immediate job, of course, is to talk the distraught person out of committing suicide. Many suicide prevention centers also provide long-term counseling. (*Michal Heron.*)

cally diagnosed psychologic disorders. Curiously, both one-time threats and repeated warnings had the same effect of reducing the expectation of the suicide on the part of the receiver. The one-time threat was "so unlike him (or her)" that it was ignored, while the multiple threat was treated as "crying wolf."

Our earlier discussion of the statistics of suicide gave the demographic factors associated with high risk.

Tabachnick and Farberow (1961) have devised a test of self-destructive potentiality as a means of identifying potential repeat attempters. It includes objective measures to evaluate the degree of lethality of the attempt and also various interpersonal and intrapersonal factors that indicate high risk of repetition. Shneidman (1975) offers a scale of lethality that yields ratings (from 1 to 9) of absent, low, medium, high, indicating the patient's probability of committing suicide. Change is the key factor in determining lethality on this scale—change in interests, habits, attitudes, eating patterns, and so on.

Management of high-risk patients calls for a well-integrated program that involves a team of collaborators headed by the therapist. Significant others in the person's life should also be included. While it is best to try to maintain the person in his or her home setting with the support of family and friends, hospitalization must be readily available in the event of signs of crisis or an attempted suicide.

A number of suicide prevention agencies maintain centers where people contemplating suicide and those who have attempted it are given professional counsel and social services. One such agency is Rescue, Inc., in Boston, sponsored by the Catholic Church. A 70-member staff includes psychiatrists, psychologists, physicians, clergy, and nurses, all unpaid. Patients are self-referred, occasionally by calling to announce that they have just taken drugs, slashed their wrists, or turned on the gas. Emergency aid is dispatched, followed by long-term counseling service.

An organization called FRIENDS operates a 24-hour answering service, with medical, psychiatric, employment, and welfare help as needed. Churches in various cities maintain 24-hour telephone answering services that put the caller in immediate touch with professional counselors and social workers. While there is no simple way to evaluate the effectiveness of such operations, they are easily justified when one considers that the alternative is death for the people who cannot find support at the critical moment in their lives.

Summary

In this chapter, we have the affective, or mood, disorders. Depression is the principal component of the affective disorders. It varies in intensity and occasionally alternates with manic (highly excited) states. The most prominent aspects of depression are the altered mood state and a sense of guilt that evokes harsh self-criticism and feelings of worthlessness. Mania, which involves a pathologically heightened mood state, is seen as the same process at work with a different psychological manifestation.

The psychodynamic interpretation of depression is based on a sequence in which (1) the person experiences loss, (2) the ego is identified with the lost object, and (3) the ego is then punished as the object of hostility.

Behavioral explanations of depression propose a model based on extinction of appropriate social behavior. This lack of positive reinforcement induces depression, which perpetuates inappropriate behaviors, and so on. "Learned helplessness" is another behavioral effect that is often involved in depression.

Psychodynamic therapy seeks to relieve the patients of the psychological conflicts that produce their guilt feelings. Behavior therapy attempts to induce the patients to emit behaviors that will elicit more positive reinforcers. Drug treatments have had some success in alleviating depression.

There are a number of myths about suicide that have been discredited. Suicide is usually the result of interpersonal tension.

Antisocial behavior and society's response

When people act against society in some manner, their behavior is considered to be antisocial. Behaviors that violate society's formal or informal rules, such as rape, assault, shoplifting, bookmaking, forgery, and rioting can all be seen as antisocial.

Antisocial behaviors have always posed a problem of classification for mental health professionals. Do they represent an individual's personal *psychological* problems being expressed in an antisocial way, or are they the result of complex *sociological* factors that influence an individual to act against society? In other words, should criminal behavior be included or excluded from the umbrella of abnormal psychological functioning? Either choice will have important ramifications both for the individuals involved and for the field of abnormal psychology itself.

In an attempt to discriminate antisocial behavior due to psychological factors from antisocial behavior not considered the result of direct psychological factors, the DSM-II has reached a compromise of sorts. It introduces the label "antisocial personality" as part of the larger group of personality disorders and thus as a form of abnormal psychological behavior. *Antisocial personality* is defined in terms of:

> . . . individuals who are basically unsocialized and whose behavior patterns bring them repeatedly into conflict with society. They are incapable of significant loyalty to individuals, groups, or social values. They are grossly selfish, callous, irresponsible, impulsive, and unable to feel guilt or learn from experience and punishment. . . . (American Psychiatric Association, 1968, p. 43)

A second type of antisocial behavior is referred to as "dyssocial behavior," which is part of the category labeled "conditions without manifest disorders." The placement of dyssocial behavior in this category implies that psychologically "normal" individuals act against society due to factors unrelated to their psychological makeup. The DSM-II defines *dyssocial behavior* in terms of:

> . . . individuals who are not classifiable as antisocial personalities, but who are predatory and follow more or less criminal pursuits, such as racketeers, dishonest gamblers, prostitutes, and dope peddlers. (p. 52)

There is yet a third category of antisocial behavior, namely, *juvenile delinquency*. This category involves many of the same behaviors as the others, but it is considered a childhood disorder and therefore is treated as a totally separate category.

While three distinct categories exist, the actual *behavior* may be similar in each. Other factors such as the causes and context of the behavior will determine the particular label according to the DSM-II.

We will return to these issues later in the chapter. But, as our initial focus, we must understand that these questions of definition and classification are not an idle academic exercise. They relate to the complex issues of responsibility for our actions and "moral" behavior. That is, if criminal behavior is a function purely of psychological factors, can anyone be held responsible for his or her actions? Can we have moral and immoral behavior? These issues are of great concern throughout our society.

Types of Antisocial Reactions

Antisocial Personality (Psychopathy)

Background of Label

Pinel made the first important statement about the antisocial personality as the result of one of his cases. When a French woman used offensive language in speaking to a peasant, the peasant became furious and threw her down a well. Since the man's violent behavior did not include the traditional symptoms of psychiatric classification, Pinel labeled his condition as *manie sans délire* (mania without delirium).

In 1835, J. C. Prichard introduced the phrase "moral insanity" to describe individuals in whom "the moral and active principles of the mind are strongly perverted or depraved" (Maughs, 1941, p. 329). This classification was extremely popular in the late nineteenth century.

In 1876, Lombroso offered a new classification of the "born criminal," which was later linked to the concept of moral insanity. But many lawyers and clergymen were disturbed by this formulation, since it seemed to suggest that such individuals were insane and thus not responsible for their actions. As a result, Koch introduced the term "constitutional psychopathic inferiority" in 1888. These individuals were said to suffer from severe behavior disorders, and yet were seen as mentally competent and legally responsible.

The diagnosis of "psychopathic personality"—a modification of Koch's concept—became an important category in the first half of the twentieth century. Unfortunately, the term was used too broadly for too many problems (including affective disorders and deviant sexual patterns), and thus it eventually became useless (Rappeport, 1974).

The DSM-I, published in 1952, refined diagnostic thinking. The concept of "sociopathic personality disturbances" was legitimized, but antisocial personality and dyssocial behavior were subcategories of this one group; they were still seen as part of the same process. Not until 1968 were these two conditions separated into distinct categories. As we noted earlier, the DSM-II made the distinction between the presumed clinical entity (the antisocial personality) and behavior that deviates from social rules without psychological disorder (dyssocial behavior).

Behavioral Description

The standard description of the antisocial personality includes the clinical features first put forth by Cleckley in his landmark work, *The Mask of Sanity* (1964). Cleckley lists 16 characteristic behaviors of the antisocial personality:

1. Superficial charm and good intelligence.
2. Absence of delusions and other signs of irrational thinking.
3. Absence of "nervousness" or psychoneurotic manifestations.
4. Unreliability.
5. Untruthfulness and insincerity.
6. Lack of remorse or shame.
7. Inadequately motivated social behavior.
8. Poor judgment and failure to learn by experience.
9. Pathologic egocentricity and incapacity for love.
10. General poverty in major affective reactions.
11. Specific loss of insight.
12. Unresponsive in general interpersonal relations.

"I can vouch for my client, Your Honor—I've been defending him ever since he was a juvenile." (*L. Herman.*)

13. Fantastic and uninviting behavior when under the influence of alcohol, and sometimes even when not.

14. Suicide rarely carried out.

15. Sex life impersonal, trivial, and poorly integrated.

16. Failure to follow any life plan. (1964, pp. 362–363)

According to Cleckley, psychopaths seem interested only in themselves. Their perceptions rarely go beyond their own immediate needs. They show a marked inability to feel loyalty to any individual or group, or to feel affection, deep emotion, or love. They can be aware of hurting others without experiencing any significant guilt or shame.

Psychopaths often fool people because they can display superior intelligence and persuasive charm. Although unreliable and insincere, they are skillful at presenting an *image* of genuine feeling and concern. Cleckley (1959) writes that the psychopath's "disregard for truth is remarkable. . . . While committing the most serious of perjuries, it is easy for him to look anyone calmly in the eye" (p. 581).

When confronted with clear evidence of their antisocial acts, psychopaths often admit their wrongdoing and make impressive apologies and commitments to change. But these eloquent moral statements do not result in any alteration in behavior. In the opinion of Hare (1970), the psychopath "knows the words but not the music" (p. 6).

Such individuals demonstrate a consistent failure to learn from their actions and mistakes, even when they have superior reasoning ability. As Cleckley (1959) observes: "No matter how many times he comes to frustrations or disaster, he does not learn by such experience to avoid the type of conduct responsible for his failures" (p. 582). This may reflect the inability of antisocial personalities to see themselves as others see them, or it may reflect their inability to understand the effects of their actions on family, friends, and co-workers.

Childhood characteristics are considered most important in predicting the development of the adult psychopath. Robins (1967) points

to an early age of onset (probably before age 12) for behaviors typical of the antisocial personality. This harks back to the late 1800s, when "constitutional" factors (such as the "bad seed" idea) were seen as central to the psychopathic personality.

Table 13-1 presents the results of a study of 524 children who were treated at a child guidance clinic and then followed up as adults. As the data indicate, the most common behaviors among the children who later became antisocial were theft, incorrigibility, truancy, running away, keeping bad companions, staying out late, and physical aggression. Studies suggest that the *number*, *frequency*, and *serious-*

Table 13-1 Childhood Symptoms Predictive of Antisocial Personality

Symptom	Percentage of Adult Antisocials Who Had Symptom	Percentage of Children with Symptom Who Became Antisocial
Theft	83	31
Incorrigibility	80	30
Truancy	66	34
Running away	65	33
Bad companions	56	30
Staying out late	54	30
Physical aggression	45	32
Poor employment record	44	32
Impulsivity	38	35
Recklessness, irresponsibility	35	29
Slovenly appearance	32	34
Enuresis	32	29
Lack of guilt	32	38
Premarital intercourse	28	31
Pathological lying	26	39

Data from Robins, L. N. *Deviant children grown up: A sociological and psychiatric study of sociopathic personality.* Baltimore: Williams & Wilkins, 1966.

ness of these childhood behaviors all serve as useful factors in predicting the adult psychopath (Winokur and Crowe, 1975).

The following case example illustrates antisocial behavior during childhood:

By all accounts Donald was considered a willful and difficult child. When his desire for candy or toys was frustrated, he would begin with a show of affection, and if this failed he would throw a temper tantrum; the latter was seldom necessary because his angelic appearance and artful ways usually got him what he wanted. . . .

Donald's misbehavior as a child took many forms including lying, cheating, petty theft, and the bullying of smaller children. As he grew older, he became more and more interested in sex, gambling, and alcohol. When he was 14, he made crude sexual advances toward a younger girl, and when she threatened to tell her parents he locked her in a shed. It was about 16 hours before she was found. Donald at first denied knowledge of the incident, later stating that she had seduced him and the door must have locked itself. He expressed no concern for the anguish experienced by the girl and her parents, nor did he give any indication that he felt morally culpable for what he had done. (Hare, 1970, pp. 2–3)

Psychopathic individuals like Donald generally do not become violent criminals in their adult years. The antisocial acts they commit tend more toward embezzlement, fraud, and other "white-collar" crimes. Mr. P., the bigamist whose case was discussed in Chapter 2, is an example of an antisocial personality.

The adult life style of the psychopath has distinct antisocial features even when the behaviors are not necessarily illegal. Often the individual "lives by his (or her) wits," as opposed to making a more typical adaptation to life. Here is some more information about Donald:

When he was 17, Donald left the boarding school, forged his father's name to a large check, and spent about a year travelling around the world. He apparently lived well, using a combination of charm, physical attractiveness, and false pretenses to

finance his way. During subsequent years, he held a succession of jobs, never staying at any one for more than a few months. Throughout this period he was charged with a variety of crimes, including theft, drunkenness in a public place, assault, and many traffic violations. In most cases he was either fined or given a light sentence. (Hare, 1970, pp. 3–4)

Causal, Contributing, and Maintaining Factors

Biological factors A large body of research over the last two decades has demonstrated that there may be differences in the functioning of the central nervous system in antisocial personalities. The following are among the distinctive CNS characteristics of psychopaths.

1. *Slower EEG rate.* Several studies have detected abnormal electroencephalographic rates (EEGs) in individuals with antisocial personalities.

2. *Lower level of cortical arousal.* Cleckley (1964) described the psychopath in the following manner: "Being bored, he will seek to cut up more than the ordinary person in order to relieve the tedium of his existence" (p. 426). Cleckley's description is important in light of Rose's finding (1964) that psychiatric patients with a low level of cortical arousal tend to be impulsive and psychopathic. This correlation implies that the antisocial personality may have an abnormal need for stimulation, excitement, and sensory input in order to alleviate routine and boredom (which result from a low level of cortical arousal).

3. *Different responsiveness to anxiety.* Hare (1970) summarizes a number of important studies by suggesting that "given the choice between an activity that is normally thought of as frightening and one that is safe but dull, the psychopath, more than the nonpsychopath, would prefer the former" (p. 67).

4. *Insensitivity to social cues.* Hare (1970) also observes that the psychopath has a "general tendency to attenuate sensory input." (p. 69). In searching for intense or exciting environmental stimulation, the individual might not perceive normal social cues for expected behavior, ones that tend to be subtle rather than startling.

The role of *genetics* and *environment* as factors in psychopathic behavior has been long debated. The interaction of these elements is perhaps most clear in adoption studies, such as those of Schulsinger (1972) and Hutchings and Mednick (1974). An adopted child is most likely to engage in antisocial behavior if *both* the biological and adopted parents have prior criminal records. Thus, although twin studies and adoption studies all suggest some evidence of genetic involvement, environmental factors cannot be dismissed.

Psychological factors Some observers discount biological factors altogether, and point to the *chaotic home environment* of the antisocial personality as a central causal factor. Several relevant findings support this position.

Many studies suggest that antisocial behavior is more likely to develop in homes affected by *separation* or *divorce* than in stable, two-parent families. Furthermore, Greer (1964) found that 60 percent of the psychopathic individuals in his survey showed an early *parental loss* (often before the child was 5), as opposed to 28 percent of neurotics and 27 percent of normal individuals. Loss of fathers was especially prevalent among psychopaths.

Even when both parents are present, circumstances can lead to the development of antisocial personality. Studies have found that many antisocial personalities had suffered *early deprivation* of emotional ties with significant individuals (such as parents, guardians, or older siblings) during childhood years.

Robins (1966) conducted an important study of more than 600 adults who had been treated in a psychiatric clinic for children 30 years earlier. She found that one critical factor in the development of psychopathy was in the area of discipline. *Inconsistent discipline* or lack of adequate discipline during childhood was an often-cited occurrence.

One way to interpret these findings is to emphasize the poor modeling role of the absent or inconsistent parent. In such a home, the child might receive inconsistent discipline and less training in social behavior. Winokur and Crowe (1975) report:

Children who had suffered severe deprivation in infancy were found as adolescents to exhibit lack of control over their behaviors, hunger for attention and affection, emotional imperviousness, superficial relationships, absence of normal tension and anxiety, and lack of social maturity. (p. 1288)

These behaviors coincide significantly with our description of the antisocial personality.

A serious problem with such environmental theories of causation, however, is that they fail to explain why some children from chaotic homes become psychopathic while others do not.

A *psychodynamic* interpretation of these findings points to the absence of the father (physically or emotionally) during childhood as an influence on the development of the superego. Without a disciplinarian (traditionally a role of the father) in the home, children may learn to play out their primary impulses with little fear of punishment. Thus they might be expected to emerge as adults with little ability to control immediate desires. This, of course, is a prime characteristic of the antisocial personality.

Solomon and his colleagues (Solomon, 1960; Solomon, Turner, and Lessac, 1968) have offered a *behavioral* viewpoint that focuses on the psychopath's lack of "conscience." They see the key elements of conscience as *resistance to temptation* and *guilt*. Psychopaths may be significantly lacking in each quality because of delayed and inconsistent reinforcement in their family life.

A second behavioral viewpoint centers on the inability of the psychopath to delay gratification. The work of Mischel (1966) pinpoints expectancy for future rewards as a determining factor in the ability to delay gratification. Psychopaths may find it difficult to delay gratification since they have often had poor impulse-control training as children, and cannot easily fantasize the future.

We have not highlighted *sociological* factors in this brief review of psychopathy, despite the fact that there is a strong correlation between socioeconomic status and application of the clinical label. Generally, when sociological factors are considered dominant, the behavior is more likely to be categorized as criminal (dyssocial) rather than psychopathic.

Criminal or Dyssocial Behavior

The category of dyssocial behavior, as noted above in the DSM-II, includes "predatory" individuals who "follow more or less criminal pursuits." It is further presumed that such behavior is not due to factors associated with a "personality disorder."

Is This Category Based on a Real Distinction?

The specific behaviors of criminal (or dyssocial) individuals are not necessarily different from those of antisocial personalities. Each group exhibits poor social judgment and a strong need for easy and quick gratification. The distinction drawn in the DSM-II between the two categories is based on the presumed causal factors. Dyssocial individuals are more likely to be viewed as products of their environments.

This distinction raises difficult questions, however, about the normality or abnormality of the criminal. In part, this reflects underlying uncertainties of Western law. The typical criminal is portrayed as mentally capable, responsible, and thus accountable for his or her actions. Yet it is not simple to distinguish the "sane" murderer from the "insane" murderer, the "sane" rapist from the "insane" rapist.

This confusion is noticeable in the DSM-II discussion of dyssocial behavior. It is unclear whether dyssocial behavior is considered psychologically normal or abnormal, whether it is or is not a form of "mental illness," and whether it can be an unhealthy psychological condition without being a "manifest psychiatric disorder" (Stojanovich, 1969).

Manipulative Behavior

Bursten (1972) has made an important contribution to current thinking by introducing a new classification that blends elements of antisocial and dyssocial individuals: the *manipulative personality*. This label is not intended to replace the others. It is meant merely to suggest a unique category for those individuals whose primary goal is *manipulation itself* (rather than personal gain or need satisfaction).

Manipulative personalities actually enjoy deceiving people. They are exhilarated when they can "put something over" on other individuals. The key to such behavior is their "intense but fragile narcissism" (Bursten, 1972, p. 320). Manipulative personalities have a shaky self-image. Because of this, they are compelled to create situations in which they can feel superior to others. Through skillful intrigues, they convince themselves of the gullibility and worthlessness of their victims. In believing that their victims are contemptible, manipulative personalities convince themselves that they must be powerful and good.

The Sociocultural Base of Criminal Behavior

A wide variety of social factors contributes to criminal or dyssocial behavior. In some cultures, there is a virtual *tradition* of organized crime; the existence of powerful criminal networks may be an unwritten law of community life. *Poverty* is also a significant influence on criminal behavior. When individuals are unemployed, homeless, or hungry, they may be more likely to lash out in anger, or to take what they feel is rightfully theirs. Other sociological factors such as race, age, peer pressures, area of residence (e.g., ghetto versus suburb), crowding, broken homes, and so on, all have been discussed. Is is beyond the scope of this book to explore the enormous sociological literature on criminality. What we must note is that sociological factors are of primary importance as correlates of criminal behavior. It will take much more research, however, before we are able to establish whether, and in what way, these factors actually cause criminal behavior.

The XYY Gene Syndrome

The cells of a normal male have 46 chromosomes and an XY genotype. A very small percentage of males have an extra Y chromosome and show an XYY genotype. An important study by Jacobs et al. (1965) linked this abnormality to tall stature, aggressive behavior, and criminality. Later research seemed to substantiate this view. It was learned that the frequency of the XYY male in the criminal population is 15 times that of the normal (XY) adult male (Jarvik, Klodin, and Matsuyama, 1973).

The following is a typical case of an XYY male.

He had a history of antisocial behavior dating back to early childhood when, according to his mother's recollection, he was so uncontrollable that she finally tied him to a tree when doing outdoor chores in order to prevent him from harming himself and others. Admitted to school at the age of 6, he created so much trouble that his parents were asked to remove him. Readmitted at the age of 7, he again beat up the other children and remained a disciplinary problem . . . until, at the age of 10, he was transferred to a boarding school for disturbed children. Ever since then he has been in institutions of one sort or another. He would escape whenever possible and invariably get into trouble on the outside. . . .

At the age of 20, he was committed to a mental hospital because of increasingly abnormal behavior. . . . Several years later, after nearly killing an attendant and another patient, he was transferred to a hospital for the criminally insane, where he was regarded as the most difficult management problem. (Jarvik et al., 1973, p. 676)

Jarvik and his co-workers (1973) see a possible genetic association between maleness and violence. If an extra Y chromosome leads to unusually aggressive behavior, the single Y chromosome in the normal male could be the root of violent conduct. But more recent findings by Witkin et al. (1976) cast doubt upon this viewpoint. In a study of more than 4,000 Danish men, these researchers determined that XYY males tended to commit crimes against *property* rather than *people*. XYY males did not show significantly greater evidence of aggressive behavior than did the normal XY control group.

The Danish study did substantiate the

higher mean crime rate among XYY males. But this genetic abnormality is so rare that it cannot serve as a widely applicable explanation for criminality. Of 4,293 criminals analyzed in 20 separate chromosome studies, only 61 individuals (less than 2%) were found to have the XYY genotype (Jarvik et al., 1973).

Juvenile Delinquency

Behavioral Description

Juvenile delinquency typically is defined as any behavior in violation of the law committed by a person who is legally of juvenile age (17 or below in most states). The behavior of the juvenile delinquent may include stealing, truancy, cruelty to animals, fire setting, sexual promiscuity, vandalism, and aggressive assault. Occasionally, juvenile assaults lead to deaths, and therefore juvenile crime contributes to the national homicide statistics.

Many investigators have noted the possibility of different types of juvenile delinquency. The most popular division is between the disturbed adolescent who commits delinquent acts due to psychological factors, and the "social" delinquent who conforms to social norms that encourage delinquent acts against the larger society. This distinction directly parallels the division noted above, in which the adult psychopathic personality is differentiated from the predatory, dyssocial individual.

Scope of the Problem

The incidence of juvenile delinquency can only be estimated since, in most states, juvenile courts are not required to make full disclosure of the names of offenders. Stephens (1973) reports that juvenile delinquents represent roughly 3 percent of all American youths aged 10 through 17.

It seems clear that juvenile delinquency is on the rise. Excluding traffic incidents, American courts are now handling more than one million juvenile delinquency cases per year. The age of the average youthful offender at the time of his or her first court appearance seems to be steadily declining.

In the past, juvenile delinquency was conventionally considered a male phenomenon. But in 1971, female cases increased by 11 percent, while male cases increased by only 6 percent (Stephens, 1973).

The school has become a principal focus of juvenile delinquent behavior. Almost every community reports a major problem of school vandalism. Attacks on teachers and other students have created alarm in many school systems, and have resulted in elaborate security arrangements (including, in some cases, police officers on duty in the halls).

Causal, Contributing, and Maintaining Factors

Biological factors As with adult antisocial behavior, various biological theories have been proposed to account for juvenile delinquency. In 1883, the Anthropometric Committee of the British Association for the Advancement of Science studied the physical characteristics of roughly 2,000 delinquent children and 50,000 nondelinquent children. The committee learned that delinquent children tended to be shorter and to weigh less. Similar findings in the early twentieth century led to a popular view that small and slight body type had some correlation to juvenile delinquency (O'Leary and Wilson, 1975). But more recent evidence does not support this view. Sheldon (1949) found that delinquents had more athletic body types than nondelinquents. The conflict between these findings dramatizes some of the inherent weaknesses of biological theories of causation.

Psychological factors Psychodynamic efforts have focused on the inability of the delinquent child (like the psychopath) to develop an adequate, inhibiting superego. Some theorists point to coldness and rejection from parents as a major contributing factor in poor superego development. Others believe that the delinquent has often lost a significant love object through illness, abandonment, or death. The child's pain over the absence or loss of the parent may lead to an angry and explosive search for the missing figure, which is expressed in the form of antisocial behavior (Stubblefield, 1967).

Still other psychodynamic theorists have focused on the hidden antisocial impulses of the parent or parents as a prime cause of the delinquent child's superego problems. In their view, many parents unconsciously encourage children to act out their (the parents') own forbidden wishes. Parents communicate these messages to the child in a variety of subtle ways, including facial expression, body language, permissive tone, and innuendo (Johnson and Szurek, 1952).

Children have a deep drive to please their parents, even if this will lead to punishment. As a result, they internalize the parents' antisocial messages and engage in delinquent behavior. The children's actions seem to stimulate the parents' unconscious antisocial feelings (including hostility toward their child). While the parent may sternly warn the child never to repeat such behavior, the parent will often describe the child's actions to others with obvious relish and admiration (Johnson, 1959).

In some cases, the father serves as an aggressive model for the delinquent son (Bandura and Walters, 1959). The harsh, punitive father generally runs his home like a tyrant, demanding unquestioning obedience from his son at all times. However, he will encourage his child to "beat the daylights" out of anyone who gets in his way. The parent will also rely on physical punishment as a means of discipline, thus reinforcing the model of aggressive behavior. If the youth is constantly exposed to physically aggressive models in his home, and is not reinforced in other ways of relating to people, it is only natural that he would engage in aggressive delinquent behavior.

Sociocultural factors The above theories of individual development are useful in understanding the inner drives of the lone delinquent. But what of the delinquent *gang*? Sociological delinquency cannot be explained by full reliance on psychological analysis.

One explanation for gang delinquency is the *social disorganization* model. According to this viewpoint, sociological delinquency is most prevalent in slum areas of larger cities, in which the population changes frequently and there is no solid social organization. But the social disorganization model seems to rest on a dubious assumption: that the cultural life of an economically depressed neighborhood is chaotic and disorganized. In fact, such areas may have very distinctive organizational forms—such as the numbers racket—that are not fully understood by the outside observer (Johnson, 1959).

An alternative explanation is the *cultural origin* or cultural transmission view. Shaw and McKay (1931), in a study of gang delinquency in Chicago, found that such behavior was almost a subcultural tradition in the lowest socioeconomic neighborhoods of the city. In other words, if Poles were residing in the poorest neighborhood during a given decade, delinquency might be most common among Polish gangs. If Poles moved out of the neighborhood and were replaced by low-income Norwegians, the Norwegian youths would become the principal delinquents.

The cultural origin theory specifically rejects the notion that particular racial, religious, or national groups are prone to antisocial behavior. Instead, it is argued that whatever groups are on the bottom of the socioeconomic ladder will form delinquent subcultures among their youth (Johnson, 1959).

The cultural origin theory states further that delinquent youths immerse themselves in a subculture that consciously rejects the values and norms of the larger society. Within the gang, there is explicit support for antisocial behavior such as stealing, fighting, or even killing. Johnson (1959) expresses the feelings of these youths: "It is their world against 'our' world. . . . It is all right to steal or betray the other world" (p. 851). There is unity *within* the members of the subculture; each feels strong resentment toward "outsiders" and has little guilt about acting on these feelings.

Cohen (1955) has pointed out an important *rational* element in the development of

Schools are frequent targets of juvenile delinquents. (*Wide World Photos.*)

sociological delinquency. Youths from poor socioeconomic backgrounds face a conflict between their home environments and the middle-class mores of the schools and other societal institutions. Often this conflict leads to feelings of confusion, frustration, inferiority, and even self-hatred.

Given these difficulties, youths from economically deprived environments naturally form groups to build an alternate community where their feelings are understood and respected. Inside the gang, no one will feel inadequate because of where he or she lives or because of the kind of accent he or she speaks with. Of course, some of these subcultures may

go even further and reward members who directly violate and attack the rules (or people) of the middle-class socioeconomic system (Johnson, 1959).

Society's Response to Antisocial Behavior

The Criminal-Legal System and Mental Health

The antisocial behaviors of the psychopathic personality, the dyssocial individual, and the juvenile delinquent often involve the breaking of laws. As a result, both the mental health and the criminal-legal systems are called on to deal with these problems. While ideally these two systems might enhance each other's work, in practice their goals and methods of treatment are often in conflict. The criminal-legal system is concerned primarily with retribution and imprisonment of lawbreakers; the mental health system focuses on the rehabilitation and return of people to better (more socially acceptable) functioning within the larger society.

The traditional liberal approach to criminal behavior has been to characterize the criminal as a neurotic individual who needs some form of mental health assistance. Menninger (1968), for example, criticized society's portrayal of the criminal as evil and immoral, and instead spoke of our notions of punishment as a "crime" against the disturbed individuals who need help.

This type of reformist thinking led to the proposal of many innovations, including the substitution of informal proceedings for criminal trials, and the practice of giving indeterminate sentences at treatment centers instead of fixed prison terms. Most of the reform measures noted that the criminal was in need of psychotherapy and treatment (Silber, 1974).

An increasing number of civil libertarians have begun to challenge these "reforms." These individuals argue against the rise of what they refer to as the "Therapeutic State." Essentially, they fear the use of mental health professionalism as a subtle and unrestricted means of social control. Szasz (1963) and others point out that people committing antisocial acts may actually be better off when labeled as criminals (and thus responsible for their actions) than they are when labeled "psychologically disturbed" and therefore not responsible for their actions.

Individuals labeled as disturbed, like criminals, are subject to informal, civil proceedings. But unlike criminals, "disturbed" individuals are not assured of basic constitutional rights, such as the right to counsel, to specific charges, and to a trial by jury. Ironically, their period of incarceration will often be longer while undergoing "treatment" than if they are labeled as criminals and are imprisoned. Perhaps the most serious result of the "disturbed" label is that mental patients have no recognized civil liberties once they enter the treatment center. They are even more vulnerable to infringements on their rights than are jailed criminals (Silber, 1974).

Prisons and Prisoners

Historical Perspective

Sellin (1972) separates the history of punishment into a number of periods. In the first phase of punishment, the *retaliatory element* was the primary emphasis. Corporal punishments, such as branding, mutilation, and flogging, and capital punishments, such as the hangman's rope and the executioner's sword, were used mainly as instruments of public revenge and retaliation.

The *exploitative* element in punishment also has a long history. As far back as the Roman Empire, criminals were forced to work in mines and quarries to serve as a cheap labor pool. Until recent decades, the American "chain gang" functioned similarly as a means of exploiting the prison population.

The *humanitarian* element in punishment represented the first progressive step toward a more understanding approach to the criminal. Religious beliefs were usually the

motivating force in campaigns to reform prison practices. Organizations to improve prisons were created to introduce medical services and libraries into prisons. Many of these reformers also fought against the use of corporal and capital punishment.

In the last two centuries, the *treatment* element in punishment has become increasingly important. As Sellin (1972) observes:

> The criminal anthropologists, the hereditarians, the psychoanalysts, . . . the Marxians, the sociologists, . . . all pointed in the same direction as far as the penal system was con-

Even in the nineteenth century, the primary emphasis in many prisons was on retaliation. Here, a convict at the State Prison at Auburn, New York is being subjected to water torture. (*Culver Pictures.*)

cerned: they all demanded that the punishment be fitted to the punished and not to the crime, broadly speaking. (p. 14)

All of these observers came to favor flexible correctional treatment with an emphasis on *individual* assistance for the criminal.

Statistical View of Prisons

Support for correctional institutions is always a difficult issue for state legislation to deal with. With the many social services demanding their share of the budget, it is difficult to justify increased expenditures for criminals. The result has been that every state has serious problems with its prison system. Overcrowding, inadequate facilities, far fewer personnel than are necessary, a lack of programming—all have created a situation that is dismal at its best, and explosive at its worst. The several examples in recent years of brutal and bloody prison riots attest to the fact that something is very wrong with our prison systems. The less dramatic finding that most prisoners eventually return to prison would seem to indicate that "correctional" institution is hardly an appropriate label for prisons.

Overcrowding is also a problem in juvenile institutions. In theory, juvenile institutions are training facilities that prepare youths for productive lives in their home communities. But due to the shortages of qualified personnel and remedial programs, the goal of "juvenile training" is rarely achieved. Often it is not even attempted.

Qualitative Description of Prisons

Prison life is a bleak reality that those who have never "done time" find difficult to understand. Keve (1974) writes of the daily humiliations of even the best prisons:

It isn't necessary to have a callous or inept warden to have a riot. It isn't necessary to have sadistic guards, bad food, or any of the other classic grievances that supposedly provoke a riot. . . . The real problem is that even

in a prison with good food and humane custodians life is still a put-down, day after day after day. Boredom, pettiness, and repetitive meaningless activities are inherent in prison existence, and it should be no surprise that at some point the inmate population has had all it can stand. (p. 15)

Prison *regimentation* is a consequence of the many problems prisons have. We already noted how badly understaffed most prisons are, with only a small number of officers available at any time to supervise the inmates. As a result, careful and continuous regimentation is an essential technique in keeping track of all prisoners.

For inmates, regimentation leads to almost intolerable *boredom*. Convicts eat every meal, every day, in the same room. They wear the same uniform every day—and so does everyone around them. They walk to their "job" every morning along the exact same route. Their cells, in which they spend every evening, are identical to as many as 500 other cells in the same block. There is no break from the routine. It goes on and on, for days, weeks, months, years.

Adding to this stress on the prisoner is the difficulty of a life without privacy. As Keve (1974) notes:

The convict ordinarily can achieve complete privacy only illicitly. If the prisoner is out of everyone's sight, it becomes a risk situation. He might be engaged in some activity that threatens the security of the institution, so the prison building and its operation are designed to keep each man always in view. (p. 21)

Prisoners' one "private" space—their cell—is open to the view of any guard or visitor walking by. Even the toilets are constructed to allow for clear supervision.

Under such conditions, many inmates engage in behaviors that would make little sense in the outside world. Some pretend to be ill in order to have a consultation with the prison doctor, since this will at least represent a momentary break from the monotony of prison life. Others will engage in more extreme reactions. During a prison riot in Minnesota, a large group of inmates broke into the prison's drug cabinets and swallowed pills at random. Within an hour, more than 20 men were unconscious, and a few nearly died. Keve summarizes the motives of the inmates: "Taking pills and having something crazy happen to one's body or mind is a sad substitute for more normal satisfaction, but it is better than no kicks at all" (p. 26).

In this respect, the life of the prisoner is similar to the life of the mental patient. Each becomes quite capable of "irrational" acts that represent a desperate response to a pervasive boredom, depression, and hopelessness.

Adaptation to the Prison Environment

Clemmer (1958) was the first to introduce the concept of "prisonization." In his view, as inmates become more familiar with the prison culture, they take on its folkways, mores, and customs in order to assimilate and survive. The effectively "prisonized" convict can easily make friends, learn the workings of the prisoners' social system, and "con" prison officials. Sandhu (1974) believes that prisonization "may be inversely related to a positive relationship with the immediate family and other relatives" (p. 142). The inmate who has little satisfactory contact with the outside world will be forced to turn to the prison subculture for friendship, status, and other rewards.

The comparison between male and female institutions is worth noting. In the female prison, many women form intense relationships with a best friend. Lovemaking and homemaking are common themes of prison life. The work of Giallombardo (1966) suggests that women in prison build a substitute universe with familiar roles such as lover, wife, and mother.

They date, select mates, write love letters, and court each other. The women prisoners marry each other, act as husband and wife, adopt younger girls as children, and raise *pseudo-*

families in the prison. They copy the fashions of the outside society, quarrel with each other, and separate from and divorce each other, just like families outside the prison. (Sandhu, 1974, p. 143)

In men's prisons, the pattern is somewhat different. Only about 20 percent of the inmates enter into a primary-group relationship with a clique of friends. Glaser (1964) reports that "inmates are far from an integrated social body; for most inmates, strong ties with other inmates seemed either entirely absent, or were limited to a few other inmates only" (p. 91).

Prisoners adapt to their environment in a number of ways. Some become leaders and come to feel more comfortable inside the prison than they did in the outside world. Others simply pass the time, avoiding any trouble, but never really make a place for themselves in the prison. Still others decide to take advantage of their circumstances and improve themselves. These inmates try to spend time learning, reading, and studying. But often, they are thwarted in their efforts. Malcolm X, for example, was an avid reader while in jail:

When I had progressed to really serious reading, every night at about ten P.M. I would be outraged with the "lights out." It always seemed to catch me right in the middle of something engrossing.

Fortunately, right outside my door was a corridor light that cast a glow into my room. The glow was enough to read by, once my eyes adjusted to it. So when "lights out" came, I would sit on the floor where I could continue reading in that glow. (cited in Irwin, 1972, p. 185)

Outcome of the Prison Experience

The traditional method for measuring the success of prison rehabilitation efforts is the rate of *recidivism*, that is, the probability that the offender will commit further crimes and eventually return to prison.

An analysis (Martinson, 1974) of over 200 studies on the effect of educational and vocational training, counseling, probation, and pa-

(Arthur Tress, Woodfin Camp & Associa

(*Marcia Keegan, Woodfin Camp & Associates.*)

(*Charles Gatewood.*)

The regimentation, boredom, and lack of privacy of prison life as depicted here often lead to behavior that would make little sense in the outside world.

role provides a gloomy picture of prison rehabilitation efforts. In fact, the author found little reason to assume that *any* rehabilitation scheme would achieve good results:

> This is not to say that we found no instances of success or partial success; it is only to say that these instances have been isolated, producing no clear pattern to indicate the efficacy of any particular method of treatment. (Martinson, 1974, p. 49)

If rehabilitation efforts don't affect recidivism rates, what does? In an attempt to determine which prisoners would be most likely to benefit from parole, the California Department of Corrections developed a statistical index known as the Base Expectancy Score or BES (Kassebaum, Ward, and Wilner, 1971). This index represents the likelihood that an inmate will become a successful parolee. Among the BES findings were:

The younger a man is at the time of his first arrest, the more likely he is to become a parole failure.

White parolees have the *best* chance of staying out of prison, while black parolees are the most likely to return. Mexican-Americans fall somewhere in the middle.

Individuals who were convicted of robbery and assault are among the most successful parolees; individuals who were convicted of serious narcotics offenses, forgery, and burglary are among the most likely to return to prison.

Group counseling treatment appears to have no significant impact on an inmate's success in dealing with parole.

Improving Prisons

One important alternative for making prison life a more useful and productive experience for inmates is the *therapeutic community* model, similar to those described in Chapter 11 for hospitalized schizophrenics (Sandhu, 1974). This type of community can be created in a small, treatment-oriented prison, or even in a special cell block of a large prison.

The basic concept behind the therapeutic community is to "therapeutize the environment" of a total institution. Among the techniques employed are frequent community meetings and the creation of a democratic structure for inmates. The therapeutic environment depends on continuous and warm contacts between prisoners and staff members. The staff must be cooperative, sincere, sympathetic, and honest. The use of punishment is discouraged in the therapeutic community. Instead, problems and grievances are aired openly, and attempts are made to build a workable consensus among all participants.

The therapeutic community model requires the active involvement of inmates in the community's decision making and goals. Even the most intelligent and committed staff cannot make the program work without full cooperation from the prisoners. Inmates must feel that the community is "theirs" in some meaningful way. They must believe that their views are important and that their participation is essential. If the staff is able to help construct an environment where inmates feel this way, the prisoners may develop a strong sense of responsibility for themselves and for others. It is hoped that this sense of responsibility will remain with the inmates after they are released.

Synanon is one of the best-known examples of such a therapeutic community. It was originally created as a voluntary care center for drug addicts who wanted to "kick the habit." Ex-addicts have often served as staff members. A Synanon house is governed by strict rules that must be observed by all members of the community. The central focus of community life is the small group meeting at which the strengths and weaknesses of each individual are examined. The atmosphere of these meetings is personal and intense, often resembling an encounter group. Some Synanon houses have demonstrated dramatic success in helping addicts to get off and stay off hard drugs.

Partial-release and *post-release* programs have become of increasing interest to mental health workers and corrections officials. A good example is the "halfway house," which represents a kind of supervised transitional stage for the offender. While living in the "halfway house," the offender, with the help of family members and counselors, can begin adjusting to greater freedom and the demands of the outside world. Unfortunately, there are few aftercare correctional programs to assist inmates. When he or she is released, the ex-offender typically still faces an immediate and sometimes traumatic adjustment from the total regimentation of prison life to the uncertainties of life outside.

Treatment Approaches

Psychodynamic Approaches

Psychodynamic approaches have not been particularly successful in treating the psychopathic individual. This is not surprising, given what we know about antisocial individuals. They usually see nothing wrong with their actions, and instead find them stimulating and rewarding. They are present-oriented and have little interest in the long-range consequences of their actions. Finally, they are incapable of the empathy and warmth needed for a serious, long-term relationship. All of these characteristics make antisocial people unlikely candidates for success in psychodynamic psychotherapy.

Thorne (1959) has offered a number of useful guidelines for successful psychodynamic therapy with the individual displaying antisocial behavior. Among these are:

1. The therapist must retain full control over the client's finances.
2. Relatives and close friends must not be allowed to "bail out" the client when he or she gets into trouble.
3. The client must be continually pressured to control his or her own behavior.
4. The therapist must not protect the client from the consequences of his or her actions—even legal consequences.
5. The therapist must take a clear stand that only the client's *actions* to change—and not *words*—will be taken seriously.

6. The therapist must be alert to point out the client's self-destructive behaviors.

Behavioral Approaches

In recent years, behavioral approaches to criminal offenders and other groups of difficult clients have had somewhat better success than psychodynamic approaches. As a result, the behavioral techniques have received increasing attention from mental health workers and criminologists. Among the most important of these experiments in behavioral techniques are Achievement Place, Case I and Case II, and community care prevention programs.

Achievement Place One of the most influential attempts at behavioral treatment of disturbed youths, Achievement Place, was begun in Lawrence, Kansas, in 1967. A small, family-style home was opened for adolescent boys who had been involved in academic failure, theft, vandalism, drug abuse, or aggressive actions. Since then, at least 15 such centers for adolescent boys and girls have been established across the nation. In most cases, the homes are supervised by two live-in "teaching parents."

The theory behind Achievement Place is that delinquent adolescents have not received the instructions, models, and feedback that they need in order to learn appropriate behavior patterns. It is hoped that in a program with clear and tangible behavior rewards, these youths will become more aware of the likely consequences of their actions.

The principal technique for reinforcing target behaviors is the token economy. Appropriate behaviors that the adolescents need to learn are identified. These behaviors are then operationalized, that is, stated in measurable terms. A point system is established to reward youths who exhibit these behaviors. O'Leary and Wilson (1975) report that one Achievement Place manual outlined 188 behaviors for which an individual could earn points.

Inappropriate behaviors are fined (see Table 13-2). The Achievement Place economy thus has both positive elements (earnings) and negative elements (fines). This allows for a

Box 13-2 The Variety of Treatment Approaches to Antisocial Behavior

A great many forms of training and therapy have been used in dealing with criminal offenders. Some of these forms are described below.

Educational Programs. Many imprisoned criminals are school dropouts with few learning skills. Their lack of education constitutes a serious liability in the outside world, which often results in unemployment and a return to crime. As a response to this problem, prisons may offer formal educational programs, as well as lectures, discussion groups, and films. Prison libraries can also serve as a crucial resource for inmates who wish to further their education.

Vocational Training Programs. Some prisons combine academic and vocational programs. In theory, this might be the ideal combination for many inmates. However, too many prison vocational training efforts fail to teach employable skills. The prison with training programs in computer key punching and data processing may be providing inmates with a genuine opportunity to find decent work after release. The prison that only instructs inmates in how to make road signs or license plates is not really helping them.

Reality Therapy. Reality therapy focuses on two basic needs of every individual: the need to feel love and be loved, and the need to feel worthwhile. The reality therapist works actively to help the client meet these needs. Instead of concentrating on interpretations of past events, the reality therapist is most interested in the "here-and-now." The goal is the development of a *sense of responsibility*, which is defined as the ability to satisfy one's own needs without interfering with the needs of others.

Rachin (1974) suggests that inmates who have not responded to other forms of therapy may find reality therapy much more suitable to their needs. This may be because the reality therapist attempts to show active concern for the client. Or it may reflect the therapist's refusal to label the client. Instead of categorizing the individual being treated, the reality therapist simply views particular behaviors as "responsible" or "irresponsible."

Logotherapy. The basic thinking underlying logotherapy is that life is worthwhile when an individual feels it has *meaning*, when the individual has a sense of *purpose*. This sense, of course, is not a common characteristic of prison inmates. Logotherapy uses special encounter techniques to assist the offender to find a deeper meaning in life.

Family Therapy. The problems of disturbed individuals often have roots in the family, and they certainly affect every family member in an important way. For these reasons, family therapists have elected to treat the individual's difficulties within the context of the entire family unit. Family therapy can help promote a supportive atmosphere for the inmate, which will be vitally important when he or she must reenter the outside world.

Rational-Emotive Therapy. The main premise of rational-emotive therapy is that the disturbed individual is acting out many illogical and self-destructive beliefs. The rational therapist attempts to assist the offender in seeing the illogic of his or her ideas and in developing a more realistic and healthy way of thinking.

Offender Therapy. Offender therapy is a branch of psychotherapy that centers specifically on the problems and needs of the *offender*. It is thus different from most therapies, whose methods were developed for the *neurotic* individual.

The goals of offender therapy are (1) cessation of law-breaking activities and (2) readjustment of the offender to a harmonious and productive life. The therapist generally takes a firm posture with the client, and avoids a permissive stance that may confuse him or her.

Based on Sandhu, H. S. *Modern corrections: The offenders, therapies and community reintegration.* Springfield, Ill.: Charles C Thomas, 1974.

Table 13-2 Behaviors and the Number of Points That They Earned or Lost

Behaviors That Earned Points	Number of Points Earned	Behaviors That Lost Points	Number of Points Lost
1. Watching news on TV or reading the newspaper	300 per day	1. Failing grades on the report card	500–1,000 per grade
2. Cleaning and maintaining neatness in one's room	500 per day	2. Speaking aggressively	20–50 per response
3. Keeping one's person neat and clean	500 per day	3. Forgetting to wash hands before meals	100–300 per meal
4. Reading books	5–10 per page	4. Arguing	300 per response
5. Aiding houseparents in various household tasks	20–1,000 per task	5. Disobeying	100–1,000 per response
6. Doing dishes	500–1,000 per meal	6. Being late	10 per minute
7. Being well dressed for an evening meal	100–500 per meal	7. Displaying poor manners	50–100 per response
8. Performing homework	500 per day	8. Engaging in poor posture	50–100 per response
9. Obtaining desirable grades on school report cards	500–1,000 per grade	9. Using poor grammar	20–50 per response
10. Turning out lights when not in use	25 per light	10. Stealing, lying, or cheating	10,000 per response

From Phillips, E. L. Achievement Place: Token reinforcement procedures in a home-style rehabilitation setting for "predelinquent" boys. *Journal of Applied Behavior Analysis*, 1968, *1*, 215.

very flexible reinforcement system (Phillips et al., 1971).

The purpose of collecting points is to buy privileges, such as a small monetary allowance; access to games, the television, or sporting equipment; special snacks; and permission to go home or downtown. When the youths accumulate sufficient net points (earnings minus fines), they can purchase a privilege for a specified amount of time. The economy is weighted so that typical house members can expect a satisfying amount of privileges if they demonstrate a good assortment of desirable behaviors and keep undesirable behaviors to a minimum.

Research on Achievement Place has demonstrated the effectiveness of this type of behavioral treatment. Phillips (1968) found that the point system acted to improve verbal behavior, bathroom tidiness, punctuality, homework preparation, and grammar. Phillips et al. (1971) noted significant improvement in promptness, room cleaning, saving of money, and accuracy of answers on a new quiz. A review by Burchard and Harig (1976) of 30 separate studies on Achievement Place concluded: "In over 90 percent of the experiments there was a significant change in the target behavior, and in each case that change was demonstrated to be a function of a particular intervention" (p. 425).

Trotter (1973) did a follow-up study of 16 adolescent boys from Achievement Place to assess the overall value of the program. The Achievement Place youths were contrasted with 15 boys from the Kansas Boys School (an institution with 250 youths) and with 13 boys placed on formal probation. Striking differences were found in terms of offenses per year after treatment ended, recidivism, and school attendance. In each category, the youths from Achievement Place were far superior to other groups of boys. Two years after release, the recidivism rate for Achievement Place boys was 19 percent, as compared with 53 percent for boys from the Kansas Boys School and 54 percent for those on probation.

A further advantage of Achievement Place is its relatively low cost. The yearly operating cost of a traditional institution in Kansas is roughly $9,800 per youth; for Achievement Place, the cost is approximately $4,100 per youth (O'Leary and Wilson, 1975).

Case I and Case II Case I was established at the National Training School for Boys in Washington, D.C., by architect Harold Cohen and his colleagues. It represented one of the first behavior modification programs attempted within an institutional setting (Burchard and Harig, 1976).

Cohen's belief was that traditional academic reinforcers (grades, promotions, etc.) would not motivate the high school dropouts with serious criminal records who populated the National Training School. He hoped to encourage academic learning through a system of rewards that would be meaningful to the inmates. Among these were time in the lounge (which had a jukebox and television), use of the telephone, and picking out items from a Sears, Roebuck catalog. To receive points that would lead to privileges, the youths had to demonstrate 90 percent accuracy on programmed academic materials.

Case I proved to be an effective pilot project. The youths developed more favorable attitudes toward learning and made significant academic advances. As a result, the Case staff expanded the Case I model into a 24-hour per day, seven-day per week supervised program known as Case II.

The primary objective of Case II was to "develop procedures that could be used to establish and maintain educational behaviors in a controlled penal setting" (Cohen and Filipczak, 1971, p. 182). Twenty-five adolescent inmates from the National Training School were immersed in a totally controlled educational environment based on extrinsic reinforcements. Among the rewards that "students" could earn for academic performance were private rooms, special meals, clothing, and room furnishings.

The Case II educational program was voluntary and tailored to the individual's particular needs. As Cohen and Filipczak (1971) described it: "The model for the project was that of a student research employee who checks in and out of the various activities for which he is paid or for which he pays. The boys were actually hired to do a job" (p. 184). In most situations, the payoff (points) depended on 90 percent performance on the material, but students could also earn points simply by studying or participating in academic seminars.

A number of encouraging findings in areas such as standardized testing and mean IQ scores were reported for the Case II experiments. In each case, the students registered significant gains, averaging an improvement of one or two grade levels during their eight months in the program.

Cohen and Filipczak (1971) offer important conclusions on what they see as the "intangible results" of Case II. In their view, the program was successful with National Training School inmates because it gave them an opportunity to make decisions on their own. Students developed a new sense of self-worth. In part, this was a result of the pride of ownership that was enhanced by the "privileges" earned in the program. Furthermore, the inmates came to the realization that they *could* change their lives. The frequent question, "What's in it for me?" was, for once, answered for these youths. There *was* "something in it for them" in Case II. Through academic learning, they could earn material privileges that made a real difference in their lives. And in the process of earning and learning, they could build up internal strengths, self-control, and a belief in their own abilities.

Case II students had a much lower recidivism rate than typical inmates of the National Training School during their first year after release. But by the third year after release, the differential between the two groups had narrowed greatly (O'Leary and Wilson, 1975). This may reflect the need for follow-up programs for youths who have been successful in controlled behavior modification environments.

Community care prevention programs
Achievement Place and the Case programs are examples of behavioral treatment approaches within controlled institutional environments. Community care prevention programs also rely on behavioral methods, but they attempt to alter youths' undesirable behaviors within their natural environment.

The Social Learning Project developed by Patterson and his associates (1968, 1973) is one of the best-known community care programs. Younger children, aged 6 through 13, are the targets of this behavioral program. The goal is to help them change their behavior *before* they become delinquents, rather than to rehabilitate these youths *afterward*.

Typical of Patterson's social engineering approach is the case of an 11-year-old hyperactive boy (Patterson, Ray, and Shaw, 1968). Patterson first taught the boy's father to use positive reinforcers (such as praise and approval) to control his son's behavior. Other members of the family were instructed to observe the father's behavior and to reward him for interacting appropriately with his son. In addition, Patterson asked the father to withhold criticism of other family members. Thus, instead of isolating the son's behavior and treating it directly, Patterson attempted to reorient the behaviors of *all* family members and involve each of them in the son's behavior training.

These "social engineering" methods were later applied in dealing with a few families of aggressive and coercive young boys (Patterson, Cobb, and Ray, 1973). The parents went through a four-stage training process:

1. They studied a programmed textbook to gain a basic understanding of the behavior theory.

2. They were taught to pinpoint target behaviors and to collect data on the boys' behaviors.

3. A parent group was established to teach management techniques, practice role-playing exercises, and reinforce the parents' data-keeping work.

4. After 10–12 weeks in the group, parents received home consultations from the project staff.

Parents were trained both in the use of token point systems and in the negotiation of behavior contracts with their children. Each parent group included three or four sets of parents and met weekly for about two hours. During this time, a specified period (generally 30 minutes) was devoted to each child and family.

Patterson and his colleagues were able to gather follow-up data on 9 of the 13 families. They found a significant decline in the frequency of the targeted undesirable behaviors. However, this positive change did not carry over into untargeted undesirable behaviors.

Evaluative review
Davidson and Seidman (1974) conducted a wide-ranging survey of the use and effect of behavior modification techniques with juvenile delinquents. In general, they found that such approaches have improved the educational behaviors, program behaviors, and nondelinquent behaviors of disturbed youths.

These researchers suggest, however, that behavior modification studies must be examined with extreme caution. There are many serious methodological weaknesses in the behavioral experiments. Eighty-two percent of the programs failed to include equivalent delinquent control groups who were *not* receiving behavioral treatment. Only 18 percent of the studies presented follow-up data. Furthermore, few researchers have examined seriously the possibility that they may be biased in their data collection.

These and other methodological flaws severely limit the usefulness of behavior modification research. It can be asserted with some justification that behavioral technology has led to noticeable (and in some cases impressive) improvements in the behavior of juvenile delinquents. Yet, as Davidson and Seidman argue, "Research of better quality is sorely needed" (p. 1009).

Interestingly, there is evidence that the behavior of antisocials may improve spontaneously with age. Research by Robins (1966) indicates that the range and severity of antisocial behaviors may diminish when the individual is between 30 and 40 years of age. This finding brings to mind the surveys discussed in Chapter 6 that suggested that disturbed individuals who undergo psychotherapy may have no better prognosis than those who are *not* treated. Until more systematic data are available, it will be impossible to make definitive statements about which programs, if any, work.

Summary

There are three principal categories of antisocial behavior—*antisocial personality* (or psychopathy), *dyssocial behavior*, and *juvenile delinquency*. Various biological, sociological, and psychological theories have been advanced to account for each of these types of behavior.

The psychopath, the dyssocial individual, and the juvenile delinquent are all likely to violate the law at some point in their lives. Such actions will bring them into contact with the *criminal-legal system*. In the past, the criminal-legal system tended toward retaliatory or exploitative forms of punishment. In recent decades, a more treatment-oriented approach to the offender has emerged.

Prison life is characterized by extreme boredom and regimentation. The inmate has virtually no privacy. Many rehabilitative efforts have been introduced to assist inmates, but few have significantly altered the rate of recidivism.

Because of the failures of psychodynamic treatment approaches for the offender, there has been an increasing interest in behavior modification programs such as Achievement Place and Case II. While certain behavioral experiments seem to have registered impressive results, there are enough methodological weaknesses in the research to make the results more suggestive than definitive.

Addiction and dependence: Alcoholism, drug abuse, overeating, and smoking

For most people, pleasurable activities such as eating, drinking alcohol, and smoking are recreations that they indulge in with moderation. Most of us overindulge in at least one of these occasionally and suffer the consequences. For some, however, the overindulgence becomes a way of life. For these people, the activity emerges as *central* to their existence, and a source of difficulty for themselves and those around them.

Many people wonder how an intelligent person can become "hooked" on alcohol or drugs. In some ways, it is harder to understand how anyone avoids overindulgences of one sort or another. Haven't we all overdone it at times? Fortunately (although we may not think so at the time), the morning after eventually arrives and with it the aftereffects of our overindulgence. It is these unpleasant aftereffects, however, that usually encourage us not to overindulge again. They serve as negative consequences that modify our future behavior.

Unfortunately, some individuals continue and even increase their consumption *despite* the enormous discomforts, losses, pain, and guilt. The negative outcomes *do not* moderate their behavior. These are the people who eventually become dependent on what were once simply pleasurable ways of passing the time.

Alcoholism

It is extremely difficult to make accurate estimates of the incidence and prevalence of alcoholism. When you think of an alcoholic, your first thought is probably of a "skid-row bum." But most American alcoholics are not "winos" who live on the streets. Many live in traditional family arrangements and continue to function within the work force. Thus the most visible alcoholics are only the "tip of the iceberg" of a far more extensive social problem.

One frequently cited estimate is that there are 10 million alcoholics in the United States. There are both higher and lower estimates offered by various observers. The differences in the statistics reflect the absence of reliable sources of information. Nevertheless, the 10 million figure seems to be a reasonable guess.

It is believed that 5 percent of the nation's work force are alcoholics, while another 5 percent can be categorized as "serious abusers of alcohol." Nearly half of the arrests that occur each year involve public intoxication, drunken driving, disorderly conduct, and other offenses affected by alcohol usage.

Nature of Alcoholism

Alcoholic behavior would seem to be simple to describe—the taking in of excessive amounts of alcohol with resulting inebriation, or drunkenness, and related problems. But it is much more complicated than this. The "falling down" drunk is the exception rather than the rule among alcoholics.

Physiological Effects of Alcohol

When people drink, alcohol enters their bloodstream through the mucous membranes and lungs. The blood then transmits the alcohol to the brain and other organs of the body. Most of the alcohol will be broken down (metabolized) in the liver.

Alcohol acts as a *depressant* on the central nervous system. Common effects of drinking depend primarily on the concentration of alcohol in the body, as well as the individual's familiarity with high levels of alcohol. At a level of 0.05 percent alcohol in the blood (2 average-sized drinks), thought, judgment, and restraint can be disrupted. At 0.10 percent (4 drinks, the definition of an intoxicated driver in most states), voluntary motor actions become more difficult to control. At 0.20 percent, the entire motor area of the brain is adversely affected. At a level of 0.40 or 0.50 percent, the person will enter a coma.

How to Define Alcoholism

What are the most appropriate and meaningful definitions of *normal drinking, excessive drinking,* and *alcoholism?* Chafetz and his co-workers (1974) offer a wide-ranging definition: "Alcoholism is any drinking behavior that is associated with dysfunction in a person's life" (p. 368).

The DSM-II describes alcoholics as those patients "whose alcohol intake is great enough to damage their physical health, or their personal or social functioning, or when it has become a prerequisite to normal functioning" (American Psychological Association, 1968, p. 45).

Following along these lines, Nathan (1976) provides five detailed criteria for determining the severity of a drinking problem:

1. Individuals exhibit a "loss of control" of drinking behavior.

2. They have an almost overwhelming need for alcohol to start the day or get through it (psychological dependence).

3. They have painful withdrawal symptoms (such as nausea or vomiting) when they stop drinking (physical dependence).

4. They have lost jobs, family, or friends as a result of their drinking.

5. They experience "blackouts" or a growing tolerance for alcohol.

Clinical Effects of Alcoholism

The most common biological consequences of alcoholism include brain damage and liver damage. Cirrhosis of the liver, a disease that does irreversible damage, frequently results from heavy drinking over a long period of time. Studies are underway to examine possible correlations with various types of cancer and heart disease.

The psychological consequences of alcoholism vary widely. They can include guilt, aggressive behavior, remorse, apathy, irresponsibility, impaired thinking, fear, and self-loathing. Often, alcoholics exhibit *denial* and will go to great lengths to prove that they do not have a drinking problem. Alcoholism can lead to particularly destructive consequences within the family, such as violent behavior against a spouse or child, strained sexual relationships, and ultimately, separation or divorce.

In certain cases, alcoholism may coincide with the appearance of acute psychotic-like states. The following are among the most significant of these "alcoholic psychoses."

1. *Blackouts.* Chronic drinkers often experience blackouts. These are states of amnesia in which the individuals function quite normally, but once the state is over, they remember nothing of what happened during it. Periodic blackouts may be an early symptom of alcoholism. The drinkers may regain consciousness in a bar or club and be unable to remember having gone there in the first place!

2. *Korsakoff's psychosis.* This alcoholic syndrome is related to nutritional deficiencies, particularly of thiamine and niacin. Korsakoff patients suffer from amnesia, falsification of memory, and time disorientation. When asked questions about events in the distant past, they will cheerfully produce coherent but fabricated answers.

3. *Delirium tremens (D.T.'s).* Chronic alcoholics may experience "D.T.'s" after a long period of drinking. The condition generally occurs over a three- to ten-day period. The individuals cannot sleep and are confused about time and place. They are restless and irritable, and show unusual motor activity. At the worst moments of delirium, they have frequent and terrifying hallucinations. They may see menacing animals or insects, such as rats or crawling bugs. The patients will become panicky and may make desperate efforts to "escape" the pursuit of these creatures.

4. *Wernicke's syndrome.* This syndrome is an unusual condition that is most likely to occur in chronic alcoholics. The symptoms include delirium, memory loss, and, in some cases, coma. Like Korsakoff's psychosis, Wernicke's syndrome is related to nutritional deficiencies—especially lack of thiamine.

5. *Alcoholic deterioration.* Heavy drinking over a period of many years leads to noticeable personality disintegration. At first, the alcoholics may tend toward impulsive behavior and feelings of resentment and hostility. Eventually, they lose ambition and any sense of responsibility to themselves or others. Their mood can instantly swing from unjustified joviality to violent outbursts. The patients become irritable and cannot focus their attention for long. Their memory begins to deteriorate, and extreme loss of mental powers may result.

Stages of Alcoholism

Many investigators of alcohol addiction have suggested that there may be stages in the development of full-scale alcoholism (see Box 14–1). Knowledge of such stages could aid attempts to intervene at an early point in an individual's emerging drinking problem.

Jellinek (1952) developed a four-stage model of alcoholism: prealcoholic, prodromal, crucial, and chronic. In the *prealcoholic* phase,

Box 14-1   The Phases of Alcoholism

Prealcoholic Phase
Prodromal (Precursory) Phase

1. Alcoholic amnesias
2. Surreptitious drinking
3. Preoccupation with alcohol
4. Avid drinking
5. Guilt feelings
6. Reference to alcohol avoided
7. Alcoholic amnesias more frequent

Crucial Phase

8. Uncontrolled alcoholic intake
9. Drinking behavior rationalized
10. Prohibitionary appeals countered
11. Grandiose behavior
12. Marked aggressive behavior
13. Persistent remorse
14. Temporary total abstinence
15. Drinking pattern modified
16. Friends avoided
17. Job left
18. Alcohol-centered behavior
19. Outside interests abandoned
20. Interpersonal relations avoided
21. Marked self-pity
22. Escape from home

23. Family abandoned
24. Unreasonable resentments
25. Alcohol hoarded
26. Nutrition neglected
27. First hospitalization
28. Decreased sexual interest
29. Unfounded jealousies
30. Regular morning drinking

Chronic Phase

31. Prolonged intoxications ("benders")
32. Ethical code deterioration
33. Thinking impaired
34. Alcoholic psychoses (delirium tremens)
35. Low-status drinking partners
36. Poisonous alcoholic substitutes
37. Partial reduction of tolerance
38. Undefined fears
39. Tremors
40. Psychomotor inhibition
41. Obsessive drinking
42. Vague religious feelings
43. Rationalization system failure, addiction admitted

From Cohen, J. *Secondary motivation. 1. Personal motives.* Chicago: Rand McNally, 1970; based on Jellinek, E. M. Phases of alcohol addiction. *Quarterly Journal of Studies on Alcohol,* 1952, 13, 673–684.

the drinkers are usually in the company of others. They show psychological dependence on alcohol. Their thoughts are clouded while drinking, and their inhibitions disappear. In the *prodromal* phase, the drinkers have developed a high tolerance for alcohol. They often drink from hidden bottles in an intense pursuit of the "jolts" of an alcoholic "high."

In the *crucial* phase of alcoholism, the drinker generally is alone, and consistently imbibes more than he planned. He experiences frequent hangovers, and turns to even more alcohol to "cure" his hangover symptoms. By the end of this phase, he needs a drink just to start the day. Once he reaches this point, he is near the *chronic* phase. In this last phase of alcoholism, the drinker may be intoxicated for weeks. He suffers extreme symptoms of physiological dependence, such as tremors, violent vomiting fits, spasms, and the hallucinations of *delirium tremens.* These symptoms usually lead to hospitalization.

Patterns of Alcohol Abuse

Another focus in the study of alcoholism has been on different *styles* of drinking. Chafetz and his colleagues (1974) present four common patterns of drinking. The *fluctuating state* is the most common drinking pattern in the United States. Drinkers may get intoxicated only on weekends, only during parties, or only during periods of stress. Whatever their off-and-on pattern, their drinking is primarily an escape valve for built-up tensions. In the *downward spiral*, individuals develop an increasing psychological and physiological dependence on alcohol. Their work and family life deteriorate. They run the risk of total collapse or emergence as derelicts. By contrast, *steady state* drinkers show no such downward spiral. They may drink large quantities of alcohol as a routine while functioning adequately at work and at home. Some observers might categorize them as social drinkers, yet alcohol plays a vital and potentially dangerous role in their lives.

Spontaneous recovery is experienced by as many as one-third of all heavy drinkers. At some time, for a variety of reasons, they may simply stop drinking, or they may successfully restrict themselves to social drinking.

One study (Nathan and O'Brien, 1971) compared the social and drinking behavior of four skid-row alcoholics and four nonalcoholics over 33-day periods. Alcoholics were found to drink almost twice as much as nonalcoholics. The skid-row alcoholics were found to be social isolates who were depressed and hostile during drinking. Whether drunk or sober, they were usually alone, whereas the nonalcoholics were more likely to drink while talking and eating at bars.

Causal, Contributing, and Maintaining Factors of Alcoholism

As with most of the abnormal behaviors we discuss in this text, there are widely divergent theories about the factors that are influential in causing, contributing to, and maintaining alcoholism. Since alcoholism is such a serious social problem, with complex medical, economic, legal, and moral dimensions, it is essential to understand these factors if we are to respond appropriately to this problem.

Psychodynamic Theories

Freud saw alcoholism as the culmination of severe oral dependency problems. Alcohol serves as a means of escaping the problems that result from oral fixation: sexual immaturity, depression, and wishes to be dependent.

Kolb (1973) expanded Freud's theory, stating that the alcoholic generally had an overprotective parent and was allowed to become a passive-dependent child, and thus fixated at the oral stage. In some cases, the *mother* was overindulgent, as one response to the father's coldness and brutality toward her. In other families, the *father* may have been inconsistent in his treatment of the child: sometimes strict, sometimes permissive.

Adler (1941) explained alcoholism as a reaction to a pervasive feeling of inferiority. In this view, alcoholics are often shy, isolated, depressed, and hypersensitive. They experience constant anxiety because of the demands of adult life, and use alcohol as one way of avoiding responsibility.

Others (e.g., Menninger, 1938) have viewed alcoholism as a hostile, aggressive, self-destructive act. Alcoholics are seen as experiencing intense anger toward their parents for failing to satisfy their need for oral gratification. They are unable to come to terms with their anger, and feel guilty about their desire to destroy their parents. The guilt is channeled into angry and self-destructive actions through the stimulus of alcohol.

Behavioral-Learning Approaches

The main emphasis of the social learning approach to alcoholism has been to examine the learning contingencies that contribute to the drinking behavior of the alcoholic.

As we noted, alcohol is a central nervous system depressant. It reduces the drinker's anxiety, frustration, and depression. The individual's self-critical responses are also diminished. The anxiety reduction then has a reinforcing effect. Furthermore, the immediate effects of the alcohol tend to be pleasant, whereas many of the negative consequences of alcoholism (family problems, loss of employment, arrests) are delayed. Finally, because of "blackouts," many alcoholics do not remember the aversive consequences that occur while they are drinking.

A number of important studies have been conducted on the effects of alcohol in "conflict" situations. Masserman and his associates (Masserman, Jacques, and Nicholson, 1945; Masserman and Yum, 1966) trained cats to feed themselves by throwing a switch to gain access to food. When they threw the switch, however, they were punished with shocks and blasts of air. This created a conflict for the cats between their hunger and their fear of punishment. Various neurotic behaviors resulted, including feeding problems and phobic responses to light and sound. When the cats were given alcohol, they overcame their fears and were again able to operate the switch system on a normal schedule for feeding.

However, more recent research casts doubts on the tension-reducing quality of alcohol. Studies by Nathan and O'Brien (1971) and by Okulitch and Marlatt (1972) have found that alcohol leads to an eventual *increase* in the alcoholic's level of anxiety (after a modest decrease during the initial 12 to 24 hours of drinking). These findings suggest that the anxiety-reduction theory of alcoholism is more complex than was previously believed.

Nathan and his co-workers (1970) studied experimentally induced drinking among chronic alcoholic patients. A programmed laboratory ward environment was created with closed-circuit television surveillance of all rooms, and space for either isolation or group interaction. When the subjects were sober, they claimed that they used alcohol to decrease anxiety and depression. However, after drinking for a number of hours, the patients exhibited *increased* anxiety and depression, and even reported these feelings themselves.

Biophysical Factors

Alcohol is an addictive drug. When individuals drink large quantities of alcohol over a long period of time, they develop both tolerance and physical dependence. By *tolerance*, we mean that they need increasing amounts of alcohol to achieve the same effects. *Physical dependence* means simply that the individuals will react physically if they cease drinking, that is, they will suffer withdrawal symptoms. Tolerance and physical dependence are important indicators of addiction to any drug or foreign substance.

Many researchers have speculated about the possibility of a genetic metabolic base for alcoholism. It has been theorized, for example, that alcoholism might result from a genetically transferred nutritional deficiency (Williams, 1951). An inherited metabolic defect could possibly account for the alcoholic's abnormal craving for liquor.

Goodwin and his colleagues (Goodwin and Guze, 1974; Goodwin et al., 1973; Schukit, Goodwin, and Winokur, 1972) conducted an instructive study of adopted children in Denmark who showed a high-risk potential for alcoholism. The children whose natural parents were alcoholics were found to have a significantly *greater* likelihood of becoming alcoholics than a control group of adopted children whose natural parents did not have drinking problems. However, the impact of this finding was diminished somewhat because the control group included a higher incidence of people classified as "heavy drinkers" than the experimental group (Chafetz et al., 1974).

Sociocultural Factors

A number of studies have suggested particular religious and ethnic patterns with respect to alcoholism. For example, Catholics appear to drink more heavily than Protestants, and liberal Protestants seem more inclined to alcohol than fundamentalist Protestants. Jews, Italians, Chinese, and Greeks are less prone to alcoholism.

There are many stages and patterns of alcoholism. In the crucial stage, the alcoholic generally drinks alone and needs a drink just to start the day. In the chronic phase, the drinker may be intoxicated for weeks and, through a downward spiral, end up a skid-row bum.

(*Joel Gordon.*)

(*Jim Anderson, Woodfin Camp & Associates.*)

In the past 15 years, there have been increasing signs that American women are becoming more frequent victims of alcoholism. Research data indicate that female alcoholics begin heavy drinking at a later age than male alcoholics, but become alcoholics more quickly (Chafetz et al., 1974). Furthermore, for alcoholic women the intoxicated behavior is more intense and its effect more devastating than for alcoholic men (Hirsh, 1962). More female than male alcoholics make suicide attempts, and, unlike nonalcoholics, more female than male alcoholics succeed in ending their lives.

Treatment Approaches

The Acute Treatment Phase

The treatment approaches described in this section are principally those designed for long-term change in the alcoholic's drinking problem. The first phase of treatment is vitally important. The alcoholic may experience severe withdrawal symptoms during the initial period. If these are not handled properly, the individual may return to drinking to reduce the unpleasant effects of withdrawal.

Therefore, the so-called "drying-out" phase of treatment requires a combination of biological and psychological supports that will correspond to the physiological and psychological dependences that have characterized alcohol abuse. A supportive therapeutic contact at this early stage of treatment may encourage individuals to seek out rehabilitative assistance if they need it in the future.

Two critical priorities in the acute treatment phase are the prevention of Wernicke's syndrome and the prevention of delirium tremens. If the alcoholic is undernourished, massive doses of thiamine and other B vitamins will be helpful in preventing Wernicke's syndrome. Management of delirium tremens involves giving special attention to the patient during the time of onset—roughly 72 to 96 hours after alcohol is withdrawn. The patient must drink a good deal of liquid to avoid dehydration, and electrolyte imbalances must be corrected. There is a chance of death unless these measures are taken. In fact, about 15 percent of all untreated victims of the "D.T.'s" die (Chafetz et al., 1974).

Drug therapy is commonly used in the acute phase of treatment. If the patient does not need to be institutionalized, a minor tranquilizer such as Librium may be recommended.

Psychodynamic Approaches

The basic psychodynamic approach to long-term treatment of alcoholism is to view alcoholism as "a psychic illness rooted in a personality disorder or immaturity" (Kolb, 1973, p. 219). In this view, the problem is largely unconscious. Patients are unaware of the deep-rooted problems that have led to alcoholism as an intended escape and relief. The solution to the patients' problem is not simply to restrain them from the use of alcohol, but to relieve them of the desire to drink. To achieve

this goal, the therapist must successfully treat the personal problems that created the desire for alcohol.

This does not mean, however, that the patients must undergo psychoanalysis. In fact, almost all psychodynamic therapists, including Freud, advise against the use of orthodox analytic techniques in treating alcoholics. Alcoholics are thought to be unstable and unable to deal with stress. When alcoholics remember painful experiences, they are likely to resume drinking. Thus alternatives to orthodox techniques must be found for treating such patients. In general, most successful therapists seem to share characteristics such as empathy and unconditional warmth, qualities we noted in Chapter 6 as central to all good therapy.

Behavioral Approaches

Behavioral approaches to alcoholism can be separated into two categories—respondent approaches and operant approaches. A comprehensive treatment program usually involves several different procedures from both groups.

Respondent approaches The principal respondent approach to alcoholism involves *aversion therapy*. The goal of this procedure is to make the pleasant stimulus of alcohol become *unpleasant* by associating it with noxious stimuli. Three common types of aversion therapy are chemical aversion therapy, electrical aversion procedures, and covert sensitization.

In *chemical aversion therapy*, a connection is made between alcohol and the unpleasant physical effects of a chemical. One of the best-known examples of chemical aversion therapy is the work of Voegtlin and his associate (Voegtlin, 1940; Lemere and Voegtlin, 1950).

The treatment procedures were spread over a ten-day period. The alcoholic was given a dose of a nausea-producing drug and was asked to concentrate on the sight, smell, and thought of an ounce of whiskey. The subject next tasted and drank the whiskey, and then was given additional whiskey mixed with warm water until vomiting occurred. Finally, the subject was given a glass of beer mixed with a drug that prolonged the nausea. The entire procedure was then repeated. All treatment sessions were held in a darkened, soundproof room with an absolute minimum of other stimuli.

A detailed and long-term follow-up study was conducted (Lemere and Voegtlin, 1950). The researchers reported an overall abstinence rate of 51 percent over a follow-up period of 1 to 10 years. Further breakdown of the statistics indicates, however, that while 60 percent of the subjects abstained for 1 to 2 years, only 23 percent were still "dry" 10 to 13 years later.

Using similar techniques, Raymond (1964) injected alcoholics with nausea-producing drugs and then had them drink a small amount of alcohol just before nausea set in. Once the nausea subsided, the patient was prevented from drinking and was told repeatedly of the harmful consequences of alcohol abuse. Some indications of aversive reaction to alcohol generally appeared after ten days of treatment. At this point, certain "choice" situations were introduced into the procedure. The patient was allowed to select a soft drink instead of an alcoholic beverage. Later, patients were placed on *Antabuse therapy*. Antabuse is a drug that causes discomfort when combined with alcohol. We will discuss antabuse therapy shortly.

In a controversial use of aversion therapy, Sanderson, Campbell, and Laverty (1963) injected unknowing patients with a paralyzing drug. The timing of the drug coincided with the offering of alcohol. Just as the patients were about to start drinking, they became totally paralyzed. They were unable to move or breathe for more than a minute, although their intellectual and emotional faculties continued to function normally.

This terrifying (although medically safe) experiment has been strongly attacked by other behavioral psychologists. O'Leary and Wilson (1975) refer to this work as "a deplorable example of unacceptable ethical standards in the practice of behavior therapy in that the clients were unprepared for the intensely harrowing experience they suffered" (p. 359).

Electrical aversion experiments rely on the same basic principles as chemical aversion therapy, but here the aversive agent is electrical stimulation. This technique is more easily controlled, more quickly administered, and generally a more favorable procedure than chemical aversion.

In one study (Blake, 1965), subjects were asked to sip (but not swallow) their favorite alcoholic beverage. An electric shock of increasing intensity was paired with the sip. When the subject spit out the beverage, the shock was ended abruptly. A second group of subjects were given both electrical aversion conditioning and relaxation therapy.

The same investigator (Blake, 1967) conducted a one-year follow-up study of both sets of alcoholics. Of the clients who underwent both aversion conditioning and relaxation therapy, 46 percent were abstinent, 13 percent were improved, 30 percent had relapsed. The rest were unaccounted for. Of those who received only aversion conditioning, 23 percent were abstinent, 27 percent were improved, 27 percent had relapsed, and 23 percent were unaccounted for. At first glance, these results may seem quite favorable, especially when both aversion and relaxation techniques are combined. However, most of the clients in this study were upper-class and fee-paying. These patients are generally the most successful in any alcoholism programs. Therefore, without a meaningful control group, it is difficult to assess the impact of Blake's findings (O'Leary and Wilson, 1975).

Wilson, Leaf, and Nathan (1975) developed a closely controlled laboratory experiment with electrical aversion procedures. Four chronic alcoholics were allowed unrestricted alcohol intake in a three-day baseline drinking period. The experimenters then used electrical aversion techniques in a number of escape conditioning trials. The results were generally unfavorable. Only one of the subjects significantly reduced his drinking after escape conditioning treatment. One week later, this drinker reverted to heavy alcoholic intake and was hospitalized.

One of the most serious problems with

aversion therapy techniques—whether electrical or chemical—is their reliance on a strong aversive stimulus. This necessarily introduces an element of medical risk, even if only a minor one, into the therapeutic treatment. Aversion therapy may also require costly machines and laboratory space.

With these problems in mind, Cautela (1966, 1967) devised the method of treatment known as *covert sensitization*, which we discussed in Chapter 7. As you will remember, the key to his technique is the use of *imagined* aversive stimuli instead of an actual chemical or electrical agent.

First, alcoholic patients are instructed in the goals and methods of the treatment program. Then they are asked to imagine in elaborate detail the pleasures of drinking alcohol and the disgusting feelings of vomiting (see Box 14-2). The aim is to establish gradually a link in the patients' minds among alcohol, nausea, and vomiting. The therapeutic staff makes a deliberate effort to induce vomiting *after* the alcohol is visualized but *before* the patient imagines reaching for it.

Ashem and Donner (1968) used covert sensitization techniques in treating 23 male long-term alcoholics who had voluntarily committed themselves for six weeks of therapy. A six-month follow-up study was then undertaken. It was determined that no members of a control group had stopped drinking; by contrast, 40 percent of the alcoholics in the treatment program had abstained.

Covert sensitization has a number of important advantages over other aversive treatment methods. Because the unpleasant stimulus is *imaginary*, it can be specifically tailored to the history and feelings of particular patients. Furthermore, covert sensitization opens up the possibility of simple self-therapy. Alcoholics who learn the technique can continue to condition themselves to an aversion to alcohol. They do not need to be hooked up to a laboratory machine. Unfortunately, long-term follow-up studies have yet to be conducted.

Operant approaches Operant approaches to treatment for alcoholism are based on the premise that drinking behavior can be modified by changing the consequences for that behavior. Hunt and Azrin (1973) originated the "community reinforcement" approach to alcoholism. The theory behind this technique is that alcoholics will stop drinking when their positive reinforcement is significantly diminished. Important relationships with family, friends, and co-workers can serve as a deterrent to alcoholism, particularly if alcoholics realize that their drinking will interfere with and possibly destroy these relationships.

To test out this approach, Hunt and Azrin selected 16 hospitalized alcoholics, who were assigned either to a community reinforcement

---

Box 14-2 Covert Sensitization—An Example

The alcoholic patient in a covert sensitization program lies down and closes his or her eyes. The therapist verbalizes an aversive scene for the patient:

You are walking into a bar. You decide to have a glass of beer. You are now walking toward the bar. As you are approaching the bar you have a funny feeling in the pit of your stomach. Your stomach feels all queasy and nauseous. Some liquid comes up your throat and it is very sour. You try to swallow it back down, but as you do this, food particles start coming up your throat to your mouth. You are now reaching the bar and you order a beer. As the bartender is pouring the beer, puke comes into your mouth. . . . As soon as your hand touches the glass, you can't hold it down any longer. You have to open your mouth and you puke. It goes all over your hand, all over the glass and the beer. You can see it floating around in the beer. . . .

From Cautela, J. R. The treatment of alcoholism by covert sensitization. *Psychotherapy: Theory, Research, and Practice,* 1970, 7, 87.

Box 14-3 Mixed Behavioral Approaches to Alcoholism

Lazarus (1965) first introduced the concept of "broad-spectrum behavior therapy," an approach to the treatment of alcoholism that has been widely accepted over the past several years. Lazarus believes that rehabilitation of the alcoholic requires a *synthesis* of various treatment approaches. Among the major elements of his broad-spectrum approach are:

1. Medical care to restore physical health.

2. Aversion therapy and anxiety relief conditioning to eliminate drinking behavior.

3. Tests and interviews to help determine the anxiety hierarchies of the patient.

4. Systematic desensitization, assertive training, behavior rehearsal, and hypnosis to encourage better "anxiety-response habits."

5. Cooperative dealings with the patient's spouse.

The broad-spectrum approach introduced by Lazarus has been further refined by McBrearty and his associates (1968). They view drinking behavior as merely one part of a complex behavior chain. In order to eliminate alcoholism, the treatment program must pinpoint the crucial links in the drinker's behavior chain and must establish reconditioning procedures.

For example, let us imagine an alcoholic housewife who always begins drinking roughly an hour before her husband returns home from work. Her anxiety about seeing him at the end of the day can be understood as an immediate antecedent to drinking behavior. Her drinking behavior must be eliminated; but to do so, she must be helped to find another way of dealing with her anxiety.

McBrearty has originated a broad-spectrum treatment program in a number of state hospitals in Pennsylvania. The principal phases of the program are:

1. Didactic training for behavioral change: Group meetings at which patients can discuss the principles of behavior modification.

2. Aversive conditioning procedures.

3. Relaxation procedures.

4. Desensitization procedures.

5. Training in areas of behavior deficit.

6. Application of contingent reinforcement procedures. This often involves the use of behavior engineering or token economy systems.

---

program or to normal hospital treatment programs. The community program included employment counseling, assistance in locating work, and training in social and behavioral skills. Most important, vocational, recreational, social, and familial reinforcers contingent on nondrinking behavior were developed for each alcoholic. Further counseling was provided after these patients left the hospital.

A six-month follow-up study indicated that the community reinforcement treatment program had tangible beneficial effects. As compared with the control group, those for whom community reinforcers were developed were much more successful in coping with day-to-day life. They were spending less time drinking, earning more money, and participating in more meaningful social activities outside the home.

Unfortunately, the results of Hunt and Azrin's study are not conclusive. Patients in the experimental group received much more therapy than those in the control group. Therefore, it is difficult to evaluate the effectiveness of the community reinforcement approach relative to normal hospital treatment programs.

Other Approaches

Alcoholics Anonymous Perhaps the most famous approach to treating the problem drinker is Alcoholics Anonymous (AA). The main emphasis is to involve alcoholics in helping each other to stop drinking. Former alcoholics serve as leaders of the group.

Alcoholics Anonymous combines certain techniques of group psychotherapy with a strong social and religious fervor. Within a local chapter, an alcoholic individual can "confess" to past difficulties with drinking and to the persisting urge to drink. The group provides emotional support, understanding, and counseling. In developing a sense of responsibility for the well-being of other group members, the alcoholic can improve his or her own self-image and build more desirable patterns of interaction. Thus the members of an AA chapter may truly find a collective solution to the problem of alcohol addiction.

Antabuse therapy In 1948, two Danish researchers, Jens Hald and Erik Jacobsen, made an important discovery. They learned that persons taking the drug Antabuse would experience symptoms of extreme discomfort if they later drank alcohol.

Patients who drink within 12 hours after taking the drug experience flushes, headaches, dizziness, chest pains, nausea, and vomiting. The entire process is so unpleasant that they generally stop drinking while the drug is still working. When patients undergo Antabuse therapy over a long period of time, the effects of the reaction to alcohol tend to become increasingly unpleasant.

Antabuse therapy should not be thought of as an aversive conditioning procedure. Actually, it is more of a maintenance drug program that keeps alcoholics from drinking by making them sick when they drink. This treatment method is probably most effective when combined with some form of psychotherapy, for unless the alcoholic sincerely *wants* to be cured, he or she may simply stop taking the Antabuse.

Emerging Approaches— Controlled Drinking

Traditionally, treatment programs for alcoholism have set *total abstinence* as their primary goal. Many professionals in the field have viewed alcoholism as a disease, and the alcoholic as someone who is totally unable to control drinking behavior. To these observers (including members of Alcoholics Anonymous), the alcoholics are always "one drink away from a drunk." Either they avoid even a single drop of liquor—or they will return to alcoholism.

More recently, this "disease" theory of alcoholism has been discredited. Certain studies—including a 1976 report by the Rand Corporation (Brody, 1976)—have indicated that alcoholics may indeed be able to learn stable and moderate patterns of social drinking. These findings cast doubt upon the "one drink away from disaster" theory.

The clash between these two opinions is no empty academic debate. It has enormous consequences for the treatment of alcoholics. Dr. Morris Chafetz, former director of the National Institute on Alcohol Abuse and Alcoholism, observes: "As long as treatment programs insist on abstinence, people who feel that alcohol must remain an integral part of their lives will be discouraged from seeking treatment early in their disease" (Brody, 1976, p. 15).

If abstinence *is* an unrealistic goal, then training in moderate or controlled drinking may serve as an appropriate alternative for treatment. A number of important studies have been conducted to evaluate the possibility of teaching "social drinking" to alcoholics.

Blood-Alcohol Level Discrimination Training

Lovibond and Caddy (1970) trained both an experimental group of alcoholics and a control group of alcoholics to estimate their blood-alcohol levels. During the treatment period, members of the experimental group were given electric shocks only when they exceeded a specific blood-alcohol level correlated with heavy drinking. Members of the control group were shocked on a noncontingent basis. The investigators found that patients in the experimental group were relatively successful in maintaining moderate drinking over a 16- to 60-week follow-up period. However, because many members of the control group dropped out of the treatment program, the research data proved to be somewhat inconclusive.

The Patton State Hospital Experiment

One of the most significant behavioral attempts to teach controlled drinking to alcoholics occurred at the Patton State Hospital in California (Sobell and Sobell, 1973). It included a 17-session treatment plan:

Sessions 1 and 2: Videotaping. Subjects were allowed to drink until they were drunk. They then talked with staff about why they drank and how they behaved when drunk. The sessions were videotaped.

Session 3: Treatment plan. The goals and methods of the program were explained to subjects.

Sessions 4 and 5: Videotape replay. Subjects viewed their drunken behavior in the first two sessions.

Session 6: Failure experience. Prior to the session, subjects were given a number of tasks that were impossible to complete. A discussion was then held on how subjects respond to the stress of failure.

Sessions 7 through 16: Stimulus control. The control group subjects were given random shocks. Subjects whose treatment goal was controlled drinking were shocked when they behaved like uncontrolled drinkers, and were given small quantities of alcohol when they behaved like controlled drinkers. All subjects were given counseling to help them identify crucial elements in their decision to drink.

Session 17: Summary and videotape contrast. Subjects viewed selected excerpts of their drunken behavior (from Sessions 1 and 2) and sober behavior (from Session 16).

The program included 70 male alcoholic patients at the state hospital. Forty were placed in a group whose treatment goal was controlled drinking, and 30 were placed in a group whose goal was total abstinence. Each group was then subdivided into an experimental group and a control group.

Follow-up data taken at 18-month and 2-year intervals indicated that experimental subjects were more likely to remain either abstinent or controlled in their drinking than were control group subjects. Furthermore, the experimental group whose goal was controlled drinking proved to be more successful in avoiding drunk days, days in the hospital, and days in jail than the experimental group whose goal was total abstinence.

These preliminary findings give hope to those who believe that controlled drinking is a viable goal in treating alcoholic patients.

Drug Addiction and Dependence

The World Health Organization (WHO) defines drug dependence as a "state arising from repeated administration of a drug on a periodic or continuous basis" (WHO, 1964). The DSM-II category of drug dependence consists of "patients addicted to or dependent on drugs other than alcohol, tobacco, and ordinary caffeine-containing beverages" (American Psychological Association, 1968, p. 46).

The prevalence of drug dependence varies greatly with the type of drug. Berg (1969) examined 38 studies on the extent of drug usage among students, young adults, and teenagers. The following findings on the extent of drug usage were reported:

Marijuana: from 5.6 to 34.9 percent

Amphetamines: from 9.5 to 21.5 percent

Barbiturates and LSD: from 1.7 to 15.7 percent

Opiates: from 1.0 to 4.7 percent

It is important to emphasize that these figures represent the *extent of drug usage* (all individuals who have ever experimented with the drug) rather than dependence or addiction.

There are many differing estimates of the number of heroin addicts in the United States. In 1969, the National Institute of Mental Health estimated that there were more than 62,000 active narcotics addicts as of December 31, 1967. However, in 1973, the Federal Bureau of Narcotics and Dangerous Drugs projected a national figure of 560,000 addicts. And in 1972, the White House offered a figure of 315,000 in January, then increased it to between 500,000 and 600,000 addicts in July of the same year (Freedman, 1975).

There are some indications that the use of heroin may be on the decline. A study of heroin addiction trends in Washington, D.C., by Greene and DuPont (1974) found that the dramatic rise in heroin use in the late 1960s had reversed itself somewhat by the early 1970s.

Figure 14-1 represents the annual incidence of the onset of heroin use among more than 15,000 patients treated by the Narcotics Treatment Administration (NTA) over a pe-

riod of nearly 20 years. It demonstrates that new heroin use increased noticeably in the late 1960s, reached its height in 1969, and fell steadily throughout the early 1970s.

Figure 14-2 was developed by Greene and DuPont because of the possibility that the decrease in addiction incidence might actually reflect a lag between onset of heroin use and entry into the NTA treatment programs. Six patient subgroups were carefully studied by the researchers; these addicts had entered treatment between 1970 and 1973. The curves for these subgroups, as illustrated in Figure 14-2, show that the peak of first use of heroin most often occurred in 1969. This finding confirmed the data presented in Figure 14-1.

Greene and DuPont concluded that two primary factors led to the decline in heroin usage: (1) the availability of treatment programs and (2) vigorous law enforcement activity that successfully reduced the supply of heroin.

One of the social costs of increased drug addiction in the United States has been a cor-

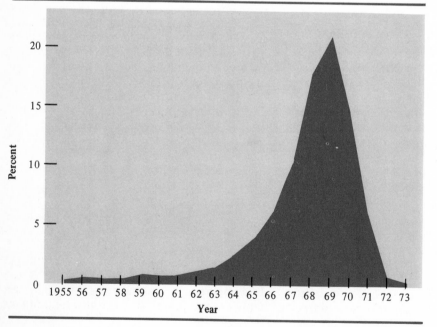

Figure 14-1 Incidence of heroin addiction: Year of first use of heroin among 15,000 NTA patients. (*Greene, M. H., and Dupont, R. L. Heroin addiction trends. American Journal of Psychiatry, 1974, 131, 546.* © *1974 by the American Psychiatric Association. Reprinted by permission.*)

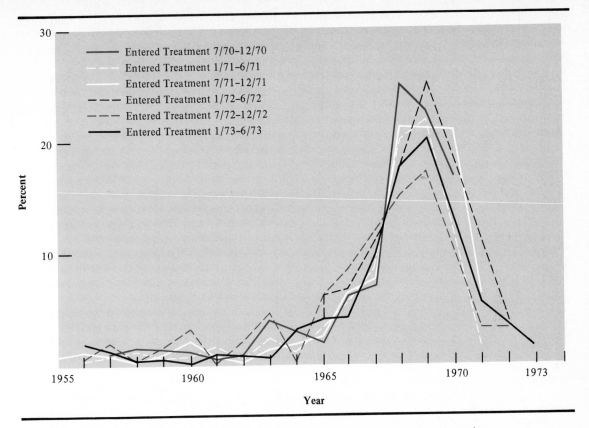

Figure 14-2 Year of first use of heroin reported by NTA patients entering treatment in six-month periods. (*Adapted from Greene, M. H., and Dupont, R. L. Heroin addiction trends.* American Journal of Psychiatry, 1974, 131, p. 546. © 1974 by the American Psychiatric Association. Reprinted by permission.)

responding increase in crime. Addicts must find a source of supply, and they must have the money necessary to pay for their costly habits. Often this leads to criminal behavior. Interestingly, in England, there has been a tradition in which physicians prescribe narcotics to help treat addicted patients. As a result, there is little correlation between addiction and crime. Addicts do not have to steal to support their habits.

Health problems are another important by-product of the use of drugs. These range from major loss of function to the now-frequent drug overdose, and death.

Nature of Drug Addiction and Dependence

Physiological Aspects

Dependence on a drug can be physical, psychological, or both. Like dependence on alcohol, physical dependence on drugs implies that the body will react if the drug is withdrawn. Withdrawal symptoms will vary depending on the nature of the drug and the frequency of usage.

Perhaps the crucial contributing factor in explaining physical dependence is the phenomenon of tolerance. Simply defined, *tolerance* means that the addict must take larger dosages of a drug in order to get the same "high" (and to avoid withdrawal symptoms).

Once an individual begins taking heroin, tolerance can build up within a few days. Unlike other addictive drugs, heroin can cause such extreme forms of tolerance that the user eventually may need more than 100 times the initial dose. The tolerant heroin addict may also experience severe withdrawal symptoms if there is an abrupt end to usage.

Clinical Effects

In this section, we will examine the psychological and physical effects of the major drugs: opiates, marijuana, amphetamines, cocaine, barbiturates, and hallucinogens.

Opiates The typical nonaddicted person, when given an injection of morphine or its derivative, heroin, both opiates, will feel nausea, giddiness, and some mental disorientation. The addict who is nontolerant, when given a single dose, will experience a state of mild euphoria. The effects of an injection may last from four to six hours.

The frequent opiate user can sometimes reach a state of chronic or acute intoxication, depending on the build-up of the chemical in his or her body. *Chronic intoxication* can lead to decreases in euphoria, nausea and vomiting, muscle spasms, impotence, and failure to menstruate. Often the addict feels extreme anxiety and guilt. *Acute intoxication* can include opiate poisoning, which causes marked unresponsiveness, slow and periodic respiration, and low blood pressure. It is associated with a high frequency of such problems as heart disease, tuberculosis, and nephritis.

Marijuana Common effects of marijuana use include a sense of lightness and airiness, periods of laughter and joviality, spurts of confused talk, lightness of limbs and body, and a drowsy and dreamless sleep. The user's sensitivity to external stimuli, such as colors or tastes, is often heightened. There tends to be a period of initial anxiety—especially for the new user. When the drug is smoked, the effects generally last from 2 to 4 hours. When it is ingested, they may last for up to 12 hours.

Unlike opiates, there is a good deal of evidence that suggests that marijuana is not addicting. Marijuana users develop neither a tolerance for nor a physical dependence on the drug. Even the psychological dependence is generally weaker than it is for other drugs, including tobacco and alcohol.

Amphetamines Amphetamines such as Benzedrine give the user a sense of well-being, exhilaration, and energy. For this reason, they are often referred to as "pep pills." After the initial period of stimulation, however, fatigue and depression return. As tolerance sets in, the individual seeking a "lift" will need larger and larger doses to fulfill his or her desire. Continued use can lead to "amphetamine psychosis," a highly disturbed state that can persist or recur despite abstinence from the drug.

Amphetamine withdrawal is a difficult and painful experience. The individuals are often confused, disoriented, demanding, and aggressive. They suffer from headaches, muscle cramps, and flashes of extreme heat and cold. They may be the victims of horrible nightmares and deep depressions.

Cocaine The cocaine "high" is similar to the euphoric feelings produced by amphetamines. The individual feels a sense of stimulation, exhilaration, and self-confidence. However, as the cocaine "high" wears off, it is replaced by feelings of weakness, depression, and irritability. The individual may experience digestive problems, tremors, palpitation, and muscular weakness.

The long-term addict may exhibit psychotic symptoms, including terrifying hallucinations and delusions of persecution. Excited and even violent behavior can result. Physical symptoms of the acutely toxic condition include rapid pulse, rising blood pressure and temperature, and irregular breathing. In some cases, these symptoms lead to respiratory arrest—and death.

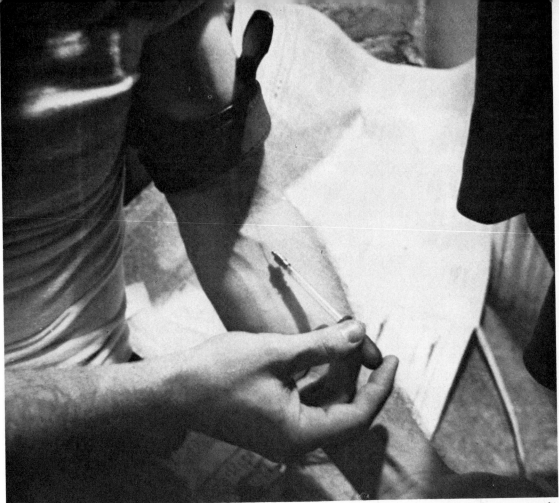

(United Press International.)

Barbiturates. Mild intoxication with barbiturates can have many of the same effects as alcohol intoxication. The user may experience sluggishness, impaired thinking, poor memory, slowness of speech, and defective motor skills. Hostile or morose moods may accompany these symptoms. Some users may become paranoid or suicidal.

Barbiturate poisoning contributes to roughly 15,000 deaths annually in the United States. This includes both suicides and accidental deaths. Often habitual users—already losing their memory as a result of the drugs—will forget whether they have already taken pills. Just to be sure, they take more pills—and kill themselves in the process.

Hallucinogens LSD, peyote, mescaline, and other hallucinogens seem to produce contradictory effects. The user may, at the same time, feel waves of relaxation and terror, happiness and sadness, frenzy and contemplation. There are often unique and intense reactions to auditory, visual, and tactile stimuli. Some users experience damaging aftereffects (without taking the drug), including "flashbacks" in which the users suddenly recall the frightening hallucinations they experienced under the influence of the drug. Occasionally, their memories lead to psychotic reactions.

Causal, Contributing, and Maintaining Factors in Drug Addiction

Psychodynamic Theories

A psychodynamic approach to drug addiction, as in the case of alcoholism, focuses on addiction as a symptom of a more deeply disturbed personality. Some observers have cited the passive-dependent individual as the most likely candidate for addiction. Yet, despite numerous investigations over the past 30 years, no clear personality pattern of the drug addict has emerged (Nyswander, 1974).

Both Freud (1905/1955) and Abraham (1960) have commented on the importance of oral erotic factors in addiction. Abraham states that morphine, like alcohol, serves to overcome sexual inhibitions, especially among men. Fenichel (1945) stresses the addict's desire to reduce tension and emotional pain.

In contrast, Glover (1956) sees aggression and sadism as central elements in the actions of the addict. Others also point to the use of needles and other painful devices as an indication of the sadomasochistic nature of addiction.

Behavioral Approaches

Cahoon and Crosby (1972) offer a useful six-part classification of behavioral contingencies that relate to drug use:

1. *Positive reinforcement involving secondary social support.* The individual may be influenced by a subculture that encourages exploration and even heavy indulgence in drugs.
2. *Positive reinforcement as a direct effect of the drug.* Some drugs do, in fact, make the user feel "good," "high," or "happy," at least for a short time.
3. *Negative reinforcement involving the removal of aversive environmental stimuli.* Many Americans—for example, residents of economically depressed inner-city areas—face an intense barrage of aversive stimuli in their daily lives. Powerful drugs such as barbiturates and opiates can counteract these aversive stimuli. As Cahoon and Crosby (1972) observe: "It is, perhaps, no coincidence that the drugs typically favored by ghetto dwellers also function as pain killers" (p. 67).
4. *Negative reinforcement involving the removal of drug-related environmental consequences.* Certain drugs lead to periods of unusual and socially disapproved behavior. This can create additional problems for the user, and, in some cases, it may cause increased consumption of the drug to reduce these upsetting consequences.
5. *Negative reinforcement involving the removal of "internal" aversive stimuli not induced by the drug itself.* People may initially take drugs because they are experiencing anxiety, fatigue, boredom, depression, or sleeplessness. The drugs alleviate or reduce these experiences.
6. *Negative reinforcement involving the removal of "internal" aversive stimuli induced by continued use of the drug itself.* As noted earlier in this chapter, addicts experience painful withdrawal symptoms when they cease taking their habitual drugs. Yet ingestion of the drug can temporarily alleviate these withdrawal symptoms (though, ultimately, it will contribute to increasing physical dependence and tolerance).

Individuals initially experiment with drugs such as heroin because of curiosity and peer pressure. After a few doses, they feel the beginnings of physical dependence. To reduce the tension and discomfort, they turn again to heroin. Thus a pattern of reinforcement develops, with immediate relief from the drug being used to counter the growing effects of withdrawal symptoms. Ultimately, physical dependence and tolerance develop, and users require larger and larger doses to obtain relief.

This observation coincides with the findings of Wikler (1965, 1971), who relied on the operant principle of negative reinforcement to explain initial drug usage. Wikler suggests that the addict's physical withdrawal symptoms become linked to specific environmental cues, such as friends, nearby streets or alleys, and music. Eventually, exposure to this conditioned environment can trigger withdrawal symptoms even *after* detoxification. The addict may return to drug usage to offset this classically conditioned withdrawal syndrome.

Sociocultural Factors

The argument has often been made that racial and ethnic minorities—such as blacks, Puerto Ricans, and Mexican-Americans—have a high-risk potential for drug dependence because of the relative poverty of their communities. In this view, such minority youths experience intense frustration because of the many social and economic problems, including discrimination, which they face.

Drugs can serve as a means of escape from the tensions and conflicts of ghetto or barrio life. But it must be remembered that many affluent suburban youths as well have fallen prey to the lures of addictive drugs. Drug dependence is by no means restricted to any racial, ethnic, or economic grouping. Thus these socioeconomic factors cannot provide a total explanation for the phenomenon of drug addiction.

Some observers point to the peer pressure that adolescents and young adults face as a critical factor in drug usage and abuse. It is certainly true that these years in one's life are filled with anxiety, uncertainty, and fear of failure—and that these feelings motivate many youths to conform to the demands of respected friends. But, again, this type of generalization is somewhat unsatisfying. It does not account for why one youth succumbs to drug-related peer pressures while another resists; or for why one peer group values drug-related behavior while another is disapproving.

Treatment Approaches

Detoxification and Replacement Drug Therapy

As with the alcoholic, the first step in treatment of the drug addict is to remove the drug and create a safe physiological situation in which other procedures can be introduced. Because methadone produces less severe withdrawal effects than other narcotics, it has traditionally been the agent used to help detoxify heroin addicts. Treatment with methadone may be administered over a period of one to two months, either within a hospital ward or on an outpatient basis.

Unfortunately, total detoxification has proven to be an unrealistic goal in treatment of heroin addicts. Nyswander (1974) reports that "about half of the patients are unable to complete detoxification and virtually all relapse after return to the street" (p. 399). For this reason, attempts have been made to devise other means of treating the heroin addict.

Since the mid-1960s, methadone maintenance therapy has become the dominant treatment for opiate addicts. Methadone seems to block the euphoric action of heroin while producing no new narcotic effects. Furthermore, researchers have determined that continued use of methadone does not require escalation of dosage. The drug is also convenient because of the relatively long duration (24 to 36 hours) of its effects and because it can be administered orally.

Methadone maintenance has become a controversial form of treatment for heroin addicts. Proponents point to the following advantages of this method:

It reduces the danger of drug overdose and the need for criminal behavior to "feed" narcotics habits.

It eliminates addicts' practice of injecting themselves daily with unsterile needles.

It is relatively inexpensive when compared to other treatment programs for heroin addicts.

A controlled form of addiction may be the only realistic alternative for many drug abusers.

These arguments are not impressive to critics of methadone maintenance therapy. They counter with the following objections to this method of treatment:

"Psst—Methadone?" (*Sidney Harris.*)

It is essentially a means of promoting "legalized addiction."

The long-term safety of methadone maintenance has not been conclusively demonstrated.

A dangerous "black market" for methadone has grown over the years.

The methadone patient may turn to other drugs in addition to methadone, including barbiturates, alcohol, and cocaine.

Many methadone-overdose deaths have been reported among users who are not tolerant of narcotics.

Although methadone maintenance relieved society of its burden, it does nothing to help addicts deal with the problems that led to their abuse in the first place.

For many critics of methadone maintenance, the only real "cure" comes when the addict is off drugs altogether. Robert Newman, head of the New York City methadone program, admitted, "If you say success is having people abusing no drugs at all, then methadone probably has a two percent success rate" (Bazell, 1973, p. 774).

Psychodynamic Approaches

There is a shortage of literature examining the intrapsychic factors contributing to drug addiction. This lack of research may be due to the fact that the socioeconomic groups involved in drug addiction are rarely found as patients in psychodynamic therapy.

Erikson (1963) has focused on the oral stage of psychosexual development in the addict. Children initially must learn a pattern of trust or distrust in their interactions with their mother. Erikson believes that addicts fail to clearly establish a point of orientation at this crucial stage of psychosexual development. As a result, they are prone to exaggerated swings of attitude and behavior, ranging from gullibility and self-deceit to massive distrust of others. It is important, therefore, for the therapist to build a relationship with the client based on trust.

Psychodynamic theorists have also pointed to addicts' deep desire to escape from depression through drug "highs." With this in mind, they have suggested that clinical depression can be expected during a period of detoxification. The addicts will need assistance in dealing with their feelings of loss, engendered by removal of the drug on which they have depended. If they are not given support from therapists, the addicts will probably resume their use of drugs (Dykens and Niswander, 1976).

Behavioral Approaches

Respondent approaches: Aversion therapy Chemical aversion, electrical aversion, and covert sensitization have all been used in treating drug addicts.[1] The same techniques that were instrumental in dealing with alcoholics have been applied with drug addicts, with many of the same issues and problems resulting.

Kraft (1968) views social anxiety as a critical factor in drug abuse. He argues that if the social anxiety of the addict can be lessened, there may be a corresponding reduction in the need for addictive drugs. In Kraft's studies, treatment procedures focus on two primary goals: (1) desensitizing the patient to being around increasingly large groups of people and (2) having the patient spend progressively greater periods of time away from the therapist.

Operant approaches Few studies have been done of a purely operant nature. There have

---

[1]For a good review of behavioral treatment approaches to drug addiction, see Callner (1975).

been some token reinforcement programs in drug rehabilitation centers, but these have been for other behaviors such as working and interpersonal skills, not for actual drug usage.

Token economy systems as a means of treating the addiction per se have been established in hospitals. In one experiment (Glicksman, Ottomanelli, and Cutler, 1971), patients could accumulate points toward their discharge from the hospital by meeting various performance goals. In another system, patients demonstrating certain desirable behaviors (such as punctuality and cleanliness) received reinforcements such as television privileges and extra visitation rights (O'Brien, Raynes, and Patch, 1971).

Therapeutic Communities

The first therapeutic community for drug addicts, Synanon, was begun in California in 1968. Synanon is based on the belief that addicts are immature and irresponsible and must be encouraged to develop more responsible behavior patterns. The methods of the community include challenging group encounters, reeducation, and hard work. The Synanon model has led to the establishment of other therapeutic communities, such as Daytop Village, Odyssey House, and Phoenix House.

The ability of these programs to help addicts is a matter of open debate. Nyswander (1974) claims that as many as half of the community members quickly drop out of the treatment programs. She also points to estimates that only 10 percent of the patients remain drug-free for more than two years. In her view, addicts who stay within the tight therapeutic communities seem to make substantial progress in changing behavior patterns, but the transition to normal life "on the outside" is rarely successful.

Some observers have cited the harsh encounter-group methods of therapeutic communities as a key factor in the high drop-out rate. Many addicts cannot cope with the intense pressures that they face in encounter groups. Furthermore, the requirement of total abstinence from drugs is difficult for most of them.

Box 14-4 Mixed Behavioral Approaches to Drug Addiction

Some researchers have combined a number of behavioral techniques in their treatment programs for drug addicts. An example is the work of Wisocki (1973) with heroin addicts.

Wisocki's treatment goals included "reinforcing thoughts and behaviors antagonistic to the use of heroin, eliminating positive thoughts and urges for heroin, and creating an aversion for all aspects of heroin usage" (p. 56). The techniques used included covert reinforcement scenes, thought-stopping techniques, and covert sensitization. There was special emphasis on improving the addict's self-concept, and on encouraging more adaptive attitudes toward society.

The following is a typical covert reinforcement scene in the Wisocki (1973) experiment:

Relax and try to imagine that you're driving in your car through the city, on your way home after work. Try to imagine the streets you're passing through; try to feel the steering wheel in your hands; try to hear the noises of the city. You suddenly see a familiar scene. You see a friend of yours, _____, in the process of making a contact for a fix. The thought immediately passes through your mind: "What a fool that guy is. Heroin is just no good. It's too bad he doesn't see it." But you feel glad you're not involved with it any longer. (p. 57)

The following is a typical covert sensitization scene from the same study:

Imagine that you're in the car, on your way to Boston to get some junk. You see a road sign indicating the distance to that city. You're thinking about how easy it will be to get drugs there. As you have that thought a wasp flies into the car. You can hear it buzzing. You can see it flying in front of your eyes. It's all brown and ugly. A fear starts to rise in you, but you shake it off and think about how you'll feel when you have the fix. Then suddenly that wasp is joined by a horde of other wasps . . . all buzzing and flying about your eyes. You keep driving to Boston, thinking about your pusher and making the contact. And then you see him—the guy who will sell you the heroin. Suddenly the wasps attack—swarms of them come crashing down on your head. They land on your hands; the steering wheel is covered with them. You can't see in front of you. The sounds are terrible. You can feel a hundred stings all over your body. They're in your clothes, on your face, all over everything. You decide it's not worth it. You decide to turn back. You think how nice it would be to be home and away from this whole scene of copping heroin and everything connected with it. And, as you turn your car away, the wasps begin to leave. The further away you get, the fewer the wasps around you. Everything is quiet, peaceful, and calm. The radio is playing your favorite song. You begin to feel happy that you resisted the urge. (pp. 57–58)

Wisocki was able to assist her client in eliminating his heroin dependence in a short time. As Wisocki points out, however, the client was not a typical addict. He was highly educated and unusually motivated to attend therapy sessions.

From Wisocki, P. A. The successful treatment of a heroin addict by covert conditioning techniques. *Behavior Therapy and Experimental Psychiatry*, 1973, 4, 55–61.

Research on the Use of Marijuana

Recent studies on marijuana are a good example of research that has introduced a note of reality into a highly charged, emotional atmosphere filled with unsubstantiated myths.

Many sweeping stereotypes about marijuana have been "sold" to the American public. Among these are that marijuana leads to violent crime, sexual indulgence, physical and mental degeneracy, and psychotic behavior. None of these myths appears to be based in fact. A body of research has grown indicating that moderate indulgence in marijuana does not lead to significant mental or physical deterioration.

One approach to treating drug addiction is the therapeutic community. These boys are taking part in a group-encounter session at Odyssey House. (*United Press International.*)

In one long-term study, chronic users of marijuana were examined over an average of eight years. The average dose for members of the sample was seven marijuana cigarettes per day, which is far above the normal amount for a moderate user. Nevertheless, the findings were that these chronic marijuana smokers had experienced no mental or physical decline after years of heavy smoking (Grinspoon, 1975).

Clark and Nakashima (1968) tested a group of adult volunteers, ages 21–40, with no previous history of marijuana use, on a variety of sensory and motor performance criteria. Although there has been some recent evidence to the contrary, their general finding was that marijuana had little effect in most performance areas. They also noted that there were marked individual differences between subjects on certain tests.

Overeating

Overeating is the behavioral event that is the primary cause of obesity. There are other (physiological) causes of obesity, but these are relatively rare conditions and account for only a small percentage of the obese population. An overinvolvement with food to the detriment of a person's well-being is similar to alcoholism and drug abuse in that an involvement with a common substance eventually gets out of hand for some individuals.

At first glance, overeating would seem to be a less serious problem than alcoholism or drug abuse. But it may, in fact, be the worst of these problems of overindulgence. It is estimated that between 40 and 80 million Americans suffer from obesity. These people must face the disabilities of various weight-related disorders, the psychological and economic costs of obesity and dieting, and the risk of a variety of diseases and shorter lives.

Nature of Obesity

Overeating is generally defined as taking in more food than the body needs. This leads to excessive body fat through storage mechanisms. Beyond that simple equation lies an extensive debate about natural mechanisms relating to the regulation of body weight. We will discuss some of these theories later. At this point, however, we need to understand that overeating is a most complex issue. There is no single view of what the mechanisms of overeating or obesity are.

Patterns of Abuse and Stages of Overeating

The actual behavior is too much eating. But there are many different patterns, styles, and food choices involved in overeating. Some individuals exhibit a "night-eating syndrome." Some are nibblers who eat continuously throughout the day; others are binge eaters who go on long eating spurts. Some people get fat on sweets, while others consume enormous quantities of meats or starches.

At one time or another, all of these patterns have been considered important in understanding obesity. More recently, it has been felt that *any* pattern can emerge. The only consistency is that the individual tends to develop one particular constellation of food choices and eating cycles and sticks to it.

One eating pattern that has been supported by observations may be one of the ways some people develop super-obesity. It is referred to as the "yo-yo" syndrome. In these cases, cycles of overeating and dieting are alternated. The individual's weight keeps going up and down over time. However, each overeating cycle peaks at a higher weight than the previous one, and each dieting cycle fails to go down to the previous low weight. Thus, over the years, there is a continual weight gain despite the short-term losses from the dieting (Mack and Harmatz, in press).

Causal, Contributing, and Maintaining Factors in Overeating

Psychodynamic Theories

The taking in of food is the earliest pleasure experienced in childhood. It can result in an oral fixation. The individual may equate food with love, and may turn to overeating when he or she is feeling unhappy, depressed, or inadequate.

There are several psychodynamic theories about the causes of obesity. One theory centers on the *symbolic meaning of food* for the overeater. Food may unconsciously represent the mother's love or the father's phallus. Another psychodynamic theory views *increased body size* as a primary concern. Obesity may represent strength, power, and physical dominance, or it may suggest a conscious or subconscious choice to become physically unattractive by conventional standards, thus avoiding normal social and sexual demand.

Bruch (1957, 1961) views obesity as an indication of deep psychological conflict, generally dating back to disturbances during childhood. In one study (1969), she examined the childhood behavior patterns of obese individuals. These children were found to be relatively bland and malleable. They rarely engaged in rough play, destructive behavior, or disobedience. Generally, they did whatever they were told by their parents. As one aspect of this behavior, they ate whatever was put in front of them. A number of mothers in the survey stated that they had always "anticipated" the needs of their children and never allowed them to "feel hungry."

Hamburger (1951) developed a four-level classification system for categorizing the overeater. Ranging from the least disturbed individuals to the most disturbed, the four levels are:

1. Those who overeat in times of anxiety or transition.
2. Those who overeat as a substitute gratification.
3. Those who overeat continually to reduce depression.
4. Those who exhibit a pathological addiction to food.

Obesity also functions for some individuals as a rationalization of failure (Kolb, 1973). It is used as a kind of defense mechanism. The individual can always fall back on the belief that "I can't do it because I am overweight." This provides an escape from taking risks and experiencing failure and disappointment.

Behavioral Approaches

Stunkard (1959) conducted one of the first significant behavioral studies on overeating.

Each obese and nonobese subject came to the laboratory in early morning after fasting during the previous evening. An experimental means was devised of testing the correlation between hunger and gastric contractions. Stunkard determined that the nonobese subjects were much more likely to experience hunger in conjunction with gastric motility, whereas obese subjects claimed to be hungry regardless of their physiological condition.

In the same vein, Schachter and Gross (1968) studied the effects of perceived time on the eating habits of obese and nonobese people. Their hypothesis before undertaking the research was that perceived time would have a greater impact on obese persons than on nonobese persons. It was learned, through use of special clocks rigged to be abnormally fast or slow, that obese subjects who believed it was not yet the normal time for dinner ate fewer crackers (when offered by the testers) than obese subjects who believed that the dinner hour had already arrived or passed. By contrast, the nonobese subjects responded to their internal state and ate crackers when they were hungry, regardless of the clock time.

To discover the relative effect of food cues, Goldman, Jaffa, and Schachter (1968) viewed a sample of obese and nonobese Jewish students at Columbia University. For Jews, the holiday of Yom Kippur is a Day of Atonement in which the observant individual fasts for a 24-hour period. The researchers found that 83.3 percent of the obese Jewish students fasted, as compared with 68.8 percent of the nonobese students. This differential suggests that the stereotype of obese persons always thinking about food may be incorrect. Without normal cues for eating (such as the presence of others who are eating), the obese Jewish students were more inclined to fast than their nonobese counterparts.

Taste appears to be another food stimulus that has a noticeable effect on obese individuals. A study by Hashim and Van Itallie (1965) tested the calorie consumption of obese and nonobese hospital patients. During an experimental period of several weeks, all subjects were placed on a bland and untasty liquid diet.

The calorie consumption level of the nonobese sample remained relatively stable. But the obese subjects—who had averaged 3,500 calories per day before hospitalization—reduced their calorie intake to an average of 500 calories per day. Thus the obese individuals were much more influenced by the taste of food than the nonobese individuals.

Goldman (1968) made an important evaluation of feedback as a factor in overeating. All subjects were given milkshakes, which they

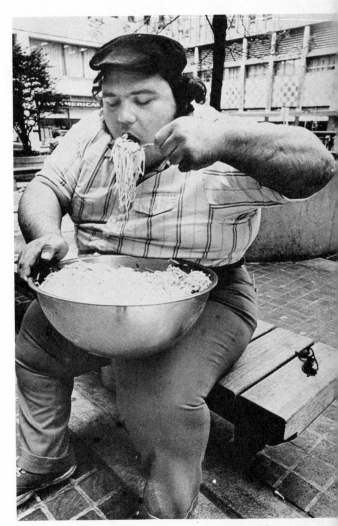

(*United Press International.*)

---

drank with straws. The liquid was provided in gallon containers. Some subjects were allowed to see how much they had ingested, while others were not. The survey results dramatized a sharp difference between obese and nonobese individuals. The obese subjects drank less when they could view their intake level, and more when they had no idea how much they had drunk. By contrast, nonobese subjects drank more when they could see how much they were drinking, and less when they could not.

Stuart and Davis (1972) speculate that when external cues to stop eating (such as feedback) are present, overweight subjects will be more influenced by these cues than by normal food cues (such as taste). However, when conflicting external cues are not available, the impact of normal food cues will be undiminished, and extreme overeating may result.

If correct, this viewpoint could explain the reported night-eating "binges" of many obese individuals. During the day, the overeater is influenced by a wide assortment of nonfood stimuli, which may counteract the attraction of food cues. For example, if a person is totally caught up in the demands of an arduous day at work, a nearby food cue may be more easily ignored. In the late evening, when the overeater is at home and may be alone, there are far fewer competing cues in the immediate environment. This may trigger more frequent notice of food cues, and may contribute to heavy night-eating.

The U.S. Public Health Service (1966) has concluded that "not all obesity can be considered the same. For this reason some investigators have come to use the plural term 'obesities' rather than 'obesity.'" (p. 33). With this in mind, it may be most helpful to look upon obesity as a behavioral problem with a variety of causes and manifestations. As with other problem behaviors we have discussed, this eliminates the need for one all-encompassing "explanation" or "answer."

Biophysical Factors

A commonly held view among the general public is that obesity is a genetically transferred phenomenon. Thus slim parents would be expected to produce slim children, whereas obese parents would be expected to produce obese children.

There is some research evidence to support this position. A study by Mayer (1957) found some interesting correlations. Roughly 80 percent of the children of two obese parents, 40 percent of the children of one obese and one nonobese parent, while only slightly more than 10 percent of the children of two nonobese parents were themselves obese. At first glance, such data might be seen as solid confirmation of the genetic hypothesis. But as Stunkard and Mahoney (1976) observe, "Such figures inevitably confuse genetic and environmental influences" (p. 50). The fact that so many nongenetic factors affect body weight makes it difficult to draw the connection between heredity and obesity. Furthermore, geneticists still have no precise explanation for the transmission of genes affecting fattening and fleshing. It may simply be that obese parents feed their children more.

Stunkard and Mahoney (1976) observe that gross metabolic abnormalities are rarely found to cause obesity. But Stuart and Davis (1972) cite important findings concerning cell counts in obese individuals. Studies have demonstrated that obesity leads to an expansion in the size of the adipose cells, which constitute an individual's "fat pads." These enlarged cells, because of a marked unresponsiveness to insulin, do not efficiently metabolize carbohydrates. This research may indicate at least one significant link between metabolism and obesity.

The correlation between lack of physical activity and obesity (or, for that matter, between increased physical activity and weight loss) has been the subject of great public interest. Traditionally, it has been assumed that physical inactivity contributed to obesity by reducing the individual's expenditure of energy. However, recent evidence suggests that inactivity may be a causal factor in increased intake of food. One study (Mayer and Thomas, 1967) found that the daily caloric intake of sedentary individuals did not necessarily decrease when their level of physical activity fell below a certain minimum. They also reported that when these individuals increased their physical activity levels, their caloric intake sometimes *decreased* (see Figure 14-3). While these results are far from conclusive, they clearly indicate a more complex relationship between exercise and eating behavior than has been conventionally assumed.

Treatment Approaches

Psychodynamic Approaches

There is no particular psychodynamic treatment method for the obese individual. Kolb (1973) notes that "successful treatment of the obese person requires a knowledge of his total personality, also that the goal of treatment be directed beyond the mere reduction of weight" (pp. 464–465). This coincides with the traditional attempt by psychodynamic theorists to treat the underlying psychological conflicts of the patient, rather than simply focusing on his or her immediate behavioral symptoms.

Careful consideration also must be given to establishing the most desirable combination and time sequence of psychotherapy, dieting, and exercise. Individuals should not begin a distasteful dieting process until they are strong enough emotionally to exist without the accustomed "rewards" of food.

There is considerable doubt—even among psychodynamic theorists—as to the usefulness of this approach in dealing with the problem of obesity. As Kolb (1973) concedes: "In individuals in whom eating provides the major satisfaction in life and other gratifications are not available, psychotherapy is often not successful" (p. 465).

Behavioral Approaches

Respondent approaches One of the first aversive conditioning experiments with food choice was conducted by Moss (1924). A child was blindfolded and fed orange juice and vinegar. Whenever vinegar was offered to the child, a clicking noise was sounded. At first, the child drank the orange juice but rejected the vinegar. In a later series of trials, the same clicking noise was paired with the orange juice and the child rejected both offerings. This suggested that children could be trained to alter their food choices through conditioning.

Meyer and Crisp (1964) attempted to use electric shock as an aversive technique with overeaters. Two subjects in the experiment

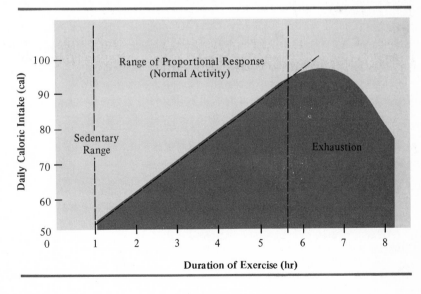

Figure 14-3 The relationship between energy expenditure and daily caloric intake. (*Adapted from Mayer, J., and Thomas, D. W. Regulation of food intake and obesity. Science, 1967, 156, 328–337.* © *1967 by the American Association for the Advancement of Science.*)

were shocked when they were given foods they regarded as particularly tempting. The treatment was quite successful in the case of one subject, whose weight fell noticeably during treatment and remained low over the next two years of follow-up. The other subject, however, chose to terminate treatment after he received the first shock.

In general, the positive effects of aversive conditioning techniques in promoting weight loss remain unproven. As Abramson (1973) observes: "Despite some early enthusiasm, there is little evidence to indicate that aversive procedures are an effective treatment for obesity. The reported outcomes of the case studies are equivocal, at best" (p. 548).

Covert sensitization methods have also been utilized as an experimental treatment procedure for obesity. Cautela (1966, 1967) described detailed and vivid scenarios in which the patient approaches high-calorie foods and becomes nauseated. Other scenes were presented in which the patient turns away from these foods and feels better. In one study (Cautela and Stuart, 1967), there was moderate success in redirecting the eating patterns of obese individuals through application of covert sensitization techniques.

Operant approaches Stuart (1967) used reinforcement procedures as a means of reducing weight in obese subjects. All eight of the obese women in the sample lost at least 26 pounds in the course of a year. The highest weight loss in the group was 47 pounds.

In a later study, Stuart (1967) again demonstrated the dramatic power of his method. The six women in the 1971 study lost an average of 28 pounds. In addition, these subjects were tested for psychodynamic "symptom substitution." It was learned that in the course of losing significant amounts of weight, the women had not developed new and destructive behavior patterns to replace their previous overeating habits.

Harris (1969) did the first controlled test of Stuart's methods for reducing obesity. She assigned 24 overweight volunteers to three groups: a control group and two experimental groups. Each experimental group received ten weeks of group treatment, which included training in the theory of reinforcement, exploration of the stimuli affecting eating behavior, and training in how to slow down the rate of eating. After the initial treatment period had been completed, one of the experimental groups was given additional training in covert sensitization techniques.

Harris found that the experimental subjects experienced a much greater weight loss than the control subjects. It was also determined that the covert sensitization procedures had little impact. There was no significant difference in the weight changes among members of the two experimental groups.

Penick and his co-workers (1970) compared the effectiveness of behavior modification techniques and group psychotherapy in contributing to weight loss. The follow-up was completed from three to six months after a three-month treatment program. The behavior modification treatment program was found to be vastly more successful than group psychotherapy methods in helping overweight patients to reduce. More than twice as many of the behavior modification patients lost 30 or 40 pounds, and nearly twice as many of the behavior modification patients lost 20 pounds.

Harmatz and Lapuc (1968) studied the impact of behavior modification, group therapy, and diet-only weight-reduction programs on a sample of 21 hospitalized schizophrenic males. The behavior modification subjects were weighed weekly. If they failed to demonstrate some loss of weight, they were not given their full $5 weekly allowance.

After six weeks of treatment, both the behavior modification and group therapy subjects showed significantly more improvement than the control group. At this point in treatment, members of the two experimental groups had registered comparable weight losses. However, another weigh-in was conducted four weeks later. It indicated that group therapy subjects weighed roughly the same as the diet-only control group, while the behavior modification group weighed less than either of the others.

Cigarette Smoking

Cigarette smoking is well known as one of the major health hazards of American society because of its link to cancer and other diseases. Yet few smokers even try to break the habit and even fewer (less than 20%) actually succeed.

The last decade has featured extensive antismoking campaigns by citizens' groups across the United States. Among the results of their actions have been television commercials warning of the dangers of smoking, legislation banning smoking in certain public facilities, and higher taxes on tobacco products. Nevertheless, these efforts have not forced any dramatic reduction in smoking.

Many lay observers think of smoking as an example of a drug addiction. However, the use of the term "addiction" in connection with smoking may be misleading. Unlike the morphine addict, the chronic smoker will not necessarily increase the dosage of nicotine if the habit is continued over a long period of time. In addition, long-term smoking does not seem to cause a spontaneous and inevitable withdrawal syndrome. It may be more appropriate to categorize smoking as a drug "habit" rather than a drug "addiction."

Nesbitt (1973) studied the physiological and psychological effects of actual and simulated cigarette smoking. He measured groups of smokers and nonsmokers for both an emotional response (pain tolerance) and a physiological response (pulse rate) under three varying test conditions. These were smoking an unlit cigarette, smoking a cigarette with a lower nicotine content, and smoking a cigarette with a higher nicotine content.

Nesbitt discovered that cigarette smoking produced definite physiological arousal for both smokers and nonsmokers. Experienced smokers showed a more *moderate* emotional response when smoking. For this group, the higher the nicotine content of the cigarettes, the greater the reduction of emotionality.

The social learning analysis of smoking is similar to social learning views of alcoholism and obesity. Smoking is understood primarily as a learned behavior, with controlling antecedent and consequent variables. The smoking habit is greatly influenced by various reinforcers, such as peer pressure, which are experienced in different ways by each individual. Other common reinforcers include the stimulant effects of smoke and nicotine; anxiety reduction in stress situations such as meetings or parties; and media images of the smokers as attractive, successful, powerful people or as people in control of their emotions.

If the social learning analysis of cigarette smoking is correct, two types of behavior modification will be needed to control or eliminate smoking. The impact of reinforcers of smoking behavior must be reduced, while new behavior reinforcers for nonsmoking must be established and encouraged. Of course, this is no easy task, given the virtually all-pervasive presence of smoking (and social reinforcers promoting smoking) in our culture.

Modification of Smoking

General Modification Approaches

Among the most commonly used modification techniques in treating smoking behavior are legislative action, public media campaigns, smoking clinics employing medication, nonmedication clinics, and antismoking drugs (Bernstein, 1969).

Legislative action to combat smoking has been a feature of antismoking efforts around the world. In the United States, cigarette manufacturers have been required to print health warnings on each pack of cigarettes. In Italy, Great Britain, and the United States, prohibitions or restrictions on tobacco advertising have been instituted. Nevertheless, there is little evidence to suggest that these legislative changes have been effective in reducing smoking.

Public media campaigns have been a fairly recent innovation in the fight against smoking. In some cases, the target population has been adult smokers. At other times, educational programs have been created to warn children or

(American Lung Association.)

within six months, and, after one year, the relapse rate was up to 70 percent.

Nonmedication clinics have also produced disappointing results. Usually, there is an immediate quitting rate of 30 to 85 percent. Unfortunately, once formal group meetings are terminated, few continue to refrain from smoking. A well-known example was the effort by McFarland in conjunction with the Seventh Day Adventists (McFarland, 1965; McFarland et al., 1964). A five-day treatment program was developed with daily sessions of 1½ to 2 hours. Medical, religious, and educational techniques were all introduced, and subjects were urged to begin special diet and exercise programs. A study of 144 subjects who finished the treatment program showed that 72.2 percent initially stopped smoking. But three months later, only 33.9 percent were still avoiding cigarettes.

A variety of *antismoking drugs* have been utilized to help smokers stop or reduce smoking. Often these drugs are one part of a multifaceted therapy program at a smoking clinic. The most commonly used drug is lobeline, which to some extent mimics the effects of nicotine. Unfortunately, most studies of lobeline treatment have indicated discouraging results. Research on other drugs has been similarly disappointing; there is no clear evidence to attest to the effectiveness of any drugs in helping to reduce habitual smoking.

Behavioral Approaches

An extensive assortment of behavioral techniques has been used to help smokers to curtail their nicotine habits. These include aversion therapy, systematic desensitization, self-control procedures, and contingency contracting. Yet, for the most part, the results have been unimpressive.

Koenig and Masters (1965) compared the results of aversive conditioning, supportive counseling, and systematic desensitization in treating smokers. Seven therapists were involved in the experiment; each treated two subjects under all of the three treatment condi-

adolescents of the dangers of cigarettes. Neither of these strategies seems to have been particularly successful thus far.

Clinics employing medication have been established as a means of helping chronic smokers break the habit. One of the most important studies of such clinics was conducted by Ejrup (1964). Smokers in Ejrup's clinics typically received ten days of treatment. A variety of techniques were combined, including antismoking educational discussions and drug therapy with such drugs as caffeine and amphetamines. Over a five-year period, 60.3 percent of the 2,271 subjects had stopped smoking. However, 50 percent of the "quitters" relapsed tions. No significant effects were found to distinguish the various treatment methods.

Marston and McFall (1971) compared two experimental therapeutic groups treating smoking problems with two control groups. One experimental group was treated with a stimulus satiation procedure that encouraged "three-at-a-time" chain smoking. The other experimental group was treated with a gradual reduction method based on counterconditioning techniques. One control group was given nondrug, spice tablets that cause an unpleasant taste after smoking begins, while the other was bluntly told to stop smoking "cold turkey."

All four groups registered a sharp drop in smoking at the end of the treatment period. The average daily smoking rate fell from 26.4 to 4.9 cigarettes. However, all four groups experienced a noticeable relapse during the six-month follow-up period. The overall mean daily smoking rate for all subjects returned to a high level of 18.3 cigarettes. Perhaps the most important finding was that no major differences were evident among any of the four experimental and control groups.

More favorable results of behavioral attempts to reduce smoking were found in a study by Chapman, Smith, and Layden (1971). Two groups of long-term smokers were treated with a number of aversive and self-control procedures. These included electric shock treatments, daily self-recording and graphing, and a monetary reward system for follow-up monitoring. Subjects were also given literature from cancer, heart, and tuberculosis associations about the hazards of smoking.

The long-range outcome data from this study suggested a dramatic difference between the two experimental groups. Group 2 subjects had received 11 weeks of posttreatment therapist monitoring, whereas Group 1 subjects had received only 2 weeks of such monitoring. At the four designated follow-up points (1 month, 3 months, 6 months, and 1 year after treatment ended), Group 2 members consistently demonstrated much greater progress in reducing smoking rates. Thus long-range therapist monitoring of posttreatment smoking behavior was found to be a vital factor in preventing relapse. In addition, the overall abstinence rate of 55 percent for Group 2 subjects was a substantial improvement over a number of earlier behavioral studies.

For smoking, as for overeating, the problem is not so much one of immediate cessation of the harmful activity. The more important goal is one of maintenance. Many individuals stop smoking for a brief period of time, but cannot truly "kick the habit." Within a month or two, they are back to two packs a day.

While it is fairly simple to teach smokers or overeaters the techniques of behavior modification, it is much more difficult to help individuals become self-conditioners over a long period of time. Maintenance methods can be a crucial factor in reinforcing the client's attempts at building self-control and new behavior patterns. Clearly, there must be new priorities for antismoking theory and research. The critical question for researchers must be "How can we help people to *maintain* nonsmoking behavior?"

Summary

There are roughly 10 million alcoholics in the United States. Alcohol use is involved in nearly half of the arrests that occur each year. The most common biological consequences of alcoholism include brain damage and liver problems. Psychological consequences include guilt, aggressive behavior, apathy, impaired thinking, and self-loathing. Alcoholism can contribute to violent behavior against family members and to separation or divorce.

The basic psychodynamic approach to treating alcoholism involves examination of the underlying personal problems of the alcoholic. Orthodox analytic techniques have proven to be generally unsuccessful in helping alcoholics. Behavioral approaches to treatment of alcoholics include chemical and electrical aversion therapy, covert sensitization, and the community reinforcement approach.

Drug addiction and dependence vary

widely depending on the particular drug. National estimates in the early 1970s suggested that there may be 500,000 to 600,000 heroin addicts in the United States. Addiction generally involves both physical and psychological dependence on a drug, as well as tolerance (which forces the individual to increase the dosage to get "high").

In recent years, the controversial method of methadone maintenance has become a widely used technique for treating the heroin addict. Therapeutic communities such as Synanon and Phoenix House have also been established to help addicts become more responsible citizens.

Between 40 million and 80 million Americans suffer from obesity. Psychodynamic approaches view overeating behavior as reflecting an equation of food with love, or a defense mechanism that allows the individual to avoid taking risks. Behavioral studies suggest that food cues have an important role in stimulating the eating behavior in obese people. When competing cues are readily available, the individual may not consume as much food. Aversion therapy and covert sensitization methods have been utilized to treat obese patients, with mixed results.

Cigarette smoking is a drug habit that is particularly difficult to quit permanently. Public antismoking campaigns thus far have been unable to significantly reduce smoking behavior. A great variety of techniques have been employed to treat smokers, including drug therapy programs and behavior modification methods. While many treatments have shown initially favorable results, few have maintained nonsmoking behavior over a long period of time.

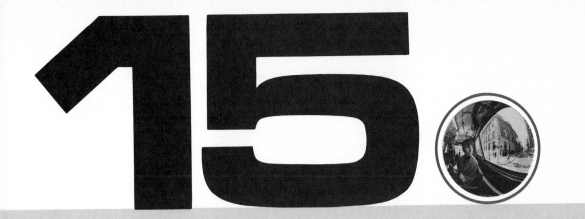

Behavior disorders
of childhood

Childhood is a time of growth, development, and change. The child is in motion, moving toward the relative stability of adulthood. This fluid state makes it difficult to draw definitive lines that distinguish abnormal from normal behavior. Yet that is what we must do in order to identify abnormal patterns in the process of development and prevent them from becoming fixed in the adult's behavior.

In response to that demand, abnormal psychology has spawned its own problem child—the study of the psychopathology of childhood. The study of abnormal behavior in childhood is such an extensive province that it has warranted its own textbooks. In this chapter, we can only survey the major behavior problems of children and the relevant theoretical notions regarding their development, maintenance, and change. The student who is especially interested in these problems will find the literature rich and stimulating and is encouraged to seek it out.

The study of the abnormal psychology of children has its roots in the study of the abnormal psychology of adults, generalized to cover the problems of children. Consequently, the labels of children's behavior patterns are borrowed from the adult pathologies (e.g., childhood "schizophrenia"). One reason for this is that there may be one or two common features. Another is that the "illness" model predisposes us to this common labeling, since similar patterns are assumed to identify similar disorders, regardless of age. Thus a physical "disease" such as pneumonia is the same in an adult and a child. As we have moved to our contemporary models, we have veered away from the practice of simply transposing labels across age boundaries in an effort to understand childhood problems. In cases where convenience dictates the use of such duplicate labels, we must be warned that the childhood versions are distinctive problems and should be treated accordingly.

The DSM-II reflects the complexity and confusion we have sketched here. The manual's labels for childhood problems are the least clearly defined and are not very helpful in organizing the thinking of practitioners in the field.

Taking a pragmatic approach, we will discuss the major clinical problems and their implications for theory and research. They include (1) the severe behavior problems of children—infantile autism and childhood schizophrenia, (2) the milder but far more frequent problems of childhood that create serious difficulties for the child and those around him or her—for example, enuresis and the phobias, (3) the hyperactive child—a major controversial issue of the day. The final sections of the chapter deal with psychotherapy with children and the family as the context of the child's abnormal behavior.

Severe Behavior Problems: Infantile Autism and Childhood Schizophrenia

Introduction: A Problem of Labels

We observed, in the case of the schizophrenias, that adults who exhibited such behaviors had a distorted view of reality. They often engaged in "primary process" thinking. But the primary process is the natural mode of infantile thinking, so how can we talk about the infant's distorted view of reality? Children below age 5 see reality differently from adults. That is a normal phase in their growing-up process. What, then, is the problem that underlies their abnormal behavior? Are there really schizophrenic children? Some psychologists say they have never seen one; others claim there are tens of thousands of them. The difference may be one of definition; that is, do these behavioral symptoms constitute genuine "syndromes"? We will proceed to discuss these syndromes as though they do exist, keeping our doubts in sight as we go along.

To sum up the state of confusion, we merely remark at this point that the names of types and subtypes indicate the differences among various diagnostic schools. Infantile autism and childhood schizophrenia are the two main categories of developmental psychosis. We will describe and discuss the behavior patterns noted by psychopathologists, keeping in mind the differences among the viewpoints and the overall questions of the viability of a concept of childhood psychosis.

Behavioral Description

Infantile Autism

Leo Kanner first identified "early infantile autism" (EIA) in 1943. He detailed 12 characteristic features of the EIA syndrome. The EIA child (1) is aloof and completely insulated, (2) looks normal and alert, (3) has normal motor coordination and often great dexterity, (4) avoids eye contact and lacks auditory responsiveness, (5) does not reach out, (6) does not initiate sounds or gestures, (7) does not use speech for communication (i.e., he or she speaks only to echo questions or repeat phrases), (8) handles objects with facility, (9) has normal or superior cognitive skills, (10) has an obsessive desire to maintain sameness, (11) rarely engages in bed-wetting, thumb-sucking, nail-biting, and masturbation, and (12) numbers less than 1 percent of the population.

In a later assessment, Kanner and Eisenberg (1956) reduced the behavioral array to two cardinal features: (1) lack of object relations, particularly in developing attachment to the parents and (2) maintenance of sameness by means of stereotyped behavior, in which the child repeats the same behavior, in exactly the same way, over and over. They felt that these two features were the only ones that were unique to EIA. To Kanner and Eisenberg's two features, others have added the failure to *use* language as a means of communication, considering this failure a central aspect of the problem.

Autistic children express these pathological characteristics in various ways. They are completely unresponsive to others. They do not even tense their bodies or orient their arms when, in infancy, they are lifted from their cribs. They refuse eye contact even when attempts are made to compel it by holding their heads. They do not cuddle or run to their parents when hurt. EIA children do not imitate adult behavior or word play, nor do they respond to adult mimicry with laughter. They play in a persistent, ritualistic manner for years with the same toys, showing preference for, and tireless interest in, toys that move in repeated patterns (pinwheels, doorknobs, balls that roll down tracks). They have considerable dexterity, which they display by endlessly twirling or flipping small objects. They make few demands and cause little fuss at meals or bedtime.

A prominent aspect of EIA behavior is an obsessive insistence on sameness. Nothing must be moved or changed in the rooms of EIA children, and they will throw a temper tantrum if anything is moved or missing. This characteristic seems related to their preoccupation with objects that move in repetitive patterns. It is as if they felt that a change in their world threatened their existence.

As we noted, the odd and limited use of language by autistic children presents a special problem. Their language development is slow, and in some cases they simply do not speak at all. When they do, they parrot questions and give no answers. In their deaf-and-dumb pose, they show no reaction to calls or noises. This lack of perception seems actually to be a conscious and deliberate denial, since they will sometimes rock rhythmically to music. Their speech is noncommunicative. It may consist of recitations of nursery rhymes, lists of names (states, presidents, animals, etc.), or prayers. They never address people, but may talk to toys in stereotyped fashion, sometimes with compulsive chatter. A curious EIA phenomenon is pronoun reversal, in which the child refers to himself (or herself) as "he" (or "she") and to the other person as "I."

Physically, autistic children appear normal, their bodies are well formed, and they are well coordinated. Their facial expression is intelligent, though not attentive to the immediate situation.

So-called "idiot savants" are an example of the exceptional development of special abilities in autistic and retarded children. This proficiency occurs particularly in such areas as music, mathematics, chess, and memorization of historical facts. All of these activities have rote learning and repetitious practice as common requirements for their mastery.

Childhood Schizophrenia

Let us look at a collection of behavioral symptoms: uncertainty of self-identity (vague ego boundaries), disturbed and bizarre speech

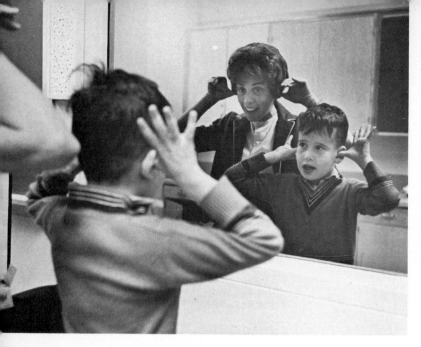

Unlike normal children, autistic children may not readily imitate adult behavior. Here a therapist works with an autistic child in an attempt to get him to mimic and respond to her. (*Allan Grant.*)

(including echolalia), motor awkwardness, poor interpersonal relations, blunted response to emotion-laden stimuli ("flat affect"), low frustration tolerance, internal preoccupations, withdrawal of interest in environment, paranoid fears, regression under stress. These are typical behaviors of both children and adults diagnosed as schizophrenic. Now you can see what we meant earlier when we spoke of similar behaviors as the basis for the same label. We could add delusions—the fantasies of childhood with the adult quality of permanence—to the list; unlike normal children, schizophrenic children do not return to the real world. Hallucinations also occur, but infrequently.

We listed blunted emotional response among the behaviors. As in the case of adult schizophrenics, many of these children are actually hypersensitive to sensory and emotional stimuli but display the characteristic "turned off" response to keep themselves at a safe, protective distance from painful reality. Table 15-1 lists typical symptoms of childhood schizophrenia in order of their observed frequency in 40 cases.

Bender (1961) provides a list of symptoms that are primarily physiological, in line with her view of childhood schizophrenia as an organic syndrome. Her diagnostic list includes:

1. Disturbance in vasovegetative (circulatory, digestive, excretory) functions.
2. Disturbance in normal rhythmic patterns (sleeping, eating, elimination).
3. Unevenness in somatic growth.
4. Faulty EEG rhythms.
5. Motor awkwardness.
6. Persistence of certain infantile reflex patterns.
7. Postural reflex responses. These are body-orienting reflexes that normally disappear in early infancy.
8. Physical dependence (leaning) on others.
9. Grimacing, expressionless speech, other neurological signs.
10. Lack of concern about body secretions.
11. Perceptual problems.
12. Language disturbances.

An actual case brings the diagnostic descriptions into sharp focus. Here is the remarkable story of Joey, age 9, whose parents had treated him with total indifference throughout his infancy and childhood. He was generally

Table 15-1 Incidence of Symptoms in 40 Cases

Rank	Symptom	No. of Cases
1	If speaks, odd quality to voice	18[1]
2	Low tolerance to frustration	36
3	Preoccupations present	32
4	Ignores other children	29
5	Attention: preoccupied or distractible	29
6	If speaks, echolalia present	14[1]
7	Stimuli excluded (pain, visual, acoustic)	27
8	Strong or unusual fears	26
9	Excessive mouth activity	26
10	Aggression self-bound	25
11	Understanding of speech uncertain	25
12	Bladder training incomplete	23
13	Bizarre movements present	23
14	Negativism high	23
15	Aggression absent	22
16	Bowel training incomplete	21
17	Object manipulation primitive	20
18	Aggression diffuse	20
19	No speech	19
20	Mother ignored	18
21	Separation problem	18
22	Affect intense	17
23	High anxiety	17
24	Afraid of other children	16
25	Avoids adults	16
26	If speaks, pronouns reversed	8[1]
27	Hyperactive	15
28	Aggression incomplete	15
29	Ignores adults	14
30	Selective food intake	11
31	Heedless of physical danger	11
32	Fleeting attention span	11
33	No social smile	11
34	Affect flat	10
35	Sleep disturbance	9
36	Biting inhibition	9
37	Identification with animals	8
38	Inhibition in amount of motor activity	7
39	Inhibition of skills in motor activity	7
40	Identification with inanimate objects	7
41	Excessive food or liquid intake	6
42	Ostentatious soiling	5
43	Avoids mother	5
44	Low food intake	5
45	Sex identification unclear or confused	4
46	Withholding of stools	2

[1] Of a total of 21.

From Brown, J. L. Prognosis from presenting symptoms of preschool children with atypical development. *American Journal of Orthopsychiatry*, 1960, 30, 386. © 1960 by the American Orthopsychiatric Association, Inc. Reprinted by permission.

ignored and seldom touched, except to be cleaned or fed. For reasons that will become obvious, Joey was called the "mechanical boy."

Joey, when we began our work with him, was a mechanical boy. He functioned as if by remote control, run by machines of his own powerfully creative fantasy. Not only did he himself believe that he was a machine but, more remarkably, he created this impression in others. Even while he performed actions that are intrinsically human, they never appeared to be other than machine-started and executed. On the other hand, when the machine was not working we had to concentrate on recollecting his presence, for he seemed not to exist. A human body that functions as if it were a machine and a machine that duplicates human functions are equally fascinating and frightening. Perhaps they are so uncanny because they remind us that the human body can operate without a human spirit, that body can exist without soul. And Joey was a child who had been robbed of his humanity. . . .

During Joey's first weeks with us we would watch absorbedly as this at once fragile-looking and imperious nine-year-old went about his mechanical existence. Entering the dining room, for example, he would string an imaginary wire from his "energy source"—an imaginary electric outlet—to the table. There he "insulated" himself with paper napkins and finally plugged himself in. Only then could Joey eat, for he firmly believed that the "current" ran his ingestive apparatus. So skillful was the pantomime that one had to look twice to be sure there was neither wire nor outlet nor plug. Children and members of our staff spontaneously avoided stepping on the "wires" for fear of interrupting what seemed the source of his very life.

For long periods of time, when his "machinery" was idle, he would sit so quietly that he would disappear from the focus of the most conscientious observation. Yet in the next moment he might be "working" and the center of our captivated attention. Many times a day he would turn himself on and shift noisily through a sequence of higher and higher gears until he "exploded," screaming "Crash, crash!" and hurling items from his ever present apparatus—radio tubes, light bulbs, even motors or, lacking these, any handy breakable object. (Joey

had an astonishing knack for snatching bulbs and tubes unobserved.) As soon as the object thrown had shattered, he would cease his screaming and wild jumping and retire to mute, motionless non-existence.

Our maids, inured to difficult children, were exceptionally attentive to Joey; they were apparently moved by his extreme infantile fragility, so strangely coupled with megalomaniacal superiority. Occasionally some of the apparatus he fixed to his bed to "live him" during his sleep would fall down in disarray. This machinery he contrived from masking tape, cardboard, wire and other paraphernalia. Usually the maids would pick up such things and leave them on a table for the children to find, or disregard them entirely. But Joey's machine they carefully restored: "Joey must have the carburetor so he can breathe." Similarly they were on the alert to pick up and preserve the motors that ran him during the day and the exhaust pipes through which he exhaled. (Bettelheim, 1959, p. 117)

How does childhood schizophrenia differ from infantile autism? Since both schizophrenic and autistic children lack contact with reality, which is manifested in poor object relations and body images, the two disorders can be confused. Kanner (1943) saw the sharp *regression* in schizophrenia as the principal feature that distinguished it from the *developmental arrest* of infantile autism. In this view, the schizophrenic child withdraws from the world while the autistic child has never been part of it.

Body images are whole but diffused to the schizophrenic child; that is, there is a fuzziness to the boundary dividing the child from other objects. Body image is fragmented to the autistic child, who can deal only in body parts, not wholes. Autistic children may think of their hands as separate from themselves and watch their performance with rapt attention.

An essential difference on which most psychiatrists agree is the presence of the EIA syndrome in the earliest stage of the infant's life, manifested by detachment from interaction with the mother and by lack of signs of physical response to the sights and sounds of the environment. Ward (1970) sums up the

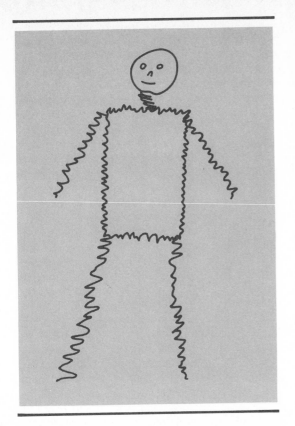

Figure 15-1 The above is an early self-portrait by Joey, the "mechanical boy." He depicts himself as a robot made of electrical wires. According to Bettelheim, "The figure symbolizes the child's rejection of human feelings. Reared by his parents in an utterly impersonal manner, he denied his own emotions because they were unbearably painful." (*Bettelheim, B. Joey: A mechanical boy. Scientific American, 1959, 200 (3), 116. © 1959 by Scientific American, Inc. All rights reserved.*)

consensus of opinions on differential diagnosis of the two disorders in four characteristics that belong to the autistic but not to the schizophrenic child:

1. Lack of object relations from birth (detachment and insulation from the environment).
2. Lack of use of speech in communication.

3. Maintenance of sameness via stereotypical behavior.
4. Lack of neurological or developmental dysfunctions (no organic defect, contrary to Bender's view).

Theoretical and Research Contributions

Psychodynamic View

As we approach the explanations for infantile autism and childhood schizophrenia, we come upon several familiar "landmarks": schizophrenogenic parents, genetic predisposition, and poorly defined ego boundary. And again, these landmarks raise more questions than they answer.

Kanner, who was the first to define autism, speaks of the "refrigerator" parent: cold, mechanical, detached, often meticulous, locked into inflexible views (rigidly scheduled feedings, strict discipline from the earliest possible moment). Others have taken up this position with variations.

A popular view points to the frustration of the child's probing and testing of reality by the mother's "symbiotic attitude." This is the smothering behavior of the overprotective mother. Related to this pattern is Bateson's double-bind hypothesis (see Chapter 4), which we noted as a possible causative factor in schizophrenia in Chapter 10. However, recall that we found little evidence for the double-bind in direct examination of parent-child interactions.

The common schizophrenogenic parent is not nurturing or attentive to the child's needs. The parents of the "mechanical boy" showed no sign of interest in him. Aside from punishing the child because his disturbing behavior fell short of their unrealistic expectations, Joey's parents treated him with machine-like indifference—and his self-mechanization was a direct response to that treatment.

Others indicate that the parent may induce the disorder in a short time by overwhelming the child with extremely negative feelings. The child may quickly develop a sense of hopelessness. This could occur at particularly sensitive periods in the developmental process, within the first year, when the child normally starts to communicate, but receives no responsive feedback to its utterances and gestures.

Childhood schizophrenia has been explained in psychodynamic terms as the consequence of failure to develop a separation between the realities of oneself and the world. Schizophrenic children are unable to discover the boundaries of their person and to experience themselves as a distinct reality, separate from the objects that are not them. Making that differentiation successfully is what determines the normal personality, according to Des Lauriers (1962), who sees the thwarted struggle for self-awareness as the cause of childhood schizophrenia.

Behavioral View

The autistic child's impoverished repertoire of behaviors is the central feature of the disorder in the behavioral view. Accordingly, the behaviorist explains the narrow range of autistic performance in terms of deficiencies in parental reinforcement patterns, with particular emphasis on ways in which large blocks of behavior can be extinguished. Ferster (1961) details an elaborate program of parent-child interactions that might account for autism.

In establishing the autistic child's range of performance, Ferster finds that it differs from the normal child's range of performance primarily in the relative infrequency of behaviors that have an influence on the environment. Autistic children spend most of their time engaged in behaviors that have a minimal effect (twirling, rubbing, flipping, chewing). Autistic children's social control of the environment (often in nonverbal or nonvocal ways) is restricted to getting their parents to respond to their demands. Since most autistic demands are presented in aversive ways and thus annoy the parent, they are not regularly reinforced, leading to strong *atavistic* (primitive) behaviors—tantrums, tugging at the parent's sleeve, and other annoyances. The aversive behavior is reinforced by the parent's satisfying the demand when the tantrum becomes intolerable.

Thus the parents tend to give positive reinforcement on a variable schedule. This results in behavior that is hard to extinguish.

Conditioned reinforcers are ordinarily not effective with autistic children, nor are generalized reinforcers such as smiles or verbal approval. Delayed reinforcement is also ineffective. However, it has been demonstrated that the autistic child can be trained gradually to respond to token and coin reinforcers, even under delay conditions.

Ferster relates aversive control and punishment to positive reinforcement. In normal situations, aversive control and punishment are usually followed by withdrawal of positive reinforcement (such as smiles). Thus aversive control and punishment are effective as extinguishers largely because of lack of positive reinforcement rather than because of direct, corporal effects. Aversive control would be less effective with autistic children, since they are not responsive to reinforcements that are unrelated to their few demands. However, punishment of particular behaviors may occasionally extinguish them when they are first performed (e.g., pulling the child away from a breakable lamp).

The parent's behavior toward the autistic child may tend to further weaken and narrow the child's behavior repertoire. The parent may be inattentive when (1) the parent is seriously disturbed or depressed, (2) the parent has "more important" interests, as do the typically well-educated parents of autistic children, and (3) the parent finds other activities more rewarding than tending to the difficult child. Under these conditions, the parent will ignore most of the child's communications, thereby extinguishing much behavior. This, of course, is exemplified by Kanner's "refrigerator" parent.

The Biological-Organic View

The deviant responses of autistic children on certain psychometric tests have persuaded some researchers of the likelihood of organic dysfunction, with possible cortical involvement. Rimland (1964) explains observations of low arousal levels in autistic children as a defect in the reticular formation in the brain stem, which serves the function of inhibition of incoming signals. The inhibition is necessary for the efficient screening and recognition of stimuli. Rimland uses arousal differential to separate autistic from schizophrenic children, since schizophrenic children show signs of high arousal. However, other researchers have generally found autistic children to be overaroused. Definitions and measurements of arousal have stirred continuing controversy in the study of both childhood and adult psychoses.

Rimland bases his hypothesis of cognitive dysfunction in childhood psychosis on the arousal concept. The reticular formation plays a key role in controlling the flow of signals through the central nervous system, thus critically affecting the efficiency of cognitive processes. Any defect could have drastic effects on perception and thinking. Rimland suggests that the defect in the reticular formation may be due to lack of oxygen (*anoxia*) during birth.

Bender (1961) finds the source of the schizophrenic disorder in the central nervous system (CNS). She postulates a correlation between the maturation of the CNS and the personality. When some biological dysfunction interferes with the development of the CNS functions, there is a corresponding lag in personality development, which manifests itself in childhood schizophrenia. This neurological defect is inherited. From this perspective, the mother's indifferent or mechanistic treatment of the child is a desperate, guilt-ridden response to the newborn child's failure to establish his or her identity and react consistently to his or her environment.

On its own, the genetic argument stands unbalanced on one leg. It does not account for autistic children who do not show organic deficits on physiological or neurological tests. There seems to be more support for the diathesis-stress model, which considers organic disorders only as predisposing factors. The genetic predisposition initiates a process involving a vicious circle in which the mother's perplexed reaction incites negative behaviors in the child,

which, in turn, disrupt the mother's normal responses to her child's needs (Mahler and Gosliner, 1955).

Thus, in these organic formulations, we see the mother-as-cause, child-as-victim relationship as more complex than originally proposed.

Treatment Approaches to Autism and Schizophrenia

Psychodynamic Approaches

In Chapter 11, we pointed out that the verbal techniques of traditional psychotherapy present a problem in dealing with schizophrenics since their language is so distorted. The same problem discourages the use of such psychotherapy for child psychotics. In dealing with autistic children, psychodynamic therapists find the verbal barrier almost insurmountable, since these children have never used language for ordinary communication. The development of techniques of communication is the main task of the therapist. This may require the use of metaphorical language or symbols from the child's own world.

Most psychotherapists emphasize the primary importance of a warm, supportive, and physically interactive role for the therapist. The physical interaction involves body contact (contrary to Freudian dictum). Some therapists use body manipulation to help psychotic children develop better body images through palpable sensations from contact with their environment.

Rank (1955) proposed a two-phase treatment program: The therapist (1) becomes a tolerant, emotionally consistent parent-substitute, and (2) helps the child acquire social skills (i.e., postponement of gratification and relating to others). However, this is difficult to achieve since the autistic child tends to limit the therapist to an impersonal relationship, in which the therapist serves as a means of satisfying the child's needs (food, candy, toys).

Bettelheim (1967) is one of a few therapists who claim success with straightforward psychoanalytical therapy directed toward ego repair. He acknowledges the importance to a good outcome of the child's "willingness to speak" before the age of 5. This would seem to place infantile autism beyond the reach of psychodynamic therapy, although Bettelheim says he has obtained "meaningful improvement" with mute children.

While occasional successes are reported with psychodynamic therapy, the diagnoses are not well defined and the cases are not carefully documented. One major problem is the painfully slow progress in obtaining even minute results, especially in EIA cases. As we noted earlier, the speech barrier is a determining factor in the prognosis of child psychotics. Eisenberg and Kanner (1956) reported that 16 out of 32 speaking children and only 1 out of 31 nonspeaking children eventually achieved some level of social adjustment. Age 5 was the cut-off point for the child's first use of speech among those who were included in the "speakers" group. The study showed no correlation between treatment and social adjustment.

Although children treated by psychotherapy have shown improvement, the record of such results is hardly better than that for untreated children whose prognostic signs (speech before 5 years of age and above-retardate intelligence) were good.

Behavioral Approaches

Lovaas (1973) sums up the arguments against psychodynamic therapy for childhood psychosis in these terms: (1) We do not know that there is really a unitary disorder that warrants a diagnostic label. (2) The psychotic child has experienced so many disturbing events that it is futile to seek a fundamental cause. (3) The initial cause may be different from the present cause, as we pointed out in Chapter 4. (4) Autistic children can be helped without knowledge of the initial cause, by treating the overt behaviors directly. The psychosis itself is not the immediate target. We showed how this was done in treating adult schizophrenics (in Chapter 11) by reinforcing appropriate, socially acceptable behaviors and extinguishing undesirable responses. Essentially, behavior therapy

is educational, based on operant conditioning principles.

Ferster's 1961 blueprint for functional analysis and behavioral treatment of childhood psychosis, which we discussed earlier, was followed by extensive work in developing speech and eliminating self-destructive behavior in autistic children. We will concentrate on the methods developed by Lovaas and his colleagues, since they were so effective and are similar to those used by other researchers.

Autistic children's self-destructive behavior is so dangerous to their very survival that it must be stopped before any other behavior is treated. The children may bang their heads so hard against the wall that concussions result. They may bite and chew their flesh until the bone is bared. Before the introduction of behavioral extinction methods to eliminate such harmful behaviors, children who were this destructive had to be confined in restraining harnesses, sometimes for years.

Lovaas et al. (1965) observed that showering autistic children with sympathy and love when they engaged in self-injurious acts caused the acts to occur more frequently. On reflection, it became clear that people working with these children were unwittingly reinforcing the destructive behavior. To test this operant hypothesis, they alternated periods of sympathetic response with periods during which each destructive act was completely ignored. The rate of such acts dropped from about 200 in ten minutes to nearly zero.

Some children, however, are so persistent and compulsive in their self-destructive behavior that more drastic measures than nonreinforcement are necessary. Lovaas (Lovaas and Simmons, 1969) discovered an effective treatment when he impulsively slapped a child on her backside immediately after he noticed her hitting her head on the wall. She stopped the behavior for a short while. Each successive headbang was punished with a hard swat. The girl soon stopped the behavior for the rest of the day.

Lovaas demonstrated the effectiveness of shock punishment on an 8-year-old autistic boy. Figure 15-2 (upper graph) shows the dramatic drop from a level of about 300 self-

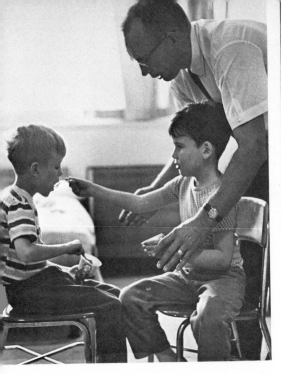

Lovaas was a pioneer in the use of behavioral techniques in the treatment of autistic children. (Left) Lovaas teaches two autistic boys social communication and sharing. (Above) An assistant attempts to teach a boy how to form words from phonemes. (*Allan Grant.*)

inflicted injuries in five minutes to zero on the sixteenth day when several shocks were given, and similar drops when shocks were given on the nineteenth, twenty-fourth, and thirtieth days. The percentage of time he spent in whining and avoiding eye contact also dropped to zero. Note the sharp rise in self-destructive behavior on days when other nurses (nos. 2, 3, 4), who did not punish the behaviors, cared for the boy. The rate dropped to zero on the twenty-eighth day, although no punishment was administered by the "punishing nurse" (no. 1), showing that the shock treatment had become associated with her. The boy's response generalized to the other nurses, and after one of them (no. 3) gave the boy several shocks on the thirtieth day, the zero rate held when the other nurses took the boy. Note that the whining and eye-avoidance behaviors also reduced to zero level along with the self-destruction. The bottom graph shows a similar result in a subsequent series of ten-minute observations during which the boy was free to move about the room. Shock punishment on the twenty-eighth and twenty-ninth days effectively extinguished

all undesirable behaviors. Self-stimulating behaviors (twirling objects, spinning oneself, etc.) were also extinguished by punishment.

Teaching the appropriate use of language to autistic children involves three stages: (1) the formation of words from phonemes (da + dee = daddy), (2) the proper use of words in labeling objects, and (3) the meaningful (semantic) use of words in correct sentences (syntax). Behavioral techniques have succeeded with echolalic children, who have obviously mastered stage 1. Sentences are built up from words and phrases by the method of successive approximation (shaping). Behavioral approaches have been the most successful method of initiating and maintaining speech. Earlier we noted the importance of speech to the outcome of the treatment of autistic children.

How effective are behavioral methods in generalizing the beneficial results to other social behaviors, especially to situations outside the treatment center? And how durable are the effects? Lovaas et al. (1973) made a follow-up study on a number of children in a behavior

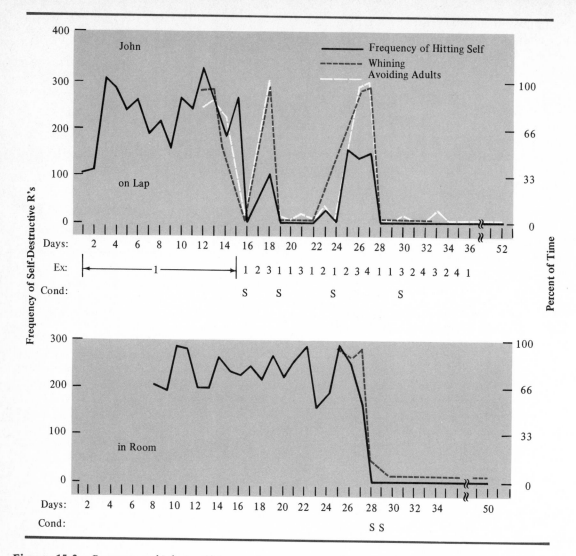

Figure 15-2 Frequency of John's self-destructive responses and percentage of time spent whining and avoiding adults during sessions with and without shock punishment. (Top: five-minute sessions when John was on nurse's lap. Bottom: ten-minute sessions in a separate room.) The abscissa gives the daily sessions, the attending experimenter, and shock sessions (S). (*Lovaas, O. I., and Simmons, J. Q. Manipulation of self-destruction in three retarded children. Journal of Applied Behavior Analysis, 1969, 2, 143–157. © 1969 by the Society for the Experimental Analysis of Behavior, Inc. Reprinted by permission.*)

therapy program, checking frequency of two undesirable behaviors (self-stimulation and echolalia) and three appropriate behaviors (see Figure 15-3). Notice the improvement in all five behaviors after treatment (A). In contrast, see how all performance advantages were lost by the children who were returned to a state institution after treatment (I)—note especially the increase of self-stimulation behavior to a level far worse even than before treatment. Children returned to their parents (P), who were instructed in continuation of the program at home, generally continued to improve or at least to maintain their previous improved level of performance. Lovaas emphasizes the necessity for maintenance of reinforcement if treated autistic children are to hold their behavior gains.[1]

Frequent Psychological Problems of Childhood

Enuresis

Bed-wetting, or enuresis, is a fairly common problem, often associated with toilet training. Because some parents are upset by the

[1] Students interested in other research developments in the treatment of autistic children may read Hingtgen and Bryson (1972), Ornitz (1973), Ross (1974), and Rutter (1971).

task of cleaning up after the child, the parent-child struggle involved in dealing with the situation, and the stigma of immaturity it casts on the child, the problem can get out of hand and become the basis for serious psychological problems.

Enuresis occurs more frequently among lower socioeconomic classes, in families with a history of bed-wetting, and about twice as often in boys as in girls. Psychoanalysts view it as a sign of maladjustment, suggesting that the child is retaliating for the way the world treats him or her ("urinating on the world").

Behaviorists have addressed the problem as a habit deficiency, possibly aggravated by a bladder with small capacity. They have developed a night wake-up system to condition appropriate habits and a bladder training program to increase the capacity.

The alarm system, developed by Mowrer and Mowrer (1938), consists of two foil sheets separated by insulation and attached to an alarm box. When the child begins to urinate in bed, the foil circuit is closed and the alarm goes off. The child wakes up, shuts off the alarm, and goes to the bathroom to complete voiding.

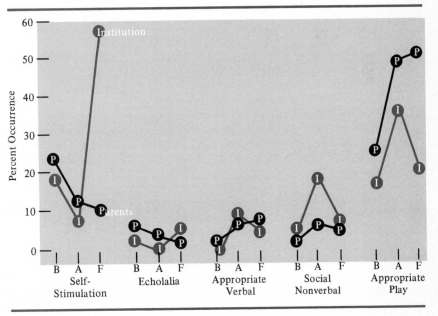

Figure 15-3 Percentage of time psychotic children engaged in five classes of behavior before treatment (B), after treatment (A), and at follow-up (F). "I" refers to the average results for children who were institutionalized after treatment; "P" refers to the average results for children who lived with parents after treatment. (*Lovaas, O. T., et al. Some generalization and followup measures on autistic children in behavior therapy.* Journal of Applied Behavior Analysis, 1973, 6, 131–165. © 1973 by the Society for the Experimental Analysis of Behavior, Inc.)

Eventually the child recognizes the internal sensations that precede the bell, awakens without it, and goes to the bathroom. The device has been effective in about 80 percent of the cases.

Bladder training is aimed at stretching the bladder by such techniques as having children retain their urine after drinking large quantities of liquid, playing family games to distract them while they are holding their urine, and attempting to interrupt their stream while they urinate. Success records for bladder training range between 40 and 45 percent.

Drug therapy has also been used. Amphetamines cause light sleep so the child is more likely to awaken. Imipramine reduces involuntary bladder contractions. However, possible side effects are objectionable features of drug therapy.

In a controlled study by Deleon and Mandell (1966), 85 children were assigned to three groups: (1) Mowrer-type conditioning, (2) psychotherapy consisting of 12 weekly sessions, and (3) a control group having no treatment. The results were 86 percent success in the Mowrer group, 18 percent success in the psychotherapy group, and 11 percent success in the control group.

In spite of the extremely good record of the conditioning treatment, psychoanalysts object to the child's dependence on mechanical aids, pointing to the threat of symptom substitution and later problems of impotence if the essential intrapsychic conflict is not resolved by psychotherapy. Behaviorists counter with test results that show lower anxiety levels and better self-image in children who feel good about the bladder control and social confidence they gain as a result of the conditioning.

Anxiety Reactions of Childhood

Children display anxiety in various ways: irritability, loss of appetite, physical symptoms. Most commonly, anxiety affects their sleeping habits, making them unable to fall asleep and causing bad dreams that awaken them during the night.

Sleeping and dreaming are as essential to the psychodynamic theories of children as they are to the theories of adults. Bedtime provides the ideal situation for the emergence of fears of separation and loss of control in sleep. Parents who use the euphemism of "sleeping" when they speak of the dead associate death with sleep in children's minds. Children's aggressions also emerge when they go to bed. Fears that their hostile wishes toward parents and siblings may become known and punished prevent them from falling asleep. During the 4–6 age interval, anxieties may be accompanied by urges to masturbate, which the children are more aware of when they are in bed. Bad dreams experienced on previous nights may discourage sleep. In some cases, these fears and anxieties amount to "night terror," from which the children awaken in a completely disoriented state.

Anthony (1975) describes the case of the 9-year-old daughter of a hypersensitive mother. The child, who had been a sickly baby, lived in a constant state of apprehension of some dire accident. Her anxieties had been magnified by her grandmother's death and her own tonsillectomy. She suffered nightmares, fear of abandonment, and guilt over masturbation. Anthony points to the complex of constitutional, familial, traumatic, and intrapsychic factors responsible for the high anxiety.

The behavioral view characterizes the anxiety reaction as overgeneralized fear, or phobia, which we will discuss next.

Phobias

We all remember certain childhood fears: animals, school, the dark, vehicles. As time passed, we outgrew the "normal" fears—the fear of animals caused by a vicious, barking dog; the fear of school induced by an overly strict teacher. But for some children the fears take hold with a morbid, irrational grip. They become clinical problems when they interfere with the normal life of the child and his or her parents.

We saw the psychodynamic view of the origins of animal phobia expressed in the case of Little Hans (Freud, 1909/1955), Freud's young patient who feared horses (in Chapters 3 and 8). The boy's phobia was presumed to be related to a classical Oedipal situation, in which intrapsychic conflict is the source of surplus anxiety. Such anxiety occurs in the process of displacing one's unacceptable impulses and fears toward a taboo object (the father) onto a symbol outside the conflict situation (the horses). The psychoanalyst sees the fear of spiders and snakes (crawling, slimy sensations) as a negative reaction to unacceptable sexual impulses.

Transportation phobia is similarly viewed as the result of the child's projection of impulses onto the vehicles, bus drivers, or conductors. The possibility of accidents provides a logical motive for the fear. A 9-year-old girl rode with women drivers but not with men. Another girl envisioned fatal school bus accidents in which her classmates all perished (Kessler, 1966).

Fear of school is one of the most common, and serious, childhood phobias. The following case of Anne shows the behavior of school phobia, and, perhaps more importantly, the parents' attempts to deal with the behavior.

They discussed with Anne the happenings of the past few days in school, and asked about the subject matter, her teachers, and her schoolmates. They tried to learn something about her recent social life, especially to discover any unfortunate emotional experience. When they found nothing to explain why Anne should have a dread of school, they suspected that she was withholding facts from them. The next morning when it was time for Anne to leave for school, her parents became anxious. Her father was annoyed by what he termed "nonsense"; there was nothing to fear. Anne admitted as much. He had to go to work, and he became angry as Anne started to cry and he insisted that she put on her wraps and come along with him to school. When the mother acted as though she felt he was doing the wrong thing, he became more annoyed; the mother's behavior increased his doubts about what he was doing. Realizing that this was no time to change his mind, however, since that would only confuse Anne more, he got into the car with her. Anne cried all the way to school, saying she knew she could not

make it. Her father assured her she would get along well as soon as she was at her desk with all her friends around her. Anne and her father walked up the school steps, but as they approached the entrance Anne grew pale and vomited.

Realizing that he had made a mistake, her father returned home with her. . . . Usually, driven by their anxiety, parents first urge their child to go back to school, beg him, and then try to bribe him with gifts. When these methods fail they often resort to punishment, in the belief that the child is being willful and stubborn. When parents become panicky about the child's not going to school, their anxiety intensifies the child's suffering. By the time they bring the child to a child guidance clinic on the advice of school or school social worker, the child feels ashamed of his helplessness and guilty about the anxiety he has caused his parents. Absence from school has made him feel that he is behind in his school work and will never be able to catch up with his classmates. (Lippman, 1956, p. 86)

For the behavioral view of the phobias, look back over our discussion in Chapters 3 and 8, where we presented a learning theory explanation for the development of phobic reactions. Watson and Rayner's experiment (1920), in which they induced a phobia in Little Albert toward furry objects, is a clear-cut model of the process. Accordingly, childhood phobias are treated by conditioning. Wolpe's desensitization procedure has been used successfully in reducing animal and transportation phobias. Bandura's modeling technique (1967) has also been applied, exposing the child to scenes in which a fearless child model makes progressively closer approaches to a dog in a pleasant situation (a birthday party, etc.).

Behavioral treatment for school phobia eliminates positive reinforcement for staying at home and reinforces attendance with candy and tokens exchangeable for privileges. Lazarus, Davison, and Polefka (1965) used a desensitization procedure in treating a boy with school phobia. The therapist conducted the boy through a sequence of steps, starting with walks to school in the therapist's company, and increasing in level of evoked anxiety (entering school, sitting at desk, spending increasing amounts of time in school with the therapist present, later with the therapist outside but still available). Rewards of comic books and tokens exchangeable for a baseball glove were then substituted for the therapist's presence. The program extended over a period of 4½ months. A 10-month follow-up showed no regression.

Other Problems of Childhood

If, indeed, "the child is father to the man," it is not surprising to find childhood counterparts of adult neuroses and psychoses. What is sometimes surprising is the fully developed pattern of an abnormal syndrome in children—as in some cases of conversion hysteria, compulsive neurosis, and the phobias—during the developmental period.

At this point, we will briefly describe the childhood versions of these problems. You may review the detailed presentation of the therapy and treatment of the corresponding adult disorders in previous chapters.

Hysteria in the conversion form is uncommon in children. When it occurs, it is marked by the typical sensory and motor disturbances of the adult version: stocking-and-glove anesthesia, tics and grimacing, paralysis of one or more body parts. Occasionally, hallucinations may be experienced, but these are distinguished from the unreal world of the schizophrenic.

Compulsive neurosis is observed as early as the second year in the incipient form of a preoccupation with sameness, although its full emergence may be delayed for several years. It may start with anxieties induced by rigorous toilet training or strict parental discipline. Many cases occur at puberty, when elaborate rituals are practiced at bedtime and on arising.

Depression in children is traced psychodynamically to the same sources as in adults: fear of loss of a love object (real or fantasized) as a result of physical separation or threatened abandonment as a punishment for misbehavior. Poor self-image and a sense of helplessness are central features. Many children experience

transitory episodes of depression that are associated with life situations. These are not considered pathological. The behavioral view of extinction of behavior as a result of a change or loss of significant others is also possible.

Several behavior patterns are specific to childhood. Among them are withdrawal, runaway, and unsocialized aggressive reactions. The DSM-II (1968) characterizes the *withdrawal reaction* by the child's "seclusiveness, detachment, sensitivity, shyness, timidity" (p. 50), when the behaviors are not definite enough to be called "schizoid." The reaction is most frequent in the 5–7 age interval when the child enters school, a time of profound change.

The *runaway reaction* is well known and the subject of some humor to everyone but the miserable child who is trying to "escape from threatening situations," according to the DSM-II definition. Cold, rejecting parents; harsh, unsympathetic discipline; failure in school are among the motivating influences. The confirmed runaway is a "loner" with a poor prognosis that includes the likelihood of delinquency.

Unsocialized aggressive reaction is sometimes covert, but usually reveals itself in "hostile disobedience, . . . physical and verbal aggressiveness, vengefulness, and destructiveness" (DSM-II, 1968, p. 51). This category contains bullies, vandals, petty thieves, and juvenile delinquents. The child is poorly socialized. The family is generally unstable. Parental discipline is nagging, brutal, and inconsistent.

The Hyperactive Child: Hyperkinesis, Minimal Brain Damage, Dyslexia

Behavioral Description

The "hyperactive" category has assumed importance since it has become the catch-all for uncontrollable children—"bad kids" whose persistent misbehavior defies ordinary disci-

A frequent problem among children is with-drawal. Some children are so timid and shy they literally wedge themselves into a corner to avoid contact with others. (*David R. White, Woodfin Camp & Associates.*)

pline. While technically the three labels above are used to describe different disorders, in real-ity they are frequently used interchangeably. And while all three have been used to describe some presumed neurological dysfunction, no "hard" signs of neurological defect have yet been found. Only the "soft" behavioral signs that are read as indications of central cortical damage have emerged. Because of its wide-spread use, we will use the term "hyperactiv-ity" to refer to all of the children included under these labels.

The behavioral characteristics of hyperac-tivity are itemized in the DSM-II (1968) as "overactivity, restlessness, distractibility, and short attention span" (p. 50). Clearly, degree is the distinguishing factor, since those terms could be used to describe most children at one time or another.

Other features of the hyperactive child include impulsivity, inability to delay gratifica-tion, inability to experience pleasure, low self-esteem, tantrums, tics, withdrawal, and resis-tance to discipline.

Since the "bad" or "difficult" child is a source of vexation to parents and teachers, we must recognize some bias in their reports and note that most diagnoses of the problem are made solely on the basis of such nonprofessional reports, unsupported by test evidence. The diagnosis may thus be as much a reflection of low parental or teacher tolerance as it is of a physical disorder.

Theory and Research

Etiology

The most common explanation for hyperactivity is that it is a biochemically based syndrome (Wender, 1972). In one study, half of the cases showing characteristic hyperactive behaviors had some neurological dysfunction (Werry, 1968). As in certain types of schizophrenia, arousal levels are also seen as symptomatic of some organic defect. Satterfield and Dawson (1971) found that half of 24 hyperactive children showed galvanic skin resistance patterns usually associated with low arousal (although two of the children showed high arousal GSR patterns). Underarousal would be consistent with the lack of attention, easy distractibility, and restlessness characteristic of hyperactive children.

One theory attempts to account for the abnormal arousal levels of these children by suggesting a deficiency in norepinephrine (NE) and serotonin, the principal neurotransmitters whose function we have described previously. The deficiency would reduce the responsiveness of postsynaptic neurons, thereby reducing the transmission of signals to and from the brain. A second hypothesis explains the low response of hyperactive children to positive and negative reinforcement (which would account for their "incorrigibility") by a deficiency in NE alone. Experiments with animals have shown a diminished rate of avoidance response in operant conditioning when NE synthesis is blocked. When the NE is replaced, response rates return to normal. Administration of antidepressants to such children improves their avoidance responses, presumably by inhibiting the reabsorption of NE, thus enhancing its effect on neuronal activity.

Are these biochemical dysfunctions inherited? Favoring the genetic hypothesis are the high concordance rates for hyperactive behaviors in siblings and near relatives: 65–90 percent for reading and writing problems and similarly high correlations for other behaviors (clumsiness, restlessness). We are aware, from our study of concordance data for schizophrenics, that we must be cautious in drawing conclusions regarding genetic causes from data on metabolic dysfunction. Even if the metabolic dysfunction is inherited, we have no direct evidence that it is responsible for the deviant behavior patterns.

Follow-up and Prognostic Studies

Hyperactive children have an uncertain prognosis. Improvement is found in some behaviors, notably the principal feature—overactivity—while other behaviors persist. One study (Menkes, Rowe, and Menkes, 1967) found that after 25 years, 6 of 14 diagnosed children were non-self-supporting and 4 were psychotic. A 20- to 30-year follow-up (Morris, Escoll, and Wexler, 1956) reported only one-fifth were "doing well," one-sixth were psychotic, and the rest had serious social and psychological problems.

A reevaluation (Weiss, Minde, and Werry, 1971) was done on 64 children out of an original group of 70 (age range 6–13) who had been diagnosed as hyperactive about five years previously. The researchers based their evaluations on parent and teacher reports. Only 5 of the children were still on medication. The hyperactivity had abated into quiet playing with pencils, etc., and other less disturbing activity. Distractibility scores were lower, although the children had difficulty in concentrating on tasks. This was the mothers' chief complaint. Excitability seemed to have decreased significantly. Reports from the mothers indicated that

30 percent of the children had no steady friends, 25 percent engaged in antisocial behavior, and 16 percent had been in court for various offenses. School performance was generally poor.

Treatment Approaches to Hyperactivity

In accordance with the assumption of neurological dysfunction in hyperactivity, drug treatment has become so popular and overused that the use of amphetamines, phenothiazines, and imipramine has been challenged by psychologists and educators. The fact that the medications have side effects and may indeed interfere with future adjustment raises doubts about their general use, especially on the unsupported request of school authorities.

Even those who are enthusiastic over the benefits of medication for hyperactivity make it clear that the drugs are symptom-reducing agents, not cures or correctives. At best, they suppress disruptive behaviors and render the child amenable to appropriate educational procedures.

Amphetamines are stimulants aimed at enhancing the child's arousal and reinforcement potential, thereby increasing his or her attention and motivation, as we indicated in the biochemical review. They involve side effects of insomnia, irritability, headache, and loss of appetite.

Methylphenidate (Ritalin) has stimulating effects similar to the amphetamines. But in addition to causing the same side effects as the amphetamines, methylphenidate causes skin rashes and, occasionally, toxic psychoses.

Tranquilizers are used to make the extremely active child manageable. They include the phenothiazines, which are usually restricted to highly disturbed children, since they produce cognitive deficits. Tranquilizers have become a common form of self-medication in our society, and so it is not surprising that they are likely to be overused to spare parents and teachers the unpleasant effects of a child with the "hyperactivity" syndrome.

Psychotherapy with Children

Children in therapy are in the midst of their developmental process. This can cause serious problems for the therapist. The children's lower level of intellectual functioning, inadequate verbal skills, lack of personal insight, and discomfort in face-to-face confrontation with a strange adult whose motives are, at first, unknown all combine to make the therapist's job a difficult one.

Psychodynamic Approaches

Individual Psychotherapy

Creative psychodynamic psychotherapists will deal with these problems and take advantage of the situation, for they are in the enviable position of being able to observe and respond to parent-child relations and reactions as they happen. Repressed emotions and events are still fresh, not buried deep under years of encrusted growth. Traumatic experiences that induce unconscious conflicts, which, in turn, lead to maladaptive behaviors, are recent or current; unwholesome family relationships are ongoing. The therapist may be able to see directly the parents' behaviors that are contributing to the child's problem and, where possible, the therapist can enlist the parents' cooperation in modifying their behavior so as to interrupt the development of the disorder.

Although the child may offer some resistance to therapy, the resourceful psychotherapist can establish the basic transference relationship, which allows the child to work out repressed thoughts and feelings on the therapist as "stand-in" for parents and siblings. In this surrogate role, the therapist provides support, insight, and interpretation in a nonthreatening manner that distinguishes him or her from the people who are enmeshed in the child's conflicts.

We suggested above that children's limited verbal skills are an obstacle to the free communication necessary for psychotherapy. However, this turns out to be a less serious problem, since children have another means of communication in which they are quite eloquent: play. The therapeutic site is set up as a playroom furnished with toys that lend themselves readily to the representation of objects and people in the child's life: dolls that take the roles of parents, siblings, and other relatives; and toy objects that serve real-life functions (dishes, furniture, etc.). With these props, the child can act out repressed hostilities, desires, and perplexing relationships.

Group Psychotherapy

Psychodynamic therapists have "borrowed" behavioral concepts in the treatment of disturbed children in groups. They speak of the reinforcement of peers along with ego structures, but they do not control reinforcement contingencies in the unstructured group situations. Tangible rewards, social reinforcers, and negative reinforcement are prominent mechanisms in the application of group dynamics to the correction of unacceptable behavior.

Once children learn how to work within the group, it offers a number of advantages in helping them to understand and deal with their problems. We will look at some of these benefits in the context of the different types and age ranges of therapy groups.

Child therapy groups are generally set up according to the developmental stages and their corresponding age ranges: preschool (to age 5),

Although they have limited verbal skills, children can communicate their feelings through play. Using props that resemble real-life situations, children can act out their repressed hostilities and desires. (*Cornell Capa, Magnum Photos.*)

early school age (5–8 years), latency age (9–11), puberty (12–13), early adolescent (13–14), middle-late adolescent (14–17). Group activity is either spontaneous or structured, with minimal intervention by a passive therapist or interactive modeling and interpretation by an active therapist. In selecting participants, efforts are made to assemble a fairly heterogeneous combination of personality types, excluding violent, sexually deviant, and psychotic children, whose needs are better served by individual psychotherapy or in homogeneous institutional groups. In some cases, however, special work on particular problems—such as those arising in disadvantaged families—dictates the grouping of children of similar background and personality.

Several assumptions have encouraged the proliferation of group therapy. One assumption is the effectiveness of peers in giving positive and negative reinforcement. Another is the emergence during permissive group activities of psychological problems that the therapist can observe. A third is the effect of the group on change of behavior by means of information exchange and decision making.

In the preschool and early school age groups, fantasy play is the vehicle of communication. We have already discussed the way this works in connection with severe behavior problems. The group play situation provides real people for acting out interpersonal conflicts. The verbal articulateness of latency age group members permits direct discussion of individual problems (social, family, intergroup) by the group members. Freedom of expression is encouraged, with minimal therapist intervention. A variation of the group structure is the club, whose goals and activities are determined by the members, avoiding the objectionable aspect of control by adults.

Unlike the lower-age groups, pubertal therapy groups usually segregate the sexes. Activity therapy involves games and defined projects in which anxieties and other neurotic responses are allowed to develop to provide more reality testing in a sympathetic milieu.

Adolescent groups are usually coed. The group becomes the sounding board and testing instrument for the individual's distorted views and behaviors. Direct feedback from peers with common interests and problems, and modeling of the therapist, aid the adolescent in recognizing and adopting successful behaviors. Discussion of common family conflicts strengthens the members in their efforts to cope with daily threats to their identities.

Behavioral Approaches

We have discussed behavior therapies at some length in connection with specific problems of children (autism, enuresis, phobias). Here we will only point up some general considerations relating the application of behavioral methods to children.

Ross (1972) distinguishes between behavior deficit (exhibited by autistic children) and maladaptive behavior (exhibited by phobic children). Operant methods are particularly suited to the replenishment of absent behaviors, as we have seen in Lovaas's treatment of autistic verbal deficiency. Combinations of operant and respondent conditioning methods are effective in modifying maladaptive behaviors. The Lazarus et al. (1965) hierarchical procedure in treating school phobia used such a combination to eliminate anxiety (respondent conditioning) and establish good habits (operant conditioning).

Wolpe-type desensitization procedures have been used successfully with children's phobias. A variation of this method is the use of *emotive imagery*. Images of positive emotional content are associated with a hierarchy of anxiety-laden situations or objects. The pleasant imagery is paired successively with stimuli of increasing anxiety potential until the most anxiety-provoking stimulus has been turned into a pleasurable event. Peer modeling (as in Bandura's treatment of animal phobia) is an example of desensitization by indirect means.

One of the principal advantages of behavioral over psychodynamic approaches is that trained aides can replace the professional in many aspects of treatment. While psychodynamic therapy has employed nonprofessional aides (notably, Little Hans's father, who received his instructions by mail from Freud), a larger part of the procedure requires direct involvement of the psychotherapist. On the other hand, a shortcoming of behavior modification is the selection and change of single behaviors. While some generalization is observed, care and insight must operate to find the crucial behavior that influences a constellation of behaviors.

The Family Context of Behavior Problems of Children

Before 1950, the individual and group therapy procedures that we have described were the only methods of therapeutic intervention. They were largely founded on the medical model, which cast the person with a problem in the role of a "patient" suffering from an "illness" that could be treated individually in an office or hospital. The improved patient could then be returned to the family and community, ready to resume his or her proper place.

After some perceptive practitioners noted the occasionally destructive effects of improved patients on their families and vice versa, they began to involve the family in the therapeutic program. At first, the family was simply "tacked on" to the therapy by means of interviews and conferences. But by the 1960s, family therapy had acquired full status among professionals and was developing theoretical and operational concepts that were a distinct advance over the earlier psychodynamic model of individual behavior.

We will now consider the dynamics of the family system—the rules that govern its interactions, and the effects of the interactions on the individual members. In particular, we are concerned with the individual viewed as a dysfunctional part of the system. Instead of the child with pathological symptoms, we now have the child as a symptom of the sick family—the "scapegoat" who is the victim of the

defective functioning of the system. Thus we move from the "sick individual" model into the "sick family" model, in which the victim has made an understandable, adaptive response to a malfunctioning system.

Methods of Studying Families

The inherent complexities of family relationships multiply the usual problems in assessing abnormalities in behavior. Existing methods and instruments have been adapted, and new ones devised for family assessment. Bodin (1968) organizes the problem into three approaches: (1) assessment of individual members, (2) assessment of joint family groupings, (3) combinations of (1) and (2).

Individual (approach 1) and joint (approach 2) interviews commonly are used to obtain a picture of the family's interactive style and the way it sees its problems. Interviews may be structured or unstructured, depending on the therapist's preference. Each offers advantages and disadvantages, but there is agreement that interviews are not only information-gathering techniques but therapeutic devices as well. Structured interviews often incorporate tests of family collaboration, decision making, and judgment of personal problems. The therapist also sees the interview as an educational opportunity, to introduce the family to the objectives, methods, and requirements for task performance that are part of the therapy (Wahler and Cormier, 1970).

Direct observation is the method of choice for most family therapists. The observation may be made of family interactions in the therapy room, in structured laboratory situations, or in the natural environment of the home. Each offers advantages and limitations. The laboratory situation permits observation of the family engaged in experimental tasks. The family's ability to agree on matching color panels or on joint decisions regarding ordinary choices of magazines, movies, and so on, is scored and analyzed. In one study (Ravich, Deutsch, and Brown, 1966), families were involved in games requiring cooperative team play in order to maximize their scores. Conflict patterns between various family members are revealed in such situations.

In-home observation presents the ideal setting for the playing-out of the family's natural roles, while responses within laboratory situations may be specific to the artificial situation. Of course, the presence of an observer has an effect on the spontaneity of family interactions, but the familiarity of the environment and the pressures inherent in real situations soon overcome awareness of the intruder, and "normal" conflicts emerge. Family members—including the problem child—also serve as observers when objective (counting) measures are used (Patterson, Ray, and Shaw, 1969).

Family Factors in Abnormal Behavior in Children

We will look first at some of the typical reciprocal interactions in which abnormal behaviors develop, and then relate them to certain types of parents and family relationships.

Our frequent references to "interaction" among family members have set the stage for the operation of family dynamics. In an operant behavior sense, the various members are sources of both discriminative stimuli and reinforcing responses for each other. In Wahler's (1976) view, the parents' behaviors induce the child's deviant responses, which in turn elicit the parents' behaviors that support the deviances, in a "continuous feedback" loop (see Figure 15-4). Interchanges between father and mother influence each other's responses to the child.

How does the child's deviance get locked into the system? Wahler describes the reciprocal reinforcements as "trap situations." Dependent (clinging) behaviors that were positively reinforcing during the infant period become aversive later, but the trap has been sprung by the earlier reinforcement patterns. The maintenance of unpleasant behavior is the common dilemma of the parent who reinforces the child's crying or nagging tantrums in order to stop them, thereby assuring their repetition. This pattern develops the "coercive" child.

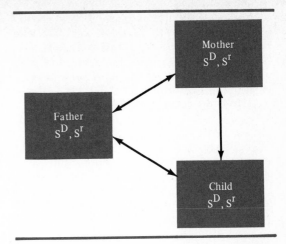

Figure 15-4 A social-learning-theory conception of the family. Each person is viewed as a source of discriminative stimuli (S^D) and reinforcing stimuli (S^r) for other family members. (*Wahler, R. G. Deviant child behavior within the family: Developmental speculation and behavior change strategies. In H. Leitenberg (Ed.), Handbook of behavior modification and behavior therapy. Englewood Cliffs, N.J.: Prentice-Hall, 1976, p. 517.* © *1976. Reprinted by permission of Prentice-Hall, Inc.*)

Parents are often responsible for the maintenance of abnormal behaviors. For example, it is easier to dress children who cannot dress themselves or wheel children who will not walk. Other abnormal behaviors are similarly reinforced by misdirected responses. The parent is unaware of the situational contingencies and so continues to reinforce the undesirable behavior whenever it occurs.

Let us take a closer look at the kinds of parent behaviors and family situations that seem to produce problem children. Child conduct disorders are often associated with absence of parents during childhood, in cases where children grew up in institutions or broken homes. Lack of self-control and inappropriate aggression are reported more often for this group. The death of a parent is less likely to cause such deviance than divorce or desertion following marital conflict.

McCord and McCord (1958) found a correlation between criminal fathers and cold mothers and the likelihood of delinquency in children. Other studies show higher incidence of delinquency among children subject to rejection and hostility by their fathers.

Hostility accompanied by severe punishment, especially when the punishment is inconsistently administered, tends to promote delinquency and aggression in boys. A combination of lax discipline by mothers and excessive discipline by fathers is found in many homes of delinquents. In fact, there is an association between parental disagreement over discipline and child maladjustment.

Neurosis has been proposed as a family trait: rigid, uncompromising fathers; anxious, overprotective mothers; inconsistent repression of impulses combined with overstimulating behavior—these are some of the familial correlates to behavior problems of childhood.

Approaches to Treatment Within the Family Context —Family Therapy

Given that so many behavior problems are a result of poor family communication and deviant interaction, treating the family as a whole rather than treating just the problem child seems to make sense. The following are the broad objectives of family therapy (Hess and Handel, 1967).

1. Defining individual separateness and group relations.
2. Identifying each member to the others in terms of personal needs and problems.
3. Developing ways of dealing with family matters.
4. Setting up boundaries within which the family lives (as distinct from its interaction with the community outside).

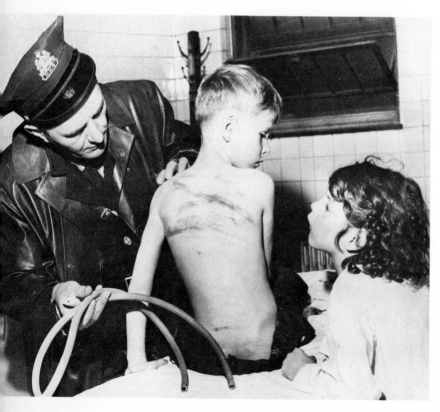

Children who are subject to severe punishment often become aggressive delinquents. (*United Press International.*)

5. Dealing with family roles of male, female, old, and young members.

Fox (1976) sums up the program goals as (1) strengthening the family system, (2) increasing separation and individuation, and (3) strengthening the marital relationship, which he considers the mainstay of the child's ego development.[2]

Open, clear, and straightforward communications are the lifeline of an efficiently functioning family system. The therapist must get the members to recognize their place in the system and abandon their image of a family with a sick patient. This is accomplished in joint sessions in which the developments that led up to the present problem are brought to light and examined. The therapist is actively involved in the process of changing destructive patterns.

Establishing individual identities and independent status requires that members acknowledge the relative autonomy of each member. The therapist emphasizes the need for separateness within the context of family collaboration. The members practice restraint until the balance between working together and respecting individual differences is achieved.

Finally, the marriage is strengthened by identifying sources of disagreement and working them out between the parents without involvement of the children.

We noted earlier that diagnosis and assessment of the family interaction patterns are conducted in the therapy room. The therapist assesses patterns of interaction, issues among family members, subgroups within the family, and so on. Assessment and therapy are intertwined in family treatment due to the complexity and changing nature of family interactions:

Therapists employ a repertoire of techniques limited only by their ingenuity and perceptiveness. Although they usually work with the family as a whole unit, bypassing individual dynamics, they will sometimes single out one member who is at the focal point of family disequilibrium. Breaking up old, pathological alliances and building new coalitions is a basic strategy for creating better patterns of interaction. Teaching communication skills is another productive practice (how to listen, how to read underlying meanings). Here the goal is to develop the family's ability to stand back and be detached observers of each other's behavior. In their therapy, Minuchin and Montalvo (1967) go so far as to place the member behind a one-way mirror where each family member can observe other family members in action.

Role-playing offers experience in relating behaviors to their effects on others. By reversing roles, the "actors" are compelled to appreciate the impact of their own behaviors on other members, especially the problem child.

Behavior modification techniques are also tools of some family therapists. We have described typical procedures in the treatment of childhood neuroses. In family therapy, the parent is instructed in contingency management and the use of positive reinforcers and punishment.

Results of Family Therapy

The complexity of family problems and the applicable programs of therapy pose great difficulties for outcome studies. As a measure of the problem, Olson (1970) qualified only 3 percent of about 250 published reports of family therapy as valid research studies! Other critics also have found an abundance of flawed methodology. We will cite here the results of one of the better studies as an example.

Wells, Dilkes, and Trivelli (1972) review a two-part, methodologically sound study. In the first part, 150 families, with one seriously disturbed member in each, were matched with a control group. The 150-family therapy cases were followed up in a second study six months after treatment. Thirteen percent of the seriously disturbed members in the experimental cases were hospitalized, against 29 percent for

[2]For those who are interested in the preconditions and procedural details of family therapy, Fox (1976) spells out the prerequisites for a successful program, including the qualifications of the family and the therapist.

the controls, and these 13 percent were less likely to be readmitted for hospitalization after discharge.

Wells also compared uncontrolled family therapy outcome studies with similarly defective psychotherapy studies. The combined "improved" and "some improvement" rates for family therapy with adults was 69 percent, and with children, 79 percent. The comparable results for psychotherapy were 66 percent and 73 percent, a close approximation. But we must reserve judgment here since the comparisons are clouded by the uncertain study methods.

Summary

Infantile autism is recognized within three to five years after birth. Its principal features are indifference to the environment and total preoccupation with the maintenance of sameness. Organic causes are suspected since autism often occurs immediately after birth. Childhood schizophrenia has a somewhat later onset and is marked by regressive behavior, resulting from a failure to make a distinction between one's self and one's object world.

Parental rejection and biological defects in the CNS arousal mechanism are blamed for the child's deficient responses. The behavioral view sees autism as the result of reduction of the child's repertoire of behaviors through failure of parents to reinforce the infant's communications. Behavioral treatment has been successful in conditioning autisic children to use language and to behave in socially appropriate ways.

Childhood neuroses—anxiety, hysteria, depression, phobias—are similar to their adult counterparts. As in the adult cases, behavioral treatment can be effective. Psychotherapy generally has to be modified to suit the child's limited verbal repertoire and insights. Playing with toys provides an alternative means of communication. The use of group therapy with children has also been successful.

The organic hypothesis as the cause of hyperactivity in children has been questioned, since there is no direct demonstration of such dysfunction on specific behaviors.

We are especially interested in the technique of family therapy, since it is directed to the very problems of faulty interaction that have been implicated in the development of neurotic and psychotic disorders.

Mental retardation

Basic Issues

On the surface, mental retardation may appear to be a less controversial topic than the types of abnormality we have discussed already. After all, unlike most psychologic disorders, mental retardation can be diagnosed on the basis of objective tests of intelligence. Somehow we are more confident in measuring intellect than in assessing psychological functions. As we study this topic, however, we will see that mental retardation offers its own special problems to our understanding and is a very complex issue in its own right.

Definitions

The definition of mental retardation and the causes and results of it have been subjects of debate since the early part of this century. In the United States, the mental retardate has been the victim of our national infatuation with the IQ score as a measure of intelligence. The development of the Stanford-Binet and Wechsler intelligence tests in this country inspired our enthusiastic commitment to objective tests as the sole basis for determining a person's intellectual potential, which presumably determines the person's potential for achievement throughout his or her lifetime. Many states established legal definitions of retardation in terms of IQ score. Intelligence was viewed as both inherited and unchangeable.

In England, by contrast, social criteria influenced the definition of retardation. In the early twentieth century, Tredgold, a British medical authority on retardation, defined mental deficiency as "a state of incomplete mental development of such a kind and degree that the individual is *incapable of adapting himself* to the normal environment of his fellows in such a way as to maintain existence independently of supervision, control, or external support" (Tredgold, 1937, p. 4; emphasis added). Notice that there is no mention of objective tests of intelligence.

Views in the United States began to change in the 1940s. Doll, the director of the Vineland Training School, proposed a definition that stressed social incompetence manifest from birth or shortly thereafter due to a "mental subnormality." Although he initially considered the condition organic and incurable, he later abandoned that view. Others concurred in the social emphasis, describing "a mentally defective person" as one "who is incapable of managing himself and his affairs, or being taught to do so" (Benda, 1954, p. 115).

Clinical definitions of mental retardation in current practice come from two influential sources. The DSM-II (1968) takes its cue from the *International Classification of Diseases* of the World Health Organization: "Mental retardation refers to subnormal general intellectual functioning which originates during the developmental period and is associated with impairment of either learning and social adjustment, or maturation, or both" (p. 14). The DSM-II manual sets up five levels of retardation based on IQ scores, from "borderline" through "profound."

The other authority is the American Association on Mental Deficiency (AAMD), whose *Manual on Terminology and Classification in Mental Retardation* (1973) offers this definition: "Mental retardation refers to significantly subaverage general intellectual functioning existing concurrently with deficits in adaptive behavior, and manifested during the developmental period."

In both definitions, we see equal importance attached to intellectual and adaptive capabilities, both of which are subject to measurement. Thus learning disability alone would not qualify the individual as a retardate if his or her social behavior were adequate. The distinction is especially important for lower-class and ethnic minority groups, who generally perform poorly on standard IQ tests, but who avoid the stigma of the retardate label because they meet the criteria for social competence and self-help capability.

Current Terminology

Labeling the problem and its victims is impeded by two complications. One is the difficulty in determining organic etiology, and the other is the offensive association that has become attached to some labels over the years.

Such phrases as "incomplete development of mind" and "subaverage intellectual functioning" appear in the accepted definitions. Which labels would suit those concepts? We have discarded old names, such as, "feeble-minded," "idiot," "moron," "imbecile," which are contaminated by outmoded, highly negative attitudes. Attempts have been made to distinguish between neurological pathology or disease and absence of organic defect. The Russians consider only neurological pathology, which they call "oligophrenia," as a special disorder involving detectable brain damage. The World Health Organization has proposed "mental subnormality" as a catch-all designation, without success. Parent groups prefer "mental retardation" to the demeaning "mental deficiency," but all names for intellectual deficits eventually acquire unpleasant connotations.

In our discussion, we will skirt the labeling controversy and use mental subnormality, mentally defective, mental retardation, and developmentally retarded interchangeably.

Incidence and Prevalence

The complications that confound estimates of prevalence of various disorders are magnified in our attempts to assess the extent of mental retardation in the United States. Criteria vary sharply among urban and rural communities, certain ethnic groups, and geographic regions. Estimates of the number of mentally retarded range from 0.05 percent to 13 percent of the population. Current estimates converge on a rate of about 3 percent of the total population, or about 6 million persons.

We noted above that one of the problems of estimating the extent of retardation relates to a community's attitude toward the signs of mental retardation. The contrasting cases that follow are clear evidence of the effect of the community's tolerance and ability to provide a place for the handicapped individual in the life of the community:

Jeanette became a ward of the juvenile court in Los Angeles, California, when she was three because of the death of her father and the inability of her widowed mother to provide a stable home for her and her four brothers and sisters. None of the several aunts, uncles, or grandparents assumed responsibility for the children, and they were placed in three separate foster homes. Jeanette reacted to this

upheaval by having inconsolable crying spells and by periodically running away from her foster home to look for her family. When she was about to start school, she had three mild convulsive seizures which greatly alarmed the foster mother. Although Jeanette had seemed possibly a little less rapid in her development than the other children, until this crisis she had presented no particular problem. On a Stanford-Binet given her by a rather inexperienced examiner hired by the court, she obtained an IQ of 68. Placement in a state institution for the mentally retarded was made by the judge on the basis of the test report and the fact that adequate care was not available in her home setting. Jeanette remained in a large custodial institution for twenty-two years. She underwent several periods of depression and schizophreniclike, bizarre behavior, which usually followed a change in the ward personnel on whom she depended. Eventually she was placed in a foster home in a community close to the institution with the hope that she might someday be able to work as a domestic servant, but she was capable of so little self-direction that this proved impractical. After several years she was returned to the institution in order to make the scarce foster-home opportunity available to someone else. (Robinson and Robinson, 1965, pp. 43-44)

Jeanette had the misfortune to live in an uncaring, urban community. Now see what a difference a more protective and adaptable community can make on the future of such a child:

Gloria was the fourth of nine children born during a twelve-year period to parents who were hardworking and deeply religious wheat farmers in Montana. The children got along well together, and Gloria was especially close to a younger sister. Gloria entered a small country school near her home at age seven. She was a consistently slow learner in reading and arithmetic but did a little better in spelling and penmanship. Despite her poor work, she was promoted every year, although she was allowed to spend most of her time with children who were in lower grades than she.

At the end of the sixth grade, all children from

this school were sent to a consolidated county junior-senior high school; in larger classes with children of her own age, Gloria's disability became more apparent. Following the advice of the school authorities, Gloria was taken to a psychological clinic at a nearby university. On the WISC, she obtained an IQ of 59, her scores on performance items being somewhat higher than those on verbal items. Gloria continued in junior high school for two years and dropped out of school when she became pregnant by a high school boy who worked for her father. The couple were married and continued to live on the farm in a cottage near the main house. Several other brothers and sisters have remained nearby with their families. At last report, Gloria was the happy mother of three healthy children and an accepted member of her family and community. (Robinson and Robinson, 1965, pp. 44-45)

Age seems to affect the detection of retardation in an inverse manner. Most cases are diagnosed during childhood, with another peak during adolescence. Children's deficiencies are revealed by the difficult challenges they face in adjusting to school requirements. Handicapped adolescents who have managed to get this far without detection collapse under the social and sexual pressures they must now deal with.

Because black children tend to obtain lower scores on intelligence tests, controversy boils around the issue of racial differences versus test bias. Other factors are the greater incidence of complications in pregnancy, depressed living conditions, poorer health care, and disrupted parent-child relations in black families. All of these factors are also associated with retardation.

Classification Approaches

Retardation is the effect of many different causes. The situation is further complicated by the fact that each of the suspected causes interacts with other aspects of the person to produce different behavioral effects. As a consequence of such multidetermined behaviors, it is virtu-ally impossible to design a single classification system that encompasses all of the possible factors. The problem is evident in the definitions we quoted, which require both intellectual and multiple social deficits to establish a diagnosis of retardation. These complications have led to a variety of schemes for classification by intellectual ability, etiology, and social adaptation.

Classification by Level of Intellectual Ability

Meaning and Measurement of Intelligence

To understand the use of intelligence tests in determining levels of mental retardation, we need to know how the various standard measures are computed and what they represent.

We start with the child's *mental age* (MA), Binet's term for the average intellectual ability of children of a given *chronological age* (CA). Thus MA should equal CA for typical children. To obtain MA, the children's scores are credited with any items they answer correctly at age levels above their *basal age* (the level at which they can pass all items). The *intelligence quotient* (IQ) is the index commonly used to compare intellectual ability among several individuals. It is obtained by dividing the mental age by the chronological age:

$$IQ = MA/CA \times 100.$$

This is the *ratio* IQ. More recently, educators have developed the deviation IQ, which is based on the distribution of the IQs at each age.

Ideal IQ distribution in the general population forms the bell-shaped curve typical of the normal distribution, in which most of the cases cluster around the mean (average score) and the number of cases tapers off as the distance from the mean increases (Figure 16-1). The distance from the mean is measured in units of standard deviation (SD).[1] You will notice that a little more than 68 percent of the scores fall

---

[1] A detailed explanation of the standard deviation is presented in most elementary statistics textbooks.

Figure 16-1 Theoretical distribution of intelligence test scores (σ = standard deviation).

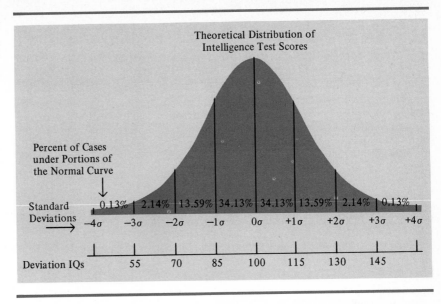

within one *SD* above and below the mean, and that between 2 and 3 percent of the population obtain scores more than two *SD* below the mean.

The lower horizontal scale in Figure 16-1 shows the distribution according to *deviation* IQ, an index that has been adopted in place of the *ratio* IQ by the two most popular intelligence tests for children, the Revised Stanford-Binet Intelligence Test (SB) and the Wechsler Intelligence Scale for Children (WISC). By setting the mean at 100 for each age's IQ distribution, the deviation IQ relates each person's score to the scores of others *of the same age*. This index has the advantage over the ratio IQ of showing the relative standing of each child against other children of his or her age. The comparison is made easily by converting the deviation IQ into a percentile rank. For example, a deviation IQ of 70 would be in the third percentile; that is, it would be exceeded by 97 percent of the children's scores in that particular age group. In fact, 70 is often used arbitrarily as the cut-off point for a designation of mental retardation.

Of course, the formulas for scoring and ranking individual intelligence, no matter how sophisticated, do not deal with questions about the validity of the tests themselves as instruments for determining intelligence. An IQ controversy was precipitated by an article on genetic influence on intelligence (Jensen, 1969). There has been a continuing storm of protest over the article's implications for certain ethnic groups, notably blacks and American Indians. Most of the objections have centered around two issues: the validity of the data on which the heredity hypothesis is based and the "cultural bias" built into the tests currently in use.

Data from a number of studies of monozygotic twins reared in separate homes indicate that 80 percent of individual variation in intelligence test scores is attributable to heredity (O'Leary and Wilson, 1975). However, these data have been rejected by some critics because of questionable procedures in the conduct of the studies and the treatment of the data.[2]

On the issue of cultural bias in tests, the debate turns on a question of what intelligence tests are supposed to do. Their purpose, accord-

[2]An extensive review and critique of this issue can be found in a paper by Kamin (1974).

ing to many educators, is to predict performance in school, and this they are acknowledged to do fairly well. The key point here is that the schools are intended to prepare students to succeed in a society that functions with certain beliefs, technological systems, and language patterns. In other words, the cultural bias is inherent in the culture in which the child must perform. "Culture-bound" tests that measure one's likelihood of success in that culture are useful instruments when they are properly utilized as guides for the improvement of the child's skills that are valued by the society. But what about the American child from a different culture—the American Indian or the Mexican-American child, for example? Can a standard IQ test truly measure this child's intelligence or potential for success? In any case, the question remains unresolved, since no "culture-free" test has yet been constructed that will stand up to all the requirements of validity and reliability.

What can the IQ itself tell us about the potential of the retardate? We must recognize first that the IQ is largely dependent on verbal skill. The test itself is composed of verbal instructions and questions. Most of the answers require some degree of verbal reasoning. Because of its verbal orientation, the IQ tells us little or nothing about "insight, foresight, originality, organization of ideas" (Robinson and Robinson, 1965, p. 40), or about capability of handling many life situations. Many childhood

retardates grow up to lead productive, independent adult lives.

At the lower levels of retardation, however, IQ does set a limit to performance. Robinson and Robinson (1965) suggest that "the greater the intellectual handicap, the wider the area of behavior it determines" (p. 402). While a moderately retarded child will be able to do many things not predicted by the IQ (motor skills, social behavior, and potential for development), a child with a very low IQ will be able to perform few social behaviors. At the lower levels, the impairment of motor behaviors is so pronounced (often due to neurological involvement) that it interferes with a wide variety of social and vocational activities. In fact, severe physiological defects (blindness, deafness, spasticity), though they may not directly impair intellectual functioning, may isolate the child sufficiently to cause learning deficiencies and emotional blockage, which will result in retarded performance.

Levels of Retardation as Indicated by Intelligence Testing

In terms of IQ ranges, the AAMD levels of retardation[3] are (see Table 16-1):

[3]The DSM-II adds one additional level of retardation—borderline (83–69). People falling in this category are capable of education and independent living when adequate educational opportunities are available.

Table 16-1 Levels of Severity of Mental Retardation by Measured Intelligence (AAMD)

Descriptive Levels	Standard Deviation Ranges	Representative IQ	
		Stanford-Binet (SD 16)	Wechsler Scales (SD 15)
Mild	−2.01 to −3.00	68–52	69–55
Moderate	−3.01 to −4.00	51–36	54–40
Severe	−4.01 to −5.00	35–20	39–25[1]
Profound	Below	19 and below	24 and below

1. Mild (68–52)—capable of self-maintenance with supervision of social and financial affairs, and gainful employment in a sheltered workshop.

2. Moderate (51–36)—can be trained in self-care and in simple, routine jobs.

3. Severe (35–20)—can be trained in a limited repertoire of self-care routines with no independent behavior; lethargic, with above-normal mortality.

4. Profound (19 and below)—restricted movement due to motor defect, often confined to bed or wheelchair, requires continuous supervision.

As we have noted, in the case of the mildly and moderately retarded, consideration must be given to adaptive behavior in making a diagnosis. This can be done with some objectivity by means of suitable tests. The Vineland Social Maturity Scale and the Gesell Developmental Schedules are examples of such tests of social adaptation performance.

Classification by Etiology

Mental retardation fits the pattern of multiple organic and psychogenic causes that we have seen in other problems of abnormal behavior. Although we know that many retardates have organic defects—the estimate runs between 10 and 25 percent of the cases—we do not find consistent correlations between specific neurological conditions and retardation patterns. Mongolism (Down's syndrome) is an exception, where an abnormal extra chromosome is associated with the retardation. Phenylketonuria (PKU), rubella (German measles), and the Rh factor are also charged with responsibility for retarded mental development. Premature birth and birth injuries are also implicated, although their cause-and-effect relationships are by no means well defined. Postnatal organic causes include diseases of the nervous system (resulting in central nervous system tissue destruction) and physical accidents causing brain injury.

The problems in relating the various causes of brain dysfunction to levels of retardation have led to several proposals for etiological differentiation. One of these is the "endog-enous" versus "exogenous" distinction. Originally proposed by Strauss and Werner (1942), the term "endogenous retardation" was applied where there was no observable brain damage. "Exogenous" described cases of retardation due to brain injury occurring before, during, or after birth.

Earlier attempts at organic versus psychological differentiation separated victims into basically the same two groups, but with different labels: "mentally defective" (caused by a neurological disorder) and "mentally retarded" (resulting from nonorganic factors). A recent variation on that theme is the "subcultural" versus "pathological" distinction. The subcultural classification is used to describe children who deviate from the norm due to some intrinsic physiological or environmental condition. The pathological cases are due to damage from disease or injury. The term "garden variety" retardation has been proposed, describing those whose natural development is limited as a result of parental deficits or environmental impoverishment. This terminology is one of several favored by supporters of the distinction between organic and cultural-familial retardation.

The unpredictable potential of higher-level retardates motivated the AAMD's consideration of "psychogenic retardation" as equivalent in effect to organically caused retardation. While emotional disturbances seriously reduce cognitive performance in all children, psychogenic retardates consistently function below their chronological age norms in all situations. This approach opens the way to recognition (and treatment) of emotional and environmental problems as causes of retardation as well as noncrippling organic defects.

"Pseudo-retardation" refers to a functional retardation without known genetic defect or physiological damage. Originally the term was related to "pseudo-feeblemindedness" and "pseudo-imbecility," both of which denoted the absence of true, inborn retardation. The hypothesis was that such children functioned as retardates for neurotic reasons. In some cases, they gained the benefits of dependency from remaining "stupid." By the use of ignorance to avoid family expectations, anxiety might be reduced. Parental neglect (as we saw in the case of the "mechanical boy" in Chapter 15) can reduce the child to a state of arrested development. Today, pseudo-retardation has lost its significance, along with the abandonment of the view of mental retardation as a disease with a specific cause and prognosis. Now all but the profoundly retarded are considered educable or trainable to some level ranging from self-care to independent living.

Classification by Adaptive Social Behavior

The emphasis on the importance of socially adaptive behavior in the AAMD and DSM-II definitions of retardation reflects the notion that the purpose of learning is to help the individual fit into society. But can we measure the individual's capacity to perform according to socially accepted standards with the same objectivity as we measure intellectual ability? In other words, can we obtain a "social quotient" (SQ) equivalent in reliability to a person's IQ?

The AAMD Adaptive Behavior Scale (ABS) classifies adaptive behavior in four levels applicable to different age ranges. Table 16-2 shows the relative criteria for placement at each level. Notice that these are all expressed in terms of self-maintenance and independent performance in social and vocational situations.

References to "educable" and "trainable" in the ABS table indicate the retardate's capability for profiting from special educational programs. *Educable retarded* children (IQs of 50–70) can learn academic subjects at a minimal level with special help. They can also acquire social skills that will enable them to live independently. *Trainable retarded* children (IQs of 25–49) cannot learn academic subjects, but may be able to acquire skills in self-care, social adjustment in a protected environment, and simple vocational tasks in a sheltered workshop. Educable retardates are usually not identified until they meet difficulties in school, while trainable retardates can be detected in

infancy or early childhood. There are some children, however, who are so severely or profoundly retarded that they cannot profit from special education programs and require complete care and supervision throughout their lives.

Types of Retardation

Cultural-Familial ("Garden Variety") Retardation

Approximately 80 to 90 percent of the retarded come from families with a history of retardation. Because their intellectual defect is not related to organic defects or brain damage, they generally fall in the borderline and mildly retarded groups, with a small portion of them moderately retarded.

Johnny is a typical case of cultural-familial retardation. Notice the unawareness and indifference of his calm mother and the almost total absence of structure and communication in his environment. Here, too, we see how the retardation emerges under the test of school requirements, explaining the high incidence of mild retardation among school-age children.

Johnny was a 6½-year-old blond, blue-eyed youngster who was spending his second year in the kindergarten of a school in a predominantly middle-class neighborhood. He was the fifth of the eight children of a rather pleasant, quiet mother who seemed not at all upset when the teacher informed her that Johnny would not be promoted. His father, a cloth man in a textile mill, provided the family living by loading finished bolts of material from weaving machines onto carts to be taken elsewhere in the mill. Johnny's mother occasionally worked in the mill while the grandmother took care of the younger children. Three of Johnny's four older brothers and sisters were in the slowest groups in their schoolrooms.

Johnny was not able to master the reading-readiness materials of the kindergarten. He had difficulty in wielding a pencil, folding paper, coloring within the lines of a coloring book, and differentiating one symbol from another. He usually had a

Table 16-2 AAMD Adaptive Behavior Classification

	Preschool Age (0–5) Maturation and Development	School Age (6–21) Training and Education	Adult (21) Social and Vocational Adequacy
Level I	Gross retardation; minimal capacity for functioning in sensorimotor areas; needs nursing care.	Some motor development present; cannot profit from training in self-help; needs total care.	Some motor and speech development; totally incapable of self-maintenance; needs complete care and supervision.
Level II	Poor motor development; speech is minimal; generally unable to profit from training in self-help; little or no communication skills.	Can talk or learn to communicate; can be trained in elemental health habits; cannot learn functional academic skills; profits from systematic habit training. ("Trainable")	Can contribute partially to self-support under complete supervision; can develop self-protection skills to a minimal useful level in controlled environment.
Level III	Can talk or learn to communicate; poor social awareness; fair motor development; may profit from self-help; can be managed with moderate supervision.	Can learn functional academic skills to approximately fourth-grade level by late teens if given special education. ("Educable")	Capable of self-maintenance in unskilled or semiskilled occupation; needs supervision and guidance when under mild social or economic stress.
Level IV	Can develop social and communication skills; minimal retardation in sensorimotor areas; rarely distinguished from normal until later age.	Can learn academic skills to approximately sixth-grade level by late teens. Cannot learn general high school subjects. Needs special education, particularly at secondary school-age levels. ("Educable")	Capable of social and vocational adequacy with proper education and training. Frequently needs supervision and guidance under serious social or economic stress.

From Sloan, W., and Birch, J. W. A rationale for degrees of retardation. *American Journal of Mental Deficiency*, 1955–1956, 60, 250–264. © by the American Association of Mental Deficiency.

pleasant smile and often seemed to be listening carefully to what the teacher told him, but half of the time, he was unable to repeat her instructions. His attention span was considerably shorter than that of his classmates, creating a special problem for the teacher, who was faced with the burden of occupying him while the rest of the class was engaged in an ongoing project. Johnny liked the other children, but they paid him little attention and usually left him out of their play at recess. At

best, he was allowed to be one of the firemen who held the ladder while the others put out the fire.

The school psychologist administered a Stanford-Binet to Johnny, who gave a rather even, cooperative performance and attained an IQ of 69 (a mental age of four years, six months). On the Goodenough Draw-a-Man Test, his drawing, a large head with arms and legs extending from it, earned a mental age of four years, nine months (IQ 73).

A home visit by the teacher, who had become

quite fond of Johnny, was revealing. Johnny and his parents, his three sisters and four brothers, and the maternal grandmother lived in a drafty four-room house made of wood shingles, with outside plumbing. It was situated on the edge of town, near a middle-class apartment development but rather isolated from other homes. The family kept a cow and several chickens. Johnny shared a bed with two older brothers; three sisters were in another bed. The house was untidy and run-down. Meals were cooked somewhat erratically, and since the whole family could not sit down at the small kitchen table, the boys often ate their meals cold while walking about the house.

His mother reported that Johnny was a very good child who played outdoors much of the day and seldom cried. His health was mediocre; he usually had a runny nose and cough throughout the winter. The mother was somewhat surprised by the interest of the teacher in Johnny's special problem, since he seemed so much like her other children and had never given her any trouble. (Robinson and Robinson, 1965, pp. 218–219)

The case we have just described is one of mild retardation, the form that clusters most densely at the bottom of the socioeconomic ladder. In contrast, the more severe forms (moderate, severe, profound) are evenly distributed across all social classes. The lopsided concentration of mild, cultural-familial retardation among poor families should give us some clue as to genetic and psychogenic causes.

To what extent are the correlations of cultural-familial retardation with socioeconomic status and familial retardation patterns the result of *genetic* inheritance? Two famous studies attempted to answer that question. In 1877, Dugdale performed a genealogical study of the "Jukes" family, whose record of criminality and mental retardation involved virtually every member. A follow-up study about 40 years later found that half of the 1,258 members were feebleminded and many of the rest were borderline. Another study by Goddard (1912) traced the "Kallikak" family through two lines of descent from the same father—one line, illegitimate—the other, the offspring of the legitimate union with a woman of "good fam-

ily." The illegitimate line was similar to the Jukes in its general level of retardation. The legitimate line was normal. We still must reserve judgment on hereditary influences, even in the face of such evidence, since we cannot separate out the effects of the wretched environment in which the retarded children were reared.

Since biological defects and brain damage are ruled out as causes of mild retardation by the AAMD definition, we would expect psychologic disorders to play a major role. We have discussed previously the contribution of parental rejection, neglect, and maltreatment to the various neurotic and psychotic dysfunctions. We will not review them here, but we will point out their relevance to cultural-familial retardation.

Parental failure to provide reinforcement and stimulation at appropriate points during the child's maturational periods upsets the pattern of development of the child's various motor and cognitive skills. Failure to develop certain motor and cognitive responses at their critical times may prevent their proper development. When the child's maturation is disrupted, the consequences can be disastrous for his or her potential growth into an effective adult. Studies of institutionalized children, deprived of adequate attention and nurturing, showed them to be extremely deficient in social and intellectual abilities. They had serious personality problems and difficulty in grasping abstract concepts, and notions of time and space, and in organizing parts into wholes. Their lack of cognitive skills will undoubtedly impede their learning of suitable social behaviors, placing them at a permanent disadvantage when they emerge into the community. In short, the low IQ and the poor adaptive behavior can be traced to sensory deprivation at critical periods during maturation.

Looking back at the normal distribution curve of IQ scores (Figure 16-1), we may ask: Are these children merely the expected lower end of the distribution of intelligence? After all, someone has to be at the bottom, just as we expect to find the statistically appropriate number of geniuses at the top. The statistics of mild mental retardation, however, are not "normal." For example, on the basis of the normal distribution, we would expect about 165,000 mild retardates, whereas the estimate is more than double that figure: 371,000 cases. To what extent is the greater number of mild retardates due to socioeconomic deprivation, seen in the form of inadequate nutrition, stimulation, and education?

A partial answer to this question can be found from studying the countereffects of preschool enrichment on the preschool and school-age, low-SES children. Kirk (1958) studied children living in their own homes and in public institutions. Some were given preschool enrichment experience for 1–3 years before entering the first grade; others (the control group) were not. Overall, 70 percent of the children given experience in mental and social development improved their intelligence and social maturity scores by 10 points, and held their gains during the 5-year follow-up period. The control children who lived in adequate homes tended to catch up within the first year of school. The experimental children living in deprived homes and institutions benefited from the preschool enrichment experience. They did not suffer the decline in ability registered by the control children living in deprived homes and institutions.

Results such as these support the views of those psychologists who challenge the entire conception of mental retardation. Braginsky and Braginsky (1971) level their attack at the social process that dooms certain lower-class children to bear the stigma of retardation through no act or defect of their own. The sequence of social events that leads to this fate is diagrammed in Figure 16-2. It starts with the poor family's separation from the mainstream of the community (mainstream = nonmenial jobs + participation in religious, political, and cultural activities + a home in a good neighborhood). The community then exploits the "surplus" family, keeping them from improving their low status. The oppressive conditions set the scene for the abuse and neglect of the child. The inevitable consequence is the discarding of the child into an institution for the mentally retarded. The final result is that the child is stigmatized as "mentally ill" or "retarded."

Organic Types of Retardation

There are strong correlations between particular kinds of neurophysiological defects and retardation. While a correlation in itself does not establish a cause-and-effect relationship, there are some biophysical disorders that are clearly responsible for retardation, including a number of gross organic abnormalities that almost invariably result in mental deterioration at, or soon after, birth.

The pathologies can be classified under the headings of *malformations* (usually associated with abnormal genes), *metabolic diseases* (malfunctioning of the biochemical system), *neurological consequences* of environmental diseases (before or after birth), *abuse* (accidents, intoxication, malnutrition). The remaining organic causes are combined under the heading *genetic factors related to hereditary deficits* (the polygenic inheritance hypothesis). We have discussed (in Chapter 10) the conception of polygenes that carry physiological and personality traits, with presumed effects on intellectual potential.

The medical pathologies can be organized into prenatal, neonatal, and postnatal events. During pregnancy, the fetal brain is vulnerable to a variety of toxic, infectious, endocrine, nutritional, X-ray, and traumatic assaults and deficiencies. At birth, cerebral hemorrhage may be caused by prematurity or difficult labor. Cortical cell degeneration follows extended periods of anoxia (lack of oxygen). After birth, diseases such as meningitis and encephalitis, head traumas, and nutritional deficiencies are responsible for some cases of retardation. Current estimates of organic causation range from 10 to 25 percent of the total retardate population.

In this section, we will look at a few of the more prominent syndromes representing various types of medical pathology. Others will be discussed in Chapter 17.

Down's syndrome is better known under the name *mongolism*, which describes the characteristic mongoloid appearance of the victim. Other physical abnormalities include protruding belly, stumpy hands, and malformed

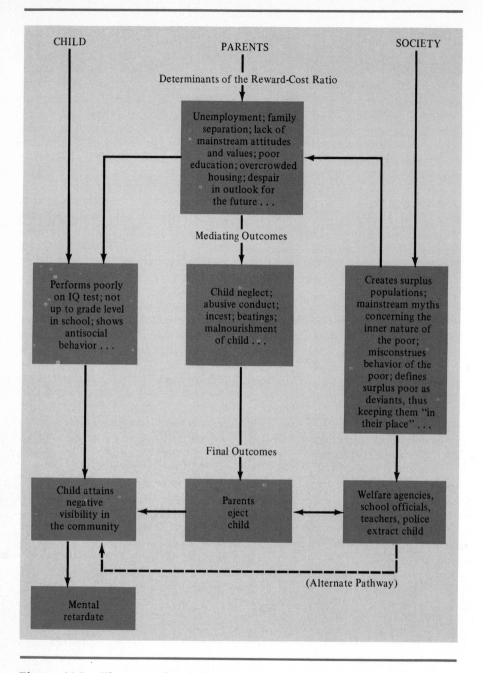

Figure 16-2 The process by which the retardate is created. (*Braginsky, D. D., and Braginsky, B. M. Hansels and Gretels: Studies of children in institutions for the mentally retarded. New York: Holt, Rinehart and Winston, 1971, p. 175.* © *1971 by Holt, Rinehart and Winston. Reprinted by permission.*)

heart. (Curiously, mongoloid fingerprints are loops instead of normal whorls.) The condition is associated with an extra chromosome, although the connection is uncertain. Mongolism occurs in 4 out of 1,000 births, and numbers approximately 10 percent of all retardates. The incidence seems to be maternal age-related, since 80 percent of mothers who bear mongoloids are between 30 and 45 years old (average age: 41). Mongoloid IQ's generally fall in the range of 15–40, sometimes reaching up to 50.

Cretinism is traced to a thyroid deficiency. Although the infant shows no signs at birth, the physical and behavioral defects appear within six months. Growth is stunted, head is disproportionately large, neck short, tongue protruding, hands stumpy, and malformed.

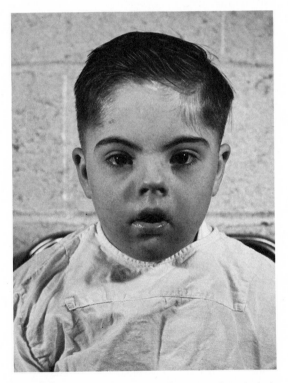

Characteristic of Down's syndrome is the victim's mongoloid appearance. Other physical abnormalities include a protruding belly, stumpy hands, and malformed heart. (*March of Dimes.*)

The infant is lethargic and slow-moving. IQ is generally below 25. Some cretins can learn simple self-care and vocational tasks. The condition is treatable by administration of desiccated (dried) thyroid extract during the first year or two of the child's life. If initiated early enough, the treatment can correct some of the physical abnormalities.

Phenylketonuria (PKU) is an inherited condition marked by faulty metabolism due to absence of an enzyme in the liver. Failure to metabolize a certain protein permits the protein to accumulate in the body fluids, where it attacks the central nervous system, causing retardation by the second year after birth. Because it can now be detected by routine urinalysis, and treated by special diet, the resulting retardation is declining.

Rubella (German measles), contracted by the mother during the first three months of pregnancy, causes congenital defects, including retardation. The likelihood of abnormality is greatest with exposure during the first fetal month and diminishes with time. Where prenatal care is practiced, the ready availability of measles vaccine has reduced this cause of retardation to a minimum.

Lead poisoning causes deterioration of the central nervous system, with consequent mental retardation and convulsions. The toxic lead is often ingested by very young children who chew on objects coated with lead-based paint. Because the lead is retained in the system, small amounts can accumulate into lethal quantities. The problem has raised controversial issues, since the older and less well-maintained homes and apartments occupied by poor families expose the children to flaking lead paint, which accounts for a higher incidence of lead poisoning among lower-class families.

Treatment of Retardation

In general, there is no cure for mental retardation, no medical procedure that will undo the arrested development that has already occurred. The treatments we speak of here consist of modification techniques designed to help the retarded achieve their maximum potential so that they can live as independent and productive lives as possible. We have repeatedly observed that the learning potential of the retarded is not bound by fixed limits. Rather, it has expanded with our growing knowledge of learning processes.

Once children's retardation is recognized and graded, what happens to them depends primarily on the level of retardation and, to a certain extent, on their family's socioeconomic status. If they are at the mild or moderate level, they may be placed in a special education class in the public school system. If they are more severely limited, they will be institutionalized in one of the residential "schools" for the retarded. We will focus our attention first on these two alternatives and then briefly survey other emerging approaches.

Institutional Care

Centuries of abuse and neglect of the retarded were followed by the "modern" era of institutional care, which may be said to have begun with Edouard Seguin in the middle of the nineteenth century. Following his lead, institutions for "mental defectives" were established in this country. The first, now known as the Fernald School, opened in Boston in 1848. Similar schools were set up in 14 states by 1890; their methods were designed to improve children's performance by means of physiological therapy, so that they could return to their community to live. Many retardates could not reach this level of independence, and as the retarded population increased, the institutions undertook lifetime custodial care. Unfortunately, as we have seen in the case of institutionalized psychotics (Chapter 11), the institution often exerts a repressive and demoralizing effect on its residents. We saw how patients were reduced to docile, dependent puppets under the hospital staff's pattern of reinforcement of conformist behaviors and punishment of troublesome signs of independence. So, too, the retarded are often rendered unfit for community living. As the Braginskys (1971) ob-

served, the retardate is "forced to act stupid" (p. 173) in order to satisfy the overly busy staff or to assure his or her continued residence in a comparatively secure environment. This conditioned response is the result of the institution's role in teaching patients how to be patients instead of how to function in their own communities (Patterson, 1963). Low staff expectations discourage progress. Ullmann and Krasner (1975) describe the pressures on the patient to assume the "good patient role" of passive, dependent child. In the process, any skill or drive toward independence that the retardate has will soon be lost under the staff's unwillingness or inability to respond favorably to the resident's assertive behavior.

Many states have started to transform the custodial institutions into educational environments. In California, they are called "developmental centers" (Rivera, 1972). In these centers, modern training methods are used to improve even the profoundly retarded. In the California plan, all but those confirmed as untrainable are moved back to smaller regional centers in the community, where sheltered workshops and programs for outside, subsidized employment of the retarded have been set up.

We have mentioned the trainability of the more severely retarded. What techniques are available for this purpose? Recall the "token economies" used in behavior therapy with schizophrenics (Chapter 11) and delinquents (Chapter 13). They work with retardates as well. Fielding (1972) reports a number of successful experiences with token economy programs. Using consumable reinforcers, the staff effectively trained severely and profoundly retarded male and female residents of a state institution to perform a series of basic self-care behaviors. After doing this, the staff reinforced a variety of useful behaviors with tokens exchangeable for store items. Initially, the tokens were exchanged instantly at the point where they were given out by the staff. At first, simple behaviors (e.g., responding to the attendant's call) were rewarded with tokens. By shaping and chaining (described in Chapter 3), more complex behaviors were developed (e.g., clean-

Institutions for the mentally retarded, sometimes providing no more than custodial care, usually encourage passive behavior. The retarded patient is often "forced to act stupid" to satisfy a busy staff. (*Bill Stanton, Magnum.*)

ing furniture, helping to dress others). Gradually, the "store" was moved farther and farther from the dispensing point (up to 120 feet), and exchange of tokens was delayed for increasing intervals (up to one hour). After five weeks, there was a very high performance of desirable behaviors. A token program was also instituted to provide compensation for industrial work. The participants earned tokens on the job and exchanged them when they got "home." This also taught them how to handle, count, and budget the spending of money. In one school, the tokens operated a vending machine containing a variety of articles, thus providing decision-making choices and motor training for the profoundly retarded.

The formidable problem in getting severely and profoundly retarded children to learn very basic behaviors has tapped the resourcefulness of clinical researchers. Azrin and Foxx (1971), for example, engaged in a "total push" program of intensive toilet training (eight hours a day), using moisture-sensitive pants, "pottying" every 30 minutes, reinforcement every five minutes (if still dry). They obtained 80 percent reduction in "misses" (urination in pants) within 1 to 14 days. Mahoney, Van Wagenen, and Meyerson (1971) eliminated the

forced pottying by sounding a tone and prompting the child to the toilet, where he was reinforced. In a three-day posttest, seven of eight subjects performed without tones or prompts after 17 to 48 hours of training.

Aggressive, injurious behavior is effectively treated by time-out (see Chapter 7). However, time-out is not effective with all behaviors; in some cases, it aggravates the offensive behaviors. It has been found that time-out is most effective when applied to single behaviors and less effective with a variety of irregularly emitted, aversive behaviors (Hamilton, Stephens, and Allen, 1967).

Shock punishment is a highly effective treatment—although it is distasteful to professionals—not only for extinguishing aversive behaviors but also for shaping desirable behaviors. Suppression is quick, often occurring in the first session. As we noted in the case of compulsive injurious behaviors in Chapter 8, shock must be administered in varied circumstances by different therapists or teachers in order to generalize the effect. Shock is used to induce desired behaviors—like holding a toy—by applying the shock while guiding the child's hand to the toy, stopping the shock when the child clutches it. The effect readily generalizes to other toys. The principal problem with all of the methods we have described is in assuring continued performance. Maintenance procedures, involving regular reinforcement, are necessary.

Special Education

Education of the retarded has been a matter of professional concern for almost two centuries. The possibility of educating or training the retarded received its first, great impetus from a dramatic experiment: the attempt to educate the Wild Boy of Aveyron undertaken by J. M. G. Itard in 1799. A 12-year-old boy was discovered living like a wild animal, with only minimal intelligence. The discovery of such a child excited general interest, which was heightened by Itard's proposal to teach the boy and raise his intellectual level, on the assumption that his deficiency was the result of lack of social stimulation. The attempt failed, possibly because the boy was too old to benefit from Itard's stimulation exercises. However, the case attracted enough professional attention to develop controversy and techniques aimed at improving the capabilities of the retarded. We have already seen how Itard's pupil, Seguin, brought about the establishment of training institutions for the retarded in this country in the mid-nineteenth century. But the big push in what became known as "special education" of the retarded did not come until after World War II. Since then, the number of handicapped children in special education programs has multiplied many times.

There has been considerable debate on and experimentation with methods of teaching the retarded, the effectiveness of various methods, and the community's responsibility for teaching both the educable and the trainable retarded. The effectiveness of such teaching has been demonstrated in studies such as the one conducted with four groups of preschool age children with IQs of 45–80 (Kessler, 1966). Some lived in institutions, others at home. Some of each group received preschool education, others did not. Of 43 in the preschool education group, 30 showed an accelerated growth rate during the preschool period and in school. Their IQs improved by 10 to 30 points. The at-home control group (no preschool education) improved after entrance into school; the institutionalized control group (no preschool education) remained static in development.

Teaching methods for the retarded have ranged from the sensory stimulation concepts introduced in this country by Seguin and expanded by Montessori, to the more recent behavior modification techniques that follow Skinnerian reinforcement principles. Maria Montessori (1912) developed a program of sense and muscle training in asylums in Rome. Retarded children engaged in "self-teaching" with materials designed to train the senses (visual discrimination, temperature, etc.). She also emphasized teaching the child by having the child perform in real-life situations. Doubt has been expressed about the generalization and transfer of Montessori training in mechanical skills to imaginative, creative activities.

Special education is provided in *residential schools* for the retarded, in *community special schools*, and in *special classes* in the public schools. The last arrangement offers the advantage of proximity to home and, for the higher-level retardates at least, some mingling and play with normal children. Some schools continue to promote the retarded, regardless of performance, to keep them close to their social age level, until they drop out.

Special classes usually follow the regular school grades in age grouping: preschool (3–6 years), elementary primary (6–10), elementary intermediate (9–13), secondary school (mid- to upper teens).

The preschool class is especially important for children from deprived, low-SES homes, since they do not attend private nurseries and often do not attend kindergarten—as middle-class children usually do—and so are not likely to be identified as retarded early enough for them to benefit from preschool education. The intermediate class "catches" the cast-offs from the regular classes where they have met with failure and contempt from teachers and classmates. Teachers at the intermediate level find the job complicated by their pupils' poor self-concepts, dislike for school, and bad behaviors acquired in other classes. They must help the students to relearn their academic subjects and improve their attitudes. The secondary school classes are increasing in number as educators find that higher-level retardates can learn more useful skills (e.g., mechanical repairs) for a productive role in society. These programs stress proper adjustment to the job. Poor behavior is a greater cause of failure on the job than poor skills. Finally, a new addition is the post-school program, conducted in sheltered workshops and rehabilitation agencies, offering continuing guidance in dealing with the complexities of daily living for those who cannot manage in regular vocational and social situations.

The particular handicaps of retardation call for modification of teaching techniques and classroom environments. Brain-injured children, for example, are distractible and require a nonstimulating environment. (The teacher is even advised to wear plain clothes and no jewelry, to minimize distraction.) At the same time, objects should be selected to provide enrichment (musical instruments, pictures, nature items) and presented in an orderly, one-at-a-time procedure, with extended opportunity for observation and manipulation.

The special classroom requires a functional arrangement that provides different areas designed for training in certain desired behaviors (Figure 16-3). One area contains desks for individual tasks, another has seats arranged in front of a chalkboard, while a third provides seats around a large table for group activities (reading aloud, etc.). A separate play area is clearly designated and isolated from the other areas. The functional arrangement reduces negative behaviors and promotes desired activities appropriate to each area.

The imaginative use of interesting teaching materials and experiences can facilitate learning by pupils with verbal deficits, improving their knowledge while increasing their vocabulary and sentence-building skills. Teaching machines have served well in rote learning where repetitive drill is the best method. They

hold attention and provide immediate corrective feedback—and they never lose their patience, a particularly important attribute where slow learners are concerned.

Teaching methods used in special education classes follow behavior modification principles. The basic operant procedures that are effective in correcting the classroom behavior of autistic and hyperactive children (Chapter 15) also work with the retarded. We will review some of the techniques and the results of their evaluation in a number of studies.

The teacher's first requirement in dealing with retardates is to hold their attention and get them to follow instructions. One successful technique is to punish disruptive behaviors

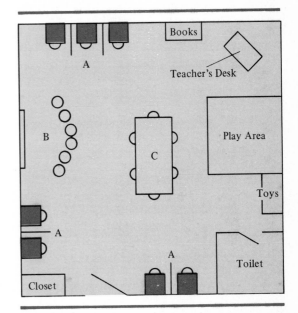

Figure 16-3 The diagram of a classroom which features three distinct study areas (A, B, and C) and a play area. Students learn behavior appropriate to each area when reinforced consistently for those behaviors. (*Fullmer, W. H. Changing the behavior of the retarded in the special education classroom. In T. Thompson and J. Grabowski (Eds.), Behavior modification of the mentally retarded. New York: Oxford University Press, 1972, p. 199.* © *1972 by Oxford University Press, Inc. Reprinted by permission.*)

with brief, immediate time-out lasting as little as two minutes and to reinforce attentive behaviors with milk and cookies or other rewards. In one study (Schutte and Hopkins, 1970), paying attention to students only when they followed instructions and ignoring them otherwise (contrary to the usual practice of most teachers) resulted in 80 percent instruction-following.

Behavior modification was also applied to the development and maintenance of "academic behaviors" by Wheeler and Sulzer (1970). They worked with an 8-year-old retardate who spoke in incomplete sentences. By reinforcing with exchangeable tokens the child's use of complete sentences in describing pictures, they increased the child's complete sentence descriptions of training pictures to 83 percent. After about 30 sessions, the child had reached a 70 percent complete sentence description rate for new pictures not included in the training set, indicating some generalization. However, such trained behaviors frequently deteriorate when reinforcement is terminated.

Ross and Ross (1969, 1972, 1973) compared modeling procedure reinforced with tokens (target groups) against reinforcement without modeling (controls). Games played outside of class were the means of teaching social, motor, listening, and problem-solving skills. Significant learning advantages were demonstrated in the target groups (educable, mildly retarded).

Disruptive behaviors have been eliminated by the ingenious use of a kitchen timer (Wolfe et al., 1970). The timer was set for intervals of 2 to 5 minutes. If the students were quiet or remained in their seats while the timer was on, they received a token at the end of the interval. If they had an outburst during the interval, the timer was set back to the starting time, with no reinforcement given.

Programmed instruction, in which students can proceed at their own rate, has been used in special education to a limited extent because of the scarcity of available materials. McCarthy and Scheerenberger (1966) reviewed the results of using programmed instruction against traditional methods and found programmed instruction superior in rate of acquiring skills and retention. A problem with programmed instruction lies in the lack of immediate reinforcement by the teacher, since the teacher does not work steadily with each pupil but circulates among the group, reinforcing appropriate behaviors as they are observed. Possibly because of such compromises, studies of programmed instruction with the retarded have not shown consistently successful results.

Other Approaches to Helping the Retarded

Parent Counseling

It seems paradoxical, but the retarded children's parents, who know all of their children's behaviors and spend the most time with them during their early developmental years, are a neglected resource in helping the retarded to reach their potential. There are reasons, of course, why this is so. The crux of the problem lies in the professional counselor's reluctance or inability to deal with the anxious, guilty, hostile reactions of the retardate's parents to the diagnosis, and also in the lack of well-defined procedures for the parents to perform in helping their child.

Poorly educated, lower-class parents often are unable to recognize their child's disabilities. Upper-class parents are inclined to minimize their child's defects, seeing them as temporary or the result of their (the parents') inattention to the child's needs. These parents tend to expect the defects to be "cleared up" with proper treatment. The label "mental retardation" evokes reactions of disbelief, shame, guilt, self-pity, and, finally, anger toward the counselor for his or her realistic but discouraging prognosis. At the outset, the counselor must relieve the parents of any expectations of miraculous drug cures, spontaneous recovery, or magical leaps forward in education methods that will wipe out the child's deficit.

The counselor must understand the reactions of the parents and the child. They are completely unprepared for such an event.

Their feelings of sorrow and hopelessness, no matter how valiantly concealed, are bound to be sensed by the retardate above the severe or profound level. As such children become aware of their limitations (through comparison with their siblings and with neighbors' children), they ask their parents what is wrong. The parents don't know how to answer, so they either ignore the questions (adding to the children's sense of stupidity) or paint unrealistic pictures of a happy future just like everyone else has.

Two alternative courses are prescribed by the counselor, depending on the degree of retardation and the family circumstances. The counselor may have to (1) prepare the parents for placement of their child in a suitable educational facility or (2) advise them of the specific things they are to do to help their child develop his or her potential skills. If the local school system has a special education program for which the child is suited, the counselor will guide the parents in preparing their child for entrance at the proper age.

Vocational Situations

Educable and trainable retardates work in three types of vocational settings: (1) as apprentices to institutional employees performing kitchen, laundry, repair jobs, (2) in sheltered workshops, where the individual is protected from the usual stresses and strains of work, (3) in transitional workshops, which provide more of the pressures and stresses of a normal job to prepare the individual for the "real world." Training, provided in vocational classes and in on-the-job experience, supplements the academic instruction. Unfortunately, much of the so-called "on-the-job" training consists of the retardates watching other workers, getting only a few instructions, and then trying to do the job the best way they can. This haphazard process screens out the very slow learners, who drop to the bottom of the labor heap where they perform only menial tasks although they may be able to learn other jobs with sufficiently patient training (Gold, 1973).

The retarded worker is often discouraged as a result of poor incentives. Generally, the pay is trivial (a few dollars a week or just some items from the canteen) and not related to the worker's productive output. This not only deprives retarded workers of experience in money management but offers no incentive to interest or motivate them. Schroeder (1972) did a careful study of the relationship between payment methods (fixed according to time intervals or number of movements per product) and individual output, with subjects in the 31–73 IQ range. As expected, output on hard jobs increased as pay rates (i.e., token reinforcements) increased in frequency. On the other hand, Gold suggests that retarded workers will do better when the job is interesting than when the pay is right. Nonetheless, as we have seen in all the research on token systems, even severely retarded people will perform the most menial jobs better when the rewards relate directly to the task.

Prevention

The ideal approach to retardation, of course, is to prevent it. Some tools and techniques are now available that promise just such a result. Advances in biological screening make it possible to eliminate or lessen the impact of some of the organic causes (e.g., the Rh factor and PKU). Newer prenatal diagnostic techniques have been developed by geneticists that permit detection of potential problems by means of *amniocentesis* (the "reading" of the genetic structure of the fetus in the uterus).

There are no "scientific" tools to prevent the problem of cultural-familial retardation. What is required for prevention are extensive changes in our society, to improve education and enrichment at the lower-SES levels, thereby eliminating the physical and psychological deprivations that contribute to retardation. In Chapter 20, we will review in detail the broad-based, social-behavioral programs designed to accomplish this objective. Present enrichment programs have produced significant benefits that encourage expansion throughout the lower-SES areas.

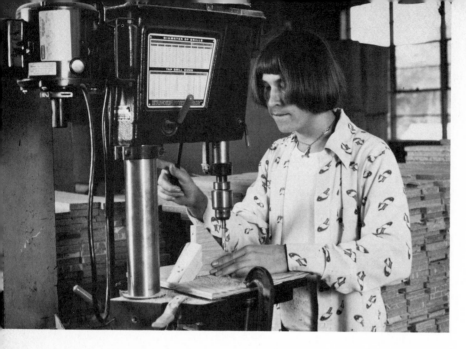

While training for the mentally retarded often consists of little more than the retardate watching other workers, most mentally retarded people can be taught skills they can use in the real world. The man in this photograph is learning how to operate a machine in a sheltered workshop. (*Michal Heron.*)

Growth of Interest in Retardation

Since the 1950s, interest in, and programs designed for, the retarded have grown at an accelerating rate. Under the pressure of sharply increased public attention to the problem (affected, in part, by the greater visibility of the retarded, no longer hidden in shame), private and government funding have increased the support of research at a rate higher than ever before.

Parents' groups have spread and grown influential in gaining special education programs in the public schools and in converting custodial institutions into educational centers. These educational changes have been reinforced by legal questions raised in the courts about the rights of the retarded to education instead of merely to custodial "storage" in institutional warehouses. Favorable decisions have compelled many states to make educational changes in their institutional programs.

New awareness of the competence and potential of the retarded has led to a greater acceptance of them as full-fledged members of our society, with civil rights, voting privileges, and rights to property ownership. As we take a more civilized and sophisticated view, we are gradually learning that the retardate is "one of us"—a complete citizen.

A happy development is the heightened interest on the part of college students in working with the retarded in rehabilitation programs. Paraprofessional training programs have become increasingly available for those who qualify and have the desire to do this challenging work.

Summary

Both the AAMD and the DSM-II have adopted definitions of mental retardation that combine IQ scores and social competence ratings in determining the diagnosis and level of retardation. There are an estimated 6 million retardates in this country—about 3 percent of the total population.

IQ is determined by tests that have been criticized for cultural bias and verbal orientation, which mask creative talents, and problem-solving and social skills. Objective tests are available to measure social competence.

While lower levels of retardation are likely to involve organic brain defects, higher levels are the result of multiple factors: biological, genetic, physical, and cultural-familial.

Virtually all retardates can learn useful behaviors. Higher-level retardates (IQ = 50–70) are considered "educable," and can learn academic subjects at a minimal level. Lower-level retardates (IQ = 25–49) are considered "trainable," and can learn skills ranging from minimal self-care up to productive skills (e.g., kitchen or laundry assistant). Some retardates can do well enough to hold paying jobs in industry that allow them to live independently. Others can work in sheltered workshops. Profoundly retarded children (IQ = 19) can be trained to perform toilet and grooming functions.

The contribution of parental neglect and impoverished environment to retardation is recognized. It accounts for the high incidence of mild retardation in the lower classes. Prenatal, neonatal, and postnatal influences include maternal diseases, metabolic disturbances, and accidents.

Behavioral techniques have been notably effective in training all levels of retardates. Token reinforcement has improved academic, self-care, and mechanical skills. Punishment procedures eliminate aversive behaviors. Special education in public schools has expanded tremendously in recent years.

Counseling the retardate's parents is a job that requires honesty combined with sensitivity to the parents' and the child's emotional reactions. Parents can be used more effectively in preparing their preschool children for special education. College students are showing considerable interest in professional roles serving the needs of the retarded.

Organic brain syndrome and aging

Thomas C., a twenty-five-year old unmarried construction worker, was brought to a small hospital in the Midwest by his father, after having behaved bizarrely for the previous two weeks. He had been living at home with his parents in a rundown neighborhood of a small community nearby. . . . His family and friends noticed that he was behaving strangely. He seemed isolated and preoccupied, and did not participate in the usual banter carried on by the workers. Moreover, he seemed very confused and mechanical in doing a job that he knew well, and required no creative effort. After a few days at work his employer noticed that Thomas was very pale and sent him home for the day. He began to complain of headaches and feverishness, although he did not have any elevated temperature, and his family doctor recommended psychiatric care. On the following day he awoke and told his family that he had just returned from winning a race at the salt flats outside Salt Lake City, and had equipped his car with new equipment from the proceeds of the race. He was then brought to the hospital, where he disclosed that he had been imagining things since his illness, but had not mentioned them to anyone.

During the initial interview he sat with a blank, preoccupied stare, gazing fixedly at a spot above the interviewer's head. At one point he reached out his hand and placed it on the doctor's shoulder, and the doctor remarked later that "It seemed almost that he was testing whether or not I was real." Thomas was disoriented for time, place, and person, being unable to tell what month it was, which hospital he was in, or who the interviewing doctor was. When asked to subtract threes serially from fifty he did very poorly and then walked to the door saying, "Is this my last visit?" Throughout the interview his affect was flat. (Zax and Stricker, 1973, pp. 278–279)

This case study demonstrates many of the abnormal behavior patterns discussed in earlier chapters. There is, however, one crucial difference:

Two weeks before his hospitalization, Thomas developed a disease that was diagnosed simply as "flu" by the family doctor. It was marked by muscular aches, weakness, poor appetite, and—most important—very high temperatures, and was treated by antibiotics. While sick he was supposed to have "talked out of his head" a considerable portion of the time. When his temperature receded he returned to work. (Zax and Stricker, p. 278)

Apparently, Thomas's illness had produced organic brain damage that, in turn, caused him to behave strangely. The behavioral manifestations of impaired *organic* functioning are hard to distinguish from the behavioral manifestations of psychological malfunction. This fact, you will recall, created the long-held presumption that all abnormal behavior was due to organic pathology.

Abnormal psychology has since moved to more sophisticated models that view behavior as multidetermined. The present chapter, however, reviews some very important problems that are, indeed, directly related to organic conditions. This chapter also examines the behavioral effects of aging, which are frequently attributed to organic changes in the brain. While not excluding the obvious physical effects of growing old, our discussion emphasizes social and psychological changes that may be more significant factors in the aging process. Since these changes are more easily reversed than biological deficits, their study may provide clues for improving the quality of later life in our society.

Clinical Features of Organic Brain Syndrome

General Behavioral Description

Organic brain syndromes are characterized by deficits in (1) orientation, (2) memory, (3) intellect, (4) judgment, and (5) affect (Sandok, 1975a). While each of these problems may be seen in nonorganic disorders, their distinctive combination immediately suggests the diagnosis of organic brain syndrome.

1. *Orientation* refers to the "who, what, when, where" relationship of an individual to his or her environment. Confusion about time and place, or about the identities of relatives and friends, all point to possible deficits in attention, perception, and memory that have an organic basis. Assessment of orientation is an important part of initial screening when organic brain syndrome is suspected.
2. *Memory* comprises the threefold tasks of registration, retention, and recall. Brain damage may affect any one or a combination of these abilities, all of which may be evaluated by objective tests.

Registration tasks usually involve presentation of short phrases or number series, which patients are asked to repeat immediately. Organically caused difficulty in perception or attention is reflected in impaired registration. *Retention* measures focus on patients' recent memory. Simply questioning them about everyday events may be sufficient to demonstrate retention deficits. The patients may not remember what they ate for breakfast or who brought them into the doctor's office. They may do well on immediate repetition of registration test phrases, but show no memory of the same phrases only minutes later. Such retention deficits are common with head injury, carbon monoxide poisoning, and Korsakoff's syndrome of alcoholism. Problems of *recall*, memory of distant past events, are usually demonstrated by directly questioning the patients. Recall deficits often appear as a progressive brain disease worsens.

3. *Intellectual* functions include comprehension, calculation, problem solving, and the ability to master new tasks. The patient's ability to understand verbal communications is the best measure of intellectual capacity. Sometimes, however, organic impairments are so circumscribed that subtle testing is required. What may appear to be generalized intellectual dysfunction may, in actuality, be speech impairment. Conversely, unimpaired attention to the details of everyday life may mask progressively declining ability to handle abstract ideas.

4. *Impaired judgment* is frequently the major reason for hospitalizing organic brain syndrome patients. Their inability to evaluate possible courses of action and to choose appropriate alternatives in everyday situations is dangerous to themselves and to others. Judgmental processes employ integrated activities of many brain centers. Thus most organic disorders produce judgment deficits. Assessment usually involves asking patients to choose correct alternatives in hypothetical problem situations.

5. *Affect* refers to an individual's emotional expressivity and thus reflects an individual's perception of his or her internal emotional state. In patients with impaired perception of external events, it is not surprising to find similar difficulties in perceiving internal events. The most frequent affect impairments are lack of affect, inappropriate affect, and generally increased instability.

Acute-Chronic Distinction

Much brain damage is *chronic*, that is, permanent and irreversible. Symptoms pre-

dominant in chronic brain syndrome include impaired consciousness, ranging from obvious loss of alert understanding to subtle decreases in sensitivity; memory defects; disorientation for time, place, or identity of self and others; impaired judgment; impaired intellectual functioning; poor control of emotions; and personality changes. Chronic disorders are associated with brain damage at birth, intracranial infections, syphilis, alcoholism, arteriosclerosis, cranial tumors, and head injury, among other causes. The management of chronic cases requires skill and understanding, since cure is not possible. While prognosis is, of course, related to the extent of damage, the patient's personality, intelligence, and cooperation play an important role in his or her ability to function at the best possible level.

Acute brain syndrome patients show many of the same symptoms of clouding of consciousness, memory defects, and disorientation common in chronic brain syndrome. The major difference, however, is that the acute condition is reversible. The causes of acute brain disorders also parallel those of chronic disorders: head trauma, alcoholism, and, as we saw in the case of Thomas C., bacterial and viral infection. Other causes include drug overdoses, poisoning, circulatory disturbances, and metabolic disorders such as uremia, diabetes, and severe vitamin deficiencies. The most important step in managing acute disorders is treatment of the basic physical disruption. Psychological support must follow to help the patient cope with the effects of brain impairment. The reassurance of familiar faces, a well-lighted room with reduced environmental stimuli, and supervised hospital care are crucial to ensure the quickest recovery and least chance of later problems.

We will discuss treatment of both acute and chronic brain syndrome patients in greater detail in the next section of this chapter.

Delirium

The most dramatic effect of organic brain syndrome is delirium, an acute state of deficient intellectual function and impaired orien-

Box 17-1 The Organismic Model of Organic Brain Syndrome

It is important to recognize that changes in orientation, memory, intellect, judgment, and affect as a result of organic brain syndrome superimpose themselves on the patient's preexisting personality. Sudden blunting of affect, for example, may be more apparent in a previously talkative extrovert than in a reserved introvert.

Kurt Goldstein (1952, 1975) has written extensively about individual adaptations of brain-injured patients. He attributes symptomatology to the combined effect of brain damage, the organism's reaction to the damage, and the organism's attempt to compensate. This has been labeled the "organismic approach to psychopathology."

Goldstein observed that patients unconsciously modify their lives to suppress and defend against psychologically threatening disabilities. Many avoid personal contacts or restrict themselves to familiar, easily managed environments. They seem particularly unaware of total impairments; indeed, adjustment to complete blindness, deafness, or paralysis is frequently better than adjustment to partial impairments.

Situations that force the individuals to confront their suppressed disability, however, produce what Goldstein labels *catastrophic reactions*. Inability to cope causes anxiety, anger, and agitation, with rising pulse and even tearful outbursts. This upset is compounded by the abnormal overreaction to external stimuli common in organic brain syndrome. Such distractibility in patients is typified by perceptual phenomena such as being unable to distinguish important elements from irrelevant elements. Patients cannot separate essentials from nonessentials.

Brain-damaged individuals operate most successfully at the concrete level of immediate, direct contact with objects and people. They are unable to handle abstractions. Patients who can use a key to unlock doors, or cut with scissors, for example, may look blank when asked to act out the movements used in these activities. This abstract notion is beyond their capacity.

Emotional reactions often seem unpredictable in these patients. They tend not to react at some times, or to respond too quickly at other times. The explanation lies in their failure to grasp situational elements that might provoke emotion, and in their restricted ability to respond only to concrete elements. Goldstein (1975) mentions the example of one of his patients, a Mr. A, who had formed a close friendship with another patient, Mr. X. Mr. A had declined Mr. X's offer to accompany him to a movie, and so Mr. X went with another man. Mr. A became terribly upset and immediately rejected his former friend. All explanations failed to convince Mr. A that Mr. X had not purposely slighted him by inviting someone else.

This example illustrates the problems of brain syndrome patients in maintaining interpersonal relationships. Because they can relate only on a concrete level, it often appears that they are unconcerned about others. One patient who never wrote to or asked about his wife and children appeared affectionate and concerned about his family during home visits. Yet, upon returning to the hospital, he seemed embarrassed and evasive when asked about his feelings. This unusual behavior represented not a deterioration of his emotional attachment, but rather his inability to picture his home relationships when he was not actually there (Goldstein, 1952).

Such lack of abstract ability makes it impossible for patients to plan for the future or to contemplate past events. They lack the capacity for initiative, fantasy, creativity, and normal social relationships. What limits their lives even more is their noticeable efforts to avoid new people or situations, and to maintain strict orderliness in every aspect of their existence. Meals and other activities must occur at exactly appointed times. Belongings must always be in definite, unchanging places. Goldstein explains this behavior as the organism's protective attempt to avoid catastrophic reactions. Since brain-damaged patients are unable to abstract the concept of fear or to plan ahead, they are not purposely avoiding anxiety-provoking situations. Their protective strategies persist simply because they are reinforcing. They prevent punishing catastrophic anxiety. It is common, therefore, even with severe organic brain damage, to see a lessening of obvious symptoms over time. Careful examination reveals no organic change in mental functioning, but merely a rearrangement of life style to accommodate diminished abilities.

tation. Delirium can run the course from slight reduction in alertness, resembling alcohol intoxication, to the complete disorientation of visual hallucinations, incoherent speech, and loss of motor control.

Delirium usually results from a transient disturbance of brain functioning. It is actually a common occurrence, seen as the confused state of patients recovering from anesthesia or overmedication, or entering or recovering from coma. Symptoms may last for moments, or weeks, but rarely longer than a month. Complete recovery may follow, or the condition may progress to an irreversible, chronic state. The behavioral manifestations of delirium are a result of the patient's previous functioning, the extent of organic damage, and the clinical treatment administered. Some people may exhibit self-blame and increased vigilance against their symptoms, while others may be so upset by their lack of control that they become incapacitated (Heller and Kornfeld, 1975).

Clinicians are careful to differentiate delirium from the clinical syndrome of *dementia*, which has similar symptomatology of failing intellectual functioning and impaired orientation. Although the end stages of dementia are quite similar to delirium, dementia shows a more slowly developing picture in which it is, at first, much less clear that there is some organic involvement. Patients are generally conscious but unaware of their changed mental functioning in dementia.

Effects of Focal Lesions

Our discussion so far has emphasized generalized symptoms of organic brain syndrome. There are, in addition, specific behavioral reaction patterns related to discrete lesions of brain tissue, that is, the area of the brain that is injured.

The view of the human brain in Figure 17-1 illustrates the four major areas of the cortex of the human brain: the frontal lobe at the front, the temporal lobe just inside the temple area of the forehead, the parietal lobe at the upper rear, and the occipital lobe at the lower back. Animal researchers commonly use mi-

nute lesions in these cortical areas to study brain function. By observing the behavior deficits produced by these lesions, they determine the functions controlled by each area. Of course, ethical considerations prevent experimental verification of these animal lesion studies in human subjects. What corroboration exists has been obtained in patients with naturally or accidentally caused lesions, and in locally anesthetized patients undergoing open-skull surgery. Such surgical patients are conscious and able to describe the sensations produced by electrical stimulation of specific brain areas. Wilder Penfield and his associate (1959) pioneered in this field. Their patients reported hearing various sounds when certain areas in the temporal lobes were stimulated. They "saw" things during occipital lobe stimulation. Their reports identified the *primary projection areas* shown on the brain "map" in Figure 17-2.

When you hear a doorbell, for example, nerve impulses from your ears must reach the specific auditory projection area in the temporal lobes. To use physiological terminology, we can say that auditory functions are *localized* in the temporal area of the cortex. Every point of your body has a corresponding cortical projection area to which messages from sensory receptors are transmitted. These projection areas account for less than one-fourth of the entire cerebral cortex. The more than three-fourths remaining cerebral cortex controls the complex organizing, processing, and storing of information that produces thinking, remembering, learning, and language-related skills so characteristic of humankind. These large *association areas*, as they are known, distinguish the brain of humans from the brains of the lower animals, where association areas are small or nonexistent. It is the association areas that are of greatest interest to psychologists studying patients with organic brain syndrome.

Before describing some characteristic discrete brain lesions, it is important to emphasize that there is not always a one-to-one relationship between brain damage and brain function. In the association cortex, for example, deficits correlate more with the extent of damage than with the specific locus of damage. To further

Figure 17-1 Lateral view of the four lobes of the cerebrum of the human brain.

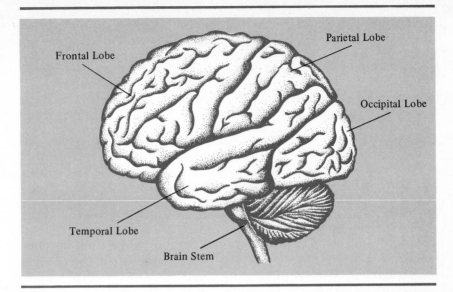

Figure 17-2 Diagram of the primary projection areas of the cortex and their functions.

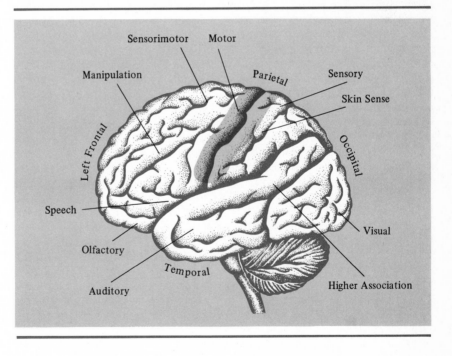

complicate matters, behavioral manifestations of organic brain damage are superimposed on the general organismic responses we described in the previous section. Thus behavioral expression of identical focal lesions often differs from patient to patient.

Remembering this, let us first consider damage to the *parietal area* (see Figures 17-1 and 17-2). This brain region is a major sensory association center. The integration of various sensory stimuli provides conscious awareness of our body parts and their ever-changing spatial orientation. Parietal damage produces left-right disorientation, and a strange inattention to anatomical features. Patients may exhibit "dressing apraxia," problems with matching left and right parts of clothing to the corresponding body parts. Parietal damage is frequently associated with disturbed topographical orientation as well: tales of getting lost on the street, or inability to find one's way around the hospital ward may suggest parietal damage (Benson and Geschwind, 1975).

Occipital lobe damage produces effects on the visual system. Commonly observed deficits include poor visual attention, disturbed color perception, and poor object recognition and localization. Occipital damage also produces visual hallucinations.

The *limbic system* encompasses portions of the temporal and frontal lobes, as well as parts of underlying cerebral areas of the hypothalamus, hippocampus, and thalamus. These interconnected cortical and subcortical areas, spread throughout so much of the brain, have been shown to control emotional behavior. Focal lesions produce characteristic disorders in what have been called the "four Fs" of the limbic system: feeding, fighting, fleeing, and the undertaking of mating activity (MacLean, 1958). Lesions in the limbic system of monkeys produce abnormal tameness, hypersexuality, and frequent shifting of attention. Some of these behaviors are seen in patients with damage in the specific areas of the limbic system. Damage involving hypothalamic limbic system areas produces flattening of affect, ranging from withdrawal to complete muteness. Other hypothalamic injuries cause eating disorders characterized by severe loss of appetite (anorexia) or the opposite, uncontrolled overeating (hyperphagia). Limbic areas have also been implicated in deficits in recent memory, often combined in an *amnestic-confabulatory*

syndrome characteristic of Korsakoff's psychosis: these patients forget the doctor's name and office location within minutes, and when questioned, reply in considerable but bizarrely incorrect detail. Careful study of these confabulatory answers reveals that they contain material from the patient's old, long-term memories, which are still intact.

Aphasia

Behavioral loss or impairment of language caused by brain damage is known as *aphasia*. Although aphasia has been studied more intensively than any other organic brain syndrome, its anatomical and psychological correlates are still in controversy.

In right-handed people, language functions are controlled almost exclusively by the left hemisphere of the brain. In left-handed people, both brain hemispheres have some language function. Thus the presence of aphasia indicates left-hemisphere damage in most patients.

Anatomical investigations of aphasia have localized specific language functions. For example, if one area of the brain is damaged, conversational speech of patients flows quickly and easily, but contains word substitutions and completely incorrect statements that sound like some strange jargon. When asked about his health, one such patient replied, "I felt worse because I can no longer keep in mind from the mind of the minds to keep me from mind and up to the ear which can be to find among ourselves" (Brown, 1975, p. 256).

Damage in another area produces motor disorders combined with characteristic hesitation, stammering, or even total loss of speech. Comprehension of spoken language is often unimpaired. Damage on yet another area results in an inability to repeat spoken language. Speech remains fluent, and comprehension is good.

Other lesions have been associated with the inability to find the correct words, particularly nouns. Patients may be able to point to a named object, or to repeat the name, but are unable to name the object directly when asked, for example, "What do you use to sweep the floor?" (Brown, 1975, p. 261).

Psychological accounts of aphasia stand in sharp contrast to these strictly anatomical explanations. Psycholinguists, for example, interpret aphasia as a cognitive impairment in the ability to put words together. They categorize aphasias according to the type of linguistic problem involved.

Psychologists view language not as the simple assembly of various anatomically localized functions, but as the complex representation of ordered cognitive functioning. Luria (1966) pictures a "system of words, behind each of which there stands not only a unitary image, but a complex system of generalizations of those things which the word signifies." This viewpoint does not necessarily negate anatomical theory. The most helpful approach to aphasic disturbances recognizes the *anatomically* proven connections between focal lesions and behavioral symptoms, which overlie the complex *cognitive* processes involved in the production of spoken language.

Organismic theory (see Box 17-1) is also relevant to discussions of aphasias. As with other organic brain syndromes we have discussed in this chapter, denial or lack of awareness of aphasias is common. Affective changes are also seen. One form of aphasia is often accompanied by apathy and depression, while another is commonly accompanied by euphoria.

Types of Organic Brain Dysfunction

Treatment of organic brain syndrome patients emphasizes quick identification of factors initiating and maintaining the clinical symptoms. We have already seen how characteristic behaviors provide clues about possible areas of organic brain injury. This section presents the opposite approach. That is, we will first identify types of organic injury, and then describe characteristic syndromes that may result.

Syndromes Associated with Different Etiological Agents

Infections

The central nervous system is as liable to infection as many other body systems. A variety of bacterial, fungal, viral, and spirochetal infections can spread to brain tissue. Toxic or allergic effects of infections outside the central nervous system may also impair brain function.

Intracranial infections take three forms: (1) meningitis, inflammation of tissues covering the brain (the meninges); (2) encephalitis, infection of brain tissue; and (3) abscess, isolated areas of infection within the meninges of the brain.

Meningitis is most frequently associated with bacterial infections. The most common form causes fever, headache, nausea and vomiting, delirium, confusion, and disorientation. Treatment with appropriate antibiotic agents is the accepted therapy. A less acute form of meningitis is found in tubercular patients. This tuberculous meningitis develops over a period of several days to several weeks during which the previously normal individual becomes increasingly lethargic, irritable, and restless. Intracranial pressure creates headache, confusion, and clouding of consciousness. Proper treatment with antituberculosis agents has reduced the mortality from this disease, but survivors commonly exhibit neurological damage such as blindness, deafness, slight facial paralysis, or intellectual impairment.

Encephalitic infections are frequently viral in nature, and may be traced to insect carriers, such as mosquitoes. Commonly observed mental and neurological symptoms include drowsiness, confusion, convulsions, aphasia, and tremor. No specific therapy exists for encephalitis; however, supportive maintenance of respiration and fluid intake is crucial.

Of all the infectious causes of meningitis and encephalitis, syphilis was, until the 1940s, the most common. At one time, 10 to 20 percent of all admissions to state hospital psychiatric wards were syphilis-related. That figure today is less than 1 percent. The reason for this change is, of course, effective penicillin treatment. The syndrome of general paresis (syphilis) remains important from the historical perspective. Much present-day knowledge of abnormal psychology was gained through observation of hospitalized syphilitic patients.

Syphilis is caused by the infectious corkscrew-like spirochete *Treponema pallidum*. The disease is spread through mucous membranes, usually during sexual contact. The spirochete reproduces rapidly in the body, eventually invading the tissues of the spinal cord and brain. The result is changes that increase pressure on brain arteries. Symptoms thus depend on which parts of the brain are served by the affected vessels. First signs usually involve slight memory impairment, increased irritability, and inattention to personal appearance. Social and moral improprieties are common early indicators. The characteristic sagging, trembling lips and slurred speech of the paretic patient are easily recognized. Slovenly physical appearance and seriously impaired intellectual functioning are typical of advanced cases.

Although penicillin treatment provides certain cure for the spirochetal infection, existing brain damage cannot be reversed. Prolonged hospitalization is frequently necessary. Interestingly, most individuals in our modern society have received sufficient penicillin and other antibiotics during their lifetime to protect them against general paresis (Dale, 1975).

The management of infection-related brain syndromes requires more than simple antibiotic therapy. As with other organic brain syndromes, organismic reactions must be treated as well. A simple, familiar environment is important, as is reassuring contact with close family members.

Intoxication

Infections are contracted unintentionally; resultant brain syndromes are totally unplanned. In contrast, human beings intentionally ingest an assortment of intoxicating substances in the conscious expectation of brain syndrome effects. Alcohol is, of course, the most obvious example of such intoxicants. Many of us have experienced acute alcohol-induced organic brain syndrome: altered mood, decreased alertness, and impaired judgment. In most cases, the symptoms disappeared the next day. It is continued overuse of alcohol that produces the chronic brain syndromes seen in alcoholics.

A wide assortment of substances can produce brain damage, if used long enough or in too high concentration. Sedatives, hypnotics, tranquilizers, antidepressants, and stimulants have such potential. Moreover, sudden withdrawal of psychoactive drugs may also produce organic brain syndrome (Peterson, 1975b).

Industrial pollutants in the form of gases, solvent vapors, chemical wastes, and heavy metal wastes can also act as intoxicants. The potential risk to large populations is truly mind-boggling.

The specific neural mechanisms that produce central nervous system intoxication are not clearly understood. Each drug appears to produce characteristic behavioral effects, which interact with the patients' existing medical problems, their personality, age, and environment. Acute reactions typically involve anxiety or depression, difficulty in concentrating, and increased irritability. Severe intoxication may produce clouding of consciousness, confusion, agitation, paranoia, and possibly hallucinations. Prolonged chronic reactions usually entail intellectual deterioration, memory disturbance, and impaired orientation.

Circulatory Disturbances

Blood flowing to the brain provides a vital supply of glucose and oxygen that enables brain cells to function. Although the brain accounts for just 2 percent of body weight, it consumes about 20 percent of the oxygen used by the body in the resting state. Thus any change in the blood supply will produce almost immediate brain damage.

In the absence of oxygen, brain cells stop

Industrial pollutants can act as intoxicants and lead to organic brain syndromes with behavioral effects such as anxiety, difficulty in concentrating, and irritability. (*United Nations.*)

functioning. If oxygen deprivation is prolonged for as little as two minutes, brain cell death (infarction) occurs. The most dramatic demonstration of oxygen deprivation occurs with cerebrovascular accidents (CVAs), known as strokes. A blood clot that obstructs a blood vessel supplying the brain with oxygen causes unconsciousness, and widespread destruction of neural tissue. In severe cases, death ensues. Patients who survive the CVA are commonly left with impairments in motor and language abilities.

Less dramatic, but still serious, changes in brain function are produced by the gradual reduction in cerebral circulation common with advancing age. Clogging and narrowing of arteries with lipid deposits account for much of this decreased blood flow. The resultant oxygen insufficiency in brain tissue leads to gradual disturbances in cellular metabolism and eventual death of cells. This arteriosclerotic condition is frequently blamed for the mental decline traditionally associated with aging. We will discuss this issue further in the final section of this chapter.

Metabolic Disturbances

Just as oxygen deprivation causes neural damage, so can deprivation of other vital substances. Glucose is particularly important for neural function, and an insufficiency of it can cause irreversible damage to nerve cells. Vitamins and hormones are important in metabolism and other activities that preserve cellular structure, maintain membrane potentials, and produce transmitter substances. Thus metabolic, nutritional, and endocrine disturbances can produce neurological and psychological changes. Since these disorders are usually correctable, proper diagnosis is crucial. This is particularly important for elderly patients whose preexisting brain impairment makes them more sensitive to metabolic disturbances. Their symptoms are frequently attributed to senility, thus preventing adequate diagnosis and effective treatment of the underlying metabolic disorder.

Endocrine disorders present a particular problem in diagnosing behavioral abnormalities. In Cushing's syndrome, for example, excessive production of adrenal hormones produces marked weakness, fatigability, and rapidly developing fat deposits particularly in the face, neck, and trunk. In women, changes in menstruation, hair growth, and masculinization of the voice are produced. Men are often impotent. Psychological effects include depression, impaired memory, irritability, and anxiety. It is difficult to determine whether resultant personality disturbances reflect neural damage or simply psychological adaptation to the endocrine-produced changes.

Vitamin deficiencies present a less complicated picture of neural involvement. In our discussion of alcoholism (Chapter 14), we mentioned Wernicke's syndrome effects such as memory loss, confabulation, dementia, clouding of consciousness, and even coma. Administration of large doses of thiamine produces prompt lessening of symptoms. Interestingly, the syndrome has disappeared almost entirely since 1942, the year in which enrichment of flour and bread was instituted.

Tumors

Psychological symptoms are often the first and occasionally the only indication of tumorous growths in the brain. Two common sites for brain tumors, the frontal and temporal lobes, are relatively *silent areas*, in which signs of the damage are seen only at late stages. Since tumors require rapid treatment to prevent permanent brain damage, many physicians first screen for possible tumors in patients with psychological symptoms.

Early psychological symptoms of neural tumors usually represent an intensification of general personality traits. A loss of inhibitions is common. Increased intracranial pressure caused by tumor growth may produce impairment of consciousness, memory defects, easy fatigability, headache, and nausea. In addition to these general symptoms, localized focal damage produces characteristic effects. Temporal lobe tumors often cause schizophrenic-type sensory hallucinations and episodes of dread, terror, and strangeness. Frontal lobe tumors produce flattening of affect, general apathy, irritability, and depression.

Diseases of Unknown Cause

Chronic brain syndromes are also seen in association with a wide variety of nervous system, vascular, and other diseases.

Multiple sclerosis produces progressive structural damage to the myelin coating of nerve axons. Abnormal behaviors are so common at the onset and during the course of this disorder that a psychiatric diagnosis is frequently made instead of a neurological one. There is, however, no characteristic behavior pattern. Abnormal manifestations often represent exaggerations of preexisting behavior patterns. Patients may compensate for the disabling effects of the disease with pathological complacency, cheerfulness, and even euphoria.

Paralysis agitans, better known as Parkinson's disease, is a degenerative disease of the brain. Neurological symptoms of muscular rigidity, difficulty in movement, and slow tremor of the extremities are well recognized. Depressive reactions are common in these patients, but may be due less to organic damage than to forced dependency on others.

Lupus erythematosus is a disease of the connective tissue of the circulatory system that produces degeneration of vessel cell walls. Physical complaints include joint and fibrous tissue symptoms similar to those of arthritis, and a characteristic "butterfly" rash across the bridge of the nose. Damage to vessels supplying the brain produces delirium and psychotic reactions, as well as neurosic-like behavior. At the onset of illness, anxiety is frequently evident. Phobic, depressive, and schizophrenic symptoms frequently necessitate hospitalization.

Huntington's chorea is an inherited degenerative disease of the central nervous system. Woody Guthrie, the folk singer and composer, was a victim of this incurable illness. Onset generally occurs between the ages of 30 and 45, with the development of jerky, involuntary muscle twitches. At first, it seems as if the patients are simply careless in their movements. However, later stages show impairment of speech, swallowing, walking, and most other movements. Irritability, or the opposite, euphoria, general emotional deterioration, and even hallucinations may occur. Kolb (1973) cites the case of R. A., a woman hospitalized at age 56, whose maternal grandmother, mother, four siblings, and other family members exhibited definite symptoms of chorea:

Prior to her illness, the patient was apparently an attractive, well-adjusted person. She was a Girl Scout leader and took part in community affairs. Shortly before she was 35 years of age she began to show an insidious change of personality. She discontinued her church, Girl Scout, card club and other activities; she lost interest in her family and at times wandered away from home, returning at night but giving no information as to where she had been. In this same period, she began to drop articles and to show twitching of her hands.

The patient became neglectful of her personal appearance, refused to comb her hair, bathe, or change her clothes. . . . The choreiform movements [jerky, involuntary muscle twitches] increased in extent, and she occasionally fell.

. . . On many occasions she threatened and even attacked her husband, sometimes with a knife. . . . She was subject to tantrums in which she would threaten to jump from a window. She came to be known to the children in the neighborhood as "the old witch on the third floor."

On arrival at the hospital, her facial expression was vacant and she showed such uncoordinated and choreiform movements of her legs that she had difficulty in walking without assistance. . . . Her constant grimacing, blinking of her eyes and twitching of her fingers were quite striking. The coordination of her hands was so poor and the movements of her head were so extreme that she had difficulty in eating. . . . Although somewhat irritable, demanding, and distrustful, she adjusted to the hospital environment without serious difficulty. (pp. 302–303)

Syndromes Associated with Head Injury

The fast pace of modern life and the pervasiveness of high speed transportation have produced a staggering incidence of accidental head injury. The automobile is the prime culprit. Vehicular accidents account for about 3 million head injuries each year, including 750,000 concussions, 150,000 skull fractures, and 150,000 significant brain injuries (Tuerk, Fish, and Ransohoff, 1975). According to esti-mates, one person in 200 will receive medical treatment for head injury each year (Peterson, 1975a).

Movement of the brain within the skull, caused by sudden acceleration, is known as *closed brain injury. Open head injury* occurs from penetration by sharp objects or bone, due to skull fractures and bullet wounds, for example. Resultant tearing of brain tissue and blood vessels, and dangers of infection, usually dictate neurosurgical intervention.

Advances in the treatment of head injury have significantly decreased patient mortality. However, many survivors are left with unfortunate psychological effects. Head trauma serious enough to produce loss of consciousness commonly causes acute symptoms of amnesia for the events immediately preceding the injury. Further deficits are correlated with the length of time the patient remains unconscious, and with the site and severity of intracranial injury.

Diffuse brain damage creates a complex picture of clinical symptoms, exemplified by the stereotype of the "punch drunk" boxer. Recurring blows to the head produce this alcoholic-like syndrome of slurred speech, staggered walk, and impaired mental function. "Explosive" outbursts, paranoia, and hallucinations are common in these individuals.

As high as the incidence of head trauma is in adults, it is astoundingly higher in children. Probably all children at some time receive potentially damaging head injuries. Fortunately, the immature skull structure of infants and very young children offers substantial protection. The skull's "growth room" acts as a cushioning shock absorber. In addition, the higher water content of young brains makes them more resistant to external forces than comparatively solid adult brains. The seemingly impossible stories of youngsters who survive falls from third and fourth floor windows attest to their remarkable tolerance for head injuries.

Physicians have learned that immediate symptoms are not necessarily predictive. Despite minimal acute damage at the time of injury, patients may experience severe delayed

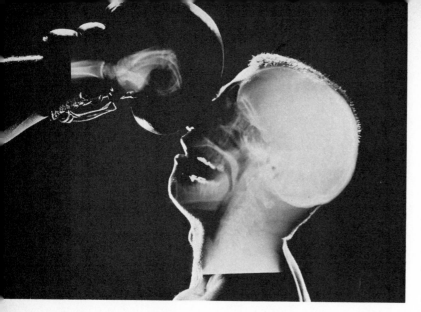

Sudden recurring blows to the head that move the brain against the skull produce a syndrome of "punch drunk" behaviors—slurred speech, staggered walk, and impaired mental functioning. (*Howard Sochurek, Woodfin Camp & Associates.*)

mental deficits. Nonspecific symptoms of tension headache, dizziness, irritability, fatigue, insomnia, and anxiety in these patients indicate that diffuse damage has occurred. However, the most obvious signs of this syndrome of "traumatic encephalopathy with deterioration" are catastrophic anxiety reactions to stress, and the development of defensive behavior patterns against this anxiety. One of the most famous cases of posttraumatic personality disorder is the woman who sued the San Francisco cable car company after an accidental head injury that, she claimed, later made her sexually promiscuous. Still another case is that of Phineas P. Gage. The dramatic nature of the accident and the personality change that occurred afterwards have made this a classic case in the psychological literature on brain damage.

The accident occurred in Cavendish, Vt., on the line of the Rutland and Burlington Railroad, at that time being built, on the 13th of September, 1848, and was occasioned by the premature explosion of a blast, when this iron, known to blasters as a tamping iron, and which I now show you, was shot through the face and head.

The subject of it was Phineas P. Gage, a perfectly

healthy, strong and active young man, twenty-five years of age. . . . Gage was foreman of a gang of men employed in excavating rock, for the road way. . . .

The missile entered by its pointed end, the left side of the face, immediately anterior to the angle of the lower jaw, and passing obliquely upwards, and obliquely backwards, emerged in the median line, at the back part of the frontal bone, near the coronal suture. . . . The iron which thus traversed the head, is round and rendered comparatively smooth by use, and is three feet seven inches in length, one and one fourth inches in its largest diameter, and weighs thirteen and one fourth pounds. . . .

The patient was thrown upon his back by the explosion, and gave a few convulsive motions of the extremities, but spoke in a few minutes. His men (with whom he was a great favorite) took him in their arms and carried him to the road, only a few rods distant, and put him into an ox cart, in which he rode, supported in a sitting posture, fully three quarters of a mile to his hotel. He got out of the cart himself, with a little assistance from his men, and an hour afterwards (with what I could aid him by taking hold of his left arm) walked up a long flight of stairs, and got upon the bed in the room where he was dressed. He seemed perfectly conscious, but was becoming exhausted from the hemorrhage, which by this time, was quite profuse, the blood pouring from the lacerated sinus in the top of his head, and also finding its way into the stomach, which ejected it as often as every fifteen or twenty minutes. He bore his sufferings with firmness, and directed my attention to the hole in his cheek, saying, "the iron entered there and passed through my head." (Harlow, 1868, pp. 330–332)

Dr. Harlow made the following observations when he followed up his patient's condition.

His physical health is good, and I am inclined to say that he has recovered. Has no pain in head, but says it has a queer feeling which he is not able to describe. Applied for his situation as foreman, but is undecided whether to work or travel. His contractors, who regarded him as the most efficient and capable foreman in their employ previous to his injury considered the change in his mind so marked that they could not give him his place again. The equilibrium or balance, so to speak, between his intellectual faculties and animal propensities, seems to have been destroyed. He is fitful, irreverent, indulging at times in the grossest profanity (which was not previously his custom), manifesting but little deference for his fellows, impatient of restraint or advice when it conflicts with his desires, at times pertinaciously obstinate, yet capricious and vacillating, devising many plans of future operations, which are no sooner arranged than they are abandoned in turn for others . . . his mind is radically changed, so decidedly that his friends and acquaintances said he was "no longer Gage." (Harlow, 1868, pp. 339–340)

Syndromes Associated with Epilepsy

Epilepsy is usually defined as a disease entity characterized by periodic, transient episodes of unconsciousness, frequently associated with convulsive movements. Actually, epilepsy is not a disease, but a group of symptoms characteristic of many brain syndromes.

Epileptic seizures are caused by the spon-

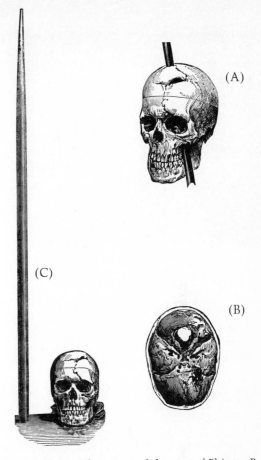

Figure 17–3 The report of the case of Phineas P. Gage was accompanied by several drawings. (A) A drawing showing where the tamping iron entered and left the skull, and a large section of the skull that was torn away as a result of the accident and later replaced. (B) An upward view of the inside of the skull illustrating the position of the hole and a new bone deposit covering part of it. (C) A size comparison between the cranium and the tamping iron that passed through it. (*The Francis A. Countway Library of Medicine.*)

taneous discharge of neurons in one area of the brain, which spreads across other areas of the brain. Discharge activity produces whatever behavior is controlled by the particular area involved. For example, discharge in visual pro-

Electroencephalograms (EEGs), such as the one pictured here, record electrical brain activity and are the primary tool in diagnosing epilepsy. (*Daily Telegraph, Woodfin Camp & Associates.*)

jection areas produces visual phenomena. Discharges in memory or association areas cause patients to have dreamlike experiences of familar past events. These characteristic sensory, motor, and association experiences provide helpful cues about the location of focal areas of discharge.

Electroencephalograms (EEGs), recordings of electrical brain activity, are the primary tool for diagnosing and localizing epileptic foci. Epi-

leptics exhibit short bursts of abnormal cortical activity that appear as interruptions in the usually rhythmic pattern of an EEG.

Grand mal epilepsy involves severe skeletal muscle convulsions, followed by coma. Many patients experience an unpleasant warning signal, or *aura*, just prior to seizure onset. The aura may take the form of hallucinations of sight, sound, or odor, obsessive thoughts, or even muscle twitches, which recur identically each time. The aura is not a premonition, but rather the first symptom of neurological discharge. The spread of discharge that follows produces falling, sudden unconsciousness, and severe muscle rigidity. This is the *tonic* phase of a grand mal seizure. In the ensuing *clonic* phase, muscle contractions produce rapid tremor and movement of the extremities. Finally, the patient sinks into the postconvulsive coma, lasting an hour or two. Upon awakening, he or she may appear bewildered, in a state of clouded consciousness that may persist for several days.

Petit mal episodes begin abruptly, without warning, but last for only several seconds. During this brief interruption of consciousness, the patient does not fall, but seems momentarily suspended in his or her activity, and unresponsive to external stimuli.

Attacks of *psychomotor* epilepsy are similar to petit mal episodes. Unconsciousness is sudden, but does not produce falling. However, psychomotor episodes may last from a half minute to several minutes or, rarely, for hours and even days. During this period, the patient performs an organized sequence of behavior quite unrelated to his or her preseizure activity. A patient may suddenly interrupt a normal conversation with an unrelated violent outburst, or with inappropriate activity such as chewing and swallowing. Because these episodes seem so purposeful and organized, they are often misdiagnosed as schizophrenia or neurosis. Incidents of psychomotor epileptics committing violent criminal acts are not uncommon, and it is difficult to accept the legal defense that the individuals had been unaware of their brutal acts. Nonetheless, patients exhibit marked clouding of consciousness during such episodes, with amnesia following return to consciousness.

Faced with such hostile, aggressive behavior, many clinicians had proposed the idea of a typical violent, irritable "epileptic personality." It is now believed that these symptoms are psychological reactions to this handicapping disease, but not characteristic of *all* epileptics.

Uncontrolled seizures seem to impair intellectual functioning. While such intellectual deterioration may also be attributed to social isolation and deprivation of normal educational opportunities, it is possible that repeated lack of oxygen and increased intracranial pressure occurring during convulsions may produce brain damage.

Fortunately, modern drug treatment has reduced the occurrence of many of these deficits by reducing the number and severity of epileptic seizures. In patients whose epilepsies are uncontrolled by drugs, surgery sometimes offers relief.

Aging

The inclusion of geriatric problems in a chapter on organic brain syndromes appears to support the traditional viewpoint that deteriorating brain function produces unavoidable deficits in older adults. On the contrary, we hope to contrast this outdated hypothesis with contemporary views on the psychological and sociological causes of behavior problems of the elderly. The changing approach to aging is the focus of this section.

Traditional Views of Aging and Senility

Forgetfulness, boredom, lack of interests, lack of pleasures—these are considered "normal" states in older people. The cerebrovascular deterioration that spares few aged individuals is often blamed in such cases of *senile dementia*. This diagnosis, however, implies *severe* loss of intellectual functioning in an elderly patient, with accompanying severe behavior problems. When such symptoms are seen in persons under the age of 65, the usual diagnosis is *pre-senile dementia*, also known as Alzheimer's disease. On autopsy, such patients show general degeneration throughout the brain. In Pick's disease, a similar pre-senile dementia, specific deterioration in the frontal lobes is observed.

Epidemiological research suggests that these dementias may be transmitted genetically, through specific enzyme defects or other biochemical abnormalities. Slow-acting viruses may also cause dementia. Investigators have reported successful transmission of senile symptoms to monkeys with the virus taken from human dementia patients (Busse, 1975).

Severe symptomatology in the elderly is usually attributed to trauma and disease. We call this *secondary aging*, or senility. This contrasts with *primary aging*, a normal process of biological deterioration that is inborn and unavoidable. This time-related deterioration is termed *senescence*. Some inevitable slowing down and decreased functioning are associated with senescence. However, this does not imply that all aged individuals exhibit signs of senility.

One early theory of aging hypothesized that living organisms are born with a fixed energy supply. As the energy runs out, function decreases. When the supply is exhausted, life ends (Busse, 1975). A more recent theory takes the cellular approach. Our bodies continuously produce new cells to replace those that die. Each newly created cell has a genetically programmed capacity for such division. However, this capacity is greater in cells produced when we are young and lessens with age. Thus the number of working cells declines with age.

Neurons never have the capacity to divide and thus reproduce. When they die, they are never replaced. Immunological theories propose that aged organisms may produce abnormal antibodies that gradually impair or destroy normal brain cells. Once they are destroyed, brain function is permanently lessened.

Psychologists and sociologists explain aging as an interpersonal process. Erik Erikson

(1959), for example, describes a basic conflict at the late stage of life between the acceptance of one's life as useful and successful, and the decline into despair and fear of death. Erikson, Neugarten, and other psychologists see old age as a turning inward of attention and a gradual withdrawal from the outside world.

Cybernetic theorists have combined the biological and psychological approaches to aging. Biological aging, they contend, involves deterioration of neuronic control. This control, however, varies with general activity levels. Early in life, neurons become activated. Repeated activation is necessary to keep them going. Thus lack of activity would combine with biological deterioration to accelerate the aging process. Conversely, maintenance of high activity levels would prevent some of this deterioration. Support for this viewpoint is visible in the many physically and socially active senior citizens who show marked preservation of intellect and personality.

It is undeniable, however, that some psychological and biological deterioration does occur in the aged. This deterioration puts them at a heightened risk for development of abnormal behavior. In one statistical study, the suicide rate for white males above 75 years of age was 54.5 per 100,000 population. For white males aged 65 to 74, the rate was 45.5. This contrasts with the 7.4 rate for subjects aged 15 to 24 (Resnik and Kantor, 1970).

Is All Senility Organic Brain Syndrome?

Western society values youth. The aged have lost something of value. And with it, they often lose their jobs, their money, their health, and the companionship of their children, now grown, or of their mates and close friends, now dead. Recognizing this, can we still conclude that organic brain damage is the prime reason for symptoms of senility?

Life styles in other cultures provide some answer. Alexander Leaf (1973) visited the Vilcabamba of Ecuador, the Hunza of West Pakistan, and the Georgians of the Soviet Union, peoples known for their amazing longevity. He returned from these surveys "convinced that a vigorous, active life involving physical activity (sexual activity included) was possible for at least 100 years and in some instances for even longer" (Leaf, 1973, p. 48). The aged of these groups shared the characteristics of physically strenuous mountain life, diets low in animal fats, and continued active involvement in community affairs. Far from retiring from active life, these elders were called upon continually to solve the problems of their societies.

Typical traits of senility—depression, anxiety, and rigidity—were absent in Leaf's subjects. Although these traits are present in many of our country's elderly, they are present in our youth as well. When normal, noninstitutionalized older subjects (average age 72) were compared with young college students (average age 20), the students scored as significantly more "senile" (Carp, 1969). The obvious conclusion is that "signs" of senility do not suddenly develop in old age. Indeed, seeking such signs *only* in the elderly creates the false impression that they alone experience impaired functioning. It is this type of faulty reasoning that dooms a large and important group of our society to a miserable and unproductive existence.

Psychological and Sociological Aspects of Aging

What are the demonstrable effects of aging? Biological changes in almost every organ system make the body weaker and less efficient in handling input from the environment (Jarvik and Cohen, 1973). The most significant result of these changes is slowing of performance on speed tasks. This slowed reaction time reflects nervous system cell loss, slowed peripheral nerve conduction, and altered synaptic conduction. Sensory and perceptual ability also decline with age. Registration deficits are apparent, too, in immediate and short-term memory. Again, the impairment seems related to speed. Older people are slower to acquire verbal learning responses. They require more time to respond to stimuli, and are more easily distracted by interference than are younger subjects. In such verbal tasks, the aged tend to make errors of omission rather than errors of commission. Such changes in speed, memory, and ability to handle perceptual input would seem to put the elderly at a disadvantage in intellectual tasks. However, research has indicated that when speed factors are carefully eliminated, performance on cognitive tasks shows no change, or even slight improvement, with age up to the eighth decade (Jarvik and Cohen, 1973).

This picture of limited behavioral effects of aging was supported by a nine-year longitudinal study of 142 aged residents of Liberty County, Pennsylvania (Britton and Britton, 1972). During the nine-year period, the group as a whole maintained a fairly stable state of health and family life, except that contact with family members declined gradually. What was most significant to the authors was the limited decline in these subjects, considering that they were in an environment in which no efforts were made to promote positive changes. The older people stressed independence and self-reliance as important social norms. For almost all subjects, however, personality and adjustment scores were lower at the final assessment than they had been nine years earlier.

Sociologists blame retirement for much of this maladjustment. Loss of social reinforcement, professional status, and financial stability comes with retirement. Inferiority feelings, reduced motivation, and withdrawal from society soon follow, regardless of the age of the individual. Becoming an observer, rather than an active contributor, causes a decreased sense of self-worth. Thus retirement may be the *cause* of sudden aging, rather than the result (Barrett, 1972).

The reduced interpersonal contact of retirement life is compounded tragically by loss of close relatives and friends through death and incapacitating illness (Chapman, 1967). Just at the time psychological health could most benefit from supportive interpersonal contact, it is suddenly cut off. When income is cut off as well, financial worries increase the sense of isolation and fear.

The unpleasant realities of old age conflict sharply with an individual's deeply ingrained self-image. Most people see themselves as dynamic forces, interacting with their environment. Of course, there is much wishful thinking in that viewpoint. Very few of us are masters of our lives. In old age, however, the evidence weighs overwhelmingly against this dynamic self-image. Is it surprising, then, that the elderly look back at their past with nostalgia, and at the future with apprehension? The transition from stabilized psychological maturity to personality decline is marked by this retreat to the past. Turning backward occurs even in those who seem to have little to look back upon. They commonly idealize the past and tend to emphasize even small triumphs.

Some individuals seem better able to survive these torments of old age. In fact, researchers have attempted to predict life span through analysis of biological and environmental factors (Botwinick, 1973). What they find is hardly surprising:

> Persons with high intelligence, sound financial status, well maintained health, and intact marriages may be expected to live significantly longer than their less intelligent and poorer brothers and sisters whose health is also declining and whose marriages are no longer intact. (Pfeiffer, 1970, p. 273)

Treatment and Prevention of Aging

During the process of senescence, individuals may become unable to function in their normal environments. Impaired hearing, inability to separate meaningful sounds from other sounds in the environment, visual and motor impediments that hamper everyday tasks such as dressing and preparing meals—these problems may dictate the need for a specially structured environment. In our society, the nursing home setting is designed to meet this need.

Nursing homes are long-term treatment centers geared to maintaining life at the most satisfactory level possible. They are frequently confused with *extended care* facilities, medical "halfway houses," which provide an extension

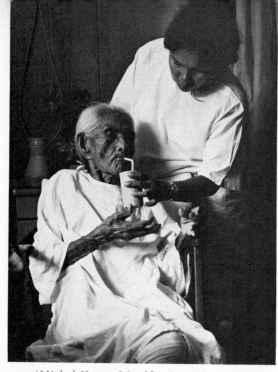

(Michal Heron, Woodfin Camp & Associates.)   (Martin Weaver, Woodfin Camp & Associates.)

(Michal Heron.)

(*Michal Heron.*)

of hospital care. Extended care provides active treatment aimed at restoring the patients' function so that they may return to their normal life. Nursing home care, on the other hand, operates on the presumption that the patients will never regain the capacity to care for themselves.

Is that presumption correct? Researchers have found encouraging evidence to the contrary. As we discussed in Chapter 16, abnormal behavior patterns of "incurable" retarded individuals have been altered by behavioral conditioning techniques. Similarly, techniques may be used to modify the low behavioral output typical of the elderly. Premack's techniques could be employed to make pleasurable activities such as eating contingent upon desirable, but less frequently performed activities. In this manner, the frequency of the desired behaviors

can be increased. Relaxation and desensitization techniques may also help to reduce fear of rejection and fear of death in the elderly (Cautela, 1969).

More traditional treatment possibilities have also been proposed. Behavior of aged individuals is a complex function of their physical abilities, their self-expectations, and the expectations of family and friends (significant others), and of society as a whole. As shown in Table 17-1, any of these four determinants can cause, or prevent, psychological disorders. If an aged person is unable to drive a car, for example, the categories suggest that this disability may have resulted from physical incapacity (poor eyesight or coordination), disturbed self-expectations (fear about driving), troubles with significant others (family attitudes about elderly people driving), or problems in society

Table 17-1 Some Possible Therapies for the Aged

Treater	Site of the Disorder					
	Self		Significant Other		Society	
	Physical capacity	Expectation	Family/friend	Therapist	Institution	Real world
Self	Adapt, medicate, use appliances	Adapt	Support, help	Teach	Reform	Initiate, agitate, support change
Family friend	Medicate, understand, ignore	Support, model, punish, understand	Model, advise, communicate	React, complain, compliment	Compliment, complain, investigate	Initiate, agitate, support change
Therapist	Medicate, use prostheses	Medicate, understand, therapy	Group therapy	Schooling, introspection	Organizational development	Initiate, agitate, support change
Institution	Contain, care for, medicate	Support, punish, understand	Inform, share care, help	Hire, train, assign	Administer, plan change	Lobby, meet, lead
Real world	Laws, social support, assistance programs	Norms	Support, limit	Support, limit	Laws, assistance programs	Legislation, evolution, revolution

Adapted from Gottesman, L. E., Quarterman, C. E., and Cohn, G. M. Psychological treatment of the aged. In C. Eisdorfer, and M. P. Lawton (Eds.). *The psychology of adult development and aging.* Washington, D.C.: American Psychological Association, 1973, p. 390. © 1973 by the American Psychological Association. Reprinted by permission.

(laws that deny insurance or licenses to the elderly). In addition, two other sites of possible disorder and therapy are listed: (1) the therapist, a significant other, and (2) treatment institutions, an extension of society.

This combination of causes and treaters poses many possible therapeutic programs. To treat the driving problem, the elderly may help themselves by getting corrective lenses, or may receive encouragement from their families. Insurance laws might change to permit them to drive. Obviously, institutionalization is not the method of choice! In fact, it is rarely the method of choice for *any* disorder. It is the most extreme form of treatment, because it alters opportunities and expectations by forcing the person into a portion of the world that is set apart from the rest of society. It sets up a treatment environment completely opposed to the self-treatment model valued by so many researchers (Gottesman, Quarterman, and Cohn, 1973). Furthermore, elderly people admitted to nursing homes and similar institutions experience a high death rate during the first year of relocation, and particularly during the first three months (Botwinick, 1973). This does not imply that care was poor. To the contrary, programs providing the most extensive services in a protected environment are associated with a higher patient mortality rate than limited service programs (Blenkner, 1967). Social and work programs are vital to help the institutionalized elderly maintain their capabilities.

At present, our society tends to ignore the mildly deviant and to incarcerate, "nurse," and infantilize the more deviant or dependent aged. With such a discouraging outlook, many older people seem to choose the "sick" role in preference to the "aged" role. Thus hypochondriasis and great concern for bodily functions achieve medical attention, where mere signs of aging are more likely to be ignored. Thus this sick role is often ascribed to old people, and accepted by them.

Since the crises of old age are so predictable—health problems, retirement, loss of loved ones, financial distress—community mental health programs appear to be an ideal treatment approach. Many researchers feel that the aged would be active if given the opportunity, but that our culture deprives them of the tools and the roles that would permit them to do so. Accepting the elderly into active community participation would be the first step in this direction. Preretirement counseling and crisis intervention for physical and emotional problems would help prevent unnecessary institutionalization (Eisdorfer, 1972).

From all the information presented in this section on aging, one conclusion is obvious: we cannot prevent old age. We can, however, prevent many of the psychological difficulties supposedly inherent in aging. Psychologists are beginning to view aging as a *developmental task*, that is, a task arising at a certain period in the life of all individuals, "successful achievement of which leads to happiness, good adjustment to society and self, and to success with later tasks" (Barrett, 1972, p. 9). When adults move into this life stage, they face a hierarchy of developmental tasks. Some are *regressive*, associated with decline in performance. Personal acceptance of inevitable losses in perceptual and motor abilities, sexual capacity, independence, social dominance, and social contacts—all are regressive tasks that must be mastered. They are interrelated with *compensatory tasks*, methods of adjustment specific to old age. Compensation is needed in developing leisure activities, learning new work skills, making dietary adjustments, adapting to changing environments, dealing with changing values in society, and adopting a new self-concept. Quite a list! What this developmental viewpoint emphasizes is the active rather than passive aspects of aging. As Barrett (1972) explains:

> Nothing remains at seventy or eighty or ninety as it was at twenty or thirty or forty. While one may resist, one cannot always prevent change. As a result, two avenues remain: (1) attempt to delay change by substituting modification, and (2) wherever a change is unavoidable, immediately accept an alternate that is personally acceptable. (p. 26)

By educating society as a whole, and the elderly in particular, to the developmental tasks faced in old age, much progress can be made toward assuring a hopeful and productive existence for the elderly in Western society.

Summary

Organic brain syndrome is characterized by deficits in orientation, memory, intellect, judgment, and affect. These symptoms of central nervous system damage are modified by the personality and response tendencies of each individual organism. *Chronic* brain syndromes are permanent, irreversible changes in behavior, usually associated with brain damage at birth, intracranial infections, alcoholism, syphilis, arteriosclerosis, cranial tumors, or head trauma. *Acute* brain syndromes have many of the same causes and signs as do chronic syndromes, however, the acute conditions are reversible. The most dramatic effect of acute brain damage is *delirium*, a temporary, unconscious or semiconscious state of deficient intellectual function combined with impaired orientation. *Dementia* is a similar chronic condition that develops slowly and is usually found without altered levels of consciousness.

Characteristic deficits in visual, auditory, and motor performance alert the physician to probable focal brain damage. Characteristic brain syndromes are also caused by infections, intoxications, circulatory disturbances, metabolic disorders, tumors, and other diseases. Head injury and epilepsy, in particular, have many well-recognized behavioral correlates. While there are characteristic organic brain syndromes related to *senility*, most older people suffer only from *senescence*, the normal decrease in neural and motor function associated with biological aging. Signs of supposed brain pathology in aged patients frequently relate to psychological and sociological pressures. Reduction of these stresses can yield significant improvement in the quality of life for aged members of our society.

Abnormal sexual behavior: Sexual dysfunction and sexual deviation

Imagine for a moment a culture on another planet, like ours in every way except for the curious attitudes they have developed around the consumption of food. In this society, the eating of food, while biologically necessary and pleasurable, has come to be constrained by legal, religious, and cultural codes.

In fact, eating is considered morally wrong except under certain prescribed rules. For example, eating in public is illicit and even pictures of the act, although quite titillating (probably because it is taboo), are deemed pornographic.

As a natural response to the restrictions

that blanket the act of eating, the language has acquired a vocabulary of "dirty words" relating to the various kinds of eating behavior and the body parts that are used in eating and digestion. The word "eat" itself is spoken with snickering and seldom in mixed company. Jokes about the subject are exchanged in private.

Engaging in the act of eating is subject to a large body of moral, religious, and legal restrictions. The religious authorities sanction eating only for nutritional purposes.

The society's views and practices in matters of eating are passed from generation to generation in rather casual and informal ways, considering the seriousness the people attach to proper behavior in this sensitive area. Some parents answer their children's questions about eating with evasive descriptions of how insects and flowers obtain nutrition. However, there is general objection to formal teaching of the subject by competent instructors. As a result, most children get their knowledge in the street, where it is confused with myths and distortions. It is not surprising that the young acquire questionable ideas and habits, such as playing with their food and chewing without swallowing (with what are believed to be dire effects on their mental stability!).

A gradual liberalization in attitudes toward eating has generated great anxiety and confusion in young and old, who cannot adjust to the growing tolerance for the public discussion and deviant practice of eating. On the other hand, many sense a healthier attitude in the community toward eating, contributing to more honest and caring relationships between couples. They believe the new climate is a vast improvement over the past. After all, they say, eating can be a beautiful experience and some day may be treated as naturally as sleeping, talking, or having sex.

A strange world indeed. Yet if you reverse the situation, you can see how that other society might view our attitudes on sexual behavior. How "abnormal" would they consider our standards of "normal" sexual practices? Although we feel we know what deviates from the "normal," in no other area of human functioning should we be more concerned about

the distortions in our view of "normal" than in the area of sexual behavior.

There is no fixed truth to point to and say what is normal sexual behavior. As in the alien culture we have been describing, recent developments leading to a loosening of restrictions offer the hope that we will see light shed on this area in the very near future. We are beginning to know what is normal from the view of physiological sexual functioning in human beings and "usual" sexual behavior in society at this time. We also can note what distortions and deviations from those norms occur and what we can do about those situations. These aspects of sexuality will be the topics of this chapter, but we should keep reminding ourselves that the whole context of our knowledge about sex may be as distorted as that alien society's view of eating.

"Normal" Sexual Behavior

The Need for Knowledge

The taboos that surround the whole area of sexual behavior have restricted the study of sexual functioning. Because the study of sexual behavior was removed for so long from the province of legitimate inquiry, we now find ourselves in a vacuum of ignorance about most aspects of the subject. For years, a handful of pioneers braved the attacks of the "Know-Nothings" and pursued knowledge in the face of hostility: ·Freud (1905/1953), Krafft-Ebing (1965), and more recently Kinsey and his colleagues (1948, 1953) in their survey of sexual behavior, and Masters and Johnson (1966, 1970) in their study of sexual response and inadequacy. The last two teams broadened the acceptance of sexual research and introduced into this work the methods of direct survey and observation as the bases of analysis of sexual activity. We are far from the final answers to many questions, but we do have a sense of having broken the ice and made substantial progress on the way to full knowledge of this once-forbidden subject.

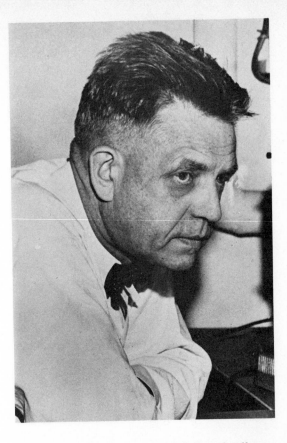

Alfred C. Kinsey's landmark studies of sexual behavior in the 1950s opened up a whole new area of investigation that previously had been taboo. (*National Library of Medicine.*)

Heterosexual Intercourse

Heterosexual intercourse has become a subject of as much controversy and analysis as the sexual deviations. Now that Kinsey and his successors have studied openly the sexual practices of the population at large, the problems that were formerly unspoken and untreated have come out of the dark. Books deal with all aspects of sexuality and its disorders. A new kind of therapeutic facility called the "sex clinic," staffed by specialists, has sprung up to provide help for those with problems in heterosexual relations. The principal problem has been a growing concern over sexual performance—in particular, failure to perform to expected "norms." We have become increasingly aware of the psychological influences on sexual satisfaction and performance. The major problem of the innumerable people who cannot

have or enjoy a full sexual life has finally attracted the attention of researchers like Masters and Johnson. Those researchers have studied the effect of a variety of factors that cause these conditions, and have developed therapeutic procedures for correcting them. Their studies of intercourse have also revealed previously obscured facts about the functioning of the clitoris (the most sensitive part of the female genital structure) and the limitations of the vagina in producing orgasm, along with the curability of psychologically based impotence. We can see the blinding effect of shame and taboo on the discovery of sexual knowledge when we note that such information about genital function remained hidden from view through all the millennia of intercourse between men and women, and indeed long after more complex anatomical functions had been discovered.

Box 18-1 Some Statistics on Sexual Behavior

We owe our statistics on sexual behavior to Kinsey's landmark studies (1948, 1953) and to those that followed his lead.

Masturbation is defined as self-stimulation of the genitals. From his sample, Kinsey determined that 95 percent of males have masturbated on one or more occasions. The incidence among women ranges from 50 percent to 80 percent in various studies. Among men, the higher the educational level, the more likely it is that they have masturbated. Even after marriage, 70 percent of male college graduates engage in it. Among single women, masturbation is the second most frequent form of sexual activity (after petting), and among married women, it ranks second to coitus.

Heterosexual petting involves erotic personal contact without intercourse. By age 25, 89 percent of men have engaged in petting, generally not with orgasmic results, while 98 percent of all women have petted at least once by the age of 25. Religious commitment tends to reduce the likelihood of petting behavior.

Homosexual relations have defied census taking because the practice is largely secret owing to legal and social sanctions. However, there are indications of more extensive homosexuality than people have generally believed. Kinsey's tallies show that about half of the men under 35 and a third of all men have had some homosexual experience. Among single men, there is a gradual increase in the homosexual part of their total sexual activity, rising to 22 percent. Homosexuality constitutes the total sexual output of an increasing number of men as they get older, possibly because of a delay in "coming out of the closet."

The known incidence of homosexuality among women (lesbianism) is substantially lower than among men. Only 28 percent of women have had a homosexual experience as compared to 50 percent of men, while only about 1 percent to 3 percent of women between 20 and 35 are known to be exclusively homosexual. Women's practice of homosexuality tends to be of shorter duration and less promiscuous than that of men. Half of the women are lesbians for one year or less, and most lesbians limit their homosexual attachments to one or two partners, while 22 percent of men have 10 or more partners. We repeat our doubts about the reliability of these Kinsey figures on homosexual activity in view of the special problems involved in obtaining credible information.

The incidence of *heterosexual intercourse* reflects increasing social tolerance, especially among women. The experience of premarital sex by males relates inversely to level of education. The percentages are 98 percent of those who have attended only grade school, 84 percent for those who have attended only high school, and 67 percent for college graduates. In frequency, too, the grade schooler had intercourse seven times as frequently between ages 16 and 20 as the college group.

Kinsey found that almost 50 percent of married women had premarital intercourse, although most of their orgasms resulted from masturbation. The frequency of premarital coitus among females was much lower than among men—reaching a peak of once every three weeks. (The past tense is used in reporting these figures since Kinsey's studies are about 25 years old, and the upward trend may well have continued.)

Surprisingly, coitus provides the exclusive sexual outlet for only about 85 percent of married men, and, perhaps more surprisingly, half of the male population engages in illegal or illicit sexual activity of various kinds. Marital coitus increases from 80 percent of total sexual outlet for men of lower education in the early years of marriage to 90 percent in the later years. In contrast, marital coitus among college-educated men drops from 85 percent of total sexual output to only 62 percent by age 55. Age does not set the absolute limits to sexual activity, as many suppose. Satisfactory intercourse (with orgasm) is experienced by three-quarters of all married men between 65 and 69, by about 60 percent between 70 and 74, and almost half of the men between 75 and 92.

Virtually all married women have sexual intercourse, although its percentage of total sexual outlet declines to 72 percent by age 70. Masturbation generally fills the woman's unabated sexual needs as her husband's sex drive wanes.

Extramarital intercourse is surprisingly common given the time at which Kinsey was gathering his data. Married men (50%) are twice as likely as their wives (26%) to engage in it by age 40. The rate for men and women increases with age.

While men and women have been reluctant to study the dynamics of the genitalia, they have been quite open in contemplating the mechanics of intercourse—positions and technique. Graphic representations of such positions decorated Greek, Roman, and Hindu buildings and artifacts. The fact that these ancient works of art exhausted all of the possible ways in which two human bodies could place themselves in the act of intercourse provides the strongest support for the axiom "There is nothing new under the sun." The one improvement we have introduced is in the recognition of the part that change plays in the build-up of excitement to the point of orgasm, and the importance of the progressive lovemaking process with its reciprocal stimulation of the partners.

Since Freud identified the so-called "sex instinct" as a main force in motivating our behavior, we can understand our erotic (sexual) impulses in terms of psychological needs and responses. These include the need and capacity for gratification by sexual or other means.

Human sexual functioning is an example of the purpose and operation of the "pleasure principle" postulated by Freud. Experiments with electrical stimulation of the brain have demonstrated the existence of "pleasure centers" that provide highly satisfying sensations to humans and other animals. Recent studies have suggested that the sensory impulses caused by stimulation of the genitals reach the pleasure centers, assuring that the various species will engage in sexual behavior and thereby perpetuate their kind. But physical gratification is not all there is to sexual interplay—although some use it solely for that purpose. The need to be nurtured and cared for—dependency—also influences our sexual behavior.

Another basic motivation is self-esteem, which is closely associated with recognition of one's identity. We run into problems when self-esteem is related to sexual performance. The preoccupation with *machismo* can become a man's way of carrying into bed the burdens of society's expectations of him as the producer on the job. But the burden of performance in bed is magnified by the sexual requirement of erection, which makes the man primarily responsible for enabling coitus (intercourse) to occur. And since penile erection is so susceptible to the effects of anxiety, a vicious circle is started, often resulting in impotence. The woman's role is no less complicated by social demands on her performance. But although attitudes are changing, her performance still may more likely be judged on her ability to satisfy the male.

Unfortunately, these burdensome performance roles get into bed with the couple. Furthermore, marital roles are also played out in the sexual arena. Now sex may become an instrument for imposing one's dominance on a hostile or scornful wife by means of "legal rape," or for punishing a domineering husband by feigning a "headache" or by belittling his sexual prowess. The ultimate punishment is to engage in overt "affairs" with other men or women.

Another extreme of the sexual picture is painted in bright colors, marking the joys of giving and receiving ecstatic satisfaction. This approach treats sex as a garden of delights in which better results can be obtained through the use of improved techniques. Another analogy compares intercourse to an art form in which the practice of higher skills produces virtuoso effects like masterworks of music, painting, and ballet.

Sexual response is as much a matter of situational mood as of long-term conditioning. The only thing that can assure continued success (which does not necessarily require culmination in an orgasm) is a mutual consideration of each partner's needs and sensitivities on each occasion.

Sexual Normality and Deviation

When we approach the business of deciding what is normal and what is deviant or "perverted" in sexual behaviors, we enter a hazy region. Our judgment leads us to make discriminations that collapse under critical examination. Of course, we have a socially determined aversion to certain sexual behaviors—rape and child molestation, for example. But most of the behaviors that have been condemned as offensive or self-destructive at one time or another, by one group or another, have eventually been absolved of blame for causing psychological or social harm.

What standards can we use for sorting out the abnormal from the normal in sexual behavior? We at once recall the criteria of abnormality proposed in Chapter 2: statistical grouping, personal discomfort, social conformity, health hazard, and legal definition. We discovered serious limitations in all of these criteria when they were put to the tests of consistency and reliability.

Cigarette smoking, alcohol consumption, and drug taking are all recognized as health hazards, yet by a statistical measure, they qualify as normal behavior practiced by major segments of the population. Personal discomfort gives an unreliable performance in detecting abnormality, since some of the most violent psychopaths show neither remorse nor even the slightest emotion when confronted with their gruesome crimes. Social conformity has been charged with stifling creative expression while masking real problems, as we saw in the case of the institutionalized psychotic patients. Finally, legal definitions tend to be arbitrary, since they are dictated by public notions of morality and unacceptable behavior. The legal attack on pornography is a case in point. Suppression of pornography, which offends some, but not all, of the population, conflicts with various constitutional rights to freedom of expression. What makes something "pornographic"? In the alien culture we discussed earlier, cookbooks and *Gourmet* magazine would be considered to be as legally pornographic as explicit sex novels and *Playboy* magazine are considered in our own society. In Denmark, all legal restrictions on hard-core pornography have been removed with no apparent deterioration of public morality or safety.

Just as in our view of abnormal behavior we have moved away from the medical illness model, so in our current view of sexual disorders we have moved away from the pathological diagnoses of sexual deviance developed by Krafft-Ebing and Freud. In their modern approach to sexual problems, Masters and Johnson have made a useful distinction between sexual deviation and sexual dysfunction, which we take as a reasonable alternative to futile attempts to determine abnormality in sexual behavior.

Sexual dysfunction is the term applied to a group of psychological disorders that prevent sexual arousal and/or orgasmic response in men and women. Male dysfunctions are impotence and premature or retarded ejaculation. Female dysfunctions include frigidity, orgasmic dysfunction, and vaginismus.

Sexual deviation is the term applied to the practice of variant forms of sexual activity, including homosexuality, sadomasochism, voyeurism, transvestism, and a list of other behaviors which we will describe shortly.

Human Sexual Dysfunction

Stages of Sexual Response

In their landmark study of normal sexual response, Masters and Johnson (1966) were able to delineate four discrete stages of full sexual response (Figures 18-1 and 18-2).

1. *Excitement.* The penis becomes erect and the vagina becomes lubricated as heart rate and blood pressure increase. The uterus elevates into a position that increases its accessibility for receiving semen.
2. *Plateau.* In addition to the penis, the testes are also filled with blood and are 50 percent larger than when relaxed. The lower end of the vagina enlarges, and the labia (lips of the vagina) swell and turn reddish. The clitoris becomes somewhat erect but, just before the orgasm, retracts to a flat posture.
3. *Orgasm.* The penis ejaculates in three to seven spurts at 0.8-second intervals. This stage occurs in two steps: first, an internal contraction signals "ejaculatory inevitability" (emission), and then the rhythmic contractions of the penile muscles are sensed as the orgasm itself (ejaculation). The female also experiences 0.8-second orgasmic contractions of the vaginal muscles.
4. *Resolution.* The penis loses about half of its erection immediately after orgasm and the rest within half an hour (sooner in older men). The clitoris has already flattened before the orgasm and

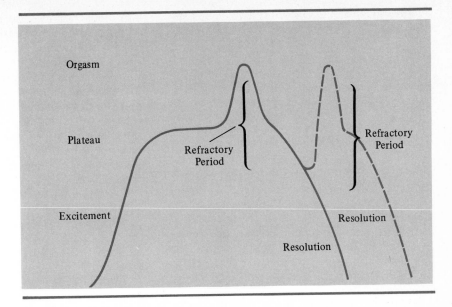

Figure 18-1 The male sexual response cycle. (*Masters, W. H., and Johnson, V. E. Human sexual response. Boston: Little, Brown, 1966, p. 5. © 1966 by Little, Brown and Company. Reprinted by permission.*)

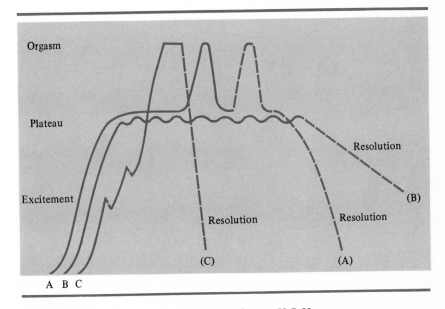

Figure 18-2 The female sexual response cycle. (*Masters, W. H., and Johnson, V. E. Human sexual response. Boston: Little, Brown, 1966, p. 5. © 1966 by Little, Brown and Company. Reprinted by permission.*)

returns to normal position within 5 to 10 seconds after orgasm. The male sexual response enters a refractory period after orgasm and is unable to generate another erection for a varying length of time. However, the female often can again be excited to an orgasmic level immediately by stimulation of the clitoris.

Types of Sexual Dysfunction

Sexual dysfunction is any deviation from any part of these four stages that the individuals find interferes with their pleasure or their ability to function. There is a superficial correspondence between male and female sexual dysfunctions. But while they share certain similarities in the sequence of coital events, their causes and psychological effects are different. The essential differences arise from the unique coital roles the male and the female play. This sets the stage for reciprocal interactions, which may range from mutually supportive, promoting regular orgasmic responses, to bitterly reproachful, inducing sexual failure. In most cases, it is impossible to find the starting point of the interactions, since the original motivation may lie in other aspects of the relationship outside the sexual area. For this reason, Masters and Johnson introduced the method of conjoint therapy, in which the couple is involved in the treatment of a problem that *seems* to belong to only one of them. Again, we see the benefits in approaching a psychologically based problem within a sociopsychological context, instead of treating the individual alone according to the "illness" model. For convenience, however, we will present the male and female problems separately, with an awareness of their interrelationship.

Problems of Male Sexual Functioning

Impotence This problem is defined as the inability to achieve and/or maintain an erection. Masters and Johnson distinguished two kinds of impotence. *Primary impotence* is a condition used to describe men who have never had an erection. It is infrequent and is considered a consequence of views of sex as sinful or dirty, or of residual sexual reactions toward a seductive mother. There are organic structural defects that can produce primary impotence, but these are rare.

Secondary impotence differs from the primary type in that the man has had normal sexual functioning but fails to achieve an erection, at least 25 percent of the times he tries. Some of the causes of this type of impotence are systemic disease (e.g., diabetes, syphilis, other infections), local disease (e.g., genital disturbances, prostatic conditions), drugs, and aging, but none of these factors is a major factor in inducing impotence. Age, in particular, seems to have no limiting effect, since some men in their seventies and beyond engage in satisfactory coitus more frequently than many men in their thirties.

Psychological influences bear the principal responsibility for secondary impotence. In the case of married men, they generally arise from problems in their marriage. Typical examples are guilt over extramarital affairs, a wife's belittling of sexual performance or reproach over the husband's indifferent treatment, fear of causing pregnancy, or fear of women.

Since the burden of making coitus possible rests on the man, and since society equates his "manhood" with his sexual performance, impotence (or even the threat of it) has a devastating effect on his ego. In no other way is he as vulnerable to humiliation by his mate as in her contempt for his inadequate performance. Depression may ensue—although in some cases, depression (induced by business or other failure) may be the cause of impotence. Of course, the depression or anxiety over the first erectile failure is just what is required to prevent erection on subsequent occasions. And, as we have pointed out, nothing is as likely to evoke such anxiety as a woman's critical reactions (real or imagined by the man) to his occasional impotence. The result of his reactions of shame, anxiety, and his feeling that he has failed to live up to his partner's expectations is the distortion of a situational impotence into a persistent inability to become erect.

Because of the tensions generated by the

expectation of sexual performance, many men suffer impotence when confronted with an aggressive partner. Ginsberg, Frosch, and Shapiro (1972) described the case of a 20-year-old man who was overwhelmed by a sexually vigorous woman on their third date. On the first attempt, he ejaculated immediately and later was unable to sustain an erection. On subsequent occasions, he was completely impotent, incurring her displeased reaction. On an earlier occasion, at age 17, he had experienced a similar failure with a prostitute a friend had gotten for him. The similarity was in the expectation that he would perform on demand in both cases although he had not chosen to do so. Women's "liberation" is charged with contributing to the incidence of impotence since women now feel free to express and satisfy their sexual needs without social stigma. This responsibility may be misplaced, however. The problem probably lies in the traditional codes that created the conflict between the man's role as the sexual aggressor and the social imperative that he perform whenever the opportunity presents itself.

Ejaculatory problems These fall into two classes: premature ejaculation and ejaculatory incompetence. *Premature ejaculation* is most precisely restricted to the release of semen before vaginal entry, although it is also applied to ejaculation shortly after entry (within 1 or 2 minutes). Of course, if his partner is satisfied rapidly, the man's rapid ejaculation is not premature. However, since most women attain orgasmic level gradually, ejaculation in less than 15 to 20 minutes is likely to be premature. This does not offer a problem to experienced partners who are skilled in accomplishing sexual satisfaction by clitoral stimulation. *Ejaculatory incompetence* is the inability to achieve orgasm after erection.

Ejaculatory problems, like impotence, are aggravated by the man's negative response to himself and any intolerant reaction from his partner. The tendency to label the problem as "impotence" evokes the socially fixed attitudes and latent anxieties he may have regarding that label. As he worries about it and constantly observes his performance, he fulfills the prophecy. A vicious cycle of fear and failure results in an unmanageable problem.

Problems of Female Sexual Functioning

Frigidity Before Masters and Johnson, women's reticence to discuss, or even to think about, their sexual needs and responses allowed the proliferation of myth and mystery concerning their sexual functioning. One of the main sources of confusion has been the matter of the "vaginal orgasm." Freud believed that "clitoral orgasm," if it persisted, was a sign of neurosis; with the development of a mature personality, the orgasmic center shifted normally to the vagina. It has become clear through recent studies that clitoral response as a result of stimulation is at the core of the orgasm. Although the lower third of the vagina is sexually responsive to friction, the rest of the internal walls are rather insensitive. In fact, orgasm can be produced by manipulation of the clitoris alone. In any case, regardless of the site of the stimulation, the female orgasm is the same, since it is always experienced as the reflex response of the same set of vaginal muscles.

The frigid woman, then, is not one who cannot achieve a vaginal orgasm (whatever it is), but one whose sexual inhibition is so strong that she does not experience erotic excitement. As a result, her vaginal passage does not lubricate, and penile entry must either be forced (with resulting pain) or facilitated by artificial lubrication. A distinction is often made between general sexual dysfunction (frigidity) and orgasmic dysfunction. Sometimes the "frigid" woman may have an orgasm even though the vagina remains dry, just as a man may ejaculate without an erection. *Orgasmic dysfunction* refers to an inability to experience orgasm although lubrication occurs.

As male impotence can be identified as primary and secondary, so may female frigidity, according to whether the woman has never reached orgasm (primary) or fails with some significant frequency (secondary). The causes for orgasmic failure among women are often different from those that affect men. They range from outright repulsion by sexual contact motivated by fear of, or hostility to, men in general, to specific distaste for intercourse with her husband because of dissatisfaction with her marital status or with his domineering behavior.

In contrast to an impotent man, the frigid woman can take part in coitus. She may find, of course, that repeated submission to her partner's demands, without compensating satisfaction, becomes increasingly offensive and intolerable. Or her difficulty in reaching orgasm may lead to a sense of inadequacy that may reduce her desire to engage in sexual activity. She may then resort to various devices in order to escape the unpleasant duty. Kaplan (1974) reports the case of a 38-year-old physician and his 29-year-old wife, married for $3\frac{1}{2}$ years, with one child. Her reluctance to have intercourse frustrated him. She imposed restrictions on their lovemaking (no fondling of her breasts). She avoided intercourse by increasingly resorting to complaints of headache, fatigue, and illness; provocation of bedtime quarrels; and criticisms of her husband's lovemaking techniques. She became less responsive sexually and only occasionally achieved orgasm. Their coital frequency dropped from nightly to once every two weeks.

Masters-and-Johnson-type therapy (which we will describe later) was employed. In the course of the therapy, the wife's internal conflict over her marriage commitment was disclosed. Her sense of responsibility to her husband was compromised by her anger at being deprived of her right to a career of her own. It was necessary to separate this issue from her sex life so it did not intrude upon her enjoyment of sexual pleasures.

Other problems Other problems of the female include dyspareunia and vaginismus. *Dyspareunia* is painful intercourse caused by vaginal irritation. When the irritation persists, it can usually be traced either to congenital deformities in the vaginal anatomy or to local injury. Painful conditions caused by various

vaginal infections carry the names of their respective diseases.

Vaginismus is a spasm of the powerful muscles that girdle the vagina. When they constrict, they either block entry of the penis or clamp it tightly after entry.

Causal, Contributing, and Maintaining Factors

Psychodynamic Factors

Freud centered his theory of personality disorders on the repression or deviation of the natural sexual impulses of the child during the oral, anal, or phallic stages of development (see Chapter 3). The focal point for the genesis of the neuroses is the Oedipal conflict, which generates the castration complex. The unconscious threat of castration by the offended father creates anxieties in the child that result in various sexual maladjustments (from impotence to various deviations). The woman is similarly motivated by anxieties arising from her childhood fantasies of sexual contact with her father, which are frustrated by her mother. The possible effects of the Oedipal conflict on a woman are presented in the following case as a basis for an explanation of her sexual dysfunction.

The patient, a divorced woman of 40, sought help for treatment of orgasmic dysfunction. She has great difficulty in achieving orgasms in the presence of a partner. Although she has sex frequently, she has climaxed with a man on only one, her first, occasion of sexual intercourse. However, she is orgastic, albeit with some difficulty, on masturbation when she is alone. During masturbation she usually fantasizes scenes of a small girl being seduced by an older man. She is only attracted to men who are attached to other women or unavailable to her for some other reason.

According to an analytic formulation, she is fixated at the Oedipal phase. A married man evokes a father "transference." The man unconsciously reminds her of the ardently desired father she could never seduce, and her relationship with this man represents an attempt to undo or compensate for this original childhood traumatic defeat and frustration. However, old Oedipal taboos inhibit her orgasm and if she succeeds in seducing the man away from her rival, she is gratified for a little while only, before quickly losing interest. Her real unconscious goal, to finally seduce her father and thereby to humiliate her mother as she had felt humiliated as a child by her mother's dominant position, has only been attained symbolically. In fact, after she really succeeds in involving the man, her unconscious fantasy that he is her father is destroyed and she now becomes angry with him for "deterring" her from her quest for her "daddy." For this reason she ultimately destroys each new relationship. The patient's life is dominated by this dynamic, which prevents her from enjoying orgasms and, more important, from forming a realistic and satisfying relationship with a man. In addition, anxiety, depression, and inhibitions in other areas of life trouble this patient. (Kaplan, 1974, p. 142)

A fundamental axiom of Freudian theory is that the child's natural sexual impulses cannot simply be blocked or turned off. When a patient deliberately or unwittingly attempts to do so, the frustration leads to repression, with pathological results.

Certain developments have presented challenges to Freud's single-track, Oedipal explanation for all kinds of sexual malfunctioning. Some cases are adequately explained by childhood events in which the classic Oedipal relations play no part. The following case, with aspects of grim humor, illustrates a situation in which the father was not involved:

Years ago, long before the [birth control] pill, a man of 40 came for consultation because of impotence. By his count he had impregnated 14 women by putting holes in his condoms. His story was that at age 13 he had discovered his mother, to whom he had been closely attached, in bed with his father's employee. He chose a unique method of gaining revenge on all women by "knocking them up." The only way he could have intense sexual excitement was when there was the danger of impregnating his female partner. It was with great glee that he would receive the news that the girl was pregnant. As a crude jest he called himself "Jack the Dripper." Over time his pleasure had begun to wane, and he no longer got an intense thrill from his vindictive triumphs. Ultimately, in a somewhat unusual example of the law of the talion, "an eye for an eye and a tooth for a tooth," he became impotent. His depression was so intense that he required psychiatric hospitalization. (Lief, 1974, p. 559)

Another objection to the strictly psychoanalytic interpretation is its bypassing of other causal factors in the child's upbringing. Negative attitudes toward sex are instilled in the child by puritanical or religious parents who, either out of ignorance or religious belief, give the child a deep sense of guilt and sinfulness with respect to sex activity. He or she is reared in an atmosphere of fears and taboos, and in some cases, revulsion toward all acts involving the genitals. Normal masturbation is prohibited and punished when discovered. "Purity"—even in one's private fantasies—is commanded. Such a strict, repressive upbringing is bound to have disturbing effects on the adult's sexual aversions, preferences, and capabilities. A further consequence of an abnormal family situation is the child's failure to develop the capacity for love and trust (Kaplan, 1974). An adult emerging from such an environment probably will be unable to engage in the close interaction that provides the basis for satisfying sexual experiences. These oppressive childhood conditions are sufficient in themselves to cripple the adult's sexual faculties without the effects of an Oedipal conflict.

Finally, the evidence against an exclusively Oedipal explanation includes the effectiveness of sex therapy that is applied only to the here-and-now responses of the client(s) with a special problem. It has been suggested that it is not the Oedipal origin of the anxiety, but the mere presence of any anxiety that causes the sexual dysfunction (Kaplan, 1974). Direct, behavioral therapies are generally adequate in relieving such anxieties. These techniques will be discussed later in the chapter.

Behavioral Factors

Behaviorists do not deny the destructive effects of childhood traumas, particularly the Oedipal conflict, on sexual functioning. They maintain, however, that psychodynamic insight alone ignores the factors and events that are directly responsible for the dysfunction. These factors, according to the behavioral conception, are learned inhibitions acquired through conditioning and maintained by reinforcement. The learned inhibitions counteract and disrupt the natural, unconditioned reactions that are motivated by the pleasurable sensations of sexual activity.

Erection and orgasm are natural reflex responses that may be inhibited by pain, guilt, hostility, or situational anxiety. These events are incompatible with the normal sexual response and thus can produce a counterconditioning of the sexual reflex to sexual stimuli. The dysfunction also can persist because it is operantly reinforced—by the frustration of a hostile spouse or by a reduction of anxiety as a result of avoidance of stressful sexual encounters.

The historical base for the problem may go back to early sexual experiences: the hasty attempt at lovemaking in an automobile or on the sofa while the girl's parents are due back momentarily; the failure to exhibit "manhood" during an episode with a prostitute as part of a peer challenge; an emission in one's pants under uncontrollable excitement during a vigorous dance. Any of the myriad of traumatic sexual experiences during puberty or early adulthood can initiate the self-perpetuating anxiety that becomes the conditioned response associated with sexual failure.

In the female, generalization of early, painful experiences may take place. A brutal defloration by a clumsy, inexperienced youth; a humiliating experience with a frustrated man who vents his anxieties in scornful abuse of a naive girl; an offensive encounter with a lustful relative—these are some of the single events that can spread their effects over a female's whole sex life.

As we will discuss in the next section, the advantage of the behavioral approach is that it permits application of treatment directly to the dysfunctional behaviors, with prompt, observable results. This can be accomplished even if knowledge of the original problem is unavailable.

Other Factors

We have considered two extreme views of sexual dysfunction. The psychodynamic view sets its sights on remote conflicts in the person's childhood. On the other hand, the behavioral view focuses on the immediate causes that occur at the point of action. Somewhere between these poles, we find the interplay of open and hidden struggles between the two players in the sexual arena. Examination of these conflicts and misunderstandings often makes more clear the causes of sexual dysfunction.

Kaplan (1974) stresses the negative effect of an antierotic environment on sexual dysfunction. She describes four inhibiting behavior patterns that contribute to that environment: (1) failure to engage in mutually stimulating behavior because of *ignorance* of or unconscious aversion to sex, (2) anxiety because of *fear of failure* in performance on demand, (3) *overconcern* with one's own reactions, to the point of "spectatoring" (i.e., viewing and evaluating oneself as if from a spectator's position), and (4) *failure to communicate sexual needs* and sensitivities to one's partner. The causes and effects of fear of failure are exemplified in the following case, which shows the lasting consequences of a single mishap in demand performance.

The patient was a handsome and successful 30-year-old businessman who had been divorced two years before. His partner was his fiancée who was 26 years of age. They were planning to get married shortly.

The chief complaint was impotence. The man

was easily aroused and achieved an erection quickly upon commencing sex play. Almost invariably, however, his erection abated when he was about to commence coitus. His fiancée had no sexual difficulty. She was easily aroused and orgastic on clitoral stimulation.

Psychiatric history was negative for serious psychopathology for both. In fact, they seemed to be very well adjusted individuals. Their relationship seemed to be excellent.

The history revealed that in his prior marriage, which had lasted five years and produced two children, the patient had experienced no sexual difficulty. He and his wife had coitus two to three times per week, and he invariably functioned well. His wife left him because she fell in love with and wished to marry a close friend of the family.

The divorce was very traumatic for the patient. He became depressed and was left with deep feelings of insecurity. He kept ruminating about why his wife had left him, and whether he was inferior to the other man.

Eight months after the separation he went to a party and met an aggressive woman who wanted to have sex with him right there. On her urging they went to an upstairs room (which did not have a lock) and attempted to have intercourse on the floor. He became excited and erect, but for the first time in his life, lost his erection. He tried to regain his erection to no avail.

He reacted with alarm to this experience. He felt depressed and extremely humiliated and embarrassed. He never saw the woman again. One month later, he tried to make love to another woman but again lost his erection when the memory of his previous failure intruded into his mind. From then on the problem escalated. He met his fiancée shortly thereafter, but initially avoided making love to her because he anticipated failure. Later, when they became more intimate, he confessed his problem to her. They attempted sex, but in most instances the patient was unable to function. Questioning revealed that he was preoccupied with thoughts about whether he would fail during lovemaking. He continued to feel humiliated and feared rejection despite his fiancée's reassurance and sensitivity. (Kaplan, 1974, pp. 128–129)

Lack of communication between lovers perpetuates the blunders and omissions that cause the dysfunction. The communication blockage results from acceptance of traditional codes of male and female sexual behavior: the performance requirement for the man and the passive, receptive attitude for the woman. Behind their masks, the partners misread each other's constrained signals, with painful, frustrating, and demoralizing results.

The antierotic coital environment is often the setting in which marital and other conflicts are acted out. Both parties bring their marital power struggles into bed with them, using their respective sexual advantages to dominate, punish, or reduce each other. The techniques employed in the struggle come under the heading of "sexual sabotage." The antierotic arsenal takes in a wide selection of devices, from making oneself sexually repulsive (body odor, unshaven face, curlers in the hair) to practicing a variety of annoying or frustrating sexual behaviors. Among the latter are such tactics as lying motionless during lovemaking, rejecting fondling of breasts or genitals, refusing to fondle breasts or genitals, plunging into sex without foreplay, and acting as if sex were a grudgingly given favor. The sexual dysfunction then becomes another grievance added to the general marital discord, which aggravates the sexual problems, and the vicious circle proceeds without end until the couple decides to deal with the problems together, often by seeking therapy.

Childhood traumas, sexual role demands and constraints, discordant marital relations, culturally sanctioned expectations, constrictive familial and religious training—all these and more combine to form one of the best examples of the multiple-factor model of causality and maintenance of dysfunction.

We mention, in passing, the possibility of *physical causes* of sexual dysfunction. These, of course, must be evaluated before proceeding with any type of therapy. However, physical disorders in genital functions are uncommon and do not account for the widespread prevalence of sexual problems.

Treatment of Sexual Dysfunction

Psychodynamic Approaches

Throughout the text, we have referred repeatedly to the traditional (i.e., psychodynamic) method of resolving early developmental conflicts through insight therapy. In cases of sexual malfunction, this involves deep probing of childhood experiences, especially during the onset of puberty, when Oedipal attachments and frustrations arise. Psychodynamic therapists believe it is necessary to reveal, recognize, and settle the conflicts of Oedipal origin, and release the inhibitions imposed by family rules and religious constraints before the immediate sexual problems can be cleared up.

Once the early conflicts and repressions have been resolved, psychotherapists hold that the sexual dysfunction will be relieved and normal responses will emerge, free of the repression that blocked them.

Practitioners of the new sex therapy recognize the inhibiting effects of Oedipal and other childhood conflicts, but they believe the here-and-now dysfunction can be addressed directly by procedures designed to change the specific antierotic responses. In cases of severe inhibition caused by early traumas, sex therapy reaches the sexual anxieties through the clients' reactions to erotic situations, as we shall see, without using extensive psychoanalysis. The object is to develop an awareness of habitual, negative behavior rather than an insight into childhood disturbances. Traditional therapy is usually not the method of choice for sexual dysfunction, although it is sometimes used as a supplement to behavioral sex therapy, providing valuable insights that suggest ways of increasing the effectiveness of the behavioral treatment.

Behavioral Approaches

The term "behavior therapy" embraces a variety of techniques for correcting sexual dysfunction. Some procedures follow classical and operant conditioning principles and are essentially behavioral applications of learning theory. Others are more recent innovations, which involve modified behavioral techniques now referred to as "sex therapy." While behavior and sex therapies spring from a common source and share a common focus on specific sexual behaviors rather than on psychodynamic origins, we separate them in this review to accent the contributions to the knowledge and improvement of sexual functioning that modern sex specialists have made.

We have studied the use of *conditioning*, *desensitization*, and *flooding* in treating phobias, schizophrenia, and other disorders. The value of these methods has also been demonstrated in the treatment of sexual dysfunctions.

Two types of desensitization have been used: *covert* (or fantasy) and *in vivo* (real-life situations). In cases where anxiety or fear prevents erection or causes premature ejaculation or frigidity, both types of desensitization have resulted in significant improvement. Obler (1973) conducted a controlled study of 64 subjects, using covert desensitization on the target group. The subjects imagined scenes that were graded in a hierarchy of increasing sexual excitement (ranging from light kissing to coitus). During the fantasizing of the erotic images, the subjects practiced muscle relaxation. While results were positive, the desensitization treatment was contaminated by other therapeutic procedures, which makes a clear-cut assessment impossible.

In vivo desensitization has produced orgasmic response in frigid women who are not susceptible to erotic fantasies. Lobitz and LoPiccolo (1972) report successful results from a nine-step, controlled masturbation program, which proceeded from the woman's examining her nude body and exploring her genitals to masturbation in the presence of her partner and his stimulation of her genitals during intercourse.

A particularly difficult case of impotence was treated successfully with both covert and in vivo desensitization by Garfield, McBrearty, and Dichter (1969). The client reported antierotic anxiety associated with events preceding a sexual encounter. The anxiety-evoking events were organized into a hierarchy starting with the most remote in place and time (leaving his business on the way to a date) and gradually approaching the sexual encounter via intermediate situations charged with increasing anxiety (bathing, shaving, driving to his lover's house, etc.). Relaxation therapy was applied to each of these situations until it was neutralized. Thought stopping and substitution were also introduced at the point where the client became preoccupied with his partner's orgasm (or lack of it). He was instructed to fantasize other exciting situations at that moment. It is interesting to note that his previous history of conflict experiences with a seductive mother, a puritanical father, an unresponsive first wife, and alcoholism was ignored in the behavioral treatment.

Special aversions that interfered with the full, mutual enjoyment of sex by both partners were treated by Lazarus (1963), using in vivo desensitization. The therapy was applied to a number of women who complained of frigidity in response to their mates' demands. In one case, the client said she was "turned off" by demands for sex in any but the "normal" man-superior position. The desensitization hierarchy ranged upward in erotic intensity from dancing with her husband (fully clothed) and kissing, through progressive caressing (from hair and face to buttocks and breasts), to genital manipulation and, ultimately, having intercourse, first in the man-superior position and then in other positions on, and away from, the bed. After completion of treatment, the client reported the coital variations "disgustingly pleasant."

Orgasmic reconditioning adapts classical conditioning principles to sexual problems. An example shows how gradual exposure in vivo is combined with conditioning in relieving vaginismus. The female client could experience orgasm only by mutual masturbation, not during intercourse. She was instructed to engage in foreplay and, just before orgasm, to imagine her fingertip inserted in her vagina. In successive sessions, she imagined more of her finger inserted at increasing intervals before

orgasm. Then she imagined her fiancé's finger in the same progressive sequence. Finally, her real finger and then his proceeded through the same sequence. Eventually, penile entry was accomplished in regular intercourse.

Shaping erection behavior by means of operant conditioning has been effective in treating clients suffering secondary impotence. The client views erotic slides. He wears a penis transducer, a device that can detect and record the degree of erectile firmness. In an adjacent room, the therapist reads the gauge and offers feedback, at first praising small erections, then reserving praise for increasingly larger, and finally, full erections. Presumably, the erections themselves are an additional reinforcement.

Sexual Therapy: Contemporary Sex Counseling and Sex Clinics

The various behavioral techniques we have just described are incorporated, with modifications, into the newer therapeutic procedures practiced by sex counselors. Since most of the programs currently in favor are based on or built around the pioneer Masters and Johnson sexual techniques, we will center our discussion around their procedures.

Masters and Johnson have developed an intensive (seven-days-a-week), rapid (two or three weeks' duration) program of sex therapy that comprises a number of operating features: sexual tasks, coital abstinence, sensate focusing, nondemand performance, and graded exposure. Clients are treated in pairs. The client pair are treated by a therapist team consisting of a man and a woman, one of whom is a physician. The reason for the double-dual arrangement is that Masters and Johnson consider faulty sexual response a result of a bad interaction between partners that must be dealt with as a mutual problem. Having a therapist of each sex eases communication with the client counterparts, although some sex counselors find the second therapist unnecessary.

Reduced to its essentials, the program provides a progressive sequence of *sexual tasks* to be performed by the client pair, under professional supervision in the clinic and at home.

Coital abstinence is imposed at the outset, eliminating all demand performance. The clients are instructed in the practice of *sensate focus*, which involves exercises in the erotic enjoyment of mutual caressing and fondling of various parts of the body. In these exercises, the whole body is treated as an "erogenous zone." Initially, each partner caresses the other's nongenital areas, while the receiver concentrates on the sensuous feelings evoked by the manipulation. The exercises progress to the genitals, without coitus at first. The couple are encouraged to communicate their sensations—pleasant and aversive—to each other during the caressing. By the prohibition of intercourse during the early phase of the program, there are *no performance pressures*. The sole objective of the mutual sensate-focusing experience is to develop the capacity for giving and receiving pleasure.

The next phase of the program deals with the act of coitus itself, treating problems of erection and orgasm. The general approach is described as *graded exposure* to the actions in the coital sequence. (Since the partners are performing acts they have attempted before, the procedure might more properly be called graded *re*exposure.)

Masturbation exercise is the prelude to lovemaking in cases of orgasmic dysfunction.

William H. Masters and Virginia Johnson were pioneers in the field of sex therapy. Most programs currently in favor are based on or built around their techniques. (*Elliott Erwift / Magnum.*)

Masters and Johnson use a nine-step masturbation procedure for women, in which self-masturbation is practiced in the first six steps. The husband takes an active part from the seventh step onward. The sexual tasks then proceed through further graded steps involving partial penile entry without orgasm, leading gradually to full entry with orgasm. Some therapists modify the basic Masters and Johnson graded exposure program by introducing orgasmic reconditioning techniques, such as those we outlined in the previous section. These generally include desensitization procedures during masturbation, with the interjection of fantasies involving the partner just prior to orgasm.

Premature ejaculation is handled by means of a "squeeze technique." When the male orgasm seems imminent, the female partner circles the tip of the penis with her forefinger and thumb, and squeezes, making ejaculation impossible. This is repeated on successive occasions, until the male develops an awareness of the oncoming orgasm in time to pause and control the impulse (Lief, 1974).

Masters and Johnson have not scored the same success in the treatment of impotence as they have with cases of orgasmic dysfunction. Apparently, the graded exposure procedure with masturbatory collaboration between the partners is not always sufficient to overcome the inhibiting effect of male anxiety. O'Leary and Wilson (1975) suggest that better results with impotence are obtainable by adding desensitization, behavior rehearsal, and assertion training to the basic Masters and Johnson program.

On the other hand, Kaplan (1974) argues for a psychodynamically oriented sex therapy with sexual behavior as "just one aspect of the total therapeutic process." She believes that an understanding of the causal factors is prerequisite to effective, long-term correction of the dysfunction. Once the source of the conflict has been determined, it is possible to design sexual tasks that relieve the anxiety and recondition successful sex behavior. With the intrapsychic information, suitable attention can also be directed toward multiple causes, including Oedipal problems, religious constraints, and marital conflicts. In this way, the Masters and Johnson learning techniques can be tailored to each individual, with improved results.

Other procedural changes and innovations have been introduced into the Masters and Johnson model by sex therapists. These include the viewing of erotic films as a prelude to sex, removal of the couple from the familiar home locale to a vacation resort or quarters near the sex clinic, videotape feedback of the clients' performance of sexual tasks with critical analysis (à la the post–football game critique of the film by the coach and players). One of the more controversial techniques is the Masters and Johnson use of a surrogate, or substitute, partner—a paid aide who serves as sexual partner for clients who have no spouse or companion who will volunteer to join in the sexual tasks. The obvious analogy to prostitution raises ethical questions for therapists who make the service available to clients. New techniques continue to emerge in this young clinical practice, which is still seeking its theoretical base.

What are the effectiveness rates for the different therapies in eliminating the several dysfunctions? Masters and Johnson's own tabulation of results with 780 clients (Table 18-1) shows success with about 60 percent of males suffering primary impotence, 70 percent of those with secondary impotence, 98 percent with premature ejaculation, and 83 percent with retarded ejaculation. They relieved 83 percent of females with primary orgasmic dysfunction and 75 percent with situational orgasmic dysfunction. Their overall success ratio was 80 percent for all male and female sexual dysfunctions. The total rates reflect a small percentage of reversals after initial success during the two-week, intensive therapy programs.

The Masters and Johnson technique for premature ejaculation is far superior in its results to psychoanalysis, marital counseling, or desensitization procedures, according to Kaplan (1974). A similar difference in results is observed for the various treatments applied to retarded ejaculation. Clinicians report virtually 100 percent cure rates, with no reversals, in the desensitization treatment of vaginismus, which we described earlier.

In analyzing the results of treatment of

Table 18-1 Overall Results of the Masters and Johnson Treatment Program (1970)

Complaint	N	F	IFR (%)	TR	OFR (%)
Primary impotence	32	13	40.6	0	40.6
Secondary impotence	213	56	26.2	10	30.9
Premature ejaculation	186	4	2.2	1	2.7
Ejaculatory incompetence	17	3	17.6	0	17.6
Male Totals	448	76	16.9	11	19.4
Primary orgasmic dysfunction	193	32	16.6	2	17.6
Situational orgasmic dysfunction	149	34	22.8	3	24.8
Female Totals	342	66	19.3	5	20.8
Male and Female Totals	790	142	18.9	16	20.0

N, marital units referred for treatment; F, immediate treatment failure; IFR, initial failure rate; TR, treatment reversal; OFR, overall failure rate.

Masters, W. H., and Johnson, V. E. *Human sexual inadequacy.* Boston: Little, Brown, 1970, p. 367. © 1970 by Little, Brown and Company. Reprinted by permission.

female sexual dysfunction, the conclusions are clouded by uncertainty in defining success. While most nonorgasmic women can be made to experience orgasm, it is not clear whether this achievement represents full sexual satisfaction. And as we discussed earlier, it is questionable whether the term dysfunctional can truly be applied to women who can achieve orgasm through clitoral stimulation, but not through vaginal stimulation alone—a conceptual vestige of the early Freudian view.

Kaplan (1974) observes that success in sex therapy often affects other areas of psychological functioning. When the sexual inadequacy is a central problem, affecting the client's self-image and attitude toward his or her life, relief of sexual problems is accompanied by resolution of other basic conflicts and disturbances.

A curious, negative result occasionally occurs after successful sex therapy. In some cases, prior to therapy, one of the partners used the spouse's dysfunction either as an instrument for domination of the spouse or as reassurance against abandonment. When the dysfunction is cured, the threat of loss becomes imminent, with disturbing effects, which must be treated by additional therapy.

Sexual Deviation

Types of Sexual Deviation

The subject of sexual deviation is beset with controversy. It is in this area that the question, "What is abnormal?" which we raised earlier, stirs up the most heated reactions. In a more puritanical phase of our culture, most of the behaviors we are about to describe were classed as "perversions" and were the objects of social contempt and legal prohibition. We have tempered our strict attitudes, however, and now make reasonable distinctions between deviations that may be practiced in normal fashion and a very small group of outright abnormalities. The DSM-II gives this definition of *sexual deviation:*

This category is for individuals whose sexual interests are directed toward objects other than people of the opposite sex, toward sexual acts not usually associated with coitus, or toward coitus performed under bizarre circumstances as in necrophilia, pedophilia, sexual sadism, and fetishism. Even though many find their practices distasteful, they remain unable to substitute normal sexual behavior for them. This diagnosis is not appropriate for individuals who perform deviant sexual acts because normal sexual objects are not available to them. (American Psychiatric Association, 1968, p. 302)

Fetishism[1]

Fetishism is the focusing of sexual interest on an object instead of a person. These objects can be virtually anything—things that have inherent erotic qualities, such as a lock of hair, undergarments, and sheer stockings, as well as those whose stimulating effect derives from an idiosyncratic association. In the psychoanalytic view, the fetishistic object is identified with the genitals. This relieves the fetishists of their anxieties evoked by the unresolved Oedipal conflict and the threat of castration. Regression is the mechanism at work. The point of regression may predate puberty, going back to the pregenital fixation on a blanket or toy as a means of establishing ego identification.

In their pursuit of substitute sexual gratification, fetishists may engage in other, more aggressive behaviors. *Kleptomania*, the compulsive stealing of objects endowed with sexual symbolism by the thief, is often practiced by women who feel unloved. *Pyromania* is another compulsive, fetishistic behavior that seems to have a curious association with sexual "heat" or, possibly, sexual purification.

We must, at the same time, acknowledge that a preoccupation with women's breasts, buttocks, and legs on the part of men is a form of fetishism that is not uncommon among men who have heterosexual relations. We see here the basis for a distinction that clinicians make between normal and abnormal sexual behavior. If the deviant behavior is enjoyed as an introduction to, or an occasional substitute for, normal heterosexual activity, or is engaged in when normal activity is not available, it is not considered abnormal.

Exhibitionism

Exhibitionism is a relatively common cause of arrest for sexual offenses. Because women may not provoke the same horrified reaction as male exhibitionists do and may, therefore, be protected from arrest, it appears on the surface to be more common among men.

According to the psychodynamic view, the urge to exhibit one's genitals to strangers, without forewarning, is a compulsive behavior motivated by feelings of inadequacy and doubts about one's sexuality. It is considered by some psychoanalysts to be a defiance of the threat of castration. Others see it as a demonstration of self-love. Often the male exhibitionist is found to be the submissive offspring of a domineering mother. The following case presents a typical history:

The patient under consideration is a 25-year-old married man of average intelligence (I.Q. 106). The elder of two boys, he recalls intense antagonism towards his brother dating from an early age. Ten years separated the two.

The parents are of Anglo-Saxon stock; artisan class; and quite puritanical in outlook. The patient reports them as domineering. He recalls his mother's early admonition against childish sexual practices which she described as "evil" and "nasty," and her frequent injunctions that he conceal his genitals from the view of females. An incident which increased his sexual guilt tremendously involved punishment by his mother for engaging in a contest with another boy to see how high up the side of a wall each could urinate. He recalls at this time feeling "hurt" by the observation that his friend's penis was the larger.

His first exposure occurred at 13 following sex play with a 10-year-old neighbour girl. He felt a desire to perform coitus, but the girl appeared indifferent to his suggestion and had refused. Her indifference hurt him; this was followed by rage, then by the exposing of his erect penis to her. . . .

---

[1] The behavioral literature avoids very general explanations for specific sexual deviations, since each is learned in a particular situation. For this reason, we refer only to psychodynamic theories for our explanation of causal factors.

Our society seems to condone many acts of female exhibitionism, yet is horrified at male exhibitionism. Therefore, statistics show that there are more male than female exhibitionists. (*United Press International.*)

Throughout adolescence he suffered feelings of inadequacy and inferiority. His exhibitionism continued, and he indulged excessively in sexual daydreams and phallic auto-erotic practices. . . .By the late teens and early twenties, his exhibitionism had reached bizarre proportions. Tension was constant and it was not unusual for him to expose several times during the day. . . .

The attack of exhibitionism was described by the patient as being preceded by a feeling of sexual excitement and dread. He would experience "a grim determination to expose, come what might." He would become tense and an erection would occur. At this time things would seem unreal, "as if watching myself doing something in a dream." He would then expose to the female usually but not always, masturbating. When the girl registered shock, "the spell would be broken" and he would flee, trembling and remorseful. His wife, often present during such an attack, described his appearance as one of being "paralyzed, with glazed eyes." . . .

The patient's police record indicated 24 charges of indecent exposure and 11 convictions with nine prison sentences of from four months to one year. (Bond and Hutchison, 1964, pp. 80–82)

This case shows the compulsive aspect quite clearly. He feels driven to engage in the behavior and feels out of control during the so-called "attack." Other characteristics of exhibitionism are the patterns of provocation by victims of a certain age range, generally children or young adolescents, and by particular locales, such as public parks, department stores, or women's washrooms.

On describing the man in the above case, Bond and Hutchison report that whenever he saw shapely female adolescents and young adults, he had the urge to expose himself. When he did so, it was usually in department stores and women's washrooms. In fact, in therapy it was necessary to desensitize him with specific reference to each of the situations in which his behavior had been provoked.

As we shall see, exhibitionism is sometimes associated with pedophilia and voyeurism.

Pedophilia

Pedophilia is a sexual deviance marked by an erotic attraction to children. Legally, the deviant acts are referred to as "child molestation," which is viewed by society—even by other felons in prison—as one of the lowest forms of criminal behavior. The pedophile, generally a man, usually seeks to uncover and play with a child's genitals. Attempts at vaginal or anal penetration may be made, accompanied by violence in about one-fifth of the cases. At times, the pedophile simply exposes himself to the child.

Often a weak and inadequate person, the molester may simply be trying to treat his victims with the love he wanted, but did not receive, from his parents. On the other hand, the concentration on children's genitals is interpreted as a response to fears of sexual inadequacy and anticipation of rejection by adult females.

Transsexualism and Transvestism

Transsexualism and transvestism are often misconstrued as the same deviation. They are easily distinguishable, as their definitions indicate. The *transsexual* has an overwhelming compulsion, often going back to early childhood, to live as a member of the opposite sex, engaging in the full pattern of life experiences—including the sexual. This orientation will probably involve a desire to wear clothing of the opposite sex. The *transvestite* enjoys dressing in female apparel (almost all known transvestites are male), and often masturbates to orgasm while so attired but generally is satisfied with heterosexual relations and has no desire to change his sex.

Transvestites enjoy dressing in female attire, but are usually oriented to heterosexual relations. (*James Motlow / Magnum.*)

Money (1974) presents a nicely detailed review of the motivations, biochemical factors, and gender identity problems involved in decisions to request sex-change operations. He distinguishes between the intersexual (a true hermaphrodite with elements of both male and female genitals) and the transsexual, whose genital structures are unmistakably recognizable and functional.

Money's central thesis is that the crucial determinant in the transsexual's gender preference is the sex assignment at, or soon after, birth. During infancy, the *gender identity* is imprinted by the attitudes of parents, and later on, by peers and teachers. Sexual impulses during childhood are associated with erotic images of one sex or the other. This early imaging process establishes the sexual orientation. Once sexual disposition has been established, later treatment with hormones and surgery will not change it. Nor will hormones change the basic structure of the reproductive organs and the secondary sexual features. Estrogens do not stop male facial and body hair growth nor change the male voice. They do promote deposits of subcutaneous fat, giving a more rounded appearance. In females, hormone treatment will lower the voice by lengthening vocal cords and will induce facial hair growth. They will not flatten the breasts nor enlarge the clitoris to penile dimensions. Most of the desired genital structures identified with the opposite sex have to be surgically constructed. While serviceable (i.e., sexually responsive) vaginas can be formed in male transsexuals, few functional penises have been made for females.

Sadism and Masochism

Sadism is the attainment of sexual gratification by inflicting pain on others; its counterpart is masochism, the attainment of sexual gratification by having pain inflicted on oneself.

Christine Jorgensen's widely publicized sex-change operation was one of the first of its kind. Here (at left) is George Jorgensen in 1943, (center) Christine Jorgensen in 1952 after a series of operations, and (right) as she looked in 1975. (*United Press International.*)

Freud saw sadism as a manifestation of male aggressiveness and desire to subjugate—the violent component of the sexual instinct. Sadistic behavior may be the acting out of repressed hostility to a parent or to society in general. It may also be used as reassurance against castration, since it establishes the absolute power of the sadist over the potentially castrating victim. The deeply disturbed sadist may commit lust murder in which the victim is murdered and mutilated, exciting the perpetrator to orgasm without coitus. The fear and revulsion generated by published accounts of lust murders are one reason for the public's abhorrence of all forms of sexual deviation.

Masochism seems to have more interest to clinicians because it is more common than sadism, its motivations are more complex, and its manifestations more varied. Freud identified masochism with an exaggeration of women's normal posture of submissiveness and an abnormal femininity in men.

The apparent gratification that masochists gain from feeling pain puzzled Freud, who found the desire for pain inconsistent with his pleasure principle. In the natural course of things, people are supposed to seek pleasure and avoid pain. He decided that masochism was sadism turned on oneself. For example, he described the girl who took sadistic pleasure in her father's beating a hated sibling. Responding to a feeling of guilt, she switched to a masochistic fantasy of herself being beaten. She imagined herself suffering punishment at the hands of her father for her sexual impulses toward him.

Some psychoanalysts believe that the masochist does not seek the pain for itself but as a symbol of the power or the punishment to which he wants to subject himself. This distinction between sources of gratification is clearly shown in the following case from Krafft-Ebing's reports:

A 29-year-old male from the age of 5 became sexually aroused by whipping himself or fantasying other boys being whipped. He masturbated with fantasies of whipping. On the first occasion that he visited a prostitute, he was flagellated [whipped]

by a pretty girl, but this did not produce arousal. The second time he fantasied the idea of subjection to the woman's will and he became sexually aroused. (Bieber, 1974, p. 319)

Masochism may also represent a means of escaping an overwhelming agony by substituting a lesser injury that is under the victim's control. The person who does the punishing serves as stand-in for the dreaded castrating parent. Nonsexual masochism is often adopted to win love or prevent rejection. Children may assume a self-critical attitude when parents are competitive with them or when parents are disapproving of certain of their creative activities. Before the era of civil rights in this country, many black mothers in the South indoctrinated their children with a submissive acceptance of white authority as a life-saving measure. Indeed, masochism is a deviation with a multiplicity of sources, not all of them sexual.

Sexual Orientation Disturbance

"Sexual orientation disturbance" is the new designation assigned to replace "homosexuality" by the American Psychiatric Association in 1973, dropping the DSM-II classification of homosexuality as an abnormality. The revised description follows:

> This [category] is for individuals whose sexual interests are directed primarily toward people of the same sex and who are either disturbed by, in conflict with, or wish to change their sexual orientation. This diagnostic category is distinguished from homosexuality, which by itself does not necessarily constitute a psychiatric disorder. Homosexuality per se is one form of sexual behavior. . . .

Note that the APA authors have separated the formerly unitary group of homosexuals into two subgroups, one of which suffers a "sexual orientation disturbance" and the other a category of homosexuals who are quite content with their sexual preference. Both subgroups prefer relations with their own sex, but one of

There is little biological, genetic, or psychological evidence that homosexuals are fundamentally different from heterosexuals. Most homosexuals are content with their sexual preference and are beginning to convince their families, friends, and communities that they deserve the same rights and respect as others. (*Charles Gatewood.*)

them is unhappy about what it feels is an uncomfortable compulsion. (Of course, the definition of "sexual orientation disturbance" technically could include heterosexuals who, because of problems with the opposite sex, might prefer to be homosexuals, but this is a rare clinical occurrence.

Some questions arise in identifying homosexuality as a clinical entity. There are circumstances in which the practice of homosexuality is indulged in for transitory or situational reasons: adolescent experimentation, disorganized behavior in psychotic states, unavailable partners of the opposite sex, and the need for ready, quick, and cost-free orgasm (by oral sex) on the part of heterosexual males with unsatisfactory marital relations. Kinsey resolved the difficulty in making clear-cut distinctions between homosexuality and heterosexuality by setting up a 7-point scale that represented sexual orientation as a continuum, ranging from 0 = exclusively heterosexual and 1 = predominantly heterosexual, through degrees 2–5, marked by an increasing proportion of homosexuality in the personality "mix," to 6 = exclusively homosexual.

Humphreys' study (1970) presents a striking demonstration of the blurring of boundaries between homosexuals and heterosexuals. (The study is a pioneering example of the effectiveness of the participant-observer method of obtaining sensitive information that might be distorted or unavailable by any less direct means.) This field survey, conducted in public restrooms (referred to in the subcultural vernacular as "tearooms"), determined that 54 percent of the participants were average husbands and fathers. About 40 percent were Roman Catholic; many were regular churchgoers. While 38 percent classed themselves in Kinsey's 5 and 6 groups, another 38 percent considered themselves solidly heterosexual except for sporadic excursions to get fast, cheap orgasms. The definition is certainly not as sharp and clear as some would have it.

If there were clear biological or genetic evidence that homosexuals are different, it would be easy to establish homosexuality as a clinical entity. But, in fact, the biological argument is extremely weak, since humans are the only animal species expected to engage exclusively in heterosexual activity. And, indeed, in many societies—64 percent of 76 societies studied by Ford and Beach (1952)—homosexual behavior is accepted as normal for certain members of the community. In our own society, Kinsey (1948) found 37 percent of males had practiced homosexuality for at least three years and 10 percent of white males reported themselves predominantly or exclusively homosexual (5 or 6 on the Kinsey scale). (Recent data indicate that these figures may have been overestimated.) Between 2 and 6 percent of

unmarried women fell into the predominantly or exclusively homosexual category, while 28 percent of all women reported experiencing arousing homosexual responses on various occasions.

The ambiguities in defining and identifying homosexuality are just as baffling when we attempt to find psychological causes for the behavior. We face two complementary questions: Is homosexuality an abnormal behavior? Is neurotic behavior more prevalent among homosexuals? Freud himself, who is associated with the medical model, did not consider homosexuality an illness. And while neurotic behavior is more prevalent among homosexuals, it has been argued that the social rejection and handicaps imposed on homosexuals could account for neurotic defenses. However, we still sense the need to seek causes for a behavior that runs counter to requirements for survival of the species, especially in the case of individuals who feel driven to that behavior against their wish to be heterosexual.

Psychodynamic explanations of homosexuality center around the classic fear of castration—in this case, by the dominant, powerful mother. A variant of this dominant mother relationship is the son's identification with the aggressive mother as the possessor of power, with a consequent assumption of the female role. This explanation is supported by a study of 106 male homosexuals made by Bieber et al. (1962). They found that the most common parental pattern comprised a detached, hostile father and a warm, seductive, dominant mother. Other studies show similar problems with distant, hostile mothers and overly close fathers. The basic, motivating factor seems to be the lack of an adequate, loving father with whom the son can identify, coupled with a mother whose ambiguous role as a seductive aggressor generates ambivalent fear responses in the son. Whereupon we collide with the rude fact that many heterosexual men come from just such upset environments.

Female homosexuality poses even more puzzling challenges to our understanding. The relatively lower prevalence of homosexuality among females than males has been ascribed to many factors, but none have proved to be reliable explanations.

Finding causes of lesbianism has thus far defied systematic investigation. Saghir and Robbins (1973) reported a great diversity of family relationships in lesbian backgrounds. A common denominator was a strong antiheterosexual attitude in parental admonitions against dating or relating to boys and, later, to men. Parents of lesbians generated overwhelming guilt and fear toward sexual contact with men, starting in the early pubescent period.

Although the American Psychiatric Association has formally disqualified homosexuality as a mental disorder, the issue is far from settled. Many argue for its restoration to the DSM-II list of disorders. Pressures from all sides are likely to speed a change, but the ultimate direction cannot be predicted—testimony that the persistent lack of definitive knowledge about this ancient sexual question still provides grounds for opposite opinions among clinicians.

Incest

Incest, the practice of family members engaging in sexual relations, is the most generally prevalent sexual taboo. With notably few exceptions, the practice has been abhorred in most cultures throughout history. There are, however, cultural differences in the degree of revulsion that attaches to incest within the various family relationships. Mother-son incest evokes the greatest abhorrence, while father-daughter and sibling incest seem to be frowned upon less in some societies. In ancient Egypt, for example, brother-sister marriages were not uncommon.

The mother-son sexual relationship is, of course, the basis of the Oedipal conflict which is at the heart of Freudian psychodynamics. By analogy, the father-daughter relationship is also the basis of Oedipal conflict in the female (though it is more properly called the Electra complex, in accordance with the Greek legends whose dramatizations provided the models for the Freudian concepts).

Since incest is a physical act and not in itself a pathologic disorder, its occurrence and psychological effects are largely determined by cultural attitudes. Here we find a variety of apparent or surmised reasons for the taboo. Fox (1962) cites several factors that affect the application of the taboo: degree of temptation, premium on a girl's virginity, codes concerning rights of illegitimate children, and lines of heritage. Some cultures may have recognized the biological disadvantages of inbreeding.

The psychological causes of incestuous behavior can be very complex, particularly in families where there are unsatisfactory natural relationships. Acts of incest can be two-sided to some degree. As an example, the mother who is hostile to the father and/or daughter rejects the father's sexual demands, forcing the father and the daughter to seek love from each other. The daughter sometimes vents her hostility toward her mother by seducing the father. The mother is often working out her hostility to her own cold, unloving mother by transferring the hostility to her daughter, forcing the daughter to assume the dependent mother's wifely duties.

This reversal of roles is seen by some psychologists as a defensive maneuver to maintain a façade of "togetherness" in a dysfunctional family. In effect, the family ridden with divisive tensions is saved from disintegration by the reversal of roles. The dysfunctional character of the incestuous family correlates well with the high prevalence of psychopathic personality disorders among the offending fathers and, to a lesser extent, among the collusive mothers.

Masturbation

Masturbation is one of the oldest sexual issues, the subject of Biblical injunction and grotesque myths. Because it is the most common of sexual behaviors (virtually all people do it in some manner at some time in their lives), it has preoccupied medical practitioners, religious moralists, and anxious parents through the ages.

Most of the myths and misconceptions about masturbation are founded on pervasive ignorance broadcast by so-called "medical authorities." It is likely that much of the horror with which masturbation has been viewed arises from its occurrence during the preadolescent period. During this period, the naive child, frightened by his or her newly experienced sexual impulses, is susceptible to suggestions of guilt and harmful effects. The hysteria stirred up by medical and religious "authorities" permitted the grossest absurdities to take root—such as the nonsense that masturbation destroyed the brain, caused epilepsy and other diseases, weakened the body to the onset of tuberculosis, and was a mortal sin. The wonder is that such irrational beliefs could persist to the present day when it is clear that masturbation provides harmless relief from sexual tension. Some psychologists question its exclusive use instead of coitus. Yet the practice of masturbation by many men and women who are celibates (individuals who do not engage in sexual intercourse) because of professional or personal inclination testifies to its suitability as a total substitute for sexual relations. Only when it reflects a compulsion or a deeply rooted fear that interferes with the person's social relationships can it be considered a harmful excess.

Other Sexual Deviations

Variety is not only the spice of life but also of sex as well. Virtually everything that can be done with or to the body provides sexual gratification to somebody. To the deviations we have just described, we add several of the more exotic variations.

Voyeurism is the surreptitious viewing of others usually by peeping through windows in homes. *Scoptophilia* refers to the same behavior directed toward genitalia and sexual acts. By observing without being observed, the voyeur enjoys sexual stimulation without threat of rejection or demand for performance.

Zoophilia is the unnatural use of animals for sexual satisfaction. *Bestiality* is the more common name and is applied especially to the act of sex with animals or of masturbating them. The behavior is most prevalent among boys who live on farms and is generally a transitory activity that ceases during adolescence when relations with girls are established.

Necrophilia is rare and is considered a true perversion with psychotic indications. The necrophile achieves orgasm by viewing or having intercourse with a corpse which is often mutilated in the process. To obtain a corpse, the necrophile may commit murder. The most straightforward explanation seems to be the need to dominate an unresisting and non-rejecting sex object.

Frottage provides sexual satisfaction by the act of rubbing against another person, usually in a crowded place (e.g., subway or elevator). Again, we see an inadequate man (women are rarely seen engaging in frottage) stealing a thrill without danger of rejection or sexual failure.

Sodomy (named after the Biblical "city of sin," Sodom) is the legal label for any "perverse" sex act that some states prohibit even between a married couple. While it is most often applied specifically to anal intercourse, it is sometimes used to describe bestiality. The act has obvious associations with the anal period of development and may reflect excessive parental preoccupation with toilet training. However, little psychoanalytic study has been addressed to it.

Nymphomania is compulsive sexual behavior by a woman whose sexual appetite is presumed to be insatiable. Although genuine cases are quite rare, many women are unjustifiably labeled as nymphomaniacs—usually by men who are either ignorant of the female's ability to enjoy multiple orgasms or who acquire a sense of inferiority in the face of the greater sexuality of their wives or lovers.

Satyriasis is the male equivalent of nymphomania. Some men may be driven to excessive sexual indulgence by the wish to achieve social status among peers by extraordinary sexual performance. Like nymphomania, professionally validated cases of satyriasis are rare.

Pornography—to keep the term from covering an overly broad area of obscenity—refers to sexually exciting material. The issue of sex-in-print (or other graphic media) is caught up in conflicting legal and moral codes.

This unsettled state of affairs led to the appointment in 1970 of the President's Commission on Obscenity and Pornography. After an extensive inquiry which included examination of research literature; opinion surveys of scientists, clinicians, law enforcement officials, and the public; a program of psychological experiments designed to test reactions to exposure to sexual materials; and a study of delinquents and sex offenders, the commission concluded that there was no "clear and present danger" from the publication of erotica. It found no evidence of a causal relationship between pornography and antisocial behavior. In fact, in Denmark, where all restrictions against pornography were removed in 1965, there has been a significant reduction in sex crimes.

There are a number of other sexual deviations of lesser interest for our purpose. If the moral sanctions that are aimed at inhibiting every sexual act except heterosexual relations in the conventional position were applied to the eating of food in that alien society, a person would be censured—and maybe jailed—for sneaking glances at a neighbor's dinner or smacking a custard pie in a sweetheart's face; and a person would be ostracized for occasionally asking for a second helping of dessert or enjoying reading cookbooks whose recipes titillated the appetite.

Treatment of Sexual Deviation

Psychodynamic Approaches

Essentially, psychodynamic treatment of sexual deviation follows the line of the classical psychoanalytic method. The theoretical basis for the approach, as we noted earlier, rests on the Freudian concept of regression, caused by some present stressful experience, to a point of fixation in the oral, anal, or genital (Oedipal) stage, at which point childhood disturbances or needs remained unsettled or unsatisfied. The adult, harboring the repressed conflict in the unconscious, makes maladaptive responses to present problems, unaware of the regressive

sources of the anxieties that interfere with sexual enjoyment.

Since the principle of multiple causation operates here, attempts to trace particular sexual "deviations" to single fixations are simplistic and misleading. Further details of general psychodynamic theory can be reviewed in Chapter 3. Specific sexual interpretations are discussed in connection with each of the deviations described earlier in this chapter.

As always in applying therapy, the psychodynamic therapist is guided by six assumptions (Meyer, 1975):

1. The problem is one manifestation of a neurotic or personality disorder.
2. Treatment is open-ended (i.e., indefinite in duration, continuing until the client is satisfied).
3. The client reports all history, thoughts, and feelings.
4. The therapist guides the client in self-exploration.
5. A cure is not promised, but the client's emerging capabilities are noted as hopeful signs.
6. The therapist must provide a secure environment in which the client's problems are the sole concern.

The essential transference relationship is especially sensitive in the treatment of sexual problems. Since the client is in the throes of a sexual disturbance, he or she is prone to develop erotic responses to the therapist. The therapist must be on guard constantly for such a possibility and muster his or her resources to maintain the transference relationship without yielding to the sexual advances of the client. For example, if a male therapist has been elected to the role of a love-object-father who failed to satisfy the female client's Oedipal needs, the therapist must resist the impulse to satisfy the reexperienced need. He must use other means to help the client understand and solve her problem. Failure to uphold the integrity of the transference may provide temporary satisfaction for the client but is likely to be followed by a sense of betrayal by the therapist.

A central cause of sexual problems is lack

of trust in potential love objects. This crippling condition is caused by repeated disappointment of the child's normal expectations and by early loss or separation. The persistent fear of loss, disappointment, or rejection keeps the mistrust alive, preventing the individual from becoming involved in an intimate relationship. The anxiety evoked in such situations becomes a barrier to erotic stimulation and sexual response. It is the therapist's function to help the client work out the anger and fear of deprivation that are the repressed reactions to the earlier loss or frustration.

An important advantage of psychodynamic therapy is that it provides an understanding of the motivating and inhibiting influences in the sexual areas. Since psychodynamic theorists believe that such neurotic influences are involved in most, if not all, sexual problems, they insist that it is necessary to work them out before short-term behavior modification can have lasting effects. Otherwise, the inhibiting anxieties are subject to recurrence, disrupting the effects of behavioral programs.

Behavioral Approaches

Behaviorists have developed empirical evidence that deviant sexual behavior can be learned. Bandura (1969) showed how parents model deviant sexual patterns, and sometimes deliberately train sons to dress and behave like the daughters they had hoped for. Rachman and Hodgson (1968) demonstrated that young males can be conditioned to produce erections to high-heeled boots when the boots are associated repeatedly with pictures of nude women.

One corrective technique for deviance suggested by classical and operant conditioning theories is *aversion therapy*, already described in Chapter 7. Two principal aversive stimuli have been used with sexual deviation: chemical and electrical. Variants of these conditioning punishments include nauseating fantasies, unpleasant smells, shaming, and the painful snapping of an elastic band against the wrist. These aversive techniques have been used with mixed results in cases of homosexuality, exhibitionism, transvestism, phobias, fetishism, and pedophilia.

Covert sensitization, a variant of aversion therapy, has also been used in treating sadistic impulses. The client imagined revolting sights in conjunction with his sadistic fantasies. Following eight sessions, the client remained free of the deviant fantasies at a 16-month follow-up (Davison, 1968).

Sexual orientation disturbance has been treated extensively by both electrical and chemical aversion therapy. Feldman and Mac-Culloch (1972) treated 43 dissatisfied homosexuals in one study, using their *anticipatory avoidance learning* technique. The procedure comprises presentation of sexually arousing male slides in an ascending hierarchy followed, after eight seconds of viewing, by painful shock, which the client can avoid by pressing a switch within eight seconds, turning off the slide. On some random occasions, either the slide goes off immediately when the switch is pressed, or the slide remains on (with shock) during a brief delay interval after switch-press, or the shock follows regardless of the avoidance response. Female slides are shown after shock avoidance response on some of the trials. Results at one-year follow-up showed success (no overt homosexual behavior) with 25 clients (58%), 11 failures, and 7 defections from therapy. We may question whether "no overt homosexual behavior" represents real success in the absence of adoption of heterosexual behavior, since suppression without satisfactory sexual alternatives may lead to other problems. However, in other studies by the same researchers, cessation of homosexual fantasies and activities was accompanied by some heterosexual interest.

One of the main shortcomings in some of the aversion therapy procedures is the lack of focus on replacement of the extinguished sexual behavior with an alternative outlet. Several special techniques have been developed or adapted to motivate the client to change from homosexual to heterosexual behavior. *Fading* develops heterosexual responses as an integral part of the process of extinguishing homosexual responses. Bancroft (1971) used it to treat a homosexual masochist. The client imagined a hierarchy of situations, starting with the fantasy of being beaten by a man in a loin cloth and proceeding through gradually less arousing images (beaten by a woman with a shorter and shorter whip, slapping by hand, etc.), eventually taking an increasingly active role in heterosexual intercourse. Eighteen sessions were required to complete the transformation.

A negative variation of the fading technique started with an aversive image of an unattractive old man, which was gradually changed to a more attractive man with an inhibiting policeman nearby, finally resolving into an attractive young man with no policeman. At each step, the client was expected to reject the urge to approach (Marks, 1976).

Fading is a variation of *pairing*. This technique associates masturbation or other pleasurable stimulation with heterosexual stimuli. Sometimes the heterosexual stimuli are paired with relief from an aversive stimulus (shock, etc.). Another version of the pairing technique is *orgasmic reconditioning*. Marquis (1970) had his homosexual clients masturbate to homosexual fantasies until orgasm was inevitable, at which point they were instructed to switch to a heterosexual fantasy. The heterosexual image would then be present during the orgasm, and as the treatment progressed, would be introduced at earlier points during masturbation. Still another version pairs the masturbatory episodes with homosexual fantasies that changed progressively into erotic heterosexual situations.

The *multifaceted treatment* of sexual deviance incorporates several of the techniques we have described into a program that deals with a complex of behaviors. Transsexualism presents just such a complex that defies techniques that focus on single behaviors. Barlow, Reynolds, and Agras (1973) used a multifaceted approach in changing gender identity in a 17-year-old male transsexual who wished to be more "male" than he felt he was. Modeling, behavior rehearsal, and videotaped feedback masculinized the subject's effeminate walking, standing, and sitting manner. His voice was retrained. Next, masculine interpersonal contacts at school were shaped by reinforcing measures. After three months, he acted like a man but still felt like a girl, responding to female arousal impulses. A female therapist then reinforced the client for fantasizing sex activity with a girl. The fantasies were not accompanied by penile erection, however, indicating that with certain behaviors, standard indices of arousal are not appropriate. Classical conditioning of arousal to female slides by connecting them with slides of attractive males (unconditioned stimulus) developed appropriate arousal responses. Remaining homosexual arousal was eliminated by means of aversion techniques. At a one-year follow-up, male behavior and arousal responses persisted. The case illustrates an important principle of relative independence of the behaviors that make up the complex pattern of a sexual deviation. This makes possible the isolation and treatment of the component behaviors in sequence.

There have been great advances in behavioral techniques in the treatment of sexual deviance. Sexual deviation was at one time considered such a strong behavior that it was incurable or, at least, so resistant to change that it required extraordinary effort and time. Because behavioral approaches have shown themselves to be most likely to succeed, they have become the treatments of choice.

Rape

Rape is a difficult behavior to classify. Should it be considered a sexual disorder, an antisocial behavior, or an act motivated by sexual politics? Our choice to treat it here reflects more the nature of the act, that is, sexual, rather than the reason for the act.

What Is Rape?

If one were to attempt a description of rape from a reading of existing laws or court procedures and decisions in rape cases, the definition would be a lengthy string of conditions, qualifications, and ambiguities that would leave the reader wondering whether anyone could ever be convicted of such a crime. And indeed, in this country, few men are. However, if we set aside our inherited, stereotyped views of woman as the eternal seductress and of man as her rightful master, we can devise a simple, straightforward definition of rape as *a violent, forcible sexual act committed on the person of an unwilling victim*. This definition equates heterosexual and homosexual rape. The only qualification is that the law assumes that a sexual act with a minor is arbitrarily classified as rape, whether or not force is used. Such an act is called statutory rape. There is a kind of rape that seems to have legal sanction and against which women believe they have no legal or social protection; this is "rape by prerogative"—the forcing of sexual acts upon a wife by her husband, or upon a woman by her friend if she is a visitor in his home.

Whether or not the rapist is convicted, we are concerned with the nature of his act, not merely as criminal behavior under cloudy legal criteria, but also as a manifestation of a possible sexual disorder. We will examine rape primarily from that aspect.

Incidence

In 1974, over 55,000 Americans reported that they were raped. Tables 18-2 and 18-3 show the high rate of occurrence of rape in U.S. cities. Note that rape is not essentially a "big city" crime. Four relatively smaller city areas had a higher incidence of rape than any city of 2 million population or larger, and at least the 10 smaller cities listed (plus many more not listed here) surpassed the New York metropolitan area in rate of occurrence. Remember also that the data cover only reported rapes. The actual figures are estimated at five times the reported assaults. Even more disturbing than the number of rapes is the sharp increase in the rate: an 80 percent national rise in reported cases between 1968 and 1974 (FBI, 1975).

Evidence of the prevailing social and legal attitudes toward rape is seen in the proportion

Table 18-2 Rape Rates (per 100,000 population)—Top Ten in Metropolitan Cities (Standard Metropolitan Statistical Areas)[1] with over 250,000 Population (1972–1973)

Number	1972–1973	Rate
1	Memphis, Tennessee; Arkansas; Mississippi	64.6
2	Las Vegas, Nevada	62.2
3	Little Rock—North Little Rock, Arkansas	57.7
4	Albuquerque, New Mexico	57.0
5	Los Angeles—Long Beach, California	55.0
6	Jacksonville, Florida	52.9
7	Orlando, Florida	51.0
8	Denver—Boulder, Colorado	48.8
9	San Francisco—Oakland, California	44.9
10	Norfolk—Virginia Beach—Portsmouth, Virginia; North Carolina	44.7

[1] Standard metropolitan statistical areas include cities and suburban areas.
From Gager, N., and Schurr, C. *Sexual assault: Confronting rape in America.* New York: Grosset & Dunlap, 1976, p. 302. © 1976 by Nancy Gager and Cathleen Schurr. Used by permission of Grosset & Dunlap, Inc.

of arrests in *reported* cases: arrests are made in only about one-half of reported rapes, with convictions in one-fifth of the cases. In fact, the rate of convictions on rape charges is lower than for any other violent crime. The lopsided graph in Figure 18-3 indicates that only 1 out of 25 rapists (including unreported assailants) is punished for his crime.

The Rapist

Depending on your source of information, the rapist is a social psychopath, a sex-starved animal, a depressed and inadequate pseudo-homosexual, or just your ordinary, next-door neighbor giving vent to his personal or familial

Table 18-3 Rape Rates (per 100,000 population)—All Metropolitan Cities (Standard Metropolitan Statistical Areas) with Over 2 Million Population (1973).

Number	1973	Rate
1	Los Angeles—Long Beach, California	55.0
2	San Francisco—Oakland, California	44.9
3	Detroit, Michigan	43.2
4	New York, New York; New Jersey	38.9
5	Washington, District of Columbia; Maryland; Virginia	38.5
6	St. Louis, Missouri; Illinois	37.4
7	Baltimore, Maryland	34.4
8	Dallas—Fort Worth, Texas[1]	33.3
9	Houston, Texas	32.5
10	Chicago, Illinois	30.2
11	Cleveland, Ohio	27.1
12	Newark, New Jersey	26.1
13	Philadelphia, Pennsylvania; New Jersey	23.5
14	Minneapolis—St. Paul, Minnesota; Wisconsin	22.3
15	Boston, Massachusetts	19.6
16	Pittsburgh, Pennsylvania	16.0

[1] Estimated by combining separate figures for Dallas and Fort Worth.

From Gager, N., and Schurr, C. *Sexual assault: Confronting rape in America.* New York: Grosset & Dunlap, 1976, p. 303. © 1976 by Nancy Gager and Cathleen Schurr. Used by permission of Grosset & Dunlap, Inc.

frustrations. An increasing number of professional efforts have been directed toward finding the rapist's basic motivations and personality traits. Amir (1971), who has produced a landmark study of rape patterns, suggests that rape is less an act of sexual expression than it is of aggression.

Police officials generally hold that the rapist, as a type, is indistinguishable from a cross-section of male society. He is a naive-looking young boy, a raging psychotic, a common thief, a clean-cut businessman, a scruffy hoodlum. Attempts have been made to separate rapists into such groupings as (1) mentally incompetent, pathological cases and (2) products of environmental conditioning or situational stresses. Members of the first group are usually put in mental hospitals; those in the second group are seldom tried or convicted. Many rapists describe themselves as being in the grip of an uncontrollable compulsion.

Another study (Guttmacher, 1951) classifies rapists as (1) sexually impelled deviants, (2) sadists, and (3) aggressive criminals bent on pillaging and robbing (viewing women as property for the taking).

Still another legal classification scheme categorizes rapists as (1) the psychotic, (2) the psychopathic delinquent, which includes the armed robber who takes what he wants, (3) the neurotic with hysterical behavior tendencies, (4) the macho man who must repeatedly demonstrate his masculine role identity, and (5) the homosexual who, because of discomfort with his sexual identity, denies it by raping women. One study showed that many of the offenders had symptoms of schizophrenia. In short, rapists exhibit most of the deviant behaviors that are found in a cross-section of men with abnormal behaviors.

Efforts to deal with the problem have been somewhat impeded by the Freudian view of the rapist as the product of maternal rejection or of incestuous Oedipal conflicts. The victim, on the other hand, is seen as motivated by masochistic urges that place her at the mercy of the assailant. Here we have the source of the ambivalent attitudes toward rape victims that have resulted in the rather tolerant treatment of rape as a crime in which the victim is a collaborator, if not a provocateur.

Gang rape is a phenomenon of surprisingly high incidence, with motivating factors that are somewhat different from those that operate in the individual rape. Amir's study of Philadelphia rapists from 1958 and 1960 police files gives some idea of the relative frequency of gang rape nationally. Pairs or gangs of assail-

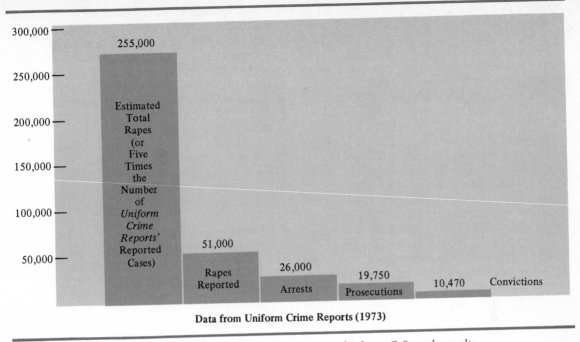

Data from Uniform Crime Reports (1973)

Figure 18-3 Rapes and rape convictions (1973). (*Gager, N., and Schurr, C.* Sexual assault: Confronting rape in America. *New York: Grosset & Dunlap, 1976, p. 301.* © *1976 by Nancy Gager and Cathleen Schurr. Used by permission of Grosset & Dunlap, Inc.*)

ants accounted for 43 percent of the 645 rapes. Of 1,292 offenders, 55 percent had participated in gang rapes and 16 percent in pairs, a total of 71 percent. Most of the offenders were between 14 and 19 years of age.

Certain differences are noted in gang rape activity. More of them are preplanned than are individual rapes. They are marked by more brutality and sadism. The leader of the gang seems to respond to the role assigned to him by the other, less decisive members. There is evidence of male cohesiveness in the recognition by all members that they must participate actively whether they want to or not.

Treatment Approaches

The lack of diagnostic agreement on the motivation, personality defects, and sexual de-

viance in the rapist is reflected in the lack of formal, carefully conceived rehabilitation programs for sex offenders. Psychological help is virtually nonexistent in prisons. A few programs, notable for their rarity, apply psychotherapeutic techniques in a limited way.

The State Prison of Southern Michigan conducts a program of group therapy designed to help the offender understand the emotional conflicts that are at the root of his sexual deviance. He is guided in the acquisition of better ways of handling his interpersonal relationships.

An interesting confrontation procedure is the main feature of the South Florida State Hospital's Sex Offender Rehabilitation Program. Rape victims and feminist women engage in personal discussion with convicted rapists in a controlled setting. Some of the men find themselves relating to women as people, not as objects, for the first time in their lives.

A Los Angeles organization, Sex Offenders Anonymous, is modeled after Alcoholics Anonymous, maintaining a "crisis line" that responds to calls by sending an associate to stay with the member who feels the urge to commit a crime. The service is strictly preventive, with no therapeutic intervention.

One study of the effect of a combination of aversion therapy and orgasmic reconditioning on the responses of 12 sexual deviates (including 2 rapists) indicates the feasibility of behavior therapy for rapists. Marshall (1973) modified the usual fantasizing procedure by verbalizing each fantasy, breaking it into six segments which started with thinking about deviant behavior and continued through approaching the situation, finding the object, approaching the object, engaging in the deviant act, experiencing orgasm. Each taped segment was accompanied by the command "Stop!" and an electric shock. The orgasmic reconditioning fantasies were each taped in three progressive segments and were listened to while the client masturbated. These orgasmic fantasies were deviant and were to be switched to "normal" fantasy just before onset of the orgasm. Results were a reduction in the client-rated attractiveness of the deviant fantasies and an absence of the deviant behavior in all of the cases up to a three-month or longer follow-up date. The correlation between deviant fantasies and the impulse to commit rape remains to be determined. If fantasies are the cue for the behavior, then the use of cognitive aversion and reconditioning therapies that interfere with the image might be best.

The Rape Victim

Much concern is focused on the rapist—his legal rights, appropriate punishment, rehabilitation, rape prevention—so that the victim is often "the forgotten woman." Her fear and shame cause her to withdraw from view, making it easy to ignore her and her feelings. Her problem is becoming known as a result of systematic interview-studies of postrape behavior.

Burgess and Holmstrom (1974) reported the psychological effects of rape on 92 adult women referred to a Victim Counseling Program in Boston. The counselors describe what they call the "rape trauma syndrome," which consists of a two-phase sequel to the rape: (1) acute disorganization and (2) long-term reorganization.

In the acute phase, the victim's life style is disrupted. She may either reveal her shocked reactions in expressed fear, anger, shame, anxiety, accompanied by crying and restlessness; or she may suppress her reactions behind a mask of composure.

The long-term reorganization process involves milder, more moderate reactions. Change of residence, travel to distant places, trips to family home are all common. During this phase, there are two principal types of psychological effects: nightmares and phobias. Nightmares replay variations of the attack or other violent incidents. The phobias—sometimes referred to by the coined term *traumatophobia*—run the gamut of fears related to the rape situation: fear of indoors, outdoors, being alone, crowds, people following, and sexual activity.

Treatment is directed to the issues that relate to the crisis. Deeper therapy is prescribed for victims whose reactions are compounded by past or present psychological or social problems.

Another condition that presents complications is the "silent rape reaction." This is the response of the victim who did not report a rape to anyone. In such cases, the fears and anxieties are held in and thus unresolved for a considerable time.

Proposed Counteraction

Age-old male and *female* biases that have institutionalized the ancient Adam-and-Eve sex roles present a barrier to measures designed to prevent rape. Our preoccupation with violence and sex tends to make heroes out of rapists and suspects out of their victims. Gager and Schurr (1976) offer a number of suggestions for rape prevention and for helping the victim emerge from her ordeal with her dignity and freedom intact.

They present a bill of rights for rape victims, which includes a broader definition of rape; sympathetic, dignified treatment by law officers; free medical and psychological treatment by specially trained professionals; legal standing as a credible witness without corroboration; no probing of prior sex life; compensation by the government. Implementation of these rights requires educational programs to change the attitudes of the police, judges, doctors, and nurses toward rape victims. Ultimately, this requires a change in society's attitudes toward women—a far more formidable problem, but one that is now being dealt with.

Compensation for victims of crimes is provided in a number of states. Federal compensation is under active consideration. Rape, of course, should not be excluded from such coverage.

Above all, education and communication are basic requisites for an antirape program—education of women regarding self-protective behavior and education of the public to develop a better understanding of the impact of rape on the victim.

Summary

Only recently, after generations of willful ignorance of human sexual functioning, have we engaged in research and begun to eliminate the myths and misconceptions about "normal" and "abnormal" sexual behavior. Masters and Johnson have suggested the four-stage model of (1) excitement, (2) plateau, (3) orgasm, and (4) resolution. The male carries a special burden in the need for penile erection to initiate coitus. Male sexual problems include primary and secondary impotence, premature and retarded ejaculation. Female problems include frigidity and general sexual dysfunction, vaginismus, and dyspareunia. Freudian theory explains the sex urge as the operation of the "pleasure principle" associated with a dependency need. Negative, inhibiting influences on sexual satisfaction and responsiveness are intrapsychic (Oedipal conflict, castration anxiety, repressive upbringing) and situational (male performance expectations, female hostility, marital power struggles).

Behaviorists see sexual dysfunction as learned behavior, which is amenable to direct reconditioning without the need for clearing up early, intrapsychic problems. Masters and Johnson techniques remove performance pressures and develop arousal responses through sexual exercises.

Sexual deviation is distinguished from dysfunction by the fact that the individual violates social norms but does not usually suffer impairment of function. Sexual deviations include: fetishism, exhibitionism, pedophilia, transsexualism, transvestism, sadomasochism, homosexuality (sexual orientation disturbance), masturbation, and incest. Homosexuals show no unique biological or psychological characteristics. Other deviations are voyeurism, necrophilia, frottage, sodomy, nymphomania, and satyriasis. Some deviations are antisocial behaviors associated with personality disturbance, while many are socially defined taboos. Multifaceted behavioral treatment is effective in many cases, in which aversive conditioning is combined with reconditioning to appropriate sexual activities.

Rape is a violent crime with mixed psychological and social motivations. The rapist is not uniquely identifiable by social, educational, or psychological characteristics. Crisis intervention therapy treats the immediate disorganization reaction of the victim and provides a base for the long-term reorganization process.

A Field in Transition: Emerging Approaches and Future Directions

PART FOUR

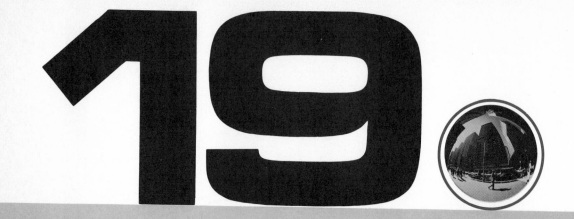

Emerging issues in conceptualizing abnormal behavior

In previous chapters, we discussed the major conceptual systems that currently serve as models for understanding abnormal behavior. We also reviewed a variety of abnormal behaviors, noting their clinical features, their possible causes, and the treatment approaches for them. Throughout the text, we have emphasized the complex nature of human behavior and the uselessness of suggesting easy solutions to complex problems. A generalization we have stressed based on all of the material covered is that any individual's behavior, whether it is normal or abnormal, is the product of the interaction of numerous factors.

In reviewing the important causal, contributing, and maintaining factors of abnormal behavior, we concentrated on those factors that have been studied most intensively in recent years: the biological, sociocultural, and psychological factors that have dominated contemporary models of abnormal behavior.

But new conceptualizations about abnormal behavior, whether they are grand theoretical schemes or simply interesting ideas, are constantly being proposed. Such proposed conceptualizations, even if they may prove to be of little lasting value, are important to scientists, whose job is to propose, counterpropose, and evaluate proposals. This work is, in fact, what the "inquiry" approach emphasized throughout this text states as the major task of psychologists in the study of abnormal behavior.

To restate that viewpoint, the prime task of the psychologist is to generate hypotheses about observed phenomena that can be tested by the scientific method. But often the methodology currently available is not sufficient for testing these hypotheses. When this is the case, the testing of interesting and potentially fruitful hypotheses must await the development of new methodological tools. For example, many years passed between the time that scientists generated hypotheses about the composition of the Martian soil and the time that the Viking explorers were able to land on Mars, sample and analyze the soil, and test the validity of the hypotheses.

In this part of the text, we will look into the future of abnormal psychology. We will review some areas of investigation that are just beginning to emerge. It is true that we are moving into relatively uncharted territory and discussing aspects of psychology that are more speculation than actual fact. But, clearly, they are areas that deserve our attention.

In Chapter 4, we reviewed many of the clearer, more readily observable factors involved in abnormal behavior. In this chapter, we will present factors that show every indication of having importance in the development of abnormal behavior, but that are as yet untested. Chapter 20 deals primarily with emerging approaches to treatment and prevention of abnormal behavior.

When reading Part IV, keep in mind that we are dealing with the frontiers of our science. Here, fact and myth become difficult to distinguish. We must constantly be aware that the breakthroughs that sound so right at this moment may evaporate in the face of harder evidence.

Four general areas of emerging importance will be discussed in Chapter 19. They are (1) the social context of abnormal behavior, (2) the stages and crises of adult life, (3) the ecological context of abnormal behavior, and (4) the aspects of the community mental health approaches that have implications for understanding abnormal behavior.

The Social Context of Abnormal Behavior

Instead of discussing individual social factors that affect behavior, in this section we will explore the total "context" of the behavior. A contextual approach recognizes that the individual's behavior is itself a series of events that produce effects on social factors. It is the interaction between the individual and the social setting that is of prime importance in this type of behavioral analysis.

In such interaction models, there is no easy way to abstract single aspects for intensive study. In fact, because of the complexity of the interrelatedness of the social context, these factors tend to be investigated less frequently. Future research and theories may well provide the models for understanding these interacting systems. For our present purposes, we will describe some of the interrelationships, as best we can, given our current limited state of knowledge.

Sociopsychological Factors

The social *subcommunity* of which the individual is a part is a critical reference point in all evaluations of behavior. The values used by individuals in assessing their behavior are usually intimately related to the values of the familiar and respected group (the subcommunity). For example, a teenage boy in a "tough," working-class neighborhood may be proud of his fighting skills and receive respect and admiration from peers for physical aggressiveness. Should this youth later become a clergyman, he may come to see these qualities as deviant and distasteful (as his church associates probably will).

In this sense, the adaptive behavior of the individual may be viewed as "healthy" or "unhealthy" depending on the cultural context of such behavior. Soldiers are rewarded for killing people during wartime. Yet, when the war is over, such behavior is considered homicide. The behavior is not fundamentally different, but the cultural context of the behavior has changed.

Maladaptive behavior is a common problem among those who migrate. Individuals who move from one geographical location to another, or from one subculture to another, must face many adjustments in meeting the norms of the new community. Such individuals are a high-risk group because of the difficulty of these transitions.

Status and role factors also influence the behavior of an individual. Certain types of behaviors may be expected from a person because of age, sex, race, religion, or occupation. The individual who experiences *role conflicts* is especially prone to maladaptive behavior. For example, a woman doctor may become accustomed to her role within medical circles as a respected, educated professional. Yet, when she walks out onto the street, she faces street harassment from men who simply view her in her role as a woman. In this manner, many individuals experience conflicts between two or more roles or statuses that they occupy within American society.

This type of role conflict is frequently severe and damaging for members of marginal groups in a society. Immigrant children at the turn of the century faced the conflict between the norms, values, and demands of two cultures: those of their European parents and those of the unfamiliar American surroundings. More recently, black Americans who have achieved middle-class status have found themselves caught between the expectations of black communities and dominant, white middle-class mores.

But status and life-style factors in abnormal behavior must not be isolated from other vital elements of society—notably money and power. Lack of money forces individuals into highly stressful living conditions characterized by poor housing, inadequate diet, and unemployment. Lack of power contributes to a person's negative self-image. An individual experiencing these difficult living conditions and feelings of self-doubt may well develop abnormal behavior.

Some members of our society, however, think this abnormal behavior results from *individual failure*. In this view, an individual's psychological problems are the result of some "personal" circumstance, such as immaturity, character defect, or maladjustment. In some cases, this ideology extends so far as to blame the victims for their own problems and failures. Typically, such stereotypes are applied in judging lower socioeconomic groups and minorities: "It's their own fault"; "They really don't want to work"; and so forth.

An alternate view is to see the individual problems as stemming from *social* causes. The broad economic, political, cultural, and social patterns of the nation and particular subcultures can be viewed as determinants of individual responses. Under this approach, the basic question is not, "What factors in the childhood and family background of Mr. X contributed to his becoming a heroin addict?" but, rather, "What economic and social factors in our culture lead thousands of youths each year to become heroin addicts?"

One result of this broader social context viewpoint is the growing feeling that the community is the place to begin if real social change is to be brought about. We will discuss this approach in depth at the close of the chapter.

Racial Issues

Racism is a major part of the social fabric of American life. While many racial and ethnic minorities have faced discrimination and hostility, the legacy of slavery has made these problems particularly devastating for generations of black Americans. The civil rights movement has been particularly important in dramatizing the oppression experienced by blacks in both the South and North.

Two critical issues of racism that affect abnormal psychology are:

1. Is racism an abnormal behavior of the racist that should be studied and treated as a psychological pathology?
2. Do victims of racism demonstrate abnormal behavior as a result of that racism?

Much debate has centered on whether racism should be understood as a psychological abnormality or as a cultural and political phenomenon. Some writers have focused on the disturbed psychological profile of the individual racist and have stressed whites' sexual fears of blacks as a contributing factor in white racism. Other social critics have suggested that, within the white community, racism is more of a "normal" than an "abnormal" reaction. But Thomas and Sillen (1972) have argued that the effect of characterizing racism as an abnormal behavior is to rationalize away the responsibility of racists for their "political crimes."

As for the so-called "abnormal behavior" of the victims, the issue is again quite controversial. Definitions of normality and abnormality that are useful in the white community may be rather distorted when used in reference to blacks. As Poussaint (1975) observes: "A black man who believes that a white policeman might shoot him for the slightest wrong move is not paranoid; such a feeling could be a sign of imbalance in a middle-class white man" (p. 2487).

Being poor in an affluent society is difficult for many to cope with. Because they are powerless, many poor people lose their self-esteem; others, such as the girl in this photograph, simply try to block out the environment around them. (*Charles Gatewood.*)

Grier and Cobbs (1968) agree that blacks must be evaluated on different psychological criteria from those used for whites. They cite a number of important adaptive personality traits that blacks have adopted in order to survive in white society, including "cultural paranoia," as in the case we just described. While white observers might classify these traits as "abnormal," Grier and Cobbs believe that these patterns are not only normal but essential for black Americans in coping with the problems stemming from racism.

In adapting to white society, many blacks have had identity conflicts. Brody (1963) conducted a classic study of the identity conflicts of black children. Eleven white boys and 19 black boys were observed during play periods with white male and black male hand puppets. The boys were asked various questions about the dolls and about themselves. At one point, they were given the choice of keeping one doll while the interviewer took the other.

Twelve of the 19 black boys were found to demonstrate a significant degree of color conflict. Some of them claimed that they or their family members resembled the white puppet more than the black puppet. Three stated that they wished they were white or were unhappy about being black. Six referred to the black puppet as "bad," while three called it "sad."

Brody (1963) interpreted these findings as possibly reflecting:

1. A reality-oriented wish to become the more powerful white male.
2. A strategy of identifying with the oppressor (the white male) as a means of survival.
3. A tendency to turn hostility toward the white world inward against oneself.

The study also found that the mothers of the black boys tended to deny the strong anxieties they felt about race and the way racism might affect their sons' lives.

Hauserman, Walen, and Behling (1973) studied the use of psychological techniques in promoting racial integration. Experiments were conducted in a first-grade classroom with 25 students. The main focus was a group of 5 black children who were functioning as a tight and exclusive social clique. A number of procedures—including positive reinforcement and teacher directives—were introduced to promote "sitting and eating with a new friend" at lunch in the school cafeteria.

The researchers learned that social reinforcement techniques did produce generalized positive effects in terms of integrated behavior. Greater mixing of blacks and whites during lunchtime was reported, and it carried over to free play periods. The researchers concluded:

Many people assume that racial integration must begin with an attitude change which, hopefully, will then result in some generalized positive behavior change. The present study, however, indicated that positive behavior changes can be brought about directly. (Hauserman et al., 1973, p. 200)

It must be stressed that this project was only an *example* of how reinforcement techniques could be used. It should not be viewed as a definitive model for achieving racial integration.

It seems clear that the mental health problems of black Americans cannot be understood outside of the context of the social problems of many black communities—high unemployment, inadequate housing, poor nutrition, and inferior educational programs. There can be no simple psychological remedies for problems that are, at the same time, economic and political. Nevertheless, individual black Americans with behavior problems must be given adequate mental health assistance.

Special Problems for Women

American women—like women across the world—must function within a society in which sex differences are considered extremely important, and in which being a woman means experiencing the results of centuries of prejudice and discrimination.

In *Women and Madness*, Chesler (1972) analyzes the ways in which women are systematically categorized as mad as a result of being rebellious, and then are literally driven mad by men and by a male-dominated society. Chesler discusses the lives of a number of women who were labeled as "mad," including Ellen West (c. 1890–c. 1926) and Zelda Fitzgerald (1900–1948).

Ellen West's childhood motto was, "Either Caesar or nothing." As a teenager, she expressed a desire to "be a soldier, fear no foe, and die joyously, sword in hand" (Chesler, 1972, p. 7), and became an avid horsewoman and poet. However, as an adult, she could not adjust

The girl in this photograph was the first black to attend previously all-white schools in Little Rock, Arkansas. Some have characterized racism as a psychological abnormality, but in some communities racism is the "norm." (*United Press International.*)

to the limits of "normal" female activities. As a result, she stopped eating and became suicidal. At the age of 21, she wrote:

> For what purpose did nature give me health and ambition? . . . I am twenty-one years old and am supposed to be silent and grin like a puppet. I am no puppet. I am a human being with red blood and a woman with a quivering heart. . . . Oh, what shall I do now, how shall I manage it?" (p. 7).

Ellen West's refusal to accept the socially approved female role marked her as "crazy," and she was institutionalized a number of times. Life in an asylum represented a change from the demands on her to be a wife and mother, but there was no real freedom inside

the asylum for Ellen West. She finally took her own life while still in her thirties.

Zelda Fitzgerald was an artist, writer, and the wife of the American novelist F. Scott Fitzgerald. Unfortunately for Zelda, it proved impossible to be all of these things at once. Scott Fitzgerald simply would not allow it. According to Chesler, he wanted Zelda to be a dependent wife and mother, not a respected creative celebrity in her own right. Scott belittled Zelda's dancing lessons and reacted with jealousy and rage when she completed an autobiographical novel before he had finished a novel of his own.

In Chesler's view, Zelda was destroyed by the conflict between her work and her marriage. She was treated by a battery of male psychiatrists who, working closely with Scott, were trying to mold her into an acceptable and pliable wife. They continually discouraged her commitment to her work and creativity. At one point, Zelda stated that she was tired of being forced into accepting Scott's opinions and decisions about everything. She declared that she would rather be hospitalized than dominated by him in that type of marital relationship. Zelda Fitzgerald spent years going in and out of mental institutions and finally died in an asylum fire.

Chesler takes a strong feminist viewpoint and suggests that both of these women were "treated and/or imprisoned by male psychiatrists—most of whom were, quite literally, agents for their husbands' 'will'" (p. 12). Both Ellen West and Zelda Fitzgerald were seen by these men as being "mad" for their attempts to defy female role expectations. And eventually, they became mad. Their madness reflected both their female powerlessness and their desperate quest for an alternative to intolerable domestic situations. But they were surrounded on all sides by male authority and power—including the mental health professionals who were supposedly there to help them. There was no way out for these women.

Although some may dismiss Chesler's view as overstated feminist rhetoric, there is no doubt that many women today face the same conflicts and pressures that were suggested as affecting Ellen West and Zelda Fitzgerald. But the last 15 years have witnessed a dramatic upsurge in movements for equal rights and liberation for women in all parts of the world. The sex-role stereotyping that confined both West and Fitzgerald is under increasing challenge from feminists in America and elsewhere.

The women's movement of the 1960s and 1970s has fought for many issues that vitally affect the lives of women. Among these are passage of the federal Equal Rights Amendment (ERA); greater representation of women at all levels of government; equal treatment on the job, including "equal pay for equal work"; federally funded child care centers to assist working mothers; an end to violent crimes against women, including rape and wife-beating; and the right of a woman to have a safe, inexpensive, and legal abortion.

Many people have confused "women's liberation" with "sexual liberation" and have assumed that the two are virtually synonymous. In fact, much of the upsurge of radical feminist activity of the late 1960s was fueled by a realization that "sexual liberation" *was not* liberation for women. Women who previously had been told that they *could not* consent to sexual relations with any man before marriage were now being told that they could not *refuse* any man.

Feminists, by contrast, have fought for a woman's right to "control over her own body." They have argued that every woman should have the right to engage in—or refuse to engage in—sexual relations with any other person *as she sees fit*. As part of this struggle, many feminist groups have supported the right of women to love and enter into sexual relationships with other women. In general, feminists have endorsed the principle that a woman has the right to choose how she will live her life—as a worker in industry or a homemaker, or both; as a single woman or a married woman; as a woman with children or without children; as a secretary, a surgeon, a high school teacher, or a university president.

The rapid growth of the women's liberation movement has contributed to the turbulent social atmosphere of the last two decades. Many men, and even some women, have reacted with confusion, patronizing humor, and outright rage to the demands of feminists for equal rights for women. The effects of the women's movement in challenging the mistreatment of women throughout American society have been felt in almost all of the key institutions of the nation—in the churches and synagogues (where women are fighting for the right to be ordained); in the media (where the sexism of broadcasters is being challenged); and in the schools (where sex-role stereotyping is under attack).

Every time of transition and social change is a time of great stress for the participants. In this case, virtually everyone has been affected in one way or another by the struggle for equal

Many men have reacted with confusion, patronizing humor, and outright rage to the demands of feminists for equal rights for women. (*Leonard Freed, Magnum Photos.*)

rights for women. Each individual—whether female or male—faces difficult adjustments in altering traditional and discriminatory assumptions and behavior patterns. Of course, the greatest burden has fallen on those women who have challenged the status quo and insisted on full human and legal rights.

Legal Aspects of Abnormal Behavior

In earlier sections of this text, we examined some of the legal aspects of abnormal behavior. In this section, we will focus on a number of emerging legal issues that relate to abnormal behavior and the responses of the legal system to these issues.

The *right to privacy* can be endangered through the process of psychological counseling. Many complex legal and ethical issues are raised when the counselor is questioned about the client by a government agency or when the counselor is required to appear in court as a witness. This situation is most serious, since the counselor may have a detailed knowledge of the client's innermost feelings and experiences.

The concept of *diminished responsibility* can have an influence in criminal trials of disturbed individuals. In certain jurisdictions, an individual accused of a serious crime may plead an "insanity defense," claiming that he or she was not "responsible" at the time of the violation. Psychiatric testimony will be introduced—often by both the prosecution and the defense—to establish whether the defendant can be held legally accountable for the crime.

In legal proceedings, defendants are considered *incompetent to stand trial* if they are unable to understand the legal charges and to participate in the defense. This is a crucial determination in actions against individuals with abnormal behavior. An unfortunate result of being incompetent to stand trial is possible involuntary commitment to a mental institution.

People enter mental hospitals through both *voluntary* and *involuntary commitment.* The voluntary patient enters freely and generally retains the right to leave. Involuntary hospitalization requires a court determination that an individual's behavior is abnormal or dangerous to himself (or herself) or dangerous to others.

Due process of law, under the Fourteenth Amendment to the Constitution, is critical in protecting the rights of the institutionalized. The American Bar Association has argued that standards of due process such as written notice and a fair hearing are required if a person is to be legally institutionalized against his or her will. An individual who is institutionalized may also be deprived of other legal rights, including the right to participate in business and professional activities and the opportunity to introduce litigation.

Institutionalized patients face other severe—and, in many cases, unfair—restrictions on their freedom. One of the most widespread and dangerous restrictions is the practice of *indefinite commitment*. Individuals may be institutionalized for long periods of time with few serious reviews of their conditions. In one Minnesota case, a man was confined for 14 years because he lacked the money to arrange for a hearing to discuss his release (Rea, 1966).

As Rea (1966) observes, "Mental hospitals are often quite isolated from society, and the right of the allegedly ill person to a hearing may become a myth once he is admitted to the institution" (p. 220). In many hospital review proceedings, the patient has no legal right to be heard, to cross-examine witnesses, or to retain counsel. In the last decade, many of these legal restrictions have been fought by civil liberties organizations on behalf of institutionalized mental patients.

A most important recent development is the suggestion that patients in mental institutions should have a "right to treatment." Birnbaum (1960) has argued:

> If the right to treatment were to be recognized, our substantive constitutional law would then include the concepts that if a person is involuntarily institutionalized in a mental hospital . . . , he needs, and is entitled to, adequate medical treatment; that being mentally ill is not a crime; that an institution that involuntarily institutionalizes the mentally ill without giving them adequate medical treatment . . . is a mental prison and not a mental hospital. . . . (p. 503)

In an important case in Alabama in 1971 (*Wyatt* v. *Stickney*, 325 F. Supp. 781, 785), the court found that the state of Alabama must provide adequate treatment for institutionalized patients in state hospitals. In an appendix to the decision, the court set down minimum standards for adequate treatment. It required that the institution develop and maintain an individualized treatment plan for each patient.

The plan would include statements about the patient's problems, needs, and treatment goals; a projected timetable for attainment of these objectives; a description of staff responsibilities in the treatment program; and specific criteria for release to less restrictive treatment conditions or discharge.

However, hospital administrators may have a conflict of interest in decisions about release of patients with abnormal behavior. Many hospitals are receiving fewer admissions as the increased availability and use of outpatient facilities and drugs reduce the need for hospitalization. As a result, the administration may have an economic interest in holding on to its patients to maintain the very existence of the hospital.

As one response to this problem, Rea (1966) advocated the establishment of a commission of experts to make determinations about the status of patients with abnormal behavior. The commissioners would serve on a long-term basis and would include lawyers, doctors, psychiatrists, social workers, and nonprofessionals. Appointments would be made by judicial authorities. This nonhospital group would not have immediate conflicts of interest and could more fairly weigh the rights of the patient against the safety of the larger society.

It is important to emphasize that many of these legal and ethical issues affect *all* patients hospitalized as a result of their abnormal behavior, not simply those who are involuntarily committed. Many individuals give seemingly "voluntary" consent to treatment, but the consent actually occurs under duress. Halleck (1974) has proposed four rules for all types of treatment of patients that would protect the rights of the individual:

1. The therapist must clearly explain the possible consequences of treatment.
2. The patient should be informed of other treatment options and allowed to make a free choice.
3. The patient must not be punished in any way for refusing treatment.
4. Any treatments forced on a nonconsenting patient should be evaluated by a special committee

that includes at least one attorney and one doctor who is not involved in the treatment.

Adult Life Stages and Crises

The traditional psychodynamic theories hold that personality development takes place in stages, the last of which occurs in a person's twenties; the remainder of life is merely a playing out of a tape recorded during these early stages of development. On the other hand, contemporary approaches have begun to view the postadolescent years much as the traditional theories viewed the preadolescent years, that is, as encompassing recognizable and definable stages of development, each with its individual issues, growth potentials, and problems that may lead to abnormal behavior.

One of the benefits of moving away from the traditional psychodynamic developmental view is that it permits us to view *all* of the adult years as an ongoing period of growth, change, and adaptation (or, in some cases, maladaptation resulting in abnormal behavior).

Life Stages and Predictable Crises

In the emerging theories of personality, the study of the *life cycle* is a critical concern. Each individual—if he or she lives a normal life span—will experience a sequence of gestation, maturation, maturity, decline, and death. One approach to the stages of development is outlined in Box 19-1. The characteristics and changes of each phase of this life cycle will depend not only on the individual's physical, emotional, and intellectual development, but also on the roles and expectations of a given society or culture. In one subculture, a 15-year-old may lead a sheltered life at home with his or her parents. In another subculture, a 15-year-old may already be a parent and wage-earner.

Under the *epigenetic principle*, certain life tasks must be accomplished or achieved before an individual can properly move on to the next stage of development. Thus, the adolescent who does not begin to establish autonomy from parental guidance and domination may have difficulty functioning as an independent adult when the adolescent years end.

Erikson (1963) presented one of the first such analyses that moved beyond adolescence. He identified eight important stages of psychosocial development, each of which has distinctive developmental tasks associated with it. In his model, late adolescence is a particularly pivotal moment in a person's life. At this time, the individual's basic ego identity must be established and solidified.

From learning about adult life stages and the psychology of normal life events, we can recognize predictable life crisis points, such as divorce or pregnancy. This allows us to anticipate and train people for the stresses of these potentially difficult periods.

Sheehy (1974) popularized the work of numerous investigators in this area. She has described and coined descriptive names for a number of these important developmental crises. Among these are:

Pulling up roots. This generally occurs between the ages of 18 and 22. The main goal of the youth is to break his or her dependence on parents. The individual may take on a distinctive peer group, life style, or ideology in order to emphasize the defiance of parental norms. Sheehy (1974) notes that "if one doesn't have an identity crisis at this point, it will erupt during a later transition, when the penalties will be harder to bear" (p. 32).

The trying twenties. In this period, some individuals choose and lock themselves into a career, a course of action, or a "life's work." They want a stable and predictable future. Others wish to explore and experiment, and adopt a more transient life pattern.

Catch-30. At age 30, many individuals experience doubts about the "lifelong" decisions they made in their twenties. The adult feels discontent with his or her career and family choices (or with the lack of choices). "What am I doing with my life?" is the common question.

Rooting and extending. In one's early thirties, there tends to be a "settling down" after the crisis of

Box 19-1 The Life Cycle: Eleven Stages of Development

Infancy. For the first 15 months, the baby is helpless and dependent. This is a stage of rapid physical growth and of motor skill development.

The toddler. The baby experiences the joys and frustrations of early attempts to walk, talk, and interact with other persons and the environment. Gender identity is first understood at this point.

The preschool child. During these years, the child moves away from heavy dependence on the primary caretaker toward greater autonomy and contact with peers.

The juvenile. The child spends increasing amounts of time within peer groups and must learn to find a fulfilling role within them.

Adolescence. This is a time of self-discovery, sexual exploration, identity crises, and strong desires for intimacy.

Youth. In this stage of life, the emerging adult must reconcile personal goals and values with the conventional expectations and pressures of society. Idealistic desires conflict with the need for financial and emotional security.

The young adult. The individual is ready to "settle down" and make commitments to career and family life. Marriage may occur at this point; it will test the young adult's ability to handle intimacy and interdependence.

Parenthood. When a couple have their first child, new and serious responsibilities enter their lives. Children may be a bond between parents or an additional source of friction and conflict.

The middle years. As adulthood continues, the individual may undergo a process of reflection and reevaluation. For some, there may be "new beginnings," especially after children have left home. For others, this may be a time of self-doubt and regret.

Old age. As adults reach old age, their physical capacities diminish somewhat. The elderly may use this time for retirement and rest, or they may prefer to pursue long-postponed interests.

Death. Death is the final and inevitable stage of the life cycle. It may be approached with intense fear or with a quiet and accepting calm.

Adapted from Lidz, T. The life cycle: Introduction. In S. Arieti (Ed.), *American handbook of psychiatry* (Vol. 1, 2nd ed.). New York: Basic Books, 1974. ©1974 by Basic Books, Inc.

"Catch 30." People buy houses, put down roots in communities, and make firm commitments to climbing career ladders.

The deadline decade. The years between 35 and 45 involve a crisis of authenticity. It is a time of uncertainty. Youth is fading, and adults may feel that it is their "last chance" to change life-style patterns and pursue long-suppressed interests and ambitions.

Renewal or resignation. The mid-forties represents a time when a new equilibrium is reached. This may be one of *resignation*—if the individual feels stale and without purpose. Or it may be a time of *renewal*—if a person has reached a more full and realistic understanding of his or her strengths and weaknesses.

Special Problem Stages and Crises

Occupational Difficulties

It is clear from the above list that a person's job is always a potential cause of crisis. In our society, we tend to identify ourselves largely by the kind of work we do. As a result, many individuals experience job-related crises as they move through their "working years." Often the psychological problems that are reflected in a person's home and family life are a direct result of pressures and conflicts at work, yet the individual may not even mention or recognize his or her work situation as a problem.

A working adult faces a variety of problems on the job. Simply performing the task itself, day after day, may be physically or emotionally draining. Then there are many associates with whom the individual must interact: co-workers, superiors, subordinates, clients, members of the general public. Also, for many working Americans, the impersonality of giant bureaucratic organizations adds to stress and alienation.

An individual's work-related difficulties are often a function of social class and job category. Blue-collar workers often perform boring and repetitive tasks in work atmospheres that can be extremely alienating. White-collar workers are affected by the stress of dependence on an employer and "office politics." Managers and administrators are generally responsible for a large number of lower-level employees. Furthermore, they are caught in a highly competitive quest for power, status, and advancement.

Marriage

Although one might expect that with the rise in the divorce rate that has occurred over the last four decades people would be more cautious about getting married, statistics show that more and more Americans are getting married (and remarried). Traditionally, society made entry into a marital relationship easy and exit difficult. But with changes in divorce laws, both entry and exit are becoming easily available courses of action.

Alger (1974) points to a number of important reasons why people choose to marry:

1. They hope for the unique and intimate closeness that a marital relationship promises.
2. Marriage gives official sanction to a couple's desire to have children and thus to assume parental roles.
3. Couple living is one means of coping with the loneliness and alienation of modern life.
4. Marriage has traditionally been the only so-cially approved means of sexual fulfillment (though this has been changing in the last decade).

Despite these incentives, the marital relationship is often unsatisfying to one or both partners. Few individuals are able to merge their distinct identities and needs into a well-adjusted "couple." Communication problems are not uncommon, and there is enormous pressure to be accountable to each other and to fulfill each other's expectations.

Many of these difficulties seem to stem from the development of the marital relationship as a *closed system*—the image of "two against the world." Married couples tend to become isolated from meaningful relationships with peers. This in turn increases the pressure on each partner to totally satisfy all of the intellectual, emotional, and sexual needs of the mate. In many marriages, this burden is simply too great to be sustained over a long period of time.

A variety of new life styles has been publicly advocated and analyzed in recent years as alternatives to the traditional marital relationship. Among these are communal living arrangements, "open" marriages, and group marriage. Most of these alternatives revolve around the desire of many Americans to find emotional and sexual intimacy without a permanent commitment to one individual. Whether these alternatives will prove viable remains to be seen.

Parenthood is a frequent consequence of marriage and results in a special crisis of its own. Parenthood occupies a distinct role in the human life cycle. In some cases, it allows parents to relive experiences from childhood and resolve lingering conflicts and fears.

But in other cases, the pressures and responsibilities of parenthood are too much to bear. Some parents cope by neglecting their children; others react by overprotecting them. Often, the stress of parenthood affects the marital relationship.

For now, however, the marital system appears to be surviving, despite all of the obvious danger signs. But if marriage is to satisfy future generations and remain a dominant social and

The repetition and boredom of an assembly line alienate many blue-collar workers. (*General Foods Corporation.*)

economic institution, there must be profound changes.

Divorce

Traditionally, divorce has been defined as a crisis, but it is becoming frequent enough that it may have to be considered as a normal stage of the life cycle. In 1974, the divorce rate reached 4.6 per 1,000 total population, while the marriage rate was only 10.5 per 1,000 total population. These figures indicate that divorce

is a social issue that is becoming more important every day.

In American society, the mystique of "romantic love" may contribute to the growing divorce rate. The acceptable reason for two people to get married is that they love each other. But the passionate attachment of romantic love does not always survive the "long haul" of marriage, which brings with it restrictions, compromises, and disappointments. And when the passion has passed, the excuse for divorce is that "we are no longer in love."

The effect of divorce on individuals is highly variable. For some, it is a tragic, life-shattering event; for others, it is the release from a destructive situation and the beginning of a better life. Marriage counselors have begun to recognize this and no longer work only to save the marriage but rather to help individuals make a rational decision.

The divorced mother may compensate for her feelings of failure by trying to become "supermom," but this will lead to her overprotecting her children. Financial needs may send her out into the working world for the first time in years, or perhaps in her life. On top of this, she is confronted with new dating and sexual demands. All of these stresses, combined with the fact that she must change her self-image, make her adjustment a difficult one.

Although instances of the father gaining custody of the children are increasing, the children usually stay with the mother when a couple divorce. The divorced father may suffer extreme guilt as a result of his separation from his children. Many spoil their children and fail to discipline them.

Children may be the most seriously injured parties in a divorce action. Common reactions of the children in a divorce may include depression, withdrawal, apathy, insomnia, and weight loss. Some children feel guilty, believing that the divorce must be their fault. Others react with anger and blame the parent who initiated the divorce. Children experience many complex problems after divorce occurs. They may develop a distorted view of the absent parent and may face unpleasant labeling in their communities as the products of a broken home. A further difficulty is adjusting to one or both parents dating and remarrying.

The "Empty Nest" Syndrome

The "empty nest syndrome" has traditionally been viewed as a crisis point for many middle-aged adults. It has been assumed that when the youngest child leaves home to begin adult life, one or both parents will experience loneliness, anxiety, or depression.

However, a study by Lowenthal and Chiriboga (1972) casts doubt on this stereotype. The researchers conducted an in-depth survey of 54 middle- and lower-middle-class women and men whose youngest child was about to leave home. Only one respondent (a man) indicated that the imminent departure of the child was a source of difficulty. The general attitude of most respondents was that the "empty nest" would not be a critical problem. In fact, many individuals anticipated the youngest child's leaving with a sense of relief. As one woman reflected: "I feel my job with them is done. I don't have to discipline them any more, it's their problem. . . . I hope I can always be a mother, but we'll treat each other as adults. I have a much more relaxed feeling now" (pp. 9–10).

It must be added that this study involved only the *anticipated* reactions of parents to the "empty nest syndrome." Some of these respondents may have experienced problems in coping with this adjustment after it actually occurred. Nevertheless, the results of this survey challenge conventional beliefs about this alleged mid-life "crisis."

The Middle Years

There is no definite agreement on what ages form the boundaries in defining the "middle years" of a person's life. Some claim the span is from 40 to 65, others 30 to 60, while still others insist it is only the forties. As this debate has continued, many psychologists have decided that middle age is simply a "state of mind"; the critical life events of the middle years occur at different chronological ages in the lives of different individuals.

For American men, the middle years traditionally represent a time for reflection and "taking stock." Generally, if a man has not achieved his career goals by this time, he is not likely to. The middle-aged male may begin feeling bored with the routine of his job; the initial excitement of the work and of career advancement is largely absent. Ironically, this sense of feeling "trapped" may set in just at the time when a man has reached a high point in his earning power and status. For many middle-aged men, these years involve significant leadership responsibilities in their occupations or in outside organizations.

The middle-aged male experiences distinctive bodily changes. There is somewhat greater likelihood of illness and a diminished sense of energy and stamina. If a man responds to these developments by lowering his level of activity, his fitness may only worsen. While sexual activity can continue on a normal basis for middle-aged men, many males experience increasing fears of loss of potency and attractiveness. But as you will recall from Chapter 18, almost all such impotence is the result of psychological rather than organic factors.

The increased probability of death has important effects on the lives of middle-aged men. As one man commented, "There is now the realization that death is very real. . . . Now you know that death will come to you, too" (Neugarten and Datan, 1974, p. 600). This can lead to reflection and a deeper understanding of oneself and others—or it can lead to desperate attempts to "prove" one's youthfulness that may be damaging physically and emotionally.

For women, the middle years often represent a time of positive change. The proportion of women entering the labor force during middle age continues to rise, as does the frequency of women returning to school for degrees. In part, this reflects the fact that many women no longer have child-rearing responsibilities. This contributes to the feelings of increased freedom reported by many middle-aged women. But for some, the loss of child-rearing responsibilities also can lead to the feeling that life has no meaning.

Menopause has commonly been cited as a key turning point in the life of middle-aged women. However, many traditional stereotypes about the effects of menopause appear to be unsubstantiated. In fact, almost no correlation has been found between menopausal symptoms and psychological well-being.

Widowhood is a frequent and difficult experience for women in their middle years. As Neugarten and Datan (1974) report: "The situation of many resembles that of a minority group who are singled out for unequal treatment and who regard themselves as objects of

social discrimination" (p. 599). Widowhood has been given an unfortunate stigma in American society; friends and relatives may stay away from the widow to escape their own feelings and fears about death.

In a society that glorifies youth, the middle-aged woman or man is often considered useless. Many times, the wisdom and understanding that have resulted from years of painful lessons are lost to future generations—simply out of lack of respect for and lack of interest in aging citizens.

Old Age

We have already discussed old age in Chapter 17. Older people experience many crises. Among these are uprooting (owing to hospitalization or relocation), death of family or friends, depression, late-life alcoholism, serious physical illness, the need for institutional care, and the humiliations and hardships of poverty. All of these crises are intensified by the demoralizing effects of society's negative attitudes toward its senior citizens. It should be stressed that the age discrimination (or agism) that affects middle-aged Americans is even more severe for the elderly. Old people are often stereotyped as senile, rigid, old-fashioned, and dull. As a result of this pervasive attitude, many elderly Americans are discarded by the rest of society. They live out their lives isolated with their peers in neighborhoods, nursing homes, or retirement communities that become virtual "senior citizens ghettos."

Statistically, seven out of ten older people live with their families, while only 5 percent live in institutions. Most older men are married, whereas most older women are widowed. One out of every four elderly people lives below the official poverty line, and as a government report indicated, many of the elderly poor actually become poor *after* becoming old (Task Force, Special Committee on Aging, 1969). Perhaps change is on its way through "Gray Power." Because nearly 90 percent of the aged are registered voters and there tends to be a high turnout among senior citizens, the elderly can be a significant force in electoral politics.

Assuming we live for the normal life span, we will all go through predictable life stages and crises. Adolescence and old age can be particularly difficult periods. (*Tim Eagan, Woodfin Camp & Associates.*)

Ecological Problems of Abnormal Behavior

Basic Principles

Ecology is an emerging science that is concerned with the total setting in which life and behavior occur. The most basic ecological principle is that the continuity and survival of any ecological system (ecosystem) depend on a deliberate balance of factors influencing the interactions between the organism and its environment. For example, in an ordinary home aquarium, there is a steady exchange of oxygen and carbon dioxide between fish and plant life. If there is a sudden change in the ecosystem—through the addition of too many fish or over-feeding of the plant life—the entire environment can be destroyed.

The core concepts of ecology include:

1. *Adaptation.* Every organism must make adjustments in order to survive and prosper within its natural environment.
2. *Interdependence.* An ecosystem is defined by the interdependence of living and nonliving elements.
3. *System change.* No form of life remains static. A species may change, or it may cease to exist, as the conditions of its environment change.
4. *Naturalistic studies.* Ecological research is not limited to the laboratory. There is a methodological concern for naturalistic study of biological phenomena.

How does this description of ecology relate to our study of abnormal behavior? At first, this question may seem difficult to answer. But, for our purposes, the focus of ecology on the *interaction of the organism and the environment* can be most instructive. The ecological method can be quite helpful in examining community mental health problems.

As Kelly (1966) suggests, the ecological method of study raises three important issues:

1. *The interrelation of social or organizational systems in the community.* This has become a growing interest of social psychologists. Ecological analysis assumes that the operations of all community services are indirectly related. Thus, if the only community mental health center in a low-income neighborhood closes down due to lack of funding, residents may turn increasingly to religious counselors or to hospitals for assistance.
2. *The relation between the physical environment and individual behavior.* Studies of overcrowding illustrate the value of this type of ecological analysis. In the cramped conditions of a New York City subway car during "rush hour," people may feel they have to avoid eye contact because of the forced physical intimacy.
3. *The relation of the individual to the immediate social environment.* It has been found that group size has definite effects on individual behavior. A smaller group tends to have a higher work output and fewer status levels than a larger group.

In simple terms, the techniques of ecological analysis allow us to examine the behavior of an individual or an organization in the context of the surrounding physical and social environment. With this knowledge, we can see that the "abnormal" behavior of an individual bears an important relationship to the particular physical, economic, and social conditions of that individual's past and present environment. Both the heroin addict from a low-income neighborhood and the "speed freak" from a middle-class community are the products of distinctive environments. Their particular forms of abnormal behavior can best be understood within the context of their day-to-day living conditions.

Kelly (1968, 1969) applied this type of ecological analysis to the study of adaptation within the environment of a high school. He contrasted one "fluid" school in Columbus, Ohio (with a 42 percent annual turnover in students), with another high school in Columbus with a more constant student body. Field observation and interviewing were conducted in each school.

In the "fluid" school, students were found to wear more varied clothing and to be noisier and more active. There were many available channels for leadership. Newcomers were welcomed into the school and helped to adjust to their new surroundings. By contrast, the "constant" school was a closed society. It was hostile to incoming students, and leadership roles were tight and highly structured. Students who proved to be "high explorers" on a specially devised paper-and-pencil test often were labeled as deviants within the "constant" school. It was interesting that the "fluid" school, which seemed to have a more open student body, had a more open physical environment (much higher ceilings and wider hallways) than the "constant" school.

"Future Shock" as an Ecological Issue

In his popular book *Future Shock* (1970), Alvin Toffler argued that many forms of social irrationality that seem to be on the rise in American society—such as random violence, serious drug abuse, and the popularity of Eastern "gurus"—are a reflection of a dangerous social and ecological spiral, which he labeled "future shock."

Toffler believes that Americans experience *overstimulation* as a crucial destructive feature of day-to-day life. This overstimulation "occurs when the individual is forced to operate above his adaptive range" (p. 306). Examples of overstimulated individuals include soldiers in battle, disaster victims, and culturally dislocated travelers. All three must respond to demanding and unpredictable stimuli. At first, they tend to be confused and disoriented, and perhaps anxious, tense, or irritable. Eventually, the overstimulated individual may pass a point of no return and experience severe emotional withdrawal.

The overstimulated individual reaches a point of shock at which the most bizarre behavioral reactions are not only possible, but common. It is the shock of overstimulation that led a soldier in Burma to fall asleep while machine gun bullets were exploding all around him. It is the shock of overstimulation that led a Texas girl to climb calmly through a broken window and buy a record in the midst of the flying debris of a tornado.

Toffler identifies three principal forms of overstimulation that are affecting contemporary America: bombardment of the senses, information overload, and decision stress.

Bombardment of the senses distorts our grip on reality. As children, we inevitably learn that looking directly into the sun for too long makes it difficult to achieve normal vision for some time afterward. Yet, the bombardment of the senses that is becoming a normal part of American life goes far beyond this one illustration. We experience an ever-growing assortment of sensory stimuli—lights, colors, sounds—coming at us constantly. Our sense organs and nervous systems simply are not equipped to cope with an infinite barrage of stimuli.

Information overload is, in many ways, similar to sensory bombardment. Information is simply one more stimulus that is being thrust at us in constantly increasing doses. Researchers of information processing among humans agree that overloads of information can cause a breakdown in normal performance. As Toffler suggests,

> Managers plagued by demands for rapid, incessant, and complex decisions; pupils deluged with facts and hit with repeated tests; housewives confronted with squalling children, jangling telephones, broken washing machines, the wail of rock and roll from the teenager's living room and the whine of the television set in the parlor—may well find their ability to think and act clearly impaired by the waves of information crashing into their senses. (p. 314)

Decision stress is the third form of overstimulation in a complex, technological society. Technological innovation is proceeding at such a rapid pace that the average American confronts almost unimaginable changes within a lifetime. With each change comes an increase in options for living. With each increase in options comes the need for more decisions, as well as the need for more information to make the decisions. This spiral has produced what Toffler calls "decisional overstimulation."

As Toffler explains, "It is impossible to produce future shock in large numbers of individuals without affecting the rationality of the society as a whole" (p. 325). He quotes Daniel P. Moynihan, now a U.S. senator from New York, as stating that America "exhibits the qualities of an individual going through a nervous breakdown" (p. 324).

Toffler insists that we live in a "future-shocked society":

Despite its extraordinary achievements in art, science, intellectual, moral, and political life, the United States is a nation in which tens of thousands of young people flee reality by opting for drug-induced lassitude; a nation in which millions of their parents retreat into video-induced stupor or alcoholic haze; a nation in which legions of elderly folk vegetate and die in loneliness; in which the flight from family and occupational responsibility has become an exodus; in which masses tame their raging anxieties with Miltown, or Librium, or Equanil, or a score of other tranquil-

One area of ecological investigation is the relationship between the physical environment and individual behavior. What effect do you think the noise and overcrowding of city life has had on the man in this photograph? (*Charles Gatewood.*)

izers and psychic pacifiers. Such a nation, whether it knows it or not, is suffering from future shock. (p. 325)

Responding to Future Shock

Toffler (1970) offers a number of suggestions (some whimsical) as to how Americans might cope with future shock.

1. *Direct coping.* We can make conscious and determined efforts to ward off future shock in our normal, day-to-day lives. The key is to limit the level of cognitive stimulation, information flow, and decision stress when we show signs of becoming overwhelmed.

2. *Personal stability zones.* We can reduce the rate of turnover in our lives by building up certain habit patterns or limited security regions that will remain stable and unchanged in the midst of other instabilities. For example, faced with the stress of constant travel, an individual can adopt a set daily routine including a morning reading hour and a late afternoon nap. This may add an element of stability and regularity to his or her life.

3. *Situational grouping.* We can establish or join "situational groups" for those who are experiencing the same profound life changes at the same time. For example, there might be situational groups for recently divorced persons, for adults with elderly relatives living in their homes, or for single mothers. Such groups could provide temporary but crucial support and understanding.

4. *Crisis counseling.* We need "crisis counselors" who will become experts in helping people through divorce, relocation, and other difficult transitional stages.

5. *Halfway houses.* At present, halfway houses are used to assist hospital and prison inmates in gradually readjusting to life in the "outside world." The same model could be used to assist other populations who are making difficult transitions from one life experience to another—for veterans returning from warfare or rural students entering large urban universities.

6. *Enclaves of the past.* In such communities, change would be intentionally limited. People could come to these areas for a "vacation" from future shock conditions for weeks or even years.

7. *Enclaves of the future.* These facilities would assist individuals and families in making adjustments *before* the actual move to a new living situation. People could be shown films and models of the community to which they will soon be moving.

8. *Global space pageants.* Toffler suggests that as the pace of change accelerates, "We need to mark off certain regularities for preservation, exactly the way we now mark off certain forests, historical monuments, or bird sanctuaries for protection. We may even need to manufacture ritual" (p. 350).

Community Mental Health View of Abnormal Behavior

The area of community mental health was introduced in Chapter 7. You will remember that the community clinician sees individual instances of psychologic disorder as a function of deeper social, economic, and cultural factors. The psychological problems of the individual are understood in light of the characteristics and conflicts of his or her community.

The themes of the community mental health movement are outlined in Box 19-2. There are a number of key factors that have contributed to the growth of a community mental health movement (Korchin, 1976). Among them are:

1. *Discouragement with existing mental health concepts, activities, and roles.* There has been increasing criticism of traditional psychotherapeutic approaches inside and outside the profession. Both the cost and effectiveness of psychotherapy have come under fire. At the same time, many professionals in the field have become dissatisfied with the medical model of mental illness, which directs its primary attention to the internal conflicts of the disturbed client (rather than to the social causes of abnormal behavior).

2. *Shortage of personnel.* In the last decade, it has become evident that our society's need for mental health services is far outrunning the availability of qualified personnel. Furthermore, it is projected

Box 19-2 Basic Themes of Community Psychology

1. *Social-environmental factors* play a major role in determining behavior.

2. *Systems-oriented interventions* can help make social institutions (such as the school or family) more effective in meeting the needs of members of the community.

3. The major concern of community psychology should be the *prevention* of abnormal behavior rather than treatment or rehabilitation.

4. One of the aims of intervention should be *building social competence* and self-sufficiency.

5. Community approaches should be applied in *familiar settings* in which the clients are comfortable.

6. Community clinicians should engage in *outreach*, instead of assisting only those persons who seek help.

7. In order to have maximum impact, the professional should work with *community resource people and nonprofessionals.*

8. The community clinician should not be made to adhere to rigid and traditional professional norms. There must be an emphasis on *experimentation* and *innovation.*

9. *Community members* must play an important role in the determination of where resources go and what strategies of prevention are needed.

10. Mental health problems must be understood and treated within a *broad social perspective* that takes into account the interplay of psychological, social, economic, and cultural factors.

11. *Public education* should be an essential element of community mental health programs.

12. The community clinician should be supportive of *social reform* efforts to deal with underlying causes of stress, such as poverty and racism.

Based on Korchin, S. J., *Modern clinical psychology: Principles of intervention in the clinic and community.* New York: Basic Books, 1976.

that the demand for psychological counseling will increase even more dramatically in the future. In part, this is due to expanded health insurance coverage from the federal government, private industry, and labor unions. As a result, the mental health professions have had to consider ways to reallocate professional time and train more individuals as mental health counselors.

3. *Poverty and mental health.* Low-income Americans have generally experienced the worst aspects of the mental health system—if they have received any supportive services at all! Traditionally, the most advanced mental health techniques have been reserved for the most affluent members of society, while the poor have been shunted off to understaffed and alienating custodial hospitals. Even when the poor *do* receive psychotherapy, they must contend with the biases of a discipline that

rewards middle-class verbal skills and introspection. Many low-income Americans have developed an understandable distrust toward the entire field of "mental health," and are unlikely to change their attitudes until they see major reforms in the mental health professions.

4. *The mental hospital.* An individual with severe psychological problems is supposedly placed in a mental hospital in order to be "helped." But as we have noted previously, the hospital is often part of the problem, rather than part of the solution. Hospitalization itself seems to induce distinct pathological symptoms. The patients perceive that they are in the midst of a total institution that defines them as being "sick." The individual eventually adjusts to the "sick role" and becomes increasingly unable to function without assistance from staff. As a reaction to these dangers of hospitalization, one of the

more ambitious goals of the community mental health movement is the elimination of total institutional care. This would require alternate services (such as halfway houses) for individuals in distress.

5. *The "spirit of the times."* The community mental health movement arose in the 1960s—a decade abundant with deep political unrest and social reform efforts. Many controversial public issues became the subjects of national attention and heated debate. Among these were poverty, racism, and the alienation of urban life. Millions of Americans became involved in attempts to *humanize* and *democratize* the social, economic, and political order of the nation. It was during this era of challenge that the community mental health concept was put forth as a response to criticisms of traditional mental health approaches.

Community mental health workers rely on *outreach* as one part of an overall strategy of "preventive medicine." They seek out and reach the individual with psychological problems *before* conditions of crisis are present. As Denner and Price (1973) observe:

> More important than the development of new techniques was the working notion that therapists cannot sit back and passively wait for the sick to request treatment. The new therapists have embraced a public health model. In short, mental illness is viewed as a health hazard, a danger to the community, and something that the community must eradicate for the sake of its own well-being. (p. 2)

Outreach is, of course, a rather general term. Even the best-staffed community mental health center lacks the resources to knock on every door and search out each individual in need of mental health counseling. How, then, does the community mental health staff actually engage in outreach?

One answer to this problem is *to work with community agencies.* The mental health worker develops cooperative relationships with other local institutions, including schools, courts, and employment agencies. Thus if a community resident visits the employment counselor and mentions the psychological problems or abnormal behavior of another family member, the mental health worker can be quickly brought in for consultation.

An additional advantage of outreach is that particular problems of disadvantaged subgroups can be addressed. For example, a community mental health center might establish special therapeutic groups to assist individuals who are approaching or beginning retirement. Such people have special needs that probably would be ignored within normal counseling programs.

In this sense, the community mental health movement is a serious and significant response to many of the issues discussed in this chapter. It has a broad social perspective that allows an enlightened understanding of the special problems faced by individuals suffering from discrimination based on sex, race, or age. At the same time, the community concept coincides in important ways with the ecological systems approach outlined earlier.

Unfortunately, there are a number of disturbing problems in the community mental health concept—and in the actual community mental health movement—that must be examined. One survey of 11 community mental health centers (Glasscote, Sanders, Forstenzer, and Foley, 1964) found that the dominant mode of treatment was individual psychotherapy. Beneath the official title of "community mental health center," most staff professionals were relying on traditional therapeutic techniques and were ignoring the goals and methods of community psychology. A follow-up study (Glasscote, Sussex, Cumming, and Smith, 1969) again indicated that there was a strong focus on individual clinical counseling within community mental health centers.

Szasz (1970) points to the dangers of state intervention into definitions of community (and individual) mental health. He recalls past historical eras in which political regimes defined what was good and evil (or, more recently, "healthy" and "unhealthy") and purged or exterminated those individuals labeled as deviant. Even Denner and Price (1973), two advocates of the community mental health concept, are forced to concede that "it is unsettling to think that public officials would concern themselves with our mental well-being" (p. 13).

On balance, however, the community mental health movement appears to be a useful and creative innovation in treatment. Denner and Price (1973) conclude that, despite certain problems of community psychology: "The alternative of having private practitioners see one voluntary client at a time is even more dismal and even less responsible" (p. 13). One of the most important underpinnings of community psychology is that community members play an important role in the determination of resource priorities and prevention strategies. If this *community control* component retains sufficient emphasis, there will be no need to worry about the power of the state or the theoretical preferences of individual professionals within community centers.

Summary

The abnormal behavior of a particular individual occurs within a social context. Ecological analysis might see that behavior as part of an interaction between individuals and their environments. Community psychology, in a somewhat similar vein, might view the individual's actions as a reflection of the social, economic, and political conflicts of the home community. The social context of an individual's behavior could also include special problems that result from membership in a disadvantaged minority group (such as blacks) or in a disadvantaged majority group (women). There are also many legal aspects of abnormal behavior. The individual's rights to privacy and due process of law are often jeopardized, regardless of whether the individual is involuntarily or voluntarily committed to a mental hospital.

Life cycle analysis constitutes an alternate means of evaluating the social context of behavior. Traditionally, the psychological literature has recognized that there are clear and definable stages of preadolescent development. More recently, mental health professionals have begun to view *all* of the adult years as a time of growth, change, and adaptation. The postadolescent years have also been broken down into various distinct stages of development. There are many special problem stages and crises. Among these are occupational difficulties, marriage and divorce, the empty nest syndrome, middle age, and old age.

Toffler has a highly original vision of the social context of abnormal behavior. He sees American society as suffering from widespread "future shock" caused by overstimulation. His analysis suggests that individual abnormal behavior is but a small part of a nationwide and collective emotional disturbance.

A number of factors have contributed to the growth of the community mental health movement, for example, discouragement with existing mental health concepts, activities, and roles; shortage of personnel; lack of mental health service for the poor; and the negative effects of hospitalization.

Emerging approaches to the treatment and prevention of abnormal behavior

Introduction—Models of Intervention

We now have some understanding of the dynamics of abnormal behavior—how it develops and how it is maintained. We have learned to question the application of the label "abnormal" to behaviors that simply may not coincide with current social attitudes and norms, and to identify behaviors that are self-destructive and socially harmful. We have seen how the psychodynamic and behavioral theories have inspired various therapeutic approaches and techniques for the elimination of abnormal behavior. It is clear that the way professionals view the development of undesirable behaviors strongly influences their choice of treatment approaches.

In Chapter 19, we reviewed some conceptions of abnormal behavior that focus on its social and ecological contexts. New therapeutic methods are emerging from these more recent views. Indeed, as the traditional interpretations and unifying theories lose their hold, the field is left open to a wide variety of treatment methods—some of which owe their substance to no theory, or to bizarre theories of dubious origin.

This proliferation of therapies presents a problem for any attempt at comprehensive coverage and critical analysis. Therefore, we will be selective in discussing those that are significant, in terms of either their theoretical importance or their large following among professionals and the public, and those that we have not discussed previously in detail. Because it provides a useful framework for organizing the various treatment approaches, we use Korchin's structure (1976) of models of treatment. Table 20-1 classifies the five models (across the top of the table) as:

Clinical Models
   Custodial
   Therapeutic

Community Models
   Clinical Pole
   Public Health Pole

Social Action Model

The first column contains the pertinent questions about treatment forms. The answers to these questions describe each of the five intervention models. Reading the column of answers under each model heading, we get an outline of the assumptions, procedures, therapists, locales, and objectives of each model.

The five models from left to right trace the progress of the treatment of abnormal behavior from the early days, when public and professional attitudes were dominated by the mental illness model, to a more contemporary view of malfunctioning social systems as important factors for abnormal behavior. The focus of attention shifts from the sick *individual* (in the three clinical approaches) to the sick *society* (in the public health and social action models). With this shift, there is a lessening of interest in the intrapsychic origins of behavioral deviations and a decrease in efforts devoted to direct treatment of specific personality disorders.

The three clinical approaches operate on the individual as patient, and deal with environmental factors only when necessary to increase or assure the effectiveness of the individual treatment. In contrast, the community public health and social action approaches devote most of their efforts to changing the person's environment in order to remove harmful stresses and distortions. In fact, the social action model in its most radical form rejects clinical treatment of the individual, since this obscures the need for change in social structures before the individual's health can be promoted.

With the knowledge you have gained from our development of the multicausal model of abnormal behavior (in Chapter 4 and in subsequent consideration of various behaviors), you will see the limitations in each of the five intervention models by scanning their side-by-side comparison in Korchin's framework. Each model seems to provide some information about the nature of the problem that can aid professionals in understanding the condition and in designing a course of therapeutic action. The traditional models certainly offer useful insights that thoughtful therapists would value in approaching a complex problem in human behavior. And they would also value the varied and extensive arsenal of intervention methods provided by the community public health and social action models. They might even wish for the development of more models to give them a greater choice of treatments for the endless diversity of problem behaviors they meet in their practices.

Recent Clinical Approaches to Treatment

Therapeutic Models

The increasing incidence of anxiety and breakdown under the intense stresses of modern living (see Chapter 19), coupled with the growing acceptance of therapy for emotional problems, has generated an explosion of new therapy approaches. Some are founded on traditional theory with innovations in procedure, while others are exotic developments without established theoretical credentials. Evaluation is made difficult by lack of formal reporting of results in psychological journals and by the suddenness of both the emergence and disappearance of some methods. We will discuss several of them in the light of their popularity.

Self-Control Techniques

The notion of self-control as a means of changing behavior has deep roots in popular views of abnormal behavior. As we noted in Chapter 1, the belief that people who behave abnormally could change if they would only make up their minds to stop their bad actions has persisted from ancient times. Today, behavior therapists have implemented the idea of self-control with specific procedures that enable the individual to treat his or her undesirable behaviors systematically as they occur.

Several techniques are employed, separately or in combination: self-monitoring, self-instruction, self-evaluation, self-reinforcement, and self-selection of standards. The most commonly used techniques are the first two.

Self-monitoring is virtually required in all self-control procedures, since it is necessary that the client be alert to detect the potential or actual onset of the target behavior and to record the outcome. It is a basic feature of programs designed to overcome such problems as obesity, alcoholism, smoking, and bad study habits. Since self-monitoring is usually combined with other procedures, such as self-instruction, it is difficult to isolate its effects from the interactive effects of the other treatments.

Self-instruction involves the covert verbalization of inhibiting or reassuring commands when the target behavior seems imminent or while the stressful condition is active. It may consist simply of the command "Stop!" Or it may proceed through internal dialogue in which the clients use reasonable arguments either to dissuade themselves from the bad behavior or to encourage themselves to engage in the desired behavior in spite of anxieties or fears. The internal dialogue usually consists of certain self-statements. These are statements in which the clients describe their own attitudes and reactions ("I am afraid . . ."), and then restate them to modify the reaction ("I am feeling calm, less afraid . . ."). Self-instruction with modifying self-statements has been used to defuse phobias (spiders, snakes, etc.), as well as for a variety of other behaviors, notably hyperactivity in children ("Slow down. I am a slow turtle"). The covert dialogues are, of course, more elaborate and more related to the particular behavior patterns than our samples are.

Self-evaluation is performed by the clients, who make comparative value judgments of their own behaviors. Children, for example, may determine the disruptiveness of their classroom behavior. Such self-evaluation may be based on standards selected either by the therapist or by the clients themselves (*self-selection*). Under *self-reinforcement* procedure, the clients immediately reinforce themselves with tokens (money) or consumable rewards for appropriate behavior.

Self-control is an attractive method because the client becomes the therapist's assistant, thus potentially expanding therapy teams to provide individual (self-) attention for every client. However, it raises theoretical and practical questions. Although self-control is a behavioral method, it violates one of the cardinal principles of behavioral doctrine. It involves the manipulation of hidden behavior

Table 20-1 Models of Mental Health Intervention

Issue	Clinical Models		Community Models		Social Action Mode
	Custodial	*Therapeutic*	*Clinical Pole*	*Public Health Pole*	
Who is recipient (R) of service?	A patient	A person	A person (and relevant others)	A population-at-risk or everyone	A population-at-risk or everyone
How is individual R's state conceived?	Diseased; unable to care for self	Psychologically disturbed; worthy of sympathy, respect, and professional effort	In psychosocial crisis; worthy of sympathy, respect, and assistance	In present crisis or potential danger; worthy of respect, but may not be motivated to change	Under present or potential social stress; all worthy of benefits of "great society"
Locus of problem?	In R (probably biologically)	In R (probably psychologically)	In R and his psychosocial situation	There or, more important, in social system	In social and political systems
Is it likely to change?	Probably not	Yes, with professional help	Yes, with help	Yes, with a change in social conditions	Yes, with a change in institutions
What is done?	Custodial care and medication	Individual, group, and family psychotherapy; milieu therapy	Crisis intervention, brief therapy, counseling, and/or direct help with jobs, school, economic, and similar problems	Various actions intended for secondary, tertiary, and primary prevention	If possible, actions directed to broad-scaled social change
Importance and purpose of clinical assessment?	Important, for diagnostic categorization	Very important, for broad-scaled personalistic understanding of R, for therapy planning and evaluation	Important, for assessing R's focal problem, strengths, and liabilities, but time-consuming and costly	Important, but mainly for survey and epidemiological purposes	Irrelevant, except in survey role as evidence of social problem
Who initiates?	Courts, family, and professionals	R, preferably self-motivated	R or family	R, social agency, health authority	Social authorities
Under what contract?	Involuntary, when need is established	Voluntary, on demand	Usually voluntary, on demand	Involuntary or voluntary when needed	Involuntary for individual, decision controlled by political process

Table 20-1 Continued

Issue	Clinical Models		Community Models		Social Action Model
	Custodial	*Therapeutic*	*Clinical Pole*	*Public Health Pole*	
At what time?	When "doctor" decides	When R requests	When R needs it (in crisis)	Whenever possible; in advance of need	All the time
Who conducts intervention?	"Doctor"	Mental health professional	Professional with nonprofessional assistance	Professionals in collaboration with nonprofessionals, other professional caretakers	Professional in collaboration with policy makers
Who else is involved?	Paramedical staff	No one, or "psychiatric team"	Team, community caretakers, and nonprofessionals	Same and community agents and leaders	Policy makers
How does the professional function?	Administratively, medically	Directly, as therapist	Directly and through supervision of nonprofessionals	Indirectly, through consultation	Indirectly, through advising policy makers
Specific role of the psychologist?	Diagnostic tester	Psychotherapist and/or clinical assessor	Therapist, counselor, community/clinician	Community change agent, organizational consultant	No specific role
Place of intervention?	Hospital	Hospital, clinic, private office	Community mental health center, day hospitals, halfway houses, community settings	In community institutions (schools, church, etc.)	In political arena, social-planning institutions
Goal of intervention?	Discharge or remission of symptoms	Personality change, positive mental health	Strengthening of coping potential, relief of distress	Reduction of social stress	An improved society
What realm of knowledge is necessary for intervention?	Descriptive and medical psychiatry	Individual psychodynamics, personality theory, psychotherapy	Personality theory, social psychology of primary institutions, organizational psychology	Social psychology, community organization, epidemiology, sociology	Sociology, policy sciences, urban planning

From Korchin, S. J. *Modern clinical psychology: Principles of intervention in the clinic and community.* New York: Basic Books, 1976. © 1976 by S. J. Korchin, Basic Books, Inc.

(self-statements, etc.), which is contrary to the behavioral rejection of "mentalistic" processes. Since therapists are not mind readers, they must rely entirely on the clients' self-reports of what they are doing covertly. However, those who accept a cognitive behavioral approach do not have such a problem with self-report measures. Thoresen and Mahoney (1974) suggest that the difference between external control and self-control is a matter of degree, and that the degree of individual responsibility for one's own behavior is a relative factor that is hard to determine.

In evaluating this technique, the first question, of course, is "How successful is it?" One review presents no clear record of effectiveness (Kazdin, 1974). In fact, it reports that self-monitoring and self-instruction are seldom effective when used alone, and that the effect of self-monitoring decreases with time. Self-control, however, does show enough promise to warrant further development, with emphasis on corroborative reporting by peers and others, and on strategies for generalizing and maintaining the therapeutic benefits.

Transcendental Meditation

Radiating the fascination of Eastern mystical rituals and the aura of its charismatic leader, Maharishi Mahesh Yogi, transcendental meditation (TM) has attracted hundreds of thousands of people to the practice of meditative techniques for the relief of stress and the improvement of personal performance. Its principal advantages are the bare simplicity and effortlessness of the procedure and the small amount of time required for its practice. Perhaps most important is the fact that, after brief training, the meditator can practice the ritual on his or her own without further consultation or professional intervention. Moreover, despite its origins in Vedic (Indian) philosophy, the TM devotee needs no knowledge of the vast literature.

The TM procedure consists in sitting in a chair with eyes closed, attending passively to the mental echo of a selected Sanskrit word (the Mantra). The mind remains in a relaxed

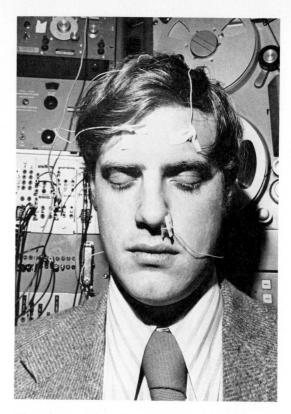

The subject of this photograph has sensors attached to his head and to a computer as studies are made of the physiological changes that occur during transcendental meditation. Tests show markedly decreased oxygen consumption, carbon dioxide production, and blood lactate. (*United Press International.*)

state until all intrusive thoughts fade away. Eventually, the meditator is expected to experience a sense of transcendent awareness, or "pure consciousness," in which subjective perception is constant and undistorted. Meditation is practiced in two 15- or 20-minute sessions a day.

Wallace and Benson (1972) and Banquet (1973) have studied the physiological effects of TM. Tests show markedly decreased oxygen consumption, carbon dioxide production, and blood lactate. Among EEG changes that have been observed, there is an increase in the correlation of certain wave frequencies between the brain hemispheres, indicating a stabilization of cortical processes.

In a recent controlled study of TM compared with merely sitting in a relaxed manner with eyes closed, Smith (1976) found no significant difference in anxiety test scores and muscle tension measurements. He concluded that TM benefits were due to the periods of passive, relaxed posture, and speculated on the likely contribution of the subject's expectation of relief. Nevertheless, TM has been introduced into institutional rehabilitation programs for psychiatric and drug abuse cases with some positive results.

Primal Therapy

This is a recent innovation by Janov (1971), who asserts that parental denial of the infant's needs causes extreme psychological pain. In defense against the pain, a split develops in the child between feeling and awareness; tensions build up in successive layers, resulting in adult neuroses.

Therapy consists of three weeks of daily sessions that last until the client is exhausted. The client is coaxed and guided to plunge into any strong feelings that are evoked by focusing on people and events in his or her early life. Immersed in such painful experiences, the client may suddenly connect with feelings locked into the "primal scene" of his or her infancy. This recall of the forgotten feeling may provoke a "primal scream," after which the client senses relief and an awareness of being "in touch with his feelings." The three-week, intensive therapy is followed by eight months of twice-weekly group sessions.

While primal therapy seems effective in evoking buried memories with cathartic (releasing) effects (an objective of traditional psychotherapy), Janov has been criticized for oversimplifying the nature and treatment of neurotic conditions. Some critics believe that the effects of primal therapy are not different from those of implosion or flooding therapy, behavioral techniques that we have described previously.

Transactional Analysis

Eric Berne's transactional analysis (TA) gained popularity largely as a result of his 1964 book, *Games People Play*, and Harris's 1969 sequel, *I'm OK—You're OK*. TA conceives the individual as a triplet of ego states: Parent, Child, and Adult. The first two (*P* and *C*) are survivors of the individual's childhood and correspond roughly to Freud's superego and id; the Adult (*A*) is the developed grown-up, Freud's reality-oriented ego.

C engages in primary process thinking, seeks immediate satisfactions, tends to be self-indulgent and irresponsible. *P* enforces "good behavior" according to the individual's possibly hazy recollection of his or her parents' rules and admonitions regarding "right" and "wrong." *A* is the mature adult, who makes reasoned judgments and reaches logical conclusions based on dispassionate analysis. The resemblance to Freudian structure is obvious, but TA treats the personality divisions quite differently, as complete ego states, each of which takes control of the individual on certain occasions. The disturbed persons are unable to distinguish their own ego states, flip-flopping from one to another under circumstantial pressures and conflicting desires ("contamination"). In effect, contamination occurs when improper ideas from *P* and *C* intrude into the *A* state.

The TA process consists of "decontaminating" the clients by teaching them to distinguish their ego states, to consistently identify the source of distorted ideas, and to change to the state that is appropriate for the present purpose. For example, *A* is the best state for choosing a career goal, while *C*'s carefree zest for fun makes recreation more enjoyable, although *P* is a necessary chaperone to see that the fun does not get out of hand.

People's interactions are called "transactions," which are stimulus-response couplings in social relations. Normally, the Adult-Adult relation should govern most transactions between people. When transactions are *complementary*, both parties are satisfied. This occurs either when both ego states are the same (e.g.,

Child-Child) or when a pair of ego states are related properly to serve mutual needs (e.g., Parent-Child) in an appropriate way. Complementary transactions are commonly found in ordinary working and social relationships, rituals, and pastimes. *Crossed* transactions occur when one person's ego state brings on a response from an ego state other than the one addressed in the second person (e.g., the child in the first person (*C1*) addresses the child in the second person (*C2*) but receives a response from the parent in the second person (*P2*). Such transactions lead to conflict.

Besides these overt transactions, covert transactions may be exchanges at the same time (the TA equivalent of the "double bind"). The simultaneous, two-level communications are called "ulterior" and constitute the basis for "games." In this mode, the agent cons the respondent with an appeal to the respondent's weakness (fear, sentimentality, greed). The agent solicits a response under some pretext (e.g., a need for advice), but in reality has an ulterior motive (e.g., a desire for sympathy). After an interchange of some length, the respondent "catches on" and ends the game as both take their respective "payoffs" (good or bad feelings).

The relative dominance of the *P*, *A*, and *C* roles a person plays in the games are determined by the "script" he (or she) adopts early in life (between the ages of 3 and 7). At this point, he fixes his image of himself (O.K. or not O.K.) relative to others (O.K. or not O.K.). Parents and others will influence the casting of the lifescript, the identification of the *P*, *A*, and *C* states, and the dominance of the *A* state.

By its transactional view of behavior, TA is basically a group therapy method (usually eight clients and a therapist, although couples may also be treated). The therapist is observer, tutor, and monitor. Group interaction, including game playing, is encouraged. The group participants learn to monitor and identify each other's transactional behaviors under the therapist's guidance. When they have been "decontaminated," they attain the ideal form of social behavior: a game-free relationship called "intimacy," in which the parties give and receive spontaneously.

Gestalt Therapy

Although trained in the European psychoanalytic tradition, Fritz Perls (1967) abandoned the insight-developing techniques he had learned and undertook a method that focused on the neurotic, here-and-now behaviors that are also the concern of the behaviorists. The similarity to behavior therapy, however, ends right there. Gestalt therapy does not subscribe to learning theory nor does it apply conditioning techniques to abnormal behaviors.

According to Gestalt theory, the organism starts with an awareness of its needs and is programmed to satisfy them appropriately. Frustration of needs causes internal conflict, which results in the build-up of impulse tensions. These are compensated for by sensori-motor tensions. The effect is a blockage of awareness with a consequent division of the individual into opposing parts. The therapist's job is to restore the wholeness (Gestalt) of the person by awakening his (or her) awareness of his tension-induced behaviors.

The techniques draw the clients' attention to their body postures and movements that reflect inner tensions. Mental and physical exercises are practiced to enhance body awareness. In group therapy, the therapist actively encourages members to express freely their true feelings and to recognize their failures to show awareness of their real needs and feelings in social interactions.

As one of the "body psychotherapies," Gestalt therapy sometimes uses the exercise techniques that make up the procedures of *bioenergetics*, a therapy that deals exclusively with body tensions as the essential manifestation of the psychological disturbance. Bioenergetics, developed by Dr. Alexander Lowen (1967), provides a repertoire of exercises designed to reveal and relieve breathing irregularities and muscular tensions. This releases the energy that was tied up by emotional stresses. The exercises involve the focusing of attention on

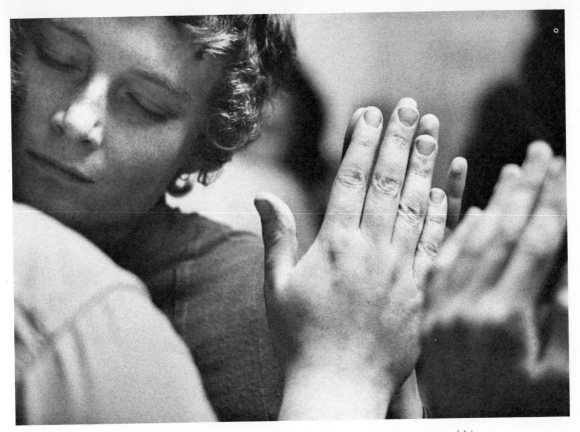

Gestalt therapy attempts to restore the wholeness of a person by making him aware of his tension-induced behavior. Mental and physical exercises are practiced to enhance body awareness and encourage individuals to express freely their true feelings. (*Ian Berry/ Magnum Photos.*)

the state of various body parts, which serves the body-awareness requirements of Gestalt therapy.

New Group-Encounter Therapies

A new and expansive development of group therapy emerged from programs designed to improve attitudes and performance among industrial and institutional personnel and servicemen during World War II. Experience with such programs enhanced professional understanding of group dynamics and the powerful effects of group participation on individual responsiveness.

One of the early programs was the work of the National Training Laboratories (NTL), using theories and techniques developed by Kurt Lewin. Starting in 1946, NTL introduced the so-called "here-and-now" encounter process. Initially, NTL and its British counterparts focused on group responses, rather than on the individual in the group.

The Esalen Institute of California applied NTL's group techniques to enhance individual self-realization and growth. Esalen exposed its clients to imaginative combinations of psychodrama (role-playing), Eastern mysticism, the Gestalt principles of Fritz Perls, and the client-centered approach of Carl Rogers. Under

William Schutz, and with the prestige lent by the endorsement of professionals of the stature of Perls and Rogers, Esalen inspired a multiplication of encounter programs during the late sixties and early seventies. The key concepts common to most of them were defined by Schutz as the psychologically, physically, and spiritually unified person, self-awareness, voluntary participation, responsibility for oneself, contact by the leader, naturalness of behavior, and encounter as a way of life. Esalen perfected structured exercises (reciprocal massages, telling each other participant what you think of his or her behavior, making grimaces at each other) as a means of encouraging communication and interaction.

One of the interesting variations of encounter programs is the marathon group. In a continuous session lasting from 18 to 48 hours, marathon participants eventually drop their social facades. They lose their reluctance and embarrassment as they share an extended experience with others. The intensity of the experience creates greater self-awareness.

Lieberman, Yalom, and Miles (1973) studied a number of encounter groups and found that their leaders depended on structured exercises to develop group cohesiveness, but this factor was not effective in improving individual learning. In fact, they concluded that the groups encourage overly optimistic expectations of personal happiness as a result of participation, but "the change is modest when compared to . . . psychotherapy" (p. 98). They also criticize the effort of encounter group leaders to induce members to concentrate entirely on feelings, to the exclusion of intelligent thinking about what is going on.

As a psychotherapist who endorses encounter groups, Burton (1970) commends them as a service to the "normal" population who labor under the stresses of modern living with no help for their "quiet desperation," their joyless lives, their alienation, and their loneliness. The encounter group invites them in from their "existential limbo" to interact with people who share their frustrations, to be a part of a social group that will pay attention to their needs and allow them to express their bottled-up feelings. Most of all, it offers them the opportunity to learn how to open up and relate to real people.

est

Erhard Seminars Training (est) is a phenomenon of the times: a strikingly packaged product, designed by a salesman to exploit a deep public need, and marketed with the most powerful "hard-sell" techniques. The therapy is administered in two successive weekend sessions that last all day. Large groups of participants are harangued, belittled, and browbeaten into confronting the realities of themselves and the world. They are obliged to think about their shortcomings and their potentials for hours on end. Rationalization is forbidden. Finally, they are given a message of hope, and exhorted to be honest with themselves and take responsibility for their own lives instead of blaming others for their failures. A sense of autonomy replaces the sense of being a helpless object.

The crass money-making aspects of est, coupled with doubts about the long-term benefits of its crude techniques, have brought it under heavy critical attack by professional therapists, in spite of the merits of its reality-confrontation and the enthusiastic reports of many of its participants.

Stren Training

The concept of *stren*—the healthy effect of life experiences—was developed to serve as an antonym for *trauma*. Finkel (1975) presents the self-reports of 40 college students, in which they described positive effects (strens) and negative effects (traumas) of particular experiences. Of greater interest were their reports of self-conversion of traumas into strens by a cognitive reworking of the experience to extract positive benefits. The conversion process was generally accomplished by the individual in isolation from friends and family. Out of the resolution of the trauma comes a sense of confidence in one's ability to cope with severe crises. This suggests the possibility of training people early in life to develop strens as a means of building an inner strength. While there is no formal stren-building program currently available, the practical use of strens by many people warrants its inclusion here as a preventive technique, a kind of "therapy by anticipation."

Institutional Treatment

The Concept of Hospitalization

The treatment of patients in mental hospitals generally fits the "custodial" dimension in Korchin's models of mental health intervention. It is not a coincidence that such institutions are called "hospitals," but rather a reflection of the mental illness model that has dominated professional thinking for many years. An early movement away from the illness model in institutional approaches was Pinel's introduction of moral treatment of mental patients after the French Revolution (see Chapter 1). There was a revival of moral attitudes toward people with abnormal behavior during the 1920s.

However, the return to moral treatment under the illness model was compromised by the continuing increase in the hospital patient population. As a result, mental hospitals became (and, in most cases, still are) custodial institutions, in which the patient is subject to more administrative than therapeutic attention. In Chapter 11, we discussed the oppressive, harmful effects of this "institutionalization" on the patient in a mental hospital. How can we justify present patterns of hospital treatment? Given our claim of humane motives, we should be able to find some progressive trends evolving in response to developments in diagnostic and therapeutic techniques.

Why hospitalization at all? The 1969 report of the Group for the Advancement of Psychiatry proposes a positive view of hospitalization as a step toward mental health. Changing concepts of hospital care offer more benefits to the patient in diagnostic services, opportunity for continuous observation, and treatment with new drugs. Perhaps most important, the view of the psychiatric hospital as a fully structured, dynamically functioning community with a coherent social system came into focus in the 1950s. Social psychologists introduced the concept of the hospital as a total environment that usually functioned as a repressive, hierarchical society, but that could be organized into a therapeutic community for the benefit of the patients rather than for the convenience of the staff. The new view inspired mental health professionals to use the social forces and group interactions, along with the hospital's resources of staff and facilities, in imaginative ways for therapeutic gain. Out of this social approach came the therapeutic community in which emerging discoveries regarding the dynamics of interpersonal relations were applied in milieu therapy.

Milieu Therapy

In the therapeutic community, the social system is the instrument of treatment. The basic principle of milieu therapy, as stated by Maxwell Jones (1953), one of the originators of the concept, is that the patient's problems can best be studied and treated by placing him or her into interactive situations that approximate "normal" social situations. This determines the specifications for the milieu structure and operational rules (see Table 20-2).

The therapeutic community has an open-door policy. Locked wards do not provide the right setting for the sense of self-reliance that is at the heart of the method. The patients assume responsibility not only for their own actions but, in some measure, for those of their fellow patients. Perhaps to a greater degree than might be feasible in the "real" world, peer assessment and open communication are encouraged. Everything done, or not done, by the staff and patients is subject to discussion.

The assumption of responsibility by patients takes with it some of the staff's decision-making authority. In some larger institutions, patient government exercises control over many hospital procedures and activities. With the dismantling of the hierarchical system, the staff may find it difficult to adjust to having less

Table 20-2	Milieu Therapy Requirements

Facilities
  Open-door wards
  Noninstitutional decor and furniture
    arrangements
Personnel
  Attendants trained in milieu techniques
  High staff-to-patient ratio
Authority
  Nonhierarchical organization
  Patient government (maximum feasible)
  Democratic decision making
  Ward-staff initiative and autonomy
Relationships
  Staff interaction with patients
  Mutual responsibility among patients

than absolute control. However, it is necessary that the patients learn how to make sound decisions, since the inability to do so is one of their basic problems. Ideally, the relationship between staff and patients should reflect mutual trust and respect, not competition for power. The staff's function is neither authoritarian nor indifferent, but rather highly interactive and educational. They are an integral part of the therapeutic community.

The trend toward shorter hospitalization imposes requirements for treatment speed-up, which may call for intensive involvement of the patient's family in the milieu therapy program. The most critical problems must be corrected so that the patients can return to their families to complete the therapy, possibly working with an auxiliary outpatient program. While it is impossible to duplicate a real-world society in the hospital, the patients' interactions should be designed to teach them how to deal with their impulses and feelings in socially acceptable and effective ways. Complications arise when patients return to a community whose values are different from those they observed in the therapeutic community. (Recall our discussion of the harmful effects of distorted social values as possible causes of abnormal behavior.)

Institutional Crisis Intervention Units

These are the psychiatric equivalent of the medical intensive care units. Patients are admitted with acute symptoms precipitated by a life crisis. The objective of crisis intervention is to prevent the patient's regression into maladaptive behaviors in response to extreme stress.

Treatment is addressed mainly to the disturbed behaviors, which are suppressed with medication. Because of the brief contact time of such interventions, deeper therapy cannot be undertaken. An evaluation is made to determine the patient's need for hospitalization, family therapy, or other service. Some critics feel that the pressures to prevent hospitalization operate to discourage clinicians from recommending commitment for long-term therapy, resulting in too much reliance on superficial crisis treatment that leaves the underlying, possibly chronic, problem untouched.

Problems of Chronicity

Some hard-core psychiatric patients resist all therapeutic efforts and remain unimproved. When their behaviors are assaultive, extremely regressed, or incompetent, they cannot be discharged. In other cases, patients who have responded favorably to behavior modification (token economy and other programs) may relapse some time after discharge and return as chronic rejects from a society that has no place for them outside the institution. Is custodial care the end of the line for them?

We noted previously the recent court rulings that state that all patients have the "right to treatment." These rulings pose problems when therapy does not help chronic patients. Some reasonable means of determining adequate care for such patients must be developed.

Behavioral Approaches in Acute Wards

In our previous discussions of milieu therapy and token economy (Chapters 7 and 11), we noted their application to chronic, long-term patients. These and other behavioral techniques have also been used with some success in the treatment of acute cases. Here their purpose is to minimize length of hospitalization and avoid the trap of custodial care.

The token economy is one form of milieu therapy in which definite, tangible rewards are given to reinforce or shape specific behaviors. Both types of program take as their objectives the control of behavior within socially acceptable limits and the teaching of social skills. Milieu therapy accomplishes this through feedback from peers and staff in interactive exchanges. The token economy changes behavior by rewarding desirable responses and punishing (by fines or time-out) undesirable behaviors. Thorough staff training is necessary to prevent sabotage of the program when the prescribed treatment is not in agreement with the staff's notions of what is "really" wrong with each patient.

In line with the behavioral view of target symptoms as the proper object of treatment, there has developed a problem-oriented approach to abnormal behavior. The diagnostic procedure starts with a dissection of the problem into specific, identifiable behaviors. This then presents a practical basis for direct application of corrective measures to each well-defined problem. In one case example (Kass, Silvers, and Abroms, 1972), five young women were diagnosed as hysterical personalities, which was defined as a complex of specific behaviors including tantrums, suicidal threats, somatic complaints, and suppression of communication. Each of the maladaptive behaviors was dealt with by a system of granting or withdrawing privileges for appropriate or inappropriate behavior in following a prescribed daily schedule of social activity.

The problem-oriented approach is also applied in individual treatment. Depressions and somatic complaints—two of the most frequent presenting disorders—have been treated by the same types of contingent reinforcement (tokens, privileges, and fines) as in group programs. Patients diagnosed as psychotic depressives had their condition broken down into talking, smiling, and other motor activity. The positive behaviors were then reinforced while the negative ones were ignored. Similarly, in the case of somatic complaints, the patient's references to aches and pains were ignored while attention was given to the patient's other communications, which were encouraged. The somatic complaints, and the accompanying drug taking, were reduced to acceptable levels (Agras, 1976).

Similar behavioral techniques, both individual and in milieu groups, have been used in treating phobias, obsessive-compulsive neuroses, and anxiety reactions. In the acute cases, the programs are designed to speed the patient's return to the community, where the procedures can be continued, on a modified basis, by the patient's family. For this reason, the family is often involved in training programs, which we will discuss in the following section.

Return to the Community and Aftercare

More important than getting out of the hospital is staying out. With this objective in mind, some of the most significant innovations are emerging from current approaches to aftercare. Hertz (1976) defines aftercare as "the total treatment program for the psychiatric patient after his discharge from the hospital" (p. 228).

One measure of the need for adequate aftercare and the inadequacy of current services is the high return rate among discharged psychiatric patients. Wren (1973) describes the "revolving door" syndrome, citing the record of readmission within six months of their release of 28 percent of patients discharged from New York State mental hospitals. It is expected that 50 percent of discharged patients will eventually be readmitted.

The growing practice of turning patients out into the community more rapidly tends to increase rates of return while reducing or limiting mental hospital populations. The problem lies in the lack of community aftercare resources prepared to maintain the improvement the patient may have made in the hospital program.

Predischarge planning is an essential step in the rehabilitation process. It begins soon after admission to the hospital. The patients are told that they will return to their community as soon as possible. They are then helped to look upon their treatment as limited in duration and eventually to give up their dependence on the hospital and staff.

The transition period is critical. Liberman (1971) adapted the milieu setting in the hospital to approximate more closely the outside situation, so that patients would become adjusted to community living.

Current emphasis on preventing or minimizing hospitalization points up the important services performed by special, limited-function hospitals. These include institutions that provide partial hospitalization, notably the *day hospital*. Designed for the patient who requires daily treatment but can be taken care of at home during the night, the day hospital relieves the full-time hospital of a large segment of its potential population. The day hospital permits earlier discharge of partially recovered or chronic patients who need regular therapy without residence or "round-the-clock" supervision. Day programs include family therapy, group sessions, electroshock, and other somatic therapies.

Living outside the hospital is another key aspect of effective aftercare. We can only guess how many chronic patients remain in the hospital because neither their families nor the community has a place where they can live. This is especially true for patients who are not ready for full assumption of social roles and responsibilities.

Although the family is the natural refuge for the patient, financial or interpersonal problems may rule against his or her return. In such cases, the patient may go to a *halfway house*. This is a homelike establishment that provides professional supervision and readjustment help in a "family" setting for patients returning to the community. Residents enjoy the reassurance of a supportive, therapeutic environment while they get used to social and vocational activities. The principal advantage of a halfway house is its family-like atmosphere, without the familiar conflicts and hostilities that divide many families. The location in a residential neighborhood brings the residents (not "patients") into contact with the community and gives them progressive experience with social requirements.

The halfway house is in a state of development motivated by the enthusiasm of those who have worked with it. It has attracted the cooperation of college undergraduates, like those at Harvard and Radcliffe, who have established a halfway house in which students share residence with ex-patients (Greenblatt and Kantor, 1962). Another development is the use of a halfway house in predischarge programs. Brooklyn State Hospital (New York City) has a halfway house on the hospital grounds for patients who are preparing for their return to their communities.

Family care placement is the closest approach to care by the patient's own family, when the patient's family is unavailable or cannot provide a harmonious environment. Placement of the ex-patient in a healthy foster family provides the benefits of normal family life. In addition to family placement of psychiatric patients, many mental retardates are permanently accommodated in such settings. This valuable aftercare resource can be expanded to assume a far greater share of the patient load, with maximum benefits to individuals who would otherwise be condemned to permanent institutionalization.

Outpatient hospital services are a traditional means of continuing to provide the patient with therapy. They enable the professional staff to check and support the patient's progress and to determine whether regression warrants readmittance.

Professional care outside the hospital serves a particularly important aftercare function for patients with more severe disorders, such as the psychoses (including schizophrenics in remission). Psychiatric clinics operate group programs in which 10 to 20 ex-patients attend 60- to 90-minute sessions several times a week. One of the services of the clinic is to continue necessary therapy, which may include medication. Patients who continue to attend such clinics show lower readmission rates than those who abandon therapy upon discharge from the hospital.

Social clubs are a kind of self-help, aftercare resource. In general, the clubs are non-structured organizations that engage in varied social activities: discussion groups, outings, movies, sports, hobbies, and crafts. The members provide mutual support and a sense of "belonging," which are vitally important. Furthermore, they provide an awareness that others have similar problems. Some clubs have experienced difficulty in retaining the more competent members to balance the numbers of the less competent. A comparatively new development in aftercare resources, the social club shows excellent prospects for success in keeping ex-patients in the community.

Emerging Approaches to Community Mental Health

Clinical-Community Intervention

The clinical-community model (see Korchin's framework, Table 20-1) views the individual's abnormal behavior in the context of social interaction. (We discussed the social context dimension in Chapter 19.) The psychosocial interpretation of the behavior as a product of social interactions leads to the design of treatments based on those interactions and, logically, to the use of the social environment (that is, the community) as the instrument for therapy. Korchin's framework notes the community resources and professional roles that operate when intervention is called for. We will now consider these community services for mental health.

Community Mental Health Services

The movement toward the treatment of mental health problems on the community level received its major impetus from the passage of the Mental Health Studies Act of 1955. With this legislation, the federal government for the first time assumed responsibility for doing something about abnormal behavior. From studies supported by that act came the incentive for the Community Mental Health

Centers Act of 1963, which established the concept of community responsibility for the delivery of mental health services.

At the heart of the program is the *community mental health center.* Operated under the joint authority of the advisory board and the professionals, the center may be associated with a hospital or an academic institution. It is responsible for developing and supervising the program of mental health services, which are funded by the National Institute of Mental Health (in the Department of Health, Education and Welfare—HEW).

A comprehensive community mental health program is composed of five essential services: inpatient, outpatient, and emergency care, partial hospitalization, and education and consultation programs. Ideally, a community advisory board works with the mental health professionals in setting up the program.

Briefly, this is how the five essential services are implemented (Weston, 1975):

Inpatient services are performed in a mental hospital, which may be a part of a regular medical hospital when separate facilities are not available.

Partial hospitalization embraces both inpatient and outpatient services. Day hospitals generally serve this limited function. In some communities, the day hospital shares facilities with the regular inpatient hospital.

Outpatient services play a large role in community programs. They may involve group therapy, the use of paraprofessionals, and even activities outside the clinic (store-front centers, mobile units, community volunteers).

Emergency care applies crisis intervention techniques as an alternative to hospitalization, as we discussed earlier. The service is available on a round-the-clock basis.

Consultation and education are directed toward prevention of psychological problems and also toward the education of the community to its obligations and opportunities for helping its members who have psychological problems. Various community agencies are brought into the program: police, social services, schools, clergy. Through them, the mental health professionals generate support for

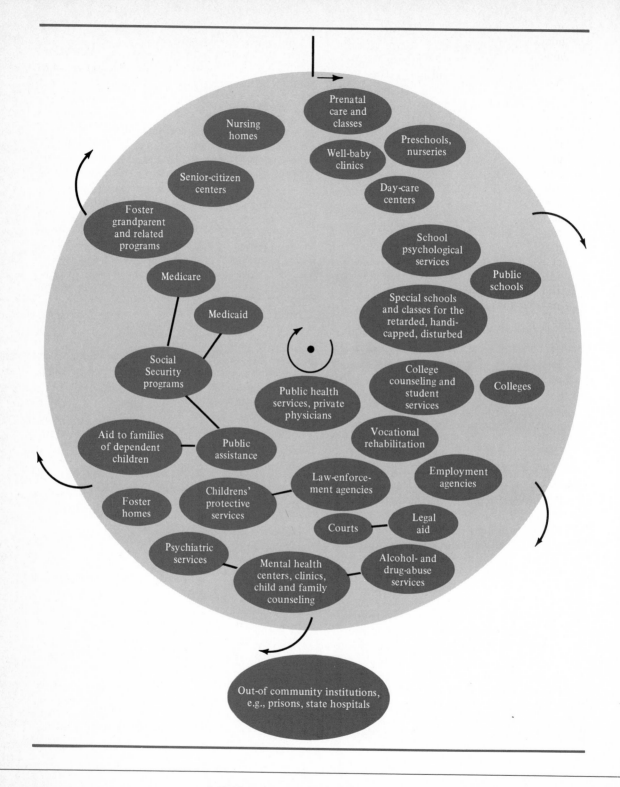

new programs. Educational lectures before community groups and seminars for interested individuals are conducted by the center's staff.

Occasionally, explosive community pressures in this highly sensitive area of social action disrupt the best-laid plans of well-intentioned professionals. This is a natural consequence of the interaction of the diverse interests, purposes, and attitudes that comprise the fabric of the community. We will not explore here the complex structure and dynamics of the community, but will merely observe the interaction of the community's mental health services with each other and with the individual citizen. Figure 20-1 is a visualization of the impact of the community's agencies on the individual as he or she moves through life (starting with birth at "12 o'clock" and proceeding clockwise). Notice the relationships between mental health and other agencies. This picture will give you an idea of the problems faced by the community's mental health professionals in developing and fitting their programs into the complex network of services.

Crisis Intervention in Community Clinics

We can distinguish between two kinds of crises: (1) the normal, landmark events in the human developmental process (discussed in Chapter 19), which contribute to healthy maturation when the individual responds with proper adaptation; and (2) extremely stressful events that present a massive threat to the individual's ability to function, and overwhelm his or her coping resources (Korchin, 1976). Crises, by their nature, are self-limiting, but if not wholly resolved, tend to return under similar circumstances. Prompt treatment can prevent maladaptive responses from becoming fixed into behavior patterns that interfere with good social relations.

Crisis intervention is basically short-term treatment. Its immediate goals are (1) relief of the critical behavioral manifestations, (2) restoration of previous functioning, (3) guidance to the client in finding and using community resources, (4) relating of the present crisis to earlier problems, and (5) development of personal attitudes and coping techniques to deal with future crises. To accomplish these objectives, a special clinical facility is needed in the community at the point where crises occur.

Being close to the community implies not only geographical nearness to the neighborhood but staffing by people familiar with and to the community (same ethnic background, same language). Service must be available immediately on a walk-in basis, without the red tape of admission procedures or the requirement of financial capacity to afford treatment. These imperatives have given impetus to the free clinic movement.

The free clinic, offering no-fee services for the treatment of life-stress disorders, drug abuse, and medical problems, emerged from the counterculture movement of the 1960s. It started as a self-help response to the failure of the "establishment" to provide sympathetic, freely available health services to the poor and the alienated segments of society. Early clinics were and, to an extent, still are run by nonprofessional, neighborhood people. Their activities range from professional counseling to informal "rap sessions," which are a form of mutual group therapy whose effectiveness for the individuals comes from the sharing of practical experiences with common problems.

The initial assessment of the problem presented may indicate a referral to other agencies (family counseling, social services, police, senior citizens agencies, drug treatment centers, etc.). Advice and guidance are given when the problem requires the use of community services other than psychological.

Short-term psychological treatment deals primarily with the disordered behaviors. The focus is placed on the precipitating factors, rather than on the early, unconscious conflicts and intrapsychic disorders. The therapist's

Figure 20-1 (Opposite page) "Community clock" of services through the life cycle. (*Sundberg, N. D., Tyler, L. E., and Taplin, J. R. Clinical psychology: Expanding horizons, 2nd ed., New York: Prentice-Hall (ACC), 1973, p. 422. © 1973. Reprinted by permission of Prentice-Hall, Inc.*)

The belief that behavior is a product of social interaction logically leads to the use of the community as the instrument for therapy. Pictured here is a community mental health center. (*George W. Gardner.*)

mode is more active and directive. He or she quickly determines the client's coping resources and tries to bring them into play in terms of the immediate crisis. The object is to induce the client's active participation in the restoration of psychological stability. Since the crisis client is in a weakened, vulnerable state, he or she tends to look to the professional expert for a magical cure, and will fall into a passive, expectant posture. This can lead to his

or her complete dependency on the therapist, which is incompatible with brief crisis intervention.

Some conditions are amenable to "crash" techniques: depressive reactions, acute psychotic episodes, panic reactions, hysteria, grief, aftermath of sexual attack, acute psychophysiologic disorders. Short-term crisis techniques are not appropriate for obsessive or phobic neuroses, schizophrenic psychosis, endogenous depression, and most chronic pathologies. When any of these are background problems in the crisis situation, referral is made to long-term psychiatric facilities.

A special type of emergency is created by the ultimate crisis: the suicidal impulse. In Chapter 12, we discussed the nature of this crisis and the special resources necessary to deal with the problem.

Some of the tactics of the crisis therapist are basic to all psychotherapy. Others are motivated by the special aspects of the crisis situation, including the availability of only partial information for assessment. (Often the therapy must start immediately and proceed along with the assessment interview.) The key tactics employed by the therapist are summarized in Box 20-1.

Community Consultation

Mental health consultation involves two parties, the consultant and the consultee (who may be an individual or a group). Both are professionals. The consultees may be physicians (general practitioners or specialists), medical administrators, nurses, lawyers, teachers, members of the clergy, social workers, or police officers. In their work, consultees encounter problems with psychological aspects but they do not have the knowledge or experience necessary to deal with such problems.

In providing advice and guidance, the consultant engages in *indirect* activity instead of *direct* therapy. The consultative function is generally an educational one. It is the consultant's purpose to make current information, derived from various sources and personal experiences, available to consultees. This is what makes the consultation a community service. The consultant's effective reach is extended throughout the community by the consultees in their various roles in the community service network.

Four types of consultation have been defined (Caplan, 1970): (1) Client-centered case consultation, in which the consultant advises the best method of dealing with the client's particular problem. This is analogous to the general practitioner's consultation of a medical

---

Box 20-1 Crisis Therapy Tactics

In crisis therapy, the therapist must:

1. Offer emotional support with a show of sensitivity and acceptance.

2. Provide opportunity for catharsis (release) through free expression of intense emotions.

3. Communicate hope and optimism by reassurance without guarantee.

4. Be actively involved, to set a model of positive action for the client.

5. Listen selectively for pertinent material for assessment.

6. Provide factual information about the client's condition to correct misconceptions, and provide interpretations and feedback.

7. Formulate the problem in terms of precipitating factors, background problems, and available coping mechanisms.

8. Advise and suggest suitable attitudes and actions to be taken by the client.

9. Set limits to acting-out behavior.

10. Identify and reinforce adaptive mechanisms, mobilizing the client's coping resources.

11. Confront the client with challenges to faulty ideas and maladaptive behaviors.

12. Make concrete demands for the performance of specific tasks, to engage the client actively in working out his or her problems.

13. Work out a contract that states clearly the treatment objectives and behavior changes to be undertaken by the client.

14. Terminate the session abruptly if the client is unreceptive, suggesting a subsequent appointment when he or she is ready to cooperate.

15. Enlist the aid of significant others to deal with economic, social, vocational, and familial aspects of the problem.[1]

---

[1]A more detailed discussion of these tactics is presented in J. N. Butcher and G. R. Maudal's review (1976) (Crisis intervention. In I. B. Weiner (Ed.), *Clinical methods in psychology*, New York: Wiley) of crisis intervention procedures.

specialist about a particular patient. (2) Consultee-centered case consultation, in which the consultant deals with the consultee's own lack of objectivity or knowledge in handling his or her client. This involves education of the consultee, improvement of his or her knowledge and skills, and change of his or her approach to the client's problem. (3) Program-centered administrative consultation, in which the areas of interest are planning and administration. This may involve a critique of existing programs and suggestions for modification of plans now under consideration. Mental health consultants may find themselves advising the medical staff on services to patients, to assure that medical personnel and hospital milieu are responsive to patients' psychological needs and personal problems. Their counseling may relate to selection and training of ward personnel with a view to instilling enlightened attitudes about the effects of the institutional environment on the patients' response to medical treatment. (4) Consultee-centered administrative consultation, in which the consultant aids with administrative problems interfering with program development and implementation. The problems may be the result of authority overlap, faulty organization, communication blocks, and similar handicaps to efficient operation.

The consultative process comprises a series of stages, which must be negotiated with care and understanding in view of the sensitive nature of the consultant-consultee relationship (Caplan, 1970). At the point of *entry*, the relationship is established—its objectives (statement of the problem) and its limits. This is done by explicit, though not necessarily formal, contract. *Definition* of the problem is the next step, but the initial definition is subject to modification as the study proceeds (the *diagnosis* stage). *Analysis* develops alternative actions in appropriate terms (cost-benefit, etc.). *Dispelling interference* to action is a delicate matter, since the consultant is barred from dealing directly with the consultee's personal attitudes and shortcomings, and from becoming involved in institutional politics. The consultant must use the leverage of his or her objectivity and professional status to get around such barriers to action. *Termination* is often a matter of judgment, since treatment of the original problem may have uncovered other issues that make the continuation of consultation desirable.

Use of Nonprofessionals

We have referred several times to the great discrepancy between the number of mental health professionals and the vast population of clients and potential clients with neglected problems. One of the chief advantages of behavior therapy, we pointed out, is that it can be administered by nonprofessionals who have had minimal training. However, there are many functions that nonprofessionals can perform besides carrying out prescribed behavioral procedures.

When we list the various types of nonprofessional groups that have served well on diverse mental health jobs, we are struck by how these human resources are unused or underused. They include volunteers (students, delinquents, ex-drug users), enlisted aides (patients, family), career paraprofessionals (psychiatric and social service workers), and professionals in other fields (clergy, physicians, public health nurses, teachers, and guidance counselors). Those in the first three groups generally participate as aides to clinicians in programs designed to prepare difficult patients for therapy (the so-called "softening up" process), to apply prescribed therapeutic procedures, and to work with those at risk in preventive activities (e.g., as companions to young people in difficulty). Those in the fourth group are in strategic positions to detect people with problems or in danger of developing them. They may make referrals for psychological evaluation, or they may call for professional consultation (see previous section).

Nonprofessional workers offer important values in the field of mental health. First and foremost, their numbers and their willingness to work within limited budgets (especially the volunteers, who work for nothing) make it feasible to serve the mental health needs of the poor and the powerless, whose problems are severe but who are usually deprived of adequate preventive and aftercare services. The nonprofessionals bring a fresh view to old problems, a flexible attitude that is not locked into narrow conceptions of what is needed and what will work, and a willingness to try unorthodox approaches in baffling situations. Unlike many professionals, the volunteers have a commitment that manifests itself in a sincere interest in the client's daily concerns and feelings. This warm interest is not lost on clients who are used to being treated indifferently as staff burdens or experimental subjects.

A sampling of programs implemented with nonprofessionals presents a fair estimate of their use, effectiveness, and shortcomings. The Harlem Hospital Center paraprofessional program (Christmas, Wallace, and Edwards, 1973) is a good example of a comprehensive undertaking, involving selection, training, and employment of "outsiders."

The Harlem paraprofessional program was part of a broad-gauged, community-oriented, sociopsychiatric approach to mental health problems in an inner-city ghetto. Applicants (over age 30) drawn from the community were interviewed for positions as psychiatric rehabilitation trainees. In-service training was geared to the background and learning styles of the participants, using a variety of techniques, including field trips, role-playing, interaction groups, and team teaching. The program was designed to attack mental health disabilities with a wide range of interventions aimed at social, psychological, educational, and vocational activities, employing individual and group services. The paraprofessionals have established themselves as a productive and versatile resource, prepared not only to serve the rehabilitative needs of their clients, but to engage in public campaigns as community activists fighting for better mental health services.

Another type of nonprofessional program uses nonpaid volunteers. The Harvard-Radcliffe Program is a model of volunteer services, in which 2,000 college students performed varied functions in the Metropolitan State Hospital in Boston (Rappaport, Chinsky, and Cowen, 1971). The students were involved in companionship activities with adult and child patients, efforts to improve the physical appearance of facilities, communal living in halfway houses, and several educational programs. Two measures of their effectiveness were (1) less behavioral withdrawal among student-attended patients and (2) a 37 percent discharge rate (compared with a 3 percent hospital discharge rate).

The range of sociopsychological problems to which nonprofessionals have been assigned covers most of the diagnostic categories, including depressive neurosis, schizophrenia (one study showed that chronic schizophrenics benefited *more* from untrained students' verbal and social interaction than from professional therapy!), drug abuse, and delinquency.

Public Health—Community Intervention

Our attention now shifts from individual clients to high-risk populations that produce individual casualties unless preventive measures are taken. These measures and their objectives come under the community public health model in Korchin's framework (Table 20-1). Some of the issues have been discussed in Chapter 7 and in other chapters relating to the detection and treatment of specific abnormal behaviors. We will mention them here to show how they fit into the public health approach. For case and treatment details, you may refer to the earlier discussions.

Prevention

Preventive intervention can be applied at any of three times in the development of abnormal behavior. *Primary prevention* is undertaken before the onset of the behavior. This is total prevention since the efforts are directed toward removing or correcting the conditions that are potential causes of abnormal behavior. *Secondary prevention* is aimed at early detection of beginning abnormal behaviors, in order to take steps that will minimize the duration or seriousness of the condition and prevent its development into a chronic disability. *Tertiary prevention* uses therapeutic intervention to reduce the harmful effects of the fully developed disorder and to rehabilitate the client. Here prevention is directed toward reducing the incapacitating consequences of the abnormal behavior.

Primary prevention appears as a noble conception whose inspiring assumptions promote exaggerated expectations. Among the assumptions are these (Caplan, 1964): (1) lack of provision for the individual's physical, psychosocial, and sociocultural needs causes maladaptive behaviors; (2) environmental deficits influence the course of development of genetically predisposed conditions (e.g., schizophrenia); (3) correction of environmental deprivations and personal malfunctions will avoid psychological problems. Disappointing results have emerged not because the assumptions are wrong, but because they tend to be applied with more faith than science.

In the area of genetic factors, biochemical manipulation has achieved success in preventing the mental retardation that results from PKU and thyroid deficiency (see Chapter 16). Ongoing investigations now seek similar biochemical imbalances in schizophrenia (see Chapter 11).

Environmental manipulation proceeds on three levels: the society, the community, and the family. Korchin's framework (Table 20-1) identifies these primary preventive activities as the social action model. On the social level, they involve such broad social programs as urban renewal, an end to job discrimination, school desegregation, improved welfare provisions. A large-scale example was President Lyndon Johnson's short-lived "Great Society" program.

On the community level, we find school enrichment programs, collective action groups designed to give power to the powerless, prenatal care for ghetto mothers, and neighborhood facilities for potential delinquents. An important community investment is the program of mental health education, which takes a two-pronged approach (1) to establish better public

attitudes toward abnormal behavior (e.g., greater receptivity to returning patients) and (2) to encourage use of mental health agencies in dealing with family and personal problems.

On the family level, the public health focus is on dealing with family problems in family counseling agencies, pediatric clinics, and parent-teacher associations. On this level also are the peer groups, a powerful force in determining the direction of the child's development, for better or for worse. Work with these groups is directed toward the threat of drug abuse and delinquent behavior.

Secondary prevention centers on early detection and diagnosis of abnormal behaviors. The "early warning system" for public health maintenance is operated by physicians, teachers, members of the clergy, police officers, juvenile court officials, social workers, and the family. Each of these agents is in a strategic position to observe the behavior of young people and to note deviations that warn of trouble. Training in detection of abnormal behavior has become a regular part of the education of practitioners in the medical, teaching, religious, and social work professions. While the detection function of these professionals is essential, it overlooks the considerable numbers of people suffering from psychological problems of varying degree who do not come into professional view. As we pointed out in Chapter 1, a substantial percentage of the population is either in need of psychological attention or is likely to need it at some time. Population screening programs move out into the community to uncover the hidden cases. One of the earliest examples of massive screening occurred in the operation of the Selective Service system during World War II. A large number of males 18 years old or over were subjected to psychiatric examination, and the public was surprised to learn how many of its youth had psychological problems that rendered them unfit for military service. Further evidence of the prevalence of mental disturbance was provided by a study of Westchester County (New York) families, in which 60 percent of the children were found to be in need of mental health intervention (Zusman, 1975).

Crisis intervention is another means of detection that is part of the community's public health detection network. We have discussed this function in some detail previously.

It follows, of course, that large-scale detection programs are of little practical value unless treatment facilities are readily available in the community. Experience has shown that as such services become available, utilization increases. Inadequate mental health center facilities, limited staffing, red tape, and lack of coordinated referral services discourage usage, especially among those who find the services strange and intimidating.

Tertiary prevention encompasses the various therapeutic processes we have discussed in connection with the treatment of various types of abnormal behavior during their active course. Intervention here is pointed toward correction and rehabilitation, using the appropriate psychodynamic, behavioral, and somatic techniques that we have described. Recognizing the shortcomings and risks in institutional care, we reemphasize the significance of predischarge planning and transitional facilities in preparing the patient for the earliest possible return to his or her community.

School-based Programs

Cowen and his co-workers (1975) point to the frequently observed fact that after the family, the school is the most influential social institution during the child's formative years. This places teachers in a strategic position to affect the child's social adjustment. It has been observed that performance in school is both a reflection of the child's personal resources and deficits and an influential factor in determining his or her future performance in academic, vocational, and social activities.

In handling the problems presented by children who experience difficulty in adapting to the demands of the school community, teachers have several options, depending on the intensity and persistence of the behavior. After applying mild classroom discipline, they may look into family situations and enlist parental help (if the parents are ready and able to im-

Box 20-2 Prevention of Abnormal Behavior

Primary prevention	Efforts directed toward removing or correcting the conditions that are potential causes of abnormal behavior.
Secondary prevention	Efforts to detect and treat abnormal behaviors before they become serious problems or develop into chronic disabilities.
Tertiary prevention	Therapeutic intervention to reduce the noxious effects of fully developed disorders and to rehabilitate clients.

prove the home environment); they may invite professional consultation (school psychologist); they may change the classroom environment (transfer the child to another class); or they may send the child to a special class. Since the effects of their choices can mark the child as dysfunctional, with lasting consequences, the least drastic alternative is the preferable one.

It is generally agreed that the child's success or failure patterns in the early school years carry over into later life. And since success and failure in school are measurable in terms of academic achievement, the effects of manipulation of school experiences are clearly observable. "Project Success Environment" (Rollins et al., 1974) shows how effective behavior modification can be in the classroom. Over a period of two years, 730 disadvantaged black students in grades 1–6 in Atlanta schools were treated with positive reinforcements (good conduct or academic behavior rewarded by exchangeable tokens) and extinction (disruptive behavior ignored) in a controlled experiment. From a 100 percent schedule of tangible rewards, the reinforcement contingency was gradually phased to intangible, intermittent rewards. The only difference between the experimental and control groups was the special training in operant techniques given to the experimental teachers. The posttest results showed that the experimental pupils gained in IQ, arithmetic, and general academic achievement scores, with a significant superiority to control pupils. Further, the control teachers, who used mostly punishment, with very little use of positive reinforcers, had a high rate of disruptions (see Figure 20-2). Clearly, proper training of teachers in behavior modification assures successful results in establishing pupil success patterns.

Increasing use of behavior modification has developed radical techniques that might never have been attempted without an understanding of operant reinforcement. For example, Solomon and Wahler (1973) trained sixth-grade students as "therapists" to modify the behavior (decrease problem behaviors, increase appropriate behaviors) of disruptive classmates.

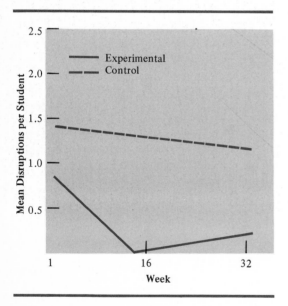

Figure 20-2 Mean number of disruptions by elementary school students over a 32-week period. (*Adapted from Rollins, H. A., et al. Project success environment: An extended application of contingency management in inner-city schools. Journal of* Educational Psychology, 1974, 66, 167–178. © 1974 *by the American Psychological Association. Reprinted by permission.*)

The peers used reinforcement and extinction procedures effectively in accomplishing the experimental objectives.

Police Work

The police are one of the most visible and controversial of the community's social agencies. Their chief function—protection against crime—tends to obscure their positive actions in family crisis intervention. The work of New York City's Family Crisis Intervention (FCI) Unit, described in graphic detail by Sullivan (1973), shows how far the police have come from the strong-arm tactics with which they used to (and in some areas, still do) respond to social deviance.

The FCI unit was set up to deal with the violent family quarrels that occur in ghetto life (note that such incidents also occur at higher socioeconomic levels, although less frequently). From the dismal statistics of intrafamily homicides and assaults on police, it was clear that a better method of handling such situations was necessary. Psychologists with a background in police work were given the assignment of developing a new approach to the problem. Out of their studies came a training program for police officers who were selected for a special unit equipped to respond to family crisis calls.

The police officers have learned how *not* to provoke the threatening, often drunken man or woman into a violent act. They have gained some insight into the frustrations and stresses of ghetto life that generate fierce conflict and violent behavior. Instead of raw discipline, they apply practical psychology in defusing explosive situations. Separating the combatants, relaxing tensions, using reasonable persuasion, and providing face-saving escape routes are part of the FCI unit's "arsenal," replacing guns and nightsticks.

Cooling inflamed tempers is not the end of the job. The police intervention continues through referrals to social service, health, and welfare agencies. It involves the careful reporting of case observations, which serve as data for professional studies. Perhaps the most important value of the FCI unit's work is that it has changed both the police's image in the eyes of the community and the community's image in the eyes of the police. Moreover, it has made the police a more productive element in the community's social resources.

Social Action Approaches

The fifth column in Table 20-1 outlines the elements that make up the social action model of intervention. This approach operates almost entirely at the primary intervention level. Here the focus moves from the individual to the high-risk population, from psychologic disorders to social stresses, and from behavioral dysfunction to the malfunctioning of social systems. In this view, "therapeutic" actions are more likely to be directed toward legislation, the mechanisms of power, and social structures than toward the individual. The psychologist becomes the agent of social change instead of just individual change. Of course, social action offers the ultimate solution to the manpower shortage in therapeutic intervention.

How much substance—in the form of empirical evidence—do we have to back up the social causation thesis? Ryan (1973) gives the pro arguments in a plea for a "universalist" approach to the treatment of psychological problems. He distinguishes this approach from the "exceptionalist" view, which assumes that such problems consist of deviations by individuals who either cannot or will not engage in normal behavior. In spite of our moving away from the medical model of "mental illness" as it affects the individual, we still "blame the victims" for their behavioral failures when we seek the causes in their inherited predisposition or in the defects in their parents' child-rearing practices. Since, according to statistics, low socioeconomic status families are most prone to faulty child rearing, this formulation leads to the indictment of social class as the culprit. Thus the intrapsychic causes are built into the environmental circumstances, which lead to family and milieu therapy without touching the causes implicit in our social sys-

tem itself. Ryan maintains that an "ideological transformation" is required before mental health professionals will deal with the harmful effects of powerlessness, rather than of deficient mothering, on self-esteem.

On the other side of the controversy, Wagenfeld (1972) protests the lack of empirical evidence for the social causation theory. A high correlation between poverty and abnormal behavior does not establish economic deprivation as a causative factor. Similarly, we can acknowledge the harmful effects of racism without, at the same time, including psychopathology among those effects. What seems to be an etiological question may be a problem in delivery of mental health services at lower social levels. The danger in the social causation model, according to Wagenfeld and others, is that its concentration on changing the system offers a promise that overlooks the reality of inherent personality disorders. This promise can lead to eventual disillusionment and disappointment in worthwhile social programs. We have already seen such "backlash" effects when the promised benefits of social welfare and juvenile delinquency programs failed to materialize on schedule.

One overriding conclusion emerges from all of the controversies we have examined: no single model will explain the entire range of deviant human behavior. We need the insights of psychodynamics, the demonstrable results of behavior modification, and the undeniable effects of social systems to account for the many different problems embraced by what we call abnormal psychology. The theory of multiple causation, described in Chapter 4, offers the best basis for a multipronged attack on the various psychological dysfunctions. We would properly implement a program of (1) primary prevention, involving social changes and improvements in education; (2) secondary prevention, involving the coordination of each community's social service agencies with the mental health center; (3) tertiary prevention—or more properly, intervention—involving the provision of hospitalization designed to prepare patients for the earliest possible return to the community via transition and aftercare programs and facilities. Since some stresses seem to be inevitable in modern living, we need to develop individual resistance to them, as we do to pervasive infection by innoculations and vitamins. The little research that has begun on *strens* suggests that people's natural resources can be trained to handle life's crises so that they pass without lasting psychological injury. When necessary, a "booster shot" would be available at the community's crisis intervention center to reinforce one's strens, assuring prompt and unscarred recovery. As in medicine, prevention offers the best hope for raising the level of mental health for the entire population.

Summary

Current treatment approaches can be organized into five intervention models: clinical (custodial, therapeutic), community (clinical, public health), and social action. Their objectives range from changing individual behavior to changing society's institutions and laws. Therapeutic techniques include: self-control techniques, transcendental meditation, primal therapy, transactional analysis, Gestalt therapy, group encounter, est, and strength training (strens versus traumas).

Institutional treatment now makes use of the therapeutic community as the setting for behavioral techniques. Milieu therapy uses the social system as an instrument for treatment. Transition facilities (day hospitals, outpatient clinics, halfway houses) help the patient return to the community faster. Foster homes and social clubs enable ex-patients to survive in the community.

Community resources are used for clinical intervention. The central dispensary for mental health services is the community health center. Crisis intervention aims to minimize the duration and effects of overwhelming stress situations.

Community consultation extends the reach of the mental health professional, who consults with physicians, teachers, social workers, the police, and others who are in a position to detect, and apply recommended treatment to, incipient problems. The professional's intervention is further implemented by nonprofessional, trained aides and field workers, who bring mental health services to the disadvantaged.

Primary prevention attempts to avoid the disorder by correcting the environmental causes. This is the principle that motivates the social action model. School-based programs are designed to establish the student's pattern of success by means of positive reinforcement and extinction techniques, thereby preventing the acquisition of self-defeating attitudes. *Secondary prevention* involves early detection and treatment of beginning conditions, in order to block their development into chronic problems. Crisis intervention belongs in this phase of prevention. *Tertiary prevention* consists of therapeutic intervention to relieve existing disorders. It involves hospitalization, therapy, and aftercare.

Glossary

Abreaction The re-experiencing of an emotional event that occurred at a previous time, as in the recall of a repressed childhood memory.

Acting Out The practice of expressing hostility, frustrations, and anxieties in overt, demonstrative behavior (e.g., tantrums, aggressive and disruptive acts).

Acute Marked by sudden onset and more active behavioral features.

Acute Undifferentiated Schizophrenia A diagnostic category of schizophrenia in which onset is sudden and behaviors are bizarre, but patterns are not clearcut enough for a specific diagnosis.

Adaptation The modification of one's own behavior to suit the requirements of the environment.

Adaptive Behavior Scale A four-level classification of social adaptability according to age level (developed by AAMD).

Adjustment See adaptation.

Affect The emotional reaction or response evoked by stimuli (distinguished from the cognitive, or rational, response).

Affective Disorders A comprehensive classification that comprises a number of disorders—neurotic depression, psychotic depression, manic-depressive psychosis, involutional melancholia—that have a common central symptom: abnormal emotional behavior or mood.

Aftercare The treatment required after discharge from the hospital, to complete the patient's recovery and to maintain him in a satisfactory condition in the community.

Agitated Depression A state of depression marked by a highly animated manner and restless motion. See retarded depression.

Agnosia Loss of ability to recognize objects or people; associated with aphasia.

Agraphia Loss of ability to write; associated with aphasia.

Alcoholism A physiological or psychological dependence on alcohol.

Alliance A cooperative arrangement in which two or more people join in serving mutually compatible interests.

Alpha Waves Electrical activity of the brain that occurs during a state of restfulness.

Amnesia   A general term for loss of memory.

Amniocentesis   An obstetrical procedure in which fluid is extracted from the fetus *in utero* and subjected to tests of genetic factors.

Anal-Sadistic Period (or Stage)   In psychodynamic theory, the developmental period during the child's second and third years, in which the anus—its retentive and excretory functions—is the center of tension and gratification.

Androgens   Male hormones.

Anhedonia   An inability to experience the sensation of pleasure.

Anorexia Nervosa   Loss of appetite due to psychological disturbance or nervous disorder.

Anoxia   Lack of requisite oxygen.

Antabuse (Disulfiram) Therapy   A therapeutic technique for the treatment of alcoholism in which the patient is given a drug (Antabuse) which reacts with alcohol to produce extreme discomfort.

Antecedent Event   See antecedent stimulus.

Antecedent Response   A conditioned response that becomes the stimulus evoking an associated response or behavior.

Antecedent Stimulus   A stimulus marking the time and place for reinforcement. See discriminative stimulus.

Anticipatory Avoidance Learning   A form of therapy in which the subject receives an aversive treatment (e.g., an electric shock) after engaging in some undesirable behavior for a limited time, but he can avoid the aversive treatment by stopping the behavior before the time limit.

Antigen   A substance (usually protein) that, when introduced into the body, stimulates production of antibodies that fight infection or foreign matter.

Antisocial Personality   A style of behavior described as grossly selfish, irresponsible, and callous to the needs, rights, and interests of others; also inclined toward criminal actions and marked by an absence of guilt over wrongdoing. See dyssocial behavior.

Anxiety   A vague sense of dread or apprehension over some uncertain, threatening event.

Anxiety Management Training (AMT)   A therapeutic technique in which the client is trained to respond to the anxiety provoked by certain stimuli ("cues") by immediately engaging in muscle relaxation followed by visualizing a success scene.

Anxiety Relief Conditioning   A general term for therapeutic procedures designed to reduce tension caused by specified stimuli or experiences (e.g., anxiety management training, desensitization).

Aphasia   Loss of ability in comprehension or use of language resulting from brain damage. See organic brain syndrome.

Approach-Avoidance Conflict   A psychological disturbance caused when approach to an attractive object is punished by an aversive stimulus, which induces an avoidance reaction.

Apraxia   Loss of control of motor functions. See organic brain syndrome.

Assertion Training   A behavior therapy technique that develops effective, direct responses to previously intimidating social situations.

Association Areas   Cortical areas adjacent to the primary projection areas in which the primary percepts are combined and integrated into meaningful representations of objects and concepts—the components of cognition and expression.

Asthenic Personality   A personality type characterized by low energy, fatigability, anhedonia, and sensitivity to stress. See neurasthenia.

Ataractic Drugs   A class of tranquilizing drugs.

Attention   A state of alertness in which the cognitive faculties are focused on a selected stimulus or combination of related stimuli in the environment. See cortical arousal.

Attribution Therapy   A technique in which subjects are persuaded to change their view of the location of the cause of their problem (e.g., from an internal to an environmental cause).

Autism   An early childhood disorder marked by virtually complete withdrawal and lack of communication; occasionally a symptom in adult disorders (e.g., schizophrenia).

Autoeroticism   Literally, self-loving—referred to in Freudian terminology as "narcissism," the infantile preoccupation with oneself and one's needs.

Autokinetic Movement   The apparent movement of stationary objects due to fatigue effect on the retina.

Autonomic Nervous System (ANS)   The section of the nervous system, consisting principally of portions of the brain stem and spinal cord, that innervates and regulates the body organs.

Autonomic Response   An automatic, involuntary response or reaction of an organism that is not under the conscious control of the organism.

Aversion Therapy   See aversive conditioning.

Aversive Conditioning   A behavior therapy technique that associates attractive but undesirable stimuli with unpleasant stimuli in order to inhibit undesirable behavior.

Basal Age (BA) An age index associated with intelligence test questions that most people of a given chronological age are capable of answering.

Baseline The level of performance of a target behavior before experimental treatment is administered to modify that behavior.

Behavior The response made by an organism to an external or internal stimulus.

Behavior Modification The change of characteristic or habitual patterns of response to particular situations or impulses by means of operant or respondent conditioning techniques.

Behavior Therapy See behavior modification.

Behavioral Deficit Lack of a behavior or adequate behavioral repertoire to serve one's personal needs or social requirements.

Behaviorism A view of psychology that considers observable or measurable behavior as the only legitimate data for scientific study.

Bestiality See zoophilia.

Beta Waves Electrical activity of the brain that occurs in an alert adult. Associated with problem solving and feelings of tension.

Biochemical Functions The electrochemical reactions involved in the natural processes by which the body organs perform their specific functions. See biophysical functions.

Biofeedback A conditioning technique that develops operant control over autonomic responses by reinforcing the subject's efforts to effect visceral changes with feedback signals when such changes are made observable. See autonomic nervous system, operant conditioning.

Biophysical Functions The processes specific to the various body organs by which they perform their natural functions.

Bipolar-Unipolar Depression A diagnostic distinction based on the differences in certain characteristics of those who suffer both manic and depressive reactions (bipolar) and those who experience only the depressive reaction (unipolar).

Brain Stem The lower portion of the brain adjacent to the spinal cord and containing the mechanisms for arousal and attention, and the cerebellum, a structure that is responsible for many basic body processes.

Cardiovascular System The heart and blood vessels.

Case Study Integration of biographical description of current and past events (case history) with observation, testing, and interview data.

Castration Complex A fear among males of having one's genitals cut off.

Catalepsy A state in which the patient assumes a fixed posture that he holds for extended periods or until someone moves him; sometimes called "waxy flexibility."

Catatonia A condition associated with certain types of schizophrenia in which the patient either moves in a contorted or stereotyped manner, assumes rigidly immobile postures (stuporous state), or engages in wildly excited behavior (manic state).

Catchment Area The geographical area (comprising one or more communities) served by a mental health facility or by a mental health complex (hospital, community clinic, mental health center).

Catecholamines A class of neurotransmitter substances (including epinephrine and norepinephrine).

Catharsis The release or letting out of pent-up emotions or anxieties, generally accomplished through some form of abreaction.

Cathexis In Freudian theory, the investment of psychic energy in an object as a means of gaining gratification or resolving a conflict.

Central Nervous System (CNS) The part of the nervous system that is composed of the brain and spinal cord.

Cerebrovascular Accident (CVA) Commonly known as "stroke," a sudden loss of some brain function as a result of obstruction of a blood vessel causing deprivation of oxygen to brain cells.

Cerebrum The upper portion of the brain consisting of the higher cortical systems responsible for the reception, processing, and storage of sensory information. See central nervous system.

Chaining An operant conditioning procedure in which each successive response in a series serves as reinforcement of its predecessor response thereby developing an extended set of behaviors.

Chromosomes Structures within the germ cells containing the genes.

Chronic Marked by persistent or repeated occurrence.

Chronic Undifferentiated Schizophrenia A deteriorated schizophrenic condition of long duration in which specific symptoms have degenerated into a conglomerate of depressed behaviors.

Classical Conditioning See respondent conditioning

Client-Centered Therapy The nondirective approach to psychotherapy, developed by Carl Rogers, in which the therapist acts as a mirror for the client putting into words the emotions that the patient is experiencing.

Clinical Assessment The analysis and evaluation of the client's history and psychological examination results as the basis for diagnosis.

Clinical Inventory The array of traits, behaviors, interests, and values manifested by the patient.

Clinical Psychologist An academically trained doctor of philosophy or psychiatry (Ph.D. or Psy.D.) skilled in research and clinical methods in the assessment and treatment of abnormal behavior.

Closed Ward A psychiatric ward in which patients are restricted to the ward by locked doors, in contrast to the open ward, where patients are permitted to visit other parts of the hospital and grounds.

Cognitive Dysfunction A deficit, deviation, or failure of mental processes involved in the analysis, storage, and organization of information into logical constructs (i.e., thinking process).

Coitus Sexual intercourse.

Community Mental Health The view that the social context is critical in the development and change of behavior patterns.

Community Reinforcement A form of therapy in which social, familial, and vocational reinforcers are made to be contingent on display of desired behavior.

Compartmentalization The separation of two incompatible aspects of the psyche from one another to prevent the anxiety and disruption of their clashing.

Compensation The ability of the ego to make up for a lack in one area with overachievement in another.

Concordance The occurrence of the same characteristic or condition in two or more family relatives.

Concurrent Validity The correspondence, or correlation, between the results of two different tests of the same variable, where the validity of one of the tests has already been established.

Conditioned Reflex In classical (Pavlovian) conditioning, the learned connection of a response with a stimulus. See respondent conditioning.

Conditioned Stimulus (CS) A stimulus that is administered simultaneously with, or in close proximity to, an unconditioned stimulus (UCS), whose ability to elicit a particular response it then acquires.

Confabulation A disordered style of speech into which the patient injects irrelevant references and invented "facts."

Conjoint Therapy A therapeutic technique involving simultaneous participation of both partners in cases of marital or sexual problems, and of family members in cases of other psychologic disorders.

Conscious In Freudian terms, that part of a person's sensory and cognitive processes of which he is fully aware and which is readily accessible on recall.

Consensual Validation The ability of a number of observers to see and agree on the accuracy of observed measurements or evaluations.

Constellation of Behaviors A group of related behaviors arising from, or associated with, a common source or cause.

Construct Validity The relative correlation between an observed measure and some hypothesized construct, or attribute that cannot be measured directly.

Contingency Management The deliberate control and scheduling of reinforcements contingent on a certain target behavior. See contingency schedule.

Contingent Reinforcement A stimulus (S^R) whose presentation or withdrawal following the emission of an operant response increases the likelihood of the repetition of that response.

Contingency Schedule The pattern of frequency and regularity of reinforcement that is presented upon repeated emission of an operant response (e.g., intermittent, continuous, variable, ratio, interval).

Control (or Control Group) In experimental procedures, a group that is matched with the target group in all critical characteristics but is not given the experimental treatment as a basis for determining the effectiveness of the treatment.

Conversion A psychological process by which a person transforms, or converts, an intolerable response or impulse into a more acceptable one (as in conversion hysteria).

Conversion Hysteria A neurotic reaction involving sensory malfunction (blindness, pain, anesthesia, etc.) and/or disruption of motor function (paralysis, erratic movements) without organic disorder.

Correlation A consistent relation between the respective occurrence, changes, or distribution of two or more variables either parallel (positive correlation) or opposite (negative correlation).

Cortex The upper part of the brain in which the higher perceptual and cognitive processes are performed, including the lobes and association areas.

Cortical Arousal The responsiveness of the central nervous system to external or internal stimuli, usually measured in terms of EEG levels.

Countercathexis In Freudian theory, the application of psychic energy to repress an unacceptable impulse or desire.

Counterconditioning See systematic desensitization.

Countertransference A development in the psychoanalytic relationship in which the therapist experiences an emotional response to the patient.

Coverant Covert mental image or fantasy.

Covert Sensitization A therapeutic technique in which the client imagines the aversive stimuli (unpleasant images or situations), which are associated with an undesirable target behavior. See aversion therapy.

Cretinism A biochemical defect marked by physical malformations and profound mental retardation, caused by a thyroid deficiency in newborn infants.

Crisis Intervention Emergency assessment, guidance and, where indicated, short-term treatment of an abnormal behavior of sudden onset.

Cross-Modal Stimulation (Synesthesia) The apparent perception of a stimulus by a sensory modality other than the one to which the stimulus is directed (e.g., visualizing colors while hearing tones).

Cue A stimulus that is associated with a certain behavior. See conditioned stimulus, discriminative stimulus, unconditioned stimulus.

Cultural-Familial Retardation Nonorganically-based mental retardation. Generally borderline or mildly retarded.

Cunnilingus A technique for inducing sexual excitement in females by stimulating the vagina and clitoris with the tongue.

Cushing's Syndrome An endocrine disorder involving excessive secretion of adrenal hormones.

Cyclothymic Characterized by swings between extremes in mood or behavior (e.g., manic-depressive).

Cyclothymic Personality A personality type characterized by mood swings between depression and elation, with high risk of eventual manic-depressive psychosis.

Day Hospital A type of partial hospitalization that provides treatment for patients who go home each night.

Decompensation The tendency toward disintegration of appropriate patterns of behavior when normal ego defenses are subjected to life stresses, proceeding through increasingly severe reactions: exaggerated use of defenses, neurotic reactions, psychotic reactions.

Defense Mechanism Unconscious ego processes used to control the demands of the id and the superego.

Delirium An acute state of gross mental dysfunction marked by incoherent raving and loss of motor control.

Delirium Tremens A pathological condition resulting from continued, excessive drinking of alcohol, whose prominent symptoms are tremors, spasms, and hallucinations (often composed of "attacks" by animals).

Delusion A belief or conception that is held persistently in the face of contradictory evidence.

Dementia A state of mental disorientation and derangement involving severely impaired intellectual functioning of which the patient is generally unaware.

Dementia Praecox An older term for schizophrenia used to describe a demented or deranged condition occurring earlier than would be attributable to aging.

Denial The refusal to acknowledge unacceptable impulses, unpleasant facts, or undesirable behaviors.

Dependency An exaggerated tendency to look to others for satisfaction of one's needs, occasionally amounting to outright parasitism; may be a mutual reaction in cases of symbiosis.

Dependent Variable A factor or characteristic that is affected in a systematic manner by changes in the value of another factor on which it is dependent. See independent variable.

Depersonalization The blocking or loss of a sense of oneself as a distinct individual; an impersonal, detached view of oneself.

Depersonalization Neurosis A feeling of unreality and loss of sense of personal identity and body awareness, usually experienced in association with other abnormal behaviors.

Depressant A drug that acts to reduce the responsiveness of the central nervous system, thereby slowing speed and degrading control of response.

Depression A state of gloom and general misery accompanied by a feeling of helplessness and hopelessness, and commonly, somatic disturbances. See agitated depression, retarded depression.

Depression (Neurotic) A type of depression which is distinguished by association with precipitating events and absence of sharp mood changes.

Desensitization A general term for behavior therapy techniques that seeks to extinguish anxiety reactions by reducing the client's sensitivity to certain stimuli.

Developmental Period (or Process) The several stages comprising infancy and childhood during which the child develops his perceptual and cognitive skills, as well as his psychic structure (ego, sense of reality, social adaptation, etc.).

Deviation IQ An alternative index of intelligence obtained by computing the standard deviation of all IQ scores at a given age from their mean (as a basis of comparison within each age group).

Diathesis-Stress Model A model of pathology that explains abnormal behavior as a consequence of the interaction between the life stresses and genetic predisposition.

Differential Diagnosis A diagnosis that distinguishes between two clinical conditions that have some symptoms in common.

Diffuse Brain Damage Injured neural tissue involving several areas of the brain; not localized.

Discriminative Stimulus (S^D) A stimulus that marks the time and place for a reinforcement.

Displacement A neurotic process of resolving a frustrated impulse or avoiding a threatening event by transferring it to another object or substituting another response.

Dissociative Hysteria A (neurotic) reaction of consciousness and memory, involving amnesia, hallucinations, loss of personal identity, or other forms of dissociation from reality.

Dissociative Reaction A neurotic reaction characterized by isolation of, or detachment from, mental processes, and marked by such symptoms as amnesia, fugue state, multiple personality, and schizoid behavior.

Dizygotic Twins Twins who come from two different eggs that have been fertilized simultaneously (i.e., fraternal twins).

Dominant Gene One of a pair of genes that will determine the presence of a hereditary trait regardless of whether the other gene is dominant or recessive.

Double Bind A situation in which the child receives contradictory messages from one or both parents that, inescapably, require opposite or conflicting responses.

Double-Blind Method An experimental method in which neither the subject nor the experimenter knows which drug or which treatment is active and which is the placebo.

Down's Syndrome See mongolism.

Drug Addiction Physiological or psychological dependence on a drug.

DSM-II Diagnostic and statistical manual of the American Psychiatric Association published in 1968.

Dyad A pair of individuals who share a formal relationship (mother-child, boss-employee) or are involved in a situational relationship in which they interact with each other (dyadic relationship).

Dysfunction Impairment or disturbance in the functioning of an organ.

Dyslexia Loss (alexia) or impairment (dyslexia) of reading ability, usually associated with aphasia.

Dyspareunia A condition in which pain is felt by the woman during coitus.

Dysphagia Disturbance in eating such as inability to swallow or nauseous reaction to certain foods.

Dyssocial Behavior Antisocial behavior that is not associated with a personality disorder; criminal behavior arising from sociocultural problems (e.g., prostitution, dope peddling).

Echolalia A deviant behavior, characteristic of some autistic children and adult schizophrenics, consisting of repetition of what the other person has just said.

Echopraxia The imitation of movements made by others.

Ecosystem The total environment—physical, social, biological—in which the organism interacts with other organisms inhabiting the system in accordance with their mutual needs and functions.

Educable Retardate A mentally retarded person (with an IQ in the range of approximately 50–70) who can learn academic subjects at some level (e.g., arithmetic, reading, writing), as well as certain higher skills (e.g., mechanical repairs). See trainable retardate.

Ego The psychoanalytic construct referring to the directing mechanism that mediates between the libido's impulse toward instant gratification and the limitations of reality; the individual's means of self-identification and distinction from others in the environment.

Ego Defense See defense mechanism.

Ejaculation Emission of sperm-bearing material from the penis during orgasm.

Ejaculatory Incompetence Inability to achieve orgasm after erection.

Electroconvulsive Shock (ECS) Electric shock applied to the brain through electrodes placed on the temples as a form of therapy for certain types of psychosis.

Electroencephalogram (EEG) A method for measuring and graphing the patterns of various types of brain function by means of the electrical currents generated by neuronal activity.

Electromyogram (EMG) A method for measuring muscular activity by graphing electrical impulses generated by various muscles when they are active.

Electroshock See electroconvulsive shock.

Emotive Imagery Images that evoke emotional reactions, used in controlled associations in behavior therapy.

Empathy The sensing of another person's responses as if they were one's own by projecting oneself into the other person's mind.

Encephalitis An infectious inflammation of neural tissue in the encephalon part of the brain.

Encounter Group See group encounter.

Endocrine System The ductless glands that secrete the chemical substances, principally hormones, involved in various body functions.

Endogenous-Exogenous A distinction applied especially to depression in which *endogenous* describes the condition resulting from internal (i.e., organic) causes, and *exogenous* refers to external, circumstantial factors.

Enuresis Bed-wetting.

Environment The objects, organisms, institutions, and materials that surround the individual in his daily life. See ecosystem.

Epidemiology The study of the occurrence and distribution of illnesses and other problems in relation to population and environmental characteristics associated with their incidence.

Epigenetic Principle A developmental concept that asserts the necessity of making adjustments appropriate to each stage of life in order to develop a sound basis for adjusting to the problems of successive stages.

Epileptic Syndromes (Epilepsy) Disturbances of brain functioning in which spontaneous neural discharges in one area of the brain spread to other areas causing convulsions and loss of consciousness.

Erotogenic (Erogenous) Zones Areas of the body associated with the satisfaction of basic needs and instincts (e.g., mouth, anus, genitals).

EST An acronym for "Erhard Seminars Training," an intensive therapeutic technique that uses a variation of flooding to induce the individual (treated in large groups) to assume responsibility for controlling his own life.

Estrogens Female hormones.

Etiology The history of a disturbance which traces the condition through a sequence of causal and maintaining factors.

Euphoria A sense of well-being and exhilaration.

Evoked Response A response generated in the cortex as a result of the application of a stimulus.

Exhibitionism A compulsion to expose one's body to others.

Existential Neurosis Disorder characterized by feelings of alienation, meaninglessness, and apathy.

Existential Theory A theoretical approach that emphasizes that people must come to terms with their existence or "being" in the world.

Experimental Analogue A laboratory situation set up to duplicate a real-life situation for experimental purposes.

External Validity The degree to which the results of an experimental treatment can be generalized to the population represented by the sample of subjects in the target group. See nomothetic analysis.

Extinction In operant conditioning, the reduction or disappearance of a behavior as a result of continued absence of reinforcement.

Fading A variation of systematic desensitization in which the subject views or imagines a succession of scenes, changing in gradual progression from those evoking extremely undesirable responses, to those evoking less objectionable responses, finally to those exciting the most suitable responses.

Family Dynamics The relationships and interactions among family members whose interpersonal responses reflect their respective needs, goals, and attitudes.

Family Therapy A class of therapeutic programs that focuses principally on family relationships and interactions as they affect the individual members.

Fellatio A technique for inducing sexual excitement in males by stimulating the penis with the mouth, lips, and/or tongue.

Fetishism Sexual gratification focused on objects or body parts other than the genitals.

Fixation A compulsive behavior that is emitted repeatedly without visible external reinforcement. In Freudian theory, a point at which unresolved conflict occurs in the developmental process.

Flat Affect An emotional reaction pattern in which there is virtually no emotion expressed to any stimuli.

Flight of Ideas Rapid succession of ideas, not necessarily in logical order.

Flooding A type of desensitization that exposes the patient to the object, pictures of the object, or the therapist's recital of situations that provoke anxiety, with continuous presentations until the object or situation loses its aversive effect. See implosion therapy.

Focal Lesion Damage to a limited area of the brain (generally referred to as specific *locus* or *site*).

Folie À Deux (À Trois) A situation in which two (or three) members of the same household manifest similar schizophrenic behavior, although only one actually may be a schizophrenic who has imposed his delusional system on the others.

Free Association A technique of psychoanalysis in which the client says whatever comes to mind, without censoring or editing, as a means of evoking repressed thoughts that are linked to conscious thoughts by association.

Free Floating Anxiety Anxiety not associated with any specific, identifiable cause.

Frequency Distribution A tabulation or graphical diagram of the relative frequency of items or members belonging to each of a number of classes or intervals.

Freudian Theory (or Model) An elaborate, formal theory of personality based on the result of the interactions of the ego, id, libido, and superego, and of their conflicts during the successive developmental stages. See developmental period, psychic conflict.

Frigidity Inability of a female to experience orgasm; sometimes limited specifically to inability to generate lubrication of the vaginal walls although able to experience orgasm nonetheless. See orgasmic dysfunction.

Frontal Lobe A cortical area at the front of the brain containing the left and right motor control, speech control, and emotional response centers.

Frustration Tolerance Relative capability for accepting and adjusting to failure to gain satisfaction of one's needs and desires.

Fugue State A form of memory loss (amnesia) in which the victim forgets his identity and the life he has been leading, his other intellectual functions remaining normal.

Functional Analysis First step in operant behavior therapy in which the subject's behavior patterns are broken down into individual components related to situational provocations and reinforcements.

Functional Autonomy The independence of an abnormal behavior from its original cause in which the behavior is maintained by other factors. See etiology.

Gender Identity The self-image of one's sex, established in early childhood.

Gene The units that carry the code for inherited characteristics and join in pairs, one gene from each parent, in the fetus chromosomes.

Generalized Reinforcer Reinforcer such as money or tokens that can be used to reinforce a wide range of behavior.

Genetic Predisposition Innate (i.e., inherited) organic characteristics that make the organism especially sensitive or responsive to certain stimuli resulting in particular behavior patterns or syndromes. See genotype.

Genital Stage In psychodynamic theory, the period when puberty is reached and sexual impulses are reactivated, now centering on responses in the genital area.

Genitalia The genital, or sexual, organs.

Genotype The composition of inherited characteristics carried by the genes. See phenotype.

Germ Cells The sperms in the male and eggs in the female which combine to produce the fetus.

Gestalt Theory A conception of perceptual response that suggests objects are seen as whole forms (i.e., *gestalt*, the German word) rather than as component parts.

Gestalt Therapy Developed by Fritz Perls, a form of psychotherapy aimed at the reintegration of attention and awareness that has been blocked or fragmented in the individual.

Graded Exposure Viewing situations or experiencing stimuli in a sequence in which each successive exposure presents an increasing value or intensity of a particular attribute (or a progressively decreasing value of that attribute) until a maximum (or minimum) value is reached.

Group Encounter A general type of therapy in which people interact with each other in a group setting under professional guidance, as a means of increasing individual awareness of one's responses to others and of their needs.

Halfway House A residential facility, generally located in the community, that provides a partially sheltered therapeutic environment designed to help the patient prepare for return to the community.

Hallucination A fantasy state in which one experiences a realistic sensation of stimuli and events that are not occurring.

Hallucinogen A drug capable of producing hallucinations.

Halo Effect The tendency of observers to judge specific traits or behaviors favorably or unfavorably according to the overall impression given by the subject.

Hawthorne Effect Changes in the behavior of a subject under observation resulting from his awareness that he is being observed.

Hebephrenic Behavior A regression of the individual, marked by childlike behavior, characteristic of a specific type of schizophrenia. See hebephrenic schizophrenia.

Hebephrenic Schizophrenia A form of schizophrenia marked by regression to childhood responses and behaviors.

Hermaphrodite A genetically malformed person whose genitalia share male and female features.

Heterosexuality A preference for sexual activity with members of the opposite sex.

Heterozygous Describing genetic characteristics inherited from only one parent. See genotype.

High-Risk Method A method of studying groups who have high-risk probability as a result of environmental or genetic factors later becoming abnormal.

Homeostasis The inherent function of body processes to maintain a state of equilibrium consistent with the requirements for survival. (In Freudian theory, the functioning of the ego to maintain the integrity and continuity of the organism.)

Homosexuality A preference for sexual activity with members of one's own sex.

Homozygous Describing genetic characteristics inherited from both parents. See gene.

Hormones Chemical substances secreted by the endocrine glands and responsible for the proper functioning of various organs and the conversion of food into forms usable by body cells. See androgens, estrogens.

Humanistic Theory A conception of personality development that focuses on personal actualization and self-direction.

Huntington's Chorea An inherited disease causing degeneration of the central nervous system and marked primarily by erratic movements and twitchings. (Commonly called St. Vitus' Dance.)

Hyperactivity Behavior marked by a high level of

excitement, excessive and disruptive activity, and (in the case of hyperactive children) short attention span.

Hyperphagia Gluttonous eating compulsion.

Hyperventilation A condition in which excess oxygen, beyond current metabolic requirements, is forced into the lungs by rapid, deep breathing (usually under stress).

Hypnosis A trance-like state in which the subject is susceptible to suggestion, particularly in his ideas or responses.

Hypochondriacal Neurosis (Hypochondria) An obsessive preoccupation with body functioning manifested by an excessive concern over real or imagined discomforts and diseases.

Hysterical Neurosis (Hysteria) A general term for a group of neurotic reactions resulting from intense anxiety and marked by blocking or displacement defenses. Specific types include conversion and dissociative hysterias.

Hysterical Personality An emotionally unstable personality type given to histrionic behavior and subject to immature dependency needs.

Id In the Freudian structural conception of the psyche, the representation of the instinctual processes, or drives and, as such, the source of the libido's psychic energy.

Ideas of Reference A delusional belief that other people are talking about, or taking action directed toward, the individual. See delusion.

Idiot Savant An autistic or retarded child who demonstrates exceptional proficiency in a single intellectual skill (e.g., mathematics) but is a functional retardate in other areas.

Illusion Perceptual misinterpretation of sensory stimuli (as in optical illusion). Compare with delusion.

Implosion Therapy A type of desensitization in which the patient is required to imagine the object that provokes his anxiety, fantasizing a continuous series of such images until they lose their power to cause aversive reactions. See flooding.

Impotence Inability of a male to produce and/or maintain an erection of his penis.

Inadequate Personality A personality type that is unable to make effectual responses to social, psychological, and physical demands; marked by incompetence, disinterest, and resentfulness.

Incest Sexual relations between close relatives (e.g., father-daughter, mother-son, brother-sister).

Incidence The number of cases (per thousand people) of a disease or disorder that occurs in a given population during a designated period (usually limited to new occurrences or first admissions).

Independent Variable A factor or characteristic whose changes in value affect the values of other factors (dependent variables) and that can be manipulated by the observer. See dependent variable.

Individuation The process by which the infant distinguishes himself from his mother and the objects in his environment thereby developing his self-identity.

Infantile Autism See autism.

Inhibition The prevention or stopping of an overt or covert response. In the nervous system, the prevention of transmission of a neural impulse at a synapse.

Innervate To provide neuronal paths into a body part, as in the transmission of impulses to the muscles via the motor nerves.

Insight Therapy A general term for psychodynamic therapies that lead the client through an exploration of internal conflicts and fixations, so that he may gain intellectual insight into the nature of his problem, resulting in an emotional catharsis.

Insomnia Inability or difficulty in sleeping.

Instrumental Conditioning See operant conditioning.

Intelligence Quotient (IQ) An index of intellectual ability obtained by dividing the mental age (MA) by the chronological age (CA) and multiplying by 100: $IQ = MA/CA \times 100$. (Also referred to as ratio IQ.)

Internal Validity The ability of a test to predict the occurrence of a characteristic or an event.

Intervention (Therapeutic Intervention) The treatment of a psychological problem by a professional psychotherapist.

Intrapsychic Causes In Freudian theory, the factors that influence or determine abnormal behavior arising from unresolved psychic conflict.

Introjection A process in which an external object or person is "taken in" and identified with the person's own ego; in effect becoming an internalized part of the individual.

Introversion A mode of thinking in which the person is preoccupied with private thoughts focusing on personal concerns.

In Vivo Real-life situations in the field as distinguished from specially structured situations under experimental controls (usually in the laboratory or private office).

Involuntary Nervous System See autonomic nervous system.

Involutional Melancholia A type of depression that occurs during middle or late-middle age and is associated with drastic life changes.

Juvenile Delinquency Criminal behavior by minors.

Kinesthetic Referring to the sense of position and movement of the body parts.

Korsakoff's Syndrome A mental disorder marked by severe impairment of recent memory which the patient attempts to repair by confabulation (i.e., faking the forgotten details by substituting irrelevant earlier memories).

Lability Changability or fluctuation in some personality characteristic, symptom, or behavior.

Latency Period (or Stage) In psychodynamic theory, the period during the child's development when the sexual urges are inactive and quiescent.

Law of Effect The principle that behavior is controlled by its consequences, a basic assumption of operant conditioning.

Learned Behavior Behavior that is acquired and maintained by conditioning processes.

Learned Helplessness A state in which the subject reacts to situations with hopeless passivity as a result of conditioning experiences in which attempted escape or avoidance behavior failed to end an aversive stimulus.

Lesbian Female homosexual.

Libido In Freudian theory, the repository of psychic energy and the mechanism that directs the energy toward desired objects and goals.

Limbic System A group of interrelated brain structures, including portions of the frontal and temporal lobes, the hypothalamus, thalamus, and hippocampus, which control, or are responsive to, emotional stimuli and survival impulses (e.g., fear, hunger, sex).

Lobe Any of the four regions in the cerebrum—frontal, parietal, occipital, and temporal—that contain neural structures involved in processing sensory information and controlling motor responses. See central nervous system, cortex.

Lobotomy Brain surgery performed as a means of relieving intolerable sensations or uncontrollable behaviors.

Logotherapy A form of therapy that seeks to find meaning and purpose in life.

Longitudinal Study A study of a target individual or group that records the stability or change in some characteristic(s) over an extended period (generally, a number of years).

Machismo (Spanish) The combination of attributes commonly associated with extreme masculinity, often used to characterize excessive emphasis on sexual dominance and prowess.

Maladaptive Behavior Responses to social situations and events that are not appropriate or socially acceptable.

Manic-Depressive Psychosis A cyclothymic disorder characterized by extreme mood changes, alternating between manic and depressed states. See depression, psychotic depression, manic reaction.

Manic Reaction (or State) The excited stage of the manic-depressive cycle in which the patient's mood soars to extreme heights of exuberance and frenzied activity.

Manipulative Personality A style of behavior that is directed toward gaining control over others, by deception or skillful persuasion, in order to get them to respond or perform in a desired way.

Masochism A sexual deviation in which the person experiences sexual gratification from receiving painful treatment or personal mortification.

Masturbation Self-stimulation of the genitals to achieve sexual gratification.

Medical Model A view of abnormal behavior that considers its various manifestations as mental illnesses, with a nosology that identifies each mental illness according to a syndrome whose specific symptoms are caused by internal malfunctions that can be isolated and treated.

Meningitis An infectious inflammation of tissues covering the brain (meninges).

Mental Age (MA) A measure of intellectual ability determined by the score obtained on an intelligence test in which credit is given for items answered above the Basal Age level.

Mental Retardation Significantly subaverage, general intellectual functioning existing concurrently with deficits in adaptive behavior and manifested during the developmental period. (AAMD definition.)

Metabolic Dysfunction Faulty functioning of the body's metabolic processes. See metabolism.

Metabolism The biochemical processes by which the body converts the products of digestion into energy forms that can be absorbed and used by the cells.

Metamorphosis Sudden changes in the perceived size of objects; size fluctuation.

Milieu Therapy An institutional therapy technique that organizes the patient's "society" (staff and co-patients) according to rules and procedures that encourage and reinforce appropriate behaviors. Milieu therapy takes place in a "therapeutic community."

Modeling A variation of the conditioning process, in which the individual's behavior is modified by observing someone else's response in that situation.

Mongolism (Down's Syndrome) A genetic brain defect identified with characteristic mongoloid features and mental retardation at severe to profound levels.

Monozygotic Twins Twins who come from the same egg which has been doubly fertilized (i.e., identical twins).

Motor Nerves The nerves that transmit impulses from

the motor cortex in the brain to the various members of the body causing the appropriate muscles to perform desired movements. (Sometimes referred to as *efferent* neurons.)

Multiple Personality Coexistence of two or more relatively independent personalities in the same person as a result of a dissociative reaction.

Mutism The inability or refusal to speak.

Necrophilia A sexual perversion in which the individual achieves orgasm by viewing or copulating with corpses.

Negative Identity Self-identification with beliefs, attitudes, and roles that are contrary to those one has been brought up to accept.

Negative Reinforcement A reinforcing stimuli whose withdrawal or cessation immediately after an operant response increases the probability that the response will recur; not to be confused with punishment. See contingent reinforcement, positive reinforcement.

Nerve A bundle of neurons encased in an insulating sheath.

Neural Impulse (or Nerve Impulse) A pulse of electric current generated in the nerve cells by a chemical process which was initiated by a stimulus applied to a sensory receptor or by a neurotransmitter exciting a nerve ending.

Neurasthenia A general feeling of weakness and fatigue without apparent anxiety or physiological basis.

Neuroanatomy The study of the structure and organization of the brain, spinal cord, and peripheral nervous system. See neurophysiology.

Neuroleptic Drugs A class of psychoactive drugs that operate directly on the transmission function of the nerve synapses to inhibit or facilitate the action of the neurotransmitters; used in treatment of psychosis.

Neuron A nerve cell, the basic component of the nervous system.

Neurophysiology The study of the functions of the various components of the nervous system in terms of the mechanical, electrical, and biochemical processes that accomplish those functions. See neuroanatomy.

Neurotransmitter Substances Chemical agents secreted in the synapses necessary for the transmission of nerve impulses.

Nondemand Performance A form of sex therapy in which the partners engage in various kinds of sexual activity exclusive of coitus and in which erection or orgasm are not required for satisfaction.

Norm In psychology, a standard of performance which is characteristic or typical of the general population. In statistical terms, the mean or average.

Nosology A system for classifying and naming diseases.

Objective Anxiety A feeling of anxiety that is evoked by actual threats in the environment; closely identified with fear of specific, real dangers.

Objective Test A standardized, structured test whose answers (usually true-false or multiple-choice) are scored according to a predetermined formula. See projective test.

Obsessive-Compulsive Neurosis A neurotic disturbance marked by the persistent, continual intrusion of unwanted thoughts and the irresistible impulse to perform certain actions repeatedly.

Obsessive-Compulsive Personality A personality type whose behavioral style is marked by preoccupation with regularity, punctuality, and cleanliness and a persistent effort to meet very high standards, but without the neurotic intensity that prevents efficient living.

Occipital Lobe A cortical area in the lower posterior part of the brain, containing the primary visual projection area.

Oedipal Conflict (or Complex) The male child's desire to enjoy sexual gratification with his mother, an impulse that brings him into competition with his father, leading to the child's fears of castration by his father (according to Freudian theory). The female child's desire to enjoy sexual gratification with her father is called the Electra Complex.

Offender Therapy A program of therapy designed to correct or eliminate law-breaking behavior.

Oligophrenia A neurological defect associated with brain damage and marked by mental retardation.

Onset The point at which the symptoms or behaviors that mark a disorder are first experienced by the patient or observed by others.

Operant Conditioning A method of conditioning in which a behavior emitted by an organism is reinforced (positively or negatively) thereby changing the likelihood that such behavior will be repeated.

Operational Definition A definition of a concept in terms of the operations or manipulations performed by the scientist in investigating the concept.

Oral Fixation A neurotic or deviant behavior involving a regression to the oral stage of development.

Oral Stage (or Period) In psychodynamic theory, the period during the child's first year when satisfaction is obtained primarily from the sucking and eating functions of the mouth.

Organic Brain Syndrome Deficits in orientation, memory, intellect, judgment, and affect resulting from damage or deterioration involving neural tissue in the brain. See agnosia, agraphia, aphasia, dyslexia.

Organic Dysfunction A deficit, deviation, or failure of some mental or body mechanism in the performance of its function as a result of an inherited defect or physiological damage.

Orgasm The culminating stage in the cycle of sexual responses in which rapid, rhythmic contractions occur in the penis and the vagina accompanied by sensations of ecstasy and, in the male, ejaculation of semen.

Orgasmic Dysfunction Inability to experience orgasm or excessive delay in orgasmic response.

Orgasmic Reconditioning A general term for various behavioral techniques designed to reduce negative responses to sexual activity and to promote positive responses at the point at which orgasm would normally occur.

Orienting Reflex The sudden switching of attention to an object in the environment in response to a visible or audible signal projected by that object.

Outcome Research Studies of the effectiveness of psychotherapy.

Overgeneralization The perception of close similarity in stimuli that have only minor attributes in common; grouping objects with remote resemblances into the same category.

Overinclusion Erroneous grouping of unrelated objects on the basis of common properties that are not salient, or critical, in defining the category. See Von Domarus Principle.

Paired Association Task A test of memory and learning in which target words are paired in memorization trials with other words or nonsense syllables (associates). The subject is then asked to recall the target words when the corresponding associates are presented alone.

Pairing A therapeutic technique that associates some pleasurable stimulation with stimuli representing desirable behaviors. See systematic desensitization.

Paralysis Agitans (Parkinson's Disease) A degenerative disease of the brain tissues marked by muscular rigidity and tremors.

Paranoia (Paranoid State) A pattern of behavior (hallucinations, grandiosity, exaggerated suspicions, hostility) associated with the paranoid personality, but not severe or incapacitating enough to be classed as schizophrenic.

Paranoid Personality A personality whose features include hypersensitivity, rigidity, and suspiciousness.

Paranoid Schizophrenia A type of schizophrenia marked by delusions of grandeur and persecution by others, or illusions of being "possessed."

Paraprofessional A trained technician who serves as an aide to a professional clinician.

Parasympathetic Nervous System Part of the autonomic nervous system responsible for controlling dilation of pupils and blood vessels, the pace of the heart, and the activity of the endocrine, digestive, and reproductive systems.

Parenteral Medication Medication administered by injection.

Paresis An organic disorder caused by syphilis, marked by progressive brain deterioration and resulting in speech dysfunction, paralysis, and eventual death.

Parietal Lobe (or Area) A cortical association area at the upper posterior part of the brain between the frontal and occipital lobes.

Parkinson's Disease See paralysis agitans.

Participant-Observer Method An experimental method in which the experimenter becomes an actual participant in the experience he is studying as an observer.

Passive-Aggressive Personality A dependency-prone personality whose frustrated needs are expressed in stubbornness and obstructive tactics.

Pathogen The agent or factor that causes an illness.

Pedophilia A sexual deviation in which children are the objects of sexual interest, ranging from exhibitionistic behavior to child molestation.

Peer Group A social, vocational, or academic group whose members are in the same age-range, at the same educational level, and/or in the same vocation.

Peptic Ulcer Open sore in the mucosa lining of the stomach.

Percept The mental representation into which a perceived stimulus is coded in the primary projection area.

Perseveration The compulsive repetition of the same behavior when it is no longer appropriate.

Personality Disorder Behavioral malfunction of indefinite pattern and origin, not clearly identifiable as a neurosis or psychosis.

Phallic Stage In Freudian theory, the period when the libido is active in the genital area and the Oedipal conflict occurs.

Phenomenological Analysis The study of individual psychological problems based on self-report of subjective views of experiences and on evaluations of one's life.

Phenotype The observable physical and behavioral inherited characteristics of the individual. See genotype.

Phenylketonuria (PKU) A metabolic disorder in° newborn infants marked by unmetabolized protein in the body fluids that, if untreated, attacks the central nervous system, causing mental retardation.

Phobia An irrational, excessive fear of some object or situation. (See the list of phobias in Box 8-2.)

Phrenology The pseudoscience that attempts to relate contours and bumps on the head to specific mental functions as the basis for personality analysis.

Placebo An inert, or neutral, substance or procedure that can relieve the patient's distress or change his behavior through his belief in its active effect on his condition.

Pleasure Center An area in the brain that responds to a stimulus by developing a feeling of satisfaction or exhilaration. See pleasure principle.

Pleasure Principle In Freudian theory, the force that motivates the organism to seek gratification; associated with the id.

Polygenic Hypothesis A genetic explanation for psychosis that ascribes it to the predisposing effect of a combination of genes (polygenes) when the organism is subjected to stresses. See diathesis-stress model.

Positive Reinforcement A reinforcing stimuli whose presentation immediately after an operant response increases the probability that the response will recur. See contingent reinforcement, negative reinforcement.

Precipitating Event An incident or experience that triggers a severe reaction, which may mark the onset of a pathological condition.

Preconscious In Freudian theory, the part of mental processes of which the person is not aware, but which can be brought into consciousness with concentration.

Predictive Validity The high correlation between a variable and some associated attribute or characteristic whose presence is predicted by the value of the variable.

Predisposition An inherent or organic characteristic of the organism that makes a certain response or pattern of behavior likely under specified environmental conditions. See diathesis-stress model.

Premack Principle A behavioral concept based on the fact that low-probability behavior is reinforced, and thereby increased, by association with high-probability behavior.

Premature Ejaculation The early release of semen either before vaginal entry, or before the partner achieves orgasm.

Premorbid Adjustment The relative effectiveness and maturity of an individual's adaptation in social relations and personal crises prior to the onset of a disorder; applied especially to schizophrenia.

Presenting Symptoms The symptoms, or complaints, reported by the patient at the time of the initial clinical interview.

Prevalence The number of cases (sometimes stated as percent of population) of a diagnosed illness under treatment at a given time or during a designated period. Prevalence = incidence + existing cases − discharges.

Primal Therapy A pseudo-Freudian type of therapy that develops a cathartic effect by inducing the client to reexperience traumatic childhood frustrations, thereby resolving the earlier conflicts. See abreaction, catharsis.

Primary Prevention Efforts to prevent the occurrence of disorders before their onset. See secondary prevention, tertiary prevention.

Primary Process In Freudian theory, the immature mode of the child's thinking and reacting in which libidinal energy seeks discharge through immediately available sources of pleasure. See pleasure principle, secondary process.

Primary Projection Areas Cortical areas of the brain in which neural signals from the peripheral sensory receptors are processed into specific percepts (e.g., lines, musical tones).

Process-Reactive Dimension A diagnostic distinction based on time and type of onset. *Process:* early, insidious onset. *Reactive:* sudden onset with no previous history of similar illness. Applied especially to schizophrenia.

Prodrome (Prodromal Phase) The phase in the development of a disorder immediately preceding the manifestation of the active symptoms and during which warning signs may be observed.

Prognosis The expected course and outcome of a disease.

Programmed Instruction A method of presenting information based on operant principles, in which the items are presented in question-and-answer sequences with correct learning reinforced by correct answers.

Projection Attributing one's own attitudes, characteristics, or behavior to another person.

Projective Test An unstructured test that elicits the subject's interpretation or reaction to ambiguous stimuli (usually pictorial), as a means of determining his thought processess, perceptions, and emotional responses. See Rorschach test, Thematic Apperception Test.

Pseudoretardation Functional retardation not resulting from genetic or physiological defects; sometimes applied to retardation motivated by secondary gain for neurotic reasons.

Psyche The Freudian conception of the dynamic system in which the id, libido, ego, and superego interact to satisfy instinctual needs and defend against psychological threats.

Psychiatrist A medical doctor who is specially trained in psychological problems, with particular focus on pathological conditions of the mind.

Psychic Conflict The Freudian concept of conflict centered around the components of the id, superego, and ego.

Psychic Determinism In Freudian theory, the concept of internal causation of all behaviors and reactions by unconscious processes.

Psychic Energy The forces generated by the drives, or

instinctual needs, in their efforts to gain satisfaction. See libido.

Psychoactive Drugs Drugs that affect psychological functions, reactions, and behavior (e.g., neuroleptic drugs, hallucinogens).

Psychoanalysis The orthodox Freudian method of psychotherapy based on the Freudian theory of intrapsychic causes, using techniques such as transference, free association, and abreaction to gain insight into the childhood origins of neurosis. See insight therapy, psychodynamic therapy.

Psychodynamic Theory A conception of personality development that explains all behavior in terms of intrapsychic conflicts and defensive maneuvers; generally based on the Freudian model or a modified version of it.

Psychodynamic Therapy A class of psychotherapeutic approaches that are based, in whole or in part, on the Freudian model of intrapsychic conflict. (Includes psychoanalysis, primal therapy, existential analysis, transactional analysis, and others.)

Psychogenic Of psychological origin, as distinguished from organic causes.

Psychomotor Response The process by which a person's voluntary nervous system motivates and directs his motor controls to activate the muscles required for performing an intended movement. See motor nerves.

Psychopath See antisocial personality.

Psychophysiologic Disorder Physical pathology, or sickness, resulting from excessive psychological response to stress or anxiety. (Sometimes referred to as psychosomatic disorders.)

Psychosis An extreme disruption of mental functioning involving impairment of perceptions, severe alterations of mood, inability to cope with life situations, and a loss of contact with reality.

Psychosurgery Operations performed on the brain to reduce or eliminate undesirable sensations or behaviors. See lobotomy.

Psychotherapy The intervention by a trained therapist using psychological measures to change behavior that is socially unacceptable or to modify responses that are personally disturbing.

Psychotic Depression Severe depression accompanied by delusional, distorted thinking and occasionally by manic mood swings.

Psychotomimetic Literally, mimicking psychosis. Applied to drugs that produce symptoms characteristic of psychosis.

Psychotropic Having an effect on psychological mechanisms and reactions.

Punishment Any unpleasant stimulus that is meant to reduce the probability that the preceding event will recur.

Pyromania An excessive fascination with fires; considered a form of neurosis or fetishism and usually involving a compulsion to set fires.

Rape A violent, forcible sexual act committed on the person of an unwilling victim.

Rape Trauma Syndrome The general pattern of emotional responses and disturbed behaviors manifested by rape victims after the assault.

Rapport Referring to good interpersonal feelings. An important component of psychotherapy.

Rational-Emotive Therapy A therapeutic method that seeks to establish a rational basis for feelings and attitudes by teaching the client to recognize emotional responses that are inappropriate to his real needs and best interests.

Rationalization Interpretation of one's real motives in acceptable terms.

Reaction Formation The transformation of an unconscious, unacceptable impulse into its conscious opposite.

Reality Principle The process by which the ego limits or delays gratification of the id in accordance with external realities. See reality testing, pleasure principle.

Reality Testing In Freudian theory, a function of the ego in which the person initiates behaviors that test the limitations and reinforcements of the environment in the process of learning how to satisfy and constrain his needs. See reality principle.

Recessive Gene One of a pair of genes that will determine a hereditary trait only if the other member of the pair is also recessive.

Recidivism The tendency of a patient or a criminal to repeat his deviant behavior and be reinstitutionalized after discharge from the institution where he was treated or incarcerated.

Reciprocal Inhibition The process by which a new response, which is incompatible with a previous response to a given stimulus, inhibits or extinguishes the previous response. See systematic desensitization.

Referral Questions Questions asked by the referral source (i.e., general practitioner, judge, etc.) when a referral is made for diagnosis and treatment of a client.

Reflex An automatic motor response to a stimulus involving only the lower levels of the nervous system.

Reliability The accuracy, appropriateness, and consistency of instruments or variables used in the measurement of behavior and the consistency in the subject's performance of the behavior. See replicability.

Remission An improved condition in which the critical symptoms of a problem are no longer present; may be partial or complete.

Reparative Response An operant response that is used to compensate or atone for some unconsciously perceived offense; developed as a means of avoiding punishment.

Replicability The ability to obtain the same or consistent results in two experiments designed to test the same variables. See concurrent validity.

Repression In psychoanalytic theory, a process by which unpleasant events or conflicts are blocked from consciousness; the principal cause of neurosis.

Resistance In psychoanalysis, the patient's active blocking, forgetting, or evading the revelation of unpleasant or intolerable early experiences.

Respondent Conditioning Classical, or Pavlovian, conditioning, in which a conditioned stimulus (CS) is associated with an unconditioned stimulus (UCS), imparting to CS the ability to elicit a response previously elicited by UCS.

Response The behavior emitted by an organism when a certain stimulus is presented (in classical conditioning), or in order to gain a desired reinforcement (in operant conditioning). Generally, the behavior of any part of the nervous system reacting to a stimulus.

Response Prevention The prevention of a target behavior by removing the means of performing it.

Retarded Depression A state of depression marked by withdrawal and slowness of movement. See agitated depression.

Reticular Activating System (RAS) (Reticular formation) A structure located in the brain stem, a source of alerting and inhibiting responses that enhance the fine control of higher attentional, cognitive, and motor functions.

Rorschach Test A projective test in which the subject describes what he sees in a series of inkblots, as an indication of his idiosyncratic perceptions.

Runaway Reaction The impulse to run away from home manifested by some children in response to threatening situations.

Sadism A sexual deviation in which the individual derives sexual gratification from inflicting pain on others. See masochism.

Sample A group representative of the population under study.

Schema A way of viewing the world and one's role and relations with others that determines one's attitudes and behaviors.

Schizo-Affective Manifesting some symptoms of schizophrenia with particular focus on emotional responses, notably depression or uncontrolled excitement and anxiety.

Schizoid See schizoid personality.

Schizoid Personality A personality type whose behavioral style is marked by a withdrawn, apathetic manner with persistent fantasizing and inability to cope with stressful emotions, but not developed to the schizophrenic state of personality disintegration.

Schizophrenia A group of psychoses marked by severe thought disturbance which manifests itself in misinterpretation of reality, leading to delusions and hallucinations.

Schizophrenogenic Tending to cause or promote the development of schizophrenia.

Schizotaxia An inherited neural defect that some theories propose as an essential schizophrenogenic factor when the person is exposed to aversive social interaction. See schizotype.

Schizotype A person with a schizotaxic defect who is predisposed to the development of schizophrenia when exposed to aversive social learning experiences. See schizotaxia.

Scoptophilia A form of voyeurism which focuses on genitalia and sexual acts.

Secondary Gain The overt advantage that the neurotic or psychotic person gets from his disorder, in addition to the primary defense against intrapsychic conflict.

Secondary Prevention Efforts directed toward early detection and intervention of incipient abnormal behaviors after onset. See primary prevention, tertiary prevention.

Secondary Process The mode in which the mature ego functions to delay gratification and channel the libido into socially acceptable sources of pleasure. See reality principle, primary process.

Sedatives Drugs used in low doses to decrease the restlessness and instability of rage, anxiety, and emotional stress of crisis situations.

Self-Actualization A humanistic concept of personal identity in which the individual experiences himself fully and without restraint or distortion.

Self-Instruction The covert expression of self-commands to stop or to encourage a target behavior; also the covert restatement of a reaction in a more desirable form. See self-statement.

Self-Monitoring The focusing of attention on a person's own behaviors to detect the onset of target behavior and note its frequency, in order to tally and/or engage in some action designed to modify the behaviors. See self-instruction.

Self-Reinforcement The reinforcement of one's own behavior by tangible rewards or by covert self-statement.

Self-Statement A covert statement made by an individual in anticipation of, or in response to, a target behavior or reaction. See self-instruction, self-reinforcement.

Senescence Biological aging process accompanied by normal decrease in neural function and motor response. See senility.

Senile Dementia Cerebrovascular deterioration causing degeneration of nerve tissue in the brain, with consequent mental dysfunction; associated with aging.

Senility Severely impaired intellectual functions resulting from neural degeneration caused by cerebrovascular deterioration, which is in turn the effect of various diseases; generally associated with old age, but occasionally occurring in young people. See senescence.

Sensate Focus A series of exercises included in Masters and Johnson type sex therapy in which each partner practices caressing and fondling of various parts of the other's body while he or she focuses on the feelings. It is employed in an effort to induce erotic enjoyment of the entire body.

Sensitivity Group See group encounter.

Sensory Deprivation Absence or patterning of stimuli to the senses for an extended period, especially with reference to environmental stimuli during an organism's developmental period.

Sensory Nerves The nerves that transmit sensations of vision, sound, touch, taste, and smell from the sensory perceptors to the appropriate cortical regions that process the signals into percepts. (Sometimes referred to as *afferent* neurons.)

Sensory Receptors Specially formed nerve endings and neural structures (e.g., the retina) that receive sensations from stimuli in the environment or inside the body and convert them into nerve impulses.

Serotonin A neurotransmitter chemical that is found in certain parts of the central nervous system.

Sex Therapy The treatment of sexual dysfunction principally by behavioral techniques of recent development, although psychodynamic techniques, and occasionally combinations of both types, are used.

Sexual Deviation The practice of variant forms of sexual activity other than coitus, or of coitus performed under bizarre circumstances.

Sexual Dysfunction A disorder that interferes with, or prevents, sexual arousal and/or orgasmic response in men and women. (Includes impotence, premature or delayed ejaculation, frigidity, orgasmic dysfunction, vaginismus.)

Sexual Orientation The inclination of a person to prefer sexual activity of a particular type with partners of the same sex (homosexual), the opposite sex (heterosexual), or both sexes (bisexual).

Sexual Orientation Disturbance A DSM-II designation for homosexuals who are disturbed and dissatisfied by their sexual preference for members of the same sex.

Shaping See successive approximation.

Sheltered Workshop A place where the mentally retarded are protected from the usual stresses and strains of work, but still learn a skill.

Shuttle Box A box consisting of two chambers, in one of which an animal may be exposed to an experimental treatment from which he may be allowed to escape into the second chamber.

Significant Other A person who plays an important role in one's life (e.g., parent, teacher, employer).

Skin Conductance The natural property of the skin to conduct electricity between separated electrodes. The level of conductance varies with the amount of moisture exuded in the process of sweating.

Social Action Model A therapeutic approach that focuses on the psychogenic effects of social institutions and standards on the individual, and attempts to eliminate the harmful influences by changing the way social institutions function.

Social Competence Relative ability to adjust to social requirements and to establish effective relationships with others.

Socioeconomic Status (SES) The relative position of a person, family, or group in the social structure and the economic factors (income, property, savings) correlated with that status.

Sociogenic Referring to causal conditions based on sociocultural factors.

Sodomy A sexual deviation usually associated with anal intercourse or bestiality. See zoophilia.

Somatic Referring to the body, as distinguished from the mind or the psyche.

Somnambulism Sleepwalking.

Spinal Cord Comprises the parallel tracts of sensory and motor nerves mounted on the spinal (vertibra) column, connecting the brain and the body.

Standard Deviation A measure of dispersion of data items from the mean, obtained by taking the square root of the variance. (Also called root-mean-square.)

Statutory Rape Sexual intercourse with a minor.

Stereotyped Behavior Behavior that is marked by fixed, artificial patterns, generally exaggerated or inappropriate to the performance of a useful action.

Stimulus Anything that produces a sensation when presented or applied to one of the sensory receptors (retina, skin, ear, etc.).

Stimulus Generalization The organism's performance of a conditioned behavior in response to stimuli that are similar to the originally conditioned stimulus.

Stren A concept defined as the positive, ego-strengthening result of satisfactorily resolved conflicts, as opposed to *trauma*.

Structured Test A test composed of questions requiring specific answers that can be evaluated according to norms or standards. See objective test.

Stupor A state of unconsciousness or complete detachment from which the patient can be aroused briefly.

Sublimation The substitution of a socially acceptable activity for an unacceptable desire or impulse.

Substitutive Reaction A response that the individual emits instead of one that might be more appropriate, but possibly intolerable to him.

Successive Approximation (Shaping) A technique used in operant conditioning in which a progression of behaviors that resemble or approach a desired behavior are successively reinforced until the target behavior is conditioned.

Superego The moralistic governor that demands good behavior through the medium of the ego; also the inspiration for the ego's striving to attain the perfection of the ideal person.

Superstition An operant response that has been immediately followed, and thereby reinforced, by an accidentally occurring, noncontingent event which spirals to greater frequency and more such accidental reinforcement.

Symbiosis (Smybiotic Relation) A relationship in which two dissimilar organisms (animals, humans, etc.) live in close, mutual dependency. In some cases, the dependency is one-sided, moving toward parasitism.

Symptom Substitution The generation of a new symptom by unresolved intrapsychic causes when a previous symptom arising from the same cause is reduced or eliminated.

Synapse The junction of two neurons across which a neural impulse is transmitted from one neuron to the other. See neurotransmitter substances.

Syndrome A combination of symptoms characteristic of a specific illness or psychologic disorder.

Systematic Desensitization A behavioral therapeutic technique that reduces anxiety by associating anxiety-producing stimuli with unconditioned stimuli eliciting responses that are incompatible with the anxiety response. See reciprocal inhibition.

Tarantism Dancing mania during the Middle Ages.

Target Behavior The particular behavior that is the object of an experimental treatment.

Target Group In experimental procedures, the individuals or group to which the experimental treatment is applied. (Sometimes referred to as "proband.")

Teaching Machine A mechanical device that presents programmed instruction materials automatically, and in more sophisticated models, reroutes the student through additional practice material when he gives an incorrect answer.

Temporal Lobes Two cortical areas, symmetrically located at each side of the brain just inside the cranial temples, containing the left and right auditory projection areas. See primary projection areas.

Tertiary Prevention Therapeutic intervention designed to prevent permanent damage or destructive effects of a problem after it has occurred. See primary prevention, secondary prevention.

Test-Retest Reliability The relative consistency, or regularity of target behavior between two or more repetitions of a test.

T-Group See encounter group.

Thematic Apperception Test (TAT) A projective, personality appraisal test in which the subject tells stories about pictures of people in various ambiguous situations, thereby revealing his attitudes, traits, and psychological problems.

Therapeutic Community A therapy technique in which the staff and the patients (or inmates) are organized into a community structure, with procedures designed to reinforce appropriate behaviors and discourage undesirable behaviors. See milieu therapy.

Therapeutic Contract An agreement between the therapist and the client that specifies the goals of the therapy, the time span involved, the therapist's services, the client's activities, etc.

Thought Stopping Interruption or blocking of an undesirable thought or mental image either by self-instruction or by the command of a therapist.

Thought Substitution Interruption of an undesirable thought and substitution of a suitable thought or mental image.

Time-Out A behavior therapy technique that removes the person emitting an undesirable behavior from the ongoing activity for a limited period.

Token Economy An institutional therapy program in which appropriate target behaviors are reinforced with token reinforcers exchangeable for desirable objects and special privileges.

Tolerance The capacity of the body's organs to absorb a drug without critical effects, measured by the quantity of the substance that can be administered before positive or negative effects are observed; also related to capacity to withstand stress and anxiety without abnormal reactions.

Trainable Retardate A mentally retarded person (with an IQ in the range of approximately 25-49) who is unable to learn academic subjects but can acquire simple skills with proper training. See educable retardate.

Trait A predisposition to respond to certain stimuli or

situations with a particular behavior that is characteristic of the individual's personality.

Transactional Analysis A therapeutic method that trains the individual to recognize and adopt mature, complementary "ego states" (i.e., views of one's role) in "transactions" (i.e., interactions) with others.

Transcendental Meditation A technique in which the subject engages in deep meditation as a means of escape from vexing thoughts, thereby relaxing tensions, relieving stresses, and reaching a state of heightened perception.

Transference In psychoanalytic therapy, the development of strong, personal feelings in the client toward the therapist, involving the transfer to the therapist of attitudes previously directed toward significant others in the client's life (e.g., father).

Transsexualism A sexual deviation which consists in a compulsion to live as a member of the opposite sex.

Transvestism A sexual deviation manifested as a compulsive desire to wear clothing of the opposite sex.

Trauma A psychic injury or shock caused by conflict, frustration, or other painful experience. See stren.

Traumatic Neurosis A condition of severe distress, involving personality disorder, precipitated by an extremely stressful event or catastrophe.

Trephining A primitive surgical technique in which a hole is cut in the skull.

Unconditioned Stimulus (UCS) A stimulus that elicits a particular response as a natural function of the organism.

Unconscious In Freudian theory, the inaccessible repository of repressed thoughts and impulses that influence conscious thinking and behavior. See conscious, preconscious.

Undoing A thought or motor act that cancels or nullifies the significance of an unconscious previous thought or act.

Unipolar-Bipolar Distinction A diagnostic distinction that groups those who suffer both manic and depressive reactions under the "bipolar" label and those who suffer only only one of the two reactions under the "unipolar" label. See manic-depressive psychosis.

Unitary Disorder A syndrome whose individual symptoms, or behaviors, may vary among patients, but all of whose variations have a common cause or etiology.

Unsocialized Aggressive Reaction Uncontrolled aggressiveness and destructiveness characteristic of some disturbed adults and juveniles.

Vaginismus A spasm of the muscles around the vaginal entry, making sexual intercourse very painful or impossible.

Variance A statistical measure of dispersion of data items from the mean obtained by taking the average of the squared differences of the items from their mean. See standard deviation.

Vegetative Functions The somatic functions of ingestion, digestion, and excretion.

Verbigeration The senseless repetition of words and phrases characteristic of certain thought disorders.

Viscera Referring to the internal organs of the body.

Vocational Rehabilitation A program of therapy for medical and psychiatric patients, designed to restore normal function through training in manual crafts, and to prepare for jobs in the community.

Voluntary Nervous System The system of nerves that transmits impulses to and from the skeletal muscles enabling the conscious control of movement.

Von Domarus Principle A faulty procedure in deductive reasoning by which objects or concepts are judged identical on the basis of a common property (identity of predicates). See overinclusion.

Voyeurism A sexual deviation in which sexual gratification is obtained from surreptitiously viewing nude members of the opposite sex (usually women).

Waxy Flexibility See catalepsy.

Withdrawal Reaction A pattern of avoidance response to social interaction characterized by detachment, seclusion, and extreme shyness.

Working Through In psychoanalysis, the process of dealing with an area of difficulty until a satisfactory resolution is achieved.

Zoophilia (Bestiality) An excessive, sexual love of animals which involves acts of sex with animals, considered a sexual deviation.

Zygosity The relationship of siblings in a multiple birth with respect to common or separate eggs. See monozygotic twins, dizygotic twins.

Bibliography

Abraham, K. The first pregenital stage of the libido (1916). In *Selected papers on psychoanalysis.* New York: Basic Books, 1960.

Abraham, K. Notes on psychoanalytic investigation and treatment of manic-depressive insanity and allied conditions (1911). In *Selected papers on psychoanalysis.* New York: Basic Books, 1960.

Abraham, K. The psychological relation between sexuality and alcoholism. In *Selected papers of Karl Abraham.* New York: Basic Books, 1960.

Abrams, R. Miscellaneous organic therapies. In A. M. Freedman, H. I. Kaplan, & B. J. Sadock (Eds.), *Comprehensive textbook of psychiatry-II* (Vol. 2, 2nd ed.). Baltimore: Williams & Wilkins, 1975.

Abramson, E. E. A review of behavioural approaches to weight control. *Behaviour Research and Therapy,* 1973, *11,* 547–556.

Abroms, G. F. Persuasion in psychotherapy. *American Journal of Psychiatry,* 1968, *124,* 1214.

Adler, A. *The practice and theory of individual psychology.* London: Routledge & Kegan Paul, 1923.

Adler, A. Individual psychiatry of alcoholic patients. *Journal of Criminal Psychopathology,* 1941, *3,* 74.

Agras, W. S. Behavior modification in the general-hospital psychiatric unit. In H. Leitenberg (Ed.), *Handbook of behavior modification and behavior therapy.* Englewood Cliffs, N. J.: Prentice-Hall, 1976.

Agras, W. S., Chapin, H. N., & Oliveau, D. C. The natural history of phobia. *Archives of General Psychiatry,* 1972, *26,* 315–317.

Alexander, F., & French, T. M. *Psychoanalytic therapy: Principles and application.* New York: The Ronald Press, 1946.

Alexander, F. *Psychosomatic medicine.* New York: Norton, 1950.

Alger, I. Marriage and marital problems. In S. Arieti (Ed.), *American handbook of psychiatry* (Vol. 1, 2nd ed.). New York: Basic Books, 1974. © 1974 by Basic Books, Inc.

American Association on Mental Deficiency. *Manual on terminology and classification in mental retardation* (Rev. ed.). H. J. Grossman (Ed.). (Special Publication Series No. 2, 1973, 11+). Washington, D. C., 1973.

American Psychiatric Association. *Diagnostic and statistical manual of mental disorders* (1st ed.) (DSM-I). Washington, D. C., 1952.

American Psychiatric Association. *Diagnostic and statistical manual of mental disorders* (2nd ed.) (DSM-II). Washington, D. C., 1968.

Amir, M. *Patterns in forcible rape*. Chicago: University of Chicago Press, 1971.

Anastasi, A. *Psychological testing* (3rd ed.). New York: Macmillan, 1968.

Anthony, E. J. The mutative impact of serious mental and physical illness in a parent on family life. *Canadian Psychiatric Association Journal*, 1969, 14, 433–453.

Anthony, E. J. Neurotic disorders. In A. M. Freedman, H. I. Kaplan, & B. J. Sadock (Eds.), *Comprehensive textbook of psychiatry-II* (Vol. 2, 2nd ed.). Baltimore, Md.: Williams & Wilkins, 1975.

Apter, N. S. Bilateral adrenalectomy in chronic schizophrenic patients. *American Journal of Psychiatry*, 1958, 115, 55–59.

Arieti, S. *Interpretation of schizophrenia* (1st ed.). New York: Brunner, 1955.

Arieti, S. Individual psychotherapy of schizophrenia. In S. Arieti & E. B. Brody (Eds.), *American handbook of psychiatry* (Vol. 3, 2nd ed.). New York: Basic Books, 1974(a).

Arieti, S. *Interpretation of schizophrenia* (2nd ed.). New York: Basic Books, 1974.(b) © 1974 by Silvano Arieti, © 1955 by Robert Brunner, Basic Books, Inc.

Arieti, S. An overview of schizophrenia from a predominantly psychological approach. *American Journal of Psychiatry*, 1974, 131, 241–249.(c)

Arieti, S. Schizophrenia: The psychodynamic mechanisms and the psychostructural forms. In S. Arieti & E. B. Brody (Eds.), *American handbook of psychiatry* (Vol. 3, 2nd ed.). New York: Basic Books, 1974.(d)

Ashem, B., & Donner, L. Covert sensitization with alcoholics: A controlled replication. *Behaviour Research and Therapy*, 1968, 6, 7–12.

Asher, R. Respectable hypnosis. *British Medical Journal*, 1956, 1, 309–313.

Atthowe, J. M., Jr., & Krasner, L. Preliminary report on the application of contingent reinforcement procedures (token economy) on a "chronic" psychiatric ward. *Journal of Abnormal Psychology*, 1968, 73, 37–43.

Ayllon, T. Intensive treatment of psychiatric behavior by stimulus control. *Behaviour Research and Therapy*, 1963, 1, 53–61.

Ayllon, T., & Azrin, N. H. *The token economy: A motivational system for therapy and rehabilitation*. Englewood Cliffs, N. J.: Prentice-Hall (ACC), 1968.

Ayllon, T., & Azrin, N. H. The measurement and reinforcement of behavior of psychotics. *Journal of the Experimental Analysis of Behavior*, 1965, 8, 357–383.

Ayllon, T., & Haughton, E. Control of the behavior of schizophrenic patients by food. *Journal of the Experimental Analysis of Behavior*, 1962, 5, 343–352.

Azrin, N. H., & Foxx, R. M. A rapid method of toilet training the institutionalized retarded. *Journal of Applied Behavior Analysis*, 1971, 4, 89–99.

Bachrach, A. J. *Psychological research*. New York: Random House, 1962.

Bachrach, A. J., Erwin, W., & Mohr, J. P. The control of eating behavior in an anorexic by operant conditioning techniques. In L. P. Ullmann & L. Krasner (Eds.), *Case studies in behavior modification*. New York: Holt, Rinehart and Winston, 1965.

Baker, B. L. Symptom treatment and symptom substitution in enuresis. *Journal of Abnormal Psychology*, 1969, 74, 42–49.

Bancroft, J. H. J. The application of psychophysiological measures to the assessment and modification of sexual behavior. *Behaviour Research and Therapy*, 1971, 9, 119–130.

Bandura, A. *Principles of behavior modification*. New York: Holt, Rinehart and Winston, 1969.

Bandura, A., & Barab, P. G. Processes governing disinhibitory effects through symbolic modeling. *Journal of Abnormal Psychology*, 1973, 82, 1–9.

Bandura, A., Blanchard E., & Ritter, B. The relative efficacy of desensitization and modeling approaches for inducing behavioral, affective and cognitive change. *Journal of Personality and Social Psychology*, 1969, 13, 173–199.

Bandura, A., Grusec, J. E., & Manlove, F. L. Vicarious extinction of avoidance behavior. *Journal of Personality and Social Psychology*, 1967, 5, 16–23.

Bandura, A., & Walters, R. H. *Adolescent aggression*. New York: The Ronald Press, 1959.

Banquet, J. P. Spectral analysis of the EEG in meditation. *Electroencephal Clinical Neurophysiology*, 1973, 35, 143.

Barlow, D. H., Reynolds, E. J., & Agras, W. S. Gender identity change in a transsexual. *Archives of General Psychiatry*, 1973, 28, 569–579.

Barrett, J. H. *Gerontological psychology*. Springfield, Ill.: Charles C Thomas, 1972.

Barton, R. *Institutional neurosis*. Bristol, England: John Wright & Sons, 1959.

Bateson, G., Jackson, D. D., Haley, J., & Weakland, J. H. A note on the double bind—1962. *Family Process*, 1963, 2, 154–161.

Bazell, R. J. Drug abuse: Methadone becomes the solution and the problem. *Science*, 1973, *179*, 772–775.

Bazelon, D. The right to treatment: The courts' role. *Hospital and Community Psychiatry*, 1969, *20*, 129–135.

Beck, A. T. Thinking and depression. I: Idiosyncratic content and cognitive distortions. *Archives of General Psychiatry*, 1963, *9*, 324–333.

Beck, A. T. *Depression: Clinical experimental, and theoretical aspects.* New York: Hoeber, 1967.

Beck, A. T. The core problem in depression: The cognitive triad. *Science and Psychoanalysis*, 1970, *17*, 47–55.

Beck, A. T. Cognition, affect, and psychopathology. *Archives of General Psychiatry*, 1971, *24*, 495–523.(a)

Beck, A. T. Psychoanalytic research in depression. In R. R. Fieve (Ed.), *Depression in the 1970's: Modern theory & research.* Amsterdam: Excerpta Medica, 1971.(b)

Beck, A. T., Laude, R., & Bohnert, M. Ideational components of anxiety neurosis. *Archives of General Psychiatry*, 1974, *31*, 319–325.

Becker, W. C. A genetic approach to the interpretation and evaluation of the process-reactive distinction. *Journal of Abnormal and Social Psychology*, 1956, *47*, 489–496.

Becker, W. C. The process-reactive distinction: A key to the problem of schizophrenia? *Journal of Nervous and Mental Disease*, 1959, *129*, 442–449.

Becker, W. C. Consequence of different kinds of parental discipline. In M. L. Hoffman & L. W. Hoffman (Eds.), *Review of child development research.* New York: Russell Sage Foundation, 1964.

Becker, W. C., Peterson, D. R., Hellmer, L. A., Shoemaker, D. J., & Quay, H. C. Factors in parental behavior and personality as related to problem behavior in children. *Journal of Consulting Psychology*, 1959, *23*, 107–118.

Bemporad, J. R. Perceptual disorders in schizophrenia. *American Journal of Psychiatry*, 1967, *123*, 971–978.

Benda, C. E. Psychopathology of childhood. In L. Carmichael (Ed.), *Manual of child psychology* (2nd ed.). New York: Wiley, 1954.

Bender, L. The brain and child behavior. *Archives of General Psychiatry*, 1961, *4*, 531–548.

Benson, A. C. *Thy Rod and Thy Staff.* London: Smith Elder, 1912.

Benson, D. F., & Geschwind, N. Psychiatric conditions associated with focal lesions of the central nervous system. In S. Arieti & M. F. Reiser (Eds.), *American handbook of psychiatry* (Vol. 4, 2nd ed.). New York: Basic Books, 1975.

Berg, D. F. *Extent of illicit drug use in the United States.* Division of Drug Sciences, Bureau of Narcotics and Dangerous Drugs, U. S. Department of Justice, 1969.

Bergin, A. E. Some implications of psychotherapy research for therapeutic practice. *Journal of Abnormal Psychology*, 1966, *71*, 235–246.

Berne, E. *Games people play.* New York: Grove Press, 1964.

Bernstein, A. The psychoanalytic technique. In B. B. Wolman (Ed.), *Handbook of clinical psychology.* New York: McGraw-Hill, 1965.

Bernstein, D. A. Modification of smoking behavior: An evaluative review. *Psychological Bulletin*, 1969, *71*, 418–440.

Bettelheim, B. Joey: A mechanical boy. *Scientific American*, 1959, *200*(3), 116–127. © 1959 by Scientific American, Inc. All rights reserved.

Bettelheim, B. *The empty fortress: Infantile autism and the birth of the self.* London: Collier-Macmillan, 1967.

Bexton, W. H., Heron, W., & Scott, T. H. The effects of decreased variation in the sensory environment. *Canadian Journal of Psychology*, 1954, *8*, 70.

Bianchi, G. N. Patterns of hypochondriasis: A principal components analysis. *British Journal of Psychiatry*, 1973, *122*, 541–548.

Bieber, I. Sadism and masochism: Phenomenology and psychodynamics. In S. Arieti & E. B. Brody (Eds.), *American handbook of psychiatry* (Vol. 3, 2nd ed.). New York: Basic Books, 1974.

Bieber, I., Dain, H. J., Dince, O. R., Drellich, M. G., Grand, H. G., Grundlack, R. H., Kremer, M. W., Rifkin, A. H., Wilbur, C. B., & Bieber, T. B. *Homosexuality: A psychoanalytic study.* New York: Basic Books, 1962.

Binswanger, L. *Being-in-the-world.* New York: Basic Books, 1963.

Biofeedback in action. *Medical World News*, 1973, *14* (11), 47–60.

Birnbaum, M. Right to treatment. *American Bar Association Journal*, 1960, *46*, 499–505.

Blake, B. G. The application of behaviour therapy to the treatment of alcoholism. *Behaviour Research and Therapy*, 1965, *3*, 75–85.

Blake, B. G. A follow-up of alcoholics treated by behaviour therapy. *Behaviour Research and Therapy*, 1967, *5*, 89–94.

Blanchard, E. B., & Young, L. D. Self control of cardiac functioning. *Psychological Bulletin*, 1973, *79*, 145–163.

Blanchard, E. B., & Young, L. D. Clinical applications of biofeedback training: A review of evidence. *Archives of General Psychiatry*, 1974, *30*, 573–589.

Blashfield, R. K. An evaluation of the DSM-11 classification of schizophrenia as a nomenclature. *Journal of Abnormal Psychology*, 1973, *82*, 382–389.

Blashfield, R. K., & Draguns, J. G. Evaluative criteria for psychiatric classification. *Journal of Abnormal Psychology*, 1976, *85*, 140–150.

Bleuler, E. [*Dementia Praecox or the group of the schizophrenias*] (J. Zinkin, trans.). New York: International Universities Press, 1950. (Originally published, 1911.)

Bleuler, M. The offspring of schizophrenics. *Schizophrenia Bulletin*, 1974, 8, 93–107.

Bockoven, J. S. *Moral treatment in American psychiatry.* New York: Springer, 1963.

Bodin, A. M. Conjoint family assessment. In P. M. McReynolds (Ed.), *Advances in psychological assessment.* Palo Alto, Calif.: Science and Behavior Books, 1968.

Bolgar, H. The case study method. In B. B. Wolman (Ed.), *Handbook of clinical psychology.* New York: McGraw-Hill, 1965.

Bond, E. Results of treatment in psychosis. *American Journal of Psychiatry*, 1954, 110, 881.

Bond, I. K., & Hutchison, H. C. Application of reciprocal inhibition therapy to exhibitionism. In H. J. Eysenck (Ed.), *Experiments in behaviour therapy.* New York: Pergamon Press, 1964.

Böök, J. A. Genetical aspects of schizophrenic psychoses. In D. D. Jackson (Ed.), *The etiology of schizophrenia.* New York: Basic Books, 1960.

Bootzin, R. R. Stimulus control treatment for insomnia. *Proceedings of the 80th Annual Convention of the American Psychological Association*, 1972, 7, 395–396.

Boss, M. *Psychoanalysis and Daseinanalysis.* New York: Basic Books, 1963.

Botwinick, J. *Aging and behavior: A comprehensive integration of research findings.* New York: Springer, 1973.

Bowers, M. B. Pathogenesis of acute schizophrenic psychosis. *Archives of General Psychiatry*, 1968, 19, 348–360. © 1968, American Medical Association.

Brady, J. V. Ulcers in "executive" monkeys. *Scientific American*, 1958, 199 (4), 94–100.

Braginsky, B., Braginsky, D., and Ring, K. *Methods of madness: The mental hospital as a last resort.* New York: Holt, Rinehart and Winston, 1969.

Braginsky, D., & Braginsky, B. *Hansels and Gretels: Studies of children in institutions for the mentally retarded.* New York: Holt, Rinehart and Winston, 1971.

Breger, L., & McGaugh, J. L. Critique and reformulation of "Learning Theory" approaches to psychotherapy and neurosis. *Psychological Bulletin*, 1965, 63, 338–358.

Brenner, C. *An elementary textbook of psychoanalysis.* New York: International Universities Press, 1955.

Breuer, J., & Freud, S. Studies on hysteria (1893–1895). In *The Standard edition of the complete psychological works of Sigmund Freud* (Vol. 2). London: Hogarth Press and the Institute of Psychoanalysis, 1962.

Britton, J. H., & Britton, J. O. *Personality changes in aging.* New York: Springer, 1972.

Brody, E. B. Color and identity conflict in young boys. *Psychiatry*, 1963, 26, 188–201.

Brody, J. E. Alcoholism treatment: Rand finding on resumption of drinking sets off dispute on new therapies. *New York Times*, June 17, 1976, p. 15.

Broen, W. E., & Storm, L. H. Lawful disorganization: The process underlying a schizophrenic syndrome. *Psychological Review*, 1966, 73, 265–279.

Brown, B. Forward. In B. B. Wolman (Ed.), *The therapist's handbook.* New York: Van Nostrand Reinhold, 1976.

Brown, F. Depression and childhood bereavement. *Journal of Mental Science*, 1961, 107, 754–777.

Brown, J. L. Prognosis from presenting symptoms of preschool children with atypical development. *American Journal of Orthopsychiatry*, 1960, 30, 386.

Brown, J. W. The neural organization of language: Aphasia and neuropsychiatry. In S. Arieti & M. F. Reiser (Eds.), *American handbook of psychiatry* (Vol. 4, 2nd ed.). New York: Basic Books, 1975. © 1975 by Basic Books, Inc.

Bruch, H. *The importance of overweight.* New York: Norton, 1957.

Bruch, H. Transformation of oral impulses in eating disorders: Conceptual approach. *Psychiatric Quarterly*, 1961, 35, 458–481.

Bruch, H. Hunger and instinct. *Journal of Nervous and Mental Disease*, 1969, 149, 100–101.

Buhler, C. Basic theoretical concepts of humanistic psychology. *American Psychologist*, 1971, 26, 378–386.

Buchwald, A. Psyching out. *The Washington Post*, June 20, 1965.

Buchwald, A. M., & Young R. D. Some comments on the foundations of behavior therapy. In C. M. Franks (Ed.), *Behavior therapy: Appraisal and status.* New York: McGraw-Hill, 1969.

Burchard, J. D., & Harig, P. T. Behavior modification and juvenile delinquency. In H. Leitenberg (Ed.), *Handbook of behavior modification and behavior therapy.* Englewood Cliffs, N. J.: Prentice-Hall, 1976.

Burgess, A. W., & Holmstrom, L. L. Rape trauma syndrome. *The American Journal of Psychiatry*, 1971, 131, 981–986.

Bursten, B. The manipulative personality. *Archives of General Psychiatry*, 1972, 26, 318–321.

Burton, A. (Ed.). *Encounter.* San Francisco: Jossey-Bass, 1970.

Butcher, J. N. *Abnormal Psychology.* Belmont, Calif.: Brooks/Cole, 1971. Excerpts on pp. 190, 240. © 1971 by Wadsworth Publishing Company, Inc. Reprinted by permission of the publisher, Brooks/Cole Publishing Company, Monterey, California.

Butcher, J. N. *Objective personality assessment.* New York: General Learning Corporation. 1974.

Butcher, J. N., & Maudal, G. R. Crisis intervention. In I. B. Weiner (Ed.), *Clinical methods in psychology.* New York: Wiley, 1976.

Busse, E. W. Aging and psychiatric diseases of late life. In S. Arieti & M. F. Reiser (Eds.), *American handbook of psychiatry* (Vol. 4, 2nd ed.). New York: Basic Books, 1975.

Byck, R. Drugs and the treatment of psychiatric disorders. In L. S. Goodman & A. Gilman (Eds.), *The pharmacological basis of therapeutics* (5th ed.). New York: Macmillan, 1975.

Cahoon, D. D., & Crosby C. C. A learning approach to chronic drug use: Sources of reinforcement. *Behavior therapy,* 1972, 3, 64–71.

Calhoun, J. Ecological factors in the development of behavioral anomalies. In J. Zubin & H. Hunt (Eds.). *Comparative psychopathology: Animal and human.* New York: Grune & Stratton, 1967.

Callner, D. A. Behavioral treatment approaches to drug abuse: A critical review of the research. *Psychological Bulletin,* 1975, 82, 143–164.

Cameron, N. Experimental analysis of schizophrenic thinking. In J. S. Kasanin (Ed.), *Language and thought in schizophrenia.* Berkeley, Calif.: University of California Press. 1946.

Cannon, W. B. *Bodily changes in pain, hunger, fear, and rage* (2nd ed.). New York: Appleton, 1929.

Cannon, W. B. "Voodoo" death. *American Anthropologist,* 1942, 44, 169.

Caplan, G. *Principles of preventive psychiatry.* New York: Basic Books, 1964.

Caplan, G. *The theory and practice of mental health consultation.* New York: Basic Books, 1970.

Carlson, G. A., & Goodwin, F. K. The stages of mania. *Archives of General Psychiatry,* 1973, 28, 221–228.

Carp, F. M. Senility or garden-variety maladjustment? *Journal of Gerontology,* 1969, 24, 203–208.

Cautela, J. R. Treatment of compulsive behavior by covert desensitization. *Psychological Record,* 1966, 16, 33–41.

Cautela, J. R. Covert sensitization. *Psychological Reports,* 1967, 20, 459–468.

Cautela, J. R. A classical conditioning approach to the development and modification of behavior in the aged. *The Gerontologist,* 1969, 9, 109–113.

Cautela, J. R. The treatment of alcoholism by covert sensitization. *Psychotherapy: Theory, Research, and Practice,* 1970, 7, 86–90.

Cautela, J. R., & Stuart, R. B. Behavioural control of overeating. *Behaviour Research and Therapy,* 1967, 5, 357–65.

Chafetz, M. E., Hertzman, M., & Berenson, D. Alcoholism: A positive view. In S. Arieti & E. B. Brady, *American handbook of psychiatry* (Vol. 3, 2nd ed.). New York: Basic Books, 1974.

Chapman, A. H. *Textbook of clinical psychiatry: An interpersonal approach.* Philadelphia: Lippincott, 1967.

Chapman, J. The early symptoms of schizophrenia. *British Journal of Psychiatry,* 1966, 112, 225–251.

Chapman, L. J. Distractibility in the conceptual performance of schizophrenics. *Journal of Abnormal and Social Psychology,* 1956, 53, 286–291.(a)

Chapman, L. J. The role of type of distracter in the "concrete" conceptual preformance of schizophrenics. *Journal of Personality,* 1956, 25, 286–291.(b)

Chapman, R. F., Smith, J. W., & Layden, L. A. Elimination of cigarette smoking by punishment and self-management training. *Behaviour Research and Therapy,* 1971, 9, 255–264.

Chesler, P. *Women and madness.* New York: Doubleday, 1972.

Christmas, J. J., Wallace, H., & Edwards, J. New careers and new mental health services: Fantasy or future? In B. Denner & R. H. Price (Eds.), *Community mental health: Social action and reaction.* New York: Holt, Rinehart and Winston, 1973.

Clark, L. D., & Nakashima, E. N. Experimental studies of marijuana. *American Journal of Psychiatry.* 1968, 125, 379–384.

Clausen, J. A. Sociology and psychiatry. In A. M. Freedman, H. I. Kaplan, & B. J. Sadock (Eds.), *Comprehensive textbook of psychiatry-II* (Vol. 1, 2nd ed.). Baltimore: Williams & Wilkins, 1975.

Cleckley, H. M. *The mask of sanity.* St. Louis: C. V. Mosby Co., 1964.

Cleckley, H. M. Psychopathic states. In S. Arieti (Ed.), *American handbook of psychiatry.* New York: Basic Books, 1959.

Clemmer, D. *The prison community.* New York: Holt, Rinehart and Winston, 1958.

Cohen, A. K. *Delinquent boys: The culture of the gang.* Glencoe, Ill.: The Free Press, 1955.

Cohen, H. L., & Filipczak, J. A. Programming educational behavior for institutionalized adolescents. In H. C. Rickard (Ed.), *Behavioral intervention in human problems.* New York: Pergamon Press, 1971.

Cohen, J. *Secondary motivation, 1. Personal motives.* Chicago: Rand McNally, 1970.

Cohen, M. B., Baker, G., Cohen, R. A., Fromm-Reichmann, F., & Weigert, E. V. An intensive study of twelve cases of manic-depressive psychosis. *Psychiatry,* 1954, 17, 103–137.

Conger, J. J., Sawrey, W. L., & Turrell, E. S. The role of social experience in the production of gastric ulcers in hooded rats placed in a conflict situation. *Journal of Abnormal and Social Psychology*, 1958, 57, 214–220.

Conley, R. W., Conwell, M., & Arrill, M. R. An approach to measuring the cost of mental illness. *American Journal of Psychiatry*, 1967, 124, 755–762.

Cowden, R. C., & Ford, L. I. Systematic desensitization with phobic schizophrenics. *American Journal of Psychiatry*, 1962, 119, 241–245.

Cowen, E. L. Social and community interventions. *Annual Review of Psychology*, 1973, 24, 423–472.

Cowen, E. L., Trost, M. A., Lorion, R. P., Dorr, D., Izzo, L. D., & Isaacson, R. V. *New ways in school mental health: Early detection and prevention of school maladaptation.* New York: Human Sciences Press, 1975.

Craik, K. H. Environmental psychology. In K. H. Craik, B. Kleinmuntz, R. Rosnow, R. Rosenthal, J. Cheyne, & R. Walters (Eds.), *New directions in psychology 4.* New York: Holt, Rinehart and Winston, 1970.

Cronbach, L. J. *Essentials of psychological testing* (3rd ed.). New York: Harper & Row, 1970.

Dale, A. J. Organic brain syndromes associated with infections. In A. M. Freedman, H. I. Kaplan, & B. J. Sadock (Eds.), *The comprehensive textbook of psychiatry-II* (Vol. 1, 2nd ed.). Baltimore: Williams & Wilkins, 1975.

Daniels, R. S. Psychotherapy of depression. *Postgraduate Medicine*, 1962, 32, 436–441.

Davidson, W. S., & Seidman, E. Studies of behavior modification and juvenile delinquency: A review, methodological critique, and social perspective. *Psychological Bulletin*, 1974, 81, 998–1011.

Davison, G. C. Differential relaxation and cognitive restructuring in therapy with a "paranoid schizophrenic" or "paranoid state." *Proceedings of the 74th Annual Convention of the American Psychological Association*, 1966, 2, 177–178.

Davison, G. C. Elimination of a sadistic fantasy by a client-controlled counterconditioning technique. *Journal of Abnormal Psychology*, 1968, 73, 84–90.

Dekker, E., Pelser, H. E., & Groen, J. Conditioning as a cause of asthmatic attacks. *Journal of Psychosomatic Research*, 1957, 2, 97–108.

Deleon, G., & Mandell, W. A comparison of conditioning and psychotherapy in the treatment of functional enuresis. *Journal of Clinical Psychology*, 1966, 22, 326–330.

Denner, B., & Price, R. H. *Community mental health: Social action and reaction.* New York: Holt, Rinehart and Winston, 1973.

Des Lauriers, A. M. *The experience of reality in childhood schizophrenia.* New York: International Universities Press, 1962.

Dinoff, M., & Rickard, H. D. Learning that privileges entail responsibility. In J. D. Krumboltz & C. E. Thoresen (Eds.), *Behavior counseling: Cases and techniques.* New York: Holt, Rinehart and Winston, 1969.

Dobson, W. R. An investigation of various factors involved in time perception. *Journal of General Psychology*, 1954, 50, 277–298.

Dobzhansky, T. Genetics and the diversity of behavior. *American Psychologist*, 1972, 27, 523–530.

Dragstedt L. R. A concept of the etiology of duodenal ulcer. *American Journal of Roentgenology*, 1956, 75, 219–229.

Dunbar, H. F. *Psychosomatic Diagnosis.* New York: Hoeber, 1943.

Dunham, H. W. Social class and schizophrenia. *American Journal of Orthopsychiatry*, 1964, 34, 634–642.

Dunlap, K. *Habits: Their making and unmaking.* New York: Liveright, 1932.

Dykens, J. W., & Niswander, G. D. The treatment of drug addiction. In B. B. Wolman (Ed.), *The therapist's handbook.* New York: Van Nostrand Reinhold, 1976.

Eaton, J., & Weil, R. J. *Culture and mental disorders: A comparative study of the Hutterites and other populations.* Glencoe, Ill.: The Free Press, 1955.

Eisdorfer, C. Mental health in later life. In S. E. Golann & C. Eisdorfer (Eds.), *Handbook of community mental health.* Englewood Cliffs, N. J.: Prentice-Hall, 1972.

Eisenberg, L., & Kanner, L. Early infantile autism. *American Journal of Orthopsychiatry*, 1956, 26, 556–566.

Ejrup, B. Treatment of tobacco addiction: Experiences in tobacco withdrawal clinics. In *Can we help them stop?* Chicago: American Cancer Society, Illinois Division, 1964.

Ellis, A. Psychoanalysis as science: A critique. *Genetic Psychology Monographs*, 1950, 41, 147–212.

Ellis, A. *Reason and emotion in psychotherapy.* New York: Lyle Stuart, 1962.

Engel, C. Sudden and rapid death . . . stress. *Annual of Internal Medicine*, 1971, 74, 771–782.

Engle, G. L. Psychological aspects of gastrointestinal disorders. In S. Arieti & M. F. Reiser (Eds.), *American handbook of psychiatry* (Vol. 4, 2nd ed.). New York: Basic Books, 1975. © 1975 by Basic Books, Inc.

Epstein, S. Toward a unified theory of anxiety. In B. A. Maher (Ed.), *Progress in experimental personality research* (Vol. 4.). New York: Academic Press, 1967.

Erikson, E. *Childhood and society* (1st ed.). New York: Norton, 1950.

Erikson, E. *Childhood and society* (2nd ed.). New York: Norton, 1963.

Erikson, E. Identity and the life cycle. *Psychological Issues* (Vol. 1, No. 1). New York: International Universities Press, 1959.

Eysenck, H. J. The effects of psychotherapy: An evaluation. *Journal of Consulting Psychology,* 1952, *16,* 319–324.

Eysenck, H. J. (Ed.). *Handbook of abnormal psychology.* New York: Basic Books, 1961.

Eysenck, H. J. The non-professional psychotherapist. *International Journal of Psychiatry,* 1967, *3,* 150–153.

Eysenck, H. J., & Rachman, S. *The causes and cures of neurosis.* London: Routledge & Kegan Paul, 1965.

Fancher, R. E. *Psychoanalytic psychology: The development of Freud's thought.* New York: Norton, 1973.

Faris, R. E. L., & Dunham, H. W. *Mental disorders in urban areas: An ecological study of schizophrenia and other psychoses.* Chicago: University of Chicago Press, 1939.

Federal Bureau of Investigation (FBI). *Uniform Crime Reports.* Washington, D. C.: U. S. Department of Justice, November 19, 1975.

Federn, T. *Ego psychology and the psychoses.* New York: Basic Books, 1952.

Feighner, J., Robins, E., Guze, S. B., Woodruff, R. A., Winokur, G., & Munoz, R. Diagnostic criteria for use in psychiatric research. *Archives of General Psychiatry,* 1972, *26,* 57–68.

Feldman, M. P., & MacCulloch, M. J. *Homosexual behavior: Therapy and assessment.* Oxford: Pergamon, 1972.

Fenichel, O. *The psychoanalytic theory of neurosis.* New York: Norton, 1945.

Fenichel, O. Remarks on the common phobias (1944). In *Collected papers* (Vol. 2.). New York: Norton, 1954.

Fenz, W. D., & Velner, J. Physiological concomitants of behavioral indexes in schizophrenia. *Journal of Abnormal Psychology,* 1970, *76,* 27–35.

Ferster, C. B. Positive reinforcement and behavioral deficits of autistic children. *Child Development,* 1961, *32,* 437–456.

Ferster, C. B. Animal behavior and mental illness. *Psychological Record,* 1966, *16,* 345–356.

Ferster, C. B. A functional analysis of depression. *American Psychologist,* 1973, *28,* 857–870.

Fiedler, F. E. A comparison of therapeutic relationships in psychoanalytic, nondirective and Adlerian therapy. *Journal of Consulting Psychology,* 1950, *14,* 436–445.(a)

Fiedler, F. E. The concept of an ideal therapeutic relationship. *Journal of Consulting Psychology,* 1950, *14,* 239–245.(b)

Fielding, L. Initial ward-wide behavior modification programs for retarded children. In T. Thompson & J. Gra-

bowski (Eds.), *Behavior modification of the mentally retarded.* New York: Oxford University Press, 1972.

Finkel, N. J. Strens, traumas, and trauma resolution. *American Journal of Community Psychology,* 1975, *3,* 175–178.

Ford, C. S., & Beach, F. A. *Patterns of sexual behavior.* New York: Harper, 1952.

Ford, H. Involutional melancholia. In A. M. Freedman, H. I. Kaplan, & B. J. Sadock (Eds.), *Comprehensive textbook of psychiatry-II* (Vol. 1, 2nd ed.). Baltimore, Md.: Williams & Wilkins, 1975.

Forrest, A. D., Fraser, R. H., & Priest, R. G. Environmental factors in depressive illness. *British Journal of Psychiatry,* 1965, *111,* 243–253.

Fox, J. R. Sibling incest. *British Journal of Sociology,* 1962, *13,* 128.

Fox, R. E. Family therapy. In I. B. Weiner (Ed.), *Clinical methods in psychology.* New York: Wiley, 1976.

Frank, G. H. The role of the family in the development of psychopathology. *Psychological Bulletin,* 1965, *64,* 191–205.

Frank, J. D. *Persuasion and healing: A comparative study of psychotherapy.* Baltimore, Md.: Johns Hopkins Press, 1961.

Fredricks, C., & Goodman, H. *Low blood sugar and you.* New York: Grosset & Dunlap, 1969.

Freedman, A. M. Opiate dependence. In A. M. Freedman, H. I. Kaplan, & B. J. Sadock (Eds.), *Comprehensive textbook of psychiatry-II* (Vol. 2, 2nd ed.). Baltimore: Williams & Wilkins, 1975.

Freedman, L. Z. Forensic Psychiatry. In A. M. Freedman & H. I. Kaplan (Eds.), *Comprehensive textbook of psychiatry* (1st ed.). Baltimore: Williams & Wilkins, 1967.

Freud, S. *A general introduction to psycho-analysis.* New York: Simon & Schuster, 1935.

Freud, S. [*An autobiographical study*] (J. Strachey, trans.) New York: Norton, 1952. (Originally published, 1935.)

Freud, S. Three essays on the theory of sexuality (1905). In *Standard edition of the complete psychological works of Sigmund Freud* (Vol. 7). London: Hogarth Press, 1953.

Freud, S. Analysis of a phobia in a five-year-old boy (1909). In *Standard edition of the complete psychological works of Sigmund Freud* (Vol. 10). London: Hogarth Press, 1955.

Freud, S. Mourning and melancholia (1917). In *Standard edition of the complete psychological works of Sigmund Freud* (Vol. 4). London: Hogarth Press, 1956.

Freud, S. Analysis terminable and interminable (1937). In *Standard edition of the complete psychological works of Sigmund Freud* (Vol. 23). London: Hogarth Press, 1964.

Friedman, M., Rosenman, R. H., Straus, R., Wurm, M., & Kositchek, R. The relationship of behavior pattern A to the state of coronary vasculature. *The American Journal of Medicine,* 1968, *44,* 525–537.

Friedrich, O. *Going crazy: An inquiry into madness in our time.* New York: Simon & Schuster, 1976.

Fromm-Reichmann, F. *Principles of intensive psychotherapy.* Chicago: University of Chicago Press, 1950.

Fullmer, W. H. Changing the behavior of the retarded in the special education classroom. In T. Thompson & J. Grabowski (Eds.), *Behavior modification of the mentally retarded.* New York: Oxford University Press, 1972.

Gager, N., & Schurr, C. *Sexual assault: Confronting rape in America.* New York: Grosset & Dunlap, 1976.

Garfield, Z. H., McBrearty, J. F., & Dichter, M. A case of impotence successfully treated with desensitization combined with *In Vivo* operant training and thought substitution. In R. D. Rubin & C. M. Franks (Eds.), *Advances in behavior therapy, 1968.* New York: Academic Press, 1969.

Garmezy, N. Children of risk: The search for the antecedents of schizophrenia. Part II: Ongoing research programs, issues and intervention. *Schizophrenia Bulletin,* 1974. *9,* 55–124.

Gauren, E., & Dickenson, J. K. Diagnostic decision-making in psychiatry. *Archives of General Psychiatry,* 1966, *14,* 233–237.

Geer, J. H. Phobia treated by reciprocal inhibition. *Journal of Abnormal and Social Psychology,* 1964, *69,* 642–645.

Giallombardo, R. *Society of women: A study of a women's prison.* New York: Wiley, 1966.

Ginsberg, G. L., Frosch, W. A., & Shapiro, T. The new impotence. *Archives of General Psychiatry,* 1972, *26,* 218–220.

Gittelman, R. K., Klein, F. D., & Pollack, M. Effects of psychotropic drugs on long term adjustment: A review. *Psychopharmacologia,* 1964, *5,* 317–338.

Glaser, D. *The effectiveness of a prison and parole system.* Indianapolis: Bobbs-Merrill, 1964.

Glass, D. C., Snyder, M. L., & Hollis, J. F. Time urgency and the type A coronary-prone behavior pattern. *Journal of Applied Social Psychology,* 1974, *4,* 125–140.

Glasscote, R., Sanders, D., Forstenzer, H. M., & Foley, A. R. (Eds.). *The community mental health center: An analysis of existing models.* Washington, D. C.: American Psychiatric Association, 1964.

Glasscote, R., Sussex, J. N., Cumming, E., & Smith, L. H. *The community mental health center: An interim appraisal.* Washington, D. C.: Joint Information Service, 1969.

Glicksman, M., Ottomanelli, G., & Cutler, R. The earn-your-way credit system: Use of a token economy in narcotic rehabilitation. *International Journal of the Addictions,* 1971, *6,* 525–531.

Glover, E. On the etiology of drug addiction. In *On the early development of mind.* New York: International Universities Press, 1956.

Goddard, H. H. *The Kallikak family.* New York: Macmillan, 1912.

Goffman, E. Characteristics of total institutions. In Walter Reed Army Institute of Research, *Symposium on Preventive and Social Psychiatry,* Washington, D. C., April 15–17, 1957.

Gold, M. W. Research on the vocational habilitation of the retarded: The present, the future. In N. R. Ellis (Ed.), *International review of research in mental retardation* (Vol. 6). New York: McGraw-Hill, 1973.

Goldfarb, W. Psychological privation in infancy and subsequent adjustment. *American Journal of Orthopsychiatry,* 1945, *15,* 247–255.

Goldman, R., Jaffa, M., & Schachter, S. Yom Kippur, Air France, dormitory food, and the eating behavior of obese and nonobese persons. *Journal of Personality and Social Psychology,* 1968, *10,* 117–123.

Goldman, R. L. The effects of the manipulation of the visibility of food on the eating behavior of obese and normal subjects. Unpublished doctoral dissertation, Columbia University, 1968.

Goldstein, A. P. *Therapist-patient expectancies in psychotherapy.* New York: Pergamon Press, 1962.

Goldstein, K. The effect of brain damage on the personality. *Psychiatry,* 1952, *15,* 245–260.

Goldstein, K. Functional disturbances in brain damage. In S. Arieti & M. F. Reiser (Eds.), *American handbook of psychiatry* (Vol. 4, 2nd ed.). New York: Basic Books, 1975.

Goodwin, D. W., & Guze, S. B. Genetic factors in alcoholism. In B. Kissin & H. Begleiter (Eds.), *Clinical Pathology* (Vol. 3), 1974.

Goodwin, D. W., Schulsinger, F., Hermansen, L., Guze, S. B., & Winokur, G. Alcohol problems in adoptees raised apart from alcoholic biological parents. *Archives of General Psychiatry,* 1973, *28,* 238–243.

Gottesman, L. E., Quarterman, C. E., & Cohn, G. M. Psychological treatment of the aged. In C. Eisdorfer & M. P. Lawton (Eds.), *The psychology of adult development and aging.* Washington, D. C.: American Psychological Association, 1973.

Gottschalk, L. A., & Pattison, E. M. Psychiatric perspectives on T-groups and the laboratory movement: An overview. *American Journal of Psychiatry,* 1969, *126,* 823–839.

Grace, W. J., & Graham, D. T. Relationship of specific attitudes and emotions to certain bodily diseases. *Psychosomatic Medicine,* 1952, *14,* 242–251.

Greenberg, J. A. Schizophrenia: Heretical notes on a diagnostic category. *Schizophrenia Bulletin*, 1975, *12*, 10–14.

Greenblatt, M., & Kantor, D. Student volunteer movement and the manpower shortage. *American Journal of Psychiatry*, 1962, *118*, 809–814.

Greene, M. H., & Dupont, R. L. Heroin addiction trends. *American Journal of Psychiatry*, 1974, *131*, 545–550.

Greenson, R. R. *The technique and practice of psychoanalysis*. New York: International Universities Press, 1967.

Greer, S. Study of parental loss in neurotics and sociopaths. *Archives of General Psychiatry*, 1964, *11*, 177–180.

Grier, W. H., & Cobbs, P. M. *Black rage*. New York: Basic Books, 1968.

Grinspoon, L. Drug dependence: Non-narcotic agents. In A. M. Freedman, H. I. Kaplan, & B. J. Sadock (Eds.), *Comprehensive textbook of psychiatry-II* (Vol. 2, 2nd ed.). Baltimore: Williams & Wilkins, 1975.

Group for the Advancement of Psychiatry. *Crisis in psychiatric hospitals*. Report No. 72, 1969.

Gruenberg, E. M. Discussion of critical reviews of Pueblo, Western, and Denver tri-county divisions. In B. Stone (Ed.), *A critical review of treatment progress in a state hospital reorganized toward the communities served*. Pueblo, Colo.: Pueblo Association for Mental Health, 1963 (mimeo.).

Gruenewald, D. A psychologist's view of the borderline syndrome. *Archives of General Psychiatry*, 1970, *23*, 180–184. © 1970, American Medical Association.

Gullick, E. L., & Blanchard, E. B. The use of psychotherapy and behavior therapy in the treatment of an obsessional disorder: An experimental case study. *Journal of Nervous and Mental Disease*, 1973, *156*, 427–431.

Gunderson, J. G., & Singer, M. T. Defining borderline patients: An overview. *American Journal of Psychiatry*, 1975, *132*, 1–10.

Guttmacher, M. S. *Sex offenses*. New York: Norton, 1951.

Halleck, S. L. Legal and ethical aspects of behavior control. *The American Journal of Psychiatry*, 1974, *131*, 381–385.

Hamburger, W. W. Emotional aspects of obesity. *Medical Clinics of North America*, 1951, *35*, 483–499.

Hamilton, J., Stephens, L., & Allen, P. Controlling aggressive and destructive behavior in severely retarded institutionalized residents. *American Journal of Mental Deficiency*, 1967, *71*, 852–856.

Hare, R. D. *Psychopathy: Theory and research*. New York: Wiley, 1970. Excerpts on p. 316. © 1970 by John Wiley & Sons, Inc. Reprinted by permission.

Harlow, H. F. Love in infant monkeys. *Scientific American*, 1959, *200*, 68–74.

Harlow, H. F., & Zimmermann, R. R. Affectional responses in the infant monkey. *Science*, 1959, *130*, 421–432.

Harlow, J. M. Recovery from the passage of an iron bar through the head. *Publication of the Massachusetts Medical Society*, 1868, *2*, 327–340.

Harmatz, M. G., & Lapuc, P. Behavior modification of overeating in a psychiatric population. *Journal of Consulting and Clinical Psychology*, 1968, *32*, 583–587.

Harmatz, M. G., Mendelsohn, R., & Glassman, M. L. Gathering naturalistic, objective data on the behavior of schizophrenic patients. *Hospital and Community Psychiatry*, 1975, *26*, 83–86.

Harris, M. B. Self-directed program for weight control: A pilot study. *Journal of Abnormal Psychology*, 1969, *74*, 263–270.

Harris, T. A. *I'm OK—you're OK*. New York: Harper & Row, 1969.

Hashim, S. A., & Van Itallie, T. B. Studies in normal and obese subjects with a monitored food dispensary device. *Annals of the New York Academy of Science*, 1965, *131*, 654–661.

Hauserman, N., Walen, S. R., & Behling, M. Reinforced racial integration in the first grade: A study in generalization. *Journal of Applied Behavior Analysis*, 1973, *6*, 193–200.

Hawkins, D., & Pauling, L. *Orthomolecular psychiatry: Treatment of schizophrenia*. San Francisco: W. H. Freeman, 1973.

Hawkins, D. R. Implications of knowledge of sleep patterns in psychiatric conditions. In E. Hartmann (Ed.), *Sleep and dreaming*. Boston: Little, Brown, 1970.

Heath, R. G. Physiological and biochemical studies in schizophrenia with particular emphasis on mid-brain relationships. *International Review of Neurobiology*, 1959, *1*, 299–331.

Heath, R. G. Reappraisal of biological aspects of psychiatry. *Journal of Neuropsychiatry*, 1961, *3*, 1–11.

Heath, R. G., & Krupp, I. M. Schizophrenia as an immunologic disorder. I: Demonstration of antibrain globulins by fluorescent antibody techniques. *Archives of General Psychiatry*, 1967, *16*, 1–9.

Heath, R. G., Martens, S., Leach, B. E., Cohen, M., & Feigley, C. A. Behavioral changes in nonpsychotic volunteers following administration of taraxein, the substance obtained from serum of schizophrenic patients. *American Journal of Psychiatry*, 1958, *114*, 917–920.

Heller, S. S., & Kornfeld, D. S. Delirium and related problems. In S. Arieti & M. F. Reiser (Eds.), *American handbook of psychiatry* (Vol. 4, 2nd ed.). New York: Basic Books, 1975.

Henle, M. On the relation between logic and thinking. *Psychological Review*, 1962, *69*, 366–378.

Henry, W. E. *The analysis of fantasy.* New York: Wiley, 1956.

Herrick, C. J. *The evolution of human nature.* Austin, Tex.: University of Texas Press, 1956.

Herron, W. G. The process-reactive classification of schizophrenia. *Psychological Bulletin,* 1962, *59,* 329–343.

Herson, M., Eisler, R. M., Smith, B. S., & Agras, W. S. A token reinforcement ward for young psychiatric patients. *American Journal of Psychiatry,* 1972, *129,* 233–242.

Hertz, D. N. Aftercare. In B. B. Wolman (Ed.), *The therapist's handbook.* New York: Van Nostrand Reinhold, 1976.

Hess, R. D., & Handel, G. The family as a psychosocial organization. In G. Handel (Ed.), *The psychosocial interior of the family.* Chicago: Aldine, 1967.

Heston, L. L. Psychiatric disorders in foster home reared children of schizophrenic mothers. *British Journal of Psychiatry,* 1966, *112,* 819–825.

Hilgard, E. R. *Introduction to psychology* (3rd ed.). New York: Harcourt Brace Jovanovich, 1962.

Hilgard, J. R. Sibling rivalry and social heredity. *Psychiatry,* 1951, *14,* 375–385.

Hingtgen, J. N., & Bryson, C. Q. Recent developments in the study of early childhood psychoses: Infantile autism, childhood schizophrenia and related disorders. *Schizophrenia Bulletin,* 1972, *5,* 8–54.

Hiroto, D. S., & Seligman, M. E. P. Generality of learned helplessness in man. *Journal of Personality and Social Psychology,* 1975, *31,* 311–327.

Hirsh, J. Women and alcoholism. In W. C. Bier (Ed.), *Problems in addiction: Alcohol and drug addiction.* New York: Fordham University Press, 1962.

Hogan, R. A. The implosive technique. *Behaviour Research and Therapy,* 1968, *6,* 423–431.

Hogarty, G. E., Goldberg, S. C., & Collaborative Study Group. Drug and sociotherapy in the aftercare of schizophrenic patients. *Archives of General Psychiatry,* 1973, *28,* 54.

Hogarty, G. E., Goldberg, S. C., Schooler, N. R., & Ulrich, R. F., & Collaborative Study Group. Drug and sociotherapy in the aftercare of schizophrenic patients. II. Two year relapse rates. *Archives of General Psychiatry,* 1974, *31,* 603–608.

Holden, C. Psychosurgery: Legitimate therapy or laundered lobotomy? *Science,* 1973, *179,* 1109–1112.

Hollingshead, A. B., & Redlich, F. C. *Social class and mental illness: A community study.* New York: Wiley, 1958.

Holmes, T. H., & Rahe, R. H. The social readjustment rating scale. *Journal of Psychosomatic Research,* 1967, *11,* 213–218.

Holt, R. R. Experimental methods in clinical psychology. In B. B. Wolman (Ed.), *Handbook of clinical psychology.* New York: McGraw-Hill, 1965.

Holt, R. R. *Methods of research in clinical psychology.* Morristown, N. J.: General Learning Press, 1973.

Homme, L. F. Perspectives in psychology: XXIV. Control of coverants, the operants of the mind. *The Psychological Record,* 1965, *15,* 501–511.

Horney, K. *The neurotic personality in our time.* New York: Norton, 1937.

Hoskins, R. G. *The biology of schizophrenia.* New York: Norton, 1946.

Hudgens, R. W., Morrison, J. R., & Barchha, J. Life events and primary affective disorders. *Archives of General Psychiatry,* 1967, *116,* 134–145.

Humphreys, L. *Tearoom trade: Impersonal sex in public places.* Chicago: Aldine-Atherton, 1970.

Hunt, G. M., & Azrin, N. H. A community reinforcement approach to alcoholism. *Behaviour Research and Therapy,* 1973, *11,* 91–104.

Hutchings, B., & Mednick, S. A. Registered criminality in the adoptive and biological parents of registered male adoptees. In R. R. Fieve, H. Brill, & L. D. Rosenthal (Eds.), *Genetic research in psychiatry.* New York: International Universities Press, 1974.

Irwin, J. The prison experience: The convict world. In R. M. Carter, D. Glaser, & L. T. Wilkins (Eds.), *Correctional institutions.* Philadelphia: Lippincott, 1972.

Isaacs, W., Thomas, J., & Goldiamond, I. Application of operant conditioning to reinstate verbal behavior in psychotics. *Journal of Speech and Hearing Disorders,* 1960, *25,* 8–12.

Itard, J. M. G. *The wild boy of Aveyron* (*1799*). New York: Appleton-Century-Crofts, 1932.

Ittelson, W., Proshansky, H., Rivlin, L., & Winkler, G. *An introduction for environmental psychology.* New York: Holt, Rinehart and Winston, 1970.

Jacobs, P. A., Brunton, M., Melville, M. H., Brittain, R. P., & McClemont, W. F. Aggressive behavior, mental subnormality, and the XYY male. *Nature,* 1965, *208,* 1351–1352.

Jacobson, E. *Progressive relaxation.* Chicago: University of Chicago Press, 1938.

James, H. *The letters of William James* (2 vols.). Boston: The Atlantic Monthly Press, 1920.

Janet, P. *Les obsessions et la psychasthenie* (2 vols.). Paris: Félix Alean, 1903.

Janet, P. *The major symptoms of hysteria.* New York: Macmillan, 1907.

Janis, I. L. *Stress and frustration.* New York: Harcourt Brace Jovanovich, 1971.

Janov, A. *The anatomy of mental illness: The scientific basis of primal therapy.* New York: Putnam, 1971.

Jarvik, L. F., & Cohen, D. A biobehavioral approach to intellectual changes with aging. In C. Eisdorfer & M. P. Lawton (Eds.), *The psychology of adult development and aging.* Washington, D. C.: American Psychological Association, 1973.

Jarvik, L. F., Klodin, V., & Matsuyama, S. S. Human aggression and the extra Y chromosome. *American Psychologist,* 1973, 28, 674–682.

Jellinek, E. M. Phases of alcohol addiction. *Quarterly Journal of Studies on Alcohol,* 1952, 13, 673–684.

Jensen, A. R. How much can we boost IQ and scholastic achievement? *Harvard Educational Review,* 1969, 39, 1–123.

Johnson, A. M. Juvenile delinquency. In S. Arieti (Ed.), *American handbook of psychiatry.* New York: Basic Books, 1959.

Johnson, A. M., & Szurek, S. A. The genesis of antisocial acting out in children and adults. *Psychoanalytic Quarterly,* 1952, 21, 323.

Jones, M. *The therapeutic community: A new treatment method in psychiatry.* New York: Basic Books, 1953.

Jones, M. C. The elimination of children's fears. *Journal of Experimental Psychology,* 1924, 7, 382–390.

Jung, C. G. [*The psychology of the unconscious*] (B. M. Hinkle, trans.) New York: Dodd, Mead, 1927.

Jung, C. G. *The psychology of dementia praecox.* New York: Journal of Nervous and Mental Diseases Publishing Company, 1936.

Kalinowsky, L. B. Psychosurgery. In A. M. Freedman, H. I. Kaplan, & B. J. Sadock (Eds.), *Comprehensive textbook of psychiatry-II* (Vol. 2, 2nd ed.). Baltimore: Williams & Wilkins, 1975.

Kamin, L. J. *Science and politics of IQ.* Baltimore, Md.: Lawrence Erlbaum Associates, 1974.

Kanfer, F. H. Self management methods. In F. H. Kanfer & A. P. Goldstein (Eds.), *Helping people change: A textbook of methods.* New York: Pergamon Press, 1975.

Kanner, L. Autistic disturbances of affective contact. *Nervous Child,* 1943, 2, 217–240.

Kanner, L., & Eisenberg, L. Early infantile autism: Childhood schizophrenia symposium. *American Journal of Orthopsychiatry,* 1956, 26, 556–564.

Kantor, R. E., Wallner, J. M., & Winder, C. L. Process and reactive schizophrenia. *Journal of Consulting Psychology,* 1953, 17, 157–162.

Kaplan, A. A philosophical discussion of normality. *Archives of General Psychiatry,* 1967, 17, 325–330.

Kaplan, H. S. *The new sex therapy: Active treatment of sexual dysfunctions.* New York: Brunner-Mazel, 1974.

Kaplan, H. S., & Kaplan, H. I. Current concepts of psychosomatic medicine. In A. M. Freedman, H. I. Kaplan, & B. J. Sadock (Eds.), *Comprehensive textbook of psychiatry.* Baltimore, Md.: Williams & Wilkins, 1967.

Karoly, P. Operant Methods. In F. H. Kanfer & A. P. Goldstein (Eds.), *Helping people change: A textbook of methods.* New York: Pergamon Press, 1975.

Karush, A., Daniels, G. E., O'Connor, J. F., & Stern, L. O. The response to psychotherapy in chronic ulcerative colitis. II. Factors arising from the therapeutic situation. *Psychosomatic Medicine,* 1969, 31, 201–226.

Kass, D. J., Silvers, F. M., & Abroms, G. Behavioral group treatment of hysteria. *Archives of General Psychiatry,* 1972, 26, 42–50.

Kassebaum, G., Ward, D., & Wilner, D. *Prison treatment and parole survival: An empirical assessment.* New York: Wiley, 1971.

Kazdin, A. E. Self-monitoring and behavior change. In M. J. Mahoney & C. E. Thoresen (Eds.), *Self control: Power to the person.* Monterey, Calif.: Brooks/Cole, 1974.

Kazdin, A. E. *Behavior modification in applied settings.* Homewood, Ill.: The Dorsey Press, 1975.

Kazdin, A. E., & Bootzin, R. R. The token economy: An evaluative review. *Journal of Applied Behavioral Analysis,* 1972, 5, 343–372.

Kelly, G. *The psychology of personal constructs.* New York: Norton, 1955.

Kelly, J. G. Ecological constraints on mental health services. *American Psychologist,* 1966, 21, 535–539.

Kelly, J. G. Towards an ecological conception of preventive intervention. In J. W. Carter (Ed.), *Research contributions from psychology to community mental health.* New York: Behavioral Publications, 1968.

Kelly, J. G. Naturalistic observations in contrasting social environments. In E. P. Willems & H. L. Raush (Eds.), *Naturalistic viewpoints in psychological research.* New York: Holt, Rinehart and Winston, 1969.

Kenyon, F. Hypochondriasis: A survey of some historical, clinical and social aspects. *British Journal of Psychiatry,* 1965, 38, 117.

Kerckhoff, A. C., & Back, K. W. *The june bug.* New York: Appleton-Century-Crofts, 1968.

Kessler, J. W. *Psychopathology of childhood.* Englewood Cliffs, N.J.: Prentice-Hall, 1966.

Kety, S. S. Biochemistry of the major psychoses. In A. M. Freedman, H. I. Kaplan, & B. J. Sadock (Eds.), *Comprehensive textbook of psychiatry-II* (Vol. 1, 2nd ed.). Baltimore: Williams & Wilkins, 1975.

Kety, S. S., Rosenthal, D., Wender, P. H., & Schulsinger, F. The types and prevalence of mental illness in the biological and adoptive families of adopted schizophrenics. In

D. Rosenthal & S. S. Kety (Eds.), *The transmission of schizophrenia*. London: Pergamon Press, 1968.

Kety, S. S., Woodford, R. B., Harmel, M. H., Freyhan, F. A., Appel, K. E., & Schmidt, C. F. Cerebral blood flow and metabolism in schizophrenia. *American Journal of Psychiatry*, 1948, *104*, 765–770.

Keve, P. *Prison life and human worth*. Minneapolis: University of Minnesota Press, 1974.

Kick, S. A. *Early education of the mentally retarded: An experimental study*. Urbana, Ill.: University of Illinois Press, 1958.

Kiesler, D. J. Experimental designs in psychotherapy research. In A. E. Bergin & S. L. Garfield (Eds.). *Handbook of psychotherapy and behavior change: An empirical analysis*. New York: Wiley, 1971.

Kiev, A. Psychiatric disorders in minority groups. In P. Watson (Ed.), *Psychology and race*. Baltimore: Penguin Education, 1973.

Kimble, G. A. *Hilgard and Marquis' conditioning and learning* (2nd ed.). Englewood Cliffs, N. J.: Prentice-Hall, (ACC), 1961.

Kimble, G. A. (Ed.). *Foundations of conditioning and learning*. New York: Appleton-Century-Crofts, 1967.

Kinsey, A. C., Pomeroy, W. B., & Martin, C. E. *Sexual behavior in the human male*. Philadelphia: Saunders, 1948.

Kinsey, A. C., Pomeroy, W. B., Martin, C. E., & Gebhard, P. H. *Sexual behavior in the human female*. Philadelphia: Saunders, 1953.

Klerman, G. L. Overview of depression. In A. M. Freedman, H. I. Kaplan, & B. J. Sadock (Eds.), *Comprehensive textbook of psychiatry-II* (Vol. 1, 2nd ed.). Baltimore, Md.: Williams & Wilkins, 1975.

Koenig, K. P., & Masters, J. Experimental treatment of habitual smoking. *Behaviour Research and Therapy*, 1965, *3*, 235–243.

Kohn, M. L. Social class and schizophrenia: A critical review and reformulation. *Schizophrenia Bulletin*, 1973, *7*, 60–79.

Kolb, L. C. *Modern clinical psychiatry* (8th ed.). Philadelphia: Saunders, 1973. Excerpts on pp. 172–173, 183, 241, 243, 292–293, 425. © 1973 by W. B. Saunders Company. Reprinted by permission.

Korchin, S. J. *Modern clinical psychology: Principles of intervention in the clinic and community*. New York: Basic Books, 1976.

Knapp, P. H. Current theoretical concepts in psychophysiological medicine. In A. M. Freedman, H. I. Kaplan, & B. J. Sadock (Eds.), *Comprehensive textbook of psychiatry-II* (Vol. 2, 2nd ed.). Baltimore, Md.: Williams & Wilkins, 1975.

Knauth, P. A season in hell. *Life*, June 9, 1972, 74–76. © 1972 Time, Inc. Reprinted with permission.

Knight, J. A. Suicide among students. In H. L. P. Resnik (Ed.). *Suicidal behaviors*. Boston: Little, Brown, 1968.

Kraepelin, E. *Clinical psychiatry* (6th ed.). New York: Macmillan, 1937. (Originally published, 1899.)

Krafft-Ebing, R. von [*Psychopathia sexualis*] (Translated from the 12th German Edition by F. S. Klaf.) New York: Stein and Day, 1965.

Kraft, T. Social anxiety and drug addiction. *British Journal of Psychiatry*, 1968, *2*, 192–195.

Krasner, L. The operant approach in behavior therapy. In A. E. Bergin & S. L. Garfield (Eds.), *Handbook of psychotherapy and behavior change: An empirical analysis*. New York: Wiley, 1971.

Kubie, L. S. *Neurotic distortion of the creative process*. Lawrence, Kan.: University of Kansas Press, 1958.

Kuhn, T. S. *The structure of scientific revolution*. Chicago: University of Chicago Press, 1962.

Lachman, S. J. *Psychosomatic disorders: A behavioristic interpretation*. New York: Wiley, 1972.

Laing, R. D. *The divided self: An existential study in sanity and madness*. Baltimore, Md.: Penguin, 1965.

Laing, R. D. Is schizophrenia a disease? *International Journal of Social Psychiatry*, 1964, *10*, 184–193.

Lakin, M. *Experiential groups: The uses of interpersonal encounter, psychotherapy groups, and sensitivity training*. Morristown, N. J.: General Learning Press, 1972.

Lambo, T. A. The role of cultural factors in paranoid psychosis among the Yoruba tribe. *Journal of Mental Science*, 1955, *101*, 239–266.

Lambo, T. A. Schizophrenic and borderline states. In A. V. S. DeRueck & R. Porter (Eds.), *Transcultural psychiatry*. Boston: Little, Brown, 1965.

Lamy, R. E. Social consequences of mental illness. *Journal of Consulting Psychology*, 1966, *30*, 450–455.

Lang, P. J., & Lazovik, A. D. Experimental desensitization of a phobia. *Journal of Abnormal and Social Psychology*, 1963, *66*, 519–525.

Langfeldt, G. *The schizophreniform states*. Copenhagen: Munksgaard, 1939.

Langsley, D. G., Enterline, J. D., & Hickerson, G. X. A comparison of chlorpromazine and ECT in treatment of acute schizophrenic and manic reactions. *Archives of Neurological Psychiatry*, 1959, *81*, 384.

Laubscher, B. J. F. *Sex, custom and psychopathology*. London: Routledge & Sons, 1937.

Laughlin, H. P. *The neuroses in clinical practice*. Philadelphia: Saunders, 1956. © 1956 by the W. B. Saunders Company.

Lazarus, A. A. Group therapy of phobic disorders by systematic desensitization. *Journal of Abnormal and Social Psychology*, 1961, 63, 504–510.

Lazarus, A. A. The treatment of chronic frigidity by systematic desensitization. *Journal of Nervous Mental Disease*, 1963, 136, 272–280.

Lazarus, A. A. Towards the understanding and effective treatment of alcoholism. *Psychosomatic Medicine*, 1965, 28, 651–666.

Lazarus, A. A. Learning theory and the treatment of depression. *Behaviour Research and Therapy*, 1968, 6, 83–89.

Lazarus, A. *Behavior therapy and beyond.* New York: McGraw-Hill, 1971.

Lazarus, A. A., & Davison, G. C. Clinical innovation in research and practice. In A. E. Bergin & S. L. Garfield (Eds.), *Handbook of psychotherapy and behavior change: An empirical analysis.* New York: Wiley, 1971.

Lazarus, A. A., Davison, G. C., & Polefka, D. A. Classical and operant factors in the treatment of school phobia. *Journal of Abnormal Psychology*, 1965, 70, 225–229.

Leaf, A. Getting old. *Scientific American*, 1973, 229 (3), 45–52.

Lehmann, H. E. Physical therapies of schizophrenia. In S. Arieti & E. B. Brody (Eds.), *American handbook of psychiatry* (Vol. 3, 2nd ed.). New York: Basic Books, 1974.

Lehmann, H. E. Schizophrenia: Introduction and history. In A. M. Freedman, H. I. Kaplan, & B. J. Sadock (Eds.), *Comprehensive textbook of psychiatry-II* (Vol. 1, 2nd ed.). Baltimore, Md.: Williams & Wilkins, 1975.

Lehrman, N. S. Precision in psychoanalysis. *American Journal of Psychiatry*, 1960, 116, 1097–1103.

Leitenberg, H., Agras, W. S., & Thomson, L. E. A sequential analysis of the effect of selective positive reinforcement in modifying anorexia nervosa. *Behaviour Research and Therapy*, 1968, 6, 211–218.

Lemere, F., & Voegtlin, W. L. An evaluation of the aversion treatment of alcoholism. *Quarterly Journal of Studies on Alcoholism*, 1950, 11, 199–204.

Lemkau, P. V., & Crocetti, G. M. Vital statistics of schizophrenia. In L. Bellak (Ed.), *Schizophrenia: A review of the syndrome.* New York: Logos, 1958.

Levitsky, A., & Perls, F. S. The rules and games of gestalt therapy. In J. Fagan & I. L. Shepherd (Eds.), *Gestalt therapy now: Theory, techniques, applications.* Palo Alto, Calif.: Science and Behavior Books, 1970.

Levitt, E. E., & Lubin, B. *Depression.* New York: Springer, 1975.

Lewinsohn, P. M., & Shaffer, M. Use of home observations as an integral part of the treatment of depression: Preliminary report and case studies. *Journal of Consulting and Clinical Psychology*, 1971, 37, 87–94.

Liberman, R. P. Behavior modification with chronic mental patients. *Journal of Chronic Diseases*, 1971, 23, 803–812.

Liberman, R. P. Behavior modification of schizophrenia: A review. *Schizophrenia Bulletin*, 1972, 6, 37–48.

Lidz, T. The life cycle: Introduction. In S. Arieti (Ed.), *American handbook of psychiatry* (Vol. 1, 2nd ed.). New York: Basic Books, 1974.

Lieberman, M. A., Yalom, I. D., & Miles, M. B. *Encounter groups: First facts.* New York: Basic Books, 1973.

Liebert, R. M., & Spiegler, M. D. *Personality: Strategies for the study of man* (Rev. ed.). Homewood, Ill.: The Dorsey Press, 1974.

Liebson, I. Conversion reaction: A learning theory approach. *Behaviour Research and Therapy*, 1969, 7, 217–218.

Lief, H. I. Sexual functions in men and their disturbances. In S. Arieti (Ed.), *American handbook of psychiatry* (Vol. 1, 2nd ed.). New York: Basic Books, 1974. © 1974 by Basic Books, Inc.

Lindsley, O. R. Characteristics of the behavior of chronic psychotics as revealed by free-operant conditioning methods. *Diseases of the Nervous System*, 1960, 21, 66–78 (Monograph Supplement).

Lippman, H. S. *Treatment of the child in emotional conflict.* New York: McGraw-Hill, 1956. © 1956 by McGraw-Hill, Inc. Used with permission of McGraw-Hill Book Company.

Lipowski, L. J. Psychophysiological cardiovascular disorders. In A. M. Freedman, H. I. Kaplan, & B. J. Sadock (Eds.), *Comprehensive textbook of psychiatry-II* (Vol. 2, 2nd ed.). Williams & Wilkins, 1975.

Lobitz, W. C., & LoPiccolo, J. New methods in the behavioral treatment of sexual dysfunction. *Journal of Behavior Therapy and Experimental Psychiatry*, 1972, 3, 265–271.

London, P. *The modes and morals of psychotherapy.* New York: Holt, Rinehart and Winston, 1964.

Lorr, M., Klett, C., & McNair, D. *Syndromes of psychosis.* London: Pergamon Press, 1963.

Lovaas, O. I. *Behavioral treatment of autistic children.* Morristown, N. J.: General Learning Press, 1973.

Lovaas, O. I., Freitag, G., Gold, V. J., & Kassorla, I. C. Experimental studies in childhood schizophrenia: Analysis of self-destructive behavior. *Journal of Experimental Child Psychology*, 1965, 2, 67–84.

Lovaas, O. I., Koegel, R. L., Simmons, J. Q., & Long, J. S. Some generalization and followup measures on autistic children in behavior therapy. *Journal of Applied Behavior Analysis*, 1973, 6, 131–165.

Lovaas, O. I., & Simmons, J. Q. Manipulation of self-destruction in three retarded children. *Journal of Applied Behavior Analysis*, 1969, *2*, 143–157.

Lovibond, S. H., & Caddy, G. Discriminated aversive control in the moderation of alcoholics' drinking. *Behavior Therapy*, 1970, *1*, 437–444.

Lowen, A. *The betrayal of the body.* New York: Macmillan, 1967.

Lowenthal, M. F., & Chiriboga, D. Transition to the empty nest. *Archives of General Psychiatry*, 1972, *26*, 8–14.

Luby, E. D., & Gottlieb, J. S. Sleep deprivation. In S. Arieti (Ed.), *American handbook of psychiatry* (Vol. 3). New York: Basic Books, 1966.

Ludwig, A. M., Brandisma, J. M., Wilbur, C. B., Bendfelt, F., & Jameson, D. H. The objective study of a multiple personality: Or, are four heads better than one? *Archives of General Psychiatry*, 1972, *26*, 298–310.

Lunde, D. T. *Murder and madness.* San Francisco: San Francisco Book Co., 1976.

Luria, A. *Higher cortical functions in man.* New York: Basic Books, 1966.

Mack, D. T., & Harmatz, M. G. A weight loss program aimed at the facilitation of weight loss maintenance. *Current Concepts in Psychiatry.* (In press)

MacLean, P. D. Contrasting functions of limbic and neocortical systems of the brain and their relevance to psychophysiological aspects of medicine. *American Journal of Medicine*, 1958, *25*, 611–626.

Maddi, S. R. The existential neurosis. *Journal of Abnormal Psychology*, 1967, *72*, 311–325.

Maher, B. A. *Principles of psychopathology.* New York: McGraw-Hill, 1966.

Maher, B. A. *Introduction to research in psychopathology.* New York: McGraw-Hill, 1970.

Mahler, M. S., & Gosliner, B. J. On symbiotic child psychosis. In *Psychoanalytic study of the child* (Vol. X). New York: International Universities Press, 1955.

Mahoney, K., Van Wagenen, R. K., & Meyerson, L. Toilet training of normal and retarded children. *Journal of Applied Behavior Analysis*, 1971, *4*, 173–182.

Mai, F. M. M. Personality and stress in coronary disease. *Journal of Psychosomatic Research*, 1968, *12*, 275–287.

Malan, D. H. The outcome problem in psychotherapy research. *Archives of General Psychiatry*, 1973, *29*, 719–729.

Malmo, R. B. Physiological concomitants of emotion. In A. M. Freedman & H. I. Kaplan (Eds.), *Comprehensive textbook of psychiatry.* Baltimore: Williams & Wilkins, 1967.

Malmo, R. B., & Shagass, C. Physiologic studies of reaction to stress in anxiety and early schizophrenia. *Psychosomatic Medicine*, 1949, *11*, 9–24.

Malzberg, B. Important statistical data about mental illness. In S. Arieti (Ed.), *American handbook of psychiatry.* New York: Basic Books, 1959.

Marks, I., & Lader, M. Anxiety states (anxiety neuroses): A review. *Journal of Nervous and Mental Disease*, 1973, *156*, 3–18.

Marks, M. Management of sexual disorders. In H. Leitenberg (Ed.), *Handbook of behavior modification and behavior therapy.* Englewood Cliffs, N. J.: Prentice-Hall, 1976.

Marlatt, G. A., & Perry, M. A. Modeling methods. In F. H. Kanfer & A. P. Goldstein (Eds.), *Helping people change: A textbook of methods.* New York: Pergamon Press, 1975.

Marquis, J. N. Orgasmic reconditioning: Changing sexual object choice through controlling masturbation fantasies. *Journal of Behavior Therapy and Experimental Psychiatry*, 1970, *1*, 263.

Marshall, W. L. The modification of sexual fantasies: A combined treatment approach to the reduction of deviant behavior. *Behaviour Research and Therapy*, 1973, *11*, 557–564.

Marston, A. R., & McFall, R. M. Comparison of behavior modification approaches to smoking reduction. *Journal of Consulting and Clinical Psychology*, 1971, *37*, 80–86.

Martin, D. G. *Introduction to psychotherapy.* Belmont, Calif.: Brooks/Cole, 1971.

Martin, D. V. Institutionalisation. *Lancet*, 1955, *2*, 1188–1190.

Martinson, R. What works?—questions and answers about prison reform. *The Public Interest*, 1974, *35*, 22–54.

Maslow, A. H. *Motivation and personality.* New York: Harper, 1954.

Maslow, A. H. *The farther reaches of human nature.* New York: Viking, 1971.

Masserman, J. H., Jacques, M. G., & Nicholson, M. R. Alcohol as preventive of experimental neuroses. *Quarterly Journal of the Study of Alcoholism*, 1945, *6*, 281–299.

Masserman, J. H., & Yum, K. S. An analysis of the influence of alcohol on experimental neuroses in cats. *Psychosomatic Medicine*, 1966, *8*, 36–52.

Masters, W. H., & Johnson, V. E. *Human sexual response.* Boston: Little, Brown, 1966.

Masters, W. H., & Johnson, V. E. *Human sexual inadequacy.* Boston: Little, Brown, 1970.

Matarazzo, R. G. Research on the teaching and learning of psychotherapeutic skills. In A. E. Bergin & S. L. Garfield

(Eds.), *Handbook of psychotherapy and behavior change: An empirical analysis.* New York: Wiley, 1971.

Mather, M. D. Obsessions and compulsions. In C. G. Costello (Ed.), *Symptoms of psychopathology.* New York: Wiley, 1970.

Maughs, S. Concept of psychopathy and psychopathic personality: Its education and historical development. *Journal of Criminal Psychopathology,* 1941, *2,* 329, 465.

May, P. R. A. Schizophrenia: Evaluation of treatment methods. In A. M. Freedman, H. I. Kaplan, & B. J. Sadock (Eds.), *Comprehensive textbook of psychiatry-II* (Vol. 1, 2nd ed.). Baltimore, Md.: Williams & Wilkins, 1975.

May, R. The emergence of existential psychology. In R. May (Ed.), *Existential psychology* (2nd ed.). New York: Random House, 1969.

May, R., Angel, E., & Ellengberg, H. *Existence: A new dimension in psychiatry and psychology.* New York: Basic Books, 1958.

Mayer, J. Correlation between metabolism and feeding behavior and multiple etiology of obesity. *Bulletin of the New York Academy of Medicine,* 1957, *22,* 744–761.

Mayer, J., & Thomas, D. W. Regulation of food intake and obesity. *Science,* 1967, *156,* 328–337.

McBrearty, J. F., Dichter, M., Garfield, Z., & Heath, G. A behaviorally oriented treatment program for alcoholism. *Psychological Reports,* 1968, *22,* 287–298.

McCarthy, J. J., & Scheerenberger, R. C. A decade of research on the education of the mentally retarded: A selected review. *Mental Retardation Abstracts,* 1966, *3,* 481–501.

McConaghy, N. The use of an object sorting test in elucidating the hereditary factor in schizophrenia. *Journal of Neurology, Neurosurgery, and Psychiatry,* 1959, *22,* 243–246.

McCord, J., & McCord, W. The effects of parental role model on criminality. *Journal of Social Issues,* 1958, *14,* 66–75.

McCord, W., McCord, J., & Howard, A. Familial correlates of aggression in non-delinquent male children. *Journal of Abnormal and Social Psychology,* 1961, *62,* 79–93.

McCulloch, J. W., & Philip, A. E. *Suicidal behaviour.* New York: Pergamon Press, 1972.

McFall, R. M. The effects of self-monitoring on normal smoking behavior. *Journal of Consulting and Clinical Psychology,* 1970, *35,* 135–142.

McFarland, J. W. Physical measures used in breaking the smoking habit. *Archives of Physical Medicine and Rehabilitation,* 1965, *64,* 323–327.

McFarland, J. W., Gimbel, H. W., Donald, W. J., & Folkenberg, E. J. The 5-day program to help individuals stop smoking. *Connecticut Medicine,* 1964, *28,* 885–890.

McGaughran, L. S. Differences between schizophrenia and brain-damaged groups in conceptual aspects of object sorting. *Journal of Abnormal and Social Psychology,* 1957, *54,* 44–49.

McGhie, A., & Chapman, J. Disorders of attention and perception in early schizophrenia. *British Journal of Medical Psychology,* 1961, *34,* 103–116.

McKinley, J. C., & Hathaway, S. R. A multiphasic personality schedule (Minnesota). II. A differential study of hypochondriasis. *Journal of Psychology,* 1940, *10,* 255–268.

McLean, P. D., Ogston, K., & Graver, L. A behavioral approach to the treatment of depression. *Journal of Behavior Therapy and Experimental Psychiatry,* 1973, *4,* 323–330.

McNeil, E. B. *The psychoses.* Englewood Cliffs, N. J.: Prentice-Hall, 1970. Excerpts on pp. 240–241, 287, 290, 294. © 1970. Reprinted by permission of Prentice-Hall, Inc.

McReynolds, W. T., & Coleman, J. Token economy: Patient and staff changes. *Behaviour Research and Therapy,* 1972, *10,* 29–34.

Mead, M. *Coming of age in Samoa.* New York: Mentor, 1949.

Mednick, S. A. A learning theory approach to schizophrenia. *Psychological Bulletin,* 1958, *55,* 316–327.

Mednick, S. A., & Schulsinger, F. Some premorbid characteristics related to breakdown in children with schizophrenic mothers. In D. Rosenthal & S. S. Kety (Eds.), *The transmission of schizophrenia.* London: Pergamon Press, 1968.

Meehl, P. E. Schizotaxia, schizotypy, schizophrenia. *American Psychologist,* 1962, *17,* 827–838.

Meichenbaum, D. H. Effects of social reinforcement on the level of abstraction in schizophrenics. *Journal of Abnormal and Social Psychology,* 1966, *71,* 354–362.

Meichenbaum, D. H. The effects of instructions and reinforcement on thinking and language behavior of schizophrenics. *Behaviour Research and Therapy,* 1969, *7,* 101–114.

Mendels, J. *Concepts of depression.* New York: Wiley, 1970.

Mendels, J., & Cochrane, C. The nosology of depression: The endogenous-reactive concept. *American Journal of Psychiatry,* 1968, *124* (Supp.), 1–11.

Menkes, M., Rowe, J. S., & Menkes, J. H. A 25-year follow-up study on the hyperkinetic child with minimal brain dysfunction. *Pediatrics,* 1967, *39,* 393–399.

Menninger, K. A. *The crime of punishment.* New York: Viking, 1968.

Menninger, K. A. *Man against himself.* New York: Harcourt Brace, 1938.

Mental health statistics: *Utilization of mental health resources by persons diagnosed with schizophrenia* (Series B, No. 3). Rockville, Md.: National Institute of Mental Health, 1973.

Meyer, A. *Psychobiology: A science of man.* Springfield, Ill.: Charles C Thomas, 1957.

Meyer, J. K. Individual psychotherapy of sexual disorders. In A. M. Freedman, H. I. Kaplan, & B. J. Sadock (Eds.), *The comprehensive textbook of psychiatry-II* (Vol. 2, 2nd ed.). Baltimore: Williams & Wilkins, 1975.

Meyer, V. Modification of expectations in cases of obsessional rituals. *Behaviour Research and Therapy,* 1966, *4,* 273–280.

Meyer, V., & Crisp, A. H. Aversion therapy in two cases of obesity. *Behaviour Research and Therapy,* 1964, *2,* 143–147.

Meyer, V., & Gelder, M. G. Behaviour therapy and phobic disorders. *British Journal of Psychiatry,* 1963, *112,* 367–381.

Miles, H., Waldfogel, S., Barabie, E., & Cobb, S. Psychosomatic study of 46 young men with coronary heart disease. *Psychosomatic Medicine,* 1954, *16,* 455.

Miles, H. W. M., Barrabee, E. L., & Finesinger, J. E. Evaluation of psychotherapy with a follow-up study of 62 cases of anxiety neurosis. *Psychosomatic Medicine,* 1951, *13,* 83–105.

Miller, D., & Schwartz, M. County lunacy commission hearings: Some observations of commitments for a state mental hospital. *Social Problems,* 1966, *14,* 26–35.

Miller, D. H. Psycho-social factors in the aetiology of disturbed behaviour. *British Journal of Medical Psychology,* 1961, *34,* 43–52.

Miller, N. E. Chemical coding of behavior in the brain. *Science,* 1965, *148,* 328–338.

Miller, N. E. Learning of visceral and glandular responses. *Science,* 1969, *163,* 434–445.

Miller, N. P. Interaction between learned and physical factors in mental illness. In C. P. Frank & G. Wilson (Eds.), *Annual review of behavior therapy.* New York: Brunner-Mazel, 1973.

Mills, H. L., Agras, W. S., Barlow, D. H., & Mills, J. R. Compulsive rituals treated by response prevention. *Archives of General Psychiatry,* 1973, *28,* 524–529.

Minc, S. Psychological factors in coronary heart disease. *Geriatrics,* 1965, *20,* 747–755.

Minuchin, S., & Montalvo, B. Techniques for working with disorganized low socioeconomic families. *American Journal of Orthopsychiatry,* 1967, *37,* 880–887.

Mirsky, I. A. Physiologic, psychologic, and social determinants in the etiology of duodenal ulcer. *American Journal of Digestive Diseases,* 1958, *3,* 285–314.

Mischel, W. Theory and research on the antecedents of self-imposed delay of reward. In B. A. Maher (Ed.), *Progress in experimental personality research* (Vol. 3). New York: Academic Press, 1966.

Mischel, W. *Personality and assessment.* New York: Wiley, 1968.

Mischel, W. Toward a cognitive social learning reconceptualization of personality. *Psychological Review,* 1973, *80,* 252–283.

Mitchell, K. R. The treatment of migraine: An exploratory application of time limited therapy. *Technology,* 1969, *14,* 50–55.

Mitchell, K. R. A psychological approach to the treatment of migraine. *British Journal of Psychiatry,* 1971, *119,* 533–534.

Money, J. Intersexual and transsexual behavior and syndromes. In S. Arieti & E. B. Brody (Eds.), *American handbook of psychiatry* (Vol. 3, 2nd ed.). New York: Basic Books, 1974.

Montessori, M. *Montessori method.* New York: Stokes, 1912.

Moody, H. *British Journal of Medical Hypnosis,* 1953, *5,* 23.

Morris, H. H., Escoll, P. J., & Wexler, R. Aggressive behavior disorders of childhood: A followup study. *American Journal of Psychiatry,* 1956, *112,* 991–997.

Morris, L. W., & Thomas, C. R. Treatment of phobias by a self-administered desensitization technique. *Journal of Behavior Therapy and Experimental Psychiatry,* 1973, *4,* 397–399.

Morrison, J. R. Catatonia: Retarded and excited types. *Archives of General Psychiatry,* 1973, *28,* 39–41.

Moss, F. A. Note on building likes and dislikes in children. *Journal of Experimental Psychology,* 1924, *7,* 475–478.

Mowrer, O. H., & Mowrer, W. M. Enuresis: A method for its study and treatment. *American Journal of Orthopsychiatry,* 1938, *8,* 436–459.

Mowrer, O. H. Learning theory and behavior therapy. In B. B. Wolman (Ed.), *Handbook of clinical psychology.* New York: McGraw-Hill, 1965.

Murray, H. A. *Explorations in personality: A clinical and experimental study of fifty men of college age.* New York: Oxford University Press, 1938.

Nathan, P. E. Alcoholism. In H. Leitenberg (Ed.), *Handbook of behavior modification and behavior therapy.* Englewood Cliffs, N. J.: Prentice-Hall, 1976.

Nathan, P. E., & O'Brien, J. S. An experimental analysis of the behavior of alcoholics and nonalcoholics during prolonged experimental drinking: A necessary precursor of behavior therapy? *Behavior Therapy,* 1971, *2,* 455–476.

Nathan, P. E., Titler, N. A., Lowenstein, L. M., Solomon, P., & Rossi, A. M. Behavioral analysis of chronic alcoholism. *Archives of General Psychiatry*, 1970, 22, 419–430.

National Institute of Mental Health. *Distribution of patient care episodes in mental health facilities, 1969, Statistical Note No. 58.* Washington, D. C.: U.S. Government Printing Office, 1972.

Nemiah, J. C. Anxiety: Signal, symptom and syndrome. In S. Arieti & E. B. Brody (Eds.), *American handbook of psychiatry* (Vol. 3, 2nd ed.). New York: Basic Books, 1974.

Nemiah, J. C. Depersonalization neurosis. In A. M. Freedman, H. I. Kaplan, & B. J. Sadock (Eds.), *Comprehensive textbook of psychiatry-II* (2nd ed.). Baltimore, Md.: Williams & Wilkins, 1975.

Nesbitt, P. D. Smoking, physiological arousal, and emotional response. *Journal of Personality and Social Psychology*, 1973, 25, 137–144.

Neugarten, B. L., & Datan, N. The middle years. In S. Arieti (Ed.), *American handbook of psychiatry* (Vol. 1, 2nd ed.). New York: Basic Books, 1974. © 1974 by Basic Books.

Nunnally, J. C. *Popular conceptions of mental health.* New York: Holt, Rinehart and Winston, 1961.

Nyswanders, M. Drug addiction. In S. Arieti & E. B. Brody (Eds.), *American handbook of psychiatry* (Vol. 3, 2nd ed.). New York: Basic Books, 1974.

Obler, M. Systematic desensitization in sexual disorders. *Journal of Behavior Therapy and Experimental Psychiatry*, 1973, 4, 93–101.

O'Brien, J. S., Raynes, A. E., & Patch, V. D. An operant reinforcement system to improve ward behavior in inpatient drug addicts. *Journal of Behavior Therapy and Experimental Psychiatry*, 1971, 2, 239–242.

Offer, D., & Sabshin, M. Normality. In A. M. Freedman, H. I. Kaplan, & B. J. Sadock (Eds.), *Comprehensive textbook of psychiatry-II* (Vol. 1, 2nd ed.). Baltimore: Williams & Wilkins, 1975.

Office of Program Planning and Evaluation. *Patient care episodes in psychiatric services, United States, 1971, Statistical Note No. 92.* Rockville, Md.: National Institute of Mental Health, 1973.

Okulitch, P. V., & Marlatt, G. Effects of varied extinction conditions with alcoholics and social drinkers. *Journal of Abnormal Psychology*, 1972, 79, 303–309.

O'Leary, K. D., & Wilson, G. T. *Behavior Therapy: Application and outcome.* Englewood Cliffs, N. J.: Prentice-Hall, 1975.

Olson, D. H. Marital and family therapy: Integrative review and critique. *Journal of Marriage and the Family*, 1970, 32, 501–538..

Orgel, S. Z. Effect of psychoanalysis on the course of peptic ulcer. *Psychosomatic Medicine*, 1958, 20, 117–123.

Orne, M. Implications for psychotherapy as derived from current research on the nature of hypnosis. *American Journal of Psychiatry*, 1962, 118, 1097.

Ornitz, E. M. Childhood autism: A review of the clinical and experimental literature. *California Medicine*, 1973, 118, 21–47.

Parkes, C. M. *Bereavement: Studies of grief in adult life.* New York: International Universities Press, 1972.

Parkes, C. M., Benjamin, B., & Fitzgerald, R. G. Broken heart: A statistical study of increased mortality among widowers. *British Medical Journal*, 1969, 1, 740–743.

Parloff, M. B. Analytic group psychotherapy. In J. Marmor (Ed.), *Modern psychoanalysis.* New York: Basic Books, 1968.

Parloff, M. B. Group therapy and the small-group field: An encounter. *International Journal of Group Psychotherapy*, 1970, 20, 267–304.

Parry-Jones, W., Santer-Weststrate, H. C., & Crawley, R. C. Behaviour therapy in a case of hysterical blindness. *Behaviour Research and Therapy*, 1970, 8, 79–85.

Patterson, C. H. *Theories of counseling and psychotherapy.* New York: Harper & Row, 1973.

Patterson, G. R. State institutions as teaching machines for delinquent behavior. Unpublished manuscript, University of Oregon, 1963.

Patterson, G. R., Cobb, J. A., & Ray, R. S. A social engineering technology for retraining the families of aggressive boys. In H. E. Adams & I. P. Unikel (Eds.), *Issues and trends in behavior therapy.* Springfield, Ill.: Charles C Thomas, 1973.

Patterson, G. R., Ray, R. S., & Shaw, D. A. Direct intervention in families of deviant children. *Oregon Research Institute Bulletin*, 1968, 8 (9), 1–47.

Patterson, G., Ray, R., & Shaw, D. Direct intervention in families of deviant children. *Oregon Research Institute Bulletin* (Rev. ed.), 1969.

Paul, G. L. Chronic mental patient: Current status—future directions. *Psychological Bulletin*, 1969, 71, 81–94.(a)

Paul, G. L. Outcome of systematic desensitization I & II. In C. M. Franks (Ed.), *Behavior therapy: Appraisal and status.* McGraw-Hill, 1969.(b)

Pavlov, I. P. [*Conditioned reflexes*] (G. V. Anrip, trans.) London: Oxford University Press, 1927.

Paykel, E. S., Myers, J. K., Dieneet, M. N., Lindenthal, J. J., & Pepper, M. P. Life events and depression: A controlled study. *Archives of General Psychiatry*, 1969, 21, 753–760.

Penfield, W., & Roberts, L. *Speech and brain mechanisms.* Princeton: Princeton University Press, 1959.

Penick, S. B., Filion, R., Fox, S., & Stunkard, A. J. *Behavior modification treatment of obesity.* (Paper presented at the annual meeting of the American Psychosomatic Society, Washington, D. C., March 1970.)

Perls, F. S. *Gestalt therapy verbatim.* Moab, Utah: Real People Press, 1967.

Perls, F. S. Four lectures. In J. Fagan & I. L. Shepherd (Eds.), *Gestalt therapy now: Theory, techniques, applications.* Palo Alto, Calif.: Science and Behavior Books, 1970.

Perris, C. A study of bipolar (manic-depressive) and unipolar recurrent depressive psychosis. *Acta Psychiatrica Et Neurologica Scandinavica*, 1966, 42, (Supp. 194), 1–89.

Perrucci, R. *Circle of madness: On being insane and institutionalized in America.* Englewood Cliffs, N. J.: Prentice-Hall, 1974.

Peterson, E. *Psychopharmacology.* Dubuque, Iowa: William Brown, 1966.

Peterson, G. C. Organic brain syndromes associated with brain trauma. In A. M. Freedman, H. I. Kaplan, & B. J. Sadock (Eds.), *The comprehensive textbook of psychiatry-II* (Vol. 1, 2nd ed.). Baltimore: Williams & Wilkins, 1975.(a)

Peterson, G. C. Organic brain syndromes associated with drug or poison intoxication. In A. M. Freedman, H. I. Kaplan, & B. J. Sadock (Eds.), *The comprehensive textbook of psychiatry-II* (Vol. 1, 2nd ed.). Baltimore: Williams & Wilkins, 1975.(b)

Pfeiffer, E. Survivor in old age: Physical, psychological and social correlates of longevity. *Journal of the American Geriatric Society*, 1970, 18, 273–285.

Pfister, H. O. Disturbances of autonomic function in schizophrenia. *American Journal of Psychiatry*, 1938, 94, 109–118.

Phillips, D. L. Rejection: A possible consequence of seeking help for mental disorders. *American Sociological Review*, 1963, 28, 963–972.

Phillips, E. L. Achievement Place: Token reinforcement procedures in a home-style rehabilitation setting for "predelinquent" boys. *Journal of Applied Behavior Analysis*, 1968, 1, 213–223.

Phillips, E. L., Phillips, E. A., Fixsen, D. L., & Wolf, M. M. Achievement place: Modification of the behaviors of predelinquent boys with a token economy. *Journal of Applied Behavioral Analysis*, 1971, 4, 45–60.

Phillips, L. Case history and prognosis in schizophrenia. *Journal of Nervous and Mental Disease*, 1953, 117, 515–525.

Phillips, L., & Zigler, E. The action-thought parameter and vicariousness in normal and pathological behaviors. *Journal of Abnormal and Social Psychology*, 1961, 63, 137–146.

Pitts, F. N., Meyer, J., Brooks, M., & Winokur, G. Adult psychiatric illness assessed for childhood parental loss and psychiatric illness in family members. *American Journal of Psychiatry*, 1965, 121 (Suppl.), i–x.

Piotrowski, Z. A. Psychological testing of intelligence and personality. In A. M. Freedman & H. I. Kaplan (Eds.), *Comprehensive textbook of psychiatry.* Baltimore: Williams & Wilkins, 1967.

Pokorny, A. D. Myths about suicide. In H. L. P. Resnik (Ed.), *Suicidal behaviors.* Boston: Little, Brown, 1968.

Pollin, W. The pathogenesis of schizophrenia. *Archives of General Psychiatry*, 1972, 27, 29–37.

Post, F., Rees, W. L., & Schurr, P. H. An evaluation of biomedical leucotomy. *British Journal of Psychiatry*, 1968, 114, 1223.

Poussaint, A. F. Interracial relations. In A. M. Freedman, H. I. Kaplan, & B. J. Sadock (Eds.), *Comprehensive textbook of psychiatry-II* (Vol. 2, 2nd ed.). Baltimore: Williams & Wilkins, 1975.

Premack, D. Toward empirical behavior laws: I. Positive reinforcement. *Psychological Review*, 1959, 66, 219–233.

Premack, D. Reinforcement theory. In D. Levine (Ed.), *Nebraska Symposium on Motivation.* Lincoln, Nebr.: University of Nebraska Press, 1965.

Price, R. *Abnormal behavior: Perspectives in conflict.* New York: Holt, Rinehart and Winston, 1972.

Prince, M. *The dissociation of a personality.* New York: Longmans, Green, 1906.

Rabin, A. I. The estimation of schizophrenics and non-psychotics. *Journal of Clinical Psychology*, 1957, 13, 88–90.

Rabkin, J. G. Opinions about mental illness: A review of the literature. *Psychological Bulletin*, 1972, 77, 153–171.

Rachin, R. L. Reality therapy: Helping people help themselves. *Crime and Delinquency*, January 1974, pp. 45–53.

Rachman, S. Sexual fetishism: An experimental analogue. *Psychological Record*, 1966, 16, 293–296.

Rachman, S., & Hodgson, R. J. Experimentally induced "sexual fetishism": A replication and development. *Psychological Record*, 1968, 18, 25–27.

Rachman, S., Hodgson, R., & Marks, I. M. The treatment of chronic obsessive-compulsive neurosis. *Behaviour Research and Therapy*, 1971, 9, 237–247.

Rahe, R. H., & Lind, E. Psychosocial factors and sudden cardiac death: A pilot study. *Journal of Psychosomatic Research*, 1971, 15, 19–24.

Raimy, V. C. (Ed.). *Training in clinical psychology.* Englewood Cliffs, N. J.: Prentice-Hall, 1950.

Rainer, J. D. New topics in psychiatric genetics. In S. Arieti (Ed.), *American handbook of psychiatry* (Vol. 3). New York: Basic Books, 1966.

Ramsay, R. A., Witkower, E. D., & Warnes, H. Treatment of psychosomatic disorders. In B. B. Wolman (Ed.), *The therapist's handbook.* New York: Van Nostrand Reinhold, 1976.

Rank, B. Intensive study and treatment of pre-school children who showed marked personality deviations or "atypical development," and their parents. In G. Caplan, *Emotional problems of early childhood.* New York: Basic Books, 1955.

Rappaport, J., Chinsky, J. M., & Cowen, E. L. *Innovations in helping chronic patients: College students in a mental institution.* New York: Academic Press, 1971.

Rappeport, J. R. Antisocial behavior. In S. Arieti & E. B. Brody (Eds.), *American handbook of psychiatry* (Vol. 3, 2nd ed.). New York: Basic Books, 1974.

Raush, H. L., & Bordin, E. S. Warmth in personality development and in psychotherapy. *Psychiatry,* 1957, *20,* 351–363.

Ravich, R., Deutsch, M., & Brown, B. An experimental study of marital discord and decision making. In I. Cohen (Ed.), *Family structure dynamics and therapy.* Psychiatric Research Report No. 20, Washington, D. C.: American Psychiatric Association, 1966.

Raymond, M. J. The treatment of addiction by aversion conditioning with apomorphine. *Behavior Research and Therapy,* 1964, *1,* 287–291.

Razani, J. Treatment of phobias by systematic desensitization: Comparison of standard vs methohexital-aided desensitization. *Archives of General Psychiatry,* 1974, *30,* 291–293.

Rea, R. B. The rights of the mentally ill: A proposal for procedural changes in hospital admission and discharge. *Psychiatry,* 1966, *29,* 213–226.

Rees, W. D., & Lutkins, S. G. Mortality of bereavement. *British Medical Journal,* 1967, *4,* 13–16.

Reiser, M. F. Changing theoretical concepts in psychosomatic medicine. In S. Arieti & M. F. Reiser (Eds.), *American handbook of psychiatry* (Vol. 4, 2nd ed.). New York: Basic Books, 1975.

Reisinger, J. J. The treatment of "anxiety-depression" via positive reinforcement and response cost. *Journal of Applied Behavior Analysis,* 1972, *5,* 125–130.

Resnik, H. L. P., & Kantor, J. M. Suicide and aging. *Journal of the American Geriatric Society,* 1970, *7,* 152–158.

Richter, C. P. On the phenomenon of sudden death in animals and man. *Psychosomatic Medicine,* 1957, *19,* 191–198.

Rickard, H. C., Dignam, P. J., & Horner, R. F. Verbal manipulation in a psychotherapeutic relationship. *Journal of Clinical Psychology,* 1960, *16,* 364–367.

Rimland, B. *Infantile autism: The syndrome and its implications for a neural theory of behavior.* Englewood Cliffs, N. J.: Prentice-Hall (ACC), 1964.

Rimm, D. C., & Masters, J. C. *Behavior therapy: Techniques and empirical findings.* New York: Academic Press, 1974.

Ringuette, E. L., & Kennedy, T. An experimental study of the double-bind hypothesis. *Journal of Abnormal Psychology,* 1966, *71,* 136–141.

Rivera, G. *Willowbrook.* New York: Random House, 1972.

Robbins, L. L. A historical review of classification of behavior disorders and one current perspective. In L. D. Eron (Ed.), *The classification of behavior disorders.* Chicago: Aldine, 1966.

Robertson, J., & Bowlby, J. Responses of young children to separation from their mothers. *Courr. Cent. Internat. l'Enfance,* 1952, *2,* 131–142.

Robins, E. Personality disorders II: Sociopathic type: Antisocial disorders and sexual deviations. In A. M. Freedman & H. I. Kaplan (Eds.). *Comprehensive textbook of psychiatry.* Baltimore: Williams & Wilkins, 1967.

Robins, E., Gassner, S., Kayes, J., Wilkinson, R. H., & Murphy, G. E. The communication of suicidal intent: A study of 134 consecutive cases of successful (completed) suicide. *American Journal of Psychiatry,* 1959, *115,* 724–733.

Robins, L. N. *Deviant children grown up: A sociological and psychiatric study of sociopathic personality.* Baltimore: Williams & Wilkins, 1966.

Robinson, H. B., & Robinson, N. M. *The mentally retarded child: A psychological approach.* New York: McGraw-Hill, 1965. Excerpts on pp. 395–396, 400–402. © 1965 by McGraw-Hill, Inc. Used with permission of McGraw-Hill Book Company.

Robinson, J. C., & Lewinsohn, P. M. Behavior modification of speech characteristics in a chronically depressed man. *Behavior Therapy,* 1973, *4,* 150–152.(a)

Robinson, J. C., & Lewinsohn, P. M. Experimental analysis of a technique based on the Premack Principle changing verbal behavior of depressed individuals. *Psychological Reports,* 1973, *32,* 199–210.(b)

Roen, S. R. Evaluative research and community mental health. In A. E. Bergin & S. L. Garfield (Eds.). *Handbook of psychotherapy and behavior change: An empirical analysis.* New York: Wiley, 1971.

Roff, J. D. Adolescent schizophrenia: Variables related to differences in long-term adult outcome. *Journal of Consulting and Clinical Psychiatry,* 1974, *42,* 180–183.

Rogers, C. R. The necessary and sufficient conditions of therapeutic personality change. *Journal of Consulting Psychology,* 1957, *21,* 95–103.

Rogers, C. R. A theory of therapy, personality, and interpersonal relationships, as developed in client-centered framework. In S. Koch (Ed.), *Psychology: A study of a science* (Vol. 3). New York: McGraw-Hill, 1959.

Rogers, C. R. *On becoming a person.* Boston: Houghton Mifflin, 1961.

Rogers, C. R. Client-centered therapy. In S. Arieti (Ed.), *American handbook of psychiatry* (Vol. 3). New York: Basic Books, 1966.

Rogers, C. R. A theory of personality. In T. Millon (Ed.), *Theories of psychopathology.* Philadelphia: Saunders, 1973.

Rollins, H. A., McCandless, B. R., Thompson, M., & Brassell, W. R. Project success environment: An extended application of contingency management in inner-city schools. *Journal of educational psychology,* 1974, 66, 167–178.

Rose, R. J. Preliminary study of three incidents of arousal: Measurement, interrelationships, and clinical correlates. Unpublished doctoral dissertation, University of Minnesota, 1964.

Rosen, J. N. The treatment of schizophrenic psychosis by direct analytic therapy. *Psychiatric Quarterly,* 1947, 2, 3.

Rosen, J. N. *Direct analysis: Selected papers.* New York: Grune & Stratton, 1953.

Rosenhan, D. L. On being sane in insane places. *Science,* 1973, 179, 250–258.

Rosenhan, D. L. On being sane in insane places. In T. J. Scheff (Ed.), *Labeling madness.* Englewood Cliffs, N. J.: Prentice-Hall, 1975.

Rosenthal, D. A program of research on heredity in schizophrenia. *Behavioral Science,* 1971, 16, 191–201.

Rosenthal, D. The genetics of schizophrenia. In S. Arieti & E. B. Brody (Eds.), *American handbook of psychiatry* (Vol. 3, 2nd ed.). New York: Basic Books, 1974. © 1974 by Basic Books, Inc.

Rosenthal, R., & Jacobson, L. *Pygmalion in the classroom.* New York: Holt, Rinehart and Winston, 1968.

Rosenthal, S. H. Electrosleep: A double-blind clinical study. *Biological Psychiatry,* 1972, 4, 179.

Ross, A. O. Behavior therapy. In H. C. Quay & J. S. Werry (Eds.), *Psychopathological disorders of childhood.* New York: Wiley, 1972.

Ross, A. O. *Psychological disorders of children: A behavioral approach to theory, research, and therapy.* New York: McGraw-Hill, 1974.

Ross, D. M., & Ross, S. A. The efficacy of listening training for educable mentally retarded children. *American Journal of Mental Deficiency,* 1972, 77, 137–142.

Ross, D. M., & Ross, S. A. Cognitive training for the EMR child: Situational problem solving and planning. *American Journal of Mental Deficiency,* 1973, 78, 20–26.

Ross, H. Orthomolecular psychiatry: Vitamin pill for schizophrenia. *Psychology Today,* 1974, 7, 82.

Ross, S. A. Effects of an intensive motor skills training program on young educable mentally retarded children. *American Journal of Mental Deficiency,* 1969, 73, 920–926.

Rowe, C. J. *An outline of psychiatry* (6th ed.). Dubuque, Iowa: Wm. C. Brown Company, 1975.

Rutter, M. (Ed.). *Infantile autism: Concepts, characteristics, and treatment.* London: Churchill Livingstone, 1971.

Ryan, W. Emotional disorder as a social problem: Implications for mental health programs. In B. Denner & R. H. Price (Eds.), *Community mental health.* New York: Holt, Rinehart and Winston, 1973.

Saghir, M. T., & Robbins, E. *Male and female homosexuality.* Baltimore: Williams & Wilkins, 1973.

Salzman, L. Other character-personality syndromes: Schizoid, inadequate, passive-aggressive, paranoid, dependent. In S. Arieti (Ed.), *American handbook of psychiatry* (Vol. 3, 2nd ed.). New York: Basic Books, 1974. © 1974 by Basic Books, Inc.

Sanderson, R. E., Campbell, D., & Laverty, S. G. An investigation of a new aversive conditioning treatment for alcoholism. *Quarterly Journal of the Study of Alcoholism,* 1963, 24, 261–275.

Sandhu, H. S. *Modern corrections: The offenders, therapies and community reintegration.* Springfield, Ill.: Charles C Thomas, 1974.

Sandler, J., & Davidson, R. S. *Psychopathology: Learning theory, research, and applications.* New York: Harper & Row, 1973.

Sandok, B. A. Organic brain syndromes: Introduction. In A. M. Freedman, H. I. Kaplan, & B. J. Sadock (Eds.), *The comprehensive textbook of psychiatry-II* (Vol. 1, 2nd ed.). Baltimore: Williams & Wilkins, 1975.(a)

Sarbin, T. R. The scientific status of the mental illness paradigm. In S. C. Plog & R. B. Edgerton (Eds.), *Changing perspectives in mental health.* New York: Holt, Rinehart and Winston, 1969.

Sarbin, T. R., & Mancuso, J. C. Failure of a moral enterprise: Attitudes of the public toward mental illness. *Journal of Consulting and Clinical Psychology,* 1970, 35, 159–173.

Satterfield, J. H., & Dawson, M. E. Electrodermal correlates of hyperactivity in children. *Psychophysiology,* 1971, 8, 191–197.

Sawrey, W. L., Conger, J. J., & Turrell, E. S. An experimental investigation of the role of psychological factors in the production of gastric ulcers in rats. *Journal of Comparative and Physiological Psychology,* 1956, 49, 457–461.

Sawrey, W. L., & Weisz, J. D. An experimental method of producing gastric ulcers. *Journal of Comparative and Physiological Psychology*, 1956, 49, 269–270.

Schachter, A., & Gross, L. P. Manipulated time and eating behavior. *Journal of Personality and Social Psychology*, 1968, 10, 98–106.

Schachter, S. *The psychology of affiliation*. Stanford, Calif.: Stanford University Press, 1959.

Schaefer, H. H., & Martin, P. L. Behavioral therapy for "apathy" of hospitalized schizophrenics. *Psychological Report*, 1966, 19, 1147–1158.

Schaefer, H. H., & Martin, P. L. *Behavioral therapy*. New York: McGraw-Hill, 1969.

Scheff, T. J. The role of the mentally ill and the dynamics of mental disorder. *Sociometry*, 1963, 26, 436–453.

Schiele, B. C., & Brozek, J. Experimental neurosis resulting from semistarvation in man. *Psychosomatic Medicine*, 1948, 10, 31–50.

Schmidtz, H. O., & Fonda, C. The reliability of psychiatric diagnosis. *Journal of Abnormal and Social Psychology*, 1956, 52, 262–267.

Schofield, W. *Psychotherapy: The purchase of friendship*. Englewood Cliffs, N. J.: Prentice-Hall, 1964.

Schooler, N. R., Goldberg, S. C., Boothe, H., & Cole, J. O. One year after discharge: Community adjustment of schizophrenic patients. *American Journal of Psychiatry*, 1967, 123, 986–995.

Schroeder, S. R. Parametric effects of reinforcement frequency, amount of reinforcement, and required response force on sheltered workshop behavior. *Journal of Applied Behavior Analysis*, 1972, 5, 431–442.

Schukit, M. A., Goodwin, D. W., & Winokur, G. A study of alcoholism in half siblings. *American Journal of Psychiatry*, 1972, 128 (9), 1132–1136.

Schulsinger, F. Psychopathy: Heredity and environment. *International Journal of Mental Health*, 1972, 1, 190.

Schutte, R. C., & Hopkins, B. L. The effects of teacher attention on following instructions in a kindergarten class. *Journal of Applied Behavior Analysis*, 1970, 3, 117–122.

Schuyler, D. Treatment of depressive disorders. In B. B. Wolman (Ed.), *The therapist's handbook*. New York: Van Nostrand Reinhold, 1976.

Schwartz, A. H., & Swartzburg, M. Hospital care. In B. B. Wolman (Ed.), *The therapist's handbook*. New York: Van Nostrand Reinhold, 1976.

Schwartz, G. E. Biofeedback as therapy. *American Psychologist*, 1973, 28, 666–673.

Schwartz, G. E., Shapiro, D., & Tursky, B. Learned control of cardiovascular integration in man through operant conditioning. *Psychosomatic Medicine*, 1971, 33, 57–62.

Scott, W. A. Research definitions of mental health and mental illness. *Psychological Bulletin*, 1958, 55, 29–45.

Sechehaye, M. A. *Symbolic realization*. New York: International Universities Press, 1951.

Sechehaye, M. A. *A new psychotherapy in schizophrenia*. New York: Grune & Stratton, 1956.

Seiden, R. H. Campus tragedy: A study of student suicide. *Journal of Abnormal Psychology*, 1966, 71, 389–399.

Seligman, M. E. P. *Helplessness*. San Francisco: W. H. Freeman, 1975.

Sellin, T. Correction in historical perspective. In R. M. Carter, D. Glaser, & L. T. Wilkins (Eds.). *Correctional institutions*. Philadelphia: Lippincott, 1972.

Selye, H. The general adaptation syndrome and the diseases of adaptation. *Journal of Clinical Endocrinology*, 1946, 6, 117–128.

Selye, H. *The stress of life*. New York: McGraw-Hill, 1956.

Shapiro, A. K. Placebo effects in medicine, psychotherapy, and psychoanalysis. In A. E. Bergin & S. L. Garfield (Eds.), *Handbook of psychotherapy and behavior change*. New York: Wiley, 1971.

Shapiro, D., Tursky, B., Gershon, E., & Stern, M., Effects of feedback and reinforcement on the control of human systolic blood pressure. *Science*, 1969, 163, 588–589.

Shapiro, M. B. The single case in clinical-psychological research. *The Journal of General Psychology*, 1966, 74, 3–23.

Shaw, C. R., & McKay, H. D. Social factors in juvenile delinquency. *National Commission on Law Observance and Enforcement, Report on the Causes of Crime* (Vol. 2). Washington, D. C.: Government Printing Office, 1931.

Sheehy, G. *Passages: Predictable crisis of adult life*. New York: Dutton, 1974.

Sheldon, W. (with the collaboration of E. M. Hartl & E. McDermott). *Varieties of delinquent youth*. New York: Harper, 1949.

Shenger-Krestovnikova, N. R. Contributions to question of differentiation of visual stimuli and the limits of differentiation by the visual analyzer of the dog. *Bulletin of Lesgaft Institute of Petrograd*, 1921, 3, 11–43.

Shneidman, E. S. Projective techniques. In B. B. Wolman (Ed.), *Handbook of clinical psychology*. New York: McGraw-Hill, 1965.

Shneidman, E. S. Suicide, lethality, and the psychological autopsy. In E. S. Shneidman & M. Ortega (Eds.), *Aspects of depression*. Boston: Little, Brown, 1969.

Shneidman, E. S. Suicide notes reconsidered. *Psychiatry*, 1973, 36, 379–394. Excerpt pp. 307–308. © 1973 by The William Alanson White Psychiatric Foundation, Inc. Reprinted by special permission of *Psychiatry*. Excerpt

p. 308, Frombley, L. E. A psychiatrist's response to a life-threatening illness. *Life-Threatening Behavior*, 1972, 2, 26–34 (original source).

Shneidman, E. S. Suicide. In A. M. Freedman, H. I. Kaplan, & B. J. Sadock (Eds.), *Comprehensive textbook of psychiatry-II* (Vol. 2, 2nd ed.). Baltimore, Md.: Williams & Wilkins, 1975.

Shoben, E. J., Jr. Toward a concept of the normal personality. *American Psychologist*, 1957, 12, 183–189.

Sifneos, P. E. Is dynamic psychotherapy contraindicated for a large number of patients with psychosomatic diseases? *Psychotherapy and Psychosomatics*, 1972, 21, 133–136.

Silber, D. E. Controversy concerning the criminal justice system and its implications for the role of mental health workers. *American Psychologist*, 1974, 29, 239–244.

Simon, W., Wirt, A. L., Wirt, R. D., & Halloran, A. V. Long-term follow-up study of schizophrenic patients. *Archives of General Psychiatry*, 1965, 12, 510–515.

Skinner, B. F. *Science and human behavior.* New York: Macmillan, 1953.

Skinner, B. F. Critique of psychoanalytic concepts and theories. *Scientific Monthly*, 1954, 79, 300–305.

Slater, E., & Roth, M. *Clinical psychiatry* (3rd ed.). Baltimore, Md.: Williams & Wilkins, 1969.

Slavney, P. R., & McHugh, P. R. The hysterical personality. *Archives of General Psychiatry*, 1974, 30, 325–329.

Sloan, W., & Birch, J. W. A rationale for degrees of retardation. *American Journal of Mental Deficiency*, 1955–1956, 60, 258–264.

Smith, J. C. Psychotherapeutic effects of transcendental meditation with controls for expectation of relief and daily sitting. *Journal of Consulting and Clinical Psychology*, 1976, 44, 630–637.

Smith, K., Pumphrey, M. W., & Hall, J. C. The "last straw": The decisive incident resulting in the request for hospitalization in 100 schizophrenic patients. *American Journal of Psychiatry*, 1963, 120, 228–233.

Smith, M. B. "Mental Health" reconsidered: A special case of the problem of values in psychology. *American Psychologist*, 1961, 16, 229–306.

Sobell, M. B., & Sobell, L. C. Individualized behavior therapy for alcoholics. *Behavior Therapy*, 1973, 4, 49–72.

Solomon, R. L. Letter quoted by O. H. Mowrer. *Learning theory and ten symbolic processes.* New York: Wiley, 1960.

Solomon, R. L., Turner, L. H., & Lessac, M. S. Some effects of delay of punishment on resistance to temptation in dogs. *Journal of Personality and Social Psychology*, 1968, 8, 233–238.

Solomon, R. W., & Wahler, R. G. Peer reinforcement control of classroom problem behavior. *Journal of Applied Behavior Analysis*, 1973, 6, 49–56.

Sommer, R., & Witney, G. The chain of chronicity. *American Journal of Psychiatry*, 1961, 118, 111–117.

Sperling, M. The neurotic child and his mother: A psychoanalytic study. *American Journal of Orthopsychiatry*, 1951, 21, 351–362.

Spitz, R. A., & Wolf, K. Anaclitic depression. *Psychoanalytic Study of the Child*, 1946, 2, 313–342.

Srole, L., Langer, T. S. Michael, S. T., Opler, M. K., & Rennie, T. A. C. *Mental health in the metropolis: The Midtown Manhattan Study* (Vol. 1). New York: McGraw-Hill, 1962.

Stampfl, T. G., & Levis, D. J. Essentials of implosive therapy: A learning-theory-based psychodynamic behavioral therapy. *Journal of Abnormal Psychology*, 1967, 72, 496–503.

Stephens, T. M. Using reinforcement and social modeling with delinquent youth. *Review of Educational Research*, 1973, 43, 323–340.

Stieper, D. R., & Wiener, D. N. *Dimensions of psychotherapy: An experimental and clinical approach.* Chicago: Aldine, 1965.

Stojanovich, K. Antisocial and dyssocial: Entities or shibboleths? *Archives of General Psychiatry*, 1969, 21, 561–567.

Stokvis, B. Possibilities et limitations de la relaxation dans la medecine psychosomatique. *Revue de Medecine Psychosomatique*, 1960, 2, 142–147.

Stoler, N. Client likability: A variable in the study of psychotherapy. *Journal of Consulting Psychology*, 1963, 27, 175–181.

Stone, S. Psychiatry through the ages. *Journal of Abnormal and Social Psychology*, 1937, 32, 131–160.

Strauss, A. A., & Werner, H. Disorders of conceptual thinking in the brain-injured child. *Journal of Nervous and Mental Disease*, 1942, 96, 153–172.

Stuart, R. B. A three dimensional program for the treatment of obesity. *Behaviour Research and Therapy*, 1971, 9, 177–186.

Stuart, R. B. Behavioral control of overeating. *Behaviour Research and Therapy*, 1967, 5, 357–365.

Stuart, R. B., & Davis, B. *Slim chance in a fat world: Behavioral control of obesity.* Champaign, Ill.: Research Press, 1972.

Stubblefield, R. L. Sociopathic personality disorders. I: Antisocial and dyssocial reactions. In A. M. Freedman & H. I. Kaplan (Eds.), *Comprehensive textbook of psychiatry.* Baltimore: Williams & Wilkins, 1967.

Stunkard, A. J. Obesity and the denial of hunger. *Psychosomatic Medicine*, 1959, 21, 281–289.

Stunkard, A. J., & Mahoney, M. J. Behavioral treatment of eating disorders. In H. Leitenberg (Ed.), *Handbook of* behavior modification and behavior therapy. Englewood Cliffs, N. J.: Prentice-Hall, 1976.

Suinn, R. M., & Richardson, F. Anxiety management training: A nonspecific behavior therapy program for anxiety control. *Behavior Therapy*, 1971, *2*, 498–510.

Sullivan, H. S. *Conceptions of modern psychiatry*. New York: Norton, 1953.

Sullivan, H. S. *Schizophrenia as a human process*. New York: Norton, 1962.

Sullivan, R. Violence, like charity, begins at home. In B. Denner & R. H. Price (Eds.), *Community mental health: Social action and reaction*. New York: Holt, Rinehart and Winston, 1973.

Sundberg, N. D., & Tyler, L. E. *Clinical psychology: An introduction to research and practice*. New York: Appleton-Century-Crofts, 1962.

Sundberg, N. D., Tyler, L. E., & Taplin, J. R. *Clinical psychology: Expanding horizons* (2nd ed.). Englewood Cliffs, N.J.: Prentice-Hall (ACC), 1973.

Szasz, T. S. *The manufacture of madness*. New York: Hoeber, 1970.

Szasz, T. S. The myth of mental illness. *American Psychologist*, 1960, *15*, 113–118.

Szasz, T. S. *Law, liberty, and psychiatry*. New York: Macmillan, 1963.

Tabachnick, N. D., & Farberow, N. L. The assessment of self-destructive potentiality. In N. L. Farberow & E. S. Shneidman (Eds.), *The cry for help*. New York: McGraw-Hill, 1961.

Task Force, Special Committee on Aging, U. S. Senate. *Economics of aging: Toward a full share in abundance*. Washington, D. C.: U.S. Government Printing Office, 1969.

Taylor, J. A., & Spence, K. W. Conditioning level in the behavior disorders. *Journal of Abnormal Psychology*, 1954, *49*, 497–502.

Taylor, V. O., & Brown, G. D. The use of swift, brief isolation as a control device for institutionalized delinquents. *Behaviour Research and Therapy*, 1967, *5*, 1–9.

Tharp, R. G., & Wetzel, R. J. *Behavior modification in the natural environment*. New York: Academic Press, 1969.

Thigpen, C. H., & Cleckley, H. A case of multiple personality. *The Journal of Abnormal and Social Psychology*, 1954, *49*, 135–151.

Thomas, A., & Sillen, S. *Racism and psychiatry*. New York: Brunner-Mazel, 1972.

Thoresen, C. E., & Mahoney, M. J. *Behavioral self-control*. New York: Holt, Rinehart and Winston, 1974.

Thorndike, E. L. *The elements of psychology*. New York: A. G. Seiler, 1905.

Thorne, F. C. The etiology of sociopathic reactions. *American Journal of Psychotherapy*, 1959, *13*, 319–330.

Toffler, A. *Future shock*. New York: Random House, 1970. © by Random House, Inc. Reprinted by permission.

Torrey, E. F. Is schizophrenia universal? An open question. *Schizophrenia Bulletin*, 1973, *7*, 53–59.

Tredgold, A. F. *A textbook of mental deficiency* (6th ed.). Baltimore: Wood, 1937.

Trotter, R. J. Behavior modification: Here, there, and everywhere. *Science News*, 1973, *103*(16), 260–263.

Tuerk, K., Fish, I., & Ransohoff, J. Head injury. In S. Arieti & M. F. Reiser (Eds.), *American handbook of psychiatry* (Vol. 4, 2nd ed.). New York: Basic Books, 1975.

Turnbull, J. W. Asthma conceived as a learned response. *Journal of Psychosomatic Research*, 1962, *6*, 59–70.

Ullmann, L. P., & Krasner, L. (Eds.). *Case studies in behavior modification*. New York: Holt, Rinehart and Winston, 1965.

Ullmann, L. P., & Krasner, L. *A psychological approach to abnormal behavior* (1st ed.). Englewood Cliffs, N. J.: Prentice-Hall, 1969.

Ullmann, L. P., & Krasner, L. *A psychological approach to abnormal behavior* (2nd ed.). Englewood Cliffs, N. J.: Prentice-Hall, 1975.

U. S. Public Health Service, *Obesity and health* (U. S. Public Health Service Publication No. 1485). Washington, D. C.: U.S. Government Printing Office, 1966.

Van der Valk, J. M., & Groen, J. J. Personality structure and conflict situation in patients with myocardial infarction. *Journal of Psychosomatic Research*, 1967, *11*, 41–46.

Venables, P. H., & Wing, J. K. Level of arousal and the subclassification of schizophrenia. *Archives of General Psychiatry*, 1962, *7*, 114–119.

Voegtlin, W. L. The treatment of alcoholism by establishing a conditioned reflex. *American Journal of Medical Science*, 1940, *199*, 802–810.

Vogel, E. F., & Bell, N. W. The emotionally disturbed child as the family scapegoat. In N. W. Bell & E. F. Vogel (Eds.), *A modern introduction to the family*. New York: The Free Press, 1968.

von Domarus, E. The specific laws of logic in schizophrenia. In J. S. Kasanin (Ed.), *Language and thought in schizophrenia*. Berkeley, Calif.: University of California Press, 1944.

von Domarus, E. The specific laws of logic in schizophrenia. In J. S. Kasanin (Ed.), *Language and thought in schizophrenia*. New York: Norton, 1964.

Wagenfeld, M. O. The primary prevention of mental illness: A sociological perspective. *Journal of Health and Social Behavior*, 1972, *13*, 195–203.

Wahler, R. G. Deviant child behavior within the family: Developmental speculations and behavior change strategies. In H. Leitenberg (Ed.), *Handbook of behavior modification and behavior therapy*. Englewood Cliffs, N. J.: Prentice-Hall, 1976.

Wahler, R. G., & Cormier, W. H. The ecological interview: A first step in out-patient child behavior therapy. *Journal of Behavior Therapy and Experimental Psychiatry*, 1970, 1, 293–303.

Wallace, R. K., & Benson, H. The physiology of meditation. *Scientific American*, 1972, 226, 84.

Walton, D. The application of learning theory to the treatment of a case of bronchial asthma. In H. J. Eysenck (Ed.), *Behavior therapy and the neuroses*. New York: Pergamon Press, 1960.

Ward, A. J. Early infantile autism: Diagnosis, etiology, and treatment. *Psychological Bulletin*, 1970, 73, 350–362.

Ward, C. H., Beck, A. T., Mendelson, M., & Mock, S. E. The psychiatric nomenclature. *Archives of General Psychiatry*, 1962, 7, 198–205.

Watson, A. S. Forensic Psychiatry. In A. M. Freedman, H. I. Kaplan, & B. J. Sadock (Eds.), *Comprehensive textbook of psychiatry-II* (Vol. 2, 2nd ed.). Baltimore: Williams & Wilkins, 1975.

Watson, J. B., & Rayner, R. Conditioned emotional reactions. *Journal of Experimental Psychology*, 1920, 3, 1–14.

Watt, N. F. Longitudinal changes in the social behavior of children hospitalized for schizophrenia as adults. *Journal of Nervous and Mental Disease*, 1972, 155, 42–54.

Weckowicz, T. E. Size constancy in schizophrenia patients. *Journal of Mental Science*, 1957, 103, 475–486.

Weiner, H., Thaler, M., Reiser, M. F., & Mirsky, I. A. Etiology of duodenal ulcer: I. Relation of specific psychological characteristics to rate of gastric secretion (Serum Pepsinogen). *Psychosomatic Medicine*, 1957, 19, 1–10.

Weinstock, H. J. Successful treatment of ulcerative colitis by psychoanalysts. *Journal of Psychosomatic Research*, 1962, 6, 243–249.

Weiss, G., Minde, K., Werry, J. S., Douglas, V., & Nemeth, E. Studies of the hyperactive child: Five year follow-up. *Archives of General Psychiatry*, 1971, 24, 409–414.

Weiss, J. M. Affects of coping response on stress. *Journal of Comparative Physiological Psychology*, 1968, 65, 251–260.

Weissman, M. N. The epidemiology of suicide attempts. *Archives of General Psychiatry*, 1974, 30, 737–745.

Wells, R. A., Dilkes, T. C., & Trivelli, N. The results of family therapy: A critical review of the literature. *Family Process*, 1972, 11, 184–207.

Wender, P. H. The minimal brain dysfunction syndrome in children. *Journal of Nervous and Mental Disease*, 1972, 155, 55–71.

Werry, J. S. Studies on the hyperactive child: An empirical analysis of the minimal brain dysfunction syndrome. *Archives of General Psychiatry*, 1968, 19, 9–16.

Weston, W. D. Development of community psychiatry concepts. In A. M. Freedman, H. I. Kaplan, & B. J. Sadock (Eds.), *Comprehensive textbook of psychiatry-II* (Vol. 2, 2nd ed.). Baltimore: Williams & Wilkins, 1975.

Wheeler, A. J., & Sulzer, B. Operant training and generalization of verbal response form in a speech deficient child. *Journal of Applied Behavior Analysis*, 1970, 3, 139–147.

Wheeler, E. O., White, P. D., Reed, W. E., & Cohen, M. E. Neurocirculatory asthenia (anxiety neurosis, effort syndrome, neurasthenia). *Journal of the American Medical Association*, 1950, 142, 878–888.

Wikler, A. Conditioning factors in opiate addiction and relapse. In D. M. Wilner & G. G. Kassebaum (Eds.), *Narcotics*. New York: McGraw-Hill, 1965.

Wikler, A. Some implications of conditioning theory for problems of drug abuse. *Behavioral Science*, 1971, 16, 92–97.

Will, O. A. Changing styles in the treatment of schizophrenia. *American Journal of Psychiatry*, 1973, 130, 152–155. © 1973, the American Psychiatric Association. Reprinted by permission.

Will, O. A. Jr. Schizophrenia: Psychological treatment. In A. M. Freedman, H. I. Kaplan, & B. J. Sadock (Eds.), *Comprehensive textbook of psychiatry-II* (Vol. 1, 2nd ed.). Baltimore, Md.: Williams & Wilkins, 1975.

Williams, E. B. Deductive reasoning in schizophrenia. *Journal of Abnormal and Social Psychology*, 1964, 69, 47–61.

Williams, R. J. *Nutrition and Alcoholism*. Norman, Okla.: University of Oklahoma Press, 1951.

Wilson, G. T., Leaf, R. C., & Nathan, P. E. The aversive control of excessive alcohol consumption by chronic alcoholics in the laboratory setting. *Journal of Applied Behavior Analysis*, 1975, 8, 13–26.

Winder, C. L. Some psychological studies of schizophrenia. In D. D. Jackson (Ed.), *The etiology of schizophrenia*. New York: Basic Books, 1960.

Wing, J. K. Institutionalism in mental hospitals. *British Journal of Social and Clinical Psychology*, 1962, 1, 38–51.

Winokur, G. The types of affective illness. *Journal of Nervous and Mental Disease*, 1973, 156 (2), 82–95.

Winokur, G., & Crowe, R. Personality Disorders. In A. M. Freedman, H. I. Kaplan, & B. J. Sadock (Eds.), *Comprehensive textbook of psychiatry-II* (Vol. 2, 2nd ed.). Baltimore: Williams & Wilkins, 1975.

Wirt, R. D., & Simon, W. *Differential treatment and prognosis in schizophrenia.* Springfield, Ill.: Charles C Thomas, 1959.

Wisocki, P. A. The successful treatment of a heroin addict by covert conditioning techniques. *Journal of Behavior Therapy and Experimental Psychiatry,* 1972, 4, 55–61.

Wisocki, P. A. The successful treatment of a heroin addict by covert conditioning techniques. *Behavior Therapy and Experimental Psychiatry,* 1973, 4, 55–61.

Witkin, H. A., Mednick, S. A., Schulsinger, F., Bakkestrøm, E., Christiansen, K. O., Goodenough, D. R., Hirschorn, K., Lundsteen, C., Jwen, D. R., Philip, J., Rubin, D. B., Stocking, M. Criminality in XYY and XXY men. *Science,* August 13, 1976, p. 4253.

Wittkower, E. D., & Fried, J. A cross-cultural approach to mental health problems. *American Journal of Psychiatry,* 1959, 116, 423–428.

Wolberg, L. R. *The technique of psychotherapy* (Part 1, 2nd ed.). New York: Grune & Stratton, 1967. Reprinted by permission.

Wolf, S., & Wolff, H. G. Evidence on the genesis of peptic ulcer in man. *Journal of the American Medical Association,* 1947, 120, 670–675.

Wolfe, M., Hanley, E., King, L., Lachowicz, J., & Giles, D. The timer game: A VI contingency for the management of out-of-seat behavior. *Exceptional Children,* 1970, 37, 113–117.

Wollersheim, J. P. The effectiveness of group therapy based upon learning principles in the treatment of overweight women. *Journal of Abnormal Psychology,* 1970, 76, 462–474.

Wolman, B. B. The process of treatment. In B. B. Wolman (Ed.), *The therapist's handbook.* New York: Van Nostrand Reinhold, 1976.(a)

Wolman, B. B. Treatment of schizophrenia. In B. B. Wolman (Ed.), *The therapist's handbook.* New York: Van Nostrand Reinhold, 1976.(b)

Wolpe, J. Experimental neuroses as a learned behavior. *British Journal of Psychiatry,* 1952, 43, 243–268.

Wolpe, J. *Psychotherapy by reciprocal inhibition.* Stanford, Calif.: Stanford University Press, 1958.

Wolpe, J. *The practice of behavior therapy.* Oxford: Pergamon Press, 1969.

Wolowitz, H. M., & Wagonfeld, S. Oral derivatives in the food preference of peptic ulcer patients: An experimental test of Alexander's psychoanalytic hypothesis. *Journal of Nervous and Mental Disease,* 1968, 146, 18–23.

World Health Organization. Expert committee on addiction-producing drugs. *Thirteenth report* (WHO Technical Report Series No. 273) Geneva: World Health Organization, 1964.

World Health Organization. *International Classification of Diseases* (8th ed.). Geneva, Switzerland, 1968.

Wotzlawick, P. A review of the double bind theory. *Family Process,* 1963, 2, 132–153.

Wren, C. S. 28% of state's mental patients return within 6 months after being released. *New York Times,* July 12, 1973, p. 43.

Yarrow, L. J. Separation from parents during early childhood. In M. L. Hoffman & L. W. Hoffman (Eds.), *Review of child development research.* New York: Russell Sage Foundation, 1964.

Young, M., Benjamin, B., & Wallis, C. The mortality of widowers. *Lancet,* August 31, 1963, pp. 454–456.

Zax, M., & Stricker, G. *Patterns of psychopathology.* New York: Macmillan, 1963. Excerpts on pp. 180–181, 190–191, 239, 245–246, 291, 414–415. © 1963 by Macmillan Company, Inc. Reprinted by permission.

Ziegler, F. J., & Imboden, J. B. Contemporary conversion reactions. *Archives of General Psychiatry,* 1962, 6, 279–287.

Zigler, E., & Phillips, L. Social effectiveness and symptomatic behaviors. *Journal of Abnormal and Social Psychology,* 1960, 61, 231–238.

Zigler, E., & Phillips, L. Psychiatric diagnosis: A critique. *Journal of Abnormal and Social Psychology,* 1961, 63, 607–618.

Zilboorg, G., & Henry, G. W. *A history of medical psychology.* New York: Norton, 1941.

Zimmerman, J., Stuckey, T. E., Garlick, B. J., & Miller, M. Effects of token reinforcement on productivity in multiply handicapped clients in a sheltered workshop. *Rehabilitation Literature,* 1969, 30, 34–41.

Zubek, J. E. (Ed.) *Sensory deprivation: Fifteen years of research.* New York: Appleton-Century-Crofts, 1969.

Zubin, J. Vulnerability—a new view of schizophrenia. *The Clinical Psychologist,* 1975, 29, 16–21.

Zuckerman, M., & Coan, N. Is suggestion the source of reported visual sensations in perceptual isolation? *Journal of Abnormal and Social Psychology,* 1964, 68, 655–660.

Zung, W. W. K., & Green, R. L. Seasonal variation of suicide and depression. *Archives of General Psychiatry,* 1974, 30, 89–91.

Zusman, J. Some explanations of the changing appearance of psychotic patients: Antecedents of the social breakdown syndrome concept. In E. M. Gruenberg (Ed.), *Evaluating the effectiveness of community mental health services.* New York: Milbank Fund, 1966.

Zusman, J. Secondary prevention. In A. M. Freedman, H. I. Kaplan, & B. J. Sadock (Eds.), *Comprehensive textbook of psychiatry-II* (Vol. 2, 2nd ed.). Baltimore: Williams & Wilkins, 1975.

Name index

Rifkin, A. H., 543
Rimland, B., 375
Rimm, D. C., 142, 146, 154
Ring, K., 258
Ringuette, E. L., 265
Ritter, B., 157, 178
Rivera, G., 406
Rivlin, L., 550
Robbins, E., 462
Robbins, L. L., 32
Roberts, L., 557
Robertson, J., 83
Robins, E., 547
Robins, L. N., 310, 315, 317, 334
Robinson, H. D., 395, 396, 398, 402
Robinson, J. C., 303
Robinson, N. M., 395, 396, 398, 402
Roen, S. R., 158, 159
Roff, J. D., 259
Rogers, Carl, 51, 52, 121, 124, 134, 137, 505, 506
Rogers, Linda, 84
Rollins, H. A., 519, 520
Rose, R. J., 316
Rosen, J. N., 119, 274
Rosenhan, D. L., 38–39, 255
Rosenman, R. H., 548
Rosenthal, D., 39, 164, 261
Rosenthal, R., 560
Rosenthal, S. H., 560
Ross, A. O., 80, 387
Ross, D. M., 410
Ross, H., 379
Ross, S. A., 410
Rossi, A. M., 557
Roth, M., 244
Rowe, C. J., 190
Rowe, J. S., 384
Rubin, D. B., 565
Rutter, M., 379
Ryan, W., 521

Sabshin, M., 26
Saghir, M. T., 462
Salzman, L., 200
Sanders, D., 495
Sanderson, R. E., 343
Sandhu, H. S., 325, 328, 330
Sandler, J., 560
Sandok, B. A., 415
Santer-Westrate, H. C., 184
Sarbin, T. R., 37, 38
Satterfield, J. H., 384
Sawrey, W. L., 225, 546
Schachter, A., 359
Schachter, S., 86
Schaefer, H. H., 118, 280
Scheerenberger, R. C., 555
Scheff, T. J., 89
Schiele, B. C., 80
Schmidt, C. F., 552
Schmidtz, H. O., 38n

Schofield, W., 120, 124
Schooler, N. R., 259
Schroeder, S. R., 411
Schukit, M. A., 561
Schulsinger, F., 262, 266, 317
Schurr, C., 467, 468, 470
Schurr, P. H., 163
Schutte, R. C., 410
Schutz, William, 506
Schuyler, D., 306
Schwartz, A. H., 281
Schwartz, G. E., 220, 221
Schwartz, M., 253–254
Scott, T. H., 80
Scott, W. A., 561
Sechehaye, M. A., 272
Seguin, Edouard, 406, 408
Seiden, R. H., 309
Seidman, E., 333, 334
Seligman, M. E. P., 297–298
Sellin, T., 323
Selye, Hans, 212
Shaffer, M., 298, 304
Shagass, C., 263
Shapiro, D., 108, 125, 220, 221
Shapiro, M. B., 561
Shapiro, T., 445
Shaw, C. R., 321
Shaw, D., 333, 389
Sheehy, G., 483
Sheldon, W., 320
Shenger-Krestovnikova, N. R., 60
Shneidman, E. S., 106, 307, 311
Shoben, E. J., Jr., 25
Shoemaker, D. J., 543
Sifneos, P. E., 217
Silber, D. E., 322, 323
Sillen, S., 477
Silvers, F. M., 509
Simmons, J. Q., 376, 378
Simon, W., 259
Singer, M. T., 202
Skinner, B. F., 54, 57, 62, 63, 141
Slater, E., 244
Slavney, P. R., 185
Sloan, W., 401
Smith, B. S., 550
Smith, J. C., 503
Smith, J. W., 365
Smith, K., 251, 253
Smith, L. H., 495
Smith, M. B., 26
Snyder, M. J., 228
Sobell, L. C., 347
Sobell, M. B., 347
Solomon, P., 557
Solomon, R. L., 317
Solomon, R. W., 520
Sommer, R., 258
Spence, K. W., 267
Sperling, M., 83
Spiegler, M. D., 45

Spitz, R. A., 83
Sprenger, Johann, 13, 190
Srole, L., 7, 88
Stampfl, T. G., 145
Stein, Gertrude, 98
Stephens, L., 407
Stephens, T. M., 320
Stern, L. O., 551
Stern, M., 561
Stieper, D. R., 129
Stocking, M., 565
Stojanovich, K., 318
Stokvis, B., 217
Stoler, N., 122
Stone, S., 12, 13, 15
Storm, L. H., 237
Straus, R., 548
Strauss, A. A., 399
Stricker, G., 181, 191, 223, 239, 246, 291, 415
Stuart, R. B., 150, 360, 362
Stubblefield, R. L., 321
Stuckey, T. E., 565
Stunkard, A. J., 358–359, 360
Suinn, R. M, 174
Sullivan, Harry Stack, 51, 265, 272
Sullivan, R., 520
Sulzer, B., 564
Sundberg, N. D., 99, 101, 109, 513
Sussex, J. N., 495
Swartzburg, M., 281
Szasz, T. S., 37, 233, 323, 495
Szurek, S. A., 321

Tabachnick, N. D., 311
Taplin, J. R., 99, 513
Taylor, J. A., 267
Taylor, V. O., 153
Thaler, M., 564
Tharp, R. G., 153
Thigpen, C. H., 187
Thomas, A., 477
Thomas, C. R., 154
Thomas, D. W., 360, 361
Thomas, J., 149, 278
Thompson, M., 560
Thompson, T., 409
Thomson, L. E., 218
Thoresen, C. E., 502
Thorndike, Edward L., 56, 57, 141
Thorne, F. C., 329
Titler, N. A., 557
Toffler, A., 205, 207, 491–493
Torrey, E. P., 268
Tredgold, A. F., 394
Trivelli, N., 564
Trost, M. A., 546
Trotter, R. J., 331
Tuerk, K., 425, 563
Turnbull, J. W., 218
Turner, L. H., 317
Turrell, E. S., 546

Subject index

Abnormal behavior
  behavioral approach to, 20, 21, 54–71
  biochemical factors, 78–79
  biological factors, 73, 76–81
  biological rhythms and, 80
  biophysical view of, 19
  cases of, 27
  causal factors, 72–91
    direct, 72–75
    overview of, 72–76
  child development and, 82–83, 367–392
  classification of, 15, 18, 32–37
  community mental health movement and, 157–160, 493–496
  conceptualizing, emerging issues in, 474–496
  contributing factors, 76, 80
  cost of, 7–8
  criteria, 26–31
  cross-cultural studies of, 90
  deprivations and, 80–81
  designation of, 23–32
  diet and, 80
  ecology and, 90, 490–493
  economic burdens of, 7–8

Abnormal behavior (*cont.*)
  family factors, 83–88
  genetic factors, 76–78
  historical overview of, 9–19
  hormonal factors, 79
  incidence rate, 6, 7
  inquiry about, 92–113
  isolation and, 80–81
  legal aspects of, 481–483
  maintaining factors, 76, 80
  malnutrition and, 80
  medical or illness model, 19, 20
  misconceptions about, 4
  multiple routes to, 73–76
  neurochemical factors, 78–79
  neurophysiological factors, 79–80
  organic view of, 11–12, 16, 18–19, 20
  parental factors, 83–88
  personal reactions to, 8–9
  prevalence rate, 6
  prevention of, 506–507
  problem-oriented approach to, 509
  problems caused by, 5–8
  psychoanalytic view of, 49
  psychodynamic approaches to, 20, 21, 40–54, 70–71

Abnormal behavior (*cont.*)
  racial issues and, 89–90
  research concerning, 92–113
  research definitions of, 31
  scientific approach to, 16–22
  serum factors, 79
  sexual, 437–471
  social class and, 88–89
  social context of, 475–483
  society and, 5–8, 67
  sociocultural factors, 88–90
  sociopsychological factors, 476–477
  stress and, 80
  study of, 37
    introduction to, 3–22
  treatment of, emerging approaches to, 497–522
  types of, 166
  See also Maladaptive behavior
Abortions, 480
Acceptance of clients' behavior, therapist's, 120
Achievement Place, 329, 331–332, 333
"Acting out," 133
Acute cases, behavioral approaches and, 508–509
Adaptive Behavior Scale, 400, 401

Addiction, *see* Alcoholism; Drug addiction; Overeating; Smoking
Adolescence, behavior disorders of, 36
Adult life, stages and crises of, 483–489
Affect, organic brain syndromes and, 416
Affective disorders, 283–306
  behavioral factors, 297–298, 303–304
  biological factors, 302
  causal factors, 295–302
  classification approaches, 290–295
  contributing factors, 205–302
  description of, 284–290
  family factors, 299
  genetic factors, 302
  maintaining factors, 295–302
  major, 36
  psychodynamic factors, 295–297, 302–303
  psychological factors, 298–299
  sociocultural factors, 299
  treatment, 302–306
  See also Depression, Involutional melancholia; Mania
Aftercare, 509–511
Age
  basal, 396
  chronological, 396
  mental, 102–103, 106, 396
Aging, 415, 429–436, 488
  prevention of, 431–436
  primary, 429
  psychological aspects of, 430–431
  secondary, 429
  sociological aspects of, 430–431
  traditional views of, 429–430
  treatment of, 431–436
Agoraphobia, 175
Aides, psychiatric, 122–123
Alcohol, physiological effects of, 336
Alcoholic psychoses, 337
Alcoholics Anonymous, 346
Alcoholism, 35, 147, 336–347
  behavioral approaches to, 342–345
  blood-alcohol level discrimination training and, 346–347
  clinical effects of, 337
  controlled drinking and, 346
  definition of, 336
  drinking styles and, 339
  factors involved, 339–341
  incidence of, 336
  nature of, 336
  operant approaches to, 344–345
  Patton State Hospital experiment, 347
  personality and, 337
  prevalence of, 336
  psychodynamic approaches to, 342
  psychodynamic theories, 339

Alcoholism (*cont.*)
  psychological consequences of, 337
  respondent approaches to, 342–344
  social learning approach to, 339–340
  stages of, 337–338, 341
  treatment approaches, 341–347
Alzheimer's disease, 429
Ambiguity, normative, 25
American Association on Mental Deficiency, 394, 398, 399, 400, 402
American Law Institute, 30
American Medical Association, 34
American Psychiatric Association, 16, 169, 180, 190, 195, 200, 293, 313, 455, 459, 462
  classification system, 34–37
American Psychological Association, 336, 347
Amines, biogenic, 79
Amnesia, 186, 187
Amniocentesis, 411
Amphetamines, 347, 350, 385
Anal personality, 46
Anal stage (psychosexual development), 45
Analogues, 112
Analysis
  direct, 119
  dream, 94
  factor, 111
  functional, 65, 68, 95, 170, 187, 201
  idiographic, 97–98
  nomothetic, 97
Anemia, psychogenic, 210
Angina pectoris, 217, 226, 227
Animal magnetism, 41, 42
Animism, 10
Antecedent conditions, 64
Antabuse therapy, 343, 346
Antidepressants, 162
Antisocial behavior, 312–334
  society's response to, 322–329
  treatment approaches, 329–334
  types of, 313–322
Antisocial personality, 313–318
  behavioral description of, 314–316
  biological factors, 316–317
  causal factors, 316–318
  childhood symptoms predictive of, 315–316
  contributing factors, 316–318
  maintaining factors, 316–318
  psychological factors, 317–318
Anxiety, 35, 47–48, 60, 63, 97, 169
  acute, 171, 172
  assertiveness and, 145–146
  chronic, 171
  concept of, 169, 170
  defined, 169, 171
  "free-floating," 171
  moral, 48
  muscle tension and, 144

Anxiety (*cont.*)
  neurotic, 35, 47, 169, 171–175, 196
  objective, 48
  test, 144
Anxiety management training, 174
Anxiety neurosis, 35
Aphasia, 420–421
Asocial behavior, 37
Assertion training, 145–146, 174, 195, 218
Assessment
  clinical process of, 98–99
  objective, 103–105
  projective, 105–106
  See also Evaluation; Tests
Assistants, nonprofessional, 160, 516–517
Asthma, 209, 215, 218
Asylums, 15
Attention-getting behavior, 35
Attribution therapy, 194
Autism, 36, 237, 368–379
Autoeroticism, 264
Automated procedures, 154–155
Automatic writing, 186
Automation techniques, 154–155
Autonomy, functional, 74, 75, 251
Aversion therapy, *see* Therapy, aversion
Aversive behavior, 64
Aversive conditioning, 146–147
Aversive consequences, 147–148

Baquet, 42
Barbiturates, 307, 347, 351, 352
Basal age, 396
Base Expectancy Score, 328
"Bedlam," origin of word, 15
Bed-wetting, *see* Enuresis
Behavior, definition of, 55. *See also names of various types of behavior*
Behavior change, 117
  contemporary approaches to, 140–165
Behavior modification, 65, 141, 155–156, 336, 388, 391, 508
  juvenile delinquency and, 333
  mental retardation and, 409–410
  obesity and, 362
  school-based programs and, 520
  smoking and, 365
Behavior satiation, 118
Behavior therapy, 57
Behavioral approach, 20, 21, 40, 54–71, 75, 94–95, 99, 101, 140, 141–157
  acute hospital wards and, 508–509
  affective disorders and, 297–298, 303–304
  alcoholism and, 342–345
  antisocial behavior and, 329

Renaissance, view of abnormality during, 14–15
Reparative responses, 192
Replacement drug therapy, 353–354
Replicability of research, 96
Repression, 44, 47–50, 169, 181, 186
Rescue, Inc. (Boston), 311
Research, 92–113
  approach to inquiry, 94, 106–113
  behavior therapy and, 157
  consensual validation of, 96
  descriptive, 109–110
  epidemiological, 110
  evaluating approaches to, 112–113
  experimental, 111–112
  exploratory, 108–109
  life-stress, 205–207
  neuroses and, 174–175, 178, 179–180, 185, 187–189, 194–195
  observational, 110
  proposals, checklist of questions concerning, 113
  psychotherapy and, 127–129
  relational, 110–111
  replicability of, 96
  schizophrenic, 269–270
  validity of, 96, 97
Resistance, 44, 131–132
Respiratory disorders, psychophysiologic, 209–210
Respondent behavior, 57–61, 142
Response facilitation effect, 156
Response prevention, 193, 194
Responses
  abnormal, 64
  conditioned (CR), 57–61
    extinction of, 58, 62, 142, 143, 145, 148, 152
  reparative, 192
  unconditioned (UCR), 57–59
Responsibility, criminal, 30
Restructuring, cognitive, 125
Retardation, see Mental retardation
Retirement, aging and, 431
Revised Stanford-Binet Intelligence Test, 397
"Revolving door" syndrome, 509
Ritalin, 385
Role conflicts, 476, 479
Role-playing, 391, 505
Roles, 67
Rome, ancient, views of abnormality in, 11–12
Rorschach inkblot test, 105–106
Rubella, 399, 405
Runaway reaction, children and, 382

Sadism, 35, 458–459
Sadness, 284
Sample, study, 108
Sampling bias, 70

Satiation, behavior, 118
Satyriasis, 463
Scapegoat, 86
Schizophrenia, 18, 34, 36, 37, 39, 60, 77, 79, 90, 104, 110, 200, 230–282
  acute undifferentiated, 245–246
  behavioral approaches to, 268, 276–278
  behavioral description, 233–250
  biochemical factors, 262–263
  biological factors, 261–262
  biophysical factors, 262–263
  catatonic, 242–244
  causal factors, 73, 74, 261–271
  childhood, 36, 368–379
  chronic undifferentiated, 246–247
  classification of, 232, 233, 239–247, 249
  clinical manifestations, 234–239
  concept of, 230–233
  contributing factors, 261–271
  costs of, 233
  course of, 250–259
  definitions of, 233, 270
  dimensions of behavior, 247–249
  disruptions in verbal behavior, language, and speech, 236, 237–238, 278
  disturbance of thought processes and, 235–237, 278
  double-bind theory and, 87–88, 265
  early symptoms of, 250–251, 252–253
  emotional behavior and, 236, 238–239
  epidemiology of, 233
  family factors, 265–266
  genetic factors, 261–262
  hebephrenic, 241–242
  high-risk children and, 266–267
  hospitalization and, 251–258, 278
  incidence rates, 233
  latent, 246
  learning approaches, 267–268
  maintaining factors, 261–271
  motor behavior and, 238
  mutism and, 238, 278
  onset experiences, 250–251, 252
  paranoid, 244–245, 319
  perceptual distortion and, 234–235, 236
  physiological factors, 263
  premorbid adjustment and, 266–267
  prevalence rates, 233
  prognosis, 258–259
  pseudoneurotic, 246
  psychoanalytic approaches, 272–273
  psychodynamic approaches and, 263–265, 272–274, 373–374, 376–379
  residual, 246

Schizophrenia (cont.)
  simple, 240–241
  social class and, 88, 269
  social withdrawal and, 234, 236
  sociocultural factors, 268–269
  treatment, 164, 271–282
  types of, 239–247
  universality of, 268
Schizophrenogenic parent, 83
School-based programs for prevention of abnormal behavior, 519–520
School, fear of, 381–382
Scoptophilia, 463
Sedatives, 161
Selection of subjects, 112
Self
  "ideal," 52
  "real," 52
Self-actualization, 21, 41, 51–52, 134
Self-control techniques, 150–151, 499, 502
Self-esteem, sex and, 441
Self-evaluation, 150, 499
Self-fulfilling prophecy, 63
Self-image
  aging and, 431
  lack of power and, 476
Self-instruction, 499, 502
Self-labeling, 39
Self-monitoring, 150, 499, 502
Self-reinforcement, 150, 153, 499
Self-report inventories, 95
Self-selection of standards, 499
Senescence, 429, 431
Senile dementia, 429
Senility, traditional veiws of, 429–430
Sensitization, covert, 147
  alcoholism and, 344
  drug addiction and, 355, 356
  overeating and, 362
Sensory deprivation, abnormal behavior and, 80
Sentence-completion tests, 106
Serotonin, 79, 262, 302
  deficiency of, 384
Serum factors (abnormal behavior), 79
Setting conditions, 64
Sex clinics, 439, 451–454
Sex counseling, 451–454
Sex Offenders Anonymous, 470
Sexual behavior
  abnormal, 437–471
  "normal," 438
  statistics on, 440
Sexual deviation, 35, 442, 454–466
  definition of, 454–455
  treatment of, 464–466
Sexual dysfunction, 442–454
  factors involved, 446–449
  treatment of, 450–454
  types of, 444–446
Sexual liberation, 480